READING
STATISTICS
AND
RESEARCH

READING
STATISTICS
AND
RESEARCH

SECOND EDITION

SCHUYLER W. HUCK
University of Tennessee

WILLIAM H. CORMIER
West Virginia University

HarperCollins*College*Publishers

Executive Editor: Christopher Jennison
Project Editors: Diane Williams, Elizabeth LaManna
Senior Designer: John Callahan
Text Designer: Interactive Composition Corporation
Art Studio: Vantage Art, Inc.
Electronic Production Manager: Su Levine
Desktop Administrator: Laura Leever
Manufacturing Manager: Willie Lane
Electronic Page Makeup: Interactive Composition Corporation
Printer and Binder: RR Donnelley & Sons Company
Cover Printer: Phoenix Color Corp.

Reading Statistics and Research, Second Edition

Library of Congress Cataloging-in-Publication Data
Huck, Schuyler W.
    Reading statistic and research / Schuyler W. Huck, William H. Cormier—
  2nd ed.
        p.   cm.
  Includes index.
  ISBN 0-06-500606-2
    1. Statistics.   2. Research.   3. Experimental design.
I. Cormier, William H. (William Henry), (date)   . II. Title.
QA276.H788 1995
001.4'22—dc20

95 96 97 98 9 8 7 6 5 4 3 2 1

This book is dedicated to two groups: those "consumers" of research reports who are willing to evaluate critically (and sometimes reject) the claims made by researchers, and those researchers who carefully analyze the data from thoughtfully designed studies that focus on worthy questions.

BRIEF CONTENTS

CONTENTS

PREFACE

In the first edition of *Reading Statistics and Research,* we asserted that humanity could be divided into three groups: (1) those who conduct their own research studies, (2) those who do not formally engage in the research process but nonetheless encounter the results of others' investigations, and (3) those who neither are "makers" nor "consumers" of research claims. More than two decades have passed since we made that statement. We remain convinced that every person on the face of the earth can be classified into one of those three groups. However, we have altered our views concerning the relative sizes and needs of the three groups.

Regarding the issue of size, it is now clear to us that our first group (the "doers" of research) is slightly larger than we first suspected, while our second group (the "consumers" of research) is *much* larger than we first thought. If we disregard infants and young children, monks, prisoners-of-war, and comatose hospital patients, the odds are extremely high that any randomly selected person belongs to one of these two groups. The first would be populated with lots of professors, all graduate students preparing to write a master's thesis or doctoral dissertation, most employees of the many research units located in both public and private organizations, and a handful of independent researchers. Whoever isn't a member of the first category is most likely a member of the second group. We say that because it is virtually impossible to avoid coming into contact with research findings.

In one way or another, almost everyone bumps up against the findings of empirical investigations. First of all, formal and full-length research reports are presented each year in thousands of professional journals and at countless international, national, regional, and local conventions. Summaries of such studies frequently appear in newspapers and magazines, on television and radio news programs, and within stories accessible through the Internet. And then there are innumerable advertisements and commercials containing the results of so-called scientific studies conducted to assess the worth of the product or service being hawked.

We strongly believe that everyone in the huge second group needs to become a more discerning consumer of research findings and research claims.

The individuals who are on the receiving end of research summaries cannot be *competent* consumers of what they read or hear unless they can both understand and evaluate the investigations being discussed. Such skills are needed because (1) trustworthy research conclusions come only from those studies characterized by a sound methodology and a careful analysis of the data, and (2) the screening process that is supposed to prevent poor studies from being disseminated is only partially successful in achieving its objective. Consequently, consumers must acquire the skills needed to protect themselves from overzealous or improperly trained researchers whose work leads to exaggeration, false "discoveries," and unjustified claims of "significance."

We also believe that individuals in the first group—the doers of research—need to increase their ability to evaluate research reports critically. We say this because almost every research project is supposed to be built on a foundation of knowledge gleaned from previous studies. Clearly, if a current researcher cannot differentiate legitimate from unjustified research conclusions, his or her own investigation may well be doomed from the outset because it is pointed in the wrong direction or grounded in a research base made of sand. If applied researchers could critique more adequately the studies cited within their literature reviews, they also would be able to apply such knowledge to their own investigations. The result would be more adequately designed studies containing more appropriate statistical analyses leading to more justifiable conclusions and claims.

And so, the second edition of *Reading Statistics and Research* is targeted at two groups: those who conduct their own research investigations and those who are the recipients of research-based claims. We have kept both groups in mind as we have gone about the task of revising our initial work. We hope that members of both groups will benefit from considering our expanded discussion of statistics and research design, the completely new array of excerpts taken from recently published research reports, and our end-of-chapter review questions.

The seven specific objectives of the second edition are basically the same as those of the first edition. These goals include providing the reader with (1) an understanding of statistical terms, (2) the ability to make sense out of (or to set up) statistical tables, (3) a knowledge of what specific research questions can be answered by each of a variety of statistical procedures, (4) an understanding of hypothesis testing, statistical testing, and the "hybrid" method for assessing null hypotheses, (5) the skills needed to notice the misuse of statistics, (6) a facility for distinguishing between good and poor research designs, and (7) a feeling of confidence when interacting with research reports.

The seven objectives just listed can be synthesized nicely into two words: **decipher** and **critique.** The book is designed to help people *decipher* what researchers are trying to communicate in the written or oral summaries of their investigations. Here, the goal is simply to distill meaning from the words, symbols, tables, and figures included in the research report. (To be competent in this arena, one must also be able to fill in the holes, because researchers usually assume that those receiving the research report are familiar with unmentioned details of the research process.) Beyond being able to decipher what is included, we want our readers to be able to *critique* such research reports. This is important because research claims are sometimes completely unjustified due to problems associated with the way studies are planned or implemented, or problems in the way data are analyzed, summarized, or interpreted.

In an effort to assist our readers to become better able to decipher and critique research reports, a variety of new features are built into this edition. Several of these additions are quite minor (such as the inclusion of answers to end-of-chapter review questions) and need not be discussed. There are, however, four main differences between this edition and the one published in 1974. We believe that these differences drastically improve the book's quality.

The first important way in which this edition differs from the first edition concerns breadth of coverage. Simply stated, far more topics are dealt with here as compared with what was done previously. Totally new chapters now deal with reliability and validity, with estimation, and with completely within-subjects ANOVAs. New sections focus on box-and-whisker plots, sampling, the Bonferroni technique for controlling Type I errors, tests of proportions, and Fisher's Exact Test. These and other additions will help readers gain the skills needed to understand a larger variety of research reports and more of what is found within any given report.

The second major difference between the first and second editions concerns the amount of attention devoted to the procedures used by researchers when they deal with null hypotheses. In the first edition, the only thing we discussed was the simplest strategy used by researchers in assessing an H_0. And within that earlier discussion, we did little more than list the steps that go together to make up that strategy. In this edition, we devote three full chapters to a consideration of alternative strategies used by researchers when they deal with null hypotheses. These new chapters also contain an examination of the "logic" that underlies those three strategies. As you will see, we show what researchers do when they apply hypothesis testing, statistical testing, or the "hybrid" approach to investigating an H_0. More important, however, we discuss what a null hypothesis really is and where it comes from; we clarify why a null hypothesis should not be accepted if the results of the data analysis indicate that H_0 cannot be rejected; we point out that a finding deemed to be statistically significant may very well be devoid of any practical significance; and we emphasize repeatedly the ever-present possibility of inferential error when null hypotheses are set up and evaluated.

The third major difference between the first and second editions of *Reading Statistics and Research* concerns the issue of mistakes made by researchers in the design and execution of their applied studies, mistakes made by researchers in the analysis of their data, and mistakes made by researchers in the claims they make at the end of their studies. In the first edition, we paid very little attention to such mistakes. After seeing 20 years' worth of studies often characterized by errors of omission or commission, glossed-over limitations, and exaggerated claims, we felt obliged to do more in the way of preparing our readers to assess critically the worth of the sometimes boastful claims made by applied researchers. To help accomplish this objective, we have been more clear and straightforward about what researchers should (and should not) do, we have included several excerpts that illustrate various problems, and we have positioned a set of "warnings" at the end of each chapter.

The final change we have made may not at first seem either very dramatic or necessary. Nevertheless, we consider it to be the most important change of all. At several points in the second edition, we point out that the worth of any study is limited by the quality of the questions posed by the researcher. It is extremely important for consumers of research reports (and for applied researchers as well) to recognize this fact, because fancy statistics and complex design strategies tend to both impress and intimidate many people. We argue as vigorously as we can that it is the quality of the research question(s) that determines the maximum worth of any investigation.

ACKNOWLEDGEMENTS

Several people helped move the first edition of this book into this second edition. We wish to express our sincere appreciation to these individuals, for this revision project would not have come to fruition without their kind assistance and expertise. They are not responsible, of course, for any mistakes, small or large, that inadvertently crept into this work. They *were* responsible, however, for getting this long-overdue project off the drawing boards, for moving it along, and for making the finished product far superior to what would have been the case if we had worked totally on our own.

We wish to thank most vigorously our editor (and friend) at HarperCollins, Chris Jennison. His support, guidance, and patience extended far beyond the norm. Our project editors, Diane Williams and Elizabeth LaManna, were incredibly talented and a pure joy to work with. We will miss (1) hearing Diane's wonderful laugh as she soothed our worries about format, deadlines, and other "production" concerns and (2) dealing with Elizabeth, one of the most courteous, conscientious, and caring people we have ever met. Also, our copyeditor, Katherine Hieatt, did a marvelous job in showing us how to express our thoughts in a clearer, more concise fashion.

Our handwritten manuscript was typed by three true "pros": Kirche Rogers, Diane Booker, and Marci Phillips. Also on our "end" of this project were several graduate students who helped to move this revision project along in important ways. Drafts of the typed manuscript were perused by Jan Tomlin and Teresa Garland, and library research was conducted by Carolyn Wade and Cynthia Webb.

Many of our decisions concerning what to include or to emphasize were influenced greatly by our conversations with colleagues and students. We especially want to recognize our colleagues Howard Sandler, Carl Huberty, Ben Layne, and Pat Busk; each of them helped in many ways, and none of them probably realized how much we valued (and still value) the consultation they provided. We feel the same way about the "blind" reviewers who examined initial drafts of our work. Students from our courses kept us "on target" by alerting us to places in our lectures where additional explanation was needed in order to permit them to understand tough concepts.

Finally, we wish to thank the many individuals who have granted us permission to use excerpts from their published research reports. By being able to include portions of their work, our book (we hope) comes "alive" and achieves a level of relevance rendered impossible without those excerpts.

Schuyler W. Huck

William H. Cormier

The Typical Format of a Journal Article

Almost all journal articles dealing with research studies are divided into different sections by means of headings and subheadings. Although there is variation among journals with respect to the terms used as the headings and the order in which different sections are arranged, there does appear to be a relatively standard format for published articles. Readers of the professional literature will find that they can get the most mileage out of the time they invest if they are familiar with the typical format of journal articles and the kind of information normally included in each section of the article.

We are now going to look at a particular journal article that does an excellent job of illustrating the basic format that many authors use as a guide when they are writing their articles. The different sections of our model article could be arranged in outline form as follows:

1. Abstract
2. Introduction
    a. Review of the literature
    b. Statement of purpose
3. Method
    a. Participants
    b. Materials
    c. Dependent variables
    d. Procedure
4. Results
5. Discussion
6. References

Let us now examine each of these items.

ABSTRACT

An **abstract,** or précis, summarizes the entire research study and appears at the beginning of the article. Although it normally contains fewer than 150 words, the abstract usually provides the following information: (1) a statement of the purpose or objective of the investigation, (2) a description of the individuals who served as participants, (3) a brief explanation of what the participants did during the study, and (4) a summary of the important findings.

Excerpt 1.1 is the abstract from our model journal article. As in most articles, it was positioned immediately after the title and authors' names. As you can see, this abstract was printed in italics. This was done in an effort to make the abstract stand out from the rest of the article. Often, this same objective is accomplished by printing the abstract in a smaller font size from that used in the rest of the article.

Excerpt 1.1 Abstract

Marketing claims of effectiveness in improving academic achievement through the use of commercially prepared subliminal audiotapes were investigated. Students enrolled in a career development class were randomly assigned to an active treatment group (n=25), an inactive treatment group (n=26), or a control group (n=22). Participants in the treatment group listened to tapes with subliminal affirmations masked by ocean waves. The inactive treatment group listened to placebo tapes with ocean waves but no subliminal messages. Dependent variables used were final examination scores from the class and current semester grade point average. No treatment differences on either dependent measure were found. The implications of these findings are discussed.

Source: T. G. Russell, W. Rowe, and A. D. Smouse. (1991). Subliminal self-help tapes and academic achievement: An evaluation. *Journal of Counseling and Development, 69,* p. 359.

The sole purpose of the abstract is to provide readers with an overview of the material they will encounter in the remaining portions of the article. The abstract in Excerpt 1.1 contains a few technical terms (e.g., *randomly assigned, dependent variables,* and *treatment differences*), and it may be difficult for you to understand completely what these researchers did in their study. After reading a few more chapters in this book, however, you will be able to decipher the full message of this seven-sentence abstract. After becoming familiar with the vocabulary used by researchers, you will be able to read *any* abstract in about 90 seconds and then decide whether to read the whole article. On the basis of the abstract, you can decide that the article in front of you is a veritable gold mine, that it *may* be what you have been looking for, or that it is not at all related to your interests. Regardless of how you react to this brief synopsis of the full article, the abstract serves a useful purpose.

INTRODUCTION

The **introduction** of an article usually contains two items: a **review of the literature** and a **statement of purpose.** We consider these two sections of an article to be of utmost importance. We encourage you to read them slowly and carefully.

REVIEW OF THE LITERATURE

Most authors start their articles with a description of previous research studies that have been conducted by them or by other individuals. In discussing these previous investigations, an author attempts to demonstrate how the research project being reported is related to previous ones. Sometimes, of course, an author will publish a completely new idea that is not connected to anything that anyone has investigated earlier. In the vast majority of articles, however, the author's work can be thought of as an extension of previous knowledge. The review of literature provides readers with background information or a framework within which to view the current study.

The discussion of previous research can be as short as one or two sentences or as long as several pages. Regardless of its length, this section of the journal article does not typically fall under any formal heading. Excerpt 1.2 is the review of literature from our model journal article. Take a moment to read through these five paragraphs.

Excerpt 1.2 Review of the Literature

The self-help subliminal audiocassette market is rapidly expanding. Such tapes are advertised in popular magazines including *Psychology Today*, are sold by direct mail and in local bookstores, and recently have been uncritically accepted and marketed by college- and university-owned bookstores. Sales of these items by Mind Communication, Inc., grossed $2 million in 1986; in that same year, the Joe Land Company sales topped that figure in 1 month (Dillingham, 1987). The public seems to be taken with the advertised promise of results without effort. Under relaxing music or simulated ocean waves, manufacturers have embedded subliminal messages, that is, messages that are below the threshold of subjective awareness. These messages are purported to facilitate positive behavioral changes such as losing weight, relieving pain, gaining intimacy, succeeding financially, achieving sexual confidence, and improving academic achievement.

We found, much like Levine (1986), that when we asked several tape distributors for the sources that document the effectiveness of subliminal tapes, they could provide little evidence and much of what they provided had little to

(Continued)

Excerpt 1.2 Review of the Literature (Continued)

do with practical application. Yet, tapes are being marketed in advance of any supportive research regarding variations in techniques for embedding messages, types of messages, instructions to users, or potential target behaviors. Even leaders such as the Joe Land Company, which partially supported this research effort, admit that "the industry is woefully inadequate when it comes to bona fide studies that show effectiveness" (Dillingham, 1987, p. 45).

The continuing controversy surrounding subliminal effects began in the 1950s when James Vicary claimed in a press release that subliminal messages had motivated movie viewers to increase their purchases of popcorn and Coca-Cola (Packard, 1957/1981). As a result of the ensuing public uproar, federal funding was provided for research in the area of subliminal perception. This systematic scientific scrutiny served to point out the many problems of conceptualization and methodology in the field (Eriksen, 1960; McConnell, Cutler, & McNeil, 1958). Even today, academic research psychologists tend to view subliminal perception with caution (Dixon, 1986; Holender, 1986).

Research focusing on subliminal auditory messages often has not been relevant to the claims of companies marketing subliminal audiotapes (Borgeat & Goulet, 1983; Zenhausern & Hansen, 1974). Some of the relevant research has produced negative findings (Treimer & Simonson, 1986), while other research has produced positive results that lack credibility due to experimental deficiencies (Kaser, 1986). Although Becker (1979) claimed to have reduced store theft by 37% using subliminal messages embedded in the store's background music, independent verification of this type of effect has not been forthcoming. McConnell (1989) says that he has "repeatedly challenged Hal Becker (and others) to produce one reputable scientific study showing the 'subliminal tapes' actually work under controlled conditions" (p. 428), but he has not received a satisfactory response.

Evidence remains at best inconclusive regarding the specific kinds of presentations that may be effective and what types of behavior can be influenced. Nevertheless, claims by Packard in *Hidden Persuaders* (1959/1981), by Key in *Subliminal Seduction* (1973), as well as by marketing agents and the media have led consumers to believe that effects are recognized, effective, and, perhaps, dangerous (Vokey & Read, 1985; Zanot, Pincus, & Lamp, 1983). The public acceptance of subliminal phenomena, despite the lack of support by the scientific community, presents a challenge to counselors. While the topic of many of these programs may meet the interests and needs of many of our clients, evidence to support the effectiveness of such programs is seriously lacking.

Source: T. G. Russell, W. Rowe, and A. D. Smouse. (1991). Subliminal self-help tapes and academic achievement: An evaluation. *Journal of Counseling and Development, 69,* p. 359.

STATEMENT OF PURPOSE

After having reviewed the relevant literature so as to provide a rationale for the study, an author usually states the specific purpose or goal of the investigation. This statement of purpose is one of the most important parts of a journal article since, in a sense, it explains what the author's "destination" was. It would be impossible for us to evaluate whether the "trip" was successful—in terms of research findings and conclusions—unless we know where the author was headed.

In some journal articles, the statement of purpose is found at the end of the final paragraph reviewing the literature. In other articles, a separate paragraph is devoted to the statement of purpose. In Excerpt 1.3 we see that the authors of our model article used this latter technique for pointing out the specific goal of their study.

Excerpt 1.3 Statement of Purpose

Inasmuch as counselors and student personnel specialists may be called upon for recommendations regarding the benefits of such materials, it behooves us not only to be able to communicate clearly the current status of research in the area of subliminal effects, but also to help develop credible research to assess possible positive outcomes. The current study was designed to evaluate the effect of using a commercially prepared subliminal self-help audiocassette tape to improve academic achievement.

Source: T. G. Russell, W. Rowe, and A. D. Smouse. (1991). Subliminal self-help tapes and academic achievement: An evaluation. *Journal of Counseling and Development, 69,* p. 359.

In most articles, the review of the literature and the statement of purpose are not identified by separate headings, nor are they found under a common heading. If a common heading were to be used, though, the word *Introduction* would probably be most appropriate because these two items set the stage for the substance of the article—an explanation of what was done and what the results were.

METHOD

In the **Method** section of a journal article, an author will explain in detail how the study was conducted. Ideally, such an explanation should contain enough information to enable a reader to replicate (i.e., duplicate) the study. To accomplish this goal, the author will address four questions: (1) Who participated in the study? (2) What types of materials were needed? (3) What data were collected? (4) What were the participants required to do? The answer to each of these questions is generally found under an appropriately titled subheading of the Method section.

PARTICIPANTS

Each of the individuals (or animals) who supplies data in a research study is considered to be a **subject.** (In some journals, the abbreviations *S* and *Ss* are used, respectively, to designate one subject or a group of subjects.) Within this section of a journal article, an author usually indicates how many participants, or subjects, were used, who the participants were, and how they were selected.

A full description of the participants is needed because the results of a study will often vary according to the nature of the subjects who are used. This means that the conclusions of a study, in most cases, are valid only for individuals (or animals) who are similar to the ones used by the researcher. For example, if two different types of counseling techniques are compared and found to differ in terms of how effective they are in helping clients reduce their anxiety, it is imperative that the investigator indicate whether the subjects were high school students, adults, patients in a mental hospital, or whatever. What works for a counselor in a mental hospital may not work at all for a counselor in a high school (and vice versa).

It is also important for the author to indicate how the subjects were obtained. Were they volunteers? Were they randomly selected from a larger pool of potential subjects? Were any particular standards of selection used? Did the researcher simply use all members of a certain high school or college class? As we shall see in Chapter 5, certain procedures for selecting subjects allow results to be generalized far beyond the specific subjects included in the study, while other procedures for selecting subjects limit the valid range of generalization.

Excerpt 1.4 is the section of our model journal article that deals with subjects. Labeled **Participants,** it was the first portion of the article's Method section. The authors of this article did a good job of indicating how many subjects were used, who the subjects were, how the subjects were obtained, and what potential subjects were told as an incentive to encourage participation.

MATERIALS

This section of a journal article is normally labeled in one of four ways: **Materials, Equipment, Apparatus,** or **Instruments.** Regardless of its label, this part of the article contains a description of the "things" (other than subjects) used in the study. The goal here, as in other sections that fall under the Method heading, is to describe what was done with sufficient clarity that others could replicate the investigation to see if the results remain the same.

> **Excerpt 1.4** Participants
>
> **PARTICIPANTS**
>
> Students in a career development class at a midwestern university were invited to participate in a 10-week project to evaluate the use of subliminal audiotapes designed to improve academic achievement. They were informed that some past studies had reported that those receiving certain types of messages had attained higher grades. Fifty-five women and 24 men volunteered to participate. The students were primarily freshmen and sophomores, ranging in age from 18 to 32 years (mode=19; mean=19.6). About 83% were Caucasian, 7% were Black, and 1% were Hispanic (9% did not indicate ethnicity).
>
> *Source:* T. G. Russell, W. Rowe, and A. D. Smouse. (1991). Subliminal self-help tapes and academic achievement: An evaluation. *Journal of Counseling and Development, 69,* pp. 359–360.

Suppose, for example, that a researcher conducts a study to see if males differ from females in the way they evaluate various styles of clothing. To make it possible for others to replicate this study, the researcher would need to indicate whether the subjects saw actual articles of clothing or pictures of clothing (and if pictures, whether they were prints or slides, what size they were, and whether they were in color), whether the clothing articles were being worn when observed by subjects (and if so, who modeled the clothes), what specific clothing styles were involved, how many articles of clothing were evaluated, who manufactured the clothes, and all other relevant details. If the researcher does not provide this information, it would be impossible for anyone to replicate the study.

Often, the only material involved is the measuring device used to collect data from the subjects. Such measuring devices—whether of a mechanical variety (e.g., a stopwatch) or of a paper-and-pencil variety (e.g., a questionnaire)—ought to be described very carefully. If the measuring device is a new instrument designed specifically for the study described in the article, the researcher will typically report evidence concerning the instrument's technical psychometric properties. Generally, the author accomplishes this task by discussing the reliability and validity of the scores generated by using the new instrument.[1] Even if an existing and reputable measuring instrument has been used, the researcher ought to tell us specifically what instrument was used (by indicating form, model number, publication date, etc.).

---

[1] *Later, in Chapter 4, we will talk more about the kinds of evidence researchers normally offer to document their instruments' technical merit.*

One would need to know such information, of course, before a full replication of the study could be attempted. In addition, the researcher ought to pass along reliability and validity evidence cited by those who developed the instrument. Ideally, the authors ought to provide their *own* evidence as to the reliability and validity of scores used in their study, even if an existing instrument is used.

In Excerpt 1.5, the Materials section of our model article, notice how the authors tell us how many audiotapes they used, which ones they used, where they got them, and what (presumably) was on them. The authors also do a nice job of telling us about the tape players that were used.

Excerpt 1.5 Materials

MATERIALS

The Joe Land Company, the largest marketer of subliminal audiotapes in the United States, provided the experimental tapes used in this study. The tapes selected were #23, *Improve Study Habits,* and #27, *Passing Exams.* The tapes are promoted as containing approximately 80,000 positive phrases, referred to as "affirmations," recorded below the level of awareness at varying frequencies and decibel levels and masked by the sound of ocean waves. The placebo tapes, supplied by the same company, merely duplicated the sound of the ocean waves and had no subliminal messages embedded. A Sony model #CES-220 auto-reverse tape player was provided to each student. The auto-reverse feature allowed continued playing without the inconvenience of turning the tape over or forgetting to replay it.

Source: T. G. Russell, W. Rowe, and A. D. Smouse. (1991). Subliminal self-help tapes and academic achievement: An evaluation. *Journal of Counseling and Development, 69,* p. 360.

DEPENDENT VARIABLES

In some articles, the author will set up a section that deals with the dependent variable(s) of the study. Although there are different ways to conceptualize what a **dependent variable** is, we wish to adopt a simple definition that is useful in most situations. According to this definition, a dependent variable is simply a characteristic of the subjects that (1) is of interest to the researcher; (2) is not possessed to an equal degree, or in the same way, by all subjects; and (3) serves as the target of the researcher's data-collection efforts. Thus, in a study conducted to compare the intelligence of males and females the dependent variable would be intelligence.

Excerpt 1.6 contains a discussion of the primary and secondary dependent variables associated with our model journal article. The authors of this article,

---

Excerpt 1.6 Dependent Variables

DEPENDENT VARIABLES

The primary dependent variable was scores on the final examination in the target class. This examination was a 100-item objective test focusing on the content of the textbook. Previous administrations of this instrument have yielded Kuder Richardson-20 reliability estimates in the range of .85. The mean score achieved by previous classes has been approximately 75 (out of a possible 100 points), with individual scores ranging from 48 to 96. A secondary dependent variable used was the grade point average (GPA) attained in all classes taken during that semester.

Source: T. G. Russell, W. Rowe, and A. D. Smouse. (1991). Subliminal self-help tapes and academic achievement: An evaluation. *Journal of Counseling and Development, 69,* p. 360.

---

like many others, equate their dependent variable with the data that were collected. Not everyone agrees that it is best to use such "operational definitions" to define a study's dependent variable(s), but the practice is widespread nonetheless.

In many articles, a discussion of the instrument(s) employed to collect data will appear in the Materials section, while a separate section is entitled Dependent Variable(s). As indicated earlier, some researchers like to distinguish between, on the one hand, the unseen characteristics of their subjects (e.g., level of intelligence) and, on the other hand, the observed data (e.g., score on an intelligence test) that correspond, hopefully, to what is "under the skin." Had this approach been taken by the authors of our model article, the primary dependent variable would have been described as "knowledge gleaned from the career development class," while the secondary dependent variable would have been described as "academic performance that semester."

PROCEDURE

How the study was conducted is explained in the **Procedure** section of the journal article. Here, the researcher explains what the subjects did—or what was done to them—during the investigation. Sometimes an author will even include a verbatim account of instructions given to the subjects.

It should be remembered that the Method section is included so as to permit a reader to replicate a study. To accomplish this desirable goal, the author must outline clearly the procedures that were followed, providing answers to questions such as these: Where was the study conducted? Who conducted the study? In what sequence did events take place? Did any of the subjects drop out prior to the study's completion? (In Chapter 5, we will see that subject dropout can cause the results to be distorted.)

Excerpt 1.7 is the Procedures section of our model article. As you read the two paragraphs of this excerpt, ask yourself whether the authors have provided enough information to allow you to set up and conduct the same study. Of course, to do this you would need to go back and reconsider the other parts of the Method section.

RESULTS

There are three ways in which the results of an empirical investigation will be reported. First, the results can be presented within the text of the article—that

---

Excerpt 1.7 Procedures

PROCEDURES

GPAs of the 79 students for previous academic courses at the university were ranked and divided into five levels. From each of these levels, students were randomly assigned into one of three groups: 28 to an active treatment group, 28 into an inactive treatment (placebo) group, and 23 to a no treatment group. Students in the control condition were told that if beneficial effects were found, they would have the opportunity to use a tape during the next semester. Students did not know to which treatment group they were assigned, nor did the instructors of the classes. After collection of the data, six students were eliminated for the following reasons: (a) four for insufficient number of reported listening hours, (b) one for failure to take the required final exam, and (c) and one for unavailability of the student's GPA. The groups then had 25, 26, and 22 students.

During the 6th week of the semester, a cassette player and Joe Land Tape #23 or a placebo tape were distributed with instructions on how to use the materials. At the beginning of the 11th week of the semester this tape was collected, and Tape #27 and another placebo tape were distributed for use during the remaining 5 weeks of the semester prior to final examinations. In the 4th and 8th week of the experiment, students brought the tape players to the class where the heads were cleaned and demagnetized to ensure maximum performance. Students were required to keep log sheets for recording the number of hours of listening and any activities in which they were involved while listening. These logs were collected weekly. At the end of the 10 weeks, students returned the tapes and players and completed a questionnaire requesting follow-up information regarding their participation in the study.

Source: T. G. Russell, W. Rowe, and A. D. Smouse. (1991). Subliminal self-help tapes and academic achievement: An evaluation. *Journal of Counseling and Development, 69,* p. 360.

---

is, with only words. Second, they can be summarized in one or more tables. Third, the findings can be displayed by means of a graph (which is technically called a **figure**). Not infrequently, a combination of these mechanisms for reporting results is used to help readers gain a more complete understanding of how the study turned out. In Excerpt 1.8, we see that the authors of our model article presented their results by means of two paragraphs of text and one table.

Although the **Results** section of a journal article contains some of the most crucial information about the study (if not *the* most crucial information), readers of the professional literature often disregard it. They do this because the typical Results section is loaded with statistical terms and notation not used in everyday communication. Accordingly, many readers of technical research reports simply skip the Results section because it seems as if it came from another planet.

Excerpt 1.8 Results

RESULTS

A 3 × 5 randomized block design was used for analysis in this study with five levels of GPA and three treatment conditions. Separate analyses of variance performed for the primary dependent variable (final exam score) and for the secondary variable (semester grade point average) revealed no significant treatment main effect or interaction effect. As might be expected, significant effects were found on the blocked variable (level of GPA): for final exams $F(4, 58) = 4.42$, $p < .005$; for semester GPA: $F(4, 58) = 12.62$, $p < .001$. Table 1 provides information on the means and standard deviations for the analysis of the primary and secondary dependent variables.

Although the distributor of the subliminal tapes recommended a minimum program exposure of 20 to 25 hours before expecting significant results, participants had been asked to try to listen to the tapes about 10 hours per week. A minimum of 50 hours was required during the 10-week period in order to exceed the marketer's recommendation. In order to obtain an accurate estimate of the real listening times, after the study was completed students were asked to give a best estimate of the amount of time they actually had played the tapes—in terms of a percentage of what was listed on their time logs. The mean reported was 80.8% for the active treatment group and 84.6% for the inactive treatment group. After adjusting the hours reported on the time logs by each participant's estimated percentage of real listening time, the treatment group mean was revised to 123.4 hours (range = 67 to 285) and the inactive treatment group mean became 121.4 (range = 60 to 254). The remaining questions on the questionnaire regarding perceived inconvenience and anticipated help from the tapes showed no apparent differences between groups.

(Continued)

Excerpt 1.8 Results *(Continued)*

Table 1

Means and Standard Deviations for Final Examination Scores and Semester GPAs

	Final Examination Score M and (SD)			Semester GPA M and (SD)		
GPA level	Treatment	Placebo	Control	Treatment	Placebo	Control
4.00–3.16	85.0	82.8	80.8	3.46	3.26	3.43
	(5.4)	(4.6)	(8.9)	(.38)	(.54)	(.44)
3.15–2.61	70.2	76.8	74.8	3.15	2.72	3.20
	(3.7)	(5.7)	(7.4)	(.50)	(1.00)	(.62)
2.60–2.25	75.0	72.8	73.2	2.29	2.43	1.98
	(10.1)	(2.3)	(7.8)	(.41)	(.31)	(.70)
2.24–1.80	76.2	70.8	74.0	2.88	3.12	2.73
	(6.8)	(11.3)	(5.4)	(.81)	(.64)	(.61)
1.79–0.00	74.2	75.2	70.0	1.78	2.37	1.75
	(9.7)	(12.8)	(3.7)	(.38)	(.95)	(.53)
Total	75.9	75.6	74.6	2.74	2.81	2.62
	(8.5)	(8.6)	(7.3)	(.75)	(.76)	(.86)

Source: T. G. Russell, W. Rowe, and A. D. Smouse. (1991). Subliminal self-help tapes and academic achievement: An evaluation. *Journal of Counseling and Development, 69,* pp. 360–361.

If you are to function as a discerning "consumer" of journal articles, you must develop the ability to read, understand, and evaluate the results provided by authors. Those who choose not to do this are forced into the unfortunate position of uncritical acceptance of the printed word. Researchers are human, however, and they make mistakes. Unfortunately, the reviewers who serve on editorial boards do not catch all of these errors. As a consequence, there sometimes will be an inconsistency between the results discussed in the text of the article and the results presented in the tables. At times, a researcher will use an inappropriate statistical test. More often than you would suspect, the conclusions drawn from the statistical results will extend far beyond the realistic limits of the actual data that were collected.

We believe that you do not have to be a sophisticated mathematician in order to understand and evaluate the Results section of most journal articles. However, you must become familiar with the terminology, symbols, and logic used by researchers. The major part of this text was written to help you do just this.

Look at Excerpt 1.8 once again. The first paragraph of this section of the article is literally packed with information that is intended to help you. Unfortunately, many readers miss out on the opportunity to receive this information because they lack the skills needed to decode what is being communicated and/or are intimidated by statistical presentations. One of our goals in this book is to help readers acquire (or refine) their decoding skills. In doing this, we hope to show that there is no reason for anyone to be intimidated by what is included in technical research reports.

After reading a few chapters of this text, we are confident that you will be able to decipher easily all of the information presented in Excerpt 1.8. The term *3 × 5 randomized block design* (in the excerpt's first sentence) is clarified in Chapter 14, as are the concepts of levels and treatment conditions. *Analyses of variance* (see the second sentence) are dealt with in Chapters 11–17, and within Chapter 14 you will discover exactly what is meant by the terms *main effect* and *interaction effect*. The notion of *significant effects* (see the beginning of the third sentence) is addressed in Chapter 7. By the end of Chapter 8, you will understand fully what the authors are saying (see the end of their third sentence) when they report that $F(4, 58) = 4.42$, $p < .005$ and $F(4, 58) = 12.62$, $p < .001$. And the concepts of *means* and *standard deviations* (see the fourth sentence and Table 1) are covered in Chapter 2.

DISCUSSION

The Results section of a journal article contains a technical report of how the statistical analyses turned out, while the **Discussion** section is usually devoted to a nontechnical interpretation of the results. In other words, the author will normally use the Discussion section to explain what the results mean in regard to the central purpose of the study. The statement of purpose, which appears near the beginning of the article, usually contains an underlying or obvious research question; the Discussion section ought to provide a direct answer to that question.

In addition to telling us what the results mean, many authors use this section of the article to explain *why* they think the results turned out the way they did. Although such a discussion will occasionally be found in articles where the data support the researcher's hunches, authors are much more inclined to point out possible reasons for the obtained results when those results are inconsistent with their expectations. If one or more of the scores turn out to be highly different from the rest, the researcher may talk about such serendipitous findings in the Discussion section.

Sometimes an author will use the Discussion section to suggest ideas for further research studies. Even if the results do not turn out the way the researcher had hoped they would, the study may be quite worthwhile in that it might stimulate the researcher (and others) to identify new types of studies that need to be conducted. Although this form of discussion is more typically associated with unpublished master's theses and doctoral dissertations, you will occasionally encounter it in a journal article.

It should be noted that some authors use the term **Conclusion** to label this part of the journal article rather than the term *Discussion*. These two terms are used interchangeably. It is unusual, therefore, to find an article that contains both a Discussion section and a Conclusion section.

Excerpt 1.9 contains the Discussion section that appeared in our model journal article. Notice that the first paragraph constitutes a nontechnical ex-

---

Excerpt 1.9 Discussion

DISCUSSION

The idea that subliminal messages will effortlessly change one's behavior is obviously appealing, but the results of this investigation do not support the claims made for the effectiveness of subliminal audiotapes. When college students listened to these commercially prepared tapes with subliminal affirmations purported to improve academic achievement, no differences were found between their performance and that of students receiving a placebo treatment or students in a control condition with respect to either course final examination scores or grade point average earned that semester. These findings lend further support to Moore's (1988) recent observation that "there is no evidence that subliminal messages can influence motivation or complex behavior" (p. 293).

Some potential experimental problems that could be thought to have obscured positive results relate to (a) the motivation of the participants and (b) the sensitivity of the measures used for academic achievement. The motivation of the students can be estimated by their willingness to participate as volunteers in the project and in their commitment to the time involved in playing the tapes. It seems reasonable to assume the participants were indeed motivated: they listened to the tapes, did not find the activity objectionable, and indicated that they thought participation would help "somewhat." And the other concern, that there might be an effect too small to be detected by the measures used, seems to lack practical significance since the grade one receives can be considered the ultimate arbiter of utility.

Recently, Merikle (1988) attempted to establish if in fact marketed subliminal audiocassettes contained detectable subliminal stimuli. In his spectrographic analysis of tapes marketed by four different companies, no evidence was found to indicate that embedded speech was within the background sounds. It should be noted that the tapes produced by the Joe Land Company were not evaluated by Merikle. That issue aside, the claim being tested here is whether the tapes had

(Continued)

Excerpt 1.9 Discussion *(Continued)*

a useful effect, not whether messages were present. The company's claim that the messages were present was accepted.

Thus, the intent of this study was to provide a direct assessment of the marketing claims of commercially prepared subliminal self-help tapes. The fact that no positive effect was detected is useful information for counselors and other mental health specialists as a basis for their recommendations regarding the effectiveness of this type of self-help material for improving academic achievement. Moreover, when counselors are approached for information with respect to self-help tapes, they may now use that opportunity to provide the client with sound alternatives for academic improvement such as increasing study- and time-management skills.

One testable explanation for the anecdotal reports of success with subliminal tapes is that of a placebo effect occasioned by belief and high motivation. If the degree of motivation and belief found in persons who purchase such materials could be reproduced or observed in persons under controlled conditions, the possible effects of placebo tapes could be ascertained. A more practical approach might be to compare directly the efficacy of subliminal tapes with commercially available tapes with audible messages.

In conclusion, assuming the tapes do contain subliminal messages as indicated by the company, the results of this study fail to support the use of subliminal tapes for academic improvement. And, given the lack of research supporting marketing claims and the reluctance of most manufacturers to distributors to support any evaluation of the products being marketed, an equally skeptical view of subliminal tapes targeting other behaviors may well be justified.

Source: T. G. Russell, W. Rowe, and A. D. Smouse. (1991). Subliminal self-help tapes and academic achievement: An evaluation. *Journal of Counseling and Development, 69,* pp. 360–361.

planation of the results. In the next two paragraphs, the authors deal with possible explanations of why their study produced the results it did. In the fourth paragraph, we encounter a brief discussion of why the authors believe their investigation has value and the particular individuals who can benefit from the findings. The fifth paragraph focuses on possible studies that would build upon the one reported here. The last paragraph contains a single-sentence summary of the study's major finding; then, a general warning is offered to readers based upon the specific findings derived from this investigation.

REFERENCES

A journal article normally concludes with a list of the books, journal articles, and other source material referred to by the author. Most of these items were probably mentioned by the author in the review of the literature positioned near the beginning of the article. Excerpt 1.10 is the **References** section of our model article.

The references can be very helpful to you if you want to know more about the particular study you are reading. Journal articles and convention presentations are usually designed to cover one particular study or a narrowly defined area of a subject. Unlike more extended writings (e.g., monographs and books), they include only a portion of the background information and only

---

Excerpt 1.10 References

REFERENCES

Becker, H. (1979, September). Secret voices. *Time, 71.*

Borgeat, F., & Goulet, J. (1983). Psychophysiological changes following auditory subliminal suggestions for activation and deactivation. *Perceptual and Motor Skills, 56,* 759–766.

Dillingham, S. (1987, September 14). Inaudible messages making a noise. *Insight,* pp. 44–45.

Dixon, N. F. (1986). On private events and brain events. *The Behavioral and Brain Sciences, 9,* 29–30.

Eriksen, C. W. (1960). Discrimination and learning without awareness: A methodological survey and evaluation. *Psychological Review, 67,* 279–300.

Holender, D. (1986). Semantic activation without conscious identification in dichotic listening, parafoveal vision, and visual masking: A survey and appraisal. *The Behavioral and Brain Sciences, 9,* 1–66.

Kaser, V. A. (1986). The effects of an auditory subliminal message upon the production of images and dreams. *Journal of Nervous and Mental Disease, 174,* 397–407.

Key, W. B. (1973). *Subliminal seduction.* Englewood Cliffs, NJ: Prentice-Hall.

Levine, A. (1986, February). The great subliminal self-help hoax. *New Age Journal,* 48–51, 80–81.

McConnell, J. V. (1989). Reinvention of subliminal perception. *The Skeptical Inquirer, 13,* 427–428.

McConnell, J. V., Cutler, R. L., & McNeil, E. B. (1958). Subliminal stimulation: An overview. *American Psychologist, 13,* 229–242.

Merikle, P. M. (1988). Subliminal auditory messages: An evaluation. *Psychology and Marketing, 5,* 297–316.

Moore, T. E. (1988). The case against subliminal manipulation. *Psychology and Marketing, 5,* 355–372.

Packard, V. (1957/1981). *The hidden persuaders.* New York: Pocket Books.

(Continued)

Excerpt 1.10 References *(Continued)*

Treimer, M., & Simonson, M. R. (1986, January). *Old wine in new bottles: Subliminal messages in instructional media.* Paper presented at the meeting of the Association for Educational Communications Technology, Las Vegas, NV. (ERIC Document Reproduction Service No. ED 267796).

Vokey, J. R., & Read, J. D. (1985). Subliminal messages: Between the devil and the media. *American Psychologist, 40,* 1231–1239.

Zanot, E. J., Pincus, S. D., & Lamp, E. J. (1983). Public perceptions of subliminal advertising. *Journal of Advertising, 12*(1), 39–45.

Zenhausern, R., & Hansen, K. (1974). Differential effect of subliminal and supraliminal accessory stimulation on task components in problem-solving. *Perceptual and Motor Skills, 38,* 375–378.

Source: T. G. Russell, W. Rowe, and A. D. Smouse. (1991). Subliminal self-help tapes and academic achievement: An evaluation. *Journal of Counseling and Development, 69,* pp. 361–362.

partial descriptions of related studies that would aid the reader's comprehension of the study. Reading books and articles listed in the References section will provide you with some of this information and probably give you a clearer understanding as to why and how the author conducted the particular study you have just read. Before hunting down any particular reference item, it is a good idea to look back into the article to reread the sentence or paragraph containing the original citation. This will give you an idea of what is in each reference item.

REVIEW TERMS

Abstract	Participants
Discussion	Procedure
Figure	References
Materials	Results
Method	Subject

REVIEW QUESTIONS

1. Where is the abstract usually found in a journal article, and what type of information is normally contained in the abstract?

2. What information does the author usually talk about immediately following the review of the literature?

3. What is the abbreviation for the term *subjects*?

4. Should an author take time to explain how the subjects were obtained?

5. If an author has done a good job of writing the Method section of the article, what should the reader of the article be able to do?

6. If a researcher compared the IQ scores of 100 boys with the IQ scores of 100 girls, what would this researcher's dependent variable be?

7. What are three forms in which an author can present the results of the statistical analyses?

8. Will a nontechnical interpretation of the results usually be found in the Results section of the article or in the Discussion section?

9. Why doesn't a summary usually appear at the end of the article?

10. What is the technical name for the bibliography that appears at the end of an article?

11. If an article is published, can we assume that it is free of mistakes?

12. Whereas the authors of our model article used the term *Participants* to label the Method section's first paragraph (see Excerpt 1.4), what other one-word label could they have used?

13. Look at Table 1 of our model article (see Excerpt 1.8). The final three columns are labeled "Semester GPA *M* and (*SD*)." What do the abbreviations *M* and *SD* stand for?

14. Should the authors of the model journal article presented in this chapter be commended or should they be criticized for distinguishing between their two dependent variables by saying that one was primary while the other was secondary?

15. Look again at these six parts of the model article: the first and next-to-last sentences of the abstract (see Excerpt 1.1), the last sentence of the statement of purpose (see Excerpt 1.2), the second sentence of the Results section (see Excerpt 1.8), the second sentence in the first paragraph of the Discussion (see Excerpt 1.9), and the first sentence of the last paragraph of the Discussion (again, see Excerpt 1.9). With respect to this study's purpose and findings, how many of these six sentences are consistent with each other?

DESCRIPTIVE STATISTICS: THE UNIVARIATE CASE

We will consider in this chapter descriptive techniques designed to summarize data on a single dependent variable. These techniques are often said to be **univariate** in nature because only one variable is involved. (In Chapter 3, we will look at several techniques designed for the **bivariate** case—that is, for situations where data have been collected on two dependent variables.)

We begin this chapter by looking at several ways data can be summarized using pictures. These so-called picture techniques include frequency distributions, stem-and-leaf displays, histograms, frequency polygons, and pie graphs. Next, the topic of distributional shape is considered; here, we will clarify what it means when a data set is said to be normal, skewed, bimodal, or rectangular. After that, we examine the concept of central tendency and various methods used to represent a data set's average score. We then turn our attention to how researchers usually summarize the variability, or spread, within their data sets; these techniques include four different kinds of range, the standard deviation, and the variance. Finally, we consider two kinds of standard scores: z and T.

PICTURE TECHNIQUES

In this section, we consider some techniques for summarizing data that produce a picture of the data. We use the term *picture* somewhat loosely, since the first technique really leads to a table of numbers. In any event, we begin our discussion of descriptive statistics by looking at three kinds of frequency distributions.

A **frequency distribution** shows how many subjects were similar in the sense that, measured on the dependent variable, they ended up in the same category or had the same score. Three kinds of frequency distributions are often seen in published journal articles: simple (or ungrouped) frequency distributions, grouped frequency distributions, and cumulative frequency distributions.

To help us in our discussion of frequency distributions, suppose a 100-point examination is administered to 48 students. The results of this test might resemble the data in Table 2.1.

TABLE 2.1

SCORES OBTAINED ON A 100-POINT EXAM

82	90	84	89	92	90	85	76
89	82	76	86	87	83	82	88
78	74	91	93	84	79	87	84
87	79	87	81	80	74	95	85
90	92	83	72	91	93	88	88
81	85	86	85	87	88	89	84

With the data in this form, it is quite difficult to get an accurate feel for how the class performed. In Table 2.2, we see how frequency distributions make it easy for us to understand the nature of our set of scores.

On the left side of Table 2.2, we see a **simple** (or **ungrouped**) **frequency distribution** of the 48 exam scores. The right side displays a **grouped frequency distribution** for the same data. In each case, the number in the right-hand column indicates how many (that is, the frequency, abbreviated f) individuals had an exam score equal to the value(s) specified in the left-hand column. Thus, the simple frequency distribution shows that 4 individuals earned an exam score of 84, whereas the grouped frequency distribution shows that 7 test-takers ended up with a score between 81 and 83. In each frequency distribution, the number at the bottom of the f column is simply the sum of all the frequencies. That total frequency, usually labeled N, tells us how many subjects were measured.

In Excerpt 2.1, we see an example of a simple frequency distribution. Note how easy it is to get a sense for the ages of the 135 subjects involved in that study. Also note how the third column, showing the percentage of subjects of any given age, allows us to tell quickly that one-third of the subjects were 9 years old.

In Excerpt 2.2, we see an example of how frequency distributions can help us understand the characteristics of a group relative to some categorical

TABLE 2.2 SIMPLE AND GROUPED FREQUENCY DISTRIBUTIONS

Score	f	Interval	f
95	1	93–95	3
94	0	90–92	7
93	2	87–89	14
92	2	84–86	8
91	0	81–83	·7
90	4	78–80	4
89	3	75–77	2
88	4	72–74	2
87	7	69–71	1
86	1	$N = 48$	
85	3		
84	4		
83	2		
82	3		
81	2		
80	1		
79	2		
78	1		
77	0		
76	2		
75	0		
74	2		
73	0		
72	0		
71	0		
70	1		
$N = 48$			

(rather than numerical) variable of interest. Here, instead of finding the left-hand column labeled *score* (as in Table 2.2) or *age* (as in Excerpt 2.1), we see that the variable of interest was the country from which children returned a questionnaire. Excerpt 2.2 also illustrates how two frequency distributions can be combined into one table.

In Excerpt 2.3, we see an example of how a grouped frequency distribution can help us understand better the characteristics of the subjects involved in a study. In this investigation, there were really four groups of subjects; the age distributions for all four of these groups were combined into one table.

Excerpt 2.1 Simple Frequency Distribution

Of the 135 children who participated in the study, 58 were males and 77 were females. . . . Seventy-one were ages 3 to 8 and 64 were ages 9 to 12 (see Table 1).

Table 1

Subjects by Age, $N = 135$

Age	Frequency	Percent
3	1	.7
4	1	.7
5	6	4.4
6	16	11.9
7	25	18.5
8	22	16.3
9	45	33.3
10	13	9.6
11	4	3.0
12	2	1.5

Source: K. B. Barchard and C. A. Atkins. (1991). Children's decisions about naughtiness and punishment: Dominance of expiatory punishments. *Journal of Research in Childhood Education, 5*(2), p. 112.

Excerpt 2.2 Simple Frequency Distribution for a Qualitative Variable

The resulting pool of data included returns for 10- and 13-year-olds from each of the 15 countries except Panama, which did not return data on 13-year-olds. The Institute for Educational Research in Denmark had used the instrument in its own independent study of the functions of reading with relatively large samples of students (Allerup, 1985). From these returns, a random sample of 300 questionnaires was selected from each age level. At this point, we had a pool of data from a total of 3,574 students from 15 countries. This pool of data was subjected to statistical analysis, and weights were applied for each country to correct for over- or under-sampling. Cases with missing values were eliminated from the analysis, reducing the sample size to 3,050. Table 5 summarizes the final samples from each country on which all analyses are based.

(Continued)

Excerpt 2.2 Simple Frequency Distribution for
a Qualitative Variable *(Continued)*

Table 5

**Number of Questionnaires Returned
from Children in 15 Countries**

Country	Age 10	Age 13
Australia	118	118
Austria	142	182
Bahamas	130	21
Canada	122	212
Denmark	154	146
India	120	120
Ireland	141	132
Israel	55	82
Japan	128	126
Nigeria	109	132
Panama	169	0
Philippines	125	84
Thailand	133	160
United States	108	133
Uruguay	115	57
Total	1,869	1,705

Source: V. Greaney and S. B. Newman. (1990). The functions of reading: A cross-cultural perspective. *Reading Research Quarterly, 25*(3), p. 183.

The variable of interest here is age, with each interval (except the lowest and highest) set up to span 5-year categories. Notice how this grouped frequency distribution is compact (requiring only nine rows). If the data had been summarized using an ungrouped frequency distribution, at least 34 rows would have been required and it would have been much more difficult to sense quickly the age distribution of each group.

In addition to simple and grouped frequency distributions, **cumulative frequency distributions** sometimes appear in journal articles. With this kind of summarizing technique, a researcher tells us, through an additional column of numbers labeled *cumulative frequency,* how many subjects ended up with any given score *and all other lower scores* (or how many subjects ended up in a given score interval *and all other lower intervals*). This kind of frequency distribution is shown in Excerpt 2.4, except cumulative percentages are presented rather

Excerpt 2.3 Grouped Frequency Distribution

The age and sex profile of the study subjects is reported in Table 1. The higher ratio of controls to cases in the under–50 age stratum reflects the fact that cases of gallbladder and bile duct cancer that were excluded from this analysis were generally younger than the pancreatic cancer cases.

Table 1

Numbers of study subjects: Adelaide, Australia, pancreatic cancer study, 1984–1987

| Age | *Males* | | *Females* | |
	Cases	*Controls*	*Cases*	*Controls*
<50	1	18	2	17
50–54	6	10	1	5
55–59	5	22	3	10
60–64	7	26	6	11
65–69	6	24	12	21
70–74	13	20	17	32
75–79	10	20	9	10
≥80	4	2	2	5
All ages	52	142	52	111

Source: P. A. Baghurst, A. J. McMichael, A. H. Slavotinek, K. I. Baghurst, D. Boyle, and A. M. Walker. (1991). A case-control study of diet and cancer of the pancreas. *American Journal of Epidemiology,* *134*(2), p. 167.

than cumulative frequencies. Notice how the cumulative percentage of 20.97 can be obtained by adding together 9.68 and 11.29 for the score intervals 0–19.99 and 20–39.99 (or by adding the frequencies for these two intervals, dividing the sum by 62, and then multiplying by 100); thus, 20.97 percent of the full group of subjects had scores between 0 and 39.99. From these cumulative percents, it is easy to see that about three-fourths of the scores fell between 0 and 79.99.

STEM–AND–LEAF DISPLAYS

Although a grouped frequency distribution provides information about the scores in a data set, it carries with it the limitation of "loss of information." The frequencies tell us how many data points fell into each interval of the score continuum but they do not indicate, within any interval, how large or

Excerpt 2.4 Cumulative Frequency Distribution

Table 3

Composite Customer Relations Scores

Score	Frequency	Percent	Cumulative %
0–19.99	6	9.68	9.68
20.00–39.99	7	11.29	20.97
40.00–59.99	22	35.48	56.45
60.00–79.99	12	19.35	75.81
80.00–99.99	12	19.35	95.16
100.00–160.00	3	4.84	100.00
Totals	$n = 62$	100.00	

Mean score = 58.31 (median = 56.35); SD = 24.64; Low score = 7.68; High score = 110.98.

Source: C. L. Martin. (1990). The employee/customer interface: An empirical investigation of employee behaviors and customer perceptions. *Journal of Sport Management, 4*(1), p. 12.

small the scores were. Hence, when researchers summarize their data by moving from a set of raw scores to a grouped frequency distribution, the precision of the original scores is lost.

A **stem-and-leaf display** is like a grouped frequency distribution that contains no loss of information. To achieve this objective, the researcher first sets up score intervals on the left side of a vertical line. These intervals, collectively called the "stem," are presented in a coded fashion by showing all but the last digit of the scores falling into each interval. Then, to the right of the vertical line, the final digit is given for each observed score that fell into the interval being focused upon. An example of a stem-and-leaf display is presented in Excerpt 2.5.

In the top row of this stem-and-leaf display, there is a 10 on the left (stem) side and a 0 on the right (leaf) side. This indicates that there was one score, a 100, within the interval represented by this row of the display. The bottom row has three digits on the leaf side, and this indicates that three scores fell into this row's interval. Using both stem and leaf from this bottom row, we see that those three scores were 27, 27, and 29. All other rows of our stem-and-leaf display are interpreted in the same way.

Notice that the actual attitude scores obtained by the 43 subjects in Excerpt 2.5 show up in the stem-and-leaf display. There is, therefore, no loss of information. Take another look at Excerpt 2.3 or Excerpt 2.4, where we presented grouped frequency distributions. Because of the loss of informa-

Excerpt 2.5 A Stem-and-Leaf Display

The 1990 McCall, Belli, and Madjidi Statistics Attitude Scale was administered to 43 postgraduate education students in Transkei at the end of a course on re-search methodology. . . . The distribution of attitude scores is shown by the stem-and-leaf plot in Table 4.

Table 4

Frequency Distribution of Attitude Scores

```
10 | 0
 9 | 2  3  6
 8 | 0  1  2  3  6  9
 7 | 0  0  1  3  3  5  8  8  9  9
 6 | 0  2  2
 5 | 0  2  4  5  7  9  9
 4 | 0  1  2  3  9
 3 | 0  3  4  6  8
 2 | 7  7  9
```

Source: G. Glencross and V. I. Cherian. (1992). Attitudes toward applied statistics of postgraduate ed-ucation students in Transkei. *Psychological Reports, 70,* p. 72. © *Psychological Reports.*

tion associated with grouped frequency distributions, you cannot tell what the highest and lowest earned scores were, what specific scores fell into any interval, or whether "gaps" exist inside any intervals (as was the case in Excerpt 2.5 because no student ended up with any score from 63 to 69).

HISTOGRAMS AND BAR GRAPHS

In a **histogram,** vertical columns (or thin lines) are used to indicate how many times any given score appears in the data set. With this picture tech-nique, the baseline (that is, the horizontal axis) is labeled to correspond with observed scores on the dependent variable while the vertical axis is labeled with frequencies.[1] Then, columns (or lines) are positioned above each base-line value to indicate how often each of these scores was observed. Whereas a tall bar indicates a high frequency of occurrence, a short bar indicates that the baseline score turned up infrequently.

A **bar graph** is almost identical to a histogram in both form and purpose. The only difference between these two techniques for summarizing data

---

[1] *Technically speaking, the horizontal and vertical axes of any graph are called the abscissa and ordinate, respectively.*

concerns the nature of the dependent variable that defines the baseline. In a histogram, the horizontal axis is labeled with numerical values that represent a quantitative variable. In contrast, the horizontal axis of a bar graph represents different categories of a qualitative variable. In a bar graph, the ordering of the columns is quite arbitrary, whereas the ordering of the columns in a histogram must be numerically logical.

In Excerpt 2.6, we see an example of a histogram. Notice how this graph allows us to discern quickly the age at intake of the children focused upon in these studies. Also notice that the columns must be arranged as was done (because the variable age is clearly quantitative).

Excerpt 2.6 Example of a Histogram

DEMOGRAPHIC CHARACTERISTICS

The age of the school refusing children at intake ranged from 7 to 17 years, with a mean age of 13.5 (SD = 2.4). A histogram depicting the age at intake (see Fig. 1) reveals that the peak age range for referral of this problem to the clinic is from 13 years to 15 years, 11 months. Some elevation also was noted at age 10, but before this age very few cases were assessed, despite the fact that the clinic accepts referrals for children from the age of 5. Of course, these data do not permit conclusions regarding the age distribution of school refusal in general (which only would be possible from an epidemiological sample); however, they do provide information regarding the age at which children are *referred* for clinical services.

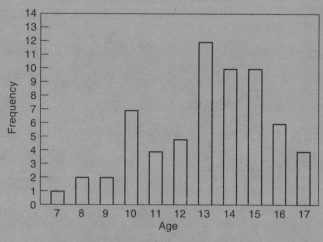

Figure 1 *Age at intake for school refusing children.*

Source: C. G. Last and C. C. Strauss. (1990). School refusal in anxiety-disordered children and adolescents. *Journal of the American Academy of Child and Adolescent Psychiatry, 29*(1), p. 32.

An example of a bar graph is presented in Excerpt 2.7. Here, the order of the bars is completely arbitrary, since the variable—type-of-skin-irritation— is qualitative in nature.

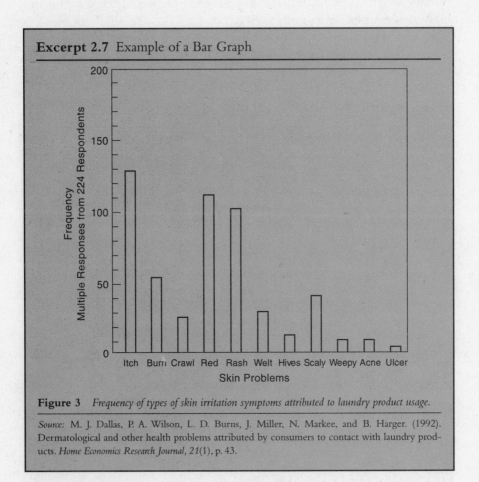

Excerpt 2.7 Example of a Bar Graph

Figure 3 *Frequency of types of skin irritation symptoms attributed to laundry product usage.*

Source: M. J. Dallas, P. A. Wilson, L. D. Burns, J. Miller, N. Markee, and B. Harger. (1992). Dermatological and other health problems attributed by consumers to contact with laundry products. *Home Economics Research Journal, 21*(1), p. 43.

FREQUENCY POLYGONS

A **frequency polygon** is the technical name for what many people refer to as a line graph. As in a histogram, this picture technique for summarizing data has a horizontal axis that is labeled with individual scores or score intervals, along with a vertical axis that is labeled with frequencies (or sometimes percents). With a frequency polygon, however, each bar is replaced with a single dot positioned where the top of the bar would have been located. Then, adjacent dots are connected with straight lines to form the final graph.

In Figure 2.1, we have built a frequency polygon for the hypothetical set of 48 examination scores presented in Tables 2.1 and 2.2. Notice how this

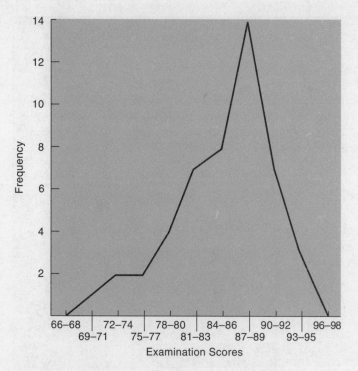

FIGURE 2.1 *Frequency polygon for the data in Tables 2.1 and 2.2.*

picture allows one to discern quickly that most of the examinees scored between 78 and 92, although three ended up in the 93–95 interval while one examinee fell into the 69–71 interval. Also notice that (1) the left and right ends of this line graph have been "tied down" to the baseline (at the interval immediately to the left of the lowest one into which scores actually fell, 69–71, and at the interval immediately to the right of the 93–95 interval), and (2) the horizontal axis is divided so as to permit our frequency polygon to fill the two-dimensional space created by the two axes.

PIE GRAPHS

A **pie graph**[2] represents an easy-to-understand way of showing how a full group is made up of subgroups—and also of showing the relative size of the subgroups. An example of a pie graph is included in Excerpt 2.8. Here, as in all pie graphs, the size of each "slice" of the pie indicates the relative size of the particular subgroup represented by that portion of the circle. Because of this feature of pie graphs, one can look at Excerpt 2.8 and quickly determine

---

[2]*Some authors refer to this particular picture technique as a pie chart or as a circle graph.*

Excerpt 2.8 Example of a Pie Graph

Our fourth question about drug use was the most general and was included mainly for comparison to the more specific questions that preceded it. Personnel managers were asked how their company's "drug problem" compared to that of other firms (see Figure 2). Not surprisingly, most of the respondents felt their organization's drug problem was either less severe than others, or about average (51% and 43%, respectively).

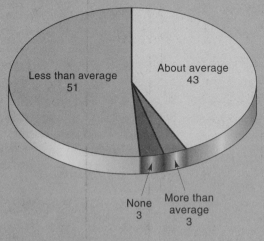

Figure 2 *Relative size of a firm's drug problems.*

Source: J. G. Rosse, D. F. Crown, and H. D. Feldman. (1990). Alternative solutions to the workplace drug problem: Results of a survey of personnel managers. *Journal of Employment Counseling, 27*(2), p. 63.

that about half of the personnel managers indicated that their company's drug problems were less than average in severity, that a very small percentage indicated having no drug problems, and that an equally small percentage indicated having more-than-average drug problems.

DISTRIBUTIONAL SHAPE

If researchers always summarized their quantitative data using one of the picture techniques we have just covered, then you could *see* whether the observed scores tended to congregate at one (or more) points along the score continuum. Moreover, a frequency distribution, a stem-and-leaf display, a histogram, or a frequency polygon would allow you to tell whether a researcher's data were symmetrical. To illustrate this nice feature of the picture techniques we have discussed, take another look at Excerpt 2.1. The frequency distribution for the 135 subjects shows nicely that (1) most subjects were clustered in the 6–10 age range and (2) the distribution of ages was not symmetrical but rather "strung out" toward the young end of the continuum.

Unfortunately, pictures of data sets do not appear in journal articles very often because they are costly to prepare and because they take up lots of space. By using some verbal descriptors, however, researchers can tell their readers what their data sets look like. To decipher such messages, you must understand the meaning of a few terms that researchers use to describe the **distributional shape** of their data.

If the scores in a data set take the form of a **normal distribution,** most of the scores will be clustered near the middle of the continuum of observed scores, and there will be a gradual and symmetrical decrease in frequency in both directions away from the middle area of scores. Data sets that are normally distributed are said to resemble a bell-shaped curve, since a side drawing of a bell will start out low on either side and then bulge upwards in the center. (If, in Excerpt 2.1, the frequencies for the 8- and 9-year-olds had been reversed, the distribution of ages would have been roughly normal.)

In **skewed distributions,** most of the scores end up being high (or low), with a small percentage of scores strung out in one direction away from the majority. Skewed distributions, consequently, are not symmetrical. If the "tail" of the distribution (formed by the small percentage of scores that is strung out in one direction) points toward the upper end of the score continuum, the distribution is said to be **positively skewed;** if the tail points toward the lower end of the score continuum, the term **negatively skewed** applies. The histogram that we looked at in Excerpt 2.6 provides a good example of a negatively skewed distribution.[3]

If the scores tend to congregate around more than one point along the score continuum, the distribution is said to be **multimodal** in nature. If there are two such places where scores are grouped together, we could be more specific and say that the data are distributed in a **bimodal** fashion. (In the grouped frequency distributions that you looked at earlier in Excerpt 2.3, the ages for the female controls illustrate a bimodal distribution.) If scores are congregated at three distinct points, the term **trimodal** would come into play.[4]

If scores are fairly evenly distributed along the score continuum without any clustering at all, then this kind of data set is said to be **rectangular.** To see

---

[3]*Following the dictionary definition of skew as "more developed on one side or in one direction than another," certain authors say that a distribution of scores is skewed toward the low end of the scale if most scores are low (or skewed toward the high end of the scale if most scores are high). This alternative notion of skewed, which focuses on the bulk of the data points rather than the minority that form the tail, appeared on page 87 of a November 1990 article published in the* British Journal of Educational Psychology *and on page A–608 of a September 1990 article published in the* American Industrial Hygiene Association Journal.

[4]*Distributions having just one "hump" are said to be unimodal in nature.*

an example of a real data set that illustrates this kind of distributional shape, take another look at Excerpt 2.3, and focus on the 142 male controls.

In Excerpts 2.9–2.11, we see a few examples of how researchers will sometimes go out of their way to describe the distributional shape of their data sets. Such researchers should be commended for indicating what their data sets looked like, because these descriptions help others to understand the nature of the data that have been collected.

Excerpts 2.9–2.11 Comments from Authors as to the Distributional Shape of Their Data Sets

---

The distribution of facial babyishness and attractiveness were each examined separately for male and female faces. Males' and females' facial babyishness ratings were both normally distributed. . . . Male attractiveness was also normally distributed . . . and female attractiveness was normally distributed.

Source: D. S. Berry. (1991). Attractive faces are not all created equal: Joint effects of facial babyishness and attractiveness on social perception. *Personality and Social Psychology Bulletin, 17*(5), p. 525.

The TRS was administered to several different samples of Educational Psychology students at a large midwestern university ($N = 211$) to collect normative data. The resulting distribution of the total scores was a very slightly positively skewed normal distribution.

Source: E. T. Dowd, C. R. Milne, and S. L. Wise. (1991). The therapeutic reactance scale: A measure of psychological reactance. *Journal of Counseling and Development, 69,* p. 544.

Statistical analysis of the distribution indicated that it was nonnormal, and visual inspection of pain tolerance times suggested that subjects were distributed in a bimodal fashion.

Source: M. E. Geisser, M. E. Robinson, and W. E. Pickren. (1992). Differences in cognitive coping strategies among pain-sensitive and pain-tolerant individuals on the cold-pressor test. *Behavior Therapy, 23,* p. 38.

As we have seen, two features of distributional shape are modality and skewness. A third feature is related to the concept of **kurtosis**. This third way of looking at distributional shape deals with the possibility that a set of scores can be nonnormal even though there is only one mode and even though there is no skewness in the data. This is possible because there may be an unusually large number of scores at the center of the distribution, thus causing the distribution to be overly peaked. Or, the "hump" in the middle of the distribution may be smaller than is the case in normal distributions, with both tails being "thicker" than in the famous bell-shaped curve.

When the concept of kurtosis is discussed in research reports, you may encounter the terms **leptokurtic** and **platykurtic.** These terms denote distributional shapes that are more peaked and less peaked (as compared with the normal distribution), respectively. The term **mesokurtic** signifies a distributional shape that is neither overly peaked or overly flat. Although you may come across one of these three terms, it is more likely that you will see kurtosis referred to by means of a numerical value. This is the case because computers can easily quantify the peakedness associated with any set of data being analyzed.

In Excerpts 2.12 and 2.13, we see examples of how researchers usually discuss the notion of kurtosis when describing a data set's distributional shape. In Excerpt 2.12, the kurtosis index was -0.14; in Excerpt 2.13, kurtosis was measured to be $-.084$. Because these values were close to 0 (the "benchmark" amount of kurtosis in a normal distribution), neither distribution was considered to be nonnormal. Each distribution, however, was slightly platykurtic (as indicated by the negative value of the kurtosis index).

Excerpts 2.12–2.13 Quantifying the Degree of Kurtosis (and Skewness)

Kurtosis and skew were, respectively, -0.14 and 0.62, suggesting a relatively normal distribution.

Source: J. Briere, D. Henschel, and K. Smiljanich. (1992). Attitudes toward sexual abuse: Sex differences and construct validity. *Journal of Research in Personality, 26*(4), p. 401.

The distribution of reading vocabulary scores under the standard condition was rather normal in shape (skewness $= .24$; kurtosis $= -.084$).

Source: A. Barona and S. I. Pfeifer. (1992). Effects of test administration procedures and acculturation level on achievement scores. *Journal of Psychoeducational Assessment, 10*(2), p. 128.

Excerpts 2.12 and 2.13 also illustrate how the degree of skewness in a data set can be quantified. It should be no surprise that negatively skewed distributions produce negative values of the skewness index while positively skewed distributions produce positive values.

When researchers quantify the degree of kurtosis or skewness within their data sets, approximate normality is generally considered to exist if the kurtosis and skewness indices are not more than 1.0 away from 0. If a data set is found to be grossly nonnormal, the researcher may opt to do further analysis of the data using statistical procedures created for the nonnormal case. Or, the data can be "normalized" by means of a formula that revises the value of each score such that the revised data set represents a closer approximation to the normal.

MEASURES OF CENTRAL TENDENCY

To help readers get a feel for the data that have been collected, researchers almost always say something about the typical or representative score in the group. They do this by computing and reporting one or more **measures of central tendency**. There are three such measures that are frequently seen in the published literature, each of which provides a numerical index of the **average** score in the distribution.

THE MODE, MEDIAN, AND MEAN

The **mode** is simply the most frequently occurring score. For example, given the nine scores 6, 2, 5, 1, 2, 9, 3, 6, and 2, the mode is equal to 2. The **median** is the number that lies at the midpoint of the distribution of earned scores; it divides the distribution into two equally large parts. For the set of nine scores just presented, the median is equal to 3. Four of the nine scores are smaller than 3; four are larger.[5] The **mean** is the point that minimizes the collective distances of scores from that point. It is found by dividing the sum of the scores by the number of scores in the data set. Thus, for the group of nine scores presented above, the mean is equal to 4.

In journal articles, authors sometimes use abbreviations or symbols when referring to their measure(s) of central tendency. The abbreviations "Mo" and "Mdn," of course, correspond to the mode and median, respectively. The letter M always stands for the mean, even though all three measures of central tendency begin with this letter. The mean is also symbolized by $\overline{X}$ and μ.

In many research reports, the numerical value of only one measure of central tendency is provided. (That was the case with the model journal article presented in Chapter 1; take a look at Excerpt 1.8 to see which one was used.) Because it is not unusual for a real data set to be like our sample set of nine scores in that the mode, median, and mean assume different numerical values, researchers sometimes compute and report two measures of central tendency, or all three, so as to help readers understand better the data being summarized.

In Excerpts 2.14 and 2.15, we see cases where two measures of central tendency were reported for the same data set. Excerpt 2.16 contains an example where the mode and the median and the mean were provided.

THE RELATIVE POSITION OF THE MODE, MEDIAN, AND MEAN

In a true normal distribution (or in any unimodal distribution that is perfectly symmetrical), the values of the mode, median, and mean will be identical.

---

[5] *When there is an even number of scores, the median is a number halfway between the two middle scores (once the scores are ordered from low to high). For example, if 9 is omitted from our sample set of scores, the median for the remaining eight scores would be 2.5—that is, the number halfway between 2 and 3.*

Excerpts 2.14–2.16 Reporting Multiple Measures of Central Tendency for the Same Data Set

---

Respondents lived in households containing from 2 to 23 people ($M = 6.77$; Mdn $= 6.0$), virtually evenly split between males ($M = 3.46$; Mdn $= 3.0$) and females ($M = 3.31$; Mdn $= 3.0$). The number of children in the households ranged from 0 to 9 ($M = 3.02$; Mdn $= 2.5$).

Source: R. B. Ruback and J. Pamdey. (1991). Crowding, perceived control, and relative power: An analysis of households in India. *Journal of Applied Social Psychology, 21*(4), p. 325.

Of the 43 subjects who completed the intervention phase of the study, 58.1% were male. The mean age was 23.1 years ($SD = 4.5$, Range $= 18.35$, Mode $= 19$ years).

Source: D. R. Kivalahan, G. A. Marlatt, K. Fromme, D. B. Coppel, and E. Williams. (1990). Secondary prevention with college drinkers: Evaluation of an alcohol skills training program. *Journal of Consulting and Clinical Psychology, 58,* p. 806.

Table 1

Descriptive Statistics for Speech Intelligibility Measures

Speech Intelligibility	Range	Mode	Median	Mean	S.D.
IsolWords	0–25	1	6	10.4	9.7
IntellWords	0–412	0	6	39.6	69.6
IntellUtts	0–34	0	0	4.3	6.6
Articulation	3–58	24	24	27.3	15.2
Nonsegmentals	0–8	0	2	3.2	3.2
Syll/Utt	0–23	3	4	5.0	4.1
LingComp	0–6	0	1	2.1	2.2

Note. The speech intelligibility measures are: number of isolated words (IsolWords), number of intelligible words (IntellWords), number of intelligible utterances (IntellUtts), number of phoneme and phoneme clusters (Articulation), number of nonsegmental features (Nonseg), average number of syllables per utterance (Syl/Utt), linguistic complexity (LingComp).

Source: C. R. Musselman. (1990). The relationship between measures of hearing loss and speech intelligibility in young deaf children. *Journal of Childhood Communication Disorders, 13*(2), p. 198.

Such distributions are rarely seen, however. In the data sets typically found in applied research studies, these three measures of central tendency assume different values. As a reader of research reports, you should know not only that this happens but also how the distributional shape of the data affects the relative position of the mode, median, and mean.

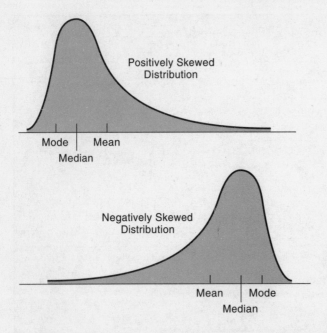

FIGURE 2.2 *Location of the mean, median, and mode in skewed distributions.*

In a positively skewed distribution, a few scores are strung out toward the high end of the score continuum, thus forming a "tail" that points to the right. In this kind of distribution, the modal score ends up being the lowest (that is, positioned farthest to the left along the horizontal axis) while the mean ends up assuming the highest value (that is, positioned farthest to the right). In negatively skewed distributions, just the opposite happens; the mode ends up being located farthest to the right along the baseline while the mean assumes the lowest value. In Figure 2.2, we see a picture showing where these three measures of central tendency are positioned in skewed distributions.

After you examine Figure 2.2, return to Table 2.2 or Figure 2.1, where we summarized the 48 scores from our hypothetical group of examinees. By looking at this data set's grouped frequency distribution or frequency polygon, you will notice that the scores are strung out slightly toward the low end of the score continuum. Because the data set has a slight negative skew, the mode, median, and mean assume the values that are only slightly different: 87, 86.5, and 85, respectively.

To see a case where the three measures of central tendency turned out to be highly dissimilar, thus implying dramatic skewness in the data, take another look at Excerpt 2.16 and focus your attention on the top row of information.

In this excerpt, the dependent variable corresponding to the top row of the table is "IsolWords" (that is, isolated words), and for this particular measure of speech intelligibility, the mode, median, and mean turned out equal to 1, 6, and 10.4, respectively. Because of this arrangement of the three measures of central tendency, you can tell that the data on isolated words were positively skewed.

In a bimodal distribution, there will be two points along the score continuum where scores tend to "pile up." If the distribution is symmetrical, the mean and median will be located halfway between the two modes. In a symmetrical trimodal distribution, the median and mean will assume a value equal to the middle of the three modes. Real data sets, however, rarely produce symmetrical bimodal or trimodal distributions. Any asymmetry (that is, skewness) will cause the median to be pulled "off center" toward the side of the distribution that has the longer tail—and the mean will be pulled even farther in that direction.

With full-fledged rectangular distributions, the mean and median will assume a value halfway between the high and low data points. In such distributions, there is no mode because all earned scores occur with equal frequency. If the distribution turns out to be only roughly rectangular, the median and mean will be located close together (and close to the halfway point between the high and low scores), but the mode could end up anywhere.

Other Measures of Central Tendency

Although the mode, median, and mean are the most popular measures of central tendency, there are other techniques for summarizing the average score in a data set. (Examples include the geometric mean and the harmonic mean.) Since these indices are rarely seen in research reports, they will not be discussed here. If you take an advanced course in statistics, however, we are confident that you will encounter these alternative methods for computing an average score.

Measures of Variability

Descriptions of a data set's distributional shape and reports as to the central tendency value(s) help us to understand better the nature of data collected by a researcher. Although terms (e.g., "roughly normal") and numbers (e.g., $M = 67.1$) help, they are not sufficient. To get a true feel for the data that have been collected, we also need to be told something about the variability among the scores. Let us consider now the standard ways that researchers summarize this aspect of their data sets.

THE MEANING OF VARIABILITY

Most groups of scores possess some degree of variability. That is, at least some of the scores differ (vary) from one another. A **measure of variability** simply indicates the degree of this **dispersion** among the set of scores. If the scores are very similar, there is little dispersion and little variability. If the scores are very dissimilar, there is a high degree of dispersion (variability). In short, a measure of variability does nothing more than indicate how spread out the scores are.

The term *variability* can also be used to pinpoint where a group of scores might fall on an imaginary homogeneous-heterogeneous continuum. If the scores are similar, they are **homogeneous** (and have low variability). If the scores are dissimilar, they are **heterogeneous** (and have high variability).

Even though a measure of central tendency provides a numerical index of the average score in a group, we need to know the variability of the scores to better understand the entire group of scores. For example, consider the following two groups of IQ scores:

Group I	Group II
102	128
99	78
103	93
96	101

In both groups the mean IQ is equal to 100. Although the two groups have the same mean score, their variability is obviously different. While the scores in the first group are very homogeneous (low variability), the scores in the second group are far more heterogeneous (high variability).

The specific measures of variability that we will now discuss are similar in that the numerical index will be zero if all of the scores in the data set are identical, a small positive number if the scores vary to a small degree, or a large positive number if there is a great deal of dispersion among the scores. (No measure of variability, no matter how computed, can ever turn out equal to a negative value.)

THE RANGE, INTERQUARTILE RANGE, SEMI-INTERQUARTILE RANGE, AND BOX PLOT

The **range** is the simplest measure of variability. It is the difference between the lowest and highest scores. For example, in Group I of the example just considered, the range is equal to 103–96, or 7. The range is usually reported by citing the extreme scores, but sometimes it is reported as the difference between the high and low scores. When providing information about the range to their readers, authors normally will write out the word *range*. Occasionally, however, this first measure of variability is abbreviated as *R*.

To see how the range can be helpful when we try to understand a researcher's data, take another look at Excerpt 2.14. If the respondents in that study had been described only by means and medians, readers probably would have misunderstood the characteristics of the 167 couples who were interviewed. With respect to the number of children per household, ask yourself what image would have come to mind as to the respondent group if you had been given only the mean and median.

Whereas the range provides an index of dispersion among the full group of scores, the **interquartile range** indicates how much spread exists among the middle 50 percent of the scores. Like the range, the interquartile range is defined as the distance between a low score and a high score; these two indices of dispersion differ, however, in that the former is based upon the high and low scores within the full group of data points whereas the latter is based upon only *half* of the data—the middle half.

In any group of scores, the numerical value that separates the top 25 percent scores from the bottom 75 percent scores is the upper **quartile** (symbolized by Q_3). Conversely, the numerical value that separates the bottom 25 percent scores from the top 75 percent scores is the lower quartile (Q_1).[6] The interquartile range is simply the distance between Q_3 and Q_1. Stated differently, the interquartile range is the distance between the 75th and 25th percentile points.

In Excerpt 2.17, we see an example of the interquartile range being used in an actual research study. The information presented here indicates that the 20 subjects who received the BRM manipulation produced preferences scores having the largest difference between Q_3 and Q_1 at the "immediately after" time. We also see that the distance between Q_3 and Q_1 remained stable for the 20 subjects who received the CRM manipulation.

Sometimes, a researcher will compute the **semi-interquartile range** to index the amount of dispersion among a group of scores. As you would guess on the basis of its name, this measure of variability is simply equal to one-half the size of the interquartile range. In other words, the semi-interquartile range is nothing more than $(Q_3 - Q_1)/2$.

With a **box-and-whisker plot**, the degree of variability within a data set is summarized using a picture. To accomplish this objective, a rectangle ("box") is drawn above a horizontal line labeled so as to correspond to scores on the dependent variable. The left and right sides of the rectangle are determined by Q_1 and Q_3, the lower and upper quartile points. On the outside of the rectangle,

---

[6] *The middle quartile, Q_2, divides any group of scores into upper and lower halves. Accordingly, Q_2 is always equal to the median.*

Excerpt 2.17 The Interquartile Range

Table 2

Medians and Interquartile Ranges (IQR) of Preference Scores for Selected Manipulated Activities by Type of Manipulation and Time of Ranking

| | Time of ranking | | | | | |
| | Before | | Immediately after | | After 2 weeks | |
Manipulation	Mdn	IQR	Mdn	IQR	Mdn	IQR
CRM (n = 20)	2.5	1.0	1.0	1.0	1.5	1.0
BRM (n = 20)	2.5	1.0	3.0	2.0	3.0	1.0
NTC, 2nd choice (n = 10)	2.0	0.0	1.5	1.5	2.0	1.5
NTC, 3rd choice (n = 10)	3.0	0.0	3.0	0.5	3.0	0.5

Note: CRM = cognitive restructuring manipulation; BRM = behavior reinforcement manipulation; NTC = no-treatment control.

Source: A. Barak, S. Shiloh, and O. Haushner. (1992). Modification of interests through cognitive restructuring: Test of a theoretical model in preschool children. *Journal of Counseling Psychology, 39*(4), p. 493.

two horizontal lines, called "whiskers" are drawn. The left line extends from Q_1 to the point that corresponds to the 10th percentile while the right line extends from Q_3 to the point that corresponds to the 90th percentile.

In Excerpt 2.18, we see a case where six box-and-whisker plots were included in a journal article. Because each rectangle's width corresponds to the interquartile range (while the distance between the whisker's end points corresponds to the range within which the middle 80 percent of the scores were located), it is easy to see the variability among the households that were measured. The dependent variable in this study was the concentration of nitrogen dioxide, and each home was measured in three rooms (kitchen, activity room, and bedroom). The box-and-whisker plots show that the homes without a gas stove or kerosene heater were far more homogeneous than were the homes that contained either of these major indoor nitrogen dioxide sources. Moreover, among the homes that did have a gas stove or a kerosene heater, there was far more dispersion among the kitchens than among the activity rooms or among the bedrooms.

Excerpt 2.18 Box-and-Whisker Plot

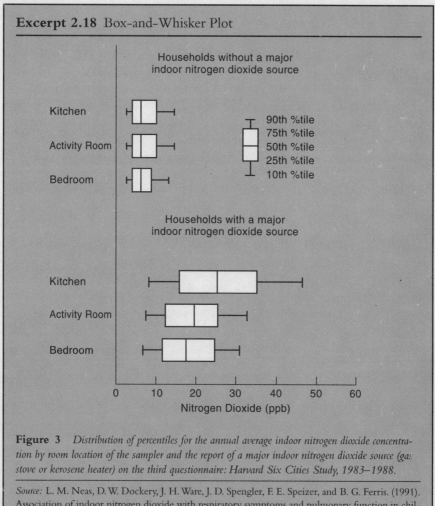

Figure 3 *Distribution of percentiles for the annual average indoor nitrogen dioxide concentration by room location of the sampler and the report of a major indoor nitrogen dioxide source (gas stove or kerosene heater) on the third questionnaire: Harvard Six Cities Study, 1983–1988.*

Source: L. M. Neas, D. W. Dockery, J. H. Ware, J. D. Spengler, F. E. Speizer, and B. G. Ferris. (1991). Association of indoor nitrogen dioxide with respiratory symptoms and pulmonary function in chil-

Although box-and-whisker plots are designed to communicate information about variability, they also reveal things about central tendency and distributional shape. Within the rectangle, a vertical line is positioned so as to correspond to Q_2, the median. If this median line appears in the center of the box and if the whiskers are of equal lengths, then we can infer that the distribution of scores is probably symmetrical. On the other hand, the median will end up off-center and the whiskers will be of unequal lengths in skewed distributions. (If the median is on the left side of the box, while the right whisker is longer, the distribution is positively skewed; conversely, negatively skewed distributions cause the median line to be on the right side of the box and the left whisker to be longer.)

STANDARD DEVIATION AND VARIANCE

Two additional indices of dispersion, the **standard deviation** and the **variance**, are usually better indices of dispersion than are the first three measures of variability that we have considered. This is due to the fact that the standard deviation and variance are each based upon all of the scores in a group (and not just the high and low scores or the upper and lower quartile points). The standard deviation is determined by (1) figuring how much each score deviates from the mean and (2) putting these deviation scores into a computational formula. The variance is found by squaring the value of the standard deviation.

In reporting their standard deviations, authors may employ the abbreviation *SD*, utilize the symbols *s* or σ, or simply write out the word **sigma**. Occasionally, authors will report the standard deviation using a "plus-and-minus" format—for example, 14.83 ± 2.51, where the first number (14.83) stands for the mean and the second number (2.51) stands for the standard deviation. The variance, being the square of the standard deviation, is symbolized as s^2 or σ^2.

Excerpts 2.19–2.20 illustrate two alternative ways authors often report information about the standard deviation within the text of their articles. In one of these articles, the abbreviation *SD* was used; in the other, the standard deviation

---

Excerpts 2.19–2.20 Reporting on the Standard Deviation within the Article's Text

---

Among the criterion group (TRC counselors) in our study, the number of actions taken varied from 4 to 14, with a mean of 9.0 actions (SD = 2.98). Among the undergraduate rehabilitation students, the number of actions taken varied from 2 to 17, with a mean of 9.21 (SD = 3.85). The number of actions taken by the graduate rehabilitation counseling students varied from 3 to 11, with a mean of 6.69 (SD = 2.5). It seemed that the undergraduates had greater variation in the number of actions taken than did the graduate students or the criterion group.

Source: C. Mecaskey, F. Chan, D. W. Wong, H. J. Parker, H. S. Carter, and C. S. Lam. (1989). Evaluating clinical problem-solving skills through computer simulations. *Journal of Rehabilitation*, July, August, September, p. 37.

The subject population consisted of 36 normal, healthy males whose age was 25.8 ± 3.4 years (range, 21 to 35 years), height was 181.3 ± 5.1 cm (range, 172 to 195 cm), and weight was 78.3 ± 10.8 kg (range, 56.7 to 113.4 kg). Based on the side used for handwriting and throwing, 34 of the subjects were right upper extremity dominant and 2 were left upper extremity dominant.

Source: J. C. Otis, R. F. Warren, S. I. Backus, T. J. Santner, and J. D. Mabrey. (1990). Torque production in the shoulder of the normal young adult male: The interaction of function, dominance, joint angle, and angular velocity. *American Journal of Sports Medicine, 18*(2), p. 120.

is presented beside the mean using the plus-and-minus reporting strategy. Notice how the last sentence in the first of these excerpts focuses on the concept of variability. (The larger the standard deviation, the greater the dispersion.)

Excerpt 2.21 shows how the standard deviation is sometimes symbolized as *s*. Based on the reported standard deviations, we can see that the 31 experimental subjects were far more homogeneous on the immediate posttest than they were on the pretest (7.13 versus 26.59); in contrast, the dispersion among the 22 control subjects decreased only slightly from the first to the second testing (22.60 versus 20.83).

Excerpt 2.21 Reporting on the Standard Deviation Within a Table

Table 1

Mean and Standard Deviation of Absolute Errors (in Newtons) for Experimental and Control Groups

	Pretest		Immediate posttest		Follow-up posttest	
Group	$\overline{X}$	s	$\overline{X}$	s	$\overline{X}$	s
Control (n = 22)	23.01	22.60	21.71	20.83	16.44	12.46
Experimental (n = 31)	32.46	26.59	9.61	7.13	10.40	8.59

Source: M. Lee, A. Moseley, and K. Refshauge. (1990). Effect of feedback on learning a vertebral joint mobilization skill. *Physical Therapy, 70*(2), p. 97.

Although the standard deviation appears in research reports far more often than does the variance, we occasionally come across this latter measure of variability. In Excerpts 2.22–2.23, we provide two illustrations of how the variance sometimes will appear in journal articles.

Before concluding our discussion of the standard deviation and variance, we would like to offer a helpful hint concerning how to make sense out of these two indices of variability. Simply stated, we suggest using an article's reported standard deviation (or variance) to estimate what the range of scores probably was. Because the range is such a simple concept, the standard deviation or variance can be demystified by converting it into an estimated range.

To make a standard deviation interpretable, just multiply the reported value of this measure of variability by 4 to obtain your guess as to what the range of scores most likely was. Thus, if an author reports that the standard deviation for a group of scores is equal to 3, you should estimate that the distance between

Excerpts 2.22–2.23 Examples Showing the Variance Being Used to Summarize Dispersion

To provide a context for discussion of mood variability and intensity, and to test hypotheses about levels of energy and restlessness, average levels of these constructs were examined. The mean levels for each mood composite, and for energy and restlessness, were calculated by averaging each girl's daily reports for the month. Variability of each mood was defined as the variance of each girl's daily mood composite over the month. Similarly, the variance of each girl's energy and restlessness composites over the month was used to indicate variability on these measures.

Source: C. M. Buchanan. (1991). Pubertal status in early adolescent girls: Relations to mood, energy, and restlessness. *Journal of Early Adolescent Girls, 11*(2), p. 191.

It was hypothesized that subjects adopting a behavioral prediction goal would display greater perceptual variability than impression formation subjects. . . . Orthogonal comparisons showed no difference in the variance of the perceptions of the control ($SD^2 = .67$) and the behavior prediction groups ($SD^2 = .93$). . . . Both of these groups, however, differed significantly from the impression-set group ($SD^2 = .29$). . . . [A]s expected, these latter subjects' perceptions showed the least amount of variability. This lack of variability in the impression formation group's perceptions provides further support for the notion that this goal resulted in a consolidation of interpersonal perceptions early in the interaction.

Source: K. Matheson, J. G. Holmes, and C. M. Kristiansen. (1991). Observational goals and the integration of trait perceptions and behavior: Behavioral prediction versus impression formation. *Journal of Experimental Social Psychology, 27*, p. 154.

the high and low scores is equal to about 12. To see how nicely this simple technique works, go back to Excerpts 2.15 and 2.16 and compare the results of your estimates with the actual ranges that are reported. Of course, if the variance is presented in the journal article, you must first take the square root (to obtain the standard deviation), then multiply by 4 to get an estimated range.[7]

OTHER MEASURES OF VARIABILITY

Of the five measures of variability discussed so far, we encounter the range and the standard deviation most often when reading research-based journal articles. We come across fewer examples of the interquartile range, the semi-

---

[7]*The procedure of multiplying by 4 works fairly well for groups that contain anywhere between 30 and 60 scores. To obtain reasonably accurate estimates with smaller or larger groups, multiply the standard deviation by 3 when N is smaller than 30, or by 5 when N is larger than 60. With tiny (N<5) or enormous (N>1000) groups, multiply by 2 or 6, respectively.*

interquartile range, and the variance. Once in a great while, we encounter some other measure of dispersion. This is what occurred when we saw the material contained in Excerpt 2.24. We doubt that you will see many examples of the wage dispersion index in your reading. Nevertheless, we wanted you to see a concrete example of an infrequently used measure of variability. More important, we wanted you to be aware of the fact that with any measure of variability (including the wage dispersion index), homogeneous groups produce small indices of variability while heterogeneous groups cause the variability index to be a big number.

Excerpt 2.24 Example of an Infrequently Used Measure of Variability

Table 2

Dispersion in Salaries within Public and Private Sectors in 1985

	United States	Sweden
Central/federal government	129	27
Industry/salaried	137	34

The wage dispersion index is computed by subtracting the earnings of the tenth percentile of the workforce from the earnings of the ninetieth percentile, dividing the difference by the median earnings and multiplying the dividend by 100.

$$\frac{P_{90} - P_{10}}{\text{Median}} \times 100$$

Sources: U.S. Office of Personnel Management, *Federal Civilian Work Force Statistics: Pay Structure of the Federal Civil Service,* various years, Table II; Statistics Sweden, Löneutvecklingen 1973–1985 (Stockholm: Statistics Sweden, 1987); U.S. Census, *Current Population Reports* (Series P–60, No 146, Table 5).

Source: L. R. Wise. (1990). Social equity in civil service systems. *Public Administration Review, 50*(5), p. 57. Reprinted with permission by the American Society for Public Administration (ASPA), 1120 G Street NW, Suite 700, Washington, D.C. 20005. All rights reserved.

STANDARD SCORES

All of the techniques covered thus far in this chapter describe features of the entire data set. In other words, the focus of attention is on all N scores whenever a researcher summarizes a group of numbers by using one of the available picture techniques, a word or number that reveals the distributional shape, a numerical index of central tendency, or a quantification of the amount of dispersion that exists among the scores. Sometimes, however, researchers want to focus their attention on a single score within the group rather than on the full data set. When they do this, they usually convert the raw score being examined into a **standard score.**

Although many different kinds of standard scores have been developed over the years, the ones used most frequently in research studies are called **z-scores** and **T-scores.** These two standard scores are identical in that each one indicates how many standard deviations a particular raw score lies above or below the group mean. In other words, the numerical value of the standard deviation is first looked upon as defining the length of an imaginary "yardstick," with that yardstick then used to measure the distance between the group mean and the individual score being considered. For example, if you and several other people took a test that produced scores having a mean of 40 and a standard deviation of 8, and if your score on this test happened to be 52, you would be one and one-half "yardsticks" above the mean.

The two standard scores used most by researchers—z-scores and T-scores—perform exactly the same function. The only difference between them concerns the arbitrary values given to the new mean score and the length of the yardstick within the revised data set following conversion of one or more raw scores into standard scores. With z-scores, the mean is fixed at zero and the yardstick's length is set equal to 1. As a consequence, a z-score directly provides an answer to the question, "How many SDs is a given score above or below the mean?" Thus a z-score of $+2.0$ indicates that the person being focused upon was 2 standard deviations above the group mean. Likewise, a z-score of -1.2 for someone else indicates that this person scored 1.2 standard deviations below the mean. A z-score close to 0, of course, would indicate that the original raw score was near the group mean.

With T-scores, the original raw score mean and standard deviation are converted to 50 and 10, respectively. Thus, a person whose raw score positioned him or her two standard deviations above the mean would receive a T-score of 70. Someone else positioned 1.2 standard deviations below the mean would end up with a T-score of 38. And someone whose raw score was near the group mean would have a T-score near 50.

Although researchers typically apply their statistical procedures to the raw scores that have been collected, they occasionally will convert the original scores into z-scores or T-scores. Excerpts 2.25 and 2.26 provide evidence that these two standard scores are sometimes referred to in research summaries.

A FEW CAUTIONS

Before concluding this chapter, we want to alert you to the fact that two of the terms discussed earlier in this chapter are occasionally used by researchers who define them differently than we have. These two terms are *skewed* and

Excerpts 2.25–2.26 Standard Scores

Children's status as popular, rejected, controversial, and average was assessed by the Coie et al. (1982) peer nomination technique. . . . This procedure required children to nominate from a class roster three children they like most and three children they liked least. . . . The number of nominations for like most (LM) and liked least (LL) were summed for each child and standardized within each classroom. Social preference (SP) z scores were derived by subtracting LL z scores from LM z scores (SP = LM − LL). . . . Popular children had SP z scores > 1.00, LM z scores > 1.00, and LL z scores < 0.

Source: F. M. Gresham and D. Stuart. (1992). Stability of sociometric assessments: Implications for uses as selection and outcome measures in social skills training. *Journal of School Psychology, 30*(3), p. 226.

The SDQ-I, which is designed for use in grades 4 through 6, consists of 76 items that respondents rate according to how true the statement is for them. These items comprise eight subscales. . . . Standard scores (*T* scores) with means of 50 and standard deviations of 10 are provided for the subscales and three total scale scores (i.e., Total Academic, Total Nonacademic, and Total Self).

Source: R. R. Delugach, B. A. Bracken, M. J. Bracken, and M. C. Schicke. (1992). Self concept: Multidimensional construct exploration. *Psychology in the Schools, 29*, p. 215.

quartile. We want to prepare you for the alternative meanings associated with these two concepts.

Regarding the term *skewed,* a few researchers use this word to describe a complete data set that is "out of the ordinary." Used in this way, the term has nothing to do with the notion of distributional shape but instead is synonymous to the term *anomaly.* In Excerpt 2.27, we see an example of how the word *skewed* was used in this fashion.

Excerpt 2.27 Use of the Term *Skewed* to Designate an Anomaly

The sample is clearly skewed. It is more educated, holds higher occupations, is more Catholic, and is racially more white than the United States as a whole. The sample has only one Black, two Hispanic, and one Asian couple. The remainder consider themselves white, though a slight majority of these express a strongly felt ethnic identity. Catholics represent 77 percent of the sample, with 16 percent being Protestant.

Source: C. T. Brockman and Y. Peterson. (1990). Marital gift giving communication. *Free Inquiry in Creative Sociology, 18*(1), p. 30.

The formal, statistical definition of *quartile* is "one of three points that divide a group of scores into four subgroups, each of which contains 25 percent of the full group." Certain researchers use the term *quartile* to designate the subgroups themselves. In this usage there are four quartiles (not three), with scores falling in the quartiles. Excerpt 2.28 provides an example of *quartile* being used in this fashion.

Excerpt 2.28 Use of the Term *Quartile* to Designate the Four
Subgroups

In the extreme groups analysis, narcissism emerged as a more decisive discriminating variable ($t = -.250, p < .05$), with couples in the lowest quartile receiving significantly higher narcissism scores than couples in the highest quartile.

Source: M. Gerson, J. Posner, and A. M. Morris. (1991). The wish for a child in couples eager, disinterested, and conflicted about having children. *The American Journal of Family Therapy, 19*(4), p. 338.

REVIEW TERMS

Average	Multimodal
Bar graph	Negatively skewed
Bimodal	Normal distribution
Bivariate	Pie graph
Box-and-whisker plot	Platykurtic
Cumulative frequency distribution	Positively skewed
Dispersion	Quartile
Distributional Shape	Range
Frequency polygon	Rectangular
Grouped frequency distribution	Semi-interquartile range
Heterogeneous	Sigma
Histogram	Simple frequency distribution
Homogeneous	Skewed distribution
Interquartile range	Standard deviation
Kurtosis	Standard score
Leptokurtic	Stem-and-leaf display
Mean	*T*-score
Measure of central tendency	Trimodal
Measure of variability	Ungrouped frequency distribution
Median	Univariate
Mesokurtic	Variance
Mode	*z*-score

REVIEW QUESTIONS

1. What does each of the following symbols or abbreviations stand for: N, $\overline{X}$, s, Mdn., Q_3, SD, R, σ, Q_2, s^2, Q_1, σ^2, μ?

2. If a cumulative frequency distribution had been used to summarize the data in Excerpt 2.1, what would the cumulative frequency be for age 6?

3. If each of several people from your town were asked to indicate his or her favorite radio station, and if the data were summarized using a picture containing vertical columns to indicate how many people voted for each radio station, what would we call this picture technique for summarizing the data?

4. Look at the fifth row of numbers in the table presented in Excerpt 2.16. Based on the information provided, what term would you use to describe the distributional shape of the "nonsegmentals"?

5. In Excerpt 2.1, what is the mode equal to?

6. (True or False) In any data set, the median is equal to the score value that lies halfway between the low and high scores.

7. Why would it be difficult to compute the range of the ages of the 52 male cases shown in Excerpt 2.3?

8. Why can't we talk about the distributional shape of the data presented in Excerpt 2.7?

9. If the variance for a set of scores is equal to 9, how large is the standard deviation for those data?

10. If the standard deviation for a set of 30 scores is equal to 5, how much greater would you estimate the highest score is than the lowest score?

11. Which measure of variability is equal to the distance between the 25th and 75th percentile points?

12. If you were reading a journal article and came across the notation 62 ± 4.1, what would you know about the data set being summarized?

13. Which of these descriptive techniques would let you see each and every score in the researcher's data set: (a) grouped frequency distribution, (b) stem-and-leaf display, (c) box-and-whisker plot?

14. (True or False) The distance between the high and low scores in any data set can be determined by doubling the value of the interquartile range.

15. If a set of scores could not be summarized by any of the picture techniques discussed in this chapter, you still could get a good feel for the data set so long as you were given information concerning the data set's central tendency, variability, and _____.

BIVARIATE CORRELATIONS

In Chapter 2, we looked at the various statistical procedures that researchers use when they want to describe single-variable data sets. We saw examples where data on two or more variables were summarized, but in each of those cases the data were summarized one variable at a time. Although there are occasions when these univariate techniques permit researchers to describe their data sets, most empirical investigations involve questions that call for descriptive techniques that simultaneously summarize data on more than one variable.

In this chapter, we will consider situations where data on two variables have been collected and summarized, with interest residing in the relationship between the two variables. Not surprisingly, the statistical procedures that we will examine here are considered to be **bivariate** in nature. In a later chapter, we will consider techniques designed for situations wherein the researcher wishes to simultaneously summarize the relationships among three or more variables.

Three preliminary points are worth mentioning as we begin our effort to help you refine your skills at deciphering statistical summaries of bivariate data sets. First, the focus in this chapter will be on techniques that simply summarize the data. In other words, we are still dealing with statistical techniques that are fully descriptive in nature. Second, this chapter is similar to Chapter 2 in that we consider ways to summarize data that involve both picture and numerical indices. Finally, the material covered in the next chapter, Reliability and Validity, draws *heavily* on the information presented here. With these introductory points now behind us, let us turn to the central concept of this chapter, correlation.

THE KEY CONCEPT BEHIND CORRELATION: RELATIONSHIP

Imagine that a researcher measures each of nine families with respect to two variables: average daily phone use in the home (measured in minutes) and the number of teenagers within each family. The data for this imaginary group of families might turn out as follows:

Family	Average Daily Phone Use (Minutes)	Number of Teenagers
Abbott	75	2
Donatelli	100	3
Edwards	60	1
Franks	20	0
Kawasaki	70	2
Jones	120	4
Lopez	40	1
Meng	65	2
Smith	80	3

While it would be possible to look at each variable separately and say something about the central tendency, variability, and distributional shape of the nine scores (first for phone use, then for number of teenagers), the key concept of correlation requires that we look at the data on our two variables *simultaneously*. In doing this, we are trying to see (1) whether there is a **relationship** between the two sets of scores and (2) how strong or weak that relationship is, presuming that a relationship does in fact exist.

On a simple level, the basic question being dealt with by **correlation** can be answered in one of three possible ways. Within any bivariate data set, it *may* be the case that the high scores on the first variable tend to be paired with the high scores on the second variable (implying, of course, that low scores on the first variable tend to be paired with low scores on the second variable). We refer to this first possibility as the *high-high, low-low* case. The second possible answer to the basic correlational question represents the inverse of our first case. In other words, it *may* be the case that high scores on the first variable tend to be paired with low scores on the second variable (implying, of course, that low scores on the first variable tend to be paired with high scores on the second variable). Our shorthand summary phrase for this second possibility is *high-low, low-high*. Finally, it is possible that little systematic tendency exists in the data at all. In other words, it *may* be the case that some of the high and low scores on the first variable are paired with high scores on the second variable while other high and low scores on the first variable are paired with low scores on the second variable. We refer to this third possibility simply by the three-word phrase *little systematic tendency*.

As a check on whether we have been clear in the previous paragraph, take another look at the hypothetical data presented earlier on the number of teenagers and amount of phone use within each of nine families. More specifically, indicate how that bivariate relationship should be labeled. Does it deserve the label *high-high, low-low*? Or the label *high-low, low-high*? Or the label *little systematic tendency*? If you haven't done so already, look again at the data presented and formulate your answer to our question.

To discern the nature of the relationship between phone use and number of teenagers, one must first identify each variable's high and low scores. The top three values for the phone use variable are 120, 100, and 80, while the lowest three values in this same column are 60, 40, and 20. Within the second column, the top three values are 4, 3, and 3; the three lowest values are 1, 1, and 0. After identifying each variable's high and low scores, the next (and final) step is to look at both columns of data simultaneously and see which of the three answers to the basic correlational question fits the data. For our hypothetical data set, we clearly have a *high-high, low-low* situation, with the three largest phone-use values being paired with the three largest number-of-teenagers values and the three lowest values in either column being paired with the low values in the other column.

The method we have used to find out what kind of relationship describes our hypothetical data set is instructive, we hope, for anyone not familiar with the core concept of correlation. That strategy, however, is not very sophisticated. Moreover, you won't have a chance to use it very often because researchers will almost always summarize their bivariate data sets by means of pictures, a single numerical index, a descriptive phrase, or some combination of these three reporting techniques. Let us now turn our attention to these three methods for summarizing the nature and strength of bivariate relationships.

SCATTER DIAGRAMS

Like histograms, bar graphs, and frequency polygons, a **scatter diagram** has a horizontal axis and a vertical axis. These axes are labeled to correspond to the two variables involved in the correlational analysis. The abscissa is marked off numerically so as to accommodate the obtained scores collected by the researcher on the variable represented by the horizontal axis; in a similar fashion, the ordinate is labeled so as to accommodate the obtained scores on the other variable. (With correlation, the decision as to which variable is put on which axis is fully arbitrary; the nature of the relationship between the two variables will be revealed regardless of how the two axes are labeled.) After the axes are set up, the next step involves placing a dot into the scatter diagram for each object that was measured, with the horizontal and vertical positioning of each dot dictated by the scores earned by that object on the two variables involved in the study.

In Excerpt 3.1, we see a scatter diagram that reveals the relationship between two methods for assessing the anterior position of the tibia (relative to the femur) in 16 patients with deficient knees. Also presented are the actual measurements derived from the two assessment methods (arthrometry and

Excerpt 3.1 Raw Data and a Scatter Diagram

Patient number	Arthrometric measurement	Radiographic measurement
1	13.0	12.5
2	17.0	16.5
3	10.5	9.5
4	8.0	9.0
5	12.5	11.5
6	18.0	16.5
7	14.0	15.5
8	10.0	7.5
9	10.0	7.5
10	11.0	14.5
11	10.0	6.5
12	8.5	5.5
13	8.0	12.5
14	12.5	8.5
15	11.5	16.5
16	16.0	8.5

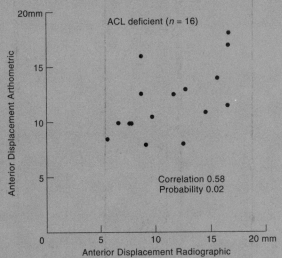

Figure 5 *Scattergram of anterior tibial position in ACL deficient knees as measured by arthrometry and by simultaneous radiography at 89 N. Patient under epidural anesthesia. Patient position supine, thigh supported, 20° of knee flexion. There was slight correlation (r = 0.58) of anterior position of the tibia as determined by arthrometric and radiographic measurements in 16 ACL deficient knees.*

Source: H. Staubli and R. P. Jakob. (1991). Anterior knee motion analysis. *American Journal of Sports Medicine, 19*(2), pp. 175–176.

radiography). The dot in the scatter diagram that is farthest to the left came from patient 12 whose scores were 8.5 and 5.5 (determined by the arthrometric and radiographic methods, respectively). Accordingly, that patient's dot was positioned 8.5 units high and 5.5 units to the right. Patient 6 is represented by the top right-hand dot in the scatter diagram; that dot was positioned by moving 18.0 units above the horizontal axis and 16.5 units to the right of the vertical axis. All other dots in this scatter diagram were positioned in a similar fashion.

A scatter diagram reveals the relationship between two variables through the pattern that is formed by the full set of dots. To discern what pattern exists, we use a simple (though not completely foolproof) two-step method. First, we draw an imaginary perimeter line, or "fence" around the full set of data points—and in so doing, we try to achieve a "tight fit." Second, we look at the shape produced by our perimeter line and examine its "tilt" and its "thickness." Depending on these two characteristics of the data set's scatter, we arrive at an answer to the basic correlational question concerning the nature and strength of the relationship between the two variables.

Consider once again the scatter diagram shown in Excerpt 3.1. Our perimeter line produces a rough oval that is tilted from lower-left to upper-right. Tilts going this direction imply a "high-high, low-low" relationship, whereas tilts going the opposite direction, from upper-left to lower-right, imply a "high-low, low-high" relationship. (In cases where there is no discernible tilt to the shape produced by the perimeter line, we conclude that there is little systematic tendency one way or the other.)

After establishing the tilt of the oval produced by our perimeter line, we then turn to the issue of the oval's thickness. If the oval is elongated and thin, then we conclude that there is a *strong* relationship between the two variables. On the other hand, if the oval is not too much longer than it is wide, then we conclude that a *weak* relationship exists. Considering one last time the scatter diagram in Excerpt 3.1, we feel that the thickness of the oval produced by the perimeter line around the 16 dots falls between these two extremes; accordingly, we feel that the term *moderate* best describes the strength of the relationship that is visually displayed. Combining the notions of tilt and thickness, we feel that the scatter diagram in Excerpt 3.1 reveals a moderate "high-high, low-low" correlation between the radiographic and arthrometric methods for assessing the anterior displacement of the tibia among these 16 patients.

THE CORRELATION COEFFICIENT

Although a scatter diagram has the clear advantage of showing the scores for each measured object on the two variables of interest, many journals are reluctant to publish such pictures because they take up large amounts of space. For that reason, and also because the interpretation of a scatter diagram involves an element of subjectivity, numerical summaries of bivariate relationships appear in research reports far more frequently than do pictorial summaries. The numerical summary is called a **correlation coefficient**.

Symbolized as *r*, a correlation coefficient is normally reported as a decimal number somewhere between −1.00 and +1.00. In Excerpt 3.2, we see an example of a researcher's data producing a correlation coefficient of −.65.

Excerpt 3.2 A Computed Correlation Coefficient

The means and standard deviations for the present sample were as follows: $M =$ 6.46, $SD = 14.6$, for the Scientist Scale, and $M = 65.4$, $SD = 20.4$, for the Practitioner Scale. These values are very similar to the SIU/OSU-sample means and standard deviations. The Scientist and Practitioner Scales were correlated at −.65.

Source: F. T. Leong, and P. Zachar. (1991). Development and validation of the Scientist-Practitioner Inventory for psychology. *Journal of Counseling Psychology, 38*(3), p. 337.

To facilitate our discussion of how to interpret correlation coefficients, we have drawn a straight horizontal line to represent the continuum of possible values that will result from researchers putting data into a correlational formula:

−1.00	0.00	+1.00

This correlational continuum will help us pin down the meaning of several adjectives that researchers use when talking about correlation coefficients and/or relationships: direct, high, indirect, inverse, low, moderate, negative, perfect, positive, strong, and weak.

First, consider the two halves of the correlational continuum. Any *r* that falls on the right side represents a **positive correlation**; this indicates a **direct relationship** between the two measured variables. (Earlier, we referred to such cases by the term "high–high, low-low.") On the other hand, any result that ends up on the left side is a **negative correlation**, and this indicates an **indirect**, or **inverse**, **relationship** (i.e., "high-low, low-high"). If *r* were to land on either end of our correlation continuum, the term **perfect** could be used to describe the obtained correlation. The term **high** comes into play when *r* assumes a value close to either end (thus implying a **strong** relationship); conversely, the term **low** is used when *r* lands close to the middle of the continuum (thus implying a **weak** relationship). Not surprisingly, any *r* that ends up in the middle area of the left or right sides of our continuum will be called **moderate**.

In Excerpts 3.3–3.5, we see examples of these adjectives being used by researchers to label their *r*s. In these excerpts, note how the researchers report on the correlations among more than just two variables; in each excerpt, however, each correlation coefficient represents a numerical summary of the relationship between just two of those variables. Also note how the low correlation of .05 reported in Excerpt 3.5 is interpreted to mean that instruments used to produce the two sets of total scores that were correlated "measure independent constructs." When r turns out very close to zero, researchers will sometimes indicate that their two variables are **independent** of each other.

Excerpts 3.3–3.5 Use of Modifying Adjectives with the Term *Correlation*

There was a moderate negative correlation of job satisfaction with both emotional exhaustion ($r = -.23$) and depersonalization ($r = -.22$). In addition, job satisfaction had a slight positive correlation with personal accomplishment ($r = .17$). These low correlations show that the two instruments measure some of the same qualities, but the overlapping is minimal, indicating that both instruments measure a unique set of behaviors.

Source: D. B. Matthews. (1990). A comparison of burnout in selected occupational fields. *The Career Development Quarterly, 38*(3), p. 233.

Individually, on-task behaviors and the number of relevance strategies were strongly correlated ($r = .607$). Conversely, a negative correlation ($r = -.496$) was shown between on-task behaviors and number of satisfaction strategies used. The comparison between confidence building strategies/on-task behaviors and attention-focusing strategies/on-task behaviors indicated relatively low positive correlations ($r = .252$ and $r = .222$, respectively).

Source: T. Newby. (1991). Classroom motivation: Strategies of first-year teachers. *Journal of Educational Psychology, 83*(2), p. 198.

Most of the correlation between the PSI and F-COPES were very low. The correlation between the PSI total score and the F-COPES total score was $r = .05$, which seems to indicate that the instruments measure independent constructs.

Source: D. W. Barnett, J. D. Hall, and R. K. Bramlett (1990). Family factors in preschool assessment and intervention: A validity study of parenting stress and coping measures. *The Journal of School Psychology, 28, p. 16.*

Before concluding our discussion of how to interpret correlation coefficients, we feel obligated to reiterate the point that when the issue of relationship is addressed, the central question being answered by r is: "To what extent are the high scores of one variable paired with the high scores of the other variable?" The term *high* in this question is considered separately for each variable. Hence, a strong positive correlation can exist even though the mean of the scores of one variable is substantially different from the mean of the scores on the other variable. As proof of this claim, consider again the data we presented earlier on nine families who had varying numbers of teenagers and also varying amounts of phone use; the correlation between the two sets of scores turns out equal to $+.96$ despite the fact that the two means are quite different (2 versus 70). Or, take another look at Excerpt 3.2, where the two means were nearly identical and yet r turned out equal to $-.65$. Together, these two examples make clear, we hope, the fact that a correlation does *not* deal with the question of whether two means are similar or different.[1]

THE CORRELATION MATRIX

When interest resides in the bivariate relationship between just two variables or among a small number of variables, researchers will typically present their rs within the text of their article. (This reporting strategy was used in Excerpts 3.2–3.5.) When interest centers on the bivariate relationships among many variables, however, the resulting rs will often be summarized within a special table called a **correlation matrix**.

In Excerpt 3.6, we see a correlation matrix that summarizes the measured bivariate relationship among five variables. If we disregard the means and standard deviations in the two columns at the far right, this correlation matrix contains 25 rs arranged in five rows and five columns. Each r indicates the correlation between the variables labeling that r's row and column. For example, the value of $-.59$ on the top row is the correlation between CTN and IND (that is, between Certainty and Indecision).

Two things are noteworthy about the correlation matrix shown in Excerpt 3.6. First, when a row and column have the same name (as is the case with the top row and the first column, the second row and the second column, etc.), the correlation coefficient positioned at the intersection of that row and column is always 1.00. This simply indicates that the relationship between any variable and itself is guaranteed to be perfect positive. Second, the set of 10 correlation coefficients that appear above the diagonal formed by the 1.00 values is a mirror image of the 10 rs presented below the diagonal. This redundant feature of such correlation matrices is brought about by the fact that correlation between any two variables is the same regardless of which variable is called the "first" variable (or the "second" variable). Because r is not sensitive to the issue of direction, the correlation coefficient at the intersection of row 1 and column 2 is identical to what ap-

---

[1]*In many research studies, the focus is on the difference between means. Later, our discussion of t-test and F-tests will show how researchers compare means.*

Excerpt 3.6 A Standard Correlation Matrix

To address the primary research question, correlational analyses were conducted to assess the relationships between self-deception, impression management, psychological distress, and career indecision. Means, standard deviations, and correlations among instruments are reported in Table 1.

Table 1

Means, Standard Deviations, and Intercorrelations Among the Variables

Variable	CTN	IND	ODQ	SDQ	SCL–10	M	SD
CTN	1.00	−.59**	.22**	.31**	−.20**	6.2	1.3
IND	−.59**	1.00	−.13**	−.22**	.33**	29.8	8.1
ODQ	.22**	−.13*	1.00	.46**	−.08	92.0	12.1
SDQ	.31**	−.22**	.46**	1.00	−.31**	96.7	12.8
SCL–10	−.20**	.33**	−.08	−.31**	1.00	13.5	6.6

Note. CTN = Certainty, IND = Indecision, ODQ = Impression Management, SDQ = Self-Deception, SCL–10 = Psychological Distress. The minimum number of participants was 175.
*p<.05.
**p<.01.

Source: S. Sabourin and J. C. Coallier. (1991). The relationship between response style and reports of career indecision. *Measurement and Evaluation in Counseling and Development, 24*(2), p. 74.

pears at the intersection of row 2 and column 1. This feature, of course, holds true across the correlation matrix.

In Excerpt 3.7, we see an example of a correlation matrix that summarizes the bivariate relationships among six variables. Note how no *r*s appear above the diagonal of the 1s. The fact that we are given *r*s only in the space beneath the diagonal keeps no information from us; we still can see every bivariate correlation that was computed. The only thing that has been eliminated is redundancy.

Because it is quite uninformative to learn that the correlation between any variable and itself is +1.00, researchers will often delete the diagonal of 1s that extends from upper left to lower right. Excerpt 3.8 provides an example of this kind of correlation matrix.

This particular correlation matrix also illustrates a reporting strategy employed by many researchers. If you compare the row names in Excerpt 3.8 with the column labels, you will notice that the variable *Personal Unconcern* corresponds to the bottom row (but to none of the columns) and that the variable *GC* corresponds to the left column (but to none of the rows). It would have been possible to set up a new first row labeled *GC* and a new final column labeled *Personal Unconcern*. However, these additions would add

Excerpt 3.7 Correlation Matrix with No Values Above the Diagonal

Table 2

Correlation matrix of independent variables.

	EDUC	STAF	CODE	TOTREN	INSP	PREN
EDUC	1					
STAF	.136	1				
CODE	.05	−.217	1			
TOTREN	.22	.389	−.091	1		
INSP	.116	.277	.06	.031	1	
PREN	.307	−.022	.588	.088	.003	1

Source: J. Laquatra. (1990). Local building officials and rental housing energy efficiency. *Housing and Society, 17*(3), p. 52.

Excerpt 3.8 Correlation Matrix with No Ones in the Diagonal, with One Row and Column Deleted

Correlations between the achievement motives of the WOFO and the IC and GC scales are presented in Table 2. Positive relationships were expected between the IC and the GC scales and the Memory and Work Orientation scales of the WOFO, because IC and GC are theorized to also be aspects of achievement motivation. Mastery was found to be positively related to both IC and GC, but Work Orientation was only positively related to GC. Work Orientation and IC were essentially uncorrelated ($r = .00$).

Table 2

Correlations Between WOFO Motives and IC and GC ($n=35$)

	GC	IC	Mastery	Work	Competitiveness
IC	−.06				
Master	.12	.35			
Work	.41	.00	.46		
Competitiveness	.07	.62	.26	.10	
Personal Unconcern	.06	.26	.43	.25	.05

Source: S. Griffin-Pierson. (1990). The Competitiveness Questionnaire: A measure of two components of competitiveness. *Measurement and Evaluation in Counseling and Development, 23*(3), p. 112.

no new information because no correlation coefficients would appear in a GC row or in a Personal Unconcern column. Occasionally, researchers will set up their correlation matrices like this one by deleting an empty row and an empty column. Knowing that this is sometimes done, you must be careful when trying to figure out how many variables were involved; simply counting the number of rows (or columns) may cause you to end up one variable short.

In Excerpt 3.9, we see a correlation matrix in which the *rs* above the diagonal do not form a mirror image of those presented below the diagonal. In cases like this, we are really being given *two* correlation matrices, one for each of two groups of subjects. As the table title in Excerpt 3.9 indicates, the two subgroups here are males and females (with the intercorrelations among the five scales based on male subjects appearing above the diagonal, those based on female subjects appearing below the diagonal). Instead of having two correlation matrices in this journal article, space was saved by putting the two sets of 10 *rs* into one table.

Excerpt 3.9 Correlation Matrix with Different Values Above and Below the Diagonal

---

As shown in Table 2, correlations among the scales were in most cases moderate, except for those with the Hunger scale which tended to be smaller.

Table 2

Correlations among Situational Appetite Measure—Urges scales for female (lower-left triangle, $n = 184$) and male (upper-right triangle, $n = 41$) dieters

			Scales		
Scales	I	II	III	IV	V
I. Relaxation		.58	.21	.61	.63
II. Food Present	.61		.27	.54	.48
III. Hunger	.24	.44		.15	−.04
IV. Reward	.50	.43	.09		.46
V. Negative Feelings	.34	.25	.05	.46	

Source: A. L. Stanton, M. E. Garcia, and S. B. Green. (1990). Development and validation of the situational appetite measures. *Addictive Behaviors, 15*(5), p. 465.

Different Kinds of Correlational Procedures

In this section, we take a brief look at several different correlational procedures that have been developed. As you will see, all of these techniques are similar in that they are designed for the case where data have been collected on two variables. These bivariate correlational techniques differ, however, in the nature of the two variables. In light of this important difference, we need to say a few things about how variables differ.

The first important distinction that needs to be made in our discussion of variables is between quantitative and qualitative characteristics. With a **quantitative variable**, the targets of the measuring process vary as to how much of the characteristic is possessed. In contrast, a **qualitative variable** comes into play when the things being measured vary from one another in terms of the categorical group to which they belong relative to the characteristic of interest. Thus, if we focus our attention on people's heights, we have a quantitative variable (because some people possess more "tallness" than others). If, on the other hand, we focus our attention on people's favorite national park, we would be dealing with a qualitative variable (because people simply fall into categories based on which park they like best).

From the standpoint of correlation, quantitative variables can manifest themselves in one of two ways in the data a researcher collects. Possibly, the only thing the researcher will want to do is order individuals (or animals, or objects, or whatever) from the one possessing the greatest amount of the relevant characteristic to the one possessing the least. The numbers used to indicate ordered position normally are assigned such that 1 goes to the person with the greatest amount of the characteristic, 2 goes to the person with the second greatest amount, and so on. Such numbers are called **ranks** and are said to represent an **ordinal** scale of measurement. A researcher's data would also be ordinal in nature if each person or thing being measured is put into one of several ordered categories, with everyone who falls into the same category given the same score. (For example, the numbers 1, 2, 3, and 4 could be used to represent freshmen, sophomores, juniors, and seniors.)

With a second kind of quantitative variable, measurements are more precise. Here, the score associated with each person supposedly reveals how much of the characteristic of interest is possessed by that individual—and it does this without regard for the standing of any other measured person. Whereas ranks constitute data that provide relative comparisons, this second (and more precise) way of dealing with quantitative variables provide absolute comparisons. In this book, we will use the term **raw score** to refer to any piece of data that provides an absolute (rather than relative) assessment of one's standing on a quantitative variable.[2]

---

[2] *Whereas most statisticians draw a distinction between interval and ratio measurement scales and between discrete and continuous variables, we believe that readers of journal articles do not need to understand the technical differences between these terms in order to decipher research reports.*

Qualitative variables come in two main varieties. If the subgroups into which people are classified truly have no quantitative connection with each other, then the variable corresponding to those subgroups is said to be **nominal** in nature. Your favorite academic subject, the brand of jelly you most recently used, and your state of residence exemplify this kind of variable. If there are only two categories associated with the qualitative variable, then the variable of interest is said to be **dichotomous** in nature. A dichotomous variable actually can be viewed as a special case of the nominal situation, with examples being "course outcome" in courses where the only grades are "pass" and "fail" (or "credit" and "no credit"), gender, party affiliation during primary elections, and graduation status following four years of college.

In Excerpts 3.10 and 3.11, we see how researchers will sometimes use the terms *nominal, ordinal,* and *dichotomous* when describing the kind of scores collected in their studies.

Excerpts 3.10–3.11 Describing the Nature of Research Data

The second independent variable, form of government, is measured dichotomously; 0 = mayor-council, and 1 = council-manager.

Source: J. D. Slack, (1990). Information, training, and assistance needs of municipal governments. *Public Administration Review, 50*(4), p. 452.

The economic, situational, and psychological variables used in the study were measured on nominal and ordinal scales.

Source: I. M. Johnson. (1992). Economic, situational and psychological correlates of the decision-making process of battered women. *Families in Society, 73*(3), p. 171.

One final kind of variable needs to be briefly mentioned. Sometimes a researcher will begin with a quantitative variable but then classify individuals into two categories on the basis of how much of the characteristic of interest is possessed. For example, a researcher conceivably could measure people in terms of the quantitative variable "height," place each individual into a "tall" or "short" category, and then disregard the initial measurements of height (that took the form of ranks or raw scores). Whenever this is done, the researcher transforms quantitative data into a two-category qualitative state. The term *artificial dichotomy* is used to describe the final data set.

PEARSON'S PRODUCT-MOMENT CORRELATION

The most frequently used bivariate correlational procedure is called **Pearson's product-moment correlation**. It is designed for the situation where (1) each of the two variables is quantitative in nature and (2) each variable is measured so as to produce raw scores. The scatter diagram presented earlier in Excerpt 3.1 provides a good example of the kind of bivariate situation that is dealt with by means of Pearson's technique.

Excerpts 3.12–3.13 illustrate the use of this extremely popular bivariate correlational technique. Note, in the second of these excerpts, that the label *Pearson* is used by itself (without the follow-up phrase *product-moment*). In this same excerpt, also note how the correlation coefficient resulting from Pearson's technique is symbolized by *r*.

Excerpts 3.12–3.13 Illustrative Use of Pearson's Product-Moment Correlation

---

Pearson product-moment correlation coefficients were calculated between MESA academic achievement and GED scores and scores produced by the DAT and TABE.

Source: T. P. Janikowski, J. E. Bordieri, and J. R. Musgrave, (1990). Construct validation of the academic achievement and general educational subtests of the Microcomputer Evaluation Screening and Assessment (MESA). *Vocational Evaluation and Work Adjustment Bulletin, 23*(1), pp. 11–16.

To assess the stability of this measure over time, we computed the Pearson correlation of the total score for the two administrations for the participants who responded to the questionnaire on both administrations of it. The scores were highly stable: $r = 0.85$.

Source: J. M. Strayhorn, C. S. Weidman, and D. Larson. (1990). A measure of religiousness and its relation to parent and child mental health variables. *Journal of Community Psychology, 18*, p. 39.

SPEARMAN'S RHO AND KENDALL'S TAU

The second most popular bivariate correlational technique is called **Spearman's rho**. This kind of correlation is similar to the one we just discussed (Pearson's) in that it is appropriate for the situation in which both variables are quantitative in nature; with Spearman's technique, however, each of the two variables is measured in such a way as to produce ranks. This correlational technique often goes by the name **rank-order correlation** (instead of Spearman's rho). The resulting correlation coefficient, if symbolized, is usually referred to as r_s or ρ.

In Excerpt 3.14, we see a table containing the actual ranks that were correlated, the term *rho*, and the symbol r_s. As the footnotes indicate, two rank-order correlations were computed here: one involving the ranks presented in the first and third columns, the other involving the ranks presented in the second and third columns. The first of these correlations ($r_s = .06$) indicates that there was not much agreement between personnel managers and line managers in how they viewed the importance of the eight human-resource criteria that were evaluated. In contrast, there was a moderate positive correlation ($r_s = .52$) between what the personnel managers thought the line

Excerpt 3.14 Example of Spearman's Rho Applied to Sets of Ranks

Table II

Comparison of Personnel Manager's Perceptions and Line Organization's Rankings of Human Resources Criteria

	Rankings		
Criteria	[a]Personnel Managers' Evaluation n = 337	[b]Perceptions of Line Organization Evaluation n = 337	[c]Line Organization Actual Evaluation n = 258
Compensation	1	1	4
Establishing and maintaining work relationships	2	2	5
Planning	5	4	1
Staffing	6	3	2
Improving work relations	7	6	3
Training and development	3	5	6
Appraising performance	4	8	7
International personnel management	8	7	8

[a]From Table I comparison using non PHR Only. Rho for Personnel Managers' Evaluation and Line Managers' Actual Evaluation (columns 1 and 3) is rs = .06.
[b]Table I comparison using non PHR Only. Rho for Personnel Managers' Perception of Line Managers' Evaluation and Line Managers' Actual Evaluation (columns 2 and 3) is rs = .52.
[c]Derived from upper and middle level managers from sample firms surveyed.

Source: A. S. King, and T. R. Bishop. (1991). Functional requisites of human resources: Personnel professionals' and line managers' criteria for effectiveness. *Public Personnel Management, 20*(3), p. 298.

managers would value and what the line managers did, in fact, view as important. Hence, the personnel managers thought they were in agreement with the line managers more than was actually the case.

Only rarely will you see the actual ranks that a researcher correlates when using Spearman's rho. Almost always, the only information you will be given will be (1) a specification of the two variables and (2) the resulting correlation coefficient. Excerpt 3.15, therefore, is much more typical of what you will see in published articles than is the material in Excerpt 3.14.

Excerpt 3.15 Typical Reporting of Spearman's Rank-Order
Correlation

Readings from the activity monitor, which is a movement sensor, were positively associated with the total number of minutes of physical activity in the complete sample (Spearman correlation = .20), and in those aged 65–74 (Spearman correlation = .28) and over age 78 (Spearman correlation = .19).

Source: R. A. Washburn, A. M. Jette, and C. Janney. (1990). Using age-neutr0al physical activity questionnaires in research with the elderly. *Journal of Aging and Health, 2*(3), p. 346.

Kendall's tau is very similar to Spearman's rho in that both of these bivariate correlational techniques are designed for the case where each of two quantitative variables is measured in such a way as to produce data in the form of ranks. The difference between rho and tau is related to the issue of "ties." To illustrate what we mean, suppose six students took a short exam and earned these scores: 10, 9, 7, 7, 5, and 3. These raw scores, when converted to ranks, become 1, 2, 3.5, 3.5, 5, and 6, where the top score of 10 receives a rank of 1, the next-best score (9) receives a rank of 2, and so on. The third-and fourth-best scores tied with a score of 7, and the rank given to each of these individuals is equal to the mean of the separate ranks that they would have received if they had not tied. (If the two 7s had been 8 and 6, the separate ranks would have been 3 and 4, respectively; the mean of 3 and 4 is 3.5, and this rank is given to each of the persons who actually earned a 7.)

Kendall's tau is simply a bivariate correlational technique that does a better job of dealing with tied ranks than does Spearman's rho. In Excerpt 3.16, we see a paragraph from a recent article wherein two sets of ranks were correlated with Kendall's tau.

Excerpt 3.16 Kendall's Tau Correlation for Two Sets of Ranks

A subject's ability to remember the order in which material was presented was assessed by using a measure computed from the protocols and a second measure computed from a cued ordering task. Each protocol statement received a code (or codes if the statement contained multiple ideas) relating it to a specific paragraph, sentence, and word. The statements then were rank ordered and a Kendall's Tau was computed by comparing the reported and "true" ranks (free recall-presentation order; range −1 to +1).

Source: C. Janiszewski. (1990). The influence of nonattended material on the processing of advertising claims. *Journal of Marketing Research, 27*(3), p. 270.

POINT BISERIAL AND BISERIAL CORRELATIONS

Sometimes a researcher will correlate two variables that are measured so as to produce a set of raw scores for one variable and a set of 0s and 1s for the other (dichotomous) variable. For example, a researcher might want to see if a relationship exists between the height of basketball players and whether they score any points in a game. For this kind of bivariate situation, a correlational technique called **point biserial** has been designed. The resulting correlation coefficient is usually symbolized as r_{pb}.

If a researcher has data on two variables where one variable's data are in the form of raw scores while the other variable's data represent an artificial dichotomy, then the relationship between the two variables will be assessed by means of a technique called **biserial correlation**. Returning to our basketball example, suppose a researcher wanted to correlate height with scoring productivity, with the second of these variables dealt with by checking to see whether each player's average is less than 10 points or some value in the double digits. Here, scoring productivity is measured by imposing an artificial dichotomy on a set of raw scores. Accordingly, the biserial techniques would be used to assess the nature and strength of the relationship between the two variables. This kind of bivariate correlation is usually symbolized by r_{bis}.

In Excerpts 3.17 and 3.18, we see examples of the point biserial and biserial correlations being discussed in published research articles. In the first of these excerpts, membership in the two groups represented a true dichotomy (and thus brought forth the point biserial correlation); in the second excerpt, qualification or nonqualification for a stress disorder diagnosis represented an artificial dichotomy (and thus brought forth the biserial correlation).

Excerpts 3.17–3.18 Point Biserial and Biserial Correlations

Point bi-serial correlation analysis indicated that items in the Information section of the Consent Screening Interview predominantly showed a high degree of correlation between the two groups.

Source: P. Lindsey, and R. Luckasson, (1991). Consent Screening Interview for community residential placement: Report on the initial pilot study data. Annual meeting of the American Association on Mental Retardation. *Mental Retardation, 29*(3), p. 122.

The biserial correlation between PTSD-I Total scores and qualification for a stress disorder diagnosis under the modified DIS standards was very high—.94.

Source: C. G. Watson, M. P. Juba, V. Manifold, T. Kucala, and P. E. D. Anderson. (1991). The PTSD Interview: Rationale, description, reliability, and concurrent validity of a DSM-III–based technique. *Journal of Clinical Psychology, 47*(2), p. 184.

PHI AND TETRACHORIC CORRELATIONS

If both of a researcher's variables are dichotomous in nature, then the relationship between the two variables will be assessed by means of a correlational technique called **phi** (if each variable represents a true dichotomy) or a technique called **tetrachoric correlation** (if both variables represent artificial dichotomies). An example calling for the first of these situations would involve, among high school students, the variables of gender and car ownership; since each variable represents a true dichotomy, the correlation between gender (male/female) and car ownership (yes/no) would be accomplished using phi. For an example of a place where tetrachoric correlation would be appropriate, imagine that we measure each of several persons in terms of height (with people classified as tall or short depending on whether or not they measure over 5'8") and weight (with people classified as "OK" or "Not OK" depending on whether or not they are within 10 pounds of their ideal weights). Here, both height and weight are forced into being dichotomies.

CRAMER'S V

If a researcher has collected bivariate data on two variables where each variable is nominal in nature, the relationship between the two variables can be measured by means of a correlational technique called **Cramer's V**. In Excerpt 3.19 we see an example of how Cramer's V was used to assess the relationship between career aspiration and ethnicity. (Career aspiration involved classifying each participant into one of Holland's six categories: investigative, artistic, scientific, etc.; ethnicity involved classifying each participant into one of three categories: Mexican-American, Black, White.)

Excerpt 3.19 Cramer's V

The association between ethnicity and career expectations was statistically significant. Cramer's V was .17 for the male subsample and .20 for the female subsample.

Source: C. Arbona, and D. M. Novy. (1991). Career aspirations and expectations of Black, Mexican American, and White students. Special Issue: Career development of racial and ethnic minorities. *The Career Development Quarterly, 39*(3), p. 234.

WARNINGS ABOUT CORRELATION

You may, at this point, be tempted to consider yourself a semiexpert when it comes to deciphering discussions about correlation. You now know what a scatter diagram is, you have looked at our correlational continuum (and know that correlation coefficients extend from -1.00 to $+1.00$), you understand what a correlation matrix is, and you have considered several different kinds of bivariate correlation. Before you assume that you know everything there is to know about measuring the relationship between two variables, we need to provide you with four warnings. These warnings deal with the issue of cause, the coefficient of determination, the possibility of "outliers," and the concept of linearity.

CORRELATION AND CAUSE

It is important for you to know that a correlation coefficient does not speak to the issue of **cause-and-effect.** In other words, whether a particular variable has a causal impact on a different variable cannot be determined by measuring the two variables simultaneously and then correlating the two sets of data. Many recipients of research reports (and even a few researchers) make the mistake of thinking that a high correlation implies that one variable has a causal influence on the other variable. To prevent yourself from making this mistake, we suggest that you memorize this simple statement: correlation $\neq$ cause.

Later in this book, you will learn how researchers often collect data in such a way as to address the issue of cause. In such situations, however, researchers typically use data-gathering strategies that help them assess the possibility that one variable actually has a determining influence on a second variable. Those strategies require a consideration of issues that cannot be discussed here; in time, however, we are confident that you will come to understand the extra demands that are placed on researchers who want to investigate causal connections between variables. For now, all we can do is ask that you trust us when we claim that correlational data alone cannot be used to establish a cause-and-effect situation.

COEFFICIENT OF DETERMINATION

To get a better feel for the strength of the relationship between two variables, many researchers will square the value of the correlation coefficient. For example, if r turns out equal to .80, the researcher will square .80 and obtain .64. When r is squared like this, the resulting value is called the **coefficient of determination**. In Excerpt 3.20 we see how a researcher not only used this term in a research report but also defined its meaning.

The coefficient of determination indicates the proportion of variability in one variable that is associated with (or explained by) variability in the other variable. The value of r^2 will lie somewhere between 0 and $+1.00$, and some researchers simply multiply by 100 so they can talk about the *percentage* of explained variability. In Excerpt 3.21, we see an example where the value of r was simply squared, thus indicating the *proportion* of explained variation.

As suggested by the material in Excerpt 3.21, the value of r^2 indicates how much (proportionately speaking) variability in either variable is explained by

---

Excerpt 3.20 The Coefficient of Determination

For quadriceps and hamstrings of both groups, the Pearson product moment correlation coefficient (r) and its square (r^2, the coefficient of determination) were calculated between PT and PW, PT and PP, and PT and PTAE.

Source: P. Kannus. (1992). Normality, variability, and predictability of work, power, and torque acceleration energy with respect to peak torque in isokinetic muscle testing. *International Journal of Sports Medicine, 13*(3), p. 250.

Excerpt 3.21 Explained Variation

Pearson correlation analysis confirms the importance of mandatory recycling . . . in accounting for higher participation in some cities. Mandatory recycling alone explained almost a third of the variation ($.56^2 = .31$) in citizen participation.

Source: D. H. Folz. (1991). Recycling program design, management, and participation: A national survey of municipal experience. *Public Administration Review, 51*(3), p. 227.

---

the other variable. The implication of this is that the raw correlation coefficient (that is, the value of *r* when not squared) exaggerates how strong the relationship really is between two variables. Note that *r* must be stronger than .70 in order for there to be at least 50 percent explained variability. Or, consider the case where *r* = .50; here, only one-fourth of the variability is explained.

OUTLIERS

Our third warning concerns the effect of one or more data points that are located away from the bulk of the scores. Such data points are called **outliers**, and they can cause the size of a correlation coefficient to understate or exaggerate the strength of the relationship between two variables. To illustrate how this can happen, take another look at the scatter diagram presented in Excerpt 3.1.

Within Excerpt 3.1, there really aren't any outliers. Nevertheless, patient 16 had scores that caused his or her dot to be farthest off the path of dots that seems to flow from the lower-left to the upper-right areas of the scatter diagram. If that dot is omitted, the value of the correlation coefficient changes from .58 to .69. Now consider what happens if we put patient 16's dot back into the scatter diagram but change its position by giving that patient radiographic and arthrometric scores of 5.5 and 18, respectively. This change in the location of just *one* data point in the scatter diagram causes *r* to change from .58 to .37. If we add a new data point to the scatter diagram and position it at the same spot where we just repositioned patient 16, the correlation coefficient for the full set of 17 data points becomes .17.

Researchers do not, of course, move data points around in their scatter diagram or add imaginary data points to their data sets. However, many researchers *do* fail to check to see if one or more outliers serve to distort the statistical summary of the bivariate relationships they study. You won't see many scatter diagrams in journal articles, and thus you will not be able to examine the data yourself to see if outliers were present. Almost always, you will be given just the correlation coefficient. Give the researcher some extra credit, however, whenever you see a statement to the effect that the correlation coefficient was computed after an examination of a scatter diagram revealed no outliers (or revealed an outlier that was removed prior to computing the correlation coefficient).

LINEARITY

The most popular technique for assessing the strength of a bivariate relationship is Pearson's product-moment correlation. This correlational procedure works nicely if the two variables have a linear relationship. Pearson's technique does not work well, however, if a curvilinear relationship exists between the two variables.

A **linear** relationship does *not* require that all data points (in a scatter diagram) lie on a straight line. Instead, what *is* required is that the *path* of the data points be straight. The path itself can be very narrow, with most data points falling near an imaginary straight line, or, the path can be very wide—so long as the path is straight. (Regardless of how narrow or wide the path is, the path to which we refer can be tilted at any angle.)

If a **curvilinear** relationship exists between two variables, Pearson's correlation will underestimate the strength of the relationship that is present in the data. Accordingly, you can place more confidence in any correlation coefficient you see when the researcher who presents it indicates that a scatter diagram was inspected to see whether the relationship was linear before Pearson's *r* was used to summarize the nature and strength of the relationship. Conversely, add a few grains of salt to the *r*s that are thrown your way without statements concerning the linearity of the data.

In Excerpt 3.22, we see a report of what was discovered after a researcher examined his data to see if linearity existed. In this study, there were several affective measures (stress, anxiety, and depression), along with data on memory performance. Several scatter diagrams were inspected, each one involving one of the affective measures and memory performance. As the researcher reports, none of these relationships appeared to be linear.

Excerpt 3.22 Checking to See Whether Relationships Are Linear

---

Because of the possibility that the relationship between affective measures and memory performance might be curvilinear, we inspected bivariate scatterplots of the relationship between the affective measures and memory performance. For all affective measures, the data appeared to fit a parabolic (inverted U) shape.

Source: Scott T. Meier, (1991). Tests of the construct validity of occupational stress measures with college students: Failure to support discriminate validity. *Journal of Counseling Psychology, 38*(1), p. 95.

REVIEW TERMS

Biserial correlation	Pearson's product-moment correlation
Bivariate	Perfect
Cause-and-effect	Phi
Coefficient of determination	Point biserial correlation
Correlation coefficient	Positive correlation
Correlation matrix	Qualitative variable
Cramer's V	Quantitative variable
Curvilinear	Ranks
Dichotomous variable	Rank-order correlation
Direct relationship	Raw score
High	Relationship
Indirect relationship	Scatter diagram
Independent	Spearman's rho
Inverse relationship	Strong
Kendall's tau	Tetrachoric correlation
Linear	Weak
Low	r
Moderate	r_s
Negative correlation	r^2
Nominal	r_{pb}
Ordinal	r_{bis}
Outlier	ρ

REVIEW QUESTIONS

1. Here are the quiz scores for five students in English (E) and History (H). Sam: E = 18, H = 4; Sue: E = 16, H = 3; Joy: E = 15, H = 3; John: E = 13, H = 1; Chris: E = 12, H = 0. Within this small group of students, what is the nature of the correlation—high-high, low-low; high-low, low-high; or little systematic tendency?

2. If 20 individuals are measured in terms of two variables, how many dots will there be if a scatter diagram is built to show the relationship between the two variables?

3. Which of the following correlation coefficients indicates the weakest relationship?

    a. $r = +.72$

    b. $r = +.41$

    c. $r = +.13$

    d. $r = -.33$

    e. $r = -.84$

4. If the correlation matrix in Excerpt 3.7 had been set up like the one in Excerpt 3.6, what number would have been positioned at the intersection of the top row (EDUC) and the right column (PREN)?

5. In Excerpt 3.9, what was the correlation between Hunger and Negative Feelings among the male dieters?

6. What is the name of the correlational procedure used when interest lies in the relationship between two variables measured in such a way as to produce:

    a. Two sets of raw scores?

    b. Two sets of ranks (with no ties)?

    c. Two sets of truly dichotomous values?

    d. One set of raw scores and one set of truly dichotomous values?

7. Look at Excerpt 3.14. If you were required to make a guess as to the numerical value of r_s if the researcher had correlated the first two columns of ranks, what numerical value would you offer as your guess?

8. What do the subscripts pb stand for in the notation r_{pb}?

9. In terms of the data for which they are intended, how does Kendall's tau differ from Spearman's rho?

10. If a researcher wanted to see if there is a relationship between people's favorite color (e.g., red, blue, orange, etc.) and their favorite TV station, what correlational procedure would you expect to see used?

11. (True or False) If a bivariate correlation coefficient is closer to 1.00 than to 0.00, this indicates that a causal relationship exists between the two variables.

12. Based upon the information presented in Excerpt 3.2, what would the coefficient of determination be equal to?

13. (True or False) If a researcher has data on two variables, there will be a high correlation if the two means are close together (or a low correlation if the two means are far apart).

14. When examining a scatter diagram, how must the dots be arranged in order for the term *linear* to apply?

15. Whose name is often paired with the term *product-moment correlation?* With the term *rank-order correlation?*

4

RELIABILITY AND VALIDITY

Empirical research articles focus on data that have been collected, summarized, and analyzed. The conclusions drawn and the recommendations made in such studies can be no better than the data on which they are based. As a consequence, most researchers describe the quality of the instruments used to collect their data. These descriptions of instrument quality normally appear in the Method section of the article, either in the portion that focuses on materials or in the description of the dependent variables.

Regardless of where it appears, the description of instrument quality typically deals with two measurement-related concepts—reliability and validity. In this chapter, we discuss the meaning of these two concepts, various techniques employed by researchers to assess the reliability and validity of their measuring instruments, and numerical indices of instrument quality that are reported. Our overall objective here is to help you refine your skills at deciphering and evaluating reports of reliability and validity.

As a simple check to see whether you can profit by studying the material in this chapter, take a look at (1) the third sentence of Excerpt 1.6 and (2) all of Excerpt 4.1. If you understand and can critique reports such as these (and if you are familiar with this chapter's review terms and can answer our end-of-chapter questions), skip this chapter and go to Chapter 5. If you are unfamiliar with the terms and cannot answer the questions, read and examine carefully the content of this chapter.

RELIABILITY

Our discussion of reliability is divided into three sections. We begin by looking at the core meaning of the term *reliability*. Next, we examine a variety of techniques that researchers use to quantify the degree to which their data are reliable. Finally, we provide five cautionary comments concerning reports of reliability that will help you as you read technical research reports.

Excerpt 4.1 A Typical Discussion of Reliability and Validity

The Watson-Glaser Critical Thinking Appraisal (GCTA) was administered as a pretest and posttest measure of critical-thinking ability (McMillan, 1987; Mitchel, 1985). The instrument measures abilities to recognize problems, evaluate evidence cited in support of claims for truth, reason inferentially, and apply these procedures to problems (Woehlke, 1985). A total of 80 multiple-choice items are divided into five subtests of 16 items each. Subtests are Inference, Recognition of Assumptions, Deduction, Interpretation, and Evaluation of Arguments. Forms A and B offer an equal number of items in each subtest so that scores from the forms can be compared directly.

Reliability was assessed by estimates of internal consistency, stability of scores over time, and correlation between scores on alternate forms. Corrected split-half reliabilities range from .69 to .85 for Form A and from .70 to .82 for Form B. A coefficient of stability over 3 months of .73 and an alternate form reliability of .75 for 228 12th-graders are reported (Watson & Glaser, 1980). With respect to validity, correlations with intelligence tests were moderate, ranging from .30 to .75. Correlations with achievement tests ranged from .20 and .65 (Woehlke, 1985).

Source: S. H. Frost. (1991). Fostering the critical thinking of college women through academic advising and faculty contact. *Journal of College Student Development, 32*(4), p. 361.

THE MEANING OF RELIABILITY AND THE RELIABILITY COEFFICIENT

The basic idea of **reliability** is summed up by the word *consistency*. Researchers can and do evaluate the reliability of their instruments from different perspectives, but the basic question that cuts across these various perspectives (and techniques) is always the same: "To what extent can we say that the data are consistent?"

As you will see, the way in which reliability is conceptualized by researchers can take one of three basic forms. In some studies, researchers ask, "To what degree does a subject's measured performance remain consistent across repeated testings?" In other studies, the question of interest takes a slightly different form: "To what extent do the individual items that go together to make up a test or inventory consistently measure the same underlying characteristic?" In still other studies, the concern over reliability is expressed in the question "How much consistency exists among the ratings provided by a group of raters?" Despite the differences among these three questions, the notion of consistency is at the heart of the matter in each case.

Different statistical procedures have been developed to assess the degree to which a researcher's data are reliable, and we will discuss some of the more frequently used procedures in a moment. Before doing that, however, we want to point out how the different procedures are similar. Besides dealing, in one way or another, with the concept of consistency, each of the reliability techniques leads to a single numerical index. Called a **reliability coefficient**, this descriptive summary of the data's consistency normally assumes a value somewhere between 0.00 and +1.00, with these two "endpoints" representing situations where consistency is either totally absent or totally present.

DIFFERENT APPROACHES TO RELIABILITY

TEST-RETEST RELIABILITY In many studies, a researcher will measure a single group of subjects twice with the same measuring instrument, with the two testings separated by a period of time. The interval of time may be as short as one day or it can be as long as a year or more. Regardless of the length of time between the two testings, the researcher will simply correlate the two sets of scores to find out how much consistency is in the data. The resulting correlation coefficient is simply renamed the **test-retest reliability coefficient**.[1]

With a test-retest approach to reliability, the resulting coefficient addresses the issue of consistency, or stability, over time. For this reason, the test-retest reliability coefficient is frequently referred to as the **coefficient of stability**. If you take another look at the first and third sentences in the second paragraph of Excerpt 4.1, you will see that the coefficient of stability turned out equal to .73 when the concern was stability of scores over a three-month time interval. In Excerpt 4.2, we see another case where the test-retest approach to reliability was used.

Excerpt 4.2 Test-Retest Reliability

Stability was measured with a test-retest technique using Pearson correlation. The reliability coefficient obtained for the knowledge subscale was 0.82.

Source: A. E. Benner, and L. S. Marlow. (1991). The effect of a workshop on childhood cancer on students' knowledge, concerns, and desire to interact with a classmate with cancer. *Children's Health Care, 20*(2), p. 104.

---

[1] *As you recall from Chapter 3, correlation coefficients can assume values anywhere between −1.00 and +1.00. Reliability, however, cannot logically turn out to be negative. Therefore, if the test-retest correlation coefficient turns out to be negative, it will be changed to 0.00 when relabeled as a reliability coefficient.*

With most characteristics, the degree of stability that exists decreases as the interval between test and retest increases. For this reason, high coefficients of stability are more impressive when the time interval is longer. If a researcher does not indicate the length of time between the two testings, then the claims made about stability must be taken with a grain of salt. Stability is not very convincing if a trait remains stable for only an hour!

ALTERNATE-FORMS RELIABILITY[2]   Instead of assessing stability over time, researchers sometimes measure subjects with two forms of the same instrument. The two forms are similar in that they supposedly focus on the same characteristic (e.g., intelligence) of the people being measured, but they differ with respect to the precise questions included within each form. If the two forms do in fact measure the same thing (and if they are used in close temporal proximity), we would expect a high degree of consistency between the scores obtained for any examinee across the two testings. With **alternate-forms reliability**, a researcher is simply determining the degree to which this is the case.

To quantify the degree of alternate-forms reliability that exists, the researcher will administer two forms of the same instrument to a single group of individuals with a short time interval between the two testings.[3] After a score becomes available for each subject on each form, the two sets of data are correlated. The resulting correlation coefficient is interpreted directly as the alternate-forms reliability coefficient.[4] Many researchers refer to this two-digit value as the **coefficient of equivalence**.

To see an example of where this form of reliability was reported, take another look at Excerpt 4.1. (There, we see that the alternate-forms reliability turned out equal to .75.) As another example, consider Excerpt 4.3. Here, coefficients ranged from .78 to .92 because the 6100 students were subgrouped by gender and grade level. Hence, a total of 10 reliability coefficients fell into this range.

INTERNAL CONSISTENCY RELIABILITY   Instead of focusing on stability across time or on equivalence across forms, researchers sometimes assess the degree to which their measuring instruments possess internal consistency. When this perspective is taken, reliability is defined as consistency across the parts of a measuring instrument, with the "parts" being individual questions or subsets of questions. To the extent that these parts "hang together" and

---

[2]*The terms* equivalent-forms reliability *and* parallel-forms reliability *are synonymous (as used by most applied researchers) with the term* alternative-forms reliability.

[3]*The two forms will probably be administered in a* counterbalanced *order, meaning that each instrument is administered first to one-half of the subjects.*

[4]*As is the case with test-retest reliability, any negative correlation would be changed to 0. Reliability by definition has a lower limit of 0.*

Excerpt 4.3 Alternate-Forms Reliability

The DAT is essentially a power test, with the exception of the Clerical Speed and Accuracy test. DAT (forms V and W) norms were derived from more than 6,100 students in grades eight through 12. . . . Alternate form reliability was reported on the Clerical Speed and Accuracy test, coefficients ranged from .78 to .92.

Source: T. P. Janikowski, J. E. Bordieri, and J. R. Musgrave. (1990). Construct validation of the academic achievement and general educational development subtests of the Microcomputer Evaluation Screening and Assessment (MESA). *Vocational Evaluation and Work Adjustment Bulletin, 23*(1), p. 13.

---

measure the same thing, the full instrument is said to possess high **internal consistency reliability**.

To assess internal consistency, a researcher need only administer a test (or questionnaire) a single time to a single group of individuals. After all responses have been scored, one of several statistical procedures is then applied to the data, with the result being a number between 0.00 and +1.00. As with test-retest and alternate-forms procedures, the instrument is considered to be better to the extent that the resulting coefficient is close to the upper limit of this continuum of possible results.

One of the procedures that can be used to obtain the internal consistency reliability coefficient involves splitting each examinee's performance into two halves, usually by determining how the examinee did on the odd-numbered items grouped together (i.e., one half of the test) and the even-numbered items grouped together (i.e., the other half). After each person's total score on each half of the instrument is computed, these two sets of scores are correlated. Once obtained, the *r* is inserted into a special formula (called **Spearman-Brown**) that makes a "correction" based upon the length of the full instrument. The final numerical result is called the **split-half reliability coefficient**.

Use of this first procedure for assessing internal consistency can be seen in Excerpt 4.1. In that study, we see that the split-half technique was employed 10 times—with each of the five subtests on each form of the WGCTA. The resulting coefficients ranged from .69 to .85 for Form A and from .70 to .82 for Form B. Another reference to this kind of reliability procedure is presented in Excerpt 4.4.

A second approach to assessing internal consistency is called **Kuder-Richardson #20**, or simply **K-R 20**. This procedure, like the split-half procedure, uses data from a single test that has been given once to a single group of respondents. After each answer is scored, the correlation between every possible pair of items is computed. The mean of those *r*s is then adjusted to take into account the fact that the full test contained more than just two

---

Excerpt 4.4 Split-Half Reliability

Reliabilities for all subtests except Writing fluency (which is timed) and for cluster scores were calculated by the split-half procedure corrected according to Spearman-Brown formula.

Source: V. K. Constenbader, and C. Perry. (1990). The Woodcock-Johnson Psychoeducational Battery-Revised. *Journal of Psychoeducational Assessment, 8*(2), p. 182.

---

items.[5] Excerpt 4.5 contains an example showing how K-R 20 results might be reported within the articles you read.

Excerpt 4.5 Kuder-Richardson 20 Reliability

The Preprimer (Grade 1 pretest), Primary II (Grade 2 posttest), and Elementary (Grade 3 posttest) levels of the test were used. Subtests included within each level of the test sampled the domains of reading, mathematics, and language. Kuder-Richardson Formula 20 reliabilities for the subtests were generally high ranging from 0.77 for mathematics (Primary II) to 0.96 for reading (Elementary) across levels of the test.

Source: C. R. Greenwood. (1991). Longitudinal analysis of time, engagement, and achievement in at-risk versus non-risk students. *Exceptional Children, 57*(6), p. 525.

A third method for assessing internal consistency is referred to as **coefficient alpha**, as **Cronbach's alpha**, or simply as **alpha**. This technique is identical to K-R 20 whenever the instrument's items are scored in a dichotomous fashion (e.g., "1" for correct, "0" for incorrect). However, alpha is more versatile because it can be used with instruments made up of items that can be scored with three or more possible values. Examples of such a situation include (1) a four-question essay test, where each examinee's response to each question is evaluated on a 0–10 scale or (2) a Likert-type questionnaire where the five response options for each statement extend from "strongly agree" to "strongly disagree" and are scored with the integers 5 through 1. Excerpt 4.6 shows how this procedure was used to assess a new rating scale developed to measure mathematics anxiety among children. The instrument contained 22 items dealing with situations that might produce math anxiety (e.g., "reading a formula in science" and "being given a math quiz that you were not told about").

---

[5]*When assessing internal consistency using the K-R 20 procedure, the researcher (or a computer) can determine the final reliability coefficient without having to (1) compute the correlation between every possible pair of items and (2) adjust r by a Spearman-Brown–like formula. A relatively simple formula produces the final result in a one-step fashion.*

Excerpt 4.6 Coefficient Alpha Reliability

Table 1 presents means, standard deviations, and coefficients alpha for the MASC with respect to grade level.

RELIABILITY

Internal consistency reliability for the MASC was estimated by computing alpha coefficients for each grade and for the total group. As can be seen in Table 1, these coefficients ranged from .90 to .93 with a median of .92.

Table 1

Means, Standard Deviations, and Reliability Coefficients for MASC

Grade	N	M	SD	Reliability (α)
4	40	36.50	10.02	.90
5	144	37.33	10.64	.92
6	171	40.26	11.39	.92
7	103	38.80	11.65	.93
8	104	30.55	7.53	.90
Total	562	37.17	11.04	.92

Source: L. H. Chiu, and L. L. Henry. (1990). Development and validation of the Mathematics Anxiety Scale for Children. *Measurement and Evaluation in Counseling and Development, 23*(3), p. 123.

Before concluding our discussion of internal consistency, we want to underscore a point made earlier. Whereas the test-retest and alternate-forms procedures for assessing reliability address the issues of stability across time and equivalence across forms, respectively, assessments of internal consistency focus on the degree to which the same characteristic is being measured. This point is illustrated nicely in Excerpt 4.7.

Excerpt 4.7 Internal Consistency as a Measure of Test Homogeneity

Nunnally (1978) has suggested that the generally accepted standard for reliability estimates is above .70. Using this criterion, four TAIS subscales (OIT, BET, NAR, RED) and one BB-TAIS subscale (NAR) failed to demonstrate acceptable levels of internal consistency. This implies that these TAIS subscales are not sufficiently homogeneous—that is, the items do not satisfactorily measure the same construct.

Source: J. J. Summers, K. Miller, and S. Ford. (1991). Attentional style and basketball performance. *Journal of Sport and Exercise Psychology, 13*(3), p. 243.

INTERRATER RELIABILITY

Researchers sometimes collect data by having raters evaluate a set of objects, pictures, applicants, or whatever. To quantify the degree of consistency among the raters, the researcher will compute an index of interrater reliability. Three popular procedures for doing this lead to Kendall's coefficient of concordance, Cohen's kappa, and the intraclass correlation coefficient.

Kendall's procedure is appropriate for situations where each rater is asked to rank the things being evaluated. If these ranks turn out to be in complete agreement across the various evaluators, then the **coefficient of concordance** will turn out equal to +1.00. To the extent that the evaluators disagree with one another, Kendall's procedure will yield a smaller value.

An interesting use of this procedure for assessing interrater reliability is presented in Excerpt 4.8. In this study, eight historians and eight students examined various written documents concerning the American Revolution. Each subject independently ranked these documents in terms of their trustworthiness. Kendall's coefficient of concordance, denoted as W, turned out to be much higher (.69) when used to summarize the historians' data as compared to its value (.25) when used to summarize the students' data. As the picture (Figure 1) of the data shows, there was more consistency in the way the historians ranked the documents than in the way the students evaluated the same documents.

Excerpt 4.8 Kendall's Coefficient of Concordance

SUBJECTS

Historians. Eight historians (H1–H8; 6 men and 2 women [H5 and H6]) were recruited from universities in the San Francisco Bay area. . . . Four of these historians (H1–H4) were "Americanists," or historians who had graduate specialization in American history and had taught history at the college level; four (H5–H8) were "non-Americanists" with specializations in other areas. Six historians possessed a doctoral degree; two others were graduate students in the advanced stages of their doctoral work.

Students. Eight students (S1–S8; M=16 years, 7 months; 4 men and 4 women [S1, S3, S5, and S8]) were recruited from two high schools in the San Francisco Bay area. Three considerations guided their selection: (a) that all students had taken 11th grade American history the previous academic year, (b) that all were reading at or above grade level (as determined by teacher recommendations and their Scholastic Aptitude Test scores), and (c) that all scored 50% or above on a pretest, administered during students' regularly scheduled history class, composed of items drawn from the National Assessment of Educational Progress (NAEP) examination in American history (Ravitch & Finn, 1987).

(Continued)

Excerpt 4.8 Kendall's Coefficient of Concordance *(Continued)*

MATERIALS

A set of eight written and three pictorial documents related to the Battle of Lexington, the opening volley of the Revolutionary War, was assembled. The written documents . . . included two diary entries, an excerpt from an autobiography, a formal deposition, a newspaper report, and a letter of protest, all of which were written fairly close to the time of the battle. Also included were two documents written much later: a selection from a historical novel (Fast, 1961) and an excerpt from a high school textbook (Steinberg, 1963).

RANKING OF DOCUMENTS

Figure 1 shows subjects' rankings of the trustworthiness of the written documents. Kendall's coefficient of concordance was used to measure the amount of agreement among each group: for historians, $W = .69$, $\chi^2(7) = 38.92$, $p < .001$; for students, $W = .25$, $\chi^2(7) = 13.83$, $\rho = .054$. The amount of agreement among historians of different specializations was virtually identical, $W = .73$ for Americanists and $W = .74$ for non-Americanists.

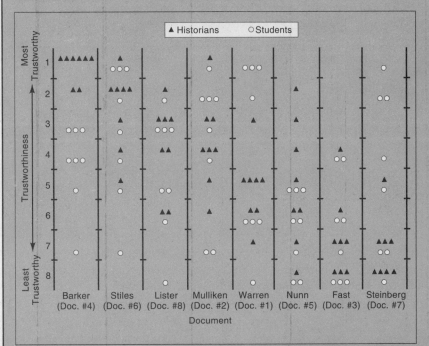

Figure 1 *Rankings of the trustworthiness of the eight written documents.*

Source: S. Wineburg. (1991). Historical problem solving: A study of the cognitive processes used in the evaluation of documentary and pictorial evidence. *Journal of Educational Psychology, 83*(1), p. 73.

Kendall's coefficient of concordance establishes how much interrater reliability exists among ranked data. **Cohen's kappa** accomplishes the same purpose when the data are nominal (i.e., categorical) in nature. In other words, kappa is designed for situations where raters classify the items being rated into discrete categories. If all raters agree that a particular item belongs in a given category, and if there is a total agreement for all items being evaluated (even though different items end up in different categories), then kappa assumes the value of +1.00. To the extent that raters disagree, kappa assumes a smaller value.

To see a case in which kappa was used to assess interrater reliability, consider Excerpt 4.9. In this study, two groups of five female undergraduates watched 236 segments of psychotherapy gleaned from videotaped sessions conducted with eight clients. Both groups were told to focus on the counselor. One group had been trained so as to become sensitive to "counselor risk intervention," and the judges (i.e., raters) in this group had to classify each of the 236 counselor comments into one of 10 possible intervention categories. The other group of judges had been trained so as to become sensitive to counselor humor, and these raters had to classify the 236 instances of counselor talk into one of 11 possible humor categories.

Excerpt 4.9 Cohen's Kappa

INTERRATER RELIABILITY

Interrater reliabilities were determined for independent ratings on the 236 events from the 8 cases. . . . Average kappas between pairs of judges were .78 (SD = .10) for counselor risk interventions and .75 (SD = .11) for counselor humor.

Source: D. R. Falk, and C. E. Hill. (1992). Counselor interventions preceding client laughter in brief therapy. *Journal of Counseling Psychology, 39*(1), p. 42.

As you can tell from the researcher's write-up, kappa was computed for each possible pair of judges from each group, with the mean of the resulting kappa coefficients reported for each group. Results indicated approximately the same degree of consistency in the classifications made by the members of each group. The authors interpreted these results to mean that the humor and risk interventions of counselors could be reliably categorized.[6]

---

[6]*As originally developed by Cohen, kappa could be used only when there were two raters. In situations where more than two raters served as judges, researchers would take the data from two judges at a time, compute kappa using only those data, and average the various kappa values to obtain a single value that represented the consistency of the ratings provided by the full set of raters. Recently, the formula for computing kappa has been revised so the researcher can compute, in one step, an index of the consistency that exists among all raters.*

The last procedure for assessing internal consistency to be considered here is called **intraclass correlation**. Abbreviated as ICC, the intraclass correlation is typically used to estimate the reliability of ratings. For example, each of 20 job applicants might be rated by each of five members of a hiring team. After analyzing the set of ratings, ICC could be used to estimate the expected reliability of either the individual ratings provided by a single rater or the mean rating provided by a group of raters.

Although originally developed for use with ratings, ICC is currently used in a wide variety of research studies wherein each subject is measured two or more times on the same characteristic. Such situations might be described using the terms *test-retest, test-retest-retest*, and so on, depending upon the number of multiple measurements taken. The simplest of these, of course, is the same as that considered earlier when we began our discussion of reliability procedures.

Intraclass correlation is similar to the other reliability procedures we have considered in terms of the core concept being dealt with (consistency), the theoretical limits of the data-based coefficient (0 to 1.00), and the desire on the part of the researcher to end up with a value as close to 1.00 as possible. It differs from the other reliability procedures in that several ICC procedures exist. The six most popular of these procedures are distinguished by two numbers put inside parentheses following the letters ICC. For example, ICC(3,1) designates one of the six most frequently used versions of intraclass correlation. The first of the two numbers indicates which of three possible statistical models has been assumed by the researchers to underlie their data. The second number indicates whether the researchers are interested in the reliability of a single rater (or one-time use of a measuring instrument) or in the reliability of the mean score provided by a group of raters (or the mean value produced by using a measuring instrument more than once). The second number within the parentheses will be a 1 for the first of these two cases; if interest lies in the reliability of means, the second number will be a value greater than 1 that designates how many scores are averaged together to generate each mean.

We will not attempt to differentiate any further among the six main cases of ICC. Instead, we simply want to point out that researchers should explain in their research reports (1) which of the six ICC procedures was used and (2) the reason(s) behind the choice made. You have a right to expect clarity regarding these two issues because the ICC-estimated reliability coefficient can vary widely depending upon which of the six available formulas is used to compute it.

In Excerpt 4.10, we see an example of how discussions of ICC ought to be presented. Note that the researchers specified the version of ICC used—(3,1)—along with the rationale behind their choice.

Excerpt 4.10 Intraclass Correlation

Intraclass correlation coefficients (ICCs) were calculated to describe the degree of intratester agreement for measurements obtained in this study. The formula chosen was (3,1) of the ICC as described by Shrout and Fleiss, . . . because only one judge evaluated the same population of subjects. The ICC, which is a measure of correlation that takes variance into account, describes the agreement between the repeated measures and therefore is an appropriate statistical means to demonstrate reliability. An ICC value of 0.8 or greater was considered acceptable for this study.

Source: D. Levine, A. Klein, and M. Morrissey. (1991). Reliability of isokinetic concentric closed kinematic chain testing of the hip and knee extensors. *Isokinetics and Exercise Science, 1*(3), p. 149.

WARNING ABOUT RELIABILITY

Before we turn to the topic of validity, there are five important "warnings" about reliability to which you should become sensitive. It would be nice if all researchers were also aware of these five concerns; unfortunately, that is not the case.

First of all, keep in mind that different methods for assessing reliability consider the issue of consistency from different perspectives. Thus, a high coefficient of stability does not necessarily mean that internal consistency is high (and vice versa). Even within the internal consistency category, a high value for split-half reliability does not necessarily mean that Kuder-Richardson 20 would be equally high for the same data. The various methods for assessing reliability accomplish different purposes, and the results do not necessarily generalize across methods. Because of this, we like to see various approaches to reliability used within the same study. (To see a case where several reliability methods were used to assess the quality of the same measuring instrument, take another look at Excerpt 4.1.)

Our second warning concerns the fact that reliability coefficients really apply to data and not to measuring instruments. To understand the full truth of this claim, imagine that a test designed for a college-level class in physics is administered twice to a group of college students, producing a test-retest reliability coefficient of .90. Now, if that same test is administered on two occasions to a group of first grade students (with the same time interval between test and retest), the coefficient of stability would not be anywhere near .90. (The first graders would probably guess at all questions, and the test-retest reliability for this younger group most likely would end up close to 0.00.) Try to remember, therefore, that reliability is conceptually and computationally connected to the data produced by the *use* of a measuring instrument, not to the measuring instrument as it sits on the shelf.

Excerpt 4.11 illustrates the fact that reliability is a characteristic of data (rather than the instrument that produces the data). Within this excerpt, the first word *(they)* refers to the developers of a test, the MVS, that was used in a later study conducted by the authors of this excerpt. Whereas the scores on the VI scale of the MVS had approximately the same K–R 20 reliability coefficients within the high school and college examinees (.86 versus .89), notice the large difference between the reliability coefficients for these two groups on the OI scale. The difference between .39 and .79 suggests that the *scores* produced by the OI portion of the MVS have varying internal consistency depending upon the nature of the group to whom it is given.

Excerpt 4.11 Different Reliabilities from Different Samples

They also cited estimates of reliability for the three scales of the MVS using the Kuder-Richardson (KR–20s) procedure with both high school and college students. The reliability estimates for the high school student sample for the VI, OI, and B scales were .86, .39, and .23. For college students and workers, the results were KR–20 correlations of .89 for the VI scale, .79 for the OI scale, and .45 for the B scale.

Source: E. B. Mauer, and N. C. Gysbers. (1990). Identifying career concerns of entering freshmen using My Vocational Situation. *The Career Development Quarterly, 39*(2), p. 157.

Our next warning calls on you to recognize that any reliability coefficient is simply an estimate of consistency. If a different batch of examinees or raters are used, we would expect the reliability coefficient to be at least slightly different—even if the new batch of examinees or raters contains people who are highly similar to the original ones. If the groups are small, there would probably be more fluctuation in the reliability coefficient than if the groups are large. Accordingly, place more faith in the results associated with large groups. Regardless of how large the group of examinees or raters is, however, we like to see researchers use the word *estimated* in conjunction with the word *reliability*. (See Excerpt 4.1 for an example of how the notion of estimation is sometimes contained in reports of reliability).

Our next-to-last warning concerns estimates of internal consistency. If a test is administered under great time pressure, the various estimates of internal consistency—split-half, K–R 20, and coefficient alpha—will be spuriously high (i.e., too big). Accordingly, do not be overly impressed with high internal consistency reliability coefficients if data have been collected under a strict time limit or if there is no mention as to conditions under which the data were collected.

Finally, keep in mind that reliability is not the only criterion that should be used to assess the quality of data. A second important feature of the data produced by measuring instruments (or raters) has to do with the concept of validity. The remaining portion of this chapter is devoted to a consideration of what validity means and how it is reported.

VALIDITY

Whereas the best one-word synonym for reliability is consistency, the core essence of **validity** is captured nicely by the word *accuracy*. From this general perspective, a researcher's data are valid to the extent that the results of the measurement process are accurate. Stated differently, a measuring instrument is valid to the extent that it measures what it purports to measure.

In this portion of the chapter, we first consider the relationship between reliability and validity. Next, we discuss several of the frequently used procedures for assessing validity. Finally, we offer a few warnings concerning published claims that you may see about this aspect of data quality.

THE RELATIONSHIP BETWEEN RELIABILITY AND VALIDITY

It is possible for a researcher's data to be highly reliable even though the measuring instrument does not measure what it claims to measure. However, an instrument's data must be reliable if they are valid. Thus, high reliability is a necessary but not sufficient condition for high validity. A simple example may help to make this connection clear.

Suppose a test is constructed to measure the ability of fifth grade children to solve arithmetic word problems. Also suppose that the test scores produced by an administration of this test are highly reliable. In fact, let's imagine that the coefficient of stability turns out equal to the maximum possible value, $+1.00$. Even though the data from our hypothetical test demonstrate maximum consistency over time, the issue of accuracy remains unclear. The test may be measuring what it claims to measure—math ability applied to word problems. On the other hand, it may be that this test really measures reading ability.

Now, reverse our imaginary situation. Assume for the moment that all you know is that the test is valid. In other words, assume that this newly designed measuring instrument does, in fact, produce scores that accurately reflect the ability of fifth graders to solve arithmetic word problems. If our instrument produces scores that are valid, then those scores, of necessity, must also be reliable. Stated differently, accuracy requires consistency.

DIFFERENT KINDS OF VALIDITY

In published articles, researchers often present evidence concerning a specific kind of validity. Validity takes various forms because there are different ways in which scores can be accurate. To be a discriminating reader of the research literature, you need to be familiar with the purposes and statistical techniques associated with the popular validity procedures. The three most frequently used procedures are content validity, criterion-related validity, and construct validity.

CONTENT VALIDITY   With certain tests, questionnaires, or inventories, an important question concerns the degree to which the various items collectively cover the material that the instrument is supposed to cover. This question can be translated into a concern over the instrument's **content validity**. Normally, an instrument's standing with respect to content validity is determined simply by having experts carefully compare the content of the test against a syllabus or outline that specifies the instrument's claimed domain. Subjective opinion from such experts establishes—or doesn't establish—the content validity of the instrument, with no statistical procedures being applied to any data.

Excerpts 4.12–4.13 contain discussions of content validity. In the first of these excerpts, the DRS had been developed specifically for the researcher's study. In contrast, Excerpt 4.13 deals with a preexisting instrument (the

---

Excerpts 4.12–4.13 Content Validity

For the content validity procedure, two therapy-experienced psychologists served as judges. They were given the DRS and asked to read it and to comment on its dimensions, categories, definitions, and examples, particularly as to whether the DRS was adequate in terms of specificity, exhaustiveness, and universality (Pinsof, 1986). Both psychologists concurred with the DRS definitions, dimensions, categories, and examples.

Source: R. D. Stinchfield, and G. M. Burlingame. (1991). Development and use of the Directives Rating System in group therapy. *Journal of Counseling Psychology, 38*(3), p. 253.

The manual cites expert opinion in item selection and states that, "important information regarding the content validity . . . may be obtained by examining the types of items and the nature of the tasks in each test. . . ." For the most part, the WJ-R ACH does appear to be measuring what it claims to measure. A notable exception to the observation is the Writing Fluency subtest, which is normed for ages 4 years, 0 months to 90+. The authors claim that this subtest measures "skill in formulating and writing simple sentences quickly." This subtest, which has a 7-minute time limit, may be used as a measure of processing speed as part of the WJ-R Cognitive Battery. It does seem to measure psychomotor speed and visual-motor dexterity, but is questionable that sentence formulation skills are measured, particularly in young subjects or in subjects with small motor delays.

Source: V. K. Constenbader, and C. Perry. (1990). The Woodcock-Johnson Psychoeducational Battery-Revised. *Journal of Psychoeducational Assessment, 8*(2), p. 182.

WJ-R ACH) and the researchers' opinions as to the content validity claims made in the test manual.

CRITERION-RELATED VALIDITY   Researchers sometimes assess the degree to which their new instruments provide accurate measurements by comparing scores from the new instrument with scores on a relevant criterion variable. The new instrument under investigation might be a short, easy-to-give intelligence test, and in this case the criterion would probably be an existing reputable intelligence test (possibly the *Stanford-Binet*). Or, maybe the new test is an innovative college entrance examination; hence, the criterion variable would be a measure of academic success in college (possibly GPA). The validity of either of those new tests would be determined by (1) finding out how various people perform on the new test and on the criterion variable and (2) correlating these two sets of the scores. The resulting *r* is called the **validity coefficient**, with high values of *r* indicating high validity.

There are two kinds of criterion-related validity. If the new test is administered at about the same time that data are collected on the criterion variable, then the term **concurrent validity** is used to designate the kind of validity being investigated. Continuing the first example provided in the preceding paragraph, if people were given the new and existing intelligence tests with only a short time interval between their administrations, the correlation between the two data sets would speak to the issue of concurrent validity. If, however, people were given the new test years before they took the criterion test, then *r* would be a measure of **predictive validity**.

In Excerpts 4.14–4.15, we see two examples of how researchers typically summarize their results after assessing the concurrent validity of their measuring instruments. In each of these excerpts, notice how the statistical technique of correlation plays a central role in this kind of validation.[7]

In Excerpt 4.16, we see a case in which the predictive validity of a single instrument (the MAP) was investigated by comparing MAP Total Scores with several "outcome criteria" measured four years after the MAP was administered. These criteria were divided into two groups, with the mean and range of the resulting validity coefficients presented for each grouping of criterion variables.

CONSTRUCT VALIDITY   Many measuring instruments are developed to reveal how much of a personality or psychological construct is possessed by the examinees to whom the instrument is administered. To establish the degree of **construct validity** associated with such instruments, the test developer will typically do one or a combination of three things: (1) provide correlational

---

[7]*Although we are not told which specific correlational procedure was used in either of these studies, we assume that the correlation coefficients presented in each excerpt are Pearson's product-moment rs.*

Excerpts 4.14–4.15 Concurrent Validity

Criterion-related validity for school-based adolescents was established between the Hamilton Depression Rating Scale clinical interview (17-item version) and RADS. Five trained interviewers assessed 111 high school students selected on the basis of sex, race, and symptom severity. . . . Correlation between the RADS and the Hamilton was .83 (p < .001), indicating a strong relationship between the two methods of assessing depression. Twelve weeks later 109 of the students were reassessed by a different interviewer (blind to previous results) with the Hamilton and RADS. Correlation was .84 (p < .001) providing strong support for the concurrent validity of RADS.

Source: N. F. Davis. (1990). The Reynolds Adolescent Depression Scale. *Measurement and Evaluation in Counseling and Development, 23*(2), p. 89.

Correlations of the *Matthews Burnout Scale for Employees* with the *Maslach Burnout Inventory* (Maslach & Jackson, 1981) and the *State-Trait Anxiety Inventory* (Spielberger, 1983) provided evidence to support the concurrent validity of the *Matthews Burnout Scale for Employees.* Comparison with the *Maslach Burnout Inventory* produced correlation coefficients on the following subscales: emotion-frequency, .65; emotion-intensity, .57; depersonalization-frequency, .46; depersonalization-intensity, .37; accomplishment-frequency, -.29; and accomplishment-intensity, -.30.

Source: D. B. Matthews, (1990). A comparison of burnout in selected occupational fields. *The Career Development Quarterly, 38*(3), p. 234.

Excerpt 4.16 Predictive Validity

The author evaluated the MAP's predictive validity in a sample of 338 children who were followed from the original standardization sample after 4 years. Outcome criteria included the Wechsler Intelligence Scale for Children-Revised; the three Woodcock-Johnson achievement clusters; program variables (grade retention and assignment to a special class); report card grades (coded as below average, average, and above average); and nonstandardized teachers' observations. The mean correlation between the MAP Total Score and school performance criteria is a modest .22 (range: .17 to .26). Correlations between the MAP Total Score and standardized achievement and IQ measures were somewhat higher, but still modest, with a mean of .42 (range: .35 to .50).

Source: P. G. Shouten, and L. A. Kirkpatrick. (1991). Miller Assessment for Preschoolers. *Journal of Psychoeducational Assessment, 9*(2), p. 182.

evidence showing that the construct has a strong relationship with certain measured variables *and* a weak relationship with other variables, with the strong and weak relationships conceptually tied to the new instrument's construct in a logical manner; (2) show that certain groups obtain higher mean scores on the new instrument than other groups, with the high- and low-scoring groups being determined on logical grounds *prior to* the administration of the new instrument; or (3) conduct a factor analysis on scores from the new instrument.

Excerpts 4.17–4.19 provide examples of how the first of these approaches to construct validity is used and reported in published articles. As alluded to by the researchers associated with Excerpts 4.17 and 4.18, the two-pronged correlational approach to construct validity provides evidence as to the convergent and discriminant validity of the new instrument. Notice how the correlation coefficients dealing with *convergent validity* are all moderate or high (with some being positive while others are negative in Excerpt 4.17) and how those dealing with *discriminant validity* are all low. The researchers connected with Excerpt 4.19 ought to be commended for calling into question the construct validity of their Love Withdrawal and Maturity Demand constructs because certain correlations turned out to be *higher* than anticipated.

Excerpts 4.17–4.19 Construct Validity Using Correlations

In support of convergent construct validity RADS was found to correlate with other self-report depression measures such as the Beck Depression Inventory (BDI; Beck, Ward, Mendelson, Mock, & Erbaugh, 1961); Center for Epidemiological Studies-Depression Scale (CES-D; Radloff, 1977); The self-Rating Depression Scale (Zung, 1965); and the Children's Depression Inventory (CDI; Kovacs, 1979) with coefficients ranging from .68 to .76 ($p < .0001$).

RADS also correlated with several constructs related to depression: self-esteem ($-.67$ to $-.75$), anxiety (.73 to .80), loneliness (.64 and .67), learned helplessness ($-.53$), suicidal ideation (.59 to .61), and hopelessness (.50 and .54). RADS was also significantly correlated to hassles, low social support, and negative life events measures.

Discriminant validity between RADS and social desirability was suggested by low magnitude negative correlations ($-.25$ and $-.24$). Academic achievement (GPA) also shared little variance with RADS (.06 to $-.24$).

Source: N. F. Davis. (1990). The Reynolds Adolescent Depression Scale. *Measurement and Evaluation in Counseling and Development, 23*(2), p. 90.

The relationship observed between STT–1 and RLT-A ($r = .60$) supports the construct validity of the STT. This substantial correlation provides evidence for convergent validity because the Rate Level Test has been designed to reflect

(Continued)

Excerpts 4.17–4.19 Construct Validity Using Correlations
(Continued)

---

how fast individuals can lexically access words and semantically encode their meaning within a sentence. Also, the Rate Level Test has been found to be valid as a measure of typical reading rate, called "rauding rate" (Carver, 1986). STT–1 also correlated .26 with ND-E Rate, a 1-minute, self-reporting sample of reading rate; this correlation also provides moderate support for convergent validity. The near zero correlation of .03 between STT–1 and ALT-A provides additional support for the construct validity of this measure of cognitive speed (discriminant validity) because the Accuracy Level Test is a power test that has been designed to be minimally influenced by a speed factor. The .07 correlation between STT–1 and ND-E Vocabulary also provides support for the discriminant validity of the STT.

Source: R. P. Carver. (1992). Reliability and validity of the Speed of Thinking Test. *Educational and Psychological Measurement, 52*(1), p. 132.

The construct validity of the Love Withdrawal and Maturity Demands constructs is somewhat questionable because these scales correlated higher with other Baumrind constructs than with the constructs that they were designed to reflect. Further research with the Parenting Style Survey on larger samples is currently being conducted to determine whether the convergence between the Parenting Style Survey subscales and the Baumrind rating scales can be replicated and whether the properties of the Parenting Style Survey Love Withdrawal and Maturity Demands scales are improved when analyses are based on larger and more representative samples of families with children who have mental retardation.

Source: C. L. Saetermoe, K. F. Widaman, and S. Borthwick-Duffy. (1991). Validation of the Parenting Style Survey for parents of children with mental retardation. *Mental Retardation, 29*(3), p. 154.

In Excerpts 4.20 and 4.21, we see two examples of the "group comparison" approach to construct validity. In each case, the group(s) that logically should have scored lower on the instruments being evaluated did, in fact, produce lower mean scores.

The third procedure frequently used to assess construct validity involves a sophisticated statistical technique called **factor analysis.** Although we will not discuss the details of factor analysis here, we want you to see an illustration of how the results of such an investigation are typically summarized. We don't expect you to understand everything in Excerpt 4.22; our only purpose in presenting it is to alert you to the fact that construct validity is often assessed statistically using factor analysis.

Excerpts 4.20–4.21 Construct Validity Using Comparison Group Differences

Lucas, Gysbers, Buescher, and Heppner (1988) provided additional evidence of construct validity for the VI scale of the MVS when they found that undeclared university freshmen, adults seeking career counseling, and displaced homemakers who were undecided all had lower VI scores than the populations of these participants, in general.

Source: E. B. Mauer, and N. C. Gysbers. (1990). Identifying career concerns of entering freshmen using My Vocational Situation. *The Career Development Quarterly,* 39(2), p. 157.

Construct validity was assessed by several methods. After 50 items were selected by discriminant analysis in the developmental phase of the final form, employees in a variety of people-oriented occupations responded to the inventory. Unknown to the employees and their immediate supervisors, top management personnel had previously identified persons who were at the two extremes of the burnout continuum. The scale differentiated between the two groups. With 80 employees in the burned-out group, the mean was 32.04, with a standard deviation of 14.65. The not-burned-out group, with 103 persons, had a mean of 23.40 and a standard deviation of 12.74. The observed t statistic was 4.26, which was significant at the .01 level.

Source: D. B. Matthews, (1990). A comparison of burnout in selected occupational fields. *The Career Development Quarterly,* 38(3), p. 234.

Excerpt 4.22 Construct Validity Using Factor Analysis

The WPPSI-R manual cites two exploratory factor-analytic studies conducted on the standardization sample as evidence for the construct validity of the test (Weschler, 1989). In the first study, all of the Verbal subtests loaded significantly on one factor and all of the Performance subtests on another. Comprehension was correlated most significantly with the Verbal factor (.75), while Block Design correlated highest with the Performance factor (.70). The second study investigated the existence of the factor structure across age levels by dividing the standardization sample into three groups: Group 1 (3 years, 0 months to 4 years, 6 months); Group 2 (4 years, 7 months to 6 years, 0 months); and Group 3 (6 years, 1 month to 7 years, 3 months). As in the first study, the second analysis demonstrated that all Verbal subtests loaded higher on the first factor and all Performance tests on the second factor with the exception of Picture Completion, at the 3 year to 4 year, 6 month age level; it loaded equally (.50) on both factors. The split loading for Picture Completion is not surprising given its verbal and visual demands, a fact examiners need to consider when they are analyzing a child's performance on this task.

(Continued)

Excerpt 4.22 Construct Validity Using Factor Analysis *(Continued)*

Because exploratory factor analytic results often are influenced by the method utilized to extract factors, a confirmatory factor analysis was performed on data from the standardization sample in order to investigate further the accuracy of the test's proposed structure (Gyurke, Stone, & Beyer, 1990). The results of this analysis were consistent with the findings of the studies reported in the manual. Data were explained best by the two-factor model, which supports the separate interpretation of the Verbal and Performance scales.

Source: R. R. Delugach. (1991). Wechsler Preschool and Primary Scale of Intelligence-Revised. *Journal of Psychoeducational Assessment, 9*(3), p. 283.

WARNINGS ABOUT VALIDITY CLAIMS

Before concluding our discussion of validity, we want to sensitize you to a few concerns regarding validity claims. Because researchers typically have a vested interest in their studies, they are eager to have others believe that their data are accurate. Readers of the research literature must be "on guard" for unjustified claims of validity and for cases where the issue of validity is not addressed at all. In an effort to help in this regard, we want to discuss a few things that you should keep in mind as you encounter reports of empirical investigations.

First, remember that reliability is a necessary but not sufficient condition for validity. Accordingly, do not be lulled into an unjustified sense of security concerning the accuracy of research data by a technical and persuasive discussion of consistency. Reliability and validity deal with different concepts, and a presentation of reliability coefficients—no matter how high—should not cause one's concern for validity to evaporate.

Next, keep in mind that validity (like reliability) is really a characteristic of the data produced by a measuring instrument and not a characteristic of the measuring instrument itself. If a so-called valid instrument is used to collect data from people who are too young or who cannot read or who lack any motivation to do well, then the scores produced by that instrument will be of questionable validity. The important point here is simply this: The subjects used by a researcher and the conditions under which measurements are collected must be similar to the subjects and conditions involved in validation studies before you should accept the researcher's claim that the research data are valid because those data came from an instrument having "proven validity."

Our third warning concerns content validity. Earlier, we indicated that this form of validity usually involves a subjective evaluation of the measuring instrument's content. Clearly, this evaluation ought to be conducted by individuals who possess (1) the technical expertise to make good judgments as to content relevance and (2) a willingness to provide, if necessary, negative feedback to the test developer. When reporting on efforts made to assess content validity, researchers should describe in detail who examined the content, what they were asked to do, and how their evaluative comments turned out.

With respect to criterion-related and construct validity, a similar warning seems important enough to mention. With these approaches to assessing validity, scores from the instrument being validated are correlated with the scores associated with one or more "other" variables. If the other variables are illogical or if the validity of the scores associated with such variables is low, then the computed validity coefficients conceivably could make a truly good instrument look as if it is defective. Thus, regarding the predictive, concurrent, or construct validity of a new measuring instrument, the researcher should first discuss the quality of the data that are paired with the new instrument's data.

Our next-to-last warning concerns the fact that the validity coefficients associated with criterion-related or construct probes are simply estimates, not definitive statements. Just as with reliability, the correlation coefficients reported to back up claims of validity would likely fluctuate if the study were to be replicated with a new batch of subjects. This is true even if the subjects in the original and replicated studies are similar. Such fluctuations can be expected to be larger if the validity coefficients are based on small groups of subjects; accordingly, give researchers more credit when their validity investigation are based on large groups.

Finally, keep in mind that efforts to assess predictive and concurrent validity utilize correlation coefficients to estimate the extent to which a measuring instrument can be said to yield accurate scores. When construct validity is dealt with by assessing an instrument's convergent/discriminant capabilities or by conducting a factor analysis, correlation again is the vehicle through which validity is revealed. Because correlation plays such a central role in the validity of these kinds of investigations, it is important for you to remember the warnings about correlation that we presented near the end of Chapter 3. In particular, do not forget that r^2 provides a better index of a relationship's strength than does r.

TWO FINAL COMMENTS

Within our discussions of reliability and validity, we have not addressed a question that most likely passed through your mind at least once as we talked about different procedures for assessing consistency and accuracy. That question is simply, "How high do the reliability and validity coefficients need to be before we can trust the results and conclusions of the study?" Before leaving this chapter, we want to answer this fully legitimate question.

For both reliability and validity, it would be neat and tidy if we could provide some absolute dividing point (say, .50) that separates large from small coefficients. Unfortunately, we cannot do this. In evaluating the reliability and validity of data, the issue of "large enough" has to be answered in a *relative* manner. The question that the researcher (and you) should ask is, "How do the reliability and validity associated with the measuring instrument(s) used in a given study compare with the reliability and validity associated with other available instruments?" If the answer to this query about relative quality turns out to be "pretty good," then you should evaluate the researcher's data in a positive manner—even if the absolute size of reported coefficients leaves lots of room for improvement.

Our next (and last) general comment about reliability and validity is related to the fact that data quality, by itself, does not determine the degree to which a study's results can be trusted. It's possible for a study's conclusions to be totally worthless even though the data analyzed possess high degrees of reliability and validity. A study can go "down the tubes" despite the existence of good data if the wrong statistical procedure is used to analyze data, if the conclusions extend beyond what the data legitimately allow, or if the design of the study is deficient. Reliability and validity are important concepts to keep in mind as you read technical reports of research investigations, but other important concerns must be attended to as well.

REVIEW TERMS

Accuracy	Factor analysis
Alpha	Internal consistency reliability
Alternate-forms reliability	Interrater reliability
Coefficient alpha	Intraclasss correlation
Coefficient of concordance	Kuder–Richardson #20 (K-R 20)
Coefficient of equivalence	Parallel-forms reliability
Coefficient of stability	Predictive validity
Cohen's kappa	Reliability
Concurrent validity	Reliability coefficient
Consistency	Spearman-Brown
Construct validity	Split-half reliability coefficient
Content validity	Test-retest reliability coefficient
Criterion-related validity	Validity
Cronbach's alpha	Validity coefficient
Equivalent-forms reliability	

REVIEW QUESTIONS

1. The basic idea of reliability is captured by what word?

2. What is the name for the reliability procedure that leads to a coefficient of stability? To a coefficient of equivalence?

3. Regardless of which method is used to assess reliability, the numerical index of the data's consistency has a maximum value of _____?

4. What piece of information should have been included along with the test-retest reliability coefficient that is reported in Excerpt 4.2?

5. Which of the reliability procedures assesses the degree to which the individual questions in a test or inventory "hang together" and measure the same thing?

6. Why is the Cronbach alpha approach to assessing internal consistency reliability more versatile than the Kuder-Richardson 20 approach?

7. What kind of data are involved in a study if the researcher uses Kendall's coefficient of concordance to quantify the consistency among raters' evaluations?

8. Look once more at Excerpt 4.5. If the internal consistency of the test data had been assessed by the split-half technique (rather than K-R 20), would the reliability coefficients have turned out equal to the same values?

9. Should a reliability coefficient be interpreted as revealing something about the measuring instrument, or should it be interpreted as revealing something about the scores produced by the measuring instrument?

10. Look again at the single sentence contained in Excerpt 4.4. What would have been a better word to use in this sentence instead of *calculated*?

11. In Excerpt 4.1, validity is discussed in the final two sentences of the second paragraph. What type of validity is being discussed: content, criterion-related, or construct?

12. If a researcher presents evidence concerning the convergent and discriminant validity of a new instrument, what main type of validity is being dealt with: content, criterion-related, or construct?

13. Look at Excerpt 4.12. Did the author provide sufficient information concerning the qualifications of the two individuals who served as judges for the content validity exercise?

14. What might cause the correlation coefficient used to assess a new test's concurrent validity to turn out very low even though the new test's scores are highly accurate?

15. Look one last time at Excerpt 4.16. What is the value of the coefficient of determination when the MAP is used to predict school performance?

5

FOUNDATIONS OF
INFERENTIAL STATISTICS

In Chapters 2–4, we considered various statistical procedures that are used to organize and summarize data. At times, the researcher's sole objective is to describe the people (or things) in terms of the characteristic(s) associated with the data. When that is the case, the statistical task is finished as soon as the data are displayed in an organized picture, are reduced to compact indices (e.g., the mean and standard deviation), are described in terms of distributional shape, are evaluated relative to the concerns of reliability and validity, and in the case of a bivariate concern, are examined to discern the strength and direction of a relationship.

In many instances, however, the researcher's primary objective is to draw conclusions that extend beyond the specific data that are collected. In this kind of study, the data are considered to represent a sample—and the goal of the investigation is to make one or more statements about the larger group of which the sample is only a part. Such statements, when based upon sample data but designed to extend beyond the sample in terms of relevance, are called *statistical inferences*. Not surprisingly, the term **inferential statistics** is used to label the portion of statistics dealing with the principles and techniques that allow researchers to generalize their findings beyond the actual data sets obtained.

In this chapter, we will discuss the basic principles of inferential statistics. We begin by considering the simple notions of sample, population, and scientific guess. Next, we take a look at five of the main types of samples used by applied researchers. Then we discuss certain problems that crop up to block a researcher's effort to generalize findings to the desired population. Finally, a few tips are offered concerning specific things to look for as you read professional research reports.

STATISTICAL INFERENCE

Whenever a statistical inference is made, a **sample** is first extracted (or is considered to have come from) a larger group called the **population.** Measurements are then taken on the people or objects that compose the sample. Once these measurements are summarized—for example, by computing a correlation coefficient—an educated guess is made as to the numerical value of the same statistical concept (which, in our example, would be the correlation coefficient) in the population. This educated guess as to the population's numerical characteristic is the **statistical inference**.

If measurements could be obtained on all people (or objects) contained in the population, statistical inference would be unnecessary. For instance, suppose the coach of the girls' basketball team at a local high school wants to know the median height of 12 varsity team members. It would be silly for the coach to use inferential statistics to answer this question. Instead of the coach's making an educated guess as to the team's median height (after seeing how tall a few of the girls are), it would be easy to measure the height of each member of the varsity team and then obtain the precise answer to the question.

In many situations, researchers cannot answer their questions about their populations as easily as could the coach in our basketball example. Two reasons seem to account for the wide use of inferential statistics. One of these explanations concerns the measurement process while the other concerns the nature of the population. Because inferential statistics are used so often by applied researchers, it is worthwhile to pause for a moment and consider these two explanations as to why only portions of populations are measured, with educated guesses being made on the basis of the sample data.

First of all, it is sometimes too costly (in dollars and/or time) to measure every member of the population. For example, the intelligence of all students in a high school cannot be measured with an individual intelligence test because (1) teachers would be upset by having each student removed from classes for two consecutive periods to take the test and (2) the school's budget would not contain the funds needed to pay a psychologist to do this testing. In this situation, it would be better for the principal to make an educated guess about the average intelligence of the high school students than to have no data-based idea whatsoever as to the students' intellectual capabilities. The principal's guess about the average intelligence is based on a sample of students taken from the population made up of all students in the high school. In this example, the principal is sampling from a **tangible population**, because each member of the student body could end up in the sample and be tested.

The second reason for using inferential statistics is even more compelling than the issue of limited funds and time. Often, the population of interest extends into the future. For example, the high school principal in our previous example probably would like to have information about the intellectual capabilities of the school's student body so improvements in the curriculum could be made. Such changes are made on the assumption that next year's students will not be dissimilar from this year's students. Even if the funds and time could be found to administer an individual intelligence test to every student in the school, the obtained data would be viewed as coming from a *portion* of the population of interest. That population is made up of students who attend the school now *plus* students who will follow in their footsteps. Clearly, measurements cannot be obtained from all members of such a population because a portion of the population has not yet "arrived on the scene." In this case, the principal creates an **abstract population** to fit an existing sample.

A few years ago, this book's first author participated as a subject in a study to see if various levels of consumed oxygen have an effect, during strenuous exercise, on blood composition. The researcher who conducted this study was interested in what took place physiologically during exercise on a stationary bicycle among non-sedentary young men between the ages of 25 and 35. That researcher's population was not just active males who were 25–35 years old at the time of the investigation. The population was defined to include active males who *would be* in this age range at the time his research summary got published—approximately 18 months following the data collection. Inferential statistics were used because the subjects of the investigation were considered to be a representative sample of a population of similar individuals that extended into the future.

To clarify the way statistical inference works, consider the two pictures in Figure 5.1. These pictures are identical in that (1) measurements are taken only on the people (or objects) that compose the sample; (2) the educated guess, or inference, extends *from* the sample *to* the population; and (3) the value of the population characteristic is not known (nor ever can be known as a result of the inferential process). While our illustration shows that the inference concerns the mean, we could have set up our pictures to show that the educated guess deals with the median, the variance, the product-moment correlation, or any other statistical concept we might wish to focus upon.

As you can see, the only differences between our two pictures involves the solid versus dotted nature of the larger circle and the black arrows. In the top picture, the population is tangible in nature, with each member within the larger circle available for inclusion in the sample. When this is the case, the researcher actually begins with the population and then ends up with the sample. In Figure 5.1, the lower picture is meant to represent the inferential setup in which the sequence of events is reversed. Here, the researcher begins with the sample and then creates an abstract population that is considered to include people (or objects) like those included in the sample.

In Excerpts 5.1–5.2, we see descriptions of the samples and populations used in two different studies. In the first excerpt, the researcher began with a tangible population (of males jailed in Chicago) and then extracted 728 of

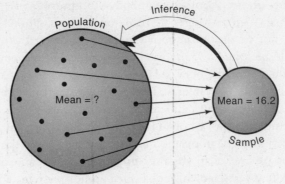

(a) Sampling from a tangible population

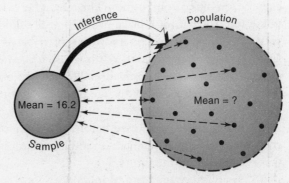

(b) Creation of an abstract population
to fit an existing sample

FIGURE 5.1 *Two kinds of sample/population situations.*

these individuals to form the sample. The sample/population situation in this study coincides with Figure 5.1a.

In Excerpt 5.2, we see a case of where the researcher began with the subjects (16 male rats) and then imagined that a larger group of similar rats, the population, corresponded to the sample that arrived one day in the mail. The sample/population situation in this rat study, therefore, coincides with Figure 5.1b.

THE CONCEPTS OF STATISTICS AND PARAMETER

When researchers engage in inferential statistics, they must deal with four questions *before* they can make their educated guess, or inference, that extends from the sample to the population:

1. If the population is tangible, how should the sample be selected?
2. What characteristic (i.e., variable) of the population is of interest?
3. How will the subjects in the sample be measured?
4. What will be the "statistical focus" of the study?

Excerpts 5.1–5.2 Tangible and Abstract Populations

SUBJECTS

Subjects were 728 male detainees, randomly selected directly from pretrial arraignment at the Cook County Department of Corrections (CCDC) in Chicago. The CCDC is used solely for pretrial detention and for offenders sentenced on misdemeanor charges for less than one year. Data were collected between November 1983 and November 1984. To include a sufficient number of persons accused of serious crimes, the sample was stratified by category of charge (50% misdemeanants, 50% felons).... All detainees, excluding persons with gunshot wounds or other traumatic injuries, were part of the sampling pool. Personnel at the jail referred all persons targeted for participation in the project, regardless of their mental state, potential for violence, or fitness to stand trial. As virtually no detainee was a priori ruled ineligible, the sample was unbiased in relation to the characteristics of the larger jail population.

Source: K. M. Abram and L. A. Teplin. (1991). Co-occurring disorders among mentally ill jail detainees: Implications for public policy. *American Psychologist, 46*(10), p. 1037.

SUBJECTS

The subjects were 16 experimentally naive male rats, 80 days old on arrival at the laboratory, purchased from the Holtzman Company, Madison, Wisconsin.

Source: E. J. Capaldi, D. J. Miller, S. Alptekin, and K. Barry. (1991). Discrimination learning. *Learning and Motivation, 22*(4), p. 443.

The first of these questions will be considered in detail in the next section. The second question, of course, is answered when the researcher decides what to study.[1] The third question—concerning the measurement of subjects—is clarified in the description of instruments used to collect data, and the issues of reliability and validity (covered in Chapter 4) are critical factors to consider when judging whether the researcher did an adequate job in measuring the subjects. This brings us to the fourth question, a concern for the "statistical focus" of the inference.

After the researcher has measured the sample subjects on the variable(s) of interest, there are many alternative ways in which the data can be summarized. The researcher could compute, for example, a measure of central tendency, a measure of variability, a measure of skewness, or a measure of

---

[1] *You may, at times, disagree with the researcher as to whether the characteristic of the people, animals, or objects in the population is important. Nevertheless, we doubt that you will ever experience difficulty determining what variables were examined. A clear answer to this question is usually contained in the article's title, the statement of purpose, and/or the discussion of dependent variables.*

relationship. But even within each of these broad categories, the researcher has alternatives as to how the data will be summarized. With central tendency, for example, the researcher might decide to focus on the median rather than on the mean or the mode. If relationship is the issue of interest, a decision might be made to compute Pearson's product-moment correlation coefficient rather than other available correlational indices. The term **statistical focus** is used simply to indicate the way in which the data are summarized.

Regardless of how a researcher decides to analyze the sample data, there will always be two numerical values that correspond to the study's statistical focus. One of these is "in" the sample—and it can be computed as soon as the sample subjects are measured. This numerical value is called the **statistic**. The second value that corresponds to the study's statistical focus is "in" the population, and it is called the **parameter**. The parameter, of course, can never be computed because measurements exist for only a portion of the people, animals, or objects that compose the population.

Because researchers often use symbols to represent the numerical values of their statistics (and sometimes use different symbols to represent the unknown values of the corresponding parameters), it is essential that you become familiar with the symbols associated with inferential statistics. To assist you in doing this, we have developed a chart (Table 5.1) showing the most frequently used symbols for the statistic and parameter that correspond to the same statistical focus. As you can easily see, Roman letters are used to represent statistics whereas Greek letters stand for parameters.

TABLE 5.1

SYMBOLS USED FOR CORRESPONDING STATISTICS AND PARAMETERS

Statistical focus	Statistic (in the sample)	Parameter (in the population)
Mean	$\overline{X}$ or M	μ
Variance	s^2	σ^2
Standard deviation	s	σ
Proportion	p	P
Product-moment correlation*	r_s	ρ
Rank-order correlation	r_s	ρ
Size of group†	n	N

*Unfortunately, the symbol ρ is used to designate the value of the product-moment correlation in the relevant population. This is the letter "rho" from the Greek alphabet. In Chapter 3, we saw that Spearman's rank-order correlation is also referred to as rho.

†In many articles, the symbol N is used to indicate the size of the *sample*. It would be better if the symbol n could be used, instead of N, when researchers give us information about their sample sizes.

Now that we have clarified the notions of statistic and parameter, we can be a bit more parsimonious in our definition of inferential statistics. When engaged in inferential statistics, a researcher uses information concerning the known value of the sample statistic to make an educated guess as to the unknown value of the population parameter. If, for example, the statistical focus is centered on the mean, then information concerning the known value of $\overline{X}$ used to make a scientific guess as to the value of μ.

Types of Samples

The nature of the sample used by a researcher as a basis for making an educated guess as to the parameter's value obviously has an influence on the inferential process. To be more specific, we can assert that the nature of the sample will influence either (1) the accuracy of the inferential guess or (2) the definition of the population toward which the inferential guess is directed. To help you understand the way in which the sample can affect the inferential process in these two ways, we need to distinguish among five different kinds of samples.

Probability Samples

If all members of the population can be specified prior to the sample's being drawn, if each member of the population has at least some chance of being included in the sample, and if the probability of any member of the population being drawn is known, then the resulting sample is referred to as a **probability sample**. The two types of probability samples that we will discuss are called *simple random samples* and *stratified random samples*. As you read about each of these samples, keep in mind the illustration presented in Figure 5.1a.

Simple Random Samples With a **simple random sample**, the researcher, either literally or figuratively, puts the names of all members of the population into a hat, shuffles the hat's contents, and then blindly selects out a portion of the names to determine which members of the total group will or won't be included in the sample. The key feature of this kind of sample is an equal opportunity for each member of the population to be included in the sample. It is conceivable, of course, that such a sample could turn out to be grossly unrepresentative of the population (because the sample turns out to contain the population members that are, for example, strongest or most intelligent or tallest). It is far more likely, however, that a simple random sample will lead to a measurement-based statistic that approximates the value of the parameter. This is especially true when the sample is large rather than small.

In Excerpt 5.3, we see a case in which a simple random sample was selected from a population. Notice that the phrase *simple random sample* does not occur in this passage, nor does the word *simple* appear. All we are told is that 52 persons were "randomly selected" from (the population of) clients registered in an Atlanta-based AIDS social services agency. Whenever researchers use the phrase *randomly selected*, you should assume that the samples being described are simple random samples.

Excerpt 5.3 Simple Random Sample

PARTICIPANTS

A total of 52 persons diagnosed with either AIDS or HIV-symptomatic infection were randomly selected from clients registered in an Atlanta-based AIDS social services agency. Of the 45 male and 7 female participants, 36 were White and 16 were Black. A total of 30 participants reported they were infected through homosexual activity only, 6 through IVDA only, 5 through homosexual activity and IVDA, 5 through heterosexual activity and IVDA, 3 through heterosexual activity only, and 3 through contaminated blood products. Four additional individuals were also selected but did not complete the individual research interview that was conducted by a White, male counselor.

Source: C. T. Allers and K. J. Benjack. (1991). Connections between childhood abuse and HIV infection. *Journal of Counseling and Development, 70*(2), p. 310.

STRATIFIED RANDOM SAMPLE To reduce the possibility that the sample might turn out to be unrepresentative of the population, researchers will sometimes select a **stratified random sample.** To do this, the population must first be subdivided into two or more parts based upon the knowledge of how each member of the population stands relative to one or more stratifying variables. Then, a sample is drawn so as to mirror the population percentages associated with each segment (or stratum) of the population. Thus, if a researcher knew that the population contained 60 percent males and 40 percent females, a random sample stratified on gender would end up containing 6 males for every 4 females.

An example of a stratified random sample was presented earlier in Excerpt 5.1. Turn back to that excerpt to see how the population was stratified. For another example of this kind of sample, take a look at Excerpt 5.4. In this study, the population of 557 graduate programs in mental health was stratified on the basis of two stratifying variables: state and status. Once this population was subdivided into the resulting 100 parts, about two programs were selected for every 11 programs that shared the same state/status classification.

Excerpt 5.4 Stratified Random Sample

A questionnaire designed for this study was sent to the chairs of 100 clinically oriented master's programs in mental health (clinical and counseling psychology, counseling, counselor education, community psychology, and marriage, family and child counseling). All such programs in the United States (N=557) were identified using *Graduate Study in Psychology and Associated Fields* (APA, 1986) and *Counselor Preparation, 1986–89: Programs, Personnel, and Trends* (Hollis & Wantz, 1986). From these a random sample of 100 programs, stratified by state and by school status (public or private), were selected.

Source: R. Olkin and S. Gaughen. (1991). Evaluation and dismissal of students in master's level clinical programs: Legal parameters and survey results. *Counselor Education and Supervision, 30*(4), p. 282.

NONPROBABILITY SAMPLES

In many research studies, the investigator does *not* begin with a finite group of persons, objects, or animals where each member has a known, nonzero probability of being plucked out of the population for inclusion in the sample. In such situations, the sample is technically referred to as a **nonprobability sample.** Occasionally, as in Excerpt 5.5, an author will tell us directly that one or more nonprobability samples served as the basis for the inferential process. Few authors do this, however, and so you need to be able to identify this kind of sample from the description of the study's subject pool.

Although inferential statistics can be used with nonprobability samples, extreme care must be used in generalizing results from the sample to the

---

Excerpt 5.5 Nonprobability Samples

PARTICIPANTS

The participants consisted of a counselor trainee group (n=125–232) and a nonclinical sample (n=312–525. . . .). Both groups were basically nonprobability samples. The counselor trainees were volunteers representing seven southern universities and were in their first or second year of graduate studies in counselor education. Additionally, they were between the ages of 22 and 64 (M=33.58) with middle-class backgrounds. . . . Participants in the nonclinical group were individuals not currently in any type of counseling or therapy. They were recruited from a southern metropolitan medical center, university community, churches, and civic organizations, representing ages 19 to 62 (M=35.57 years) with a middle-class background.

Source: D. M. Lawson and H. Gaushell. (1991). Intergenerational family characteristics of counselor trainees. *Counselor Education and Supervision, 30*(4), p. 313.

population. From the research write-up, you probably will be able to determine who (or what) was in the sample that provided the empirical data. Determining the larger group to whom such inferential statements legitimately apply is usually a much more difficult task.

We will now consider three of the most frequently seen types of nonprobability samples. These are called purposive samples, convenience samples, and quota samples.

PURPOSIVE SAMPLES In some studies, the researcher starts with a large group of potential subjects. To be included in the sample, however, members of this large group must meet certain criteria established by the researcher because of the nature of the questions to be answered by the investigation. Once these screening criteria are employed to determine which members of the initial group wind up in the sample, the nature of the population at the "receiving end" of the "inferential arrow" is different from the large group of potential subjects with which the researcher started. The legitimate population associated with the inferential process is either (1) the portion of the initial group that satisfied the screening criteria, presuming that only a subset of these "acceptable" people (or objects) were actually measured or (2) an abstract population made up of people (or objects) similar to those included in the sample, presuming that each and every "acceptable" person (or object) was measured. These two notions of the population, of course, are meant to parallel the two situations depicted earlier in Figure 5.1.

Excerpts 5.6–5.7 illustrate the way researchers will sometimes use and describe their **purposive samples**. The researchers who conducted the study from which Excerpt 5.6 was taken deserve credit for using the term *purposive sample* to describe the students used to provide data. It would have been helpful, however, if they had told us how many returning graduate students there were and whether more than 68 students met the threefold criteria for inclusion in the sample.

In Excerpt 5.7, we see another instance of a purposive sample being used in an applied study. Note here that the researcher purposefully chose not to select a probability sample from the total pool of fourth-grade students enrolled in the four schools. Specific criteria were set up to restrict which children could potentially enter the sample because the researcher's central question was whether practice in retelling of silently read discourse differentially affects the reading-comprehension performance of good and poor readers. Marginal readers were not wanted in the sample. (As with Excerpt 5.6, we wish the authors of Excerpt 5.7 had indicated how large the sample was in comparison to the total group of individuals who satisfied the selection criteria.)

Excerpts 5.6–5.7 Purposive Samples

DATA COLLECTION

A purposive sample of adult returning graduate students in two schools at a large midwestern university was selected for this study. Criteria for the sample were threefold: adult students were 25 years of age and older, were returning to school after an absence of at least 3 years, and were adding the student role to their other adult roles. Students in the sample were enrolled in a mix of day, evening, and weekend programs.

Sixty-eight students were contacted by telephone during the first semester of return to school. A one-hour meeting with the investigator was scheduled. At this meeting, students participated in an open-ended interview regarding their expectations of instructors, and completed the Canfield Learning Style Inventory and the demographic data questionnaire.

Source: D. D. Flannery. (1991). Adults' expectations of instructors: Criteria for hiring and evaluating instructors. *Continuing Higher Education Review, 55*(1&2), p. 37.

SUBJECTS

The subjects for this study were fourth-grade students from four elementary schools in Maryland. Criteria for inclusion in the study were as follows: a score at the 20th percentile or above on the Cognitive Abilities Test for all subjects, a score at the 41st percentile or below on the reading comprehension section of the California Achievement Test (CAT) for the less-proficient readers; and a score at the 68th percentile or higher on the reading comprehension section of the CAT for the proficient readers. The sample for the study consisted of 48 fourth-grade students (24 proficient readers and 24 less-proficient readers).

Source: L. B. Gambrell, P. S. Koskinen, and B. A. Kapinus. (1991). Retelling and the reading comprehension of proficient and less proficient readers. *Journal of Educational Research, 84*(6), p. 357.

CONVENIENCE SAMPLES   In many studies, the researcher does not select a small group of subjects (the sample) from a large group of potential subjects (the population). Instead, the investigator simply collects data from whoever is available or can be recruited to participate in the study. Such data-providing groups, if they serve as the basis for inferential statements, are called **convenience samples**.

The population corresponding to any convenience sample is an abstract (i.e., hypothetical) population. It is considered by the researcher to include individuals (or objects) similar to those included in the sample. Therefore, the sample-population relationship brought about by convenience samples is always like that pictured earlier in Figure 5.1b.

Excerpts 5.8–5.11 describe groups of subjects that can be considered to be convenience samples. In each case, notice how the sample was made up of individuals who were available (because they were enrolled in a college course) or who volunteered to participate (after seeing a newspaper advertisement or poster designed to produce a sample).

The material presented in Excerpts 5.8–5.11 constitutes the complete description of the convenience samples used in these four studies. Because the inference, in each case, extends from the sample to an abstract population made up of individuals similar to those included in the sample, we feel that the descriptions of the first three samples are exceedingly short. The fourth of these excerpts, in contrast, provides us with five pieces of information about the 48 members of the sample recruited to participate in a study evaluating the comparative effectiveness of self-help books focused on divorce adjustment. In that description, the authors indicate the subjects' gender, age, how long they had been involved in a relationship, who initiated the breakup, and status of the relationship prior to breakup.

Excerpts 5.8–5.11 Convenience Samples

SUBJECTS

Subjects were 49 undergraduate psychology students (39 men, 10 women) at the University of Washington. They volunteered for a study entitled "Jam Taste Test" in return for course credit and were instructed not to eat anything for 3 hours before the study.

Source: T. D. Wilson, and J. W. Schooler. (1991). Thinking too much: Introspection can reduce the quality of preferences and decisions. *Journal of Personality and Social Psychology, 60*(2), p. 183.

The subjects for the follow-up study included 38 graduate students, 31 women and 7 men, who were enrolled in either a course in adolescent development ($n=16$) or one in tests and measurement ($n=22$) during a 3-week summer session. The mean age of the sample was 32.9 years (31.4 for men and 33.2 for women), and ages ranged from 20 to 50.

Source: N. K. Parsons, G. D. P. Kanter, and H. C. Richards. (1990). Validation of a scale to measure reasoning about abortion. *Journal of Counseling Psychology, 37*(1), p. 111.

PARTICIPANTS

Because the COSE is intended for use in training, supervision, and research regarding the development of strong percepts of self-efficacy, the population of greatest interest to us was counselor trainees. Thus, beginning counselor trainees who were enrolled in introductory pre-practicum courses were sampled. The sample consisted of 159 women, 53 men, and 1 person who did not indicate

(Continued)

Excerpts 5.8–5.11 Convenience Samples *(Continued)*

gender, all of whom were enrolled in graduate-level introductory counseling courses at one of two midwestern universities or one university in Hawaii (n=83, n=94, and n=36, respectively). The age range of the sample was 20 to 50 years, with a mode age of 23 years and a mean age of 29 years. The sample was 83% White, 14% Asian, and 3% other ethnic groups.

Source: L. M. Larson, L. A. Suzuki, K. N. Gillespie, M. T. Potenza, M. A. Bechtel, and A. L. Toulouse. (1992). Development and validation of the Counseling Self-Estimate Inventory. *Journal of Counseling Psychology, 39*(1), p. 107.

PARTICIPANTS

A total of 48 women and 16 men were recruited to participate in the study after responding to a newspaper advertisement or poster stating that participants could receive a free self-help book for participating in a study. Participants ranged in age from 19 to 62 years and had recently (90% within the past 12 months) experienced a divorce or breakup. The average length of the relationship was 10.3 years ($SD = 10.1$; Mode = 3; Mdn = 5), with a range of 1 to 36 years. Twenty-five percent ($n = 16$) of the participants reported that they had initiated the breakup, whereas 52% ($n = 33$) reported that their partner had ended the relationship. The remaining 23% of the participants ($n = 15$) reported that the breakup was a mutual decision. The nature of the participant's relationship at the time of the divorce or breakup was represented by one of four categories: marriage (63%), living together (23%), engaged (5%), or separated (8%).

Source: B. M. Ogles, M. J. Lambert, and D. E. Craig. (1991). Comparison of self-help books for coping with loss: Expectations and attributions. *Journal of Counseling Psychology, 38*(4), p. 388.

QUOTA SAMPLES The final type of nonprobability sample that we will consider is called a **quota sample**. Here, the researcher decides that the sample should contain X percent of a certain kind of person (or object), Y percent of a different kind of person (or object), and so on. Then, the researcher simply continues to hunt for enough people/things to measure, within each category, until all predetermined sample slots have been filled.

In Excerpt 5.12, we see an example of a quota sample that was used to assess the perceptions of students at a particular college toward a building on their campus, the Wexner Center. In this investigation, the researcher wanted the sample to be made up of between 5 and 10 individuals from each of the various campus locations (e.g., the student union, apartments, fraternity and sorority houses) who would agree to be interviewed. After the quota was filled from any one site, the researcher moved on to another site to find additional subjects.

Excerpt 5.12 Quota Samples

The interviewer moved from site to site at various times of day and night obtaining between 5 and 10 responses per site. For passersby, the interviewer took a position and then approached the first passerby for an interview. At restaurants, the interviewer took a position and then approached the first person who sat down. In each case, for the next interview the interviewer selected the next person of the opposite sex of the first and so on. For the apartments, fraternity and sorority houses (all within several blocks from the Center), the interviewer selected buildings at random (and in the case of apartments, units at random). For the apartment, the person who answered the door was asked to participate. For the fraternity and sorority houses, up to five of those present were asked to participate.

Source: B. S. Fisher and J. L. Nasar. (1992). Fear of crime in relation to three exterior site features prospect, refuge, and escape. *Environment and Behavior, 24*(1), p. 50.

On the surface, quota samples and stratified random samples seem to be highly similar. There is, however, a big difference. To obtain a stratified random sample, a finite population is first subdivided into sections and then a sample is selected randomly from each portion of the population. When combined, those randomly selected groups make up the stratified random sample. A quota sample is also made up of different groups of subjects that are combined. Each subgroup, however, is not randomly extracted from a different stratum of the population; rather, the researcher simply takes whoever comes along until all vacant sample slots are occupied. As a consequence, it is often difficult to know to whom the results of a study can be generalized when a quota sample serves as the basis for the inference.

THE PROBLEMS OF LOW RESPONSE RATES, REFUSALS TO PARTICIPATE, AND ATTRITION

If the researcher uses a probability sample, there will be little ambiguity about the destination of the inferential statement that is made—as long as the researcher clearly defines the *population* that supplied the study's subjects. Likewise, there will be little ambiguity associated about the target of inferential statements based upon nonprobability samples—as long as the *sample* is fully described. In each case, however, the inferential process becomes murky if data are collected from less than 100 percent of the individuals (or objects) that comprise the sample. In this section, we want to discuss three frequently seen situations in which inferences are limited because only a portion of the full sample is measured.

RESPONSE RATES

In many studies, the research data are collected by mailing one or more surveys, questionnaires, or tests to members of the sample. Usually, only a portion of the individuals who receive these mailed measurement probes furnish the researcher with the data that was sought. In many cases, the recipient of the survey, questionnaire, or test simply does not take the time to read and answer the questions. In other cases, the questions are answered but the instrument is never sent back to the researcher. In any event, the term **response rate** has been coined to indicate the percentage of sample subjects who send their completed forms back to the researcher.

In Excerpt 5.13–5.14, we see two studies in which questionnaires were sent to all members of the defined populations. Because the response rate in each study was far below the optimal value of 100 percent, the statistical inferences extend only to individuals similar to those who responded to the questionnaire. Fortunately, we are given information about the individuals who returned questionnaires, thus making it a bit easier to know the appropriate group to whom inferences apply.

Excerpts 5.13–5.14 Response Rate Influence on Sample

SAMPLE

One hundred eighty-eight of 508 deliverable questionnaires were returned, yielding a return rate of 37%. Limited financial resources and a brief funding period precluded additional follow-up mailings. Of the 181 respondents whose questionnaires were usable, 52% were males and 48% females. Their ages ranged from 25 to 57 with a mean age of 31.3. Fourteen percent had been away from school two years or less, 64% had been away between three and 10 years, and 22% had been away 11 or more years. As a group the male respondents were younger, with 63% between 25 and 29 years of age, 25% between 30 and 34, and 13% age 35 or older. Thirty-eight percent of the female respondents were between 25 and 29 years of age, 31% were between 30 and 34, and 31% were 35 or older.

Source: J. M. Ross-Gordon. (1991). Critical incidents in the college classroom: What do adult undergraduates perceive as effective teaching? *Continuing Higher Education Review, 55*(1&2), p. 18.

Five hundred questionnaires were distributed to participants in events sanctioned by the New York Road Runners Club, and to members of the organization who were presently using, or had previously used, orthotic shoe inserts. Questionnaires were distributed over a period of 3 months. Included with the survey was a self-addressed, prepaid, return envelope. Participants were informed that the data would be available to them at the end of the study. . . . Of the 500

(Continued)

Excerpts 5.13–5.14 Response Rate Influence on Sample *(Continued)*

---

questionnaires distributed, 347 (69.4%) were returned. These 347 runners who had used or who were using orthotic shoe inserts comprised the primary study group. There were 245 (71%) men and 102 (29%) women. The average age of the group was 36 years (range 15 to 61) and the average distance run each week was 39.6 miles (range, 5 to 89). The mean length of time for use of orthotic inserts was 23 months (range, 1 to 96). Of the types of inserts used, 281 (63%) were flexible, 80 (23%) were semi-rigid, and 49 (14%) were rigid.

Source: M. L. Gross, L. B. Davlin, and P. M. Evanski. (1991). Effectiveness of orthotic shoe inserts in the long-distance runner. *American Journal of Sports Medicine, 19*(4), p. 410.

In some studies, questionnaires will be sent to a random sample of individuals selected from a larger population. When this is done, you may be tempted to think that the researchers are basing their inferential statements on probability samples. If, however, only a portion of the questionnaires are returned, then the resulting sample loses its status as a probability sample. In Excerpt 5.15, we see a study where 49 percent of the randomly selected individuals provided usable data. Here again, the legitimate inference extends to individuals who are similar to those who responded, not to those who were sent the questionnaire or to the larger group that was sampled.

Excerpt 5.15 A Low Response Rate

SUBJECTS

Questionnaires were mailed to 1000 members of the National Association of Black Accountants (NABA), a professional organization whose members are accountants in a variety of professional settings, including public accounting, industry, government, and academia. The 1000 participants were randomly selected from a current NABA membership of approximately 1500. Of the 1000 questionnaires mailed, 529 were returned. Incomplete surveys and late returns reduced the number of processed replies to 494, yielding a usable response rate of 49%. The average age of the respondents was 30 years, with a range of 23 to 52 years. All had undergraduate college degrees, were Certified Public Accountants (CPAs). Of the 483 respondents indicating their sex, 250 were men and 233 were women.

Source: G. O. Gamble and M. T. Mattson. (1992). Type A behavior, job satisfaction, and stress among Black professionals. *Psychological Reports, 70*(1), p. 44.

Researchers often want their results to generalize to the full group of individuals to whom questionnaires are sent, even though it is likely that only a portion of the population will respond. In an effort to do this legitimately, they will employ two strategies for which they deserve credit. First, they will send reminders and follow-up questionnaires to those who fail to respond to the initial mailing. Second, they will compare the final groups of responders and nonresponders to see if these two groups appear to be similar. Excerpts 5.16–5.17 come from two studies in which these strategies were employed.

Excerpts 5.16–5.17 Dealing with Response Rates

The first wave of mailings occurred on February 1, 1988. One week later, all departments were sent a postcard reminding them to reply. Two weeks after that, all non-respondents received a second packet containing everything they had received three weeks earlier plus a brief message saying that because we had not heard from them, we assumed they had not responded, and that they were to disregard our letter if they had responded. Two weeks after that, all nonrespondents received a third packet. No further mailings were sent after that time. There were 39 nonrespondents out of 366 departments surveyed; 22 were in the identified group, and 18 were in the anonymous group. It should also be noted that 6 anonymous and 9 duplicates were eliminated from the sample. There was no way, however, to identify the 6 duplicate anonymous surveys. Consequently, all of the anonymous responses received were analyzed, falsely inflating the sample size for anonymous surveys by 6. It should also be noted that among the respondents asked to identify themselves, there were 9 that rendered themselves anonymous by refusing to give their name or the name of their university.

FOLLOW-UP OF NONRESPONDENTS

Although an 89% return rate is excellent by survey research standards, it still leaves one wondering whether the nonrespondents differ in some important way from the respondents. To answer this question, 16 of the nonresponding department chairs or acting chairs were phoned and asked to respond to the survey verbally. The department chairs typically acknowledged receiving the survey and said that they had passed it on to their designees to fill out, and that they were surprised that we had not received it. None of the departments phoned were willing to respond to the survey verbally. Their data (which were not incorporated into the corpus of data that was analyzed and reported) did not appear to differ from those of the initial respondents. The other seven were adamant that because spring classes were over, there was no one present who was qualified to answer the survey.

Source: J. E. Sieber, and M. J. Saks. (1989). A census of subject pool characteristics and policies. *American Psychologist, 44*(7), p. 1055.

(Continued)

Excerpts 5.16–5.17 Dealing with Response Rates *(Continued)*

Of the 100 questionnaires sent, 54 usable responses were returned. Responses were checked for representativeness of the stratified random sample of 100 programs. There were no significant differences between sample and responses in proportion of public or private schools. Most programs were in state universities (67%). There were also no significant differences by region of the country (as defined by the four AACD regions). Respondents were from the four geographical regions as follows: Western (15%), Southern (37%), Midwestern (31%), and North Atlantic (17%).

Source: R. Olkin and S. Gaughen. (1991). Evaluation and dismissal of students in master's level clinical programs: Legal parameters and survey results. *Counselor Education and Supervision, 30*(4), p. 282.

REFUSAL TO PARTICIPATE

In studies where individuals are asked to participate, some people may decline. Such **refusals to participate** create the same kind of problem that is brought about by low response rates. In each case, valid inferences extend only to individuals similar to those who actually supplied data, not to the larger group of individuals who were *asked* to supply data. In Excerpt 5.18, we see a case in which about half of the group of potential subjects chose not to participate.

Excerpt 5.18 Refusals to Participate

About 50% of those to whom the study was described agreed to participate. Of the group who declined participation, some did not meet the selection criteria, while others could not obtain agreement from their husbands/partners, despite their interest in participating. A sizable minority were simply not responsive to the idea of participation in the research.

Source: P. Fonagy, H. Steele, and M. Steele. (1991). Maternal representations of attachment during pregnancy predict the organization of infant-mother attachment at one year of age. *Child Development, 62*(5), p. 893.

Just as some researchers perform a check to see whether a less-than-optimal response rate affects the generalizability of results, certain investigators will compare those who agree to participate with those who decline. If no differences are noted, a stronger case exists for applying inferential statements to the full group of individuals invited to participate (and others who are similar) rather than simply to folks similar to those who supplied data. Excerpt 5.19 illustrates this kind of comparison.

Excerpt 5.19 Comparison of Participants Versus Nonparticipants

The project continued for a period of 2 months, in which time 106 women and 104 men agreed to be involved, and 30 clients (12%) declined. Inevitably, some clients were not asked to be involved. Reasons included: because it was not remembered to ask them, because they could not understand English, or because they arrived late for their appointment. Participating clients ranged in age from 16 to 64 years (total $M = 34.99$, $SD = 6.54$; women, $M = 33.72$, $SD = 6.36$; men, $M = 36.26$, $SD = 6.49$). Of the 30 persons who declined to be involved in the study, 14 were women and 16 men (total M age $= 34.37$ years, $SD = 6.99$; women, $M = 35.19$, $SD = 6.18$; men, $M = 33.54$, $SD = 6.33$).... Data for the refusing group of clients were compared through t or χ^2 tests, with data from the 210 clients who agreed to be involved. The only significant result from these analyses concerned the proportion of couples versus individuals in each of the groups. There was a significantly greater proportion of individuals in the refusing group.... That is, a client who arrived at the Counseling Section with a spouse was more likely to agree to be involved in the study than a person who was alone.

Source: D. G. McKinnon. (1990). Client-preferred therapist sex role orientations. *Journal of Counseling Psychology, 37*(1), p. 12.

ATTRITION[2]

In many studies, less than 100 percent of the subjects remain in the study from beginning to end. In some instances, such attrition arises because the procedures and/or data-collection activities of the investigation are aversive, boring, or costly to the subject. In other cases, forgetfulness, schedule changes, or changes in home location explain why certain individuals become dropouts. Regardless of the causal forces that bring about the phenomenon of **attrition**, it should be clear why attrition can affect the inferential process.

In Excerpt 5.20, we see an example where there was about a 20 percent attrition rate. The inferences generated in this study, therefore, extend to a population made up of individuals similar to those who remained in the study until its completion. Notice how the researchers who conducted this investigation used the term *sample* only in reference to the group that provided complete data during both of the testing sessions.

A FEW WARNINGS

As we approach the end of this chapter, we want to offer a handful of warnings about the inferential connection between samples and populations. We highly suggest that you become sensitive to these issues, because many professional

---

[2]*The problem of attrition if sometimes referred to as* **mortality.**

Excerpt 5.20 Attrition

PARTICIPANTS

Initial testing was done with 163 participants drawn from introductory educational psychology courses at a large midwestern university. Approximately 3 weeks following initial testing, 141 participants were retested, the difference being accounted for by participants who did not return. Data for participants who either did not attend both testings or provided incomplete data during a testing session were deleted, resulting in a final sample of 130 participants. The majority of the participants were in their early 20s, with about 75% of the sample being women.

Source: E. T. Dowd, C. R. Milne, and S. L. Wise. (1991). The Therapeutic Reactance Scale: A measure of psychological reactance. *Journal of Counseling and Development, 69*(6), p. 542.

---

journals contain articles in which the researcher's conclusions seem to extend far beyond what the inferential process legitimately allows. Unfortunately, more than a few researchers get carried away with the techniques used to analyze their data—and their technical reports suggest that they gave little or no consideration to the nature of their samples and populations.

Our first warning has to do with *a possible mismatch between the source of the researcher's data and the destination of the inferential claims.* Throughout this chapter, we have emphasized the importance of a good match between the sample and the population. Be on guard when you read or listen to research reports, because the desired "fit" between sample and population may leave much to be desired. Consider, for example, the information presented in Excerpt 5.21.

Our major concern with this study involves the nature of the subjects who supplied the data. To be more specific, we highly suspect that the female triple jumpers who formed the sample were generally superior to the intended population of "intercollegiate women triple jumpers." Although the results of this investigation may well generalize to other triple jumpers like those who were measured in this study, we do *not* accept the suggestion that the results apply to *all* intercollegiate women triple jumpers.

Our next warning has to do with the *size of the sample.* If you don't know much about the members of the sample or how the researcher obtained the sample, then the inferential process cannot operate successfully—no matter how large the sample might be. Try to remember, therefore, that it is the quality of the sample (rather than its size) that makes statistical inference work. Proof of this claim can be seen during our country's national elections when pollsters regularly predict with great accuracy who will win elections even though the samples used to develop these predictions are relatively small.

Excerpt 5.21 Mismatch Between Intended Population and Sample

The primary purpose of this study was to investigate the following selected kinematic characteristics of intercollegiate women triple jumpers: 1) the distance of each phase of the jump; 2) the horizontal and vertical velocity components of the center of gravity at takeoff and touchdown for each phase of the jump; 3) the position of the center of gravity at takeoff and touchdown for each phase of the jump; and 4) the angle of the center of gravity at takeoff for each phase of the jump. . . . The subjects of this study were drawn from two groups of women triple jumpers. One group consisted of eight women triple jumpers who were participating in the 1986 Big Ten Track and Field Championships at the University of Wisconsin at Madison. The other group consisted of 10 women triple jumpers participating in the 1986 National Track and Field Championships in Indianapolis.

Source: M. A. Al-Kilani and C. J. Widule. (1990). Selected kinematic characteristics of intercollegiate women triple jumpers. *American Journal of Sports Medicine, 18*(3), p. 268.

Warning number 3 concerns the term *random*. Randomness in research studies is usually considered to be a strong asset, but you should not be lulled into thinking that an investigation's results can be trusted simply because the term *random* shows up in the Method section of the write-up. Consider, for example, the material presented in Excerpts 5.22–5.24.

In the study from which Excerpt 5.22 was taken, the results do *not* generalize to the full population of adults in the unnamed Southwestern city. Even though the term *random* appears twice in this passage, certain people refused to participate; as a consequence, the results generalize only to the city's adults who would agree to face-to-face interviews. In Excerpt 5.23, the first sentence might prompt you to think that the 180 participants constituted a stratified random sample of employees from the large industrial organization. However, the second sentence indicates that these participants were drawn from a different study in which *volunteers* provided the data.

In Excerpt 5.24, we see that each of 400 subjects was randomly assigned to one of 10 experimental groups. It is important to note here that random assignment is not the same thing as random selection. Both are good, but these techniques are designed to accomplish *different* research objectives. Later in this book, we will discuss random assignment. For now, however, all we want you to do is recognize that the 400 undergraduate students used in this study were not randomly selected from any larger group. Collectively, these students constitute a convenience sample (and not a probability sample).

Excerpts 5.22–5.24 Warnings Concerning the Term *Random*

SAMPLE

Data were collected in 1990 in a survey of 330 adults (18 years old or older) in a Southwestern City with a population of approximately 350,000. A simple random sample of names and address was drawn from the R. L. Polk Directory for the city. People who refused to participate or who could not be located were replaced by random selection until the target sample size of 330 was reached. Interviews were conducted face-to-face by trained interviewers.

Source: H. G. Grasmick, E. Davenport, M. B. Chamlin, and R. J. Bursik, Jr. (1992). Protestant fundamentalism and the retributive doctrines of punishment. Criminology, 30(1), p. 28.

PARTICIPANTS

A random, stratified population of Black (n=64) and White (n=116) employees affiliated with a large industrial organization were selected for this study (N=180). This sample was drawn from a larger study (N=726) designed to investigate employee's perceptions of their organization's culture. Participants in the latter project were volunteers and they were recruited by letters of announcement.

Source: L. H. Gerstein and W. Valutis. (1991). Racial differences related to potential helpers' impressions of impaired workers. *Journal of Multicultural Counseling and Development, 19*(1), p. 4.

SUBJECTS

Subjects were 400 undergraduate students enrolled in introductory social science classes (200 males and 200 females). The average age of the participants was 20.54 years (range = 17 to 51 years; approximately 82% were between 18 and 22).... Subjects participated in small groups. Each subject was randomly assigned to one of 10 experimental groups.

Source: R. A. Fabes and C. L. Martin. (1991). Gender and age stereotypes of emotionality. *Personality and Social Psychology Bulletin, 17*(5), p. 534.

Our next-to-last warning again concerns the term *random*. Unfortunately, many people (including some researchers) do not understand clearly what qualifies as a random sample. Most likely, the term *random sample* has been used more than once to describe a sample created by the researcher asking for volunteers. For this reason, give researchers some extra credit when they go beyond simply saying that they used a random sample and also explain *how* they extracted their samples in a random fashion from the relevant populations. Be on the lookout for statements, for example, indicating that dice were rolled or coins were flipped to determine which members of the population were included in the sample. A device for selecting a random sample that is somewhat better than dice or coins is a **table of random numbers**. Excerpt 5.25 contains a reference to such a table, and the authors deserve credit for clarifying how their random sample was created.

Excerpt 5.25 Use of a Table of Random Numbers

SUBJECTS

Subjects were selected randomly from a listing of all licensed day care providers in a large city metropolitan area in the midwest. Child care centers and Head Start programs from two states were represented in the study. Using a table of random numbers, 187 centers were selected with three staff members per site to be included (N = 561) in the study.

Source: P. D. Welterau and D. A. Stegelin. (1991). Daycare providers' knowledge and attitudes about AIDS: A needs assessment. *Children's Health Care, 20*(2), p. 109.

The final warning we wish to provide is really a repetition of a major concern expressed earlier in this chapter. Simply stated, an empirical investigation that incorporates inferential statistics is worthless unless there is a detailed description of the population or the sample. No matter how carefully the researcher describes the measuring instruments and procedures of the study, and regardless of the levels of appropriateness and sophistication of the statistical techniques used to analyze the data, the results will be meaningless unless we are given a clear indication of the population from which the sample was drawn (in the case of probability samples) or the sample itself (in the case of nonprobability samples). Unfortunately, too many researchers get carried away with their ability to use complex inferential techniques when analyzing their data. We can almost guarantee that you will encounter technical write-ups in which the researchers emphasize their analytical skills to the near-exclusion of a clear explanation of where their data came from or to whom the results apply. When you come across such studies, give the authors *high* marks for being able to flex their "data analysis muscles"—but *low* marks for neglecting the basic inferential nature of their investigations.

To see an example of a well-done description of a nonprobability sample, consider Excerpt 5.26. Given this relatively complete description of

Excerpt 5.26 Detailed Description of a Sample

SUBJECTS

The subjects for the present study consisted of 60 identified children and adolescents with learning disabilities (LD) evaluated at an outpatient clinic affiliated with an Arkansas children's hospital. The subjects were predominantly from lower middle class socioeconomic backgrounds and were referred to the clinic because of academic and/or behavioral difficulties. The mean age for the sample was 11.03 years (range = 9 to 15), with a standard deviation of 1.88. There were 44 boys and 16 girls in the sample. The mean Wechsler Intelligence Scale for Children-Revised (WISC-R) (Wechsler, 1974) Full Scale IQ was 90.25 (range = 74 to 120), with a standard deviation of 13.19. Means and standard deviations on the Wide Range Achievement Test-Revised (WRAT-R) (Jastak & Wilkinson, 1984) were as follows: Reading $M = 81.26$ (range = 46 to 123), $SD = 17.77$; and Arithmetic $M = 77.71$ (range = 46 to 115), $SD = 16.53$. All of the children were identified as LD based on the presence of a discrepancy between actual and expected achievement. For the purposes of this study, children were included who evidenced at least a 15-point difference between scores from the WRAT-R and an intellectual scale from the WISC-R.

The child had to have either a Verbal or Performance Scale IQ score equal to or greater than 85. Ratings completed by both parents and teachers were examined in order to rule out potential associated attention deficit-hyperactivity disorder. If an elevated hyperactivity index from the Child Behavior Checklist (Achenbach & Edelbrock, 1983) or the Conners' Abbreviated Teachers Scale (Conners, 1973) was found, the child was excluded from the sample. None of the children had any significant history of hard neurological involvement (i.e., seizures, brain tumors, or head injuries). All the children were presently identified as in need of special education services within their respective school districts and were receiving instruction in either a resource or self-contained classroom. The children were all right-hand dominant, as indicated by the Lateral Dominance Exam from the Halstead-Reitan Neuropsychological Test Battery (Reitan, 1969). This criterion was employed in order to control for expected hand advantage in motor speed.

Source: J. H. Snow. (1992). Mental flexibility and planning skills in children and adolescents with learning disabilities. *Journal of Learning Disabilities, 25*(4), p. 266.

the 60 subjects used in this study, we have a much better sense of the hypothetical population to which the statistical inferences can be directed. After reading the material in Excerpt 5.26, go back and take a look at Excerpts 5.8 and 5.9, which describe the samples used in two other studies. In which case do you have the best sense of the kind of person included in the sample?

In Excerpt 5.27, we see another example of a researcher being careful to describe the sample of individuals from whom data were gathered. Notice how this researcher acknowledges in the last sentence of the first paragraph the existence of "selection biases" caused by only a subset of the initial random sample of students actually participating. Despite the selection biases, the researcher's careful description of the participating and nonparticipating individuals puts us in a good position to sense the legitimate population to which the inferential results can be directed.

Excerpt 5.27 Another Good Description of a Sample

SUBJECTS

The study was designed to test students who had completed most of their general education requirements necessary for graduation. To accomplish this, the active student file was used to select those students at a large midwestern university who have completed between 85–110 credits (of the 180 needed for graduation) by the end of spring quarter 1988. Three further criteria were used to define a group of students whose general education experiences were less diverse and more recent: (a) U. S. high school graduate; (b) entered as a freshman with no transfer credits fall quarter 1984 or later; and (c) between the ages of 19 and 30.

From amongst the 1,820 students who met the above criteria, letters of invitation were sent in April 1988 to a random subset of 750 students. In return for participating in the testing session, students received a $25 bookstore credit, a free lunch, and a feedback session to discuss test results. A total of 328 students (43.7%) responded to the letter, of whom 248 (33.1%) were interested in participating and 80 (10.7%) were not. A second letter was sent to students asking them to sign up for one of 10 testing sessions scheduled during the last four weeks of the quarter. Not all of the students who were interested in the study signed up for a particular testing session, and less than half (N = 118, 47.6%) attended one of the four-hour testing sessions. The resulting 15.7% participation rate introduced into the study inevitable selection biases that were not detectable.

Table 1 [not included here] describes the characteristics of students for whom test data were obtained. Comparisons between participating and nonparticipating students in the original sample of 750 students indicated comparability for credits completed and high school rank, but that participating students had higher overall college grade point averages. An estimated 47.7% of the students who met the original selection criteria were female, and 88.9% were Caucasian. Although no housing data for nonparticipating students were available, the percentage of dormitory residents (55.1%) is considerably higher than that for campus undergraduates (approximately 10%).

Source: D. D. Hendel. (1991). Evidence of convergent and discriminant validity in three measures of college outcomes. *Educational and Psychological Measurement, 51*(2), p. 352.

Detailed descriptions of samples and populations not only help to clarify the nature of the legitimate inferences associated with the completed study, but also serve to guide the work of future researchers. An example of how this can happen is presented in Excerpt 5.28. As you examine this passage, notice how the authors underscore the difference between earlier studies and the one from which this passage was taken—a difference in the nature of the adolescents who formed the "earlier" and "current" samples. If the samples in those "previous studies" had not been described well, the "present study" probably would not have been undertaken.

Excerpt 5.28 Using Clearly Defined Samples to Guide Others' Research

---

The present findings add to our knowledge of adolescents designated as behaviorally disordered and enrolled in special education programs in the public school system. Previous investigators examining the moral reasoning of deviant youth have either included only institutionalized delinquents in their samples (e.g., Hains & Miller, 1980; Jurkovic & Prentice, 1977; Kohlberg, 1978) or have confounded cognitive deficits with behavioral disorders (Freeman et al., 1980; Sigman et al., 1983). As a result, the findings of these previous studies are, for the most part, only generalizable to institutionalized delinquents or BD students with cognitive deficits and not to those students given the primary label of behavioral disorders in the public school system. The results of the present study, however, provide some information to those researchers and educators specifically concerned with understanding the moral reasoning of BD students in the public school system.

Source: K. A. Schonert and G. N. Cantor. (1991). Moral reasoning in behaviorally disordered adolescents from alternative and traditional high schools. *Behavioral Disorders, 17*(1), p. 31.

REVIEW TERMS

Abstract population

Attrition

Convenience sample

Inferential Statistics

Mortality

Nonprobability sample

Parameter

Population

Probability sample

Purposive sample

Quota sample

Refusals to participate

Response rate

Sample

Simple random sample

Statistic

Statistical inference

Statistical focus

Stratified random sample

Table of random numbers

Tangible population

REVIEW QUESTIONS

1. *Statistic* is to *sample* as _____ is to *population*.

2. In which direction does statistical inference move: from population to sample *or* from sample to population?

3. If a simple random sample of 100 individuals is drawn from a population of 1000 individuals, why might the results of the inferential process *not* provide a good "educated guess" as to the parameter's value?

4. In Excerpt 5.27, how should we conceptualize the population that corresponds with the final sample of students?

5. If a researcher collects data from a group of volunteers and then engages in inferential statistics, what kind of sample exists?

6. In general, quota samples are considered to be _____ (good/poor).

7. If each member of the population has an equal chance of being included in the sample, then the resulting sample is referred to as a(n) _____ sample.

8. If a random sample of individuals from a population are contacted and asked to participate in a study, and if those who respond negatively are replaced by randomly selected individuals who indicate a willingness to participate, should the sample be considered a random subset of the original population?

9. Random assignment _____ (does/does not) mean the same thing as random selection.

10. Look at Excerpt 5.1. We are told that the sample was randomly selected and stratified by category of charge. What else could the researcher have told us about the way this sample was drawn?

11. In the study associated with Excerpts 5.4 and 5.17, how large was the researcher's sample?

12. What does it mean to say that a researcher must decide upon the study's statistical focus before any inferential procedures can be utilized?

13. What is the matter with the paragraph that appears in Excerpt 5.29?

Excerpt 5.29 The Population and Sample in a Study on Bank
Holding Companies

The population for this study consists of U.S. bank holding companies located in all 50 states and the District of Columbia. To reduce possible distortions arising from size variations in the population, the study is limited to all medium and large bank holding companies—those with $300 million or more in total assets. This results in a sample of 563 bank holding companies ranging in size from $300 million to $205,012 million with a mean level of total assets of $4,776 million. These bank holding companies (BHCs) account for 90 percent of the total assets in the U.S. banking system and are thus the key players in the industry. This sample includes a broad range of U.S. bank holding companies (BHCs), ranging from large money center BHCs to regional and local BHCs, thus the size requirement does not lead to a sample so homogeneous as to be unrepresentative of the population. However, it eliminates possible distortions in model specification that might arise if the nearly 6,000 smaller BHCs that account for the remaining 10 percent of banking system assets were included.

Source: R. K. Reger, I. M. Duhaime, and J. L. Stimpert. (1992). Deregulation, strategic choice, risk, and financial performance. *Strategic Management Journal, 13*(3), p. 195.

6

ESTIMATION

In the previous chapter, we laid the foundation for our consideration of inferential statistics. We did that by discussing the key ingredients of this form of statistical thinking and analysis: population, sample, parameter, statistic, and inference. In this chapter, we now turn our attention to one of the two main ways in which researchers use sample statistics to make educated guesses as to the values of population parameters. These procedures fall under the general heading **Estimation.**

This chapter is divided into three main sections, First, the logic and techniques of *interval estimation* are presented. Next, we examine a second, slightly different way in which estimation works; this approach is called *point estimation*. Finally, we offer a few tips to keep in mind as you encounter research articles that rely on either of these forms of estimation.

Before beginning our discussion of estimation, we need to point out that the two major approaches to statistical inference—estimation and hypothesis testing—are similar in that the researcher makes an educated guess as to value of the population parameter. In that sense, both approaches involve a form of guesswork that might be construed to involve estimation. Despite this similarity, the term *estimation* has come to designate just one of the two ways in which researchers go about making their educated guesses about population parameters. The other approach, hypothesis testing, is discussed in Chapters 7 and 8.

INTERVAL ESTIMATION

To understand how **interval estimation** works, you must become familiar with three concepts: sampling errors, standard errors, and confidence intervals. In addition, you must come to realize that a confidence interval can be used with just about any statistic that is computed on the basis of sample data. To help you acquire these skills, we begin with a consideration of what is arguably the most important concept associated with inferential statistics: sampling error.

SAMPLING ERROR

When a sample is extracted from a population, it is conceivable that the value of the computed statistic will be identical to the unknown value of the population parameter. Although such a result is possible, it is far more likely that the statistic will turn out to be different from the parameter. The term **sampling error** refers to the magnitude of this difference.

To see an example of sampling error, take a coin out of your pocket or purse and flip your coin 20 times, keeping track of the proportion of times the outcome is "heads." We'll consider your 20 coin flips to represent a sample of your coin's life history of flips, with that total life history being the population. We also will assume that your coin is unbiased and that your flipping technique does not make a "heads" outcome more or less likely than a "tails" outcome. Given these two simple assumptions, we can assert that the parameter value is known to be .50. Now, stop reading, take out a coin, flip it 20 times, and see what proportion of your flips produce a "heads" outcome.

We did not know, of course, how your little coin-flipping exercise turned out. When *we* flipped our coin (a nickel) 20 times, however, we *do* know what happened. We ended up with 13 "heads" and 7 "tails," for a statistic of .65. The difference between the sample's statistic and the population's parameter is the sampling error. In our case, therefore, the sampling error turned out to be .15.[1]

If we (or you) end up observing 10 "heads" in our 20 coin flips, the sampling error would be equal to zero. Such a result, however, is not likely to occur. Usually, the sample statistic will "contain" sampling error and fail to mirror exactly the population parameter. Most of the time, of course, the size of the sampling error will be small, thus indicating that the statistic is a reasonably good approximation of the parameter. Occasionally, however, a sample will yield a statistic that is quite discrepant from the population's parameter. That would be the case if you get 19 or 20 "heads" (or "tails") when flipping a coin 20 times.

It should be noted that the term **sampling error** does *not* indicate that the sample has been extracted improperly from the population or that the sample data have been improperly summarized. (We ended up with a sampling error of .15 even though we took a random sample from our population of interest and even though we carefully summarized our data.) When sampling error exists, it is attributable not to any mistake being made but rather to the natural behavior of samples. Samples generally do not turn out to be small mirror images of their corresponding populations, and statistics usually do not turn out equal to their corresponding parameters. Even with proper sampling techniques and data analysis procedures, sampling error ought to be expected.

---

[1] *We computed the sampling error by subtracting .50 from .65.*

In our example dealing with 20 coin flips, we knew what the parameter's value was equal to. In most inferential situations, however, the researcher will know the numerical value of the sample's statistic but not the value of the population's parameter. This situation makes it impossible for the researcher to compute the precise size of the sampling error associated with any sample, but it does not alter the fact that sampling error should be expected. For example, suppose we gave you a coin that was known *only by us* to be slightly biased. Imagine that it would turn up "heads" 55 percent of the time over its life history. If we told you to flip this coin 20 times and then make a guess as to the value of the coin's parameter value, you should expect sampling error to occur. Hence, not knowing the parameter value (and thus not being able to compute the magnitude of any sample's sampling error) should not affect our expectation that the statistic and the parameter are at least slightly unequal.[2]

Sampling Distributions and Standard Errors

Most researchers extract a single sample from any population about which they want to make an educated guess. Earlier, for example, we asked you to take a sample of 20 flips of your coin's coin-flipping life history. It is possible, however, to *imagine* taking more than one sample from any given population. Thus, we can imagine taking multiple samples from the coin we flipped that gave us, in our first sample, an outcome of .65 (that is, 65 percent "heads").

When we imagine taking multiple samples (each made up of 20 flips) from that same coin, we visualize the results changing from sample to sample. In other words, whereas we obtained a statistic of .65 in our first sample, we would not be surprised to find that the statistic turns out equal to some other value for our second set of 20 flips. If a third sample (of 20 flips) were to be taken, we would not be surprised to discover that the third sample's statistic assumes a value different from the first two samples' statistics. If we continued (in our imagination) to extract samples (of 20 flips) from that same coin, we would eventually find that values of the statistic (1) would begin to repeat, as would be the case if we came across another sample that produced 13 "heads", and (2) would form a distribution having "tails" that extend away from the distribution's modal value.

The distribution of sample statistics alluded to in the preceding paragraph is called a **sampling distribution,** and the standard deviation of the values that make up such a distribution is called a **standard error.** Thus, a standard

---

[2] *If a population is perfectly homogenous, the sampling error will be equal to 0. If the population is heterogeneous but an enormously large sample is drawn, here again the statistic will turn out equal to the parameter once that statistic is rounded to one or two decimal places. Both of these situations, however, are unrealistic. Researchers typically are involved with heterogeneous populations and base their statistical inferences on small samples where $n < 50$.*

error is nothing more than an index of how variable the sample statistic is when multiple samples of the same size are drawn from the same population. As you recall from Chapter 2, variability can be measured in various ways; the standard error, however, is always conceptualized as being equal to the standard deviation of the sampling distribution of the statistic (once we imagine that multiple samples are extracted and summarized).[3]

Figure 6.1 contains the sampling distribution that we would end up with if we took many, many samples (of 20 flips per sample) from a fair coin's population of potential flips, with the statistical focus being the proportion of "heads" that turn up within each sample. The standard deviation of this sampling distribution is equal to about .11. This standard error provides a numer-

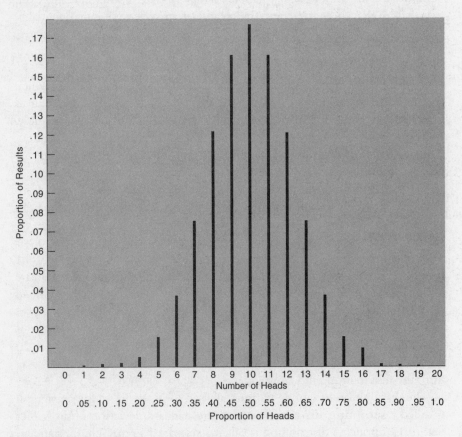

FIGURE 6.1 *Sampling distribution of number/proportion of "heads" in 20 flips of a fair coin.*

---

[3]*Even though the concepts of standard deviation and standard error are closely related, they are conceptually quite different. A standard deviation indicates the variability inside a single set of actual data points; a standard error, in contrast, indicates how variable the sample statistic is from sample to sample.*

ical index of how much dispersion exists among the values upon which the standard deviation is computed; in this case, each of those values corresponds to the proportion of "heads" associated with one of our imaginary samples.

The standard error indicates the extent to which the statistic fluctuates, from sample to sample, around the value of the parameter. The standard error, therefore, provides a measure of how much sampling error is likely to occur whenever a sample of a particular size is extracted from the population in question. To be more specific, the chances are about 2 out of 3 that the sampling error will be smaller than the size of the standard error (and about 1 in 3 that the sampling error will be larger than the size of the standard error). If the standard error is small, therefore, this would indicate that we should expect the statistic to approximate closely the value of the parameter. On the other hand, a large standard error would indicate that a larger discrepancy between the statistic and parameter is to be anticipated.

Earlier, we said that researchers normally extract only one sample from any given population. Based on our earlier statement to that effect (and now our reiteration of that same point), you may be wondering how it is possible to know what the standard error of the sampling distribution is equal to in light of the fact that the researcher cannot develop a sampling distribution like that shown earlier in Figure 6.1. The way researchers get around this problem is to use their sample data to estimate the standard error. We will not discuss the actual mechanics that are involved in doing this; rather, we simply want you to accept our claim that it *is* possible to do this.[4]

In our earlier example about a coin being flipped 20 times, our statistical focus was a proportion. Accordingly, the standard error (of .11) illustrated in Figure 6.1 is the standard error *of the proportion*. In some actual studies, the researcher's statistical focus will be a proportion, as has been the case in our coin-flipping example. In many studies, however, the statistical focus is something other than proportion. When reading journal articles, we find that the overwhelming majority of researchers focus their attention on means and correlation coefficients. There are, of course, other ways to "attack" a data set, and we occasionally come across articles in which the median, the variance, or the degree of skewness represents a study's statistical focus. Regardless of the statistical focus selected by the researcher, the standard error concept applies so long as the study involves inferential statistics.

Consider, for example, the two sentences in Excerpt 6.1. The statistical focus concerning the skiers' ages was the mean, and accordingly the index of sampling error is the standard error of the mean. This standard error is abbreviated SEM.

---

[4]*For example, when we use our single sample of 20 coin flips (13 heads, 7 tails) to estimate the standard error of the theoretical sampling distribution, we obtain the value of .1067. This estimated standard error of the proportion approximates the true value, .1118, that corresponds to the full sampling distribution shown in Figure 6.1.*

Excerpt 6.1 Standard Error of the Mean in the Text

Eight ski racers who were competitive at the provincial level took part in the study. The average age of the 5 junior and 3 senior competitors was 26.5±5.7 years ($\overline{X}$±SEM).

Source: A.E. Ready, H.R. Huber. (1990). Physiologic response of Nordic ski racers to three modes of sport specific exercise. *Canadian Journal of Sport Sciences, 15*(3), p. 214.

By providing information as to the estimated SEM associated with the skiers' mean age, the researchers who conducted this study are alerting their readers to the fact that their sample statistic should *not* be thought of as being identical to the population parameter. Stated symbolically, the estimated SEM cautions us not to consider $\overline{X}$ to μ. If a different sample of eight skiers were to be plucked out of the same population, the mean age of the skiers in this second sample would likely turn out equal to some value other than 26.5.

In Excerpt 6.2, we see another case where the researchers' statistical focus is the mean. Hence, the numbers in the third column of Table 1 correspond to the estimated standard error *of the mean*.[5] The first sentence in the second paragraph clarifies this fact.

In Excerpt 6.2, there are three standard error values presented because three samples were involved in this study, with each sample considered to have come from a different population. These values are different from one another because (1) the sample standard deviations suggest that the population corresponding to Group 2 is more homogeneous than the other two populations and (2) there were about twice as many individuals in Group 2 than in either of the other groups, a fact made clear in a different part of the research summary.

Also notice that the estimated standard errors presented in Table 1 of Excerpt 6.2 speak to the issue of the sampling error that is likely to be associated with the group *means*. Each value (9.00, 4.14, and 8.73) is an estimated standard error *of the mean*, and they help with the interpretation of the group means (99.62, 104.93, and 95.47). Even though each standard error value suggests what the *standard deviation* would be if we repeatedly sample from each population and then construct a sampling distribution of the resulting sample means, and even though the size of each group's *standard deviation* did influence the size of the values in the third column of Table 1, these estimated standard errors help us in interpreting the group *means*.

Excerpt 6.3 contains a graph of means for two groups (experimental and control), each of which was measured at three points in time: pretest, imme-

---

[5]*The term* estimated standard error *should have been used to label these numbers, not* standard error. *In each case, the data from a single sample was used to estimate the true standard error.*

Excerpt 6.2 Estimated Standard Error of the Mean in a Table

The mean, standard deviation, standard error of the mean, and the range for the Myers-Briggs sensing-intuition. . . scale. . . for each group. . . are presented in Table [1]. Private providers, facility staff, and state agency counselors are identified as Group 1, 2, and 3, respectively.

One statistic computed was the standard error of the mean. The standard error of the mean indicates, in raw score points, the amount that the mean may be expected to vary on repeated administrations of the Myers-Briggs. . . in comparison to similar populations.

Table 1

Intergroup Distribution of Myers-Briggs Sensing-Intuition Scale (N=62)

	Mean	Standard deviation	Standard error	Range
Group 1	99.62	36.03	9.00	102
Group 2	104.93	22.31	4.14	80
Group 3	95.47	36.01	8.73	106

Source: B. W. Gatlin, and C. D. Brown. (1990). Problem-solving orientations and decision-making styles among rehabilitation professionals. *Journal of Rehabilitation, 56*(2), p. 24.

Excerpt 6.3 Estimated Standard Error of the Mean in a Graph

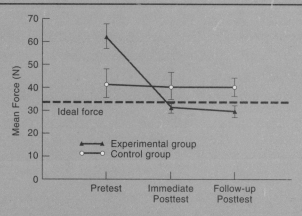

Figure 2 *Mean force level at each test for experimental and control groups. Vertical bars represent one standard error above and below mean.*

Source: M. Lee, A. Moseley, and K. Refshauge. (1990). Effect of feedback on learning a vertebral joint mobilization skill. *Physical Therapy, 70*(2), p. 100.

diate posttest, and follow-up posttest. As indicated in the graph's explanatory title, the vertical lines help us to recognize that sampling error is associated with the six sample means that are plotted. If replicated, this investigation would likely produce a new set of means that would turn out close to, but not exactly equal to, the means that were obtained.

In Excerpt 6.4, we see once again how the notion of the standard error is sometimes integrated into technical research articles. In this study, seven speed skaters were measured in terms of their blood lactate concentration immediately after participating in five 4-minute exercise sessions, where each session demanded that the skaters skate at increasing intensity levels (i.e., velocities designed to increase heart rate). Figure 2 contains a bivariate graph of the sample means presented in the final two columns of Table 2. Notice how the vertical and horizontal bars that pass through each mean in Figure 2 have end

---

Excerpt 6.4 Estimated Standard Error of the Mean in a Bivariate Graph

---

The purpose of this study was to document submaximal and maximal on-ice training intensities by monitoring both heart rate and blood lactate responses to various training programs used in speed skating and to establish a skating velocity and heart rate/lactate response. . . .

RESULTS

Mean ($\pm$SEM) heart rate, velocity and blood lactate concentration during the 5 $\times$ 4 min skating lactate curve are presented in Table 2. There was a significant increase in blood lactate concentration between level 2 and 3 with increasing velocity (Fig. 2).

Table 2

Mean ($\pm$SEM) Heart Rate, Velocity and Lactate Concentration During Five 4 min Intensities for Establishment of a Skating Lactate Curve

Intensity level	Heart rate ($b \cdot min^{-1}$)	Velocity ($m \cdot s^{-1}$)	Lactate concentration ($mmol \cdot L^{-1}$)
1	155$\pm$1	8.96$\pm$0.23	3.7$\pm$0.4
2	160$\pm$1	9.43$\pm$0.16	3.9$\pm$0.4
3	165$\pm$1	9.84$\pm$0.11	5.2$\pm$0.5
4	171$\pm$2	10.30$\pm$0.10	6.8$\pm$0.6
5	177$\pm$2	10.68$\pm$0.06	9.0$\pm$0.7

(Continued)

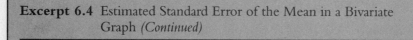

Excerpt 6.4 Estimated Standard Error of the Mean in a Bivariate Graph *(Continued)*

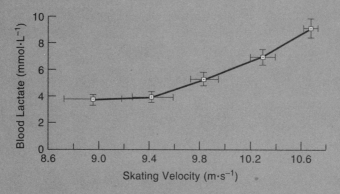

Figure 2 *Relationship between skating velocity and blood lactate concentration for five 4 min skating intensities in speed skating (n=7). Values represent the mean (SEM).*

Source: D. J. Smith, and D. Roberts. (1990). Heart rate and blood lactate concentration during on-ice training in speed skating. *Canadian Journal of Sport Science, 15*(1), p. 25.

points that are positioned precisely one SEM away from the mean. These bars alert us to the fact that the means should be expected to fluctuate in a horizontal and/or vertical fashion as we imagine replicating this study with a new sample of seven speed skaters.

In Excerpt 6.5, we see how the concept of a standard error can be applied when the statistical focus is something other than the mean. In this particular instance, the researcher computed the percentage of two kinds of questions answered correctly by each of three groups. As was the case in the previous two excerpts (in which attention was focused on means), the vertical line that extends above and below the top of each column in Excerpt 6.5 alerts us to the fact that the percentages presented in this section of the published article are statistics, not parameters. If this study were to be replicated with a new sample from each of the three populations, the percentage correct on each of the two dependent variables would probably vary at least slightly from what was computed in the original study.

CONFIDENCE INTERVALS

Researchers who report standard errors along with their computed sample statistics deserve to be commended. This practice helps to underscore the fact that sampling error is very likely to be associated with any sample mean, with any sample standard deviation, with any sample correlation coefficient, and with any other statistical summary of sample data. By presenting the numerical value of

Excerpt 6.5 Estimated Standard Error of the Percentile

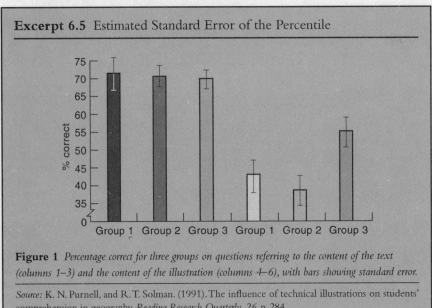

Figure 1 *Percentage correct for three groups on questions referring to the content of the text (columns 1–3) and the content of the illustration (columns 4–6), with bars showing standard error.*

Source: K. N. Purnell, and R. T. Solman. (1991). The influence of technical illustrations on students' comprehension in geography. *Reading Research Quarterly, 26,* p. 284.

the standard error (as in Excerpts 6.1–6.2) or by putting a line segment through the statistic's position in a graph (as in Excerpts 6.3–6.5), researchers help us to remember that they are only making educated *guesses* as to parameters.

Although standard errors definitely help us when we try to understand research results, a closely related technique helps us even more. As the title of this section indicates, we now wish to talk about **confidence intervals.** Our fourfold objective here is to show what a confidence interval looks like, to explain how confidence intervals are built, to clarify how to interpret confidence intervals properly, and to point out how confidence intervals carry with them a slight advantage over standard errors.

CONFIDENCE INTERVALS: WHAT THEY LOOK LIKE A confidence interval is simply a finite interval of score values on the dependent variable. Such an interval is constructed by adding a specific amount to the computed statistic (thereby obtaining the upper limit of the interval) and by subtracting a specific amount from the statistic (thereby obtaining the lower limit of the interval). In addition to specifying the interval's upper and lower limits, researchers will always attach a percent to any interval that is constructed. Most often, this percentage value will be either 95 or 99. Taken together, the interval's length and the percentage value that goes with it form the confidence interval.

In technical articles, confidence intervals are typically presented in one of three ways. Excerpt 6.6 illustrates how confidence intervals will sometimes be reported within the text of the article. (In this excerpt, note how the first

---

Excerpt 6.6 Confidence Intervals Reported in the Text of an Article

The presence of smokers in the home had a significant effect on duration of exposure across specific settings. Subjects without smokers at home reported that the majority of their exposure was in the workplace (mean = 36.1 minutes per day, 95% confidence interval [CI] = 22.7–49.5), with very little either at home (mean = 1.4 minutes per day, 95% CI = 0.05–2.75) or in other locations (mean = 13.1 minutes per day, 95% CI = 8.75–17.4).

Exposure was significantly related to education, $r(185) = -.22, \ldots 95\%$ (CI $= -.37$ to $-.08$): exposure was higher among less educated subjects.

Source: K. M. Emmons, D. B. Abrams, R. J. Marshall, R. A. Etzel, T. E. Novotny, B. H Marcus, and M. E. Karr. (1992). Exposure to environmental tobacco smoke in naturalistic settings. *American Journal of Public Health, 82*(1), p. 25.

---

group of confidence intervals pertain to the mean whereas the last one deals with a correlation coefficient.)

Confidence intervals can also be presented in an article's table. Excerpt 6.7 illustrates this reporting strategy; once again, we see that the two critical ingredients of a confidence interval—interval end points and a percentage value—are provided.

Excerpt 6.7 Confidence Intervals Reported in a Table

The survey was an anonymous, structured questionnaire which asked respondents to indicate their specialty and year of graduation from medical school. The number of adult patients with diabetes mellitus the physician cared for who required insulin and were not obese (i.e., less than 20% above their ideal body weight) were measured using a five point scale (0, 1–2, 3–5, 6–9, >10). Respondents were provided a list of 10 commonly used insulin regimens which varied according to the number of injections, the type of insulin used, and whether mixed insulins were employed. They were requested to indicate which of these regimens they used in treating their non-obese, insulin-requiring patients. . . .

Table 1 summarizes the 191 physicians' use of the 10 insulin regimens listed on the survey; respondents could indicate using more than one type of regimen. Although the majority of physicians reported using a two shot regimen of mixed insulin, at least 67 percent also used some form of a single injection regimen for a portion of their non-obese, insulin-requiring patients.

(Continued)

Excerpt 6.7 Confidence Intervals Reported in a Table *(Continued)*

Table 1

Type of Insulin Regimens Used by Physicians[*]

Insulin regimen	Proportion of physicians	95% CI
NPH or Lente alone, once per day	0.674	(0.61, 0.74)
NPH or Lente alone, twice per day	0.621	(0.55, 0.69)
NPH or Lente + Regular, once per day	0.647	(0.58, 0.71)
NPH or Lente + Regular, twice per day	0.858	(0.81, 0.91)
Lente + Semilente, once per day	0.026	(0.00, 0.05)
Lente + Semilente, twice per day	0.011	(0.00, 0.03)
Ultralente alone, once per day	0.053	(0.02, 0.08)
Ultralente alone, twice per day	0.011	(0.00, 0.03)
Ultralente + Regular, once per day	0.042	(0.01, 0.07)
Ultralente + Regular, twice per day	0.063	(0.03, 0.10)

[*]Total number of respondents, n = 191

Source: D. G. Marrero, P. S. Moore, N. S. Fineberg, C. D. Langefeld, and C. M. Clark, (1991). The treatment of patients with insulin-requiring diabetes mellitus by primary care physicians. *Journal of Community Health. 16*(5), pp. 261, 264.

Researchers sometimes report confidence intervals by putting vertical or horizontal line segments through the graphed value of the statistic. In Excerpt 6.8, we see an example where this third approach to reporting confidence intervals was used.

Before leaving this section, note that the confidence intervals reported in Excerpts 6.6–6.8 were constructed to help interpret a variety of sample statistics: means, correlation coefficients, proportions, and medians. These particular excerpts were specifically selected not only because they illustrate different procedures for reporting confidence intervals but also because they help to underscore the point that confidence intervals can be constructed around *any* sample statistic.

THE CONSTRUCTION OF CONFIDENCE INTERVALS The end points of a confidence interval are not selected by the researcher magically making two values appear out of thin air. Rather, the researcher first makes a decision as to the level of confidence that is desired (usually 95 or 99). Then, the end points are computed by means of a joint process that involves the analysis of sample

Excerpt 6.8 Confidence Intervals Reported Within a Graph

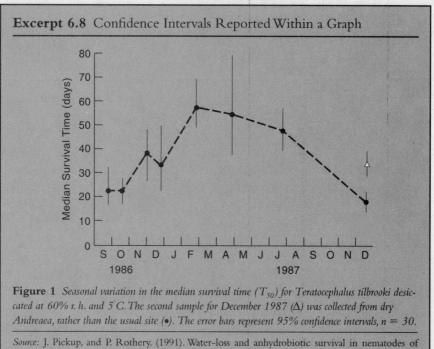

Figure 1 *Seasonal variation in the median survival time (T_{50}) for Teratocephalus tilbrooki desiccated at 60% r. h. and 5°C. The second sample for December 1987 (Δ) was collected from dry Andreaea, rather than the usual site (●). The error bars represent 95% confidence intervals, n = 30.*

Source: J. Pickup, and P. Rothery. (1991). Water-loss and anhydrobiotic survival in nematodes of Antarctic fellfields. *OIKOS, 61*(3), p. 383.

data (so as to obtain the estimated standard error of the statistic) and then multiplied by a tabled numerical value.[6]

Although you do not need to know the various formulas used to construct confidence intervals, you should be cognizant of the fact that a scientific approach is taken to the creation of any confidence interval. Moreover, you should be aware of three factors that affect the length of any confidence interval. These factors are the level of confidence selected by the researcher, the degree of homogeneity within the sample, and the size of the sample. If other things are held constant, the distance between the end points of a confidence interval will be smaller to the extent that (1) the researcher selects a lower level of confidence, (2) the sample is homogeneous, and (3) the sample is large. Because short (i.e., "narrow") intervals that have a high level of confidence associated with them are more helpful in inferential statistics, researchers typically try to base their confidence intervals on large samples.

[6] *For example, the first confidence interval in Excerpt 6.6 was established by dividing the sample standard deviation by the square root of the sample size, with the resulting value multiplied by the number 1.98, which was looked up in a t-table. The product, 13.4, was then added to and subtracted from the sample mean.*

It should be noted that the length of a confidence interval is also affected by the nature of the statistic computed on the basis of sample data. For example, confidence intervals built around the mean will be shorter than those constructed for the median. The same situation holds true for Pearson's product-moment correlation coefficient as compared with Spearman's rho. This may explain, in part, why $\overline{X}$s and rs are seen so frequently in the published literature.

THE PROPER INTERPRETATION OF CONFIDENCE INTERVALS   Confidence intervals are often misinterpreted to designate the probability that population parameters lie somewhere between the intervals' upper and lower limits. For example, many people (including more than a few researchers) would look at the end points of the first of the 95 percent confidence interval presented in Excerpt 6.6 and conclude that there is a .95 probability (i.e., a 95 percent chance) that the population parameter, μ, lies somewhere between 22.7 and 49.5 minutes per day exposure. Confidence intervals should *not* be interpreted in this fashion.

After a sample has been extracted from a population and then measured, the confidence interval around the sample's statistic either will or will not "cover" the value of the parameter. Hence, the probability that the parameter lies between the end points of a confidence interval is either 0 or 1. Because of this fact, a confidence interval should never be considered to specify the chances (or probability) that the parameter is "caught" by the interval.

The proper way to interpret a confidence interval is to *imagine* that (1) many, many samples of the same size are extracted from the same population; and (2) a 95 percent confidence interval is constructed separately around the statistic computed from each sample's data set. Some of these intervals would "capture" the parameter—that is, the interval's end points would be such that the parameter would lie within the interval. On the other hand, some of these confidence intervals would *not* capture the parameter. Looked at collectively, it would turn out that 95 percent of these 95 percent confidence intervals contain the parameter. Accordingly, when you see a 95 percent confidence interval, you should consider that the chances are 95 out of 100 that the interval you are looking at is one of those that does, in fact, capture the parameter. Likewise, when you encounter a 99 percent confidence interval, you can say to yourself that the chances are even higher (99 out of 100) that the interval in front of you is one of the many possible intervals that would have "caught" the parameter.

THE ADVANTAGE OF CONFIDENCE INTERVALS OVER ESTIMATED STANDARD ERRORS   As we indicated in a previous section, a confidence interval is determined by first computing and then using the value of the estimated standard error. Researchers should be commended for providing either one of these inferential aids to their readers, for it is unfortunately true that most researchers supply their readers with neither standard errors nor confidence intervals for any of the sample statistics that are reported. Nevertheless, confidence intervals carry with them a slight advantage that is worth noting.

When a confidence interval is computed, we can look at the interval and discern the precise probability that the interval is one of the many possible intervals (each theoretically based upon a separate random sample) that capture the parameter. Given a 95 percent confidence interval, we can say that the chances are 95 out of 100 that we are looking at one of the "successful" intervals (rather than one of these that fails to capture the parameter). This line of thinking is not possible when the estimated standard error, by itself, is added to and subtracted from the value of the statistic.

To clarify this point, consider Excerpt 6.9. With respect to the heights of the female subjects, we could form an interval, based on the data provided, that would extend from 154.9 to 169.5. This interval around the mean of 162.2 would be a 50 percent interval.[7] If the sample had included two more females and if we formed an interval in the same way, the resulting interval would have been about equal to a 60 percent interval. Thus, intervals formed by using the estimated standard error vary in their meaning in light of the size of the sample. In contrast, confidence intervals always carry with them the same meaning, regardless of how big the sample is. Simply stated, a 95 percent confidence interval designates a 95 percent interval irrespective of n.[8]

Excerpt 6.9 The Advantage of Confidence Intervals over "Standard Error" Intervals

Table 1

Physical Characteristics of the Subjects ($\overline{X} \pm$ SEM)

Sex	n	Height (cm)	Weight (kg)	Body fat (%)
M	6	172.4 ± 1.7	67.2 ± 3.4	10.4 ± 1.5*
F	2	162.2 ± 7.3	55.6 ± 7.3	18.8 ± 0.2

*Indicates 5 subjects

Source: A. E. Ready, and H. R. Huber. (1990). Physiologic response of Nordic ski racers to three modes of sport specific exercise. *Canadian Journal of Sport Sciences, 15*(3), p. 214.

---

[7]We determined that our interval is analogous to a 50 percent confidence interval by consulting a t-table.
[8]This advantage of confidence intervals is of trivial importance with large samples.

POINT ESTIMATION

When engaged in interval estimation, a researcher will (1) select a level of confidence (e.g., 95%), (2) analyze the sample data, (3) extract a number out of a statistical table, and (4) scientifically build an interval that surrounds the sample statistic. After completing these four steps, the researcher makes an educated guess as to the unknown value of the population parameter. In making this guess, the researcher ends up saying, "My data-based interval extends from _____ to _____, and the chances are _____ out of 100 that this interval is one of the many possible intervals (each based on a different sample) that would, in fact, contain the parameter between the interval limits."

A second form of estimation is called **point estimation,** and here again an educated guess is made, on the basis of sample data, as to the unknown value of the population parameter. With this second kind of estimation, however, the activities and thinking of the researcher are much simpler. With point estimation, no level of confidence needs to be selected, no statistical table needs to be consulted, and no interval needs to be created. Instead, the researcher simply computes the statistic on the basis of the sample data and then posits that the unknown value of the population parameter is the same. Thus, the researcher who uses this guessing technique ends up saying, "Since the sample-based statistic turned out equal to X, my best guess is that the value of parameter is also equal to X."

Point estimation, of course, is likely to produce statements that are incorrect. Because of the great likelihood of sampling error, the value of the statistic will rarely match the value of the parameter. For this reason, interval estimation is generally considered to represent a more logical way of making educated guesses as to parameter values than is point estimation.

Despite the fact that point estimation disregards the notion of sampling error, researchers often can be seen making pinpoint guesses as to parameter values. Consider, for example, the material contained in Excerpt 6.10.

The three sentences found in Excerpt 6.10 appear in the Discussion section of a recent article on eating disorders. The authors of this article cite per-

---

Excerpt 6.10 Point Estimation

Individuals who perceive of themselves as overweight may be prone to chronic dieting and eating disorders. Jakobovits et al. (18), for example, reported that 50 percent of female college students were chronic dieters. Rosen and Gross found that 63 percent of high school girls were on weight-reducing regimens, even though most of them were already of normal weight.

Source: J. P. Sciacca, C. L. Melby, G. C. Hyner, A. C Brown, and P. L Femea. (1991). Body mass index and perceived weight status in young adults. *Journal of Community Health, 16*(3), p. 166.

centages that appeared in two earlier studies. It should be noted, however, that the study by Jakobovits involved a *sample* of college students. To say, as is done here, that "50 percent of female college students were chronic dieters" is to make a pinpoint claim as to the parameter value. Likewise, the finding by Rosen and Gross pertains to their *sample*; the claim that they found "that 63 percent of high school girls were on weight-reducing regimens" is a clear-cut case of point estimation.

A place where *many* researchers engage in point estimation is in the discussion of the measuring instruments used to collect data. As we indicated in Chapter 4, these discussions often involve the presentation of reliability coefficients.

Give yourself a pat on the back if you recall, within that discussion, our claim that such coefficients are only estimates. If a different sample of examinees were to provide the data for the assessment of reliability and/or validity, the obtained coefficients most likely would fluctuate. Sampling error would account for such fluctuation.

Although it is possible to build confidence intervals around reliability and validity coefficients, researchers rarely do this. Instead, point estimates are typically provided. This is a common practice, even in cases where the researcher recognizes that the computed reliability and/or validity coefficients are only estimates. Consider, for example, Excerpts 6.11 and 6.12.

Excerpts 6.11–6.12 Point Estimation Concerning Reliability Coefficients

---

The reliability estimate from this technique was .81.

Source: M. Caovette and G. Reid. (1991). Physical work output. Influence of auditory stimulation on the physical work outputs of adults who are severely retarded. *Education and Training in Mental Retardation, 26,* p. 47.

The reliability estimates for the high school student sample for the VI, OI, and B scales were .86, .39, and .23.

Source: E. B. Mauer and N. C. Gysbers. (1990). Indentifying career concerns of entering freshman using *My Vocational Situation. The Career Development Quarterly, 39*(2), p. 157.

In both of these excerpts, notice how the reliability coefficients are acknowledged to be only estimates. In the second excerpt, we are even told that the examinees who provided the data were considered to be a sample. Here, we see illustrations of the common practice of point estimation being used in conjunction with reliability coefficients.

Although the likelihood of sampling error causes the practice of point estimation to seem quite ill-founded, this form of statistical inference deserves to be respected for two reasons. These two supportive arguments revolve around (1) the role played by point estimation in interval estimation and (2) the reliance on point estimation by "more advanced" scientific disciplines (such as physics). Let's consider briefly each of these reasons why it would be unwise to look upon point estimation with complete disrespect.

When engaged in interval estimation, the researcher builds a confidence interval that surrounds the sample statistic. Point estimation is relied upon in two ways when such intervals are constructed. First of all, the pinpoint value of the sample statistic is used as the best single estimate of the population parameter. The desired interval is formed by adding a certain amount to the statistic and subtracting a certain amount from the statistic. Hence, the value of the statistic, as a *point estimate* of the parameter, serves as the foundation for each and every confidence interval that is constructed.

Interval estimation draws upon point estimation in a second manner. To be more specific, the amount that is added to (and subtracted from) the statistic in order to obtain the interval's upper and lower limits is based upon a point estimate of the population's variability. For example, when a confidence interval is constructed around a sample mean, the distance between the end points of the interval is contingent upon, among other things, a *point estimate* of the population standard deviation. Likewise, whenever a confidence interval is built around a sample proportion, the length of the interval cannot be specified until the researcher first uses *point estimation* to guess how variable the population is.

From a totally different perspective, the practice of point estimation deserves to be respected. Certain well-respected scientists assert that as a discipline advances and becomes more "scientifically rigorous," point estimation is turned to with both increased frequency and greater justification.

In a recent article, for example, psychologists George Howard, Thomas Curtain, and Andy Johnson first pass along some advice provided by Paul Meehl ("that psychologists' empirical efforts might be improved if they turned to point estimation") and then discuss two of their own studies conducted with Meehl's advice in mind.[9] In this article's abstract, Howard and his colleagues assert that "one can easily conduct research using point estimation with great success"; in the discussion section, they state that "the theoretical arguments traced in this article and the point estimation techniques offered represent attempts to reframe our understanding of research in counseling psychology."[10]

At the present time, you will probably see the interval form of estimation used much more frequently than the kind that Howard et al. argue for. In the

---

[9]*G.S. Howard, T.D. Curtain, and A.J. Johnson. (1991). Point estimation techniques in psychological research: Studies on the role of meaning in self-determined action.* Journal of Counseling Psychology, *38(2), pp. 219—226.*

[10]*Ibid.*

future, however, you may find that point estimation gains respect among applied researchers.

WARNINGS CONCERNING INTERVAL AND POINT ESTIMATION

As we wrap up this chapter, we would like to provide four cautionary comments concerning the techniques of estimation. The first three of these warnings concern interval estimation while the fourth is relevant to both kinds of estimation techniques: point and interval. You will be a better consumer of the research literature if you will keep these final points in mind.

First of all, be aware that the second of two numbers separated by a plus-and-minus sign may or may not be the numerical value of the estimated standard error. In Excerpt 6.1, we saw how researchers sometimes use this format to provide readers with a feel for the sampling variability associated with a sample mean. However, the same format was considered in Chapter 2 when we looked at different ways researchers report their standard deviations. Thus, the number 8 in the notation 63 ± 8 could be a standard deviation *or* it could be an estimate of the standard error. The author will always clarify which case pertains, so take a moment to read the table's or figure's title or the explanatory information in the text. Your effort here will help you understand the author's information, for $\overline{X}\pm SD$ means something quite different from $\overline{X}\pm SEM$.

Our second warning concerns the fact that sample data allow a researcher to *estimate* the standard error of the statistic, not to *determine* that standard error in a definitive manner. Excerpts in this chapter illustrate how researchers sometimes forget to use the word *estimated* prior to the phrase *standard error.* Keep in mind that the researcher will never know for sure, based upon the sample data, how large the standard error is; it can only be estimated.

Our third warning concerns, once again, confidence intervals. The sample statistic, of course, will always be located between the upper and lower limits of the confidence interval—but it will *not* always be located halfway between the interval's end points. When confidence intervals are built around a sample mean, it is true that $\overline{X}$ will turn out to be positioned at the midpoint of the interval. When confidence intervals are constructed for many other statistics (e.g., r, s, and s^2), however, one "side" of the interval will be longer than the other "side."[11] Whenever a confidence interval is built around a proportion (or percent), the same thing will happen unless the value of the statistic is .50 (i.e., 50 percent).

Our final warning applies to both interval estimation and point estimation—and this is by far the most important of our end-of-chapter cautionary

---

[11] *The degree to which such confidence intervals appear to be "lopsided" is inversely related to sample size. If n is large enough the statistic will be positioned in the middle of the interval.*

comments. Simply stated, the entire process of estimation requires that the data used to form the inference come from a *random* sample. For the techniques of estimation to work properly, therefore, there must be a legitimate connection between the sample and population such that either (1) the former is actually extracted, randomly, from the latter (with no refusals to participate, mortality, or response rate problems); or (2) the population, if hypothetical, is conceptualized so as to match closely the nature of the sample. Without such a link between sample and population, neither form of estimation can be expected to function very well.

REVIEW TERMS

Confidence interval
Estimation
Interval estimation
Point estimation
Sampling distribution
Sampling error
Standard error

REVIEW QUESTIONS

1. The discrepancy between the value of the sample statistic and the value of the population parameter is referred to as _____.

2. If a fair die is rolled 36 times, which of these two expectations would represent a better bet: (a) that a "1" will turn up 6 times, or (b) that a "1" will turn up something other than 6 times?

3. (True or False) Sampling errors can be eliminated by selecting samples randomly from their appropriate populations.

4. If many, many samples of size n are drawn from an infinitely big population, with the data from each sample summarized so as to produce the same statistic (e.g., r), what would the resulting set of sample statistics be called?

5. The standard deviation of a sampling distribution is called the

   _____.

6. Look at Excerpt 6.2. The standard error of 9.00 for group 1 should really be thought of as the "estimated standard error of the _____."

7. The two most popular levels of confidence associated with confidence intervals are _____ and _____.

8. (True or False) If a researcher constructs a 95 percent confidence interval around a sample statistic, the chances are 95 out of 100 that the population parameter lies within the interval limits.

9. What level of confidence is associated with an interval built around a sample mean if that interval is formed by (a) adding 1 SEM to $\overline{X}$ and (b) subtracting 1 SEM from $\overline{X}$?

10. One type of estimation is called interval estimation; the other type is called _____ estimation.

11. When researchers present quantitative information regarding their instruments' reliability and validity, which type of estimation is typically used?

12. (True or False) The sample statistic will be located precisely in the middle of any confidence interval that is constructed.

HYPOTHESIS TESTING—
PART I

In Chapter 6, we saw how the inferential techniques of estimation can assist researchers when they use sample data to make educated guesses about the unknown value of population parameters. Now, we turn our attention to a second way in which researchers engage in inferential thinking. This procedure is called **hypothesis testing.**

As you will soon discover, the hypothesis testing procedure involves abstract concepts and a form of logic that strikes most learners as being somewhat topsy-turvy when they first encounter it. For these reasons, we have decided to divide our discussion of the hypothesis testing procedure into two parts. Half of this discussion is presented here; the balance appears in Chapter 8.

In this chapter, we will consider the six steps that form the simplest version of hypothesis testing that can be used. This six-step form of hypothesis testing is extremely popular. In fact, more researchers use the six-step version of hypothesis testing than either the seven-step or nine-step versions that you will learn about in Chapter 8.

In addition to clarifying each of the six steps that form the bare-bones (yet popular) version of hypothesis testing, we want to accomplish three other objectives in this chapter. First, we intend to explain not only what a null hypothesis is, but also where the null hypothesis comes from. Second, we will address a question that almost everyone poses when first exposed to this form of inferential statistics—a question concerning the apparently topsy-turvy way in which hypothesis testing functions. Finally, we will end this chapter by offering you a set of warnings that should, we hope, put you in a better position to interpret properly research results generated by the six-step version of hypothesis testing.

Before we turn our attention to the half-dozen elements of the simplest version of hypothesis testing, we must reiterate something we said near the beginning of Chapter 6. In order for inferential statistics to begin, the researcher must first answer four preliminary questions: (1) What is/are the relevant population(s)? (2) How will a sample be extracted from the population(s) of interest? (3) What characteristic(s) of the sample people, animals, or objects will serve as the target of the measurement process? (4) What is the study's statistical focus—or stated differently, how will the sample data be summarized so as to obtain a statistic that can be used to make an inferential statement concerning the unknown parameter? In the remaining portions of this chapter (and in Chapter 8 as well), we will assume that these four questions have been both raised and answered by the time the researcher starts to apply *any* version of hypothesis testing.

To help you understand the six-step version of hypothesis testing, we first will simply list the various steps in their proper order (that is, the order in which a researcher ought to do things when engaged in this form of statistical inference). After presenting an ordered list of the six steps, we then will take each step and discuss its function and logic.

AN ORDERED LIST OF THE SIX STEPS

Whenever researchers use the six-step version of the hypothesis testing procedure, they will

1. State the null hypothesis.
2. State the alternate hypothesis.
3. Select a level of significance.
4. Collect and summarize the sample data.
5. Refer to a criterion for evaluating the sample evidence.
6. Make a decision to discard/retain the null hypothesis.

It should be noted that there is no version of hypothesis testing that involves fewer than six steps. Stated differently, it is outright impossible to eliminate any of these six "ingredients" and have enough left to test a statistical hypothesis.

A DETAILED LOOK AT EACH OF THE SIX STEPS

As indicated previously, the list of steps we just presented is arranged in an ordered fashion. In discussing these steps, however, we now will look at these six component parts in a somewhat jumbled order: 1, 6, 2, 4, 5, and then 3. Our motivation in doing this is not related to sadistic tendencies! Rather, we are convinced that the function and logic of these six steps can be understood far more readily if we purposely chart an unusual path through the hypothesis testing procedure. Please note, however, that the six steps will now be rearranged only for pedagogical reasons. If we were asked to apply these six steps in an actual study, we would use the ordered list as our guide, not the sequence to which we now turn.

Step 1: The Null Hypothesis

When engaged in hypothesis testing, a researcher begins by stating a **null hypothesis.** If there is just one population involved in the study, the null hypothesis is a pinpoint statement as to the unknown quantitative value of the parameter in the population of interest. To illustrate what this kind of null hypothesis might look like, suppose that (1) we conduct a study in which our population contains all full-time students enrolled in a particular university, (2) our variable of interest is intelligence, and (3) our statistical focus is the mean IQ score. Given this situation, we could set up a null hypothesis to say that $\mu = 100$. This statement deals with a population *parameter,* it is *pinpoint* in nature, and *we* made it.

The symbol for null hypothesis is H_0, and this symbol is usually followed by (1) a colon, (2) the parameter symbol that indicates the researcher's statistical focus, (3) an equal sign, and (4) the pinpoint numerical value that the researcher has selected. Accordingly, we could specify the null hypothesis for our imaginary study by stating $H_0: \mu = 100$.

If our study's statistical focus involved something other than the mean, we would have to change the parameter's symbol so as to make H_0 consistent with the study's focus. For example, if our imaginary study were to be concerned with the variance among students' heights, the null hypothesis would need to contain the symbol σ^2 rather than the symbol μ. Or, if we were concerned with the product-moment correlation between the students' heights and weights, the symbol ρ would have to appear in H_0.

With respect to the pinpoint numerical value that appears in the null hypothesis, researchers have the freedom to select any value that they wish to test. Thus, in our example dealing with the mean IQ of university students, the null hypothesis could be set up to say that $\mu = 80$, $\mu = 118$, $\mu = 101$, or $\mu = $ any specific value of our choosing. Likewise, if our study focused on the variance, we could set up H_0, the null hypothesis, to say that $\sigma^2 = 10$ or that $\sigma^2 = $ any other positive number of our choosing. And in a study having Pearson's product-moment correlation coefficient as its statistical focus, the null hypothesis could be set up to say that $\rho = 0.00$ or that $\rho = -.50$ or that $\rho = +.92$ or that $\rho = $ any specific number between -1.00 and $+1.00$.

The only statistical restrictions on the numerical value that appears in H_0 are that it (1) must lie somewhere on the continuum of possible values that correspond to the parameter and (2) cannot be fixed at the upper or lower limit of that continuum, presuming that the parameter has a lowest and/or highest possible value. These restrictions rule out the following null hypotheses:

$$H_0: \sigma^2 = -15 \qquad H_0: \rho = +1.30$$

$$H_0: \sigma^2 = 0 \qquad H_0: \rho = -1.00$$

because the variance has a lower limit of 0 while Pearson's product-moment correlation coefficient has limits of ± 1.00.

Excerpt 7.1 contains an illustration of the kind of null hypothesis we have been discussing. In the study from which this excerpt was selected, the researchers collected data on a number of corporate firms. The study focused on these firms' "sinking funds," with an effort made by the researchers to see if they could use information on several variables to predict which of two options each firm would select regarding its sinking fund. One of the variables examined to see if it could help improve the success of this prediction effort was profit ratio. This was the third of several potentially useful explanatory variables investigated by the researchers, and the parameter value corresponding to this variable was symbolized as β_3. If profit ratio was worthless as a predictor, β_3 would be equal to zero.

Excerpt 7.1 A Null Hypothesis

A test of the null hypothesis $H_0: \beta_3 = 0$, that is, the profit ratio adds no additional explanatory power, can be carried out.

Source: C. Kao, and C. Wu. (1990). Sinking funds and the agency costs of corporate debt. *The Financial Review, 25*(1), p. 106.

So far, we have considered the null hypothesis in relation to studies in which there is a single population. The hypothesis testing procedure, however, can also be used when two or more populations are involved in the investigation. In such studies, the null hypothesis takes the form of a pinpoint statement as to the degree to which the parameter value varies in the populations of interest.

Excerpt 7.2 contains a set of three null hypotheses that were evaluated in an investigation of 141 *Fortune* 500 companies. Some of these firms had a corporate structure referred to as "CEO duality" whereas others had "independent board leadership." In the former, the CEO served as chair of the board of directors; in the latter, these roles were filled by different individuals.

In this study comparing companies with two kinds of corporate structure, each of the three null hypotheses could have been articulated, using symbols, as $H_0: \mu_1 = \mu_2$, where the subscripts 1 and 2 correspond to CEO duality and independent board leadership, respectively. Equivalent expressions include $H_0: \mu_1 - \mu_2 = 0$ and $H_0: \sigma_\mu^2 = 0$. We prefer either of these latter expressions, because the pinpoint number that specifies how much the two population means differ is now clearly visible.

In Excerpt 7.3, we see an example of how a researcher set up a two-group null hypothesis so as to include the pinpoint numerical value required of any H_0. Had this null hypothesis been set up to say $MSCPE_2 = MSCPE_1$, we would *not* have an exception to the requirement that every null hypothesis

---

Excerpt 7.2 Null Hypotheses

HYPOTHESES

On the basis of arguments noted earlier, observers argue that the choice between CEO duality versus independent board leadership will influence organizational performance. As noted, however, the literature seems to provide persuasive, but competing, predictions. Accordingly, hypotheses are stated in the null form. Also, the hypotheses reflected reliance on multiple performance indices:

H1: There will be no difference in return on investment between CEO duality firms and those with independent board leadership.

H2: There will be no difference in return on equity between CEO duality firms and those with independent board leadership.

H3: There will be no difference in profit margin between CEO duality firms and those with independent board leadership.

Source: P. L. Rechner and D. R. Dalton. (1991). CEO duality and organizational performance: A longitudinal analysis. *Strategic Management Journal, 12*(2), p. 156.

Excerpt 7.3 A Null Hypothesis Set Up to Show a Zero Difference Between Two Means

---

To detect a difference between the abnormal returns of two groups of securities, [the] hypothesis of interest may then be expressed as

$$H_0: MSCPE_2 - MSCPE_1 = 0$$

Source: C. M. Impson and I. Kara Fiath. (1992). A note on the stock market reaction to dividend announcements. *The Financial Review, 27*(2), p. 264.

---

must contain a pinpoint numerical value; instead, the pinpoint number would simply be slightly hidden by the format used to express H_0.[1]

Although researchers have the freedom to select any pinpoint number they wish for H_0, a zero is often selected when two or more populations are being compared. When this is done, the null hypothesis becomes a statement that there is no difference between the populations. Because of the popularity of this kind of null hypothesis, people sometimes begin to think that a null hypothesis *must* be set up as a "no difference" statement. This is both unfortunate and

---

[1] *MSCPE is an abbreviation for "mean standardized cumulative prediction error."*

wrong. When two populations are compared, the null hypothesis can be set up with any pinpoint value the researcher wishes to use. (For example, in comparing the mean height of men and women, we could set up a legitimate null hypothesis that stated H_0: $\mu_{men} - \mu_{women} = 2$ inches.) When the hypothesis testing procedure is used with a single population, the notion of "no difference," applied to parameters, simply doesn't make sense. How could there be a difference, zero or otherwise, when there is only one μ (or only one ρ, or only one σ^2, etc.)?

In Excerpts 7.4–7.6, we see the null hypotheses that were set up in studies dealing with three, five, and seven populations, respectively. Because there were multiple populations involved in each of the studies, the researchers had the option of setting up their null hypotheses in the "no difference" manner, and this was, in fact, the way each H_0 was stated.

The pinpoint number required of any null hypothesis is contained in Excerpts 7.4, 7.5, and 7.6—but it resides just "beneath the surface" of each H_0. When there are three or more populations involved in a study and when the H_0 is set up in a "no difference" fashion, the researcher is saying, in effect, that there is no variability among the populations. Inasmuch as the variance provides one means for measuring how much variability exists among a set of numbers, and inasmuch as the variance is equal to zero for the case of perfect homogeneity, the notion of "no difference" can be translated into the assertion that the variance is equal to zero. Thus, each of the null hypotheses in Excerpts 7.4–7.6 could have been set up to say that the variance of the pop-

---

Excerpts 7.4–7.6 Null Hypotheses in Studies Dealing with Multiple Populations

---

The null hypothesis for this study, H_0: $\mu_I = \mu_{II} = \mu_{III}$, stated that there were no differences in mean scores on the curricular need scale for each of the 30 curricular need statements among the three groups.

Source: K. W. Lambrecht. (1991). Curricular preparation needs for sport club managers. *Journal of Sports Management, 5*(1), p. 51.

A one-way Analysis of Variance was calculated for each socialization variable. The null hypothesis in each case was that the population means of each socialization variable were equal across [the five] levels of termination.

Source: D. E. Martin, and R. A. Dodder. (1991). Specialization experiences and level of terminating participation in sports. *Journal of Sport Behavior, 14*(2), p. 121.

Statistical analyses were used to test the hypotheses that the [mean] ratings at the seven vertical work locations were equal.

Source: S. S. Vlin, C. M. Ways, T. J. Armstrong, and S. H. Snook. (1990). Perceived exertion and discomfort versus work height with a pistol-shaped screwdriver. *American Industrial Hygiene Association, 51*(11), p. 591.

ulation means was equal to zero. Stated in symbols, therefore, the null hypotheses of these three excerpts could have been articulated as H_0: $\sigma_\mu^2 = 0$. If expressed in this manner, each of these null hypotheses would have had a pinpoint number that was clearly visible: zero.

Before we leave our discussion of the null hypothesis, it should be noted that H_0 does *not* always represent the researcher's personal belief, or hunch, as to the true state of affairs in the population(s) of interest. In fact, the vast majority of null hypotheses are set up by researchers in such a way as to *disagree* with what they actually believe to be the case. We will return to this point later (when we consider formally H_r, the research hypothesis). For now, however, all we want to do is alert you to the fact that the H_0 associated with any given study probably is *not* an articulation of the researcher's honest belief concerning the population(s) being studied.

Step 6: The Decision Regarding H_0

At the end of the hypothesis testing procedure, the researcher will do one of two things with H_0. One option is for the researcher to take the position that the null hypothesis is probably false. In this case, the researcher **rejects** H_0. The other option available to the researcher is to refrain from asserting that H_0 is probably false. In this case, a **fail-to-reject** decision is made.

If, at the end of the hypothesis testing procedure, a conclusion is reached that H_0 is probably false, the researcher will communicate this decision by saying one of four things: that H_0 was rejected, that a statistically significant finding was obtained, that a reliable difference was observed, or that p is less than a small decimal value (e.g., $p < .05$). In Excerpts 7.7–7.8, we provide

---

Excerpts 7.7–7.8 Expressions Indicating That H_0 Is Probably False

To test the hypothesis that no variance in adaptation to shiftwork may be predicted by the circadian type, usual coping skills, environmental factors, risk taking behaviors, injury status, and sociodemographic characteristics of workers on a rotating shift schedule, all variables were entered into a regression analysis with stepwise entry and removal. . . . The null hypothesis was rejected.

Source: J. Phillips, and K. Brown. (1992). Industrial workers on a rotating shift pattern–adaptation and injury status. *AAOHN Journal, 40*(10), p. 473.

A t test performed on the number of explanatory thoughts listed revealed that high-need-for-cognition subjects generated significantly more such thoughts (M = 5.83) than low-need-for-cognition subjects (M = 4.83), $t(195) = 2.67, p < .01$.

Source: G. D. Lassiter, M. A. Briggs, and R. D. Slaw. (1991). Need for cognition, causal processing, and memory for behavior. *Personality and Social Science Bulletin, 17*(6), p. 696.

examples of how researchers will sometimes communicate their decision to disbelieve H_0.

Just as there are different ways for a researcher to tell us that H_0 is considered to be false, there are various mechanisms for expressing the other possible decision concerning the null hypothesis. Instead of saying that a fail-to-reject decision has been reached, the researcher may tell us that H_0 was tenable, that H_0 was accepted, that no reliable differences were observed, that no significant difference was found, that the result was not significant (often abbreviated as *ns* or *NS*), or that *p* is greater than a small decimal value (e.g., $p > .05$). Excerpts 7.9–7.12 illustrate these different ways of communicating a fail-to-reject decision.

Excerpts 7.9–7.12 Failing to Reject the Null Hypothesis

Furthermore, analysis indicated that there was no significant difference in length of employment between persons with disabilities and able-bodied employees $(p > .05)$. The null hypothesis was tenable.

Source: D. Ondusko. (1991). Comparison of employees with disabilities and able-bodied workers in janitorial maintenance. *Journal of Applied Rehabilitation Counseling, 22*(2), p. 21.

No reliable differences were found among groups in terms of either age, $F(2, 153) = 0.16$, *ns*, or subjective ratings of health, $F(2, 153) = 0.31$, *ns*.

Source: P. Gratzinger, L. Friedman, J. I. Sheikh, and J. A. Yesavage. (1990). Cognitive interventions to improve face-name recall: The role of personality trait differences. *Developmental Psychology, 26*(6), p. 891.

Contrary to our prediction, differences between the two NH groups were not statistically significant.

Source: G. G. Bear, A. Clever, and W. A. Proctor. (1991). Self-perceptions of nonhandicapped children and children with learning disabilities in integrated classes. *Journal of Special Education, 24*(4), p. 417.

Performance on the keyword-recall task was uniformly high in all three mnemonic conditions (averaging better than 87% correct in each), with no statistical differences between conditions.

Source: T. M. Franke, J. R. Levin, and R. N. Carney. (1991). Mnemonic artwork-learning strategies: Helping students remember more than "Who painted what?" (1991). *Contemporary Educational Psychology, 16*(4), p. 381.

It is especially important to be able to decipher the language and notation used by researchers to indicate the decision made concerning H_0. This is because most researchers neither articulate their null hypotheses nor clearly state that they used the hypothesis testing procedure. Often, the only way to tell that a researcher has used this kind of inferential technique is by noting what happened to the null hypothesis.

Step 2: The Alternate Hypothesis

Near the beginning of the hypothesis testing procedure, the researcher must state an **alternative hypothesis**. Referred to as H_a (or as H_1), the alternative hypothesis takes the same form as the null hypothesis. For example, if the null hypothesis deals with the possible value of Pearson's product-moment correlation in a single population (e.g., H_0: $\rho = +.50$), then the alternative hypothesis must also deal with the possible value of Pearson's correlation in a single population. Or, if the null hypothesis deals with the variability among the means within three populations (e.g., H_0: $\sigma_\mu^2 = 0$), then the alternative hypothesis must also say something about the variability of the means in three populations. In general, therefore, H_a and H_0 are identical in that they must (1) deal with the same number of populations, (2) have the same statistical focus, and (3) involve the same variable(s).

The only difference between the null and alternative hypothesis is that the possible value of the population parameter included within H_a will always differ from what is specified in H_0. If the null hypothesis is set up so as to say H_0: $\rho = +.50$, then the alternative hypothesis might be set up to say H_a: $\rho \neq +.50$; or, if a researcher specifies, in Step 1, that H_0: $\sigma_\mu^2 = 0$, we might find that the alternative is set up to say H_a: $\sigma_\mu^2 > 0$.

As we indicated in the previous section, the hypothesis testing procedure terminates (in Step 6) with a decision to either reject or fail-to-reject the null hypothesis. In the event that H_0 is rejected, H_a represents the state of affairs that the researcher will consider to be probable. In other words, H_0 and H_a always represent two opposing statements as to the possible value of the parameter in the population(s) of interest. If, in Step 6, H_0 is rejected, then belief shifts *from* H_0 *to* H_a. Stated differently, if a "reject" decision is made at the end of the hypothesis testing procedure, the researcher will reject H_0 *in favor of* H_a.

In Excerpt 7.13, we see four alternative hypotheses that were specified in a study dealing with the way undergraduate students evaluate business courses. Data came from 1668 students who evaluated 63 business courses, with each course classified as "high," "mid," or "low" depending upon whether its quality was evaluated as being in the top quarter, middle half, or bottom quarter of all courses. The researchers analyzed their data to see if course evaluations were unrelated to (i.e., independent of) or related to (i.e., dependent on) grades assigned, to full- or part-time status of the instructor, to instructor gender, or to course level.

Although researchers have the flexibility to state any alternative hypothesis in various ways, most researchers will set up H_a either in a **directional** fashion or in a **nondirectional** fashion.[2] To clarify the distinction between these

---

[2]*A directional H_a is occasionally referred to as a "one-sided" H_a; likewise, a nondirectional H_a is sometimes referred to as a "two-sided" H_a.*

Excerpt 7.13 Alternative Hypotheses

HYPOTHESES

1. H_0: Rank is independent of grades. H_a: Rank is dependent on grades.

2. H_0: Rank is independent of instructor status. H_a: Rank is dependent on instructor status.

3. H_0: Rank is independent of instructor gender. H_a: Rank is dependent on instructor gender.

4. H_0: Rank is independent of course level. H_a: Rank is dependent on course level.

Source: G. F. Goldberg and J. P. Callahan. (1991). Comparative analyses of instructor ranking based on student evaluations. *College Student Journal, 25*(2), p. 199.

---

options for the alternative hypothesis, let's imagine that a researcher conducts a study to compare men and women in terms of intelligence. Further suppose that the statistical focus of this hypothetical study is on the mean, with the null hypothesis asserting that H_0: $\mu_{men} = \mu_{women}$. Now, if the alternative hypothesis is set up in a nondirectional fashion, the researcher will simply state H_a: $\mu_{men} \neq \mu_{women}$. If, on the other hand, the alternative hypothesis is stated in a directional fashion, the researcher will specify a direction in H_a; this could be done by asserting H_a: $\mu_{men} > \mu_{women}$ *or* by asserting H_a: $\mu_{men} < \mu_{women}$. In Excerpts 7.14–7.15, we show examples of how H_a can be set up in a nondirectional or a directional manner.

The directional/nondirectional nature of H_a is highly important within the hypothesis testing procedure. The researcher will need to know whether H_a was set up in a directional or nondirectional manner in order to decide whether to reject (or to fail-to-reject) the null hypothesis. No decision can be made about H_0 unless the directional/nondirectional character of H_a is clarified.

In most empirical studies, the alternative hypothesis is set up in a nondirectional fashion. Thus, if we had to guess what H_a would say in studies containing the null hypotheses presented here on the left, we would bet that the researchers would set up their alternative hypotheses as indicated on the right.

Possible H_0	*Corresponding non-directional H_a*
H_0: $\mu = 100$	H_a: $\mu \neq 100$
H_0: $\rho = +.20$	H_a: $\rho \neq +.20$
H_0: $\sigma^2 = 4$	H_a: $\sigma^2 \neq 4$
H_0: $\mu_1 - \mu_2 = 0$	H_a: $\mu_1 - \mu_2 \neq 0$

Excerpts 7.14–7.15 Nondirectional and Directional Alternative Hypotheses

The specific hypothesis is:

$$H_0: \pi = 0$$

$$H_a: \pi \neq 0$$

Source: K. C. Chan, B. E. Gup, and M. Pan. (1992). An empirical analysis of stock prices in major Asian markets and the United States. *The Financial Review, 27*(2), p. 294.

The procedure involves testing the difference between the post-event average relative turnover and the pre-event average relative turnover for the sample, defined as

$$D_J = (\text{Post-event RT}_j) - (\text{Pre-event RT}_j).$$

Because we are testing for an *increase* in trading activity, under the null hypothesis, μ_D, the average of these differences will be zero. But if the alternative hypothesis is true, then the true average difference will be positive. Stated more formally,

$$H_0: \mu_D = 0$$

$$H_1: \mu_D > 0$$

Source: G. A. Wolfe, D. P. Klein, and L. E. Bowyer. (1992). The impact on stock returns and liquidity for OTC equity issues added to the list of marginable OTC stocks. *The Financial Review, 27*(1), p. 99.

Researchers typically set up H_a in a nondirectional fashion because they do not know whether the pinpoint number in H_0 is too large or too small. By specifying a nondirectional H_a, the researcher permits the data to point one way or the other in the event that H_0 is rejected. Hence, in our hypothetical study comparing men and women in terms of intelligence, a nondirectional alternative hypothesis would allow us to argue that μ_{women} is probably higher than μ_{men} (in the event that we reject the H_0 because $\overline{X}_{women} > \overline{X}_{men}$); or such an alternative hypothesis would allow us to argue that μ_{men} is probably higher than μ_{women} (if we reject H_0 because $\overline{X}_{men} > \overline{X}_{women}$).

Occasionally, a researcher will feel so strongly (based on theoretical consideration or previous research) that the true state of affairs falls on one "side" of H_0's pinpoint number that H_a is set up in a directional fashion. So long as the researcher makes this decision prior to looking at the data, such a decision is fully legitimate. It is, however, totally inappropriate for the researcher to look at the data first and then subsequently decide to set up H_a in a directional manner. Although a decision to reject or fail-to-reject H_0 could still be made after first examining the data and then articulating a directional H_a, such a sequence of events would sabotage the fundamental logic and practice of hypothesis testing. Simply stated, decisions concerning how to state H_a (and how to state H_0) must be made without peeking at any data.

When the alternative hypothesis is set up in a nondirectional fashion, researchers sometimes use the phrase **two-tailed test** to describe their specific application of the hypothesis testing procedure. In contrast, directional H_as lead to what researchers sometimes refer to as **one-tailed tests**. Inasmuch as researchers rarely specify the alternative hypothesis in their technical write-ups, the terms *one-tailed* and *two-tailed* help us to know exactly how H_a was set up. For example, consider Excerpts 7.16–7.19. Here, we see how researchers sometimes communicate, using the term *two-tailed* or *one-tailed,* their decisions to set up H_a in a nondirectional or directional fashion.

Excerpts 7.16–7.19 One-Tailed and Two-Tailed Tests

Two-tailed t tests were performed. Normals mean $= 6.167$; dysphasic mean $= 2$; $t(10) = 4.11$; $p = .0021$. This is a significant difference.

Source: M. Gopnik and M. B. Crago. (1991). Familial aggregation of a developmental language disorder. *Cognition, 39*(1), p. 24.

When these differences were examined with a two-tailed test, American men were found to have significantly lower scores than Taiwan men ($t = 4.60$, $p <$ .001), and American women scored significantly higher than Taiwan women ($t = 3.23$, $p < .001$).

Source: Yu-Wen Ying. (1991). Validation of the California Psychological Inventory Femininity Scale in Taiwan college graduates. *Journal of Multicultural Counseling and Development, 19*(4), p. 168.

A one-tailed t-test revealed that country of origin was significantly more important to purchasers of U.S. made sweaters than to purchasers of imported sweaters ($t = 176$, $P = 0.040$).

Source: K. Gipson and S. Francis. (1991). The effect of country of origin on purchase behavior: An intercept study. *Journal of Consumer Studies and Home Economics, 15*(1), p. 40.

On the delayed test, however, only the multiple keyword/control contrast remained significant (as had been predicted), $t = 2.32$, $p < .016$ (one-tailed).

Source: R. N. Carney and J. R. Levin. (1991). Mnemonic facilitation of artists and their paintings: Effects of familiarity and correspondence. *Contemporary Educational Psychology, 16*(2), p. 162.

THE GENERAL RESEARCH QUESTION AND THE RESEARCH HYPOTHESIS

Inasmuch as the hypothesis testing procedure is focused on the null and alternative hypotheses, it is important to consider, in any given investigation, where H_0 and H_a come from. On one level, we could answer this implied question by simply responding that both H_0 and H_a come from researchers, because they decide what data will be collected, what the statistical focus of the study will be, what pinpoint number will be included in H_0, and whether H_a will be set up in a directional or nondirectional fashion. On a deeper level, however, we want to address the legitimate questions "Why is one pin-point number chosen for H_0 rather than other possible values?" and "What influences the researcher's decision to set up H_a in one way rather than in a different possible manner?" To answer these questions, we must digress from our consideration of the six main steps of hypothesis testing and consider two things that determine H_0 and H_a: the general research question and the research hypothesis.

The hypothesis testing procedure is used by researchers as an aid in obtaining answers to general questions. Often, the general research question is not directly stated but rather is implied in the introductory portion of an article. If the review of literature illuminates a "hole" in the knowledge base connected to a given line of research or if previous investigations have produced conflicting results, the implied general research question could be stated "Can a new study fill in the hole?" or "Can a new study provide insight as to why earlier studies yielded dissimilar results?" Occasionally, the introductory section of the article will contain a specific and direct articulation of the general research question. An example of such an articulation is contained in Excerpt 7.20.

Excerpt 7.20 General Research Questions

This study was undertaken to investigate the psychological context of the career development process of university students. Specifically, the research questions were (a) whether help seekers who express concerns about their careers report concerns about other areas of their lives and if so, whether the concerns reported relate to help seekers' career goal clarity and stability; (b) whether these concerns are unique to career help seekers.

Source: M. S. Lucas. (1992). Problems expressed by career and non-career help seekers: A comparison. *Journal of Counseling and Development, 70*(3), p. 417.

In most studies, the researcher will take the general research question, turn it into a more specific and testable question, and then formulate a tentative answer to this question. This is the researcher's hunch as to how the specific question will be answered after the data of the investigation are collected and analyzed. Technically referred to as the **research hypothesis,** and sometimes symbolized as H_r, these informal predictions on the part of researchers are based on their personal observation, results from earlier investigations, and/or a consideration of theoretical postulates. An example of a research hypothesis is presented in Excerpt 7.21.

Excerpt 7.21 The Research Hypothesis

What causes an individual to evaluate a certain level of density as dysfunctional? The crowding literature seems to converge on an information processing view to explain this process. It is posited that feelings of crowding emerge as a result of an excessively high number and rate of informational cues from the environment. High perceived density, for example, is related to physical qualities (such as high degree of enclosure, high activity levels, many uses) as well as social qualities (such as the number of people, nature of the group, its homogeneity, hierarchy, and so on) (Rapoport and Kantor 1967). According to Milgram (1970), under high perceived density conditions people are likely to experience information overload whereby the rate and amount of environmental stimuli exceed the capacity to cope with them. This, then, results in feelings of being confined, out of control, and constrained. Applying these arguments to the domain of shopping environments, we hypothesize:

H1: The higher the level of perceived retail density, the higher the retail crowding experienced.

Source: S. A. Eroglu, and K. A. Machleit. (1990). An empirical study of retail crowding: Antecedents and consequences. *The Journal of Retailing, 66*(2), p. 204.

The research hypothesis helps set the hypothesis testing procedure in motion because the pinpoint number needed for the null hypothesis can be fixed as soon as the research hypothesis is articulated. To obtain H_0's pinpoint number, the researcher first thinks about the numerical continuum of possible values suggested by the research hypothesis. Then, this continuum is divided into two segments: (1) numerical values that would support the research hypothesis, and (2) numerical values that would contradict the research hypothesis. The point that divides the numerical continuum into these two segments then becomes the pinpoint numerical value that goes into H_0.

To illustrate how the research hypothesis guides the formation of H_0, consider again Excerpt 7.21. In this study, the statistical focus (i.e., correlation) suggests a numerical continuum that extends from $+1.00$ to -1.00. With respect to this continuum, the research hypothesis would gain support if the sample correlation coefficient were to turn out to be positive. On the other hand, negative values of r would contradict the research hypothesis. The dividing point on this continuum that creates a "segment of support" and a "segment of nonsupport" is 0.00. Accordingly, this pinpoint value, zero, was selected for the null hypothesis.

As previously indicated, the research and null hypotheses usually disagree with each other. You may be tempted, therefore, to think that the research hypothesis is always embodied in the alternative hypothesis. Sometimes, as suggested by the content of Excerpt 7.19, this is the case. In that study, the researchers had a directional hunch and set up a directional alternative hypothesis. Thus, H_a and H_r were congruent with each other.

Although the research and alternative hypotheses occasionally correspond with each other, it is more often the case that a researcher with a directional hunch will set up a nondirectional alternative hypothesis. This is done because the typical researcher is interested in making discoveries, even if the evidence turns out to contradict his or her initial hunch. Excerpt 7.22 provides an example of this typical situation.

Excerpt 7.22 A Research Hypothesis That Is Different from Both H_0 and H_a

Although asthma is likely to exert a powerful effect on the child, the mother, and the mother-child relationship, few studies have examined maternal perceptions of self, child, and the parent-child relationship. . . . The purpose of this study was to investigate these maternal perceptions. Our general expectation was that there would be greater distress and problems reported by these mothers than mothers in the normative samples. . . . A series of t-tests (two-tailed) for independent samples were conducted to examine whether scale means between this sample of families and those in the various normed groups on which each measure was standardized were significantly different.

Source: D. K. Carson and R. W. Schauer. (1992). Mothers of children with asthma: Perceptions of parenting stress and the mother-child relationship. *Psychological Reports, 71*(3), pp. 1141, 1143.

In the study from which Excerpt 7.22 was taken, the researchers compared the way in which two groups of mothers filled out questionnaires dealing with the mother-child relationship and with maternal stress in relation to a young child. Each of the mothers in the first group had an asthmatic child while those in the second group had nonasthmatic children. A t-test was used to compare the two groups of mothers on each of several scales derived from the questionnaires (e.g., overprotectiveness), and in each case the null and alternative hypotheses were $H_0 : \mu_1 = \mu_2$ and $H_a: \mu_1 \neq \mu_2$. The researchers' hunch was directional in nature and it could be expressed as $H_r: \mu_1 > \mu_2$. Clearly, H_r was different from either H_0 or H_a.

As we have seen, the research hypothesis that stands behind the hypothesis testing procedure is, in some studies, consistent with the alternative hypothesis set up by the researcher. In other studies, the research hypothesis is not congruent with either of the two hypotheses (H_0 and H_a) articulated at the outset of the hypothesis testing procedure. In still other studies, the researcher will use the hypothesis testing procedure without having any hunch whatsoever as to the actual value of the population parameter(s). While it is true that the decision concerning H_0's pinpoint value and the decision as to how H_a is structured (directional or nondirectional) are usually guided by the research hypothesis, it is also true that the hypothesis testing procedure can produce valuable insights even in cases where no research hypothesis exists.

To see an example of a study in which the researcher had no strong hunch, consider Excerpt 7.23. In this investigation, the researchers indicate that they "did not have prior information on which to base a prediction" concerning one of the relationships focused upon in the study. They even point out how one could muster an argument one way or the other as to whether the relationship in question is more likely to be direct or indirect. Although the researchers end up making a prediction, the clear impression given here is that the null hypothesis (H_0: $\rho = 0.00$) was set up for reasons other than the researchers' having a strong hunch.

Excerpt 7.23 A Research Hypothesis That Comes After (Not Before) H_0

We did not have prior information on which to base a prediction regarding the relationship between discomfort seeking support and satisfaction with support. It is possible that those who are uncomfortable seeking support are less satisfied with support under high and low stress. It is also possible that those who feel relatively comfortable seeking support are more satisfied with the support they receive but lose this relative advantage when pressed into the vulnerable position of more prolonged need for help. Because of the lack of empirical information, we chose the more simple, straightforward prediction. Specifically, we hypothesized a direct relationship between discomfort seeking support and dissatisfaction.

Source: S. Hobfoll, S. Shoham, and C. Ritter. (1991). Women's satisfaction with social support and their receipt of aid. *Journal of Personality and Social Psychology, 61(2),* p. 334.

Before returning to our formal consideration of the six basic steps of the hypothesis testing procedure, we need to make one final comment concerning the research hypothesis. Simply stated, a researcher cannot gain support for a hunch by (1) setting up H_0 so as to be *consistent* with the research hypothesis and (2) reaching, in Step 6, a fail-to-reject decision. Near the end of this chapter, we will explain why such a strategy will not work. For now, however, all we want to do is alert you to the fact that the hypothesis testing procedure yields very murky information when H_0 is not rejected. This fact helps to explain why researchers make certain that the research hypothesis, if there is one, is *not* reflected in the null hypothesis.

STEP 4: COLLECTION AND ANALYSIS OF SAMPLE DATA

So far, we have covered Steps 1, 2, and 6 of the hypothesis testing procedure. In the first two steps, the researcher states the null and alternative hypotheses. In Step 6, the researcher will either (1) reject H_0 in favor of H_a or (2) fail-to-reject

H_0. We now turn our attention to the principal stepping-stone that is used to move from the beginning points of the hypothesis testing procedure to the final decision.

Inasmuch as the hypothesis testing procedure is, by its very nature, an empirical strategy, it should come as no surprise that the researcher's ultimate decision to reject or to retain H_0 is based upon the collection and analysis of sample data. No crystal ball is used, no Ouija board is relied upon, and no eloquent argumentation is permitted. Once H_0 and H_a are fixed, only scientific evidence is allowed to affect the disposition of H_0.

The fundamental logic of the hypothesis testing procedure can now be laid bare, because the connections between H_0, the data, and the final decision are as straightforward as what exists between the speed of a car, a traffic light at a busy intersection, and a lawful driver's decision as the car approaches the intersection. Just as the driver's decision to stop or to pass through the intersection is made after observing the color of the traffic light, the researcher's decision to reject or to retain H_0 is made after observing the sample data. To carry this analogy one step further, the researcher will look at the data and ask, "Is the empirical evidence *in*consistent with what one would expect if H_0 were true?" If the answer to this question is "yes," then the researcher has a "green light" and will reject H_0. On the other hand, if the data turn out to be consistent with H_0, then the data set serves as a "red light" telling the researcher not to discard H_0.

Because the logic of hypothesis testing is so important, let us briefly consider a hypothetical example. Suppose a valid intelligence test is given to a random sample of 100 males and a random sample of 100 females attending the same university. If the null hypothesis had first been set up to say H_0: μ_{male} − $\mu_{\text{female}} = 0$ and if the data reveal that the two sample means (of IQ scores) differ by only two points, the sample data would be consistent with what we expect to happen when two samples are selected from populations having identical means. Clearly, the notion of sampling error could fully explain why the two $\overline{X}$s might differ by two IQ points even if $\mu_{\text{male}} = \mu_{\text{female}}$. In this situation, no empirical grounds exist for making the data-based claim that males at our hypothetical university have a different IQ, on the average, than do their female classmates.

Now, let's consider what would happen if the difference between the two sample means turns out to be equal to 40 (rather than 2) IQ points. If the empirical evidence turns out like this, we would have a situation where the data are inconsistent with what one would expect, if H_0 were to be true. Although the concept of sampling error strongly suggests that neither sample mean will turn out exactly equal to its population parameter, the difference of 40 IQ points between $\overline{X}_{\text{males}}$ and $\overline{X}_{\text{females}}$ is quite improbable if, in fact, μ_{males} and μ_{females} are equal. With results such as this, the researcher would reject the arbitrarily selected null hypothesis.

To help drive home the point we are trying to make about the way sample data influence the researcher's decision concerning H_0, let's shift our attention to a real study that had Pearson's correlation as its statistical focus. In Excerpt 7.24, we see a pair of sentences that show the separate correlation coefficients obtained when a sample of 236 subjects filled out three attachment-style rating scales, with Pearson's r computed between each possible pair of scales.

Excerpt 7.24 Illustration of How H_0 Is Rejected When the Sample Data Turn Out to Be "Inconsistent" With H_0

Correlations involving ratings of the three attachment-style descriptions will be reported separately for the three styles, even though, as in previous studies, the secure and avoidant styles were fairly highly correlated: $r = -.58, p < .001$, at Time 1. (The correlation between the secure and anxious scales was $-.32$, $p < .001$; between the anxious and avoidant scales, .03, n.s.)

Source: P. R. Shaver, and K. A. Brennan. (1992). Attachment styles and the "Big Five" with personality traits: Their connections with each other and with romantic relationship outcomes. *Personality and Social Psychology Bulletin, 18*(5), p. 539.

In the study from which Excerpt 7.24 was taken, the hypothesis testing procedure was used separately to evaluate the sample correlation between the secure and avoidant scales, between the secure and anxious scales, and between the anxious and avoidant scales. In each case, the null hypothesis stated H_0: $\rho = 0.00$. The sample data, once analyzed, yielded correlations of $-.58$, $-.32$, and .03. The first two of these rs were so inconsistent with H_0 that sampling error was viewed as an inadequate explanation for the discrepancy between the pinpoint number in H_0, 0.00, and the single-value summaries of the sample data, $-.58$ and $-.32$. Accordingly, the first two null hypotheses were rejected, as indicated by the notation $p < .001$. The third sample correlation, however, was so close to the null hypothesis value of 0.00 as to make sampling error a very plausible explanation for the discrepancy between the observed sample coefficient, on the one hand, and the null value of 0.00, on the other. Accordingly, the third null hypothesis was not rejected, as indicated by the abbreviation *n.s.*

In Step 4 of the hypothesis testing procedure, the summary of the sample data will always lead to a single numerical value. Being based on the data, this number is technically referred to as the **calculated value**. (It is also called the **test statistic**.) Occasionally, the researcher's task in obtaining the calculated value involves nothing more than computing a value that corresponds to the study's statistical focus. This was the case in Excerpt 7.24, where the statistical focus was Pearson's correlation coefficient and where the researcher needed to do nothing more than compute a value for r.

In most applications of the hypothesis testing procedure, the sample data are summarized in such a way that the statistical focus becomes hidden from view. For example, consider Excerpts 7.25–7.27, in which we see that the calculated values turned out equal to 6.85, 1.231, 1.07, 0.2, and 1.41.

Excerpts 7.25–7.27 The Calculated Value

Similar to the findings in the first study, the mean for the 14 counseling values ($M = 8.36$) was significantly higher than the mean of the general-psychology values ($M = 6.93$) for the counseling psychologist, $t(50) = 6.85, p < .001$.

Source: G. S. Howard. (1992). Behold our creation! What counseling psychology has become and might yet become. *Journal of Counseling Psychology, 39*(4), p. 426.

Within the autistic group an ANOVA revealed no significant differences in overall stress scores found between mothers with 0, 1, 2, or 3 children, $F(3, 20) = 1.231, p > .05$.

Source: R. Bouma and R. Schweitzer. (1990). The impact of chronic childhood illness on family stress: A comparison between autism and cystic fibrosis. *Journal of Clinical Psychology, 46*(6), p. 727.

The analysis compared the number of suicides occurring in the seven days centered around the full moon versus the rest of the lunar cycle. No relations were evident over-all ($\chi^2_1 = 1.07, p = .30$), for the men ($\chi^2_1 = 0.2, p = 0.65$), or for women ($\chi^2_1 = 1.41, p = 0.24$).

Source: S. J. Martin. (1992). Suicide and lunar cycles: A critical review over 28 years. *Psychological Reports, 71*(3), p. 788.

In the first two of these excerpts, the statistical focus was the mean; the calculated values, however, are presented as t and F values rather than a simple measure of how different the sample means were. In the third excerpt, the statistical focus was on frequencies: how many people committed suicide within three days of a full moon as compared with the number who committed suicide at other times during the month. In later chapters, you will learn about t-tests, F-tests, and chi-square tests, and you should not worry if you currently fail to comprehend what is presented in these three excerpts. They are shown here only to illustrate the typical situation in which the statistical focus of the study is not reflected directly in the calculated value.

Although we will delay our discussion of t, F, chi-square, and other tests until later in the book, we can provide a partial explanation as to why researchers convert their sample data into these kinds of calculated values. By converting the sample data into a standardized calculated value (i.e., a calculated value that is "metric-free"), the researcher makes it much easier to determine whether the sample data are consistent or inconsistent with H_0. For example, it would have been possible, but hard, for the researcher associated with Excerpt 7.25 to evaluate the mean difference, which turned out equal to 1.43, between the two sets of values. After the data were converted into a t calculated value, however, the task of deciding whether to reject or fail-to-reject H_0 became as easy as rolling off a log.

Before computers were invented, researchers would always have a single goal in mind when they turned to Step 4 of the hypothesis testing procedure. That goal was the computation of the data-based calculated value. Now that computers are widely available, researchers still are interested in the magnitude of the calculated value derived from the data analysis. Contemporary researchers, however, are also interested in a second piece of information generated by the computer. This second item is the data-based p-value.

Whenever researchers use a computer to perform the data analysis, they will either (1) tell the computer what the null hypothesis is going to be or (2) accept the computer's built-in "default" version of H_0. The researcher will also specify whether H_0 is directional or nondirectional in nature. Once the computer "knows" what the researcher's H_0 and H_a are, it can easily analyze the sample data and compute the probability of having a data set that deviates as much or more from H_0 as does the data set being analyzed. The computer informs the researcher as to this probability by means of a statement that takes the form "$p =$ _____," with the blank being filled by a single decimal value somewhere between 0 and 1. You saw examples of such p-statements earlier in Excerpts 7.16, 7.18, and 7.27.

If the p-value associated with the data is a very small number, this indicates that the researcher's sample data set deviates greatly from what one would expect if H_0 were true. For example, the p-value in Excerpt 7.18 is equal to .04. This means that the chances were 4 out of 100 of getting sample data that deviated as much or more from H_0 as did the researcher's data, if H_0 had really been true. In Excerpt 17.16, we see an even smaller p-value, .0021. This computer-generated p told the researchers that having their two samples yield a mean difference as large or larger than 4.167 (i.e., this value coming from the difference between the means of 6.167 and 2) is quite improbable, because such an outcome would occur only 21 out of 10,000 times if the study's H_0 were true.

Step 5: The Criterion for Evaluating the Sample Evidence

After the researcher has summarized the study's data, the next task involves asking the question "Are the sample data inconsistent with what would likely occur if the null hypothesis were true?" If the answer to this question is "yes," then H_0 will be rejected; on the other hand, a negative response to this query will bring forth a fail-to-reject decision. Thus, as soon as the sample data can be "tagged" as "consistent" or "inconsistent" (with H_0), the decision in Step 6 is easily made. "But how," you might ask, "does the researcher decide which of these labels should be attached to the sample data?"

If the data from the sample(s) are in perfect agreement with the pinpoint numerical value specified in H_0, then it is obvious that the sample data are consistent with H_0. (This would be the case if the sample mean turned out equal to 100 when testing H_0: $\mu = 100$, if the sample correlation coefficient turned out equal to $+.25$ when testing H_0: $\rho = +.25$, etc.) Such a situation, however, is unlikely. Almost always, there will be a discrepancy between H_0's parameter value and the corresponding sample statistic.

In light of the fact that the summary of the sample data (produced by Step 4) is almost certain to be different from H_0's pinpoint number (specified in Step 1), the concern over whether the sample data are inconsistent with H_0 actually boils down to the question "Should the observed difference between the sample evidence and the null hypothesis be considered to be a big difference or a small difference?" If this difference (between the data and H_0) is judged to be large, then the sample data will be looked upon as being inconsistent with H_0 and, as a consequence, H_0 will be rejected. If, on the other hand, this difference is judged to be small, the data and H_0 will be looked upon as consistent with each other and, therefore, H_0 will not be rejected.

To answer the question about the sample data's being either consistent or inconsistent with what one would expect if H_0 were true, a researcher can use either of two simple procedures. As you will see, both of these procedures involve comparing a single-number summary of the sample evidence against a criterion number. The single-number summary of the data can be either the calculated value or the p-value. Our job now is to consider what each of these data-based indices is compared against and what kind of result forces researchers to consider their samples as representing a "large" or a "small" deviation from H_0.

One available procedure for evaluating the sample data involves comparing the calculated value against something called the **critical value**. The critical value is nothing more than a number extracted from one of many statistical tables developed by mathematical statisticians. Applied researchers, of course, do not close their eyes and point to just any entry in a randomly selected table of critical values. Instead, they must learn which table of critical values is appropriate for their studies and also how to locate the single number within the table that constitutes the correct critical value.

As a reader of research reports, you do not have to learn how to locate the proper table that contains the critical value for any given statistical test, nor do you have to locate, within the table, the single number that allows the sample data to be labeled as being consistent or inconsistent with H_0. The researcher will do these things. Occasionally, the critical value will be included in the research report, as exemplified in Excerpts 7.28 and 7.29.

Once the critical value is located, the researcher will compare the data-based summary of the sample data against the scientific dividing line that has been extracted from a statistical table. The simple question being asked at this

Excerpts 7.28–7.29 The Critical Value

Using an alpha of 0.05, the critical value of F for 1 and 108 degrees of freedom is 3.92.

Source: C. L. Hodges. (1992). The effectiveness of mental imagery and visual illustrations: A comparison of two instructional variables. *Journal of Research and Development in Education, 26*(1), p. 50.

The computed J-statistic for the natural gas equation was 2.56 and the computed J-test statistic for the liquefied petroleum gas equation was 3.10. The critical chi-square value at the 5 percent level is 3.84.

Source: N. D. Uri. (1991). Estimating the agricultural demand for energy in the presence of measurement error in the data. *Energy Systems and Policy, 15(2)*, p. 127.

point is whether the calculated value is larger or smaller than the critical value. With most tests (such as t, F, chi-square, and tests of correlation coefficients), the researcher will follow a decision rule that says to reject H_0 if the calculated value is at least as large as the critical value. With a few tests (such as U or W), the decision rule tells the researcher to reject H_0 if the calculated value is smaller than the critical value. You do not need to worry about which way the decision rule works for any given test, because this is the responsibility of the individual who performs the data analysis. The only things you need to know about the comparison of calculated and critical values are (1) that this comparison allows the researcher to decide easily whether to reject or fail-to-reject H_0 and (2) that some tests use a decision rule that says to reject H_0 if the calculated value is larger than the critical value, whereas other tests involve a decision rule that says to reject H_0 if the calculated value is smaller than the critical value.

Researchers who use the hypothesis testing procedure almost always indicate the magnitude of their calculated value and whether or not the null hypothesis is rejected. As we have seen, they occasionally will also indicate the size of the critical value. Every so often, we come across a research report wherein the researcher specifies the nature of the decision rule associated with the specific test used to assess the null hypothesis. In Excerpts 7.30 and 7.31, we see two examples of such a report.

In the study from which Excerpt 7.30 was pulled, several Pearson product-moment correlation coefficients were computed to assess the bivariate relationships among 11 variables. The 55 correlation coefficients obtained by correlating each variable with every other variable were presented using a correlation matrix. The sentence appearing in Excerpt 7.30 was a note beneath that correlation matrix. In Excerpt 7.31, a calculated value called Z was used to compare several groups two at a time. For any pair of groups, H_0 was rejected if Z's absolute value was equal to or larger than 1.96.

Excerpts 7.30–7.31 The Decision-Rule Concern Calculated and Critical Values

---

Correlations of .073 or greater are significant at the .05 level.

Source: A. J. Reynolds and H. J. Walberg. (1992). A structural model of high school mathematics outcomes. *Journal of Educational Research, 85*(3), p. 154.

Groups differed significantly at the .05 level when $Z \geq |1.96|$.

Source: B. Burman, G. Margolin, and R. S. John. (1993). America's angriest home videos: Behavioral contingencies observed in home reenactments of marital conflict. *Journal of Consulting and Clinical Psychology, 61,* p. 32.

When researchers make a data-versus-H_0 evaluation by comparing the calculated value against the critical value, the critical value may appear in the research summary, as was illustrated in Excerpts 7.28–7.31. Normally, however, researchers do not indicate anything at all about this criterion number that allows them to decide whether or not they should reject their null hypotheses. Even though you rarely will see critical values in published research reports, you won't have any trouble determining what decision was made by the researcher because this decision will be declared openly, as illustrated earlier in Excerpts 7.7–7.12.

The second way a researcher can evaluate the sample evidence is to compare the data-based p-value against a preset point on the 0-to-1 scale on which the p must fall. This criterion is called the **level of significance**, and it functions much as does the critical value in the first procedure for evaluating sample evidence. Simply stated, the researcher compares his or her data-based p-value against the criterion point along the 0-to-1 continuum so as to decide whether the sample evidence ought to be considered "consistent" or "inconsistent" with H_0. The decision rule used in this second procedure is always the same: If the data-based p-value is equal to or smaller than the criterion, the sample is viewed as being *in*consistent with H_0; if, on the other hand, p is larger than the criterion, the data are looked upon as being consistent with H_0.

We will discuss the level of significance in more depth in the next section, since it is a concept that must be dealt with by the researcher no matter which of the two procedures is used to evaluate the sample data. (With the second procedure, the level of significance *is* the criterion against which the data-based p-value is compared; with the first procedure, the level of significance influences the size of the critical value against which the calculated value is compared.) Before we complete this section, however, we need to point out that the same decision will be reached regarding H_0 no matter which of the two procedures is used in Step 5 of the hypothesis testing procedure. For example, suppose a researcher conducts an F-test and rejects H_0

because the calculated value is larger than the critical value. If that researcher were to compare the data-based p against the level of significance, it would be found that the former is smaller than the latter, and the same decision about H_0 would be made. Or, suppose a researcher conducts a t-test and fails to reject H_0 because the calculated value is smaller than the critical value. If that researcher were to compare the data-based p against the level of significance, it would be found that the former is larger than the latter, and the same fail-to-reject decision would be made.

Step 3: Selecting a Level of Significance

After the data of a study are collected and summarized, the six-step hypothesis testing procedure allows absolutely no subjectivity to influence, or bias, the ultimate decision that is made concerning the null hypothesis. This goal is accomplished by reliance on a scientific cutoff point to determine whether the sample data are consistent or inconsistent with H_0. By referring (in Step 5) to a numerical criterion, it becomes clear whether or not sampling error provides, by itself, a sufficient explanation for the observed difference between the single-number summary of the researcher's data (computed in Step 4) and H_0's pinpoint numerical value (articulated in Step 1). If the single-number summary of the data is found to lie on H_a's "side" of the criterion number (or if the data-based p lands on the H_a's side of the level of significance), a decision (in Step 6) is made to reject H_0 in favor of H_a (set forth in Step 2); on the other hand, if the calculated value lands on H_0's "side" of the critical value (or if the data-based p lands on H_0's side of the level of significance), a fail-to-reject decision is made.

Either the critical value or the level of significance serves as a scientific cutoff point that determines what decision will be made concerning the null hypothesis. The six-step hypothesis testing procedure not only allows the researcher to do something that affects the magnitude of this criterion—*it actually forces the researcher to become involved in determining how rigorous the criterion will be.* The researcher cannot, as we have pointed out, do anything like this after the data have been collected and summarized. However, the researcher *must* do something prior to collecting data that has an impact on how large or small the criterion number will be.

After the null and alternative hypotheses have been set up, but before any data are collected, the researcher must select a level of significance. This third step of the hypothesis testing procedure simply asks the researcher to select a positive decimal value of the researcher's choosing. Although the researcher has the freedom to select any value between 0 and 1 for the level of significance, most researchers select a small number such as .10, .05, .01, or .001. The most frequently selected number is .05.

Before explaining how the researcher-selected level of significance influences the size of the critical value, we need to alert you to the fact that not all researchers use the phrase *level of significance* to designate the decimal number that must be specified in Step 3. Instead of indicating, for example, that the level of significance is set equal to .05, some researchers will state that "the alpha level (α) is set equal to .05," others will assert that "$p = .05$," and still others will indicate that "H_0 will be rejected if $p < .05$." Likewise, a decision to use the .01 level of significance might be expressed using statements such as "alpha = .01," "$\alpha = .01$," or "results will be considered significant if $p < .01$."

In Excerpts 7.32–7.37, we see different ways in which researchers report what level of significance was selected within their studies.

If the single-number summary of the sample data is a p-value, the pragmatic value of the level of significance is clear. In this situation, p is compared directly against α to determine whether or not H_0 should be rejected. But even if the single-number summary of the sample data is a critical value, the

---

Excerpts 7.32–7.37 The Level of Significance

The level of significance was set at .05 for rejecting or failing to reject the null hypothesis.

Source: K. W. Lambrecht. (1991). Curricular preparation needs for sport club managers. *Journal of Sports Management, 5*(1), p. 50.

The alpha level for all post hoc comparisons was .05.

Source: C. Leone, and C. Wingate. (1991). A functional approach to understanding attitudes toward AIDS victims. *The Journal of Social Psychology, 131*(6), p. 764.

The rejection level of the F test was set at $\alpha = .05$ to assess differences among club groups.

Source: K. W. Lambrecht. (1991). Curricular preparation needs for sport club managers. *Journal of Sports Management, 5*(1), p. 51.

We chose the .10 level of significance.

Source: J. Kluzik, L. Fetters, and J. Coryell. (1990). Quantification of control: A preliminary study of effects of neurodevelopmental treatment on reaching in children with spastic cerebral palsy. *Physical Therapy, 70*(2), p. 71/19.

The probability level accepted for statistical significance was $P < 0.05$.

Source: T. Hortobagyi, N. Lambert, C. Tracy, and M. Shinebarger. (1992). Voluntary and electromyo-stimulation forces in trained and untrained men. *Medicine and Science in Sports and Exercise, 24*(6), p. 704.

In keeping with customary practice, the significance level was set at $p < .05$.

Source: C. A. Darling, J. K. Davidson, and L. C. Passarello. (1992). The mistique of first intercourse among college youth: The role of partners, contraceptive practices and psychological reactions. *Journal of Youth and Adolescence, 21*(1), p. 101.

---

level of significance still performs a valuable, pragmatic function. This is because a critical value cannot be located (in Step 5) unless the level of significance has first been set. As indicated in our earlier discussion of Step 4, there are many tables of critical values. Once the proper table is located, the researcher still has the task of locating the single number within the table that will serve as the critical value. The task of locating the critical value is easy, so long as the level of significance has been specified.[3] If you take another look at Excerpts 7.28–7.31, you will see that each critical value has a level of significance associated with it. These excerpts help to illustrate the point that a critical value cannot exist in the absence of a level of significance.

Although the level of significance plays an important pragmatic role within the six-step hypothesis testing procedure, the decimal number selected in Step 3 is even more important from a different perspective. When we introduced the concept of the null hypothesis, we were careful to point out that H_0 is never *proven* to be true or false by means of hypothesis testing. Regardless of the decision made about H_0 after the calculated and critical values are compared, it is possible that the wrong decision will be reached. If H_0 is rejected in Step 6, it is conceivable that this action represents a mistake, since H_0 may actually be true. Or, if H_0 is not rejected, it is conceivable that *this* action represents a mistake, since H_0 may actually be an inaccurate statement about the value of the parameter in the population(s).

In light of the fact that a mistake can conceivably occur regardless of what decision is made at the end of the hypothesis testing procedure, two technical terms have been coined to distinguish between these potentially wrong decisions. A **Type I error** designates the mistake of rejecting H_0 when the null hypothesis is actually true. A **Type II error,** on the other hand, designates the kind of mistake that is made if H_0 is not rejected when the null hypothesis is actually false. The following chart may help to clarify the meaning of these possible errors.

Is H_0 Really True?

		Yes	No
Researcher's Decision	Reject H_0	Type I Error	Correct decision
	Fail-to-Reject H_0	Correct decision	Type II Error

---

[3] *With certain tests, researchers cannot locate the critical value unless they also know (1) whether their test is one- or two-tailed in nature and (2) how many degrees of freedom are connected with the sample data. We will discuss the concept of degrees of freedom in later chapters.*

Beyond its pragmatic utility in helping the researcher locate the critical value (or in serving as the criterion against which the data-based p is compared), the level of significance is important because it establishes the probability of a Type I error. In other words, the selected alpha level determines the likelihood that a true null hypothesis will be rejected. If the researcher specifies, in Step 3, that $\alpha = .05$, then the chances of rejecting a true null hypothesis become equal to 5 out of 100. If, on the other hand, the alpha level is set equal to .01 (rather than .05), then the chances of rejecting a true null hypothesis would become equal to 1 out of 100. The alpha level, therefore, directly determines the probability that a Type I error will be committed.[4]

After realizing that the researcher can fully control the likelihood of a Type I error, you may be wondering why the researcher does not select an alpha level that would dramatically reduce the possibility that a true H_0 will be rejected. To be more specific, you may be inclined to ask why the alpha level is not set equal to .001 (where the chance of a Type I error becomes equal to 1 out of 1,000), equal to .00001 (where the chance of Type I error becomes equal to 1 out of 100,000), or even equal to some smaller decimal value. To answer this legitimate question, we must consider the way in which a change in the alpha level has an effect on both Type I error risk *and* Type II error risk.

If the alpha level is changed, it's as if there is an apothecary scale in which the two pans hanging from opposite ends of the balance beam contain, respectively, Type I error risk and Type II error risk. The alpha level of a study could be changed so as to decrease the likelihood of a Type I error, but this change in alpha will simultaneously have an opposite effect on the likelihood of a Type II error. Hence, researchers rarely move alpha from the more traditional levels of .05 or .01 to levels that would greatly protect against Type I errors (such as .0001) because such a change in the alpha level would serve to make the chances of a Type II error unacceptably high. In Excerpt 7.38, we

---

Excerpt 7.38 The Influence of the Alpha Level on Type I and Type II Error Risk

---

The .01 level was chosen over the conventional .05 to reduce the possible number of Type I errors. An even more conservative probability level was not used to help avoid committing Type II errors.

Source: C. Buehler, P. Betz, C. M. Ryan, B. H. Legg, and B. B. Trotter. (1992). Description and evaluation of the orientation for divorcing parents: Implications for postdivorce prevention programs. *Family Relations, 41*, p. 158.

---

[4]*As you will see later, the alpha level defines the probability of a Type I error only if (1) important assumptions underlying the statistical test are valid and (2) the hypothesis testing procedure is used to evaluate only* one *null hypothesis.*

see a case where a group of researchers selected the level of significance with a sensitivity for both Type I and Type II errors.

In our earlier discussion of null and research hypotheses (e.g., H_0 and H_r), we pointed out that H_0 is normally set up so as to disagree with H_r. In light of the fact that researchers typically like to reject H_0 so as to gain empirical support for H_r, and in light of the fact that a change in the level of significance has an impact on the likelihood of Type II errors, you now may be wondering why the researcher does not move alpha in the opposite direction. It is true that a researcher would decrease the chance of a Type II error by changing alpha—for example, from .05 to .40—since such a change would make it more likely that H_0 would be rejected. Researchers do not use such high levels of significance simply because the scientific community generally considers Type I errors to be more dangerous than Type II errors. In most disciplines, few people would pay attention to researchers who reject null hypotheses at alpha levels higher than .20, because such levels of significance are considered to be "too lenient" (i.e., too likely to yield "reject" decisions that are Type I errors).

The most frequently seen level of significance, as illustrated earlier in Excerpts 7.28–7.37, is .05. This alpha level is considered to represent a "happy medium" between the two error possibilities associated with any application of the six-step hypothesis testing procedure. If, however, a researcher feels that it is more important to guard against the possibility of a Type I error, a lower alpha level (such as .01 or .001) will be selected. On the other hand, if it is felt that a Type II error would be more dangerous than a Type I error, then a higher alpha level (such as .10 or .15) will be selected. Excerpts 7.39–7.41 illustrate the way in which the alpha level is sometimes set equal to a value higher than .05 because of a concern for protecting more against Type II errors.

Before concluding our discussion of the level of significance, we need to clarify three points of potential confusion. To accomplish this goal, we want to raise and then answer three questions: "Does the alpha level somehow determine the likelihood of a Type II error?" "When will you, the recipient of a research report, come to know whether the researcher's ultimate decision regarding H_0 is correct?" and "If H_0 is rejected, does the alpha level indicate the probability that H_0 is true?"

The first point of potential confusion concerns the relationship between alpha and Type II error risk. Since alpha does, in fact, determine the likelihood that the researcher will end up rejecting a true H_0, and since it is true that a change in alpha affects the chance of a Type I error *and* the chance of a Type II error (with one increasing, the other decreasing), you may be tempted to expect the level of significance to dictate Type II error risk. Unfortunately, this is not the case. The alpha level specified in Step 3 does influence Type II error risk, but so do other features of a study such as sample size, population variability, and the reliability of the measuring instrument used to collect data.

Excerpts 7.39–7.41 Alpha Levels Other than .05

Due to the exploratory nature of the present study, and the desire to reduce the risk of Type II errors, an alpha of .10 was set for the significance level.

Source: J. M. Williams and V. Crane. (1992). Coping styles and self-reported measures of state anxiety and self-confidence. *Journal of Applied Sport Psychology, 4,* p. 138.

We chose the .10 level of significance for data analysis. This choice was made to avoid the chance of committing a Type II error, that is, assuming no significant difference posttreatment when a significant difference actually does exist.

Source: J. Kluzik, L. Fetters, and J. Coryell. (1990). Quantification of control: A preliminary study of effects of neurodevelopmental treatment on reaching in children with spastic cerebral palsy. *Physical Therapy, 70*(2), p. 71/19.

Because this was an exploratory study with a small size, we set the significance level at $p < .10.$ to reduce the risk of a Type II error (Stevens, 1986).

Source: C. D. Morrison, A. C. Bundy, and A. G. Fisher. (1991). The contribution of motor skills and playfulness to the play performance of preschoolers. *American Journal of Occupational Therapy, 45*(8), p. 690.

In the next chapter, we will consider the full set of influences that determine the chances that a fail-to-reject decision will be made when H_0 is actually false. For now, however, all we can do is ask that you resist the temptation to think that alpha, by itself, determines Type II error risk.

The second point of potential confusion is connected to the question "When will you come to know whether the researcher's ultimate decision regarding H_0 is correct?" The simple answer to this question, unfortunately, is that neither you nor the researcher ever will! Regardless of the decision made at the end of the hypothesis testing procedure, neither you nor the researcher will know whether the conclusion reached within a single study is right or wrong. Although this may seem disconcerting when the hypothesis testing procedure is considered in conjunction with any one study, the beauty of this inferential procedure shines through when we consider what happens "in the long run." If the hypothesis testing procedure is used within many, many studies (as *is* the case), the majority of the decisions reached will be accurate. As we have seen in this chapter, the level of significance helps to protect against Type I errors. In Chapter 8, we will consider the concept of statistical power and mechanisms for also holding down the likelihood of Type II errors.[5]

---

[5]*Earlier we used the analogy of an apothecary scale to illustrate the fact that a change in the level of significance causes both Type I error risk and Type II error risk to change, but in opposite directions. In Chapter 8, we will illustrate how researchers can change certain features of their studies besides the alpha level so as to bring about increased protection against* both *kinds of decision errors.*

The final point of potential confusion about the alpha level again concerns the decision reached at the end of the hypothesis testing procedure. If a study's H_0 is rejected in Step 6, it is *not* proper to look back to see what alpha level was specified in Step 3 and then interpret that alpha level as indicating the probability that H_0 is true. For example, if a researcher ends up rejecting H_0 after having set the level of significance equal to .05, you cannot legitimately conclude that the chances of H_0 being true are less than 5 out of 100. The alpha level in any study indicates only what the chances are that the forthcoming decision will be a Type I error. If alpha is set equal to .05, then the chances are 5 out of 100 that H_0 will be rejected *if H_0 is actually true.* Statisticians sometimes try to clarify this distinction by pointing out that the level of significance specifies "the probability of a reject decision, given a true H_0" and *not* "the probability of H_0 being true, given a reject decision."

FAILING-TO-REJECT H_0 VERSUS ACCEPTING H_0

At the end of the hypothesis testing procedure, a decision may be made to fail-to-reject the null hypothesis. In light of the fact that a decision not to reject H_0 is made because the empirical evidence of the study is congruent with H_0, you probably have been wondering why the phrase *fail-to-reject H_0* is used to describe such a decision rather than the seemingly more sensible label *accept H_0*. Because almost every person who first learns about the hypothesis testing procedure forms this same question, we want to explain why the two decision options available at the end of the hypothesis testing procedure do not constitute flip sides of the same coin.

Whenever a null hypothesis is not rejected, it is improper to say (or think) that H_0 is accepted, because the word **accept** strongly suggests that H_0 is considered to be true. To understand why researchers should not leave a study believing in H_0 if a fail-to-reject decision is made, consider once again the nature of H_0. The first step of the hypothesis testing procedure always involves the assertion of something that is both highly specific and arbitrary. Any H_0 is specific because it must take the form of a pinpoint numerical statement, and it is arbitrary because the researcher has the freedom to select H_0's pinpoint number from a large set of possible values. This dual characteristic of H_0 stands behind the reason why it is technically wrong to "accept the null."

As you now know, the null hypothesis in any particular study is rejected only if the sample data turn out to be inconsistent with what one would expect if H_0 were true. If the sample data are not inconsistent with H_0, a fail-to-reject decision is made. In this latter situation, the sample evidence cannot be interpreted as providing support for H_0 because that same set of sample data would also be consistent with other similar yet slightly different null statements that conceivably could have been specified by the researcher. Because the sample data in any study leading to a fail-to-reject decision not only are "consistent" with the one pinpoint numerical value actually specified in H_0 but also would be "consistent" with any of several other pinpoint values that could have been inserted in H_0, the researcher has no logical basis for leaving the study believing that H_0 is true.

To drive home this important point, let's imagine that a study is conducted to investigate the intelligence of college males versus females. Within this hypothetical study, imagine further that the statistical focus is on mean IQ score, that the hypothesis testing procedure is used, that the researcher states (in Step 1) that H_0: $\mu_{males} - \mu_{females} = 0$, and that a fail-to-reject decision is reached because the two sample means turn out to be quite similar ($\overline{X}_{males} = 109$, $\overline{X}_{females} = 111$). It would be improper for the researcher (or you) to accept this study's H_0 and thus believe that there is a zero difference between the male and female populations. While the sample evidence is "consistent" with the arbitrarily selected pinpoint value of 0, this same evidence would have been "consistent" with H_0 if the researcher had said, in Step 1, that the difference between μ_{males} and $\mu_{females}$ was equal to $+1, -1, +2,$ or -2. Since the sample evidence in our hypothetical study is consistent with *many* possible null hypotheses that *could* have been set up (in addition to the one that actually *was* set up), there is no logical or statistical basis for considering any one of these null hypotheses to be true as compared with the others. For this reason, it would be improper to interpret the outcome of our hypothetical study as signifying that the mean IQ of male college students is identical to the mean IQ of female college students.

Despite the fact that most researchers have been taught that a fail-to-reject decision should not be interpreted to mean that H_0 is true, you will occasionally come across research reports wherein the words of the authors strongly suggest that they "accepted the null." Excerpt 7.42 represents a case in point. Although the word *accept* was not used by the researchers, the final sentence presented here certainly appears to claim that two populations (listen/notes/no review and listen/no notes/no review) are identical with

Excerpt 7.42 The Mistake of "Accepting the Null"

The encoding group was compared with the control group on recall and synthesis performance to determine whether it was more effective to listen and take notes during a lecture or to listen without note-taking. The groups did not differ on either the recall test or the synthesis test, $t(46) < 1$ in both cases. . . . In terms of note-taking functions, results also indicated that taking lecture notes but not reviewing them (the encoding function) is no more effective than listening to a lecture without note-taking and without reviewing.

Source: K. A. Kiewra, and N. F. Dubois (1991). Note-taking functions and techniques. *Journal of Educational Psychology, 83*(2), p. 243.

respect to the dependent variables of recall and synthesis. It would have been much better if the authors had said "results also *suggest*" rather than "results indicated that," since inferential statistics can never do anything more than suggest.

THE "BACKWARDS" NATURE OF HYPOTHESIS TESTING

On first glance, the hypothesis testing procedure seems to operate in a "backwards" fashion. After stating, at the outset, a null hypothesis that is considered to be false, the researcher then goes out and collects data that will, it is hoped, turn out to be inconsistent with H_0. By rejecting H_0, the researcher obtains scientific support for the "opposite" of what was initially stated.

When first exposed to the notion of rejecting a null hypothesis in order to gain support for the alternative hypothesis, most people wonder why the hypothesis testing procedure doesn't work in a more straightforward manner. In everyday life, people typically evaluate their tentatively held beliefs by searching for evidence that *agrees* with those beliefs. If newly found facts are consistent with hunches or hopes, then belief is strengthened; conflicting evidence, on the other hand, causes one's confidence about being right to decrease. Why doesn't hypothesis testing work in a similar fashion? In other words, why don't researchers use a simple three-step procedure involving (1) the articulation of honestly held expectations, (2) the collection of data, and (3) a decision rule that allows those expectations to be confirmed when the evidence is supportive?

Although the three-step everyday "commonsense" method for evaluating tentatively held beliefs is clearly much simpler than the six-step hypothesis testing procedure, it has a serious weakness when applied to inferences concerning the numerical value of population parameters. This weakness can be illuminated if we consider a hypothetical research study. Although our ultimate point would hold true for *any* empirical study we might concoct, we want you to imagine a very simple study.

Within our hypothetical study, let's imagine that the researcher is interested in a particular population and the relationship that exists between two specific variables. Let's also imagine that (1) our hypothetical researcher has a hunch that the two variables of interest have a direct relationship, (2) limited funds make it impossible for data to be gathered from the full population, (3) a sample ($n = 30$) *can* be extracted randomly from the population and measured, and (4) the analysis of the sample data yields a correlation coefficient equal to +.15.

If the three-step "commonsense" approach were to be taken to the evaluation of our hypothetical researcher's hunch, this study would be interpreted as providing empirical support for the initial belief. The researcher stated, in Step 1, that a direct relationship exists in the population. In Step 2, the scientific evidence was found to agree with that hunch (because r was positive). Therefore, the researcher decides, in Step 3, to believe even more strongly that the two variables of interest have a direct relationship in the population.

To understand the danger associated with our hypothetical researcher's inferential strategy, you must do three things: (1) remain sensitive to the fact that sampling error constitutes the "rule" rather than the "exception," (2) recognize that a third type of inferential error (other than a Type I or Type II error) can be committed, and (3) compare the three-step "commonsense" inferential strategy against the formal six-step hypothesis testing procedure in terms of the likelihood that incorrect conclusions will be drawn. As we hope to make clear in the following discussion, the fatal weakness of the simple, three-step inferential strategy is its inability to limit the probability that the research conclusion will be the direct *opposite* of truth.

If the relationship (in the population) between the two variables of interest is *very* strong, an accurate conclusion would be drawn regardless of whether our hypothetical researcher were to use the three-step "commonsense" inferential strategy or the formal "seemingly backwards" six-step strategy. With ρ equal to a value close to $+1.00$ (or close to -1.00), the observed value of r in the sample would likely turn out far away from zero and would have the same sign as ρ. Regardless of which inferential strategy were to be used, our researcher would leave the study thinking proper thoughts about the population (that the initial hunch was probably correct, if r is positive; or that the initial hunch was a flip-flop of reality, if r is negative).

While the two inferential strategies would lead to the same accurate conclusion in the case where there is a very strong relationship in the population, the relative effectiveness of the two strategies changes if we consider the possible situations where (1) $\rho = 0$ and (2) ρ is equal to a small nonzero value. In the first of these situations, the three-step "commonsense" inferential strategy would cause the researcher to make an inferential error with a high probability, since sampling error makes it improbable that r will equal ρ. In this same situation, the formal six-step strategy would most likely cause the researcher to avoid such a mistake. With the level of significance set equal to a small value (e.g., .05), there would be only a small chance that a Type I error would be made. Hence, the formal six-step inferential strategy would work much better than the three-step "commonsense" inferential strategy if it were the case that $\rho = 0$.

The formal six-step version of hypothesis testing also would be superior to the simple three-step inferential strategy if it were the case that the population correlation is equal to any small nonzero value. To illustrate why this is true, let's consider what would likely happen if $\rho = -.16$. With the sample size of 30 and a null hypothesis saying $\rho = 0$, the formal hypothesis testing procedure would likely lead to a fail-to-reject decision. With ρ equal to $-.16$, the sample value of r would not likely be far enough away from the null value of 0 to permit rejection of H_0. This conclusion, of course, would constitute a Type II error. Although it seems, on first glance, that the formal hypothesis testing procedure works quite poorly in this situation because the probability of a Type II error is quite high, consider now what would happen in this same situation if the simple three-step inferential strategy were to be used.

The "commonsense" inferential strategy has a decision rule stating that the researcher should let the "direction" of the sample data dictate the conclusions drawn about the population(s) being studied. In our hypothetical correlational study, the researcher would thus conclude that ρ is positive if $r > 0$ or that ρ is negative if $r < 0$. With ρ actually equal to $-.16$, sampling error would likely cause r to be different from ρ. With a sample size of 30, the sampling distribution of r would be quite wide, with the observed value of r conceivably turning out to be quite far away from the parameter value of $-.16$. Because the sampling distribution of r is not symmetrical when $\rho \neq 0$, there is a slightly greater chance that our hypothetical researcher would end up with a negative r than with a positive r. Nevertheless, the small distance between the true value of ρ ($-.16$) and the dividing point between positive and negative correlations (0.00) would cause the likelihood of getting a positive r to be just slightly under a 50–50 proposition. In other words, the three-step inferential strategy would make it almost as likely that the researcher's conclusion will have the *wrong* sign as compared with the right sign.

In this third situation that we have considered (where $\rho = -.16$), the superiority of the formal six-step inferential strategy over the simple three-step strategy is grounded in the seriousness of any wrong conclusion that is likely to be made. With the hypothesis testing procedure, there is a high probability that a Type II error will be committed—but this kind of inferential error is not considered to be very serious. This is due to the fact that failing-to-reject a null hypothesis is not equivalent to accepting (i.e., believing) H_0. With the three-step inferential strategy, there is less likelihood that a wrong conclusion will be drawn, but the seriousness of the inferential error is enormous. While it is not good to fail-to-reject a false H_0, it is *far worse* to claim that reality points in a certain direction (e.g., by claiming that ρ is positive because $r = +.15$) when reality actually points in the opposite direction (because $\rho = -.16$). Any research conclusion such as this is technically referred to as a **Type III error**.

It should be noted that our discussion comparing the simple "commonsense" inferential strategy with the hypothesis testing procedure extends to studies in which the statistical focus is on something other than the correlation between two variables. If the researcher is interested in means, variances, proportions, beta weights, indices of skewness, or anything else, the hypothesis testing procedure that operates in a seemingly "backwards" fashion works better than the simple straightforward three-step inferential strategy because of the way Type III error risk is controlled. With the hypothesis testing procedure, the probability of this worst kind of inferential error can never exceed one-half the level of significance employed. In contrast, the probability of this kind of error could be as high as .49 in a study in which the researcher simply states a nonpinpoint hunch and then checks to see if sample data support that hunch.

A FEW CAUTIONS

Now that you have considered the six-step hypothesis testing procedure from the standpoint of its various elements and its underlying rationale, you may be tempted to think that it will be easy to decipher and critique any research report in your field that has employed this particular approach to inferential statistics. We hope, of course, that this chapter has helped you become more confident about making sense out of statements such as these: "A two-tailed test was used," "A rigorous alpha level was employed to protect against the possibility of a Type I error," and "The results were significant ($p < .01$)." Before we conclude this chapter, however, it is important that we alert you to a few places where misinterpretations can easily be made by the consumers of the research literature.

ALPHA

The term *alpha* (or the symbol α) is used by researchers to refer to two different concepts. In each case, the numerical value for alpha will be a decimal value somewhere between 0 and 1. To help you avoid becoming confused when you see a numerical value attached to this term, we want to reiterate these two meanings.

Within the hypothesis testing procedure, alpha designates the level of significance selected by the researcher, and it indicates the probability that a true null hypothesis will be rejected. (This alpha is also used in a pragmatic fashion to aid the researcher in locating the critical value or in establishing the criterion against which the data-based p is compared). In discussions of measuring instruments, alpha means something entirely different. In this context, alpha refers to the estimated internal consistency of the questionnaire, inventory, or test being discussed. Note that alpha must be a small decimal number in hypothesis testing in order to accomplish the task of protecting against Type I errors. In contrast, alpha must be a large decimal number in order to document high reliability.

UNSTATED NULL AND ALTERNATIVE HYPOTHESES

Earlier in this chapter, we presented excerpts from various journal articles wherein H_0 and H_a were clearly specified. Unfortunately, most researchers do not take the time or space to indicate publicly the precise nature of these first two elements of the hypothesis testing procedure. They don't do this, we suspect, because they presume that their readers will understand what the null and alternative hypotheses were in light of the number of samples involved in the study, the nature of the measurements collected, and the kind of statistical test used to analyze the data.

After you become familiar with the various statistical tests used to analyze data, you will find that you can make a fairly good guess as to a researcher's H_0 and H_a even if they are not specifically presented. Many of the chapters in this book, beginning with Chapter 10, will help you acquire these skills. Even though you will quickly gain the ability to surmise H_0 and H_a from a research report wherein they are not stated explicitly, you should nevertheless downgrade slightly your evaluation of such studies. As indicated earlier in this chapter, the null hypothesis in a study focusing on a correlation coefficient can be set up to say something other than $H_0: \rho = 0$; likewise, the null statement in studies focusing on the means of two groups does not necessarily have to be $H_0: \mu_1 = \mu_2$. Because the null hypothesis is "flexible" despite the number of samples used, type of data collected, and kind of statistical test employed, researchers should always specify clearly their H_0 and H_a.

THE IMPORTANCE OF H_0

Although the journey of hypothesis testing ends with an important decision, you should keep in mind that this final decision always has reference to the point of departure. Researchers never end up by rejecting (or failing-to-reject) "in the abstract"; instead, they *always* will terminate the hypothesis testing procedure by rejecting (or failing-to-reject) *a specific H_0*. Accordingly, no decision to reject should be viewed as important unless we consider what specifically has been rejected.

On occasion, the hypothesis testing procedure is used in conjunction with a null hypothesis that could not possibly be true. Although it is statistically legal to test such a H_0, no real discovery is made by rejecting something that was known to be false from the outset. To illustrate such a case, consider Excerpt 7.43. In this study, Pearson's r was used to estimate test-retest reliability. Although the results turned out to be statistically significant, the null hypothesis being tested ($H_0: \rho = 0$) was not relevant to the issue being investigated. Evidence that r is significantly different from 0 is not equivalent to evidence that reliability is sufficiently high.

We cannot exaggerate the importance of the null hypothesis to the potential meaningfulness of results that come from someone using the hypothesis testing procedure. Remember that a "reject" decision, by itself, is not indicative of a useful finding. Such a result could be easily brought about simply by setting up, in Step 1, an outrageous H_0. Consequently, you should always be

---

Excerpt 7.43 Rejection of an Unimportant H_0

Additionally, a test-retest for all 20 subjects indicated a statistically significant reliability coefficient for all testing conditions ($P < 0.001$).

Source: B. H. Greenfield, R. Donatelli, M. J. Wooden, and J. Wilkes (1990). Isokinetic evaluation of shoulder rotational strength between the plane of scapula and the frontal plane. *American Journal of Sports Medicine, 18*(2), p. 127.

---

interested in not only the ultimate decision reached at the end of the hypothesis testing procedure but also the target of that decision—H_0.

THE AMBIGUITY OF THE WORD *HYPOTHESIS*

In discussing the outcomes of their data analyses, researchers will sometimes assert that their results "support the hypothesis" (or that the results "do not support the hypothesis"). But which hypothesis is being referred to? As indicated earlier in this chapter, there can be as many as three different hypotheses involved in any single application of the hypothesis testing procedure: H_0, H_a, and H_r. Usually, the full context of the research report will help to make clear which of these three hypotheses stands behind any statement about "the hypothesis." At times, however, you will need to read very carefully to understand accurately what the researcher found.

To illustrate why we offer this caution, consider the four sentences contained in Excerpt 7.44. The word *hypothesis* was used twice in this passage, but the meaning of this word changes. In the first sentence, the hypothesis being referred to is H_0; in contrast, the hypothesis referred to in the fourth sentence is H_r. Not only do different researchers use the term *hypothesis* to mean different things, but sometimes (as exemplified by Excerpt 7.44) even the same researcher will use this term to refer to different components of the hypothesis testing procedure.

Excerpt 7.44 Different Meanings of the Term *Hypothesis*

The hypothesis that the vectors of coefficients for waves 2 and 3 are equal is rejected ($p < .10$). This result implies that customers' attitude formation process is affected by the service change. . . . In the QUALITY$_2$ equation, the estimated coefficient of CHANGE$_2$ is statistically significant ($p < .05$). This result supports the hypothesis that a favorable disconfirmation experience (i.e., perceived improvement in telephone service) has a positive effect on customer attitudes.

Source: R. N. Bolton and J. H. Drew (1991). A longitudinal analysis of the impact of service changes on customer attitudes. *Journal of Marketing, 55*(1), p. 6.

THE MEANING OF THE TERM *SIGNIFICANT*

If the null hypothesis is rejected, the researcher may assert that "the results are **significant**." Since the word *significant* means something different when used in casual everyday discussions than when it is used in conjunction with the hypothesis testing procedure, it is crucial that you recognize the statistical meaning of this frequently seen term. Simply stated, a statistically significant finding may not be very significant at all.

In our everyday language, the term *significant* means "important" or "noteworthy." In the context of hypothesis testing, however, the term *significant* has a totally different meaning. Within this inferential context, a significant finding is simply one that is not likely to have occurred if H_0 is true. So long as the sample data are inconsistent with what one would expect from a "true null" situation, the statistical claim can be made that the results are significant. Accordingly, a researcher's statement to the effect that "the results are significant" simply means that the null hypothesis being tested has been rejected. It does *not* necessarily mean that the results are *important* or that the absolute difference between the sample data and H_0 was found to be *large*.

Whether or not a statistically significant result constitutes an important result is influenced by (1) the quality of the research question that provides the impetus for the empirical investigation and (2) the quality of the research design that guides the collection of data. We have come across journal articles that summarized carefully conducted empirical investigations leading to statistically significant results, yet the studies seemed to us to be quite insignificant. Clearly, to yield important findings, a study must be dealing with an important issue.

But what if statistically significant results *are* produced by a study that focuses on an important question? Does this situation mean that the research findings are important and noteworthy? The answer, unfortunately, is "no." As you will see in the next chapter, it is possible for a study to yield statistically significant results even though there is a tiny difference between the data and the null hypothesis. For example, in a recent study reported in the *Journal of Applied Psychology,* the researcher tested H_0: $\rho = 0$ within the context of a study dealing with correlation. After collecting and analyzing the sample data, this null hypothesis was rejected, with the report indicating that the result was "significant at the .001 level." The sample value that produced this finding was $-.03$!

Even if the issue being investigated is crucial, we cannot consider a correlation of $-.03$ to be very different in any meaningful way from the null value of 0. (With $r = -.03$, the proportion of explained variance is equal to .0009!) As you will soon learn, a large sample can sometimes cause a trivial difference to end up being statistically significant—and that is precisely what happened in the correlational study we were considering. In that investigation, there were

21,646 individuals in the sample. Because of the gigantic sample, a tiny correlation turned out to be statistically significant. Although significant in a statistical sense, the r of $-.03$ was clearly insignificant in terms of its importance.

REVIEW TERMS

Accept

Alpha

Alternative hypothesis

Calculated value

Critical value

Directional

Fail-to-reject

Hypothesis testing

Level of significance

Nondirectional

Null hypothesis

One-tailed test

Reject

Reliable difference

Research hypothesis

Significant

Test statistic

Two-tailed test

Type I error

Type II error

Type III error

α

H_0

H_a

H_r

ns

p

.05

REVIEW QUESTIONS

1. How could the null hypothesis in Excerpt 7.4 be rewritten so as to
   make explicit a pinpoint numerical value?

2. In Excerpt 7.8, we can see that the researcher decided to reject the null
   hypothesis. Using words, describe what the rejected null hypothesis asserted.

3. (True or False) If the alternative hypothesis is set up in a nondirectional
   fashion, this indicates that a one-tailed test is being conducted.

4. In Excerpt 7.16, is the number 4.11 the researchers' calculated value or
   is it the tabled critical value?

5. Which level of significance offers greater protection against Type I errors, .05 or .01?

6. In any single application of the hypothesis testing procedure, it _____
   (is/isn't) possible for the researcher to make both a Type I error and a
   Type II error at the same time.

7. (True or False) Suppose a researcher takes a sample from a population,
   collects data, and then computes the correlation between two variables
   of interest. If the researcher wants to conduct a nondirectional test, the
   null hypothesis will be set up to say $H_0: r = 0.00$.

8. The null hypothesis will be rejected if the sample data turn out to be
   _____ (consistent/inconsistent) with what one would expect if H_0
   were true.

9. Using symbols, write out the null hypothesis that most likely stands behind the results of Excerpt 7.25.

10. The critical value typically _____ (does/does not) appear in the technical summaries of research studies.

11. If a researcher sets $\alpha = .05$ and then determines that the data are such that $p = .03$, will the null hypothesis be rejected or not rejected?

12. If a researcher's data turn out such that H_0 cannot be rejected, why can't the researcher conclude that H_0 is most likely true?

13. If a null hypothesis is rejected because the data are extremely improbable when compared against H_0 (with $p = .000001$), why might the authors of this book dismiss the research study as unimportant?

14. If a researcher compares two sample means with a test having a null hypothesis that says $H_0: \mu_1 = \mu_2$, what is the name for the inferential mistake that would be made if H_0 is rejected because $\overline{X}_1, > \overline{X}_2$ when in fact $\mu_1 < \mu_2$?

15. The probability of making the kind of inferential mistake alluded to in Question 14 depends upon the true size of the difference between μ_1 and μ_2. With $\alpha = .05$, what is the *maximum* probability of claiming that one population mean is larger than the other when in reality it's the other way around?

HYPOTHESIS TESTING— PART II

In Chapter 7, we considered the basic six-step version of hypothesis testing procedure. Although many researchers use that version of hypothesis testing, there is a trend toward using a seven-step or nine-step procedure when testing null hypotheses. In this chapter, we will consider the extra step(s) associated with these approaches to hypothesis testing. In addition, this chapter includes two related topics: the connection between hypothesis testing and confidence intervals, and the problem of an inflated Type I error rate brought about by multiple tests conducted simultaneously.

THE SEVEN-STEP VERSION OF HYPOTHESIS TESTING

As you will recall from the previous chapter, the elements of the simplest version of hypothesis testing are as follows:

1. State the null hypothesis (H_0).
2. State the alternative hypothesis (H_a).
3. Select a level of significance (α).
4. Collect and analyze the sample data.
5. Refer to a criterion for evaluating the sample evidence.
6. Reject or fail-to-reject H_0.

To these six steps, many researchers add a seventh step. Instead of ending the hypothesis testing procedure with a statement about H_0, these researchers return to their sample data and perform one of three additional analyses. Regardless of which specific analysis is applied to the data, the purpose of the seventh step is the same: to go beyond the decision made about H_0 and say something about the *degree* to which the sample data turned out to be incompatible with the null hypothesis.

Before discussing what researchers do when they return to their data in Step 7 of this (slightly expanded) version of hypothesis testing, we want to explain why researchers take the time to do this. Simply stated, they do this because a result that is deemed to be statistically significant can be, at the same time, completely devoid of *any* practical significance whatsoever. This is because there is a direct relationship between the size of the sample(s) and the probability of rejecting a false null hypothesis. If the pinpoint number in H_0 is wrong, large samples increase the likelihood that the result will be "statistically significant"—even if H_0 is very, very close to being true. In such situations, a decision to reject H_0 in favor of H_a is no great accomplishment due to the fact that H_0 is "off" by such a small amount.

In Excerpt 8.1, we see a case in which a nice distinction is made between **statistical significance** and **practical significance**. In this study, the former was achieved whereas the latter was not because there were over 210 children included in the sample. Even though age at entering first grade was significantly related to school success in a statistical sense, it didn't explain nearly as much as other variables.

Excerpt 8.1   Statistical Significance Versus Practical Significance

In finding a significant effect of age at entrance to first grade on first grade achievement, our study is consistent with the results of several studies cited earlier. However, our findings provide a good example of the difference between statistical significance and practical significance. . . . Practically speaking in this school district, and within the ranges of the variables studied, age of entrance to first grade seemed to make no important difference with respect to school success. As an explanatory variable it pales, for example, when compared to the socioeconomic variables in our covariate set.

Source: D. Bickel, N. Zigmond, and J. Strayhorn. (1991). Chronological age at entrance to first grade: Effects on elementary school success. *Early Childhood Research Quarterly, 6*(2), p. 115.

We now turn to three ways in which a researcher can perform the seventh step of the seven-step version of hypothesis testing. These options include (1) computing a "strength-of-association index," (2) estimating the "effect size," and (3) assessing the statistical "power" of the test used to make a decision about H_0.

STEP 7A: COMPUTING A STRENGTH–OF–ASSOCIATION INDEX

In our earlier discussion of bivariate correlation (see Chapter 4), we pointed out that researchers often report the value of r^2 along with or instead of the value of r. The square of the correlation coefficient indicates the proportion of variability in one variable that is explained by or associated with variability in the other variable, and because of this fact r^2 (but not r) is considered to be an index of the "strength of association" in the data.

When engaged in hypothesis testing, researchers can compute a **strength-of-association index** in addition to making a decision to reject or fail-to-reject. By so doing, they give us information as to the *degree* to which the sample data were found to be incompatible with H_0. Various strength-of-association indices have been developed, but they are similar in that they indicate the proportion of variance in the dependent variable that is explained by the study's independent variable. Such information is conveyed by means of a decimal number between 0 and 1.00.

The three most frequently seen strength-of-association indices are **eta squared, omega squared,** and the **intraclass correlation.** In Excerpt 8.2, we see an example where eta was computed. In this study, two groups of women were compared in terms of degree of fatness, with the null hypothesis being $H_0: \mu_1 = \mu_2$. After this H_0 was rejected in Step 6 of the hypothesis testing procedure, the researcher went one step further in an effort to assess how large the obtained difference between the sample means was. The researcher provides us with the value of eta, and by squaring .21 we can see that eta squared is equal to approximately .04. This indicates that only 4 percent of the variability among the 118 BMI scores can be accounted for by means of the known classification of each person into one or the other of the two comparison groups. Therefore, even though the null hypothesis was rejected, the eta squared value indicates that the observed difference between the two sample means is, statistically speaking, relatively small.

Excerpt 8.2   Computing a Strength-of-Association Index

To measure the degree of fatness, respondents were asked to report their height and weight. From this, the body mass index (BMI), weight (kg)/(height [m]^2), was calculated. . . . The majority (100, 79.4%) of the women were supported by their families, 18 (14.3%) supported themselves, and 8 (6.3%) were classified as other and were excluded. Women who received their financial support mainly from their parents were thinner than those who received their funds mainly from other sources (BMI = 21.21 vs. 22.61), $t(116) = 2.31$, $p < .05$, eta = .21.

Source: C. S. Crandall. (1991). Do heavy-weight students have more difficulty paying for college? *Personality and Social Science Bulletin, 17*(6), p. 607.

STEP 7B: ESTIMATING THE MAGNITUDE OF THE OBSERVED EFFECT

Instead of computing a strength-of-association index after H_0 is rejected, a researcher may choose to examine the sample data so as to estimate the actual degree to which the null hypothesis is false. When doing this, most researchers utilize a procedure that yields estimates that are "standardized" in the sense that they take into consideration the amount of variability in the data. An estimate so derived will usually turn out equal to a decimal value between 0 and 1.0, but it is possible for the "observed effect" to end up larger than 1.0 if there is a giant discrepancy between the sample evidence and H_0.

In Excerpt 8.3, we see a case in which the magnitude of the observed effect was estimated. The value of 0.4 was obtained by dividing the observed difference between the two sample means by a weighted "average" of the two standard deviations; 3.0/7.0 = .42. When compared with Cohen's set of "standards" for judging magnitude of effects (.2 = a small effect, .5 = a medium effect, and .8 = a large effect), the value of 0.4 obtained in Excerpt 8.3 was considered to be between small and medium. Such information helps us when trying to make sense out of the significant difference between the sample means of 33.6 and 36.6.

Excerpt 8.3   Determination of Effect Size Following a Significant Finding

---

A significant difference was found, $t = 2.982$, $p < .0032$, in favor of the formal dress condition. Means and standard deviations are shown in Table 1. The size of the effect was measured using the standardized mean difference d, (Cohen, 1977). The standardized mean difference was 0.4. Cohen categorizes a standardized mean difference of 0.5 as a medium size difference, "one large enough to be visible to the naked eye" (p. 26).

Table 1

	Casual dress	Formal dress
mean (over 12 questions)	33.6	36.6
standard deviation	7.32	6.55
N	96	92

$t = 2.982$

$p < .0032$

Means and standard deviations on respect questionnaire.

Source: B. Davis, A. R. Clarke, J. Francis. (1992). Effect of teacher dress on student expectations of deference behavior. *Alberta Journal of Educational Research, 38*(1), p. 29.

STEP 7C: COMPUTING THE STATISTICAL TEST'S POWER

As we pointed out earlier in this chapter, the sample size used by a researcher is one of the factors that influences whether or not a false null hypothesis will be rejected. With large samples, it is possible that a false H_0 will be rejected—

even if there is no practical significance associated with the findings. Examples of that possibility were presented in Excerpts 8.1 and 8.2. In each case, the sample size was so large as to give the researcher a high probability of rejecting H_0 even if the null was "off" by a small margin.

The sample size, if too large, will make the statistical test too "powerful" in the sense that null hypotheses that are false by a trivial amount will be declared statistically significant. Such a finding has statistical significance but no practical significance. As we have seen, a small strength-of-association index or a small magnitude of effect provides a "red flag" that serves to alert the researcher and you that an *unimportant* finding has been declared statistically significant because of a large sample size.

The sample size, on the other hand, can be too small and, as a consequence, cause the findings to be misleading. Due to the fact that there is a direct relationship between the sample size and the probability of rejecting a false H_0, a statistical test based upon an insufficient amount of data will likely lead to a fail-to-reject-decision—even if the discrepancy between the arbitrary null hypothesis, on the one hand, and the reality of the population(s), on the other hand, is so large as to deserve the label *important* or *noteworthy*. If a researcher doesn't reach a reject decision when H_0 is "off-target" by a wide margin, then a major Type II error is committed.

After conducting a statistical test and reaching a fail-to-reject decision, researchers can assess the likelihood that their test would reject H_0. To do this, the researcher not only has the opportunity but is required to specify the point on a continuum that shows how false the null hypothesis must be before it ceases to be false by only a small, unimportant, trivial amount and begins to be false by a large, important, and noteworthy amount. The term **statistical power** denotes the likelihood of rejecting a false H_0 that is false to the degree specified by this point, and its complement is the probability of a Type II error. Researchers want to use sample sizes that are sufficiently large to give their tests adequate power; conversely, they don't want to use sample sizes that are so small as to make the probability of rejecting a grossly false H_0 too low.

After reaching a fail-to-reject decision, researchers will sometimes compute the power of the statistical test in an effort to find out whether the amount of sample data was sufficient to make the test sensitive to important deviations from the null. If the reported power turns out to be high enough (say .80 or higher), this would indicate that the researcher's test was likely to reject H_0—if the discrepancy between H_0 and the actual state of affairs in the population(s) is big, important, and noteworthy. When a fail-to-reject decision is supplemented by a power analysis that yields a value close to 1.0 for the test's power, researchers are simply saying that they had large enough sample sizes so as to make it unlikely that an important finding was missed due to a Type II error.

Excerpt 8.4 illustrates the manner in which a researcher can add a seventh step to the six basic steps of hypothesis testing outlined in Chapter 7. Here again, as was the case in Steps 7a or 7b, the researcher returns to the data and performs some additional computation designed to address the legitimate concern as to the likely degree to which H_0 is off-target. In Excerpt 8.4, the researchers' conclusion is that the tested H_0 is either true or only trivially false. In other words, the researchers are asserting that the sample sizes were *not* so small as to make it likely that a Type II error was committed.

Excerpt 8.4   Computing Statistical Power Following a Fail-to-Reject Decision

---

The lack of significance between BTFS and BT may arouse concern over the power for comparisons on the [dependent] measures. A power analysis for this planned comparison was conducted using the method described by Kirk (1968).... For our data, at the .05 level, a power coefficient of .78 was obtained for this comparison. While this is slightly below the typical 80% power desired, it is within the acceptable range. [This suggests] that our study findings on the self-reported measures are a consequence of minimal observed effects rather than Type II error.

Source: V. Radojevic, P. Nicassio, and M. Weisman. (1992). Behavioral intervention with and without family support for rheumatoid arthritis. *Behavior Therapy, 23*(1), p. 21.

THE NINE-STEP VERSION OF HYPOTHESIS TESTING

Although many researchers still utilize the six-step and seven-step versions of hypothesis testing, there is a definite trend toward using a nine-step approach. Six of the steps of this more elaborate version of hypothesis testing are identical to the six basic elements considered in Chapter 7, while the other three steps are related to the concepts of effect size, power, and sample size considered in the earlier portion of this chapter. Listed in the order in which the researcher will deal with them, the various elements of the nine-step version of hypothesis testing are as follows:

        1. State the null hypothesis, H_0.
        2. State the alternative hypothesis, H_a.
        3. Specify the desired level of significance, α.
(new) 4. Specify the effect size, ES.
(new) 5. Specify the desired level of power.
(new) 6. Determine the proper size of the sample(s).
        7. Collect and analyze the sample data.
        8. Refer to a criterion for assessing the sample evidence.
        9. Make a decision to discard/retain H_0.

The steps in the first third and final third of this nine-step version of hypothesis testing are identical to the six steps we discussed in Chapter 7. We will focus here only on Steps 4, 5, and 6. Although our discussion of these three steps will, in some ways, seem redundant with the material presented earlier in this chapter, there is an important way in which the seven- and nine-step versions of hypothesis testing differ. In the seven-step approach considered earlier in this chapter, the researcher executes the six basic steps and then adds a seventh step. That seventh step—regardless of whether it involves computing a strength-of-association index, estimating the size of the obtained effect, or assessing the statistical test's power—involves returning to the sample data *after* the reject/retain decision has been made. In contrast, the nine-step version of hypothesis testing requires that the researcher specify the effect size, specify the desired power, and then determine the size of the sample(s) *before* any data are collected.

STEP 4: SPECIFICATION OF THE EFFECT SIZE

In our discussion of Step 7c of the seven-step version of hypothesis testing, we discussed the option of following up a reject/fail-to-reject decision with a computation of the statistical test's power. As you will recall, such a procedure requires that the researcher specify a point that divides a hypothetical continuum of non-null effects into two segments: (1) a segment that contains all non-null possibilities that are considered, by the researcher, to be only trivial deviations from the situation articulated in H_0, and (2) a segment that contains all non-null possibilities that are judged to be important deviations from the null case. This numerical value, selected arbitrarily by the researcher, is technically referred to as the **effect size**.

To illustrate what an effect size is and how it gets selected, suppose a researcher uses the hypothesis testing procedure in a study where there is one population, where the data are IQ scores, where the statistical focus is on the mean, and where the null and alternative hypotheses are $H_0: \mu = 100$ and $H_a: \mu < 100$, respectively. In this hypothetical study, the continuum of possible false null cases, as specified by H_a, extends from a value that is just slightly greater than 100 (say, 100.1) to whatever the maximum earnable IQ score is (say 300). The researcher might decide to set 110 as the effect size. By so doing, the researcher would be declaring that (1) the true μ is judged to be only trivially different from 100 if it lies anywhere between 100 and 110, while (2) the difference between the true μ and 100 is considered to be important so long as the former is at least 10 points greater than H_0's pinpoint value of 100.

Most researchers convert their **"raw" effect sizes** into **"standardized" effect sizes** by dividing the raw effect size by the estimated standard deviation in the population. Since IQ scores are considered to have a standard deviation of about 15 points, the standardized effect size in the previous example would be equal to 10/15, or .67. Note that the resulting standardized effect size is influenced greatly by the researcher's initial judgment as to what point separates trivial from important deviations from the null case. If our hypothetical researcher had specified 105 (rather than 110) as this point, the standardized effect size would have turned out equal to .33. If 115 had been specified, the standardized effect size would have become equal to 1.00.

In many situations, a researcher will be unable to posit a reasonable guess as to the value of the standard deviation in the population. There may be no previous research relevant to the researcher's study because the researcher's study involves a new measuring instrument, a new procedure, or a different kind of subject than was used by earlier researchers. In any event, a statistician by the name of Jacob Cohen has argued that researchers can arbitrarily set the standardized effect size equal to .20, .50, or .80 depending upon whether they are interested in detecting a **small**, **medium**, or **large** deviation from the null case. When applied to our hypothetical study involving IQ scores, these standardized effect sizes translate into points along the H_a continuum of 103 (for a small effect), 107.5 (for a medium effect), and 112 (for a large effect).[1]

In Excerpts 8.5–8.6, we see two examples where the effect size was specified within the nine-step version of the hypothesis testing procedure. Notice that one of Cohen's standardized effect sizes was used in Excerpt 8.5 whereas the effect size in Excerpt 8.6 is "raw" in the sense that it is on the same scale as the instrument used to measure the dependent variable.

Excerpts 8.5–8.6   Specification of the Effect Size

A purposive sample of 52 subjects was accessed through an allergy clinic at a tertiary medical center in a mid-Atlantic metropolitan area. The sample size was based on a power analysis utilizing: alpha = .05, power = .80, and a large effect size for the Student's two-tailed t test (Cohen, 1977).

Source: K. Huss, M. Salerno, and R. W. Huss. (1991). Computer-assisted reinforcement of instruction: Effects on adherence in adult atopic asthmatics. *Research in Nursing & Health, 14*(4), p. 261.

A sample size of 30 is large enough to detect true differences of one rating point [on a 9-point scale] with paired-sample t-tests at the .05 level.

Source: M. T. Curren, V. S. Folkes, and J. H. Steckel. (1992). Explanations for successful and unsuccessful marketing decisions: The decision maker's perspective. *Journal of Marketing, 56*(2), p. 22.

---

[1]*Although it is quite easy for a researcher to select one of Cohen's standardized effect size values of .20, .50, or .80, Cohen strongly urges researchers to determine the effect size by making a judgment as to where the trivial and meaningful sections lie along the H_a continuum, and then by dividing the point of separation by a reasonable guess as to the value of σ.*

STEP 5: SPECIFICATION OF THE DESIRED LEVEL OF POWER

The researcher's next task within the nine-step hypothesis testing procedure is to specify the level of power that is desired for rejecting H_0 if H_0 is "off" by an amount equal to the previously established effect size. Being a probability value, power can range from 0 to 1.0. Only high values are considered, however, because the complement of power is the probability of a Type II error.

The researcher does not know, of course, exactly how far off-target the null hypothesis is (or even if it is wrong at all). The specified effect size is simply the researcher's judgment as to what would or wouldn't constitute a meaningful deviation from the null case. Note, however, that if the null hypothesis is wrong by an amount that is greater than the specified effect size, then the actual probability of rejecting H_0 will be larger than the specified power level. Thus, the power level selected in Step 5 represents the lowest acceptable power for any of the potentially true H_a conditions that are considered to be meaningfully different from H_0.

To see an illustration of how researchers might report specifying a desired level of power for their statistical test, take another look at Excerpt 8.5. In that study, the researchers set their power level equal to .80. By doing this, they set up their hypothesis testing procedure such that they would have an 80 percent chance of rejecting H_0, presuming that their H_0 was false and that the reality of the population corresponded to the "large" standardized effect size that was specified. (Although the researchers do not indicate precisely what numerical value was chosen for the effect size, the words *large* and *Cohen* make it quite likely that a standardized effect size of .80 was used.)

Before leaving our discussion of statistical power, we need to address a question that you may have formulated. Inasmuch as power is a good thing to have for trying to detect situations where H_0 is false by an amount at least equal to the effect size, why doesn't the researcher specify a power equal to .95 or .99 or even .999? There are two reasons why such high power values are rarely seen in applied research studies. First, they would place unreasonable demands on researchers when they move to Step 6 and compute the sample size required to provide the desired power. Second, extremely high power increases the probability that trivial deviations from H_0 will be labeled as statistically significant. For these two reasons, power levels higher than .90 are rarely seen.

STEP 6: DETERMINATION OF THE NEEDED SAMPLE SIZE

After stating H_0 and H_a, after selecting a level of significance, and after specifying the effect size and the desired power, the researcher then uses a formula or a specially prepared table to determine how many subjects will be needed in the study. No judgment or decision making comes into play at this point in the nine-step version of hypothesis testing, since the researcher simply calculates or looks up the answer to a very pragmatic question: How large should the sample be? At this point (and also in Steps 7–9), the researcher functions like a robot who performs tasks in a routine fashion without using much brain power.

Excerpt 8.7 contains an illustration of how a researcher might report the outcome of the **sample size determination**. In this excerpt, notice how the authors provide information as to the decisions they made regarding the level of significance, the effect size, and the power that would be operational in their investigation. Once these ingredients were inserted into the proper formula (along with the directional/nondirectional nature of H_a), the researchers found out that they needed to include 89 adolescents in each sample.

Excerpt 8.7   Sample Size Determination

According to Cohen and Cohen (1983), a minimum of 89 subjects was needed for each sample of adolescents based on a medium effect size of .30, a .05 level of significance, and a power of .80 for hierarchical analysis of sets.

Source: N. Mahon, and A. Yarcheski. (1992). Alternate explanations of loneliness in adolescents: A replication and extension study. *Nursing Research, 41*(3), p. 152.

Another example of sample size determination was presented earlier in Excerpt 8.5. In the study from which that excerpt was taken, the researchers determined that they needed to have a sample size of 52 as a consequence of their decisions to set alpha equal to .05, to set power equal to .80, and to use a large effect size.

On occasion, researchers will be forced to use a limited number of subjects in their studies. For example, time and/or money may dictate that a fixed number of subjects can be measured. Sometimes only a fixed number of individuals may volunteer to participate. In other studies, researchers cannot use more than the number of subjects that are at the site to which they have been given access. For any of these or other reasons, researchers who want to use the nine-step version of hypothesis testing must sometimes slightly adjust the nature and order of the step dealing with the size of the sample.

When the sample size is a "given" due to the pragmatic contingencies of the study being conducted, Steps 5 and 6 of the nine-step approach to hypothesis testing become the following:

Step 5: Specify the fixed number of available subjects.
Step 6: Determine and assess the statistical power of the planned test.

After stating H_0 and H_a, after specifying the desired level of significance and effect size, and after taking account of the available sample size, the researcher then uses a formula or a specially designed table to determine the level of statistical power associated with the intended analysis of the data. If the resulting power (i.e., the probability of detecting meaningful deviations from H_0) is sufficiently high, then the researcher will proceed to collect and evaluate the study's data. On the other hand, if the power analysis yields a value that is too low, the researcher will either (1) change one or more of the initial decisions (e.g., the alpha level) in an effort to boost the study's power or (2) put the study "on hold" until a larger number of subjects become available.

In Excerpt 8.8, we see an example of the nine-step version of hypothesis testing wherein the power of the statistical test was determined (as Step 6) for a fixed number of available subjects (specified in Step 5). Notice that the computed power for both of the planned tests turned out to be sufficiently high to allow the researcher to proceed with the study.

Excerpt 8.8 Power Computed for a Fixed Number of Subjects

Power analyses (Cohen, 1977) were conducted to determine whether the available sample size was adequate to detect medium-sized effects. . . . Power to detect such an effect size in the comparison of continuers and no-shows was .89, and power for the tests of correlations involving length of delay was .83.[1] These values signify that if a true effect exists in the population from which our sample was drawn, then our statistical tests would yield significant results 89% and 83% of the time, respectively.

[1]*Power calculations were based on an alpha level of .05 for a directional hypothesis. Directional hypotheses were appropriate here because all previous reported effects of lengthy delays were either nonsignificant or in a negative direction.*

Source: R. D. Freund, T. T. Russell, and S. Schweitzer. (1991). Influence of length of delay between intake session and initial counseling session on client perceptions of counselors and counseling outcomes. *Journal of Counseling Psychology, 38*(1), p. 5.

As we finish our discussion of the nine-step version of hypothesis testing, we want to underscore the primary advantage of this approach to evaluating any null hypothesis. The eventual results of the statistical test become easier to interpret after the researcher has successfully wrestled with the issue of what ought to be viewed as a meaningful deviation from H_0, and after the sample size has been computed so as to create the desired level of power (or the power computed on the basis of the available sample). In contrast, the six-step version of hypothesis testing can lead to a highly ambiguous finding.

If no consideration is given to the concepts of effect size and power, the researcher may end up very much in the dark as to whether (1) a fail-to-reject decision is attributable to a trivial (or zero) deviation from H_0 *or* is attributable to the test's insensitivity to detect important non-null cases due to a small sample size, or (2) a reject decision is attributable to H_0 being false by a nontrivial amount *or* is attributable to an unimportant non-null case being labeled *significant* simply because the sample size was so large. In Excerpts 8.9 and 8.10, we see examples of how murky results can be produced when the six-step approach to hypothesis testing is used. In Excerpt 8.9, the researcher tells us, in essence, that the statistically insignificant results may have been caused by insufficient power. In Excerpt 8.10, we see a researcher who obtained statistically significant results but admits, in essence, that the initial findings may have been caused by an overly large sample size making the statistical tests too sensitive. By doing the analysis a second time with only 300 subjects (rather than the full sample of 509), this researcher was trying to show that the statistically significant findings truly were reflecting a situation that deserved to be considered significant in a practical way as well.[2]

Excerpts 8.9–8.10 Problems Caused When No Consideration Is Given to the Concepts of Effect Size and Power

---

Due to the small size of the sample, it is possible that a Type II error was made in the two-factor factorial design. An increase in sample size may result in a relationship [showing up] between classification of employees and turnover.

Source: D. Ondusko. (1991). Comparison of employees with disabilities and able-bodied workers in janitorial maintenance. *Journal of Applied Rehabilitation Counseling, 22*(2), p. 23.

Because a large sample can increase the power of a statistical test and cause differences of even a very small magnitude to reach significance, all analyses were repeated with a smaller subsample ($n = 300$) of the main sample, obtained by randomly sampling the 509 participants. In no case did a result significant with the larger sample lose significance with the smaller sample.

Source: L. E. Bassman. (1992). Reality testing and self-reported AIDS self-care behavior. *Psychological Reports, 70*(1), p. 63.

The advantage of the nine-step (or seven-step) approach to hypothesis testing is *not* that the researcher will be able to know whether the decision reached about H_0 is right or wrong. Regardless of the approach used, a "reject" decision might be correct or it might constitute a Type I error, and similarly a "fail-to-reject" decision might be correct or it might be a Type II error. The advantage of researchers considering effect size and power to be "built into" the hypothesis testing procedure is twofold: On the one hand, the researchers know and control, on *a priori* basis, the probability of making a Type II error, and on the other hand, they set up the study so that no critic can allege that a significant

---

[2]*Unless the researcher considered very small deviations from H_0 to be nontrivial, the sample size of 300 used in the second set of analyses still made it likely that small and unimportant non-null cases would end as statistically significant.*

finding, if found, was brought about by an overly sensitive test (or that a non-significant result, if found, was produced by an overly insensitive test).[3]

HYPOTHESIS TESTING USING CONFIDENCE INTERVALS

Researchers can, if they wish, engage in hypothesis testing by means of using one or more confidence intervals, rather than by comparing a calculated value against a critical value or by comparing a p-level against α. Although this approach to hypothesis testing is not used as often as the approaches discussed earlier in this chapter, it is important for you to understand what is going on when a researcher uses confidence intervals within the context of hypothesis testing.

Whenever confidence intervals are used in this manner, it should be noted that everything about the hypothesis testing procedure remains the same except the way the sample data are analyzed and evaluated. To be more specific, this alternative approach to hypothesis testing involves the specification of H_0, H_a, and alpha, and the final step will involve a reject or fail-to-reject decision regarding H_0. The concepts of Type I and Type II errors are still relevant, as are the opportunities to specify effect size and power and to compute the proper sample size if the nine-step version of hypothesis testing is being used.

As indicated in Chapter 7, calculated and critical values usually are numerical values that are "metric-free." Such calculated and critical values have no meaningful connection to the measurement scale associated with the data. Although it is advantageous for the researcher to use metric-free calculated and critical values, such values provide little insight as to why H_0 ultimately is rejected or not rejected. The advantage of confidence intervals is that they help to provide that insight.

The way confidence intervals are used within hypothesis testing is easy to explain. If there is just a single sample involved in the study, the researcher will take the sample data and build a confidence interval around the sample statistic. Instead of computing a calculated value, the researcher computes an interval, with the previously specified alpha level dictating the level of confidence associated with the interval (an α of .05 calls for a 95 percent interval, an α of .01 calls for a 99 percent interval; etc.). Instead of then turning to a critical value, the researcher turns to the null hypothesis and compares the confidence interval against the pinpoint number contained in H_0. The decision rule for the final step is straightforward: If the null number is outside the confidence interval, H_0 can be rejected; otherwise, H_0 must be retained.

If the researcher's study involves a comparison of two or more samples, a confidence interval will be built around each sample-based statistic. In those cases where H_0 is a "no-difference" statement, the resulting confidence intervals will be compared to see if they overlap with each other. If two or more

---

[3]*In saying this, we assume that the hypothetical critic agrees with the researcher's decisions about H_0, H_a, alpha, and the effect size.*

do not overlap, H_0 can be rejected; on the other hand, if the confidence intervals overlap each other, the researcher must make a fail-to-reject decision.

Excerpt 8.11 illustrates the confidence-interval approach to hypothesis testing in a study involving three groups. Notice how the phrase *statistically significant* appears three times in the note beneath the table, even though no calculated and critical values were compared.

In the vast majority of studies that involve two or more comparison groups (including the study from which Excerpt 8.11 was taken), the null hypothesis is set up to say that the value of the parameter is the same in the various populations being compared. As indicated in Chapter 7, however, H_0 does not have to be set up in a "no-difference" format. When the confidence-interval approach to hypothesis testing is used in conjunction with an H_0 that contains something other than zero for its pinpoint value, the decision rule for deciding H_0's fate is simple yet slightly different from the no-difference case. If H_0 were to specify a nonzero difference between two populations, a reject decision would be made if H_0's pinpoint number could not be "positioned" so as to "extend" from inside one interval to inside the other interval. For example, if H_0 specified 50 as the pinpoint value while the two confidence intervals turned out equal to 90–110 and 170–190, H_0 would be rejected since no value in the first interval can be increased by 50 and then become equal to a value inside the second interval.

Before completing our discussion of the confidence-interval approach to hypothesis testing, we need to alert you (once again) to the difference between a confidence interval and a standard error interval.[4] Many researchers who compute calculated and critical values within one of the more traditional approaches to hypothesis testing will summarize their sample data in terms of values of the statistic plus-or-minus the standard error of the statistic. Intervals formed by adding and subtracting the standard error to the sample statistic do *not* produce alpha-driven confidence intervals. Instead, the result is a 68 percent interval. (Alpha-driven confidence intervals will typically be "95 percent" intervals.)

To illustrate the difference between true confidence intervals and standard error intervals, consider Excerpt 8.12. The intervals based on 308 ± 13 and 280 ± 13 extend from 295 to 321 and 267 to 293, respectively. Although these intervals do not overlap, the null hypothesis (of no difference between the population means) was not rejected. This potentially confusing set of results is attributable to the intervals being standard error intervals, which are approximately equivalent to 68 percent confidence intervals. If 95 percent confidence intervals had been reported, each one would have been wider, they would have overlapped each other, and the "NS" result would have been immediately understandable.

---

[4]*The difference between confidence intervals and standard errors was first covered in Chapter 6.*

Excerpt 8.11 A Confidence-Interval Approach to Hypothesis Testing

In summary, age-adjusted rates reflect smoking behavior for women grouped as 12–49 year olds. Age-specific rates group women in 10-year intervals and can expose generational differences in smoking behavior. For age-specific data, percentages, means, and 95% confidence intervals were calculated and compared. . . . Puerto Rican 20–29 year olds had significantly higher (no confidence interval overlap) smoking prevalence than the same age cohorts of the other two groups. In addition, Puerto Rican 30–39 year olds had significantly higher smoking prevalence rates than Mexican-Americans, and Puerto Rican 12–19 year olds had significantly higher rates than Cuban-Americans.

Table 1

Prevalence, Percentage, and Confidence Intervals for Current Smokers in Each Age Stratum for Three Groups of Hispanic Women

	Group					
	Mexican-American (N = 2,537)		Cuban-American (N = 542)		Puerto Rican (N = 1,189)	
Cohort	%	n	%	n	%	n
12–19	8.8 (6.4–11.2)[a]	58	5.9 (0.7–11.1)	6	15.8 (11.2–20.4)***	47
20–29	25.5 (20.4–26.6)	204	23.1 (15.2–31.0)	30	42.2 (37.1–47.3)*	153
30–39	25.8 (22.2–29.4)	168	32.1 (24.6–39.6)	54	37.3 (31.7–42.9)**	115
40–49	31.0 (25.9–36.1)	111	22.4 (15.0–29.9)	32	29.6 (23.2–36.0)	65

Note. Percentages are significantly different if there is no confidence interval overlap.

[a]95% confidence intervals.
*Statistically significant differences between PR and both groups.
**Statistically significant difference between PR and MA.
***Statistically significant difference between PR and CA.

Source: P. K. Pletsch. (1991). Prevalence of cigarette smoking in Hispanic women of childbearing age. *Nursing Research, 40,* (2), p.105. © *The American Journal of Nursing Company.* Used with permission All rights reserved.

ADJUSTING FOR AN INFLATED TYPE I ERROR RATE

In Chapter 7, we indicated that the researchers have direct control over the probability that they will make a Type I error when making a judgment

---

Excerpt 8.12   Standard Error Intervals Versus Confidence Intervals

---

Comparisons of arterial pressure, coronary blood flow, and left ventricular size between and within the normal and hypertensive dogs were made by unpaired t test and paired t test respectively. The data were presented as mean $\pm$SEM, and the level of statistical significance was $p < .05$. . . . Over the course of the experiment, coronary flow remained stable at any given perfusion pressure. For example, maximal coronary flow per left ventricular mass in the control group (at 80 mm H_G of perfusion pressure) was 308 ± 13 and 280 ± 13 ml/min/100_G ($p = $ NS) before the incision and at the end of the experiment, respectively.

Source: M. Fujii, D. W. Nuno, K. G. Lamping, K. C. Dellsperger, C. L. Eastham, and D. G. Harnson. (1992). Effect of hypertension and hypertrophy on coronary microvascular pressure. *Circulation Research: A Journal of the American Heart Association, 71*(1), p. 122.

---

about H_0. (Type I errors, you will recall, occur when true null hypotheses are rejected.) This control is exerted when the researcher selects the level of significance. So long as the underlying assumptions of the researcher's statistical test are tenable, the alpha level selected in Step 3 of the hypothesis testing procedure instantly and accurately establishes the probability that a true H_0 will be rejected.

The fact that α dictates Type I error risk holds true *only* for situations where researchers use the hypothesis testing procedure just once within any given study. In many studies, however, data on multiple dependent variables are collected, with a null hypothesis evaluated separately for each data set. Such situations are quite common, as illustrated in Excerpt 8.13.

When the hypothesis testing procedure is applied separately to each of multiple dependent variables, the alpha level used within these tests specifies the Type I error risk as if each dependent variable were the one and only dependent variable in the study. However, when multiple tests are conducted (one per dependent variable), the actual probability of making a Type I error somewhere within the set of tests *exceeds* the alpha level used within any given test. The term **inflated Type I error risk** is used to refer to this situation where the alpha level used within each of two or more separate tests understates the likelihood that at least one of the tests will cause the researcher to reject a true H_0. In Excerpt 8.14, we see a case in which a set of researchers made reference to this aspect of their study with a suggestion that readers of their report interpret their finding with caution due to the "heightened probability of a Type I error."

A simple example may help to illustrate the problem of an inflated Type I error rate. Suppose you were given a fair die and told to roll it on the table. Before you toss the die, also suppose that the person running this little game tells you that you will win $10 if your rolled die turns out to be anything but a "six." If you get a "six," however, you must fork over $50. With an unloaded

Excerpt 8.13 Hypothesis Testing with Multiple Dependent Variables

Table 2

Classroom Teachers' Evaluations on Selected Variables of Consulting Teachers with and Without Apprenticeship Training

Variables	Apprenticeship (N = 15)		No apprenticeship (N = 55)		t^a	p
	M	SD	M	SD		
Was feedback specific?	4.42	1.45	2.44	1.78	3.96	.001
Was feedback helpful?	4.28	1.49	3.24	1.85	2.00	.025
Were observations helpful?	4.86	.53	2.38	1.50	6.27	.001
Overall quality of observation and feedback	4.20	.92	3.0	1.16	3.70	.001

Note: Evaluations based on a 5-point scale where 1 5 extremely negative, 3 5 neutral, and 5 5 extremely positive.

$^a df = 68$.

Source: R. Gersten. (1991). Apprenticeship and intensive training of consulting teaching: A naturalistic study. *Exceptional Children, 57*(3), p. 231.

Excerpt 8.14 Multiple Dependent Variables and the Inflated Type I Error Risk

Analyses were performed on the individual tests and subtests that comprised the psychometric battery. Because any conclusions drawn from the individual *t* tests of group differences are cautioned by the heightened probability of Type 1 error, results must be considered exploratory in nature.

Source: S. Perrott, H. Taylor, and J. Montes. (1991). Neuropsychological sequelae, familial stress, and environmental adaptation following pediatric head injury. *Developmental NeuroPsychology, 7*(1), p. 73.

---

die, this would be a fair bet, for your chances of winning would be 5/6 while the chances of losing would be 1/6.

But what if you were handed a pair of fair dice and asked to roll both members of the pair simultaneously, with the rule being that you would win $10 if you can avoid throwing an "evil-six" but lose $50 if your role of the dice produces a bad outcome. This would not be a fair bet for you, for the chances of avoiding a "six" are 5/6 × 5/6 = 25/36, a result that is lower than the 5/6 value needed to make the wager an even bet in light of the stakes ($10 versus $50). If you were handed five pair of dice and were asked to roll them simultaneously, with the same payoff arrangement in operation (i.e., win $10 if you avoid a "six," otherwise lose $50), you would be at a terrific disadvantage. With 10 of the six-sided cubes being rolled, the probability of your winning the bet by avoiding a "six" anywhere in the full set of results is equal to approximately .16. You would have a 16 percent chance of winning $10 versus an 84 percent chance of losing $50. That would be a very good arrangement for your opponent!

As should be obvious, the chances of having an "evil six" show up at least once increase as the number of dice being thrown increase. With multiple dice involved in our hypothetical game, there would be two ways to adjust things to make the wager equally fair to both parties. One adjustment would involve changing the stakes. For example, with two dice being rolled, the wager could be altered so you would win $11 if you avoid a "six" or lose $25 if you don't. The other kind of adjustment would involve tampering with the two little cubes so as to produce a pair of loaded dice. With this strategy, each die would be weighted such that its chances of ending up as something other than a "six" would be equal to a tad more than 10/11. This would allow two dice to be used, in a fair manner, with the original stakes in operation ($10 versus $50).

When researchers use the hypothesis testing procedure multiple times— once for each of several dependent variables—an adjustment must be made somewhere in the process to account for the fact that at least one Type I error somewhere in the set of results increases rapidly as the number of dependent variables increases. Although there are different ways to effect such an adjustment, the most popular method is to change the level of significance used in conjunction with the statistical assessment of each dependent variable's H_0. If the researchers want to have a certain level of protection against a Type I error anywhere within their full set of results, then they would make the alpha level more rigorous within each of the individual tests. By so doing, it's as if the researchers are setting up a "fair wager" in that the claimed alpha level will truly match the study's likelihood of yielding a Type I error.

The most frequently used procedure for adjusting the alpha level is called the **Bonferroni technique**, and it is quite simple for the researcher to apply or for consumers of research to understand. When there is a desire on the part of the researcher to hold the Type I error in the full study equal to a selected value, the alpha levels for the various tests being conducted must be chosen such that the sum of the individual alpha levels is equivalent to the full-study alpha criterion. This is usually accomplished by simply dividing the desired Type I error risk for the full study by the number of times the hypothesis testing procedure is going to be used. Excerpts 8.15–8.16 illustrate nicely this way of using the Bonferroni technique.

Excerpts 8.15–8.16   The Bonferroni Adjustment Technique

To examine the effects of demographic and practitioner characteristics on contact time, *t* tests were performed. To avoid the problem of inflated error rates because of the number of *t* tests (nine), only results significant at the .005 are reported (obtained by dividing .05 by the number of tests, according to the Bonferroni method).

Source: M. C. Fish, and R. F. Massey. (1991). Systems in school psychology practice: A preliminary investigation. *Journal of School Psychology, 29*(4), p. 363.

The proper execution of studies, such as this one, involving numerous comparisons requires that an acceptable Type I error rate be clearly established. We guarded against Type I error through the use of the Bonferroni technique, through which we limited our study-wide Type I error rate to a .05 alpha level. This error rate was spread over 14 individual comparisons, resulting in a per-comparison alpha level of .0036.

Source: J. Blackorby, E. Edgar, and L. Kortering. (1991). A third of our youth? A look at the problem of high school dropout among students with mild handicaps. *The Journal of Special Education, 25*(1), p. 107.

In most applications of the Bonferroni technique, the desired study-wide Type I error risk is divided by the number of dependent variables to produce the same adjusted alpha level for each individual test. Excerpts 8.15 and 8.16 exemplify this popular way of adjusting alpha to guard against an inflated Type I error risk. A researcher can, however, use different alpha levels in the tests on different dependent variables—so long as the sum of the individual alpha levels does not exceed the desired study-wide alpha level. This option (of varying the individual alpha levels) would be appropriate if a researcher decides that the dependent variables varied in importance and, consequently, should be examined statistically with varying levels of Type I error control.

Regardless of whether the Bonferroni technique is used to produce a constant or a varying alpha level for use with the individual hypothesis tests to be conducted, the impact is the same. By making the level of significance more rigorous for the individual tests, the Bonferroni technique accomplishes its objective by making the critical value(s) more demanding. By using a harder-to-beat critical value, the sample data corresponding to any single dependent variable will have to be more incompatible with H_0 before a statistically significant finding can be claimed. With each of the various tests using a more rigorous critical value, the problem of an inflated Type I error risk is eliminated.

In Excerpt 8.17, we see a case of where a researcher used the Bonferroni technique and indicated the resulting critical value employed within each of the 15 applications of the hypothesis testing procedure. If the Bonferroni technique had not been used, the critical value would have been an easier-to-beat 1.97.

Excerpt 8.17   The Impact of the Bonferroni Technique on the
Critical Value

Tests of nonzero correlation were conducted using Bonferroni's correction (Dunn, 1961) to maintain an experiment-wise error rate at the .05 level across all 15 comparisons. With this adjustment the hypothesis-wise error rate for each correlation was estimated to be .003; thus a critical value of $t(339) = 3.320$ ($\alpha = .001$) was identified as the most sensitive and appropriate measure of significance (Glass & Hopkins, 1984).

Source: R. F. Ittenback and P. L. Harrison. (1990). Predicting ego-strength from problem-solving ability of college students. *Measurement and Evaluation in Counseling and Development, 23*(3), p. 131.

Although the Bonferroni procedure is widely used to deal with the inflated Type I error problem, other procedures have been developed to accomplish the same general objective. One of these is referred to as the Sidak modification of Dunn's procedure (or simply as the **Dunn–Sidak modification**). In Excerpt 8.18, we see a case where this alternative procedure was used because the data from eight dependent variables were subjected to separate analyses. In this excerpt, notice how the Dunn–Sidak modification functions like the Bonferroni procedure in that the magnitude of the critical value is increased.

Excerpt 8.18   Use of the Dunn–Sidak Procedure

Based on the hypotheses, separate analyses were conducted for each of the eight dependent variables: self-efficacy level, self-efficacy strength, outcome judgment level, outcome judgment strength, generality level, generality strength, persistence, and game score. . . . To alleviate this problem [of an inflated Type I error rate], the Sidak modification of Dunn's procedure (as described by Kirk, 1982) was used. That procedure involves upwardly adjusting the minimum value of the critical difference t ratio for each comparison to account for the number of comparisons. . . .

Source: G. D. Ellis, M. Maughan-Pritchett, and E. Ruddell. (1993). Effect of attribution based verbal persuasion and imagery on self-efficacy of adolescents diagnosed with major depression. *Therapeutic Recreation Journal, 27*(3), p. 92.

A FEW CAUTIONS

As we come to the close of our two-chapter treatment of hypothesis testing, we want to offer a few more cautions that should assist you as you attempt to make sense out of the technical write-ups of empirical investigations. These tips (or warnings!) are different from the ones provided at the end of Chapter 7, so you may profit from a review of what we said there. In any event, here are three more things to keep in mind when you come across statistical inferences based upon the hypothesis testing procedure.

TWO MEANINGS OF THE TERM *EFFECT SIZE*

When the seven-step approach to hypothesis testing is used, the researcher may opt (in Step 7) to estimate the magnitude of the observed effect. We saw an example of this in Excerpt 8.3. In that study, "the [standardized] size of the effect found" turned out equal to .4. Note that this kind of "effect size" is based entirely on a comparison of the sample evidence and the pinpoint value specified in H_0. If the data closely approximate H_0, the estimated "effect size" will turn out to be small. On the other hand, a large discrepancy between the sample evidence and H_0 will cause the estimated "effect size" to be large.

When the nine-step version of hypothesis testing is employed, a different kind of effect size comes into play. Within this strategy, researchers *specify* (rather than *estimate*) the effect size, and this is done prior to the collection and examination of any data. When researchers specify the effect size in Step 4 of the nine-step version of hypothesis testing, they are not making a predictive statement as to the magnitude of the observed effect that will be found once the data are analyzed. Rather, they are indicating through Step 4 the minimum size of an effect that they consider to have practical significance. Most researchers hope that the magnitude of the observed effect, once computed, will exceed the effect size specified prior to the collection of any data.

Because the meaning of the term *effect size* can be confusing, we prefer to use it only to describe what the researcher specifies when conducting a power analysis within the nine-step version of hypothesis testing. When the seven-step version is used, we prefer to think that the researcher is not specifying the effect size or anything else, but "estimating the magnitude of the observed effect."

COHEN'S EFFECT SIZE VALUES OF .2, .5, AND .8

When doing a power analysis, many researchers utilize one of Cohen's popular values of .2, .5, or .8 to indicate the decision to specify a small, medium, or large effect size, respectively. This is very easy for the researcher to do. However, even Cohen himself argues that it is always better for the researcher to specify the effect size by thinking about the particular study being conducted rather than to use one of the "accepted" values cited earlier in this paragraph. In other words, it is preferable for the researcher to think about the data to be collected and to specify what distinguishes trivial from meaningful deviations from H_0 in terms of the raw units associated with the measuring instrument. (For example, a researcher investigating a new diet might assert that a nontrivial effect exists if the diet brings about a mean weight loss of at least 5 pounds.) Although this is not typically a difficult task by itself, the researcher who does this must also be able to estimate how much variability exists in the population(s) to which the statistical inference is intended. In many studies, it is difficult to estimate σ.

Researchers who perform a power analysis within the nine-step version of hypothesis testing should be given high marks for doing something that helps to make their investigations superior to those that are based upon the simpler six-step or seven-step versions. However, you should give them even higher marks when they follow Cohen's recommendation to avoid selecting .2 or .5 or .8 as the value for the effect size and instead specify it after (1) deciding what is and isn't significant in a practical sense and (2) estimating the variability in the population.

INFLATED TYPE I ERROR RATES

Our final caution is simply a reiteration of something we said earlier in this chapter. This has to do with the heightened chance of a Type I error when multiple tests are conducted simultaneously. This is a serious problem in scientific research and our caution deserves to be reiterated.

Suppose a researcher measures each of several people on seven variables. Also suppose that the true correlation between each pair of these variables is exactly 0.00 in the population associated with the researcher's sample. Finally, suppose our researcher computes a value for r for each pair of variables, tests each r to see if it is significantly different from 0.00, and then puts the results into a correlation matrix. If the .05 level of significance is used in conjunction with the evaluation of each r, the chances are greater than 50–50 that at least one of the rs will turn out to be significant. In other words, even though the alpha level is set equal to .05 for each separate test that is conducted, the collective Type I error risk has ballooned to over .50 due to the fact that 21 separate tests are conducted.

Our caution here is simple. Be wary of any researcher's conclusions if a big deal is made out of an unreplicated single finding of significance when the hypothesis testing procedure is used simultaneously to evaluate many null hypotheses. In contrast, give researchers extra credit when they apply the Bonferroni technique or the Dunn-Sidak modification to hold down their study-wide Type I error risk.

REVIEW TERMS

Bonferroni technique	Omega squared
Dunn-Sidak procedure	Power
Effect size (raw and standardized)	Practical significance
Eta squared	Sample size determination

Inflated Type I error risk   Small standardized effect size
Intraclass correlation   Statistical significance
Large standardized effect size   Strength-of-association index
Medium standardized effect size   Type II error risk

REVIEW QUESTIONS

1. Is it possible for a researcher to conduct a study wherein the result *is* significant in a statistical sense but *is not* significant in a practical sense?

2. In Excerpt 8.2, how much of a difference existed between the means of the two comparison groups? Was this difference found to be statistically significant? Was it an important difference?

3. (True or False) Statistical power equals the probability of not making a Type II error.

4. In Excerpt 8.4, if the researchers had used a larger number of subjects per group but had kept everything else about their study the same (including the sample means and standard deviations), would the power of their statistical test increase or decrease?

5. In the nine-step approach to hypothesis testing, when does the researcher specify the effect size—before or after looking at the sample data?

6. In Excerpt 8.5, suppose the researchers had used a medium (or small) effect size in their power analysis rather than the large effect size actually used. If they had done this, would they have needed a smaller or larger number of subjects than the 52 actually used?

7. If a researcher conducts a study in which $H_0: \mu = 50$, $H_a: \mu > 50$, and $\sigma = 10$, how large is the standardized effect size if the researcher states that any value of μ greater than 55 is important and worth detecting?

8. What are the values of small, medium, and large standardized effect sizes suggested by Jacob Cohen?

9. (True or False) If researchers have a fixed number of subjects and cannot get additional subjects, they have no reason to conduct a power analysis.

10. Look at Excerpt 8.10. If a very large sample size had been used, would the researcher have the right to say, "Due to the large size of the sample, it is not possible that a Type II error was made"?

11. If a study is conducted to test $H_0: \mu = 30$ and if the results yield a confidence interval around the sample mean that extends from 26.44 to 29.31, will H_0 be rejected or retained?

12. Suppose a friend gave you two "fair" coins and asked you to flip them simultaneously. To make it a fair wager, how much money would you have to put up if your friend bet $30 that you would end up with at least one "tail," with you betting that no "tail" would appear?

13. If researchers used the hypothesis testing procedure five times, once for each of the five dependent variables in the study, what level of significance would they need to use in testing each dependent variable in order to have a .05 probability of ending up with one or more Type I errors somewhere in the set of five results?

14. What would the number at the end of Excerpt 8.16, need to be if the study-wide Type I error rate in that investigation had been set at .01 rather than .05?

15. If researchers divide their desired "study-wide" Type I error risk by the number of times they use the hypothesis testing procedure, what is the name of this technique for adjusting alpha?

SIGNIFICANCE TESTING AND THE HYBRID APPROACH TO TESTING H_0

In the previous two chapters, we examined several versions of the hypothesis testing procedure. Although those versions differed from one another in certain respects (e.g., whether a critical value comes into play or whether the sample size is calculated on the basis of power and effect size considerations), they were similar in many ways. To be more specific, each of the hypothesis testing procedures focused upon in Chapters 7 and 8 involved the following concepts: H_0, H_a, α, a calculated value, and a reject/fail-to-reject decision. In each version, a statistically significant result is said to come about when $p < \alpha$.

We now turn to a procedure for evaluating null hypotheses that does not involve some of the common elements associated with the various test procedures discussed in the previous two chapters. Referred to as **significance testing** (as contrasted with hypothesis testing), the inferential technique that we will now examine is not used as often as the six-, seven-, and nine-step versions of hypothesis testing covered earlier. Even though significance testing is used less frequently than other ways of evaluating null hypotheses, it is best for you to be aware of its existence and be familiar with how it works.

We first will look at the objectives, logic, and procedural steps associated with significance testing. Then, we will look at a very popular way of evaluating null hypotheses that merges together a part of hypothesis testing and a part of significance testing.

The Component Parts of Significance Testing

As compared with some of the more complicated versions of hypothesis testing, significance testing will appear to be quite simplistic. The various steps that researchers must use if they apply this inferential technique are as follows:

1. State the null hypothesis, H_0.
2. Decide whether the test will be conducted in a one-tailed or two-tailed fashion.
3. Measure the sample objects, summarize the data, and compute a calculated value (i.e., test statistic).
4. Determine the probability associated with the sample evidence, assuming H_0 to be true.
5. Consider the resulting p-value to be stronger evidence against H_0 to the extent that the data-based p is a small value.

We will consider each of these five steps in the sections that follow. Before doing that, however, we must reiterate something we said near the beginning of Chapter 7. Before researchers can turn to the first step of either hypothesis testing or significance testing, they must make four preliminary decisions. These include specifying the nature of the relevant population(s), deciding how to extract the sample(s) from the population(s), determining what variable(s) will be measured, and choosing a way to summarize the sample data so as to reflect the preferred statistical focus. Once these preliminary tasks are completed, the researcher can turn to the five basic steps of significance testing.

Step 1: Stating H_0

In significance testing, the null hypothesis is the same as it is in hypothesis testing. It must be a pinpoint numerical statement as to the possible value(s) of the parameter in the population(s) of interest. The researcher selects H_0's pinpoint number for the same reasons as indicated in Chapter 7, with H_0 set up to divide the continuum of possible values of the parameter into two segments—one that is consistent with the research hypothesis and one that is inconsistent with H_r. As before, the null hypothesis is a statement that cannot be proven true or false by means of significance testing.

If researchers were to state their null hypothesis when they engage in significance testing, each H_0 would look just like those considered in Chapter 7. For example, if a researcher felt that a positive correlation existed, in the population, between two variables of interest, the first step of significance testing would involve the statement $H_0: \rho = 0$. Unfortunately, null hypotheses rarely appear in the technical summaries of research journals, regardless of whether the inferential procedure being used is hypothesis testing or significance testing. After you read about the specific test procedures discussed in the remainder of this book, we are confident that you will be able to make reasoned guesses as to what the researcher's H_0 probably was even though it is not explicitly articulated.

Step 2: The One-Tailed Versus Two-Tailed Decision

In significance testing as in hypothesis testing, researchers must decide whether they want to conduct their tests in a one-tailed fashion or in a two-tailed fashion. This decision has an important bearing on a subsequent step in both forms of inferential testing. Our earlier comment that most researchers conduct two-tailed tests when engaged in hypothesis testing also holds true within our discussion of significance testing. If a researcher fails to state explicitly which of these options was selected, it is a fairly safe bet that a two-tailed test was conducted.

It should be noted that Step 2 in significance testing is different from the parallel step in hypothesis testing. In significance testing, no alternative hypothesis is stated. In contrast, Step 2 of hypothesis testing involves the articulation of H_a, with a nondirectional H_a leading to a two-tailed test while a directional H_a yields a one-tailed test. In significance testing, the researcher bypasses the notion of H_a and instead "jumps" directly to the choice of a one- or two-tailed test. Such a choice has implications, as you will see, for the data-based computation of a p-value in Step 4.

One final similarity should be noted between the activity in Step 2 of hypothesis testing and significance testing. The choice between conducting a one- or two-tailed test should be made prior to the time the data are examined. If the data are allowed to influence the researcher's decision at Step 2, the statistical foundation associated with either form of inferential technique is destroyed.

Step 3: Computing a Calculated Value

Step 3 in significance testing is identical to Step 4 of the basic six-step version of hypothesis testing discussed in Chapter 7. The researcher needs to measure each object in the sample(s), summarize the sample data in accordance with the study's statistical focus (e.g., by computing $\overline{X}$ if the study is focusing on the mean), and then compute a calculated value. As you may recall, the calculated value is simply a metric-free way of expressing how far the sample evidence deviates from H_0's pinpoint value. In many studies, the researcher's calculated value will be expressed as a t-value, an F-value, or a χ^2-value. There are, however, many other forms that the calculated value can take, such as U, z, H, and J.

The calculated value, whether it appears in hypothesis testing or significance testing, carries little intrinsic meaning for the reader of research reports. To be told that the researcher's calculated F turned out equal to 4.17 is unlikely to help clarify much for the typical recipient of the research finding. The calculated value is extremely important to researchers, however, because it allows them (or their computer) to compute the highly important item needed in Step 4.

STEP 4: DETERMINING THE DATA-BASED p-VALUE

After the calculated value has been obtained, the researcher will determine a probability value for the sample data. Symbolized as p, this probability will normally be computed by a computer at the same time the sample data are analyzed to obtain the calculated value. With a few test procedures, however, printed tables exist that allow the researcher to "look up" the needed p-value.

The p-value secured in Step 4 indicates the probability of obtaining, simply by chance, sample data that deviate as much or more from H_0 as do the researcher's data. In other words, the computed p-value tells how likely it is that a "true H_0 population situation" would produce a randomly selected data set that, when summarized, is at least as far away from H_0's pinpoint number as is the researcher's actual data set. The greater the discrepancy between H_0 and the data, the smaller the p-value will be.

Excerpts 9.1 and 9.2 illustrate how significance testing yields a precise p-value for any calculated value. In the first of these excerpts, the calculated

---

Excerpts 9.1–9.2   The p in Significance Testing

When delineated by race and sex, Black males accounted for 18 of the deaths (38%), with an average age at death of 65 years. Seventeen deaths (35%) occurred among White males, with an average age at death of 72 years ($t = 1.65$, $P = 0.11$).

Source: A. Cottrell, E. Schwart, R. Sokas, V. Kofie, and L. Welch. (1992). Surveillance of sentinel occupational mortality in the District of Columbia: 1980 to 1987. *American Journal of Public Health, 82*(1), p. 118.

Resistance training resulted in increases in strength and muscle fiber size. The leg press 3RM increased [$t(7) = 7.2837, P = 0.0003$] by $25 \pm 3\%$, and the knee extension 3RM by $31 \pm 6\%$ [$t(7) = 7.1901, P = 0.0004$]. Muscle hypertrophy was indicated by an increase [$t(6) = 5.59978, P = 0.0014$] of $21 \pm 5\%$ in average muscle fiber size.

Source: D. L. Tatro, G. A. Dudley, and V. A. Convertino. (1992). Carotid-cardiac baroreflex response and LBNP tolerance following resistance training. *Medicine and Science in Sports and Exercise, 24*(7), p. 791.

value of 1.65 and the *p*-value of 0.11 came about by comparing the two groups of men in terms of average age at death. In the second excerpt, three sets of calculated values and *p*-values are presented because significance testing was used to measure the effects of "resistance training" on three variables: leg press, knee extension, and muscle hypertrophy.

STEP 5: ASSESSING THE LIKELIHOOD THAT H_0 IS TRUE

The final step of significance testing is similar to the final step of hypothesis testing in that a statement is made concerning H_0. The nature of this concluding statement, however, is different in the two inferential procedures. In hypothesis testing, the researcher makes a dichotomous decision either to reject or to fail-to-reject H_0, with the level of significance playing a major role in setting up a criterion that allows the researcher to make the final reject/retain decision. In contrast, with significance testing there is no alpha-based criterion because none of the earlier steps involves the specification of an α level.

In significance testing, the researcher allows the data "to speak for themselves" regarding the likelihood that they came from a true H_0 situation. If the *p*-value associated with the calculated value turns out to be extremely small (e.g., $p = .004$), the researcher will report this outcome as an indication that the sample evidence is very, very unlikely to have come from a population situation wherein H_0 is true. On the other hand, if the *p*-value turns out to be high (e.g., $p = .68$), the researcher will report this outcome as well, indicating that the data do not deviate very much from what one would expect if H_0 were true. Between these extremes, intermediate values of *p* will be interpreted as providing stronger or weaker evidence against the null.

SIGNIFICANCE TESTING USING "*p*-LESS THAN" AND "*p*-GREATER-THAN" STATEMENTS

In reporting how strong the evidence is against H_0, a researcher will often cite the exact *p*-level associated with the sample data. Examples of this mechanism for summarizing results were presented in Excerpts 9.1 and 9.2. Frequently, however, researchers will utilize "*p*-less-than" or "*p*-greater-than" statements when communicating the extent to which the sample data turned out to be inconsistent with H_0. This is done for one of two reasons: either the researcher lacks access to a computer that can determine a precise *p*-value, or the researcher simply converts the precise *p* into a "*p*-less-than" or "*p*-greater-than" format because of the dominating influence of hypothesis testing (where results are often presented in a "$p < \alpha$" or "$p > \alpha$" manner).

In Excerpts 9.3 and 9.4, we see two examples where the "*p*-less-than" technique for reporting results was used. The researchers who conducted

---

Excerpts 9.3–9.4   Reporting Results Using "p-Less-Than" Statements

---

The correlation between the SIAS and SPS for the combined social phobic group was $r = .41$, for the community sample $r = .89$, and for the undergraduate sample $r = .52$ (all $ps < .001$).

Source: R. G. Heimberg, G. P. Muller, C. S. Holt, D. A. Hope, and M. R. Leibowitz. (1992). Assessment of anxiety in social interaction and being observed by others: The Social Interaction Anxiety Scale and the Social Phobia Scale. *Behavior Therapy, 23*(1), p. 64.

The recorded frequency of coitus among those patients who purchased the device was 0.3 per week prior to the VTCT training, and 1.5 per week at follow-up ($t = -5.7, p < 0.0001$).

Source: R. Aloni, L. Heller, O. Keren, E. Mendelson, and G. Davidoff. (1992). Noninvasive treatment for erectile dysfunction in the neurogenically disabled population. *Journal of Sex and Marital Therapy, 18*(3), p. 245.

---

these two studies are not telling us in these excerpts that they used alpha levels of .001 and .0001, respectively. Rather, they are indicating how strongly their sample evidence argues against their null hypotheses. They do this by reporting that p is less than one of the easily understood points that exist on the lower end of the p continuum.

In Excerpt 9.5, we see another example where the "p-less-than" format was used. Notice how the p associated with the comparison of the two 1988 means is "bracketed" by .05 and .10.

Excerpt 9.5   Bracketing the p Between .05 and .10

The means for the baseline year, 1985, were -1.2 and 1.8 for the two groups, $t(37) = 2.11, p < .05$, and the means for 1988 were -1.1 and 1.5, $t(37) = 1.83$, $.05 < p < .10$.

Source: G. K. Mandeville. (1992). Does achievement increase over time? Another look at the South Carolina P.E.T. program. *Elementary School Journal, 93*(2), p. 127.

A POPULAR HYBRID: SIGNIFICANCE TESTING WITH AN α-LEVEL

As indicated earlier in this chapter, true significance testing does not involve the specification of a level of significance. True hypothesis testing, on the other hand, involves an alpha level, but it does not permit the researcher to report "impressive" p-levels due to the fact that the final step in hypothesis testing is simply a dichotomous decision. Feeling that both significance testing and hypothesis testing have valuable components, many researchers utilize a procedure for testing null hypotheses that represents a merger of the two separate strategies.

This hybrid approach is identical to the six-, seven-, or nine-step version of hypothesis testing except for one thing. After a decision has been reached to either reject or fail-to-reject H_0, researchers will present the precise data-based p-value (or a "p-less-than" or "p-greater-than" statement) in order to provide evidence as to how strongly the data "argue against the null." When using this approach to dealing with H_0, researchers are not satisfied simply to end up making a reject/fail-to-reject decision; they want also to demonstrate the degree to which that decision was (or wasn't) a "close call."

In Excerpts 9.6 and 9.7, we see two examples where the hybrid approach was used. In each of these cases, the p-value indicates that the decision (to fail-to-reject in Excerpt 9.6; to reject in Excerpt 9.7) was made decisively.

Excerpt 9.6-9.7   Retaining or Rejecting H_0 by Comparing p Versus the Alpha Level

---

When the data concerning decision-making styles was compared, no significant intergroup variance was found at the .05 level of significance (F = .399, p = .672).

Source: B. W. Gatlin, and C. D. Brown. (1990). Problem-solving and orientations and decision-making styles among rehabilitation professionals. *Journal of Rehabilitation, 56*(2), p. 24.

A significance level of .05 was used [revealing that] the effects of peer tutoring were significantly different, $F(2,26) = 10.1, p = .0006$.

Source: M. Beirne-Smith. (1991). Peer tutoring in arithmetic for children with learning disabilities. *Exceptional Children, 57*, p. 334.

Often, the hybrid approach to statistical testing will be used without an explicit statement of the level of significance. An alpha level of .05 has become so commonplace that many researchers assume that others will somehow know that they set $\alpha = .05$. They end up reporting simply that their statistical test either did or did not "reach significance," that it either did or did not lead to "a significant finding," or that it either did or did not produce a "significant difference." With no indication of the alpha level, you should presume that the claim of significance came about because the calculated value "beat" the .05 critical value (or that the p turned out smaller than .05). When they also say something like $p < .001$, they are not telling us that they used $\alpha = .001$; instead, they are using the significance testing device of indicating how strongly the evidence argued against H_0.

In Excerpts 9.8–9.10, we see several cases where a term such as *significant difference* is a tip-off that a reject/retain decision was made, even though information about p is provided so as to show how improbable the data would be if H_0 was true.

Excerpts 9.8–9.10 "Significant" or "Nonsignificant" Results with Information on p

---

The accuracy of the same predicted match between emotion condition and report was not so clear when children supplied their own emotion terms, although there were significant differences between numbers of children making positive or negative reports according to condition, $\chi^2(1, N=60) = 7.02, p = .008$.

Source: R. J. Casey. (1993). Children's emotional experience: Relations among expression, self-report, and understanding. *Developmental Psychology, 29*(1), p. 124.

In all three programs results show a significant main effect for sexual status. In Teen Aid the group means were Nonvirgin mean = 2.84, Virgin Informed mean = 3.26, and Virgin Uninformed mean = 3.65, $F(2,688) = 21.86, p < .001$.

Source: J. Olsen, S. Weed, D. Daly, and L. Jensen. (1992). The effects of abstinence sex education programs on virgin versus non-virgin students. *Journal of Research and Development in Education, 25*(2), p. 73.

However, a MANOVA indicated that the effect of the subliminal slides on ratings was not significantly different across the three dependent measures, $F(2,62) = 0.47, p = .50$.

Source: J. A. Krosnick, A. L. Betz, L. J. Jussim, and A. R. Lynn. (1992). Subliminal conditioning of attitudes. *Personality and Social Psychology Bulletin, 18*(2), p. 156.

"MARGINAL SIGNIFICANCE" AND OTHER DESCRIPTIVE PHRASES FOR "NEAR MISSES"

In hypothesis testing, the researcher either rejects or fails-to-reject H_0. Regardless of whether the calculated value exceeds (or falls short of) the critical value by a giant margin or a smidgen, the same decision will be made to reject (or retain) H_0. Results are not discussed in terms of "close calls," "large discrepancies between the calculated and critical values," or "impressive p-values" because such issues are irrelevant. In hypothesis testing, the only thing that matters at the end is whether or not H_0 is rejected.

With the hybrid form of statistical testing, the researcher not only will indicate whether or not the data produce a significant finding, but also will provide evidence as to how strongly the data challenge H_0. If it turns out that the data-based p is larger than .05 but not too much larger than this commonly accepted threshold into the land of statistical significance, the researcher is likely to report that the results are **marginally significant** or of **borderline**

significance, that the findings **approach significance**, or that the evidence reveals a **trend toward significance**.

Consider Excerpts 9.11–9.15. In each case, a result that fails to beat the conventional .05 criterion is noted because the researcher felt the outcome was a "close call."

In Excerpts 9.14 and 9.15, we are told that there was "a trend toward a difference" and "a trend for men to have higher levels of exposure than women." There is really no *trend* here in the usual meaning of this term; rather, the researchers are simply interpreting their *p*s of .19 and .10 to be close enough to the .05 criterion to be worth discussing.

Excerpts 9.11–9.15 Results That Are "Marginally Significant," That "Approach Significance," and That Show a "Trend Toward Significance"

Hypothesis 1, that there would be reduced use of emergency services and nonpsychiatric clinics, was unconfirmed. The number of these visits correlated marginally with number of Axis III diagnoses ($r = 0.43, p = 0.11$).

Source: M. F. Weiner. (1992). Group therapy reduces medical and psychiatric hospitalization. *International Journal of Group Psychotherapy, 42*(2), p. 270.

In terms of teacher report of a child's social competence, the interaction term approached significance, $F(1,58) = 3.81, p \leq .10$.

Source: A. M. Thomas, L. Armistead, T. Kempton, S. Lynch, R. Forehand, S. Novisainen, B. Neighbors, and L. Tannenbaum. (1992). Early retention: Are there long-term beneficial effects? *Psychology in the Schools, 29*(4), p. 345.

The difference in the HOME score by birth order was of borderline significance ($p = .09$).

Source: N. Weintraub, and H. Palti. (1991). Comparison of the home environment of children who participated in an early intervention program = "PROD," with controls, at 5 years-of-age. *Early Child Development and Care, 66*, p. 28.

We conducted analyses to search for gender differences on dependent variables. A significant gender difference on physical symptoms was indicated by *t* tests ($t = 5.17, p < .001$) and a trend toward a difference in memory performance ($t = 1.31, p = .19$).

Source: S. T. Meier. (1991). Tests of the construct validity of occupational stress measures with college students: Failure to support discriminant validity. *Journal of Counseling Psychology, 38*(1), p. 94.

The relationship between gender and exposure was marginally significant ($p = .10$), indicating a trend for men to have higher levels of exposure than women.

Source: K. M. Emmons, D. B. Abrams, R. J. Marshall, R. A. Etzel, T. E. Novothy, B. H. Marcus, and M. E. Kane. (1992). Exposure to environmental tobacco smoke in naturalistic settings. *American Journal of Public Health, 82*(1), p. 26.

SIGNIFICANT AND HIGHLY SIGNIFICANT RESULTS

In using the hybrid approach to statistical testing, some researchers will attempt to call attention to the margin by which they rejected H_0 if the data-based *p*-value turns out to be quite small. They do this by modifying the word *significant* with an adjective such as *highly* or *clearly*. Examples of this reporting strategy appear in Excerpts 9.16–9.18.

Excerpts 9.16–9.18   Calling Attention to Results That Are Quite Improbable

---

Analyses of the results for the 375 and 500 Hz harmonics separately showed main effects of phase condition, target, and subjects in each case; interactions were highly significant (all *ps* < .01).

Source: J. D. McKeown, and C. J. Darwin. (1991). Effects of phase changes in low-numbered harmonics on the internal representation of complex sounds. *The Quarterly Journal of Experimental Psychology, 43A*(3), p. 406.

A 3 × 3 chi-square test analyzes the differences in frequencies produced by the nature of coping strategy (primary, secondary, relinquished). The result is clearly significant, $\chi^2(4, N=416) = 32.31, p \leq .01$.

Source: T. Tremewan, and K. Strongman. (1991). Coping with fear in early childhood: Comparing fiction with reality. *Early Child Development and Care, 71*, p. 31.

The data for the two components were analyzed separately. First, for phase changes of the 375-Hz component, there was a highly significant effect of subjects ($p < 0.001$), a significant effect of phase ($p < 0.05$), and a highly significant interaction between these two factors ($p < 0.001$).

Source: J. D. McKeown, and C. J. Darwin. (1991). Effects of phase changes in low-numbered harmonics on the internal representation of complex sounds. *The Quarterly Journal of Experimental Psychology, 43A*(3), p. 413.

When results are presented using a table instead of paragraphs of text, the researcher who wishes to call attention to the very low *p*-values usually does so by using multiple asterisks for any outcome that is **highly significant**. Excerpt 9.19 illustrates how this is usually done. (Note that the three columns of decimal numbers inside the table are correlation coefficients, not *p*-values; the information beneath the table provides the explanation of what it means when one, two, or three asterisks appears next to an *r*.)

Unfortunately, the meaning of a particular number of asterisks attached to *p* will vary from article to article. Excerpts 9.20–9.23 serve to document this claim, since each of these excerpts appeared as a note beneath a table. Notice how all four of these reporting schemes are different from the one used in Excerpt 9.19.

Excerpt 9.19   Use of Multiple Asterisks in a Table

Table 1

Pearson Correlation Coefficients Between Tested, Preevaluation Estimates, and Postevaluation Estimates of Client Aptitudes

Aptitude	Tested with preevaluation	Tested with postevaluation	Preevaluation with postevaluation
	r	r	r
General learning	.376**	.323**	.506***
Verbal aptitude	.274*	.372**	.515***
Numerical aptitude	.270*	.377**	.646***
Spatial aptitude	.446***	.416***	.533***
Form perception	.382**	.532***	.367**
Clerical perception	.005	.374**	.223
Motor coordination	.294*	.359**	.494***
Finger dexterity	.381**	.519***	.386**
Manual dexterity	.303*	.329**	.490***

Note. N ranged from 55 to 59.
$^{*}p<.05.$ $^{**}p<.01.$ $^{***}p<.001.$

Source: T. P. Janikowski, J. E. Bordieri, and J. Musgrave. (1992). Impact of vocational evaluation on client self-estimated aptitudes and interests. *Rehabilitation Counseling Bulletin, 36*(2), p. 75.

Excerpts 9.20–9.23   Variability in the Use of Multiple Asterisks for Results in Tables

$^{*}p \leq .05.$ $^{**}p \leq .01.$

Source: B. A. Hawkins. (1991). An exploration of adaptive skills and leisure activity of older adults with mental retardation. *Therapeutic Recreation Journal, 25*(4), p. 21.

Probabilities (Two-tailed): $^{*}p < .10;$ $^{**}p < .05;$ $^{***}p < .01.$

Source: J. L. Cotterell. (1992). The relation of attachments and supports to adolescent well-being and school adjustment. *Journal of Adolescent Research, 7*(1), p. 35.

(Continued)

Excerpts 9.20–9.23   Variability in the Use of Multiple Asterisks for
Results in Tables (Continued)

$^*p < .05.$ $^{**}p < .01.$ $^{***}p < .001.$ $^{****}p < .0001.$

Source: L. Phelps, N. Dowdell, F. Rizzo, P. Ehrlich, and F. Wilszenski. (1992). Five to ten years after
placement: The long-term efficacy of retention and pre-grade transition. *Journal of Psychoeducational
Assessment, 10*(2), p. 120.

$^*p < .05.$ $^{**}p < .005.$ $^{***}p < .001.$

Source: W. E. Snell Jr., B. R. Hampton, and P. McManus. (1992). The impact of counselor and participant gender on willingness to discuss relational topics: Development of the Relationship Disclosure
Scale. *Journal of Counseling and Development, 70*(3), p. 411.

REPORTING FAIL-TO-REJECT DECISIONS USING "p-LESS-THAN" STATEMENTS

Normally, "p-less-than" statements signify that H_0 was rejected while
"p-greater-than" statements indicate that H_0 was not rejected. When the hybrid approach to statistical testing is used, however, this general rule of
thumb can prove to be misleading. This is due to the fact that researchers
sometimes use "p-less-than" statements to indicate the degree to which the
sample evidence *failed* to beat the alpha level criterion.

Excerpt 9.24 contains an example of a situation where the researchers indicate $p < .20$ even though a fail-to-reject decision was reached concerning
the H_0 being tested. In this excerpt, the researchers are telling us that the calculated value of 1.26 was so far away from the .05 critical value that the former exceeded only the .20 critical value. Presumably, the researchers'
calculated value was not large enough to beat the .15 critical value, otherwise
they probably would have stated $p < .15$.

Excerpt 9.24   Signifying a Fail-to-Reject Decision Using a p-Less-
Than Statement

Multivariate analysis of variance (MANOVA) was used to evaluate initial differences on dependent variables between the four groups. The Wilks' Lambda was
.5259, $F(27,138) = 1.26$, $p < .20$, indicating that the groups did not differ at
pretreatment on pain, physical functioning, psychological status, depression, and
disease activity variables.

Source: V. Radojevic, P. Nicassio, and M. Weisman. (1992). Behavioral intervention with and without
family support for rheumatoid arthritis. *Behavior Therapy, 23*(1), p. 20.

In cases where H_0 is not rejected, the typical researcher will report that p is greater than the level of significance employed or that p is greater than some value higher than α. For example, the researchers who conducted the study from which Excerpt 9.24 was taken could have told us that $p > .15$. Regardless of whether a "p-less-than" or "p-greater-than" statement is used, however, the results are not entirely clear. For this reason, we prefer to see the precise p-level associated with the sample evidence.

THE "ONE-SIDED" VARIATION TO THE HYBRID APPROACH

Certain researchers use an approach to testing null hypotheses that involves a different kind of statement when $p < \alpha$ as compared to when $p > \alpha$. If p turns out to be smaller than the level of significance, these researchers will report that the results are significant and will present the precise p-level associated with the data (with smaller ps interpreted as providing stronger evidence against H_0). If, however, p turns out to be larger than α, these researchers assert that the results are not significant no matter what the value of p.

For the researchers who subscribe to this "one-sided" variation of the hybrid approach, terms such as *marginally significant result*, *trend toward significance*, and *borderline significance* are never used. From their point of view, a $p > \alpha$ outcome is the same regardless of how close p is to α. Whereas multiple asterisks and terms like *highly significant* are used to distinguish cases where p beats α by a wide margin as contrasted to cases where the results are just barely significant, these researchers consider all $p > \alpha$ outcomes to be the same—simply not significant.

In Excerpts 9.25–9.27 we see three examples where results were reported as simply being nonsignificant even though the researchers' p-values missed beating α by small margins. If you compare these three excerpts with

---

Excerpts 9.25–9.27   "Near Misses" Interpreted Simply as Not Significant

---

When the data were examined in regard to the restrictiveness of policy, there was no relationship between having very restrictive policies and the adoption of a tobacco-related curriculum ($r = -0.145$, $df = 1$, $p = .14$). That is, school districts with policies prohibiting tobacco use at all school related events and functions were not necessarily more likely to have an adopted tobacco prevention curriculum than school districts with less restrictive policies.

Source: D. W. Smith, A. B. Steckler, K. McLeroy, and R. Frye. (1990). Tobacco prevention in North Carolina public schools. *Journal of Drug Education, 20*(3), p. 263.

(Continued)

Excerpts 9.25–9.27   "Near Misses" Interpreted Simply as Not Significant *(Continued)*

To answer the second research question regarding the severity of nausea, the 965 incidents of nausea were analyzed to determine the time periods in which nausea was most severe. . . . The difference in severity by time period was not statistically significant ($\chi^2 = 16.781$, $df = 10$, $p = .079$).

Source: C. Dilorio, D. VanLier, and B. Manteufell. (1992). Patterns of nausea during first trimester of pregnancy. *Clinical Nursing Research*, 1(2), p. 133.

The results of the hypothesis tests were not significant at the .05 level; respectively, the results were $F(1,53) = 2.8$, $p = .10$ in Reading and $F(1,53) = 1.56$, $p = .21$ in Math. A 10-point difference in NCE between the two subgroups was observed on the combined first-grade measure, but this difference was also not significant at the .05 level, $F(1.53) = 3.37$, $p = .07$.

Source: M. Banerji. (1992). An integrated study of the predictive properties of the Gesell School Readiness Screening Test. *Journal of Psychoeducational Assessment, 10*(3), p. 251.

Excerpts 9.11–9.15, you will see that researchers who end up with *p*s that exceed α by small amounts interpret their results differently depending upon whether they use the "two-sided" or "one-sided" variation of the hybrid approach to testing H_0. In Excerpt 9.14, the researcher said there was "a trend toward a difference" because $p = .19$; here in Excerpt 9.26, the researchers indicate simply that their result "was not statistically significant" even though $p = .079$.

THE SEVEN-, EIGHT-, AND TEN-STEP VERSIONS OF THE HYBRID APPROACH

As we have pointed out earlier, the hybrid approach to testing a null hypothesis involves adding a step to hypothesis testing. (That "extra" step amounts to using the data-based *p*-value to show how decisively H_0 was or was not rejected.) Since hypothesis testing can be used with six, seven, or nine steps, the addition of the extra step means that there are seven-, eight-, and ten-step versions of the hybrid approach to testing null hypotheses.

Many researchers apply the six basic steps of hypothesis testing that we examined in Chapter 7 and then simply present (and possibly talk about) the *p*-value associated with the data. Doing that creates the seven-step version of the hybrid approach. Excerpts 9.6–9.27 illustrate the application of this simplest variation of the hybrid approach.

It should be noted that researchers can and do employ the available eight-step and ten-step versions of the hybrid approach. The eight-step version is created when the researcher not only computes a post hoc effect size estimate but also shows, using a p-value, how strongly the data argue against H_0. The ten-step version occurs when the researcher not only determines the appropriate sample size through a power analysis, but also shows how distant p is from α following the ultimate decision to reject/fail-to-reject H_0.

Over time, we expect the popularity of the eight- and ten-step versions of the hybrid approach to increase (as contrasted to the seven-step version). In each case, more information is provided through the research report than simply a reject/fail-to-reject decision paired with the p-value.

A FEW WARNINGS

Beginning in Chapter 10, we will focus our attention on the specific statistical tests—t, F, chi-square, U, H, and so on—that researchers apply to the null hypotheses of their applied studies. Before looking at those tests, however, we want to offer a few final warnings that will help make you an informed recipient of research reports that deal with null hypotheses.

THE IMPORTANCE OF H_0

In Chapter 7, we pointed out why the hypothesis testing procedure will yield worthless information if the null hypothesis specified by the researcher is silly, stupid, or uninteresting in the eyes of everyone except the researcher. The same point holds true for significance testing and for the hybrid approach to statistical testing. In light of the fact that H_0 is inextricably tied to any reject/fail-to-reject decision and/or to any data-based p-value, the researcher's null hypothesis must be worthy of investigation in order for the final conclusions to be worth noting.

Of course, a worthy H_0 does not guarantee that results will be important, for deficiencies in the data-collection portion of a study can ruin a study even though there is an interesting H_0 under investigation. Measuring instruments having low reliability or validity, designs lacking needed control groups, and failure to use "double-blind" procedures—these are just a few of the many pitfalls that can doom a study even if the H_0 is "perfect." Having a good H_0, therefore, should be considered to be a necessary but not sufficient condition for having a good study.

THE MEANING OF THE DATA-BASED PROBABILITY

In Chapter 7, we alerted you to the fact that a statistically significant result may or may not signify a finding with practical significance. Even if the H_0 under investigation is a good one, a decision to reject the null may well be analogous to the discovery of a very small molehill rather than a majestic mountain. This is possible because of the relationship between the amount of data and the power to reject a false H_0. Given sample sizes that are large enough, just about any study will lead to a reject decision—even if the null statement is false by a tiny amount.

In this chapter, the focus has been on the data-based p-level. If the p is very small, you may be tempted to think that there is a large effect in the data or, stated differently, that H_0 is false by a mile. Similarly, you may be tempted to think that ps that are not small turned out that way because there was a small effect in the data or, stated differently, because the null hypothesis (if false at all) was false by a small amount. Resist these temptations!

For any given degree of discrepancy between the sample evidence and H_0, there is an inverse relationship between the sample size and the data-based p-level. For example, consider a study in which a researcher is concerned with Pearson's product-moment correlation, conducts a two-tailed test of $H_0 : \rho = 0.00$, and finds that $r = .40$ for the sample. Now, if the size of that sample is 10, then p is .24. If $n = 30$, then $p = .03$. And if $n = 500$, then $p = .00006$. Now consider the same study but this time with a very small difference between H_0 and the sample evidence. For the case where $H_0: \rho = 0.00$ and $r = .03$, the p-value will turn out to be very small if the sample size is very large. If $n = 25,000$, $p < .00002$.

Our point here is that the data-based p-value does *not* indicate how big a difference exists between H_0 and the summary of the sample data but rather how likely it is that a difference as large as (or larger than) that actually observed would occur by chance—that is, if H_0 is true. If there is an enormous amount of data, the summary of the data should turn out to be very, very similar to H_0's pinpoint number, presuming that H_0 is true. In this situation, the data-based p-value will turn out to be quite small (e.g., $p < .01$) even if the difference between the data and H_0 is quite small.

It's important to understand the true meaning of p because researchers will sometimes state things in such a way as to suggest that p reflects the effect size in the data. For example, consider Excerpts 9.28 and 9.29. In these two excerpts, notice how the qualifying terms *slightly more familiarity* and *marginally higher* are used when p did not quite beat the .05 criterion but are *not* used when $p < .05$.

Excerpts 9.28–9.29   Misleading Statements Based on Misguided
Understanding of p

Consistent with our prediction, early-maturing girls in mixed-sex settings had more familiarity with delinquent peers than did their early-maturing peers who were attending all-girl schools (19.23 vs. 14.17), $t(263) = 2.12$, $p < .05$. Between school comparisons among the other two menarcheal groups yielded

(Continued)

Excerpts 9.28–9.29   Misleading Statements Based on Misguided
Understanding of *p* (Continued)

---

equivocal support for our predictions. At age 13, on-time maturers in mixed-sex settings had slightly more familiarity with delinquent peers than did their counterparts in all-girl schools (16.79 vs. 13.77), $t(263) = 1.66$, $p < .10$.

Source: A. Caspi, D. Lynam, T. E. Moffitt, and P. A. Silva. (1993). Unraveling girls' delinquency: Biological, dispositional, and contextual contributions to adolescent misbehavior. *Developmental Psychology, 29*(1), p. 23.

There was no sex difference for either of the event measures, but girls had marginally higher depression scores than boys, $t(357) = 1.77$, $p < .08$, and boys had significantly higher conduct-disorder scores than girls, $t(357) = 2.45$, $p < .02$.

Source: I. Sandler, K. Reynolds, W. Kliever, and R. Ramirez. (1992). Specificity of the relation between life events and psychological symtomatology. *Journal of Clinical Child Psychology, 21*(3), p. 244.

As we indicated earlier in this chapter, researchers who use the hybrid approach to evaluating an H_0 will sometimes use the term *marginally significant* when the *p*-value just barely misses being on the reject side of alpha. That use of the term *marginally* is acceptable. It is wrong, however, to think that a marginally significant result came about because there was a marginally sized effect in the data.

THE SUBJECTIVE INTERPRETATION OF *P*

In hypothesis testing, researchers function like robots once the data are collected. In that approach to dealing with null hypotheses, the researchers' subjective opinion (e.g., as to the appropriate level of Type I error risk) can enter the picture only during the initial stages of the inferential activity. After the data are gathered, however, researchers must be totally objective in the sense that anyone could reach the same conclusion if they abided by the decisions made regarding H_0, H_a, α, and *n*.

In significance testing and in the hybrid approach to dealing with null hypotheses, an element of subjectivity is allowed when the researcher interprets the *p*-value following the collection and analysis of the sample data. This is especially true in significance testing, since there is no alpha-based criterion against which the data-based summary can be compared. But even when the hybrid approach is used, the researcher's impressions of the results often affect the conclusions that are drawn.

In Excerpts 9.11–9.15, we saw examples of terms such as *marginally significant* and *trend toward significance* being used in conjunction with results where *p* just barely missed beating the alpha level. But how far away from α must *p* be before it stops being a "close call" worth noting? This is a question to which there is no clear-cut answer, and a given p may be interpreted by one researcher as being "of borderline significance" while the same p in a different study is interpreted by that study's researcher as simply "not significant."

In a similar fashion, subjectivity is involved when researchers who use the hybrid approach try to decide whether a "highly significant" result has been obtained. How much smaller than α must p be in order for the results to be "highly" or "clearly" significant? If you take another look at Excerpts 9.16 and 9.18, you will see that some researchers say that their results are highly significant when $p < .01$ while others use this label only when $p < .001$.

Besides simply pointing out how researcher subjectivity enters the picture when p-values are interpreted, we have some advice for readers of research articles. Simply stated, judge for yourself whether a result is or isn't marginally significant or highly significant. Because these labels are subjectively based, your opinion is just as worthy as the researcher's.

"Resetting" the Level of Significance

In describing the hypothesis testing and hybrid approaches to dealing with null hypotheses, we have indicated that the researcher is the one who specifies the level of significance. In terms of the way the data are analyzed and then summarized for dissemination, it *is* the researcher who specifies α. However, in reading research reports, you are not bound to the alpha level used by the researcher; you legitimately can apply a more stringent or more lenient α than that used in any report that you are examining. No law exists to prevent you from doing this!

For example, consider again Excerpt 9.27, where a $p = .07$ outcome was said to be "not significant at the .05 level." If you tend to be more concerned about Type II errors as compared with Type I errors, you could apply a more lenient alpha level to the results of this investigation. And were you to reset alpha equal to .20, .15, or even .10, the outcome would change from being not significant to achieving the status of a significant result. On the other hand, you may want to exert more control over Type I error than do some of the authors you read. If so, you can reset alpha so as to gain this added protection. If you were to do this in relation to the result presented in Excerpt 9.30, the claim of a significant increase would vanish.

Although you are entitled to use your own level of significance when interpreting research results, it is not proper for you to look at the outcome and *then* decide to apply a different alpha level to the results. Your decision to change to (or to accept) the researcher's alpha level must be made prior to your knowledge of how big an effect turned up in the sample data and/or how large the p-value is. You can use whatever alpha level you wish when interpreting research results, but you must "play by the same rules" as does the

> **Excerpt 9.30** A Significant Result That Would Be Nonsignificant If
> Alpha Is Made More Rigorous
>
> ---
>
> Hypothesis 2, that there would be reduced use of psychotropic and nonpsy-
> chotropic medications, was also confirmed. There was, in fact, significantly in-
> creased use of neuroleptics ($\chi^2 = 4.0$, $p = .046$) (but not other classes of
> psychotropics) and nonpsychotropic drugs.
>
> ---
>
> *Source:* M. F. Weiner. (1992). Group therapy reduces medical and psychiatric hospitalization.
> *International Journal of Group Psychotherapy, 42*(2), p. 270.

researcher—and these rules demand that α be specified before the data of
any study are examined.

REVIEW TERMS

Borderline significance   Marginal significance
Highly significant   Significance testing
Hybrid approach to testing H_0 Trend toward significance

REVIEW QUESTIONS

1. (True or False) In significance testing, the researcher neither states an alternative hypothesis nor specifies a level of significance.

2. In Excerpt 9.1, what was the null hypothesis for which the data-based p
   turned out equal to 0.11?

3. Assuming that our answer to Question 2 is correct, would the final number
   in Excerpt 9.1 have been larger or smaller if the two averages had been 68
   and 70 (rather than 65 and 72), with everything else about the study remaining the same?

4. In significance testing, why can't the researcher end up making a decision to
   reject or fail-to-reject the null hypothesis?

5. In Excerpts 9.3 and 9.4, did the sample evidence turn out consistent with
   what one would expect if H_0 were true?

6. Why aren't Excerpts 9.6 and 9.7 examples of significance testing rather than
   examples of the hybrid approach to testing null hypotheses?

7. If researchers report that they "obtained a significant result with $p < .0001$,"
   the authors of this book would guess that they used _____ within the study
   being discussed.

   a. hypothesis testing

   b. significance testing

   c. the hybrid approach to testing H_0

8. If researchers set $\alpha = .05$, which of the following data-based p-levels might prompt them to say that they obtained a result that is "marginally significant" (assuming that they use the hybrid approach to testing H_0)?

   a. $p = .003$

   b. $p = .047$

   c. $p = .054$

   d. $p = .94$

9. Which of the ps given at the end of the previous question might bring forth the term *highly significant*?

10. If a researcher's data turn out such that $p < .05$, and if the researcher puts this symbolic statement beneath a table, how many asterisks will the researcher put in front of the letter p ?

11. If researchers were to summarize their inferential work by reporting $p < .05$, how confident should you be that a decision was made to reject H_0?

12. (True or False) Because no alternative hypothesis is specified in significance testing, this form of inferential statistics (as contrasted with hypothesis testing or the hybrid approach to dealing with H_0) does not require an "interesting" H_0 in order to produce an interesting result.

13. Suppose two researchers each compare two diets in terms of average weight loss, with each study having $H_0: \mu_1 = \mu_2$. Researcher A compares two diets located in the popular media, while Researcher B compares two diets located in the technical literature of nutritional science. In terms of results, Researcher A finds that $p = .04$ while Researcher B finds that $p = .0001$. Based on these p-values, which researcher observed the biggest difference between the two sample means that were compared?

14. (True or False) It is illegal (or at least unethical) for you to decide for yourself whether or not a result is significant by using your own alpha-level standard.

Statistical Inferences Concerning Bivariate Correlation Coefficients

In Chapter 3, we discussed several descriptive techniques used by researchers to summarize the degree of relationship that exists between two sets of scores. In the present chapter, we will examine how researchers deal with their correlation coefficients inferentially. Stated differently, the techniques to be considered here are the ones used when researchers have access only to sample data but wish to make "educated guesses" as to the nature of the population(s) associated with the sample(s). As you will see shortly, the techniques used most frequently to do this include hypothesis testing, significance testing, and the hybrid approach to testing H_0. Occasionally, however, inferential "guesses" are made through the use of confidence intervals.

We begin this chapter with a consideration of the statistical tests applied to various bivariate correlation coefficients, along with an examination of the typical ways researchers communicate the results of their analyses. We will also point out how the Bonferroni technique is used in conjunction with tests on correlation coefficients, how researchers compare two (or more) correlation coefficients to see if they are significantly different, and how statistical tests can be applied to reliability and validity coefficients. Finally, we will provide a few tips designed to help you become a more discerning consumer of research claims that emanate from studies wherein inferential statistics are applied to correlation coefficients.

Statistical Tests Involving a Single Correlation Coefficient

Later in this chapter, we will consider the situation in which data are analyzed to see if a significant difference exists between two or more correlation coefficients. Before doing that, however, we want to consider the simpler situation where the researcher has a single sample and a single correlation coefficient. Although simple in nature because only one sample is involved, the inferential techniques focused upon in the first part of this chapter are used far more frequently than the ones that involve comparisons between/among correlation coefficients.

THE INFERENTIAL PURPOSE

Figure 10.1 has been constructed to help clarify what researchers are trying to do when they apply an inferential test to a correlation coefficient. We have set up this picture to make it consistent with a hypothetical study involving Pearson's product-moment correlation. However, by changing the symbols that are included, we could make our picture relevant to a study wherein any other bivariate correlation coefficient is tested.

As Figure 10.1 shows, a correlation coefficient is computed on the basis of data collected from a sample. Although the sample-based value of the correlation coefficient is easy to obtain, the researcher's primary interest lies in the corresponding value of the correlation in the population from which the sample has been drawn. However, the researcher cannot compute the value of the correlation coefficient in the population because only the objects (or persons) in the sample can be measured. Accordingly, an inference (i.e., educated guess)

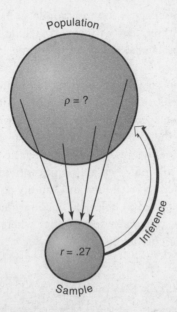

FIGURE 10.1   *The inferential purpose of a test on a correlation coefficient.*

about the parameter value of the correlation is made on the basis of the known value of the statistic.

The nature of the inference that extends from the sample to the population could take one of two forms depending upon whether the researcher wishes to use the techniques of estimation or to set up and evaluate a null hypothesis. Near the end of the chapter, we will examine the way confidence intervals are sometimes used to make inferences about correlation coefficients. We first turn our attention to the way researchers set up, evaluate, and report what happens to correlation null hypotheses.

THE NULL HYPOTHESIS

When researchers are concerned about the relationship between two variables in a single population but can collect data only from a sample taken from that population, they are likely to attack their inferential question by means of hypothesis testing, significance testing, or the hybrid approach to statistical testing. Regardless of which one of these three inferential strategies is used, a null hypothesis serves as the hub around which all other statistical elements revolve.

In dealing with a single correlation, the null hypothesis will simply be a pinpoint statement as to a possible value of the correlation in the population. Although researchers have the freedom to choose any value between -1.00 and $+1.00$ for inclusion in H_0, typical researchers will set up their correlational null hypothesis to say that there is, in the relevant population, a zero correlation between the two variables of interest. In Excerpt 10.1, we see an example where the notion of "no relationship" appeared in a stated null hypothesis.

Excerpt 10.1 The Notion of a Zero Correlation Stated in H_0

There is no relationship between level of rehabilitation counselor education and competitive closure rate of clients with severe disabilities.

Source: E. M. Szymanski. (1991). Relationship of level of rehabilitation counselor education to rehabilitation client outcome in the Wisconsin Division of Vocational Rehabilitation. *Rehabilitation Counseling Bulletin, 35*(1), p. 26.

In Excerpt 10.2, we see another example of a study in which the null hypothesis of a zero correlation is made explicit. In this study, there were really 10 null hypotheses, one for each of the possible correlations being considered. Ten correlations were involved because the single sample of third graders was measured on several variables, with 10 bivariate correlations used to evaluate the researchers' hunch that strong positive relationships existed in the population. In this study, note that the various correlation coefficients were not compared against each other; instead, each of the 10 was used in conjunction with a separate test in which H_0 was set up to say that the population correlation was zero.

Excerpt 10.2   Indication in Results That the H_0 Specified a Zero Correlation

---

We expected that all of the correlations would be fairly high. Although there are differences in students' knowledge from one topic to another, we assumed that their knowledge about any given topic would be fairly stable regardless of the test format. However, this was not the case. . . . At third grade, 4 of the 10 possible correlations with interview scores were significantly different from 0.

Source: S. W. Valencia, A. C. Stallman, M. Comeyras, P. D. Pearson, and D. K. Hartman. (1991). Four measures of topical knowledge: A study of construct validity. *Reading Research Quarterly, 26*(3), p. 221.

Because the correlational null hypothesis is usually set up to say that a zero correlation exists in the population, most researchers do not explicitly state the H_0 that is tested but rather take for granted that recipients of their research reports will know that the inferential conclusions refer to a null hypothesis of "no relationship." Consider, for example, Excerpts 10.3–10.5. In each case, the sample r presented in the report was compared against the null value of zero—even though the tested H_0 never appeared in the technical write-ups.

In light of the fact that very few researchers either state the null hypothesis when applying a test to a sample correlation coefficient or refer to H_0's pinpoint number when discussing their results, you frequently will be forced into the position of having to guess what a researcher's H_0 was. In these situations, a safe bet is that H_0 was a statement of "no relationship" in the population. If researchers set up a null hypothesis that specifies a population correlation different from zero, we are confident that they will specify H_0's pinpoint number.

Excerpt 10.3–10.5   Tests on r Without Explicit Statement That H_0 Said "No Relationship"

Correlation between the RADS and the Hamilton was .83 ($p < .001$), indicating a strong relationship between the two methods of assessing depression.

Source: N. F. Davis. (1990). The Reynolds Adolescent Depression Scale. *Measurement and Evaluation in Counseling and Development, 23*(2), p. 89.

(Continued)

Excerpt 10.3–10.5 Tests on *r* Without Explicit Statement That H_0 Said "No Relationship" *(Continued)*

As in previous studies, perceived leader power (measured as the summation of the power subscales) was significantly related to ratings of leader effectiveness (r 5 0.77, p , 0.001).

Source: B. R. Ragins. (1991). Gender effects in subordinate evaluations of leaders: Real or artifact? *Journal of Organizational Behavior, 12*(3), p. 263.

Negative affect was rated in each 10-sec epoch of the 3-min reunion episodes on a 5-point scale (0 = no overt distress; 1 = frown face; 2 = fuss/whine, which involves intermittent negative vocalization; 3 = cry, longer durations of negative vocalization; and 4 = scream, high-pitched vocalization). When these micro ratings of negative affect were summed within reunion episodes and correlated with the global resistance ratings made by independent attachment coders, the association between the two sets of measures proved to be marginally significant in Reunion I ($r = .39, p < .10$) and highly significant in the second reunion ($r = .68, p < .001$).

Source: J. Belsky and J. M. Braungart. (1991). Are insecure-avoidant infants with extensive day-care experience less stressed by and more independent in the Strange Situation? *Child Development, 62*(3), p.

THE CALCULATED VALUE, CRITICAL VALUE, AND SAMPLE SIZE

In conducting a statistical test on a single correlation coefficient, researchers usually compute a sample-based calculated value that is nothing more than a correlation coefficient. If you review Excerpts 10.3–10.5, you will see examples of this. Many researchers (when assessing a "no relationship" H_0) follow this procedure of letting the computed correlation serve as the calculated value because tables of critical values have been developed that contain, as entries, values of the correlation coefficient.

After researchers obtain the sample-based value of the correlation coefficient, all they must do is locate the proper tabled value of the critical correlation coefficient. If the sample value is equal to or greater than the critical value, H_0 will be rejected; otherwise, H_0 will not be rejected. For example, the two *r*s presented earlier in Excerpt 10.5 are the calculated values. Even though no critical values are specified in that excerpt, we can infer that (1) the critical value at the .05 level of significance was higher than .39 and (2) the critical value at the .001 level was lower than .68.

Normally, researchers do not include the critical value in their technical reports. On occasion, however, you will come across a report that includes the tabled value used by the researcher to determine whether or not the computed correlation coefficient was significant. An example of such situation is presented in Excerpt 10.6, where the abbreviation *cv* stands for critical value.

Excerpt 10.6   Specification of the Critical Value

A correlation of .78 (cv = .38, $p < .05$) among the native speaker evaluations of comprehensibility and the global ratings made by the principal investigator indicate that differences in raters should not seriously impact overall results.

Source: K. E. Schairer. (1992). Native speaker reaction to non-native speech. *The Modern Language Journal, 76*(3), p. 310.

Occasionally, researchers will use a *t*-test to evaluate the null hypothesis associated with their correlational study. When this is done, the data-based correlation coefficient is put into a *t*-formula that yields a calculated value referred to as *t*. To determine whether H_0 should be rejected, the researchers will then take the calculated *t* and compare it against the appropriate critical *t* located in a *t*-table. H_0 will be rejected if the computed *t* is equal to or larger than the critical value. Otherwise, a fail-to-reject decision will be made.

To see an example where a *t*-test was used within a correlational study, consider Excerpt 10.7. In this study, the data-based correlation coefficient of .33 was put into a formula that resulted in a calculated *t*-value of 0.99. The critical value is not provided in this study (as is typically the case), but it must have been larger than 0.99 since the null hypothesis—of a zero correlation in the population—was not rejected.

Excerpt 10.7   Using a *t*-Test to Evaluate a Correlation Coefficient

---

It is possible that nondecoders in the analogy condition were less apt to read transfer words by analogy and more apt to misread them as training words than decoders in the analogy condition because the former received more practice trials in learning to read the words ($M = 14.3$ vs. 9.3 trials to criterion by nondecoders and decoders, respectively). To check on this, the correlation coefficient was calculated between the number of misreadings produced by analogy decoders and the number of trials they took to reach criterion in reading the training words. Results revealed a slightly positive but nonsignificant correlation, $r = .33$, $t(18) = 0.99$, $p > .05$.

Source: L. C. Ehri and C. Robbins. (1992). Beginners need some decoding skill to read words by analogy. *Reading Research Quarterly, 27*(1), p. 20.

With respect to the use of a *t*-test to evaluate a correlation coefficient, two points are worth noting. First, the conclusion reached using the *t*-test will be identical to the decision about H_0 that would be made if the computed correlation coefficient serves as the calculated value (and is compared against a correlation-coefficient-type critical value). Thus, if the *t*-test used in Excerpt 10.7

had been bypassed, with the computed correlation of .33 compared against the appropriate critical value, the same decision would have been made to fail-to-reject the null hypothesis of a zero correlation in the population. Thus, the t-test applied in this situation is really an extra step that is not necessary.

Our second comment about the use of a t-test to evaluate a correlation coefficient concerns the nondecimal number that typically is reported next to the letter t. In Excerpt 10.7, this number is 18. This reported value signifies the "degrees of freedom" associated with the t-test, and it is equal to the sample size less 2 (i.e., $n - 2$). It is a useful number, because we can quickly determine the sample size from which the correlation coefficient was computed by adding 2 to the t-test's degrees of freedom. Hence, Excerpt 10.7 reveals that there were 20 analogy decoders.

Later in this chapter, we will return to the issue of sample size as it affects tests of correlational null hypotheses. For now, all we want to do is indicate that it is helpful to know the size of the sample when inferences are made concerning a correlation coefficient. When the t-test is not used, however, a researcher can still give us information about the sample size. As exemplified in Excerpt 10.8, the disclosure of the number of subjects doesn't take up very much room in the research report!

Excerpt 10.8   Indication of the Sample Size

The perceived relative importance of Behavior 15 (employees verbally complimenting bowlers) was most strongly correlated with bowling average ($r = .251$, $n = 82$, $p = 0.011$).

Source: C. L. Martin. (1990). An empirical investigation of employee behaviors and customer perceptions. *Journal of Sport Management, 4*(1), p. 10.

Before turning to a consideration of statistical tests on specific kinds of correlations, we should point out that you may come across studies in which the researchers put their correlation coefficient into a formula that produced a calculated value called something other than t. For example, Excerpt 10.9 shows a case wherein the researcher used a z-test to assess the study's null hypothesis. If you encounter such a result, there are only two things you need keep in mind. First, the number provided between the correlation coefficient and the p-value (e.g., 4.08 in Excerpt 10.9) is the test's calculated value. Second, the most important numbers will be those on the left and right sides of the calculated value (e.g., $r = .76$ and $p < .001$ in Excerpt 10.9).[1]

---

[1] *With z-tests, no degrees-of-freedom number will ever be presented next to the symbol z. This is because the concept of degrees of freedom, while tied to other tests (such as t, F, and χ^2), is fully unconnected to z-tests.*

Excerpt 10.9   Use of a z-Test to Evaluate a Correlation Coefficient

A second [correlation] was calculated to determine the extent to which male and female exercise addicts agreed on their reasons for exercising. This relationship was statistically significant ($r = .76, z = 4.08, p < .001$). Thus, male and female addicts tended to reflect highly similar rationale for their exercise habits.

Source: M. H. Anshel. (1991). A psycho-behavioral analysis of addicted versus non-addicted male and female exercisers. *Journal of Sport Behavior, 14*(2), p. 152.

TESTS ON SPECIFIC KINDS OF CORRELATION

Up until this point, we have been discussing tests of correlation coefficients in the generic sense. However, there is no such thing as a generic correlation. When correlating two sets of data, a specific correlational procedure must be used, with the choice usually being influenced by the nature of variables and/or the level of measurement of the researcher's instruments. As you will recall from Chapter 3, there are many different kinds of bivariate correlations: Pearson's, Spearman's, biserial, point biserial, phi, tetrachoric, and so on.

With any of the various correlation procedures, a researcher can apply the hypothesis testing procedure, significance testing, or the hybrid approach to testing H_0. Excerpts 10.10–10.13 present examples illustrating that many of the bivariate correlation coefficients are subjected to inferential testing.

In reading research reports, you are likely to encounter studies in which p-values are associated with rs, with no specification as to which kind of correlation was computed. In such situations, you are likely to be correct if you make a guess that the unnamed r is a Pearson's product-moment correlation coefficient. Because Pearson's r is so popular, researchers often forget to clarify that they used this specific technique for estimating the nature and strength of the relationship between their variables. If they use a correlational technique other than Pearson's, however, they are highly likely to specify the kind of correlation used (e.g., Spearman's rho, point biserial, etc.).

Excerpts 10.10–10.13   Tests on Specific Kinds of Correlation

Completed WAI-S forms were obtained from both members of 91 of the 103 dyads, an 88% return rate. . . . The Pearson product-moment correlation between client and counselor WAI-S total scale ratings was significant, $r(89) = .34$, $p < .01$.

Source: G. S. Tyron and A. S. Kane. (1993). Relationship of working alliance to mutual and unilateral termination. *Journal of Counseling Psychology, 40*(1), p. 35.

(Continued)

Excerpts 10.10–10.13 Tests on Specific Kinds of Correlation
(Continued)

Table 2 [not shown] provides a comparison of the ranks of program characteristics byparticipants and experts. A significant, positive correlation of moderate strength ($r_s = .55, p < .01$) was found.

Source: J. P. Witman. (1993). Characteristics of adventure programs valued by adolescents in treatment. *Therapeutic Recreation Journal, 27*(1), p. 47.

Two forms of analysis were performed. The first was the simple point biserial correlation between scores on the RIASEC themes (Holland, 1973, 1985) and choice of a Scientific or Technological college or university program versus some other choice (Elsworth et al. 1987). . . . The correlation between the Investigative theme score and Scientific/Technological choices is $r = .46$ ($p < .001$) and is consistent with the hypothesized relation.

Source: F. D. Naylor and G. J. Kidd. (1991). The predictive validity of the investigative scale of the Career Assessment Inventory. *Educational and Psychological Measurement, 51*(1), p. 221.

Calculation of pairwise intertask correlations for individual subjects (ø coefficients) did not reveal a significant effect of age group on the magnitude of the correlations.

Source: S. C. Levine, N. C. Jordan and J. Huttenlocher. (1992). Development of calculation abilities in young children. *The Journal of Experimental Child Psychology, 53*(1), p. 82.

TESTS ON MANY CORRELATION COEFFICIENTS (EACH OF WHICH IS TREATED SEPARATELY)

In most of the excerpts presented so far in this chapter, inferential interest was focused upon a single correlation coefficient. Although some researchers set up only one correlational null hypothesis (because each of their studies involves only one correlation coefficient), most researchers have two or more correlations that are inferentially tested in the same study. Our objective now is to consider the various ways in which such researchers present their results, to clarify the fact that a separate H_0 is associated with each correlation coefficient that is computed, and to consider the way in which the Bonferroni adjustment technique can help the researcher avoid the problem of an inflated Type I error risk.

TESTS ON THE ENTRIES OF A CORRELATION MATRIX

As we saw in Chapter 3, a **correlation matrix** is an efficient way to present the results of a correlational study in which there are three or more variables and a correlation coefficient is computed between each possible pair of variables.[2] Typically, each of the entries within the correlation matrix will be subjected to an inferential test. In Excerpt 10.14, we see an illustration of this situation.

In Excerpt 10.14, the correlation matrix presents the 28 bivariate correlations that were computed among the eight variables. Each of the resulting *r*s was subjected to a separate statistical test. And in each case, the null hypothesis was a "no relationship" statement about the population associated with the

---

Excerpt 10.14   Tests of the Elements in a Correlation Matrix

I examined the relationship between grades and scores on course examinations and class attendance using scores on four examinations and attendance from the beginning of the course until the first examination as well as attendance between subsequent examinations. Table 1 contains the correlations among these variables and shows that the intercorrelations among the four examinations were all significant, as were five of the six intercorrelations for the attendance data. Students displayed stability both on the examinations and in their attendance behavior throughout the semester. Intercorrelations among attendance during the four quarters of the course increased toward the later part of the semester.

Table 1

Correlation Matrix for Part 4

Variable	2	3	4	5	6	7	8
1. Exam 1	.45**	.48**	.46**	.05	.00	.08	-.08
2. Exam 2		.46**	.43**	.12	.02	.17	.02
3. Exam 3			.29**	.05	.09	.23*	.11
4. Exam 4				00	.01	.21*	.10
5. Attendance—1st quarter					.33**	.25**	.13
6. Attendance—2nd quarter						.64**	.50**
7. Attendance—3rd quarter							.62**
8. Attendance—4th quarter							

*p < .05.   **p < .01.

Source: M. Van Blerkom. (1992). Class attendance in undergraduate courses. *Journal of Psychology,* 126(5), p. 491.

---

[2] *Whenever a correlation coefficient is computed, it is really not the variables per se that are being correlated. Rather, it is the measurements of one variable that are correlated with the measurements of the other variable. This distinction is not a trivial one, because it is possible for a low correlation coefficient to grossly underestimate a strong relationship that truly exists between the two variables of interest. Poor measuring instruments could create this anomaly.*

single sample of subjects used in the investigation. If the unnamed correlation coefficients are Pearson's rs, as we think is the case, then each of the 28 null hypotheses could be written as H_0: $\rho = 0.00$. There would be 28 null hypotheses rather than just one because each of the rs that was tested involved a different pair of variables.

Tests on Correlation Coefficients in a Table That Is Not a Correlation Matrix

At times, researchers will summarize the results of their correlational studies by means of a table that is not a true correlation matrix. Consider, for example, Excerpts 10.15 and 10.16. The first of these tables is not a correlation matrix because the variables listed on the left are not the same as those used to label the columns. The second table of correlation results is clearly not a true correlation matrix, because it doesn't come close to having a square format or having the same number of variables listed on the side and on the top of the table.

What is important, of course, is not the label you attach to the tables in Excerpts 10.15 and 10.16 but rather your ability to understand what was done in each investigation and what results were obtained. In each of these studies, a single group of subjects was measured on multiple variables, with correlations then computed between those pairs of variables that were of particular

---

Excerpts 10.15–10.16   Tests on Correlations in a Table That Is Not a Correlation Matrix

Table 3

Correlations Among Predictors

Maternal factors	Child factors 1	2	3
1. Task orientation	.78***	−.06	.67***
2. Autonomy/reliance	.62**	−.07	.65***
3. Positive emotions	.52**	−.40**	.53**

**p < .01.
***p < .001.

Source: S. A. Denham, S. M. Renwick, and R. W. Holt. (1991). Working and playing together: Prediction of preschool social-emotional competence from mother-child interactions. *Child Development*, 62(2), p. 246.

(Continued)

Excerpts 10.15–10.16   Tests on Correlations in a Table That Is Not a Correlation Matrix (*Continued*)

Table 4 lists the correlations between the credibility ratings and the scores from the EPI. Higher neuroticism scores were significantly correlated with higher credibility ratings for self-control, cognitive, relaxation, and psychodynamic therapies. Extroversion scores were negatively correlated with credibility ratings of cognitive therapy and positively associated with activity-change therapy.

Table 4

Correlations Between Personality Measures and Credibility Ratings for Each Therapy Rationale

	EPI	
Therapy	*Neuroticism*	*Extroversion*
Interpersonal	.10	.16
Communication	−.02	−.10
Self-control	.26*	−.11
Cognitive	.24*	−.20*
Social skills	.03	.03
Relaxation	.24*	.12
Psychodynamic	.28*	.01
Activity-change	.04	.26*
Biological/drug	−.06	.01

Note. $n = 84$ for all correlations. EPI = Eysenck Personality Inventory. Therapies are arranged in order of credibility from most credible to least.
*$p < .05$.

Source: P. D. Rokke, A. S. Carter, L. P. Rehm, and L. G. Veltum. (1990). Comparative credibility of current treatments for depression. *Psychotherapy*, 27(2), p. 240.

interest to the researchers. In Excerpt 10.15, the researchers evidently were interested in the relationship between each "maternal factor" and each "child factor" (but not in the relationships among the factors within each grouping); similarly, the researchers who conducted the study from which Excerpt 10.16 was taken apparently had an interest in the relationship between the each of the nine credibility ratings and each of the two EPI personality measures (but not in the relationships among the nine credibility ratings).

The commonality between the tables in Excerpts 10.15 and 10.16 is that each of the computed correlation coefficients was dealt with inferentially, with a null hypothesis (of "no relationship" in the population) being rejected or not rejected for each pair of measures that was correlated. Note that the correlation coefficients close to zero turned out to be nonsignificant whereas those far away from zero allowed H_0 to be rejected. Also note in Excerpt 10.15 that the three highest correlations (.78, .67, and .65) were significant at $p < .001$ whereas the four next-highest correlations (.62, .53, .52, and $-.40$) were significant at $p < .01$.

TESTS ON SEVERAL CORRELATION COEFFICIENTS REPORTED IN THE TEXT

Research write-ups often present the results of tests on many correlation coefficients in the text of the article rather than in a table. Excerpts 10.17 and 10.18 illustrate this approach to revealing how the outcome of inferential tests on several correlation coefficients can be summarized.

Excerpts 10.17–10.18   Multiple Tests on Correlation Coefficients Reported in the Text

---

Since significant effects of sex were anticipated, separate Pearson correlations were derived for males and females. No significant correlations between EFT and COS measures were found in the female sample. In the male group, significant negative correlations were found between EFT latencies and the COS total score, $r(20) = -.45, p < .05$, and between EFT errors and COS "mean differentiation" (summed score), $r(20) = -.49, p < .05$. A negative correlational trend was also found between EFT latencies and COS "mean differentiation" (summed score), $r(20) = -.40, p < .10$; sex, $r(20) = -.38, p < .10$; and identity, $r(20) = -.39, p < .10$.

Source: J. Krieger and M. Reznikoff. (1992). Cognitive and projective measures of differentiation and their relationship to empathy. *Journal of Research in Personality, 26*(4), p. 328.

All respondents reported some use of drugs. Spearman rank-order correlations showed a significant negative correlation between self-esteem and drug use ($r = -.31, p < 0.05$), a significant positive correlation between trait anxiety and drug use ($r = .39, p < 0.05$), and a significant negative correlation between self-esteem and trait anxiety ($r = -.69, p < 0.01$).

Source: D. N. Taylor and J. D. Pilar. (1992). Self-esteem, anxiety, and drug use. *Psychological Reports, 71*(3), p. 897.

Normally, the results of tests on correlation coefficients will be put into a table when several correlations have been computed, while the results will usually be put into the text when only a small number of correlations have been tested. However, the final choice is a matter of author and journal editor preference. Take another look at the results in Excerpt 10.18 and notice that we are provided information concerning what happened when all possible bivariate correlations among three variables were computed and tested. The results could have been put into a correlation matrix such as this:

	(1)	*(2)*	*(3)*
Self-esteem (1)	—	−.69**	−.31*
Trait Anxiety (2)		—	.39*
Drug Use (3)			—

*p <.05.   **p <.01.

As readers of the research literature, we prefer to have the results of a multivariable correlational study presented in a correlation matrix or in some other form of table. We find it easier to "see" how the results turned out when the outcome is summarized in a chart rather than simply reported in the text of the technical write-up. If you agree with us, remember that you can always create your own correlation matrix or table in the event that the results are presented as in Excerpts 10.17 and 10.18.

THE BONFERRONI ADJUSTMENT TECHNIQUE

In Chapter 8, we explained why researchers will sometimes use the **Bonferroni technique** to adjust their level of significance. As you will recall, the purpose of doing this is to hold down the chances of a Type I error when multiple tests are conducted. We also hope that you remember the simple mechanics of the Bonferroni technique: Simply divide the desired study-wide Type I error risk by the number of tests being conducted.

In Excerpt 10.19, we see an example where the Bonferroni technique was applied within a study that relied heavily on a series of correlation coeffi-

---

Excerpt 10.19   Use of the Bonferroni Technique with Correlation
Coefficients

Two different statistical techniques were used to analyze the data. First, Pearson correlation coefficients were computed and a complete intercorrelation matrix was constructed for all possible pairwise combinations of measures. Tests of nonzero correlation were conducted using Bonferroni's correction (Dunn, 1961) to maintain an experiment-wise error rate at the .05 level across all 15 comparisons. With this adjustment the hypothesis-wise error rate for each correlation was estimated to be .003.

Source: R. Ittenback and P. L. Harrison. (1990). Predicting ego-strength from problem-solving ability of college students. *Measurement and Evaluation in Counseling and Development, 23*(3), p. 131.

cients to answer the research questions. Because 15 correlations were computed, the researcher divided .05 by 15 in order to determine the alpha level criterion for use in assessing each individual correlation coefficient.

In Excerpt 10.20, we see another example where a researcher was sensitive to the "inflated Type I error rate problem" within a large correlational study. Here, the researcher used a modification of the normal Bonferroni technique to control for false rejections of the no-relationship null hypotheses. The adjustment strategy used by this researcher is called the **Holms procedure**, and its basic operation is outlined within the excerpt.

Excerpt 10.20 The Holms Procedure (a Modified Bonferroni Adjustment Strategy)

The large number of correlations ($n = 588$ for each gender) necessitated the use of a family-wise error control procedure to prevent excessive Type I errors. The Holms procedure, a modification of a simple Bonferroni procedure, was used, and it guarantees a 95% probability of *no* Type I errors in each of the two correlation matrices (see Holland & Copenhaver, 1988). This procedure requires a varying cutoff for significance for each single correlation, depending on the rank of the correlation's absolute magnitude. A significance level of $p < .000085$ (.05/588) was required for the largest correlation in the matrix, and the required level of significance declined, as did the rank of the correlation, until a significance level of $p < .05$ was required for the smallest correlation in the matrix.

Source: R. B. Basham. (1992). Clinical utility of the MMPI research scales in the assessment of adolescent acting out behaviors. *Psychological Assessment, 4*(4), p. 486.

When you come across the report of a study that presents the results of inferential tests applied to several correlation coefficients, try to remember that the conclusions drawn can be radically different depending upon whether or not some form of Bonferroni adjustment technique is used. For example, consider once again Excerpt 10.16. In that excerpt, we see that 18 correlations were tested for significance, with six of the sample *r*s being far enough away from zero to allow the underlying null hypotheses to be rejected at the .05 level. If the Bonferroni technique had been applied, the adjusted level of significance would have become equal to .0028 (i.e., .05/18), and none of the computed *r*s would have been significant!

TESTS ON RELIABILITY AND VALIDITY COEFFICIENTS

As indicated in Chapter 4, many of the techniques for estimating reliability and validity rely totally or partially on one or more correlation coefficients. After computing these indices of instrument quality, researchers often apply a statistical test to determine whether or not their reliability and validity coefficients are significant. Illustrations of such tests, when applied to various reliability coefficients, are contained in Excerpts 10.21–10.24.

Excerpts 10.21–10.24   Tests of Reliability Coefficients

Test-retest reliability was calculated over a 3-week period using a subsample of 23 subjects in a separate mailing. Correlation coefficients were as follows: .86, .81, and .92, for the CSA-V, CSA-P, and CSB, respectively; and .87, .93, .93, .92, and .86 for the emotional, socializing, practical assistance, financial assistance, and advice/guidance subscales of the CSB, respectively. All correlations were significant at the .001 level.

Source: G. L. Caruso. (1992). The development of three scales to measure the supportiveness of relationships between parents and child care providers. *Educational and Psychological Measurement, 52*(1), p. 156.

Cronbach's alpha coefficients for the four scales, in the present sample, ranged from .72 (Too Nonassertive) to .85 (Too Cold). In the present sample, the Too Dominant and the Too Nonassertive scale also was significantly correlated with the Too Nurturant scale ($r = .50$) and with the Too Cold scale ($r = .48$). The correlations among the Too Dominant, Too Cold, and Too Nurturant scales were all small ($rs < .09$) and nonsignificant.

Source: D. M. Kivlighan Jr. and E. O. Angelone. (1992). Interpersonal problems: Variables influencing participants' perception of group climate. *Journal of Counseling Psychology, 39*(4), p. 469.

Before the experiment began, a measure of interrater consistency among the four judges was computed using the Kendall coefficient of concordance—W (Siegal, 1956). The four judges rated all 40 players on the quality of their attacks on the topspun and underspun balls. The results indicated their judgments were significantly related to one another ($W = .62$, $df = 39$, $p < .001$ on ratings of attacks to topspun balls, and $W = .63$, $df = 39$, $p < .001$ on ratings of attacks to underspun balls).

Source: L. Zhang, Q. Ma, T. Orlick, and L. Zitzelsberger. (1992). The effect of mental-imagery training on performance enhancement with 7–10-year-old children. *The Sport Psychologist, 63*(3), p. 234.

After both judges had rated the 10 training tapes, they independently rated an additional 5 hour-long audiotapes of group interaction to provide data for determining interjudge agreement. Agreement in identifying discrete PIUs, computed using coefficient kappa (Cohen, 1960), was .74 ($z = 18.50$, $p < .001$).

Source: F. A. Robinson and D. A. Hardt. (1992). Effects of cognitive and behavioral structure and discussion of corrective feedback outcomes on counseling group development. *Journal of Counseling Psychology, 39*(4), p. 476.

In Excerpt 10.25, we see an example of several correlations being tested in an effort to establish the validity of a psychological inventory called the Therapeutic Reactance Scale (TRS). As indicated in the second paragraph of

---

Excerpt 10.25   Tests of Validity Coefficients

If the TRS is a valid measure of a discrete psychological construct, it should not correlate highly with measures of other constructs. Morgan (1986) correlated scores on the TRS with scores on the Counselor Rating Form-Short (CRF), a measure of counselor social influence. Theoretically, no significant relationship would be expected between these two constructs. This hypothesis was supported, in that no significant correlations were found between the Expertness and Trustworthiness subscales of the CRF and the Total scale and Verbal and Behavioral Reactance subscales of the TRS. . . .

Further evidence for divergent validity was reported by Lukin et al. (1985), who found nonsignificant correlations of the TRS total score with the State (.11) and Trait (.06) scales of the State-Trait Anxiety Inventory (Spielberger, Gorsuch, & Lurshene, 1970) and a nonsignificant .11 correlation with the Beck Depression Inventory (Beck, 1967). Thus, the TRS does seem to measure a construct other than anxiety, depression, or counselor social influence.

Source: E. T. Dowd, C. R. Milne, and S. L. Wise. (1991). The Therapeutic Reaction Scale: A measure of psychological reactance. *Journal of Counseling and Development, 69*(6), p. 543.

---

this excerpt, the tests on the correlations reported here were applied to assess the TRS's divergent validity.

Although researchers should be commended for evaluating their correlation-based estimates of reliability and validity with statistical tests, such tests provide helpful information only if the null hypothesis is set up in a sensible manner. As exemplified by Excerpts 10.21–10.25, the tests applied to reliability and validity coefficients usually have a null hypothesis of "no relationship." At times, as in Excerpt 10.25, this kind of H_0 fits a study's purpose. When researchers statistically test reliability coefficients, however, we question whether much is gained simply by saying that a test-retest correlation (or any other kind of reliability coefficient) is significantly different from zero. We say this because it is possible for a researcher to have a very low reliability coefficient turn out to be significant, so long as the sample size is large enough. For this reason, we strongly recommend that you pay close attention to the actual values of the reliability and validity coefficients reported by researchers instead of simply the *p*-based results of any statistical test applied to such coefficients.

STATISTICALLY COMPARING TWO CORRELATION COEFFICIENTS

At times, researchers will have two correlation coefficients that they wish to compare. The purpose of such a comparison is to determine whether a significant difference exists between the two *r*s, with the null hypothesis being a statement of no difference between the two correlations in the population(s) associated with the study. For such tests, a "no difference" H_0 is fully appropriate.

Figure 10.2 is designed to help you distinguish between two similar but different situations where a pair of correlation coefficients is compared. In Figure 10.2(a), we see that a sample is drawn from each of two populations, with a bivariate correlation coefficient computed, in each sample, between the same pair of variables. In our picture, we have labeled these variables as X and Y; the two variables might be height and weight, running speed and swimming speed, or any other pair of variables. The null hypothesis is that correlation between X and Y has the same value in each of the two populations. Notice that the single inference here is based upon both groups of sample data and is directed toward the *set* of populations associated with the study.

In Figure 10.2(b), we see that a single sample is drawn from one population, but two correlation coefficients are computed on the basis of the sample data. One correlation addresses the relationship between variables X and Y while the other correlation is concerned with the relationship between variables P and Q. The null hypothesis in this kind of study is that the parameter value of the correlation between X and Y is equal to the parameter value of the correlation between P and Q. Based upon the sample's pair of correlation coefficients, a single inference is directed toward the unknown values of the pair of correlations in the population.

In Excerpts 10.26 and 10.27, we see two examples where a test between two correlations was applied. These two studies illustrate the two situations depicted in Figure 10.2. Note that a z-test was used to compare the two correlations in the first of these excerpts whereas a t-test was used in the second excerpt. The choice between these two tests was related to the sample sizes involved in the two studies. In the K-BIT/WISC-R study, there was a relatively small sample ($n = 35$); in contrast, the IHSSRLE/PSS study involved a fairly large sample ($n = 176$). However, the t- and the z-tests have the same basic objective: to determine whether the difference between the two sample correlation coefficients is greater than would be expected if H_0 is true.

Before leaving Excerpt 10.27, a final comment about the number in parentheses is in order. Earlier in this chapter, we pointed out that the non-decimal number next to the letter t, in t-tests applied to a single correlation coefficient, is equal to $n - 2$. When a t-test is used to compare two correlation coefficients, however, the researcher computes the degrees of freedom as $n - 3$. Accordingly, you must be careful when trying to figure out the size of the sample based upon the t-test's degrees of freedom. If the t-test is focused on a single correlation, add 2 to the degrees of freedom to know the size of n; on the other hand, if the t-test is focused on a comparison of two correlations, add 3 to the degrees of freedom to figure out the sample size.

$H_0: \rho_{XY(1)} = \rho_{XY(2)}$

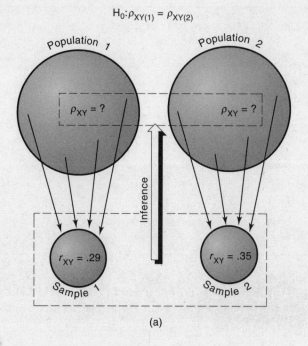

(a)

$H_0: \rho_{XY} = \rho_{PQ}$

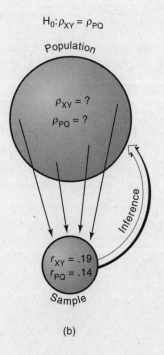

(b)

FIGURE 10.2 *Two kinds of inferential situations involving two correlations.*

Excerpts 10.26–10.27   Statistical Comparison of Two Correlation Coefficients

The correlations of the IHSSRLE against the PSS were .58, $p < .01$, for males and .69, $p < .01$, for females. The difference between correlations was non-significant, $z = -1.03$.

Source: P. M. Kohn and J. A. Milrose. (1993). The inventory of high school students' recent experiences: A decontaminated measure of adolescents' hassles. *Journal of Youth and Adolescence, 22*(1), p. 47.

The K-BIT Vocabulary subtest correlated significantly higher with the WISC-R Verbal IQ score [$r = .83$] than with the WISC-R Performance IQ score [$r = .58$], $t(32) = 4.92$, $p < .01$.

Source: P. N. Prewett. (1992). The relationship between the Kauffman Brief Intelligence Test (K-BIT) and the WISC-R with referred students. *Psychology in the Schools, 29*(1), p. 27.

THE USE OF CONFIDENCE INTERVALS AROUND CORRELATION COEFFICIENTS

When researchers subject a data-based correlation coefficient to an inferential statistical procedure, they will probably do so by applying the hypothesis testing procedure, significance testing, or the hybrid approach to dealing with H_0. All of the excerpts presented so far in this chapter have been taken from studies where one or more of these testing strategies were used. It is possible, however, for a researcher to deal inferentially with a correlation coefficient simply by placing a confidence interval around the sample value of r. Oddly, few researchers do this.

As we indicated previously, confidence intervals can be used *within* the context of hypothesis testing or the hybrid approach to testing any H_0. In applying inferential tests to correlation coefficients, most researchers do not place confidence intervals around their sample values of r, but a few do. We see an illustration of this use of confidence intervals in Excerpt 10.28.

Excerpt 10.28   Use of a Confidence Interval to Test a Correlational H_0

Correlational analyses were used to compare the exposure diary data with global estimates from the exposure questionnaire across locations (home, work, other). The correlation was strongest between global and diary estimates of exposure at home, $r(185) = .62$, $P \le .001$ (95% CI $= .58–87$), but all correlations (work, $r = .40$; other, $r = .29$; overall, $r = .44$) were significant at $P \le .01$.

Source: K. M. Emmons, D. B. Abrams, R. J. Marshall, R. A. Etzel, T. E. Novotny, B. H. Marcus and M. E. Kane. (1992). Exposure to environmental tobacco smoke in naturalistic settings. *American Journal of Public Health, 82*, p. 26.

In Excerpt 10.28, note that the 95% confidence interval extends from .58 to .87. Since this interval does not overlap with zero, the pinpoint number in H_0 for a test of "no relationship," the researcher can claim that the sample correlation coefficient of .62 is significant at the .05 level. Also note that the researcher reports $p \leq .001$. The fact that this p-value is something other than .05 indicates that this researcher was using the hybrid approach to testing the correlational null hypotheses.

CAUTIONS

We feel obligated to end this chapter by suggesting a few cautions that you should keep in mind when trying to decipher (and critique) research reports based on correlation coefficients. As you will see, our comments here constitute a reiteration of some of the points we discussed at the end of Chapter 3 as well as some of the points offered at the conclusions of Chapters 7, 8, and 9.

STRENGTH OF EFFECT (r^2)

Many researchers seem to get carried away with the p-levels associated with their correlation coefficients and thus seem to forget that the estimated strength of a relationship is best assessed by squaring the sample value of r. Discovering that a correlation coefficient is "significant" may not really be very important—even if the results indicate $p < .01$ or $p < .001$—unless the value of r^2 is reasonably high. The result may be significant in a statistical sense (thus indicating that the sample data are not likely to have come from a population characterized by H_0), but it may be quite insignificant in a practical sense.

In Excerpts 10.29 and 10.30, we see two examples where researchers did, in fact, pay attention to the estimated strength of effect associated with their correlational studies. Unfortunately, many researchers do *not* follow the good example set by the investigators who conducted these studies.

Excerpts 10.29–10.30   Correlation Coefficients That Were Significant Statistically But Not Very Significant in a Practical Sense

---

A Pearson correlation was computed between loneliness scores and sociometric acceptance scores for the entire sample. The correlation was significant, but very low, $r(352) = -.14$, $p < .01$, indicating that factors other than sociometric status account for a large proportion of the variance in loneliness.

Source: L. C. Quay. (1992). Personal and family effects on loneliness. *Journal of Applied Developmental Psychology, 13*(1), p. 103.

(Continued)

Excerpts 10.29–10.30   Correlation Coefficients That Were Significant Statistically But Not Very Significant in a Practical Sense *(Continued)*

Self-ratings of family skills were significantly correlated with the perceived value of family roles, $r = .395$, $p < .0001$, although the shared variance accounted for was only 15.6%.

Source: D. B. Bailey, S. A. Palsha, and R. J. Simeonsson. (1991). Professional skills, concerns, and perceived importance of work with families in early intervention. *Exceptional Children, 58*, p. 160.

POWER, EFFECT SIZE, AND *r*

In Chapter 8, we pointed out how researchers can apply a nine-step version of the hypothesis testing procedure by (1) specifying the desired Type II error risk (i.e., the complement of power) and the effect size and (2) determining the sample size required to make the statistical test function with known properties. In Chapter 9, we indicated how the hybrid approach to testing an H_0 can also incorporate these concerns for power and *n* prior to the collection of any data. When a researcher's study is focused on one or more correlation coefficients, it is quite easy to add these extra steps to the basic six-step version of hypothesis testing presented in Chapter 7.

Unfortunately, most researchers do not seem to consider the issues of power and effect size prior to the collection of data. It seems as if they simply set up their null hypotheses, collect as much data as time and money permit, and then apply the six-step version of hypothesis testing (or the seven-step version of the hybrid approach to testing null hypotheses). Those who do this run the risk of encountering one of two problems. A correlation coefficient can turn out to be statistically significant even though it (and especially its squared value) is close to zero. Or a correlation coefficient can appear to be far away from H_0's pinpoint number but end up being nonsignificant due to a statistical test of inadequate power.

When you come across a study in which the appropriate sample size was determined prior to the collection of any data, give the researcher some "bonus points" for taking the time to set up the study with sensitivity to both Type I *and* Type II errors. When you come across a study in which the power associated with the test(s) conducted on the correlation coefficient(s) is computed in a post hoc sense, give the researcher only a few "bonus points." And when you come across a study in which there is no mention whatsoever of statistical power, award *yourself* some "bonus points" for detecting a study that could have been conducted better than it was.

In Excerpt 10.31, we see a case in which a set of researchers did, in fact, demonstrate sensitivity to the issue of statistical power. Although these researchers had to "live with" the sample sizes produced by their recruitment effort, they combined samples and computed statistical power estimates. They are to be commended for thinking about an aspect of their study that is typically neglected by researchers who conduct similar investigations.

Excerpt 10.31   A Power Analysis Within a Correlational Study

Because of unexpected recruitment difficulties experienced by the HEP program during the period permitted for the research, the sample sizes were lower than planned. In addition, female enrollments in the HEP program are typically limited because of cultural factors and the residential nature of the program. To obtain the larger sample sizes needed for the tests of most hypotheses, we combined data from the English and Spanish versions of each instrument. . . . We computed statistical power estimates for each hypothesis to determine whether our sample sizes were sufficient to attain statistical significance for moderate-size correlations. . . . Statistical power estimates for most of the hypotheses were very acceptable (i.e., estimates of generally .75 to .95 for an alpha of .05 and moderate effect sizes of .30) but were more marginal for Hypothesis 2 (.52 to .77 for an alpha of .05 and a moderate effect size of .35; Cohen, 1988).

Source: A. T. Church, J. S. Teresa, R. Rosebrook, and D. Szendre. (1992). Self-efficacy for careers and occupational consideration in minority high school equivalency students. *Journal of Counseling Psychology, 39*(4), p. 500.

LINEARITY AND HOMOSCEDASTICITY

Tests on Pearson's *r* are conducted more frequently than tests on any other kind of correlation coefficient. Whenever tests on Pearson's *r* are conducted, two important assumptions about the population must hold true in order for the test to function as it is designed. One of these important "prerequisite" conditions is referred to as the linearity assumption. The other is referred to as the equal variance assumption (or, alternatively, as the assumption of homoscedasticity).

The assumption of **linearity** states that the relationship in the population between the two variables of interest must be such that the bivariate means fall on a straight line. The assumption of **homoscedasticity** states that (1) the variance of the Y variable around μ_y is the same regardless of the value of X being considered and (2) the variance of the X variable around μ_x is constant regardless of the value of Y being considered. If a population is characterized by a curvilinear relationship between X and Y and/or characterized by heteroscedasticity, the inferential test on Pearson's *r* will provide misleading information concerning the existence and strength of the relationship in the population.

The easiest way for a researcher to check on these two assumptions is to look at a scatter diagram of the sample data. If the data in the sample appear to conform to the linearity and equal variance assumptions, then the researcher can make an informed guess that linearity and homoscedasticity are also characteristics of the population. In that situation, the test on r can then be performed. If a plot of the data suggests, however, that either of the assumptions is untenable, then the regular test on r should be bypassed in favor of one designed for curvilinear or unequal variance conditions.

As readers of the research literature, our preference is to be able to look at scatter diagrams so we can judge for ourselves whether researchers' data sets appear to meet the assumptions that underlie tests on r. Because of space limitations, however, technical journals rarely permit such visual displays of the data to be included. If scatter diagrams cannot be shown, then it is our feeling that researchers should communicate in words what *they* saw when they looked at their scatter diagrams. In Excerpt 10.32, we see an illustration of how this can be done in a very short sentence.

Excerpt 10.32   Looking at a Scatter Diagram in Addition to Testing r

Results revealed a slightly positive but nonsignificant correlation, $r = .33$, $t(18) = 0.99$, $p > .05$. Inspection of individual scores also revealed little relationship.

Source: L. C. Ehri and C. Robbins. (1992). Beginners need some decoding skill to read words by analogy. *Reading Research Quarterly*, 27(1), p. 20.

Note that the test on r in Excerpt 10.32 resulted in a decision to not reject H_0: $[\rho] = 0.00$. The researcher looked at a scatter diagram and verified that little relationship existed in the data. If the data had been curvilinear in nature, however, a strong relationship could have existed even though the outcome of the statistical test did not permit the researcher to reject the null hypothesis. By inspecting the data, the researcher is telling us that there was *not* a strong curvilinear relationship between the two variables being correlated.

Too many researchers, we feel, move too quickly from collecting their data, to testing their rs, to drawing conclusions based upon the results of their tests. Few take the time to look at a scatter diagram as a safety maneuver to avoid misinterpretations caused by curvilinearity and/or heteroscedasticity. We applaud the small number of researchers who take the time to perform this extra step.

FAILURE TO APPLY A STATISTICAL TEST

If a study is conducted solely to describe the subjects who provide the data, no inferential statistics ought to be applied. That situation, however, is quite rare. In the vast majority of studies, the data are looked upon as having come from one or more samples, with the researcher interested in making statements about the population(s) that corresponds to the sample(s).

When correlational data are considered to have come from samples, inferential techniques ought to be applied. Researchers can choose from an array of inferential strategies (see Chapters 7–9), but they ought to set up some form of test and/or construct confidence intervals around the sample values of computed correlation coefficients. Unfortunately, inferential procedures are not applied as frequently as they should be. A representative case is illustrated in Excerpt 10.33.

Excerpt 10.33   Failure to Apply Inferential Procedures to Correlational Data

---

Measures obtained on each behavioral task included the number of atraditional behaviors engaged in and the time spent in each. These correlated at $r = .66$ ($p < .001$). The stability of each measure was assessed by readministering the behavioral tasks to one group of 40 subjects 8 weeks later. The number of atraditional behaviors showed a test-retest correlation of .76 ($p < .001$), whereas the comparable figure for the time measure was $r = .42$ ($p < .01$), suggesting that the time variable is a less stable measure.

Source: P. A. Katz and P. V. Walsh. (1991). Modification of children's gender-stereotyped behavior. *Child Development, 62*(2), p. 344.

Although three inferential tests of *r* were applied in Excerpt 10.33, look again carefully at the final sentence. Two *r*s are reported in this sentence (.76 and .42), and the final comment "suggests" that there is a difference between the stability of the two measures. It would have been possible to statistically compare these two *r*s, and we feel that the conclusion drawn about differential stability should have rested on such a comparison. Possibly, .76 and .42 are *not* significantly different from each other!

CAUSALITY

When we initially looked at correlation from a descriptive standpoint in Chapter 3, we pointed out that a correlation coefficient usually should not be interpreted to mean that one variable has a causal impact on the other variable. Now that we have considered correlation from an inferential standpoint, we want to embellish that earlier point by saying that a correlation coefficient, even if found to be significant at an impressive alpha level, normally should not be viewed as addressing any cause-and-effect question.

Later, we will consider various ways in which researchers can deal with questions of possible causal connections between variables. At that time, we will point out how the statistical tool of correlation *can* be used to provide answers to questions such as these: Does variable *A* have a causal impact on variable *B*? Which of two variables, *A* or *B*, has more of a causal impact on a third variable? To deal with these questions, we will need to move our discussion beyond a more elementary discussion of the bivariate relationship between two variables (found here and in Chapter 3) to considerations of research design principles. Until you become acquainted with the concepts dealt with in those later discussions, we advise you to remember our earlier (and current) warning about bivariate correlations. Even if found to be statistically significant, correlation coefficients normally *do not* speak to the issue of causality.

ATTENUATION

The inferential procedures covered in this chapter assume that the two variables being correlated are each measured without error. In other words, these procedures are designed for the case where each variable is measured with an instrument that has perfect reliability. While this assumption may have full justification in a theoretical sense, it certainly does not match the reality of the world in which we live. To the best of our knowledge, no researcher has ever measured two continuous variables and ended up with data that were perfectly reliable.

When two variables are measured such that the data have less than perfect reliability, the measured relationship in the sample data will systematically underestimate the strength of the relationship in the population. In other words, the computed correlation coefficient will be a **biased estimate** of the parameter if either or both of the variables are measured without error-free instruments. The term **attenuation** has been coined to describe this situation, where, using the product-moment correlation as an example, measurement error causes r to systematically underestimate $[\rho]$.

Once you come to understand the meaning (and likely occurrence) of attenuation, you should be able to see why statistical tests that yield fail-to-reject decisions are problematic in terms of interpretation. If, for example, a researcher computes Pearson's r and ends up not rejecting H_0: $[\rho] = 0.00$, this outcome *may* have come about because there is a very weak (or possibly no) relationship between the two variables in the population. On the other hand, the decision not to reject H_0 *may* have been caused by attenuation masking a strong relationship in the population.

In Chapter 4, we spent a great deal of time talking about the various techniques used by researchers to estimate the reliability of their measuring instruments. That discussion now becomes relevant to our consideration of inferential reports on correlation coefficients. If a researcher's data possess only trivial amounts of measurement error, then attenuation becomes only a small concern. On the other hand, reports of only moderate reliability coupled with correlational results that turn out nonsignificant leave us in a quandary as to knowing anything about the relationship in the population.

If researchers have information concerning the reliabilities associated with the measuring instruments used to collect data on the two variables being correlated, they can use a formula that adjusts the correlation coefficient to account for the suspected amount of unreliability. When applied, this **correction-for-attenuation** formula will always yield an adjusted *r* that is higher than the uncorrected, raw *r*. In Excerpt 10.34, we see an example where a research team conducted a correlational study and used the correction-for-attenuation formula.

Excerpt 10.34   Correlation Coefficients and Attenuation

Table 3 gives the correlation coefficients between CMA scores and various GPAs. Students with higher CMA scores tended to receive higher GPAs; all CMA-GPA correlations were positive and statistically significant, but low to moderate in magnitude. Of greater interest than the observed *r*'s is the value of *r* that would be observed if measurement error were eliminated from the CMA or GPA measures. It is well known (Hopkins, Glass, and Hopkins, 1987, p. 83) that the presence of measurement error in either of the measures causes the observed correlation to underestimate the extent of the true relationship between variables. Consequently, the correlations in Table 3 were corrected for attenuation (Hopkins, Stanley, and Hopkins, 1990, p. 359) to provide an estimate of what the correlations would have been between CMA, assuming both were measured with perfect reliability.

Table 3

Correlation Coefficients Between Academic Achievement and CMA[a] Scores for Different Grade Levels (Disattenuated Coefficients are Italicized)

Grade	n	CMA-Science	CMA-Humanities	CMA-Total GPA
9	116	.265**(*.372*)	.407***(*.571*)	.375***(*.526*)
10	92	.324**(*.457*)	.280**(*.396*)	.309**(*.436*)
11	102	.149(*.186*)	.181*(*.226*)	.176*(*.213*)
12	91	.258**(*.321*)	.294**(*.366*)	.290**(*.351*)

*$^*p < .05. ^{**}p < .01. ^{***}p < .001.$

[a]The CMA measure was administered in Grade 10 for the Grade 9–10 sample, and in Grade 12 for the Grade 11–12 sample.

Source: J. Otero, J. M. Campanario, and K. D. Hopkins. (1992). The relationship between academic achievement and metacognitive comprehension monitoring ability of Spanish secondary school students. *Educational and Psychological Measurement, 52*(2), pp. 425–426.

Attenuation, of course, is not the only thing to consider when trying to make sense out of a correlation-based research report. Several of these "other relevant considerations" have been addressed within our general discussion of "cautions." Two points are worth reiterating, each now connected to the concept of reliability. First, it is possible that a correlation coefficient will turn out to be statistically significant even though H_0 is true and even though highly reliable instruments are used to collect the sample data; do not forget that Type I errors *do* occur. Second, it is possible that a correlation coefficient will turn out to be nonsignificant even when H_0 is false and even when highly reliable data have been collected; do not forget about the notion of Type II errors and power.

REVIEW TERMS

Attenuation
Biased estimate
Bonferroni technique
Correction-for-attenuation
Correlation matrix
Holms procedure
Homoscedasticity
Linearity

REVIEW QUESTIONS

1. In Excerpt 10.10, a sample correlation coefficient of .34 was found to be statistically significant. Using symbols, what was the likely null hypothesis associated with this inferential test?

2. (True or False) Researchers typically do not state explicitly their null hypotheses when testing correlation coefficients.

3. In Excerpt 10.17, how many subjects were there in the male group?

4. When a researcher checks to see if a correlation coefficient is or isn't statistically significant, the inferential test will most likely be conducted in a _____ (one-tailed/two-tailed) fashion.

5. With respect to Excerpt 10.9, which of the three main inferential testing strategies was used: hypothesis testing, significance testing, or the hybrid approach to testing H_0?

6. With respect to Excerpt 10.15, how many null hypotheses were set up and evaluated by means of the sample data?

7. Suppose a researcher first collects data from a single group of subjects on five variables and then uses the hypothesis testing procedure to evaluate each possible bivariate correlation coefficient. If the researcher wants to have the Type

I error risk be equal to .05 for the full set of tests to be conducted, what alpha level should be used in conjunction with the test of each and every r?

8. Is it possible for a researcher to have a reliability coefficient of .25 that turns out to be statistically significant at $p < .0001$?

9. In Excerpt 10.27, what was the null hypothesis associated with the t-test used to compare .83 and .58?

10. In Excerpt 10.7, if a 95 percent confidence interval is put around the computed correlation coefficient, will one end of this confidence interval have a negative value?

11. Is it possible for r^2 to be a low value (i.e., close to zero) even though $p < .01$?

12. Which of the following two-word phrases expresses nicely the core issue associated with the term *homoscedasticity?*

    a. Equal means

    b. Equal variances

    c. Equal correlations

13. (True or False) To the extent that the p-value associated with a correlation coefficient is small (e.g., $p < .01$, $p < .001$, or $p < .0001$), the researcher has a more solid base on which to argue that a cause-and-effect relationship exists between the two variables that were correlated.

14. Attenuation makes it _____ (more/less) likely that a true relationship will reveal itself through the data by means of a statistically significant correlation coefficient.

INFERENCES CONCERNING
ONE OR TWO MEANS

In the previous chapter, we saw how inferential statistical techniques can be used with correlation coefficients. Now, we turn our attention to the procedures used to make inferences with means. A variety of techniques are used by applied researchers to deal with their sample means, and we will consider many of these inferential procedures here and in several of the following chapters. Multiple chapters are needed to deal with this broad topic because the inferential procedures used by researchers vary according to (1) how many groups of subjects are involved, (2) whether underlying assumptions seem tenable, (3) how many independent variables come into play, (4) whether data on concomitant variables are used to increase power, and (5) whether subjects are measured under more than one condition of the investigation.

In this introductory chapter on inferences concerning means, we will restrict our focus to the cases where the researcher has computed either just one sample mean or two sample means. We will illustrate how statistical tests are used in studies where interest lies in one or two means and the way interval estimation is sometimes used in such studies. Near the end of this chapter, we will talk about the assumptions that underlie the inferential procedures covered in this chapter, and we will also discuss the concept of "overlapping distributions." With this overview now under your belt, let us turn to the simplest inferential situation involving means: the case where there is a single mean.

INFERENCES CONCERNING A SINGLE MEAN

If researchers have collected data from a single sample and if they wish to focus on $\overline{X}$ in an inferential manner, one (or both) of two statistical strategies will be implemented. On the one hand, a confidence interval can be built around the sample mean. On the other hand, a null hypothesis can be set up and then evaluated by means of the hypothesis testing procedure, by means of significance testing, or by means of the hybrid approach to dealing with H_0.

THE INFERENTIAL PURPOSE

Figure 11.1 has been constructed to help clarify what researchers are trying to do when they use the mean of a sample as the basis for building a confidence interval or for assessing a null hypothesis. As this figure shows, $\overline{X}$ is computed on the basis of data collected from the sample. Although the sample-based value of the mean is easy to obtain, primary interest lies in the corresponding value of the mean in the population from which the sample has been drawn. However, the researcher cannot compute the value of μ because only the objects in the sample can be measured. Accordingly, an inference (i.e., educated guess) about the unknown value of the population parameter, μ, is made on the basis of the known value of the sample statistic, $\overline{X}$.

In summarizing their empirical investigations, many researchers discuss their findings in such a way that the exclusive focus seems to be on the sample data. The thick arrow in Figure 11.1 will help you remember that the different inferential techniques to which we now turn our attention are designed to allow a researcher to say something about the *population* involved in the study, not the sample. If concern rested with the sample, no inferential techniques would be necessary.

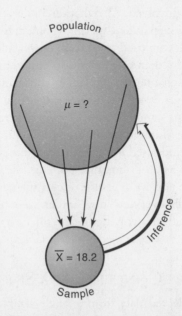

FIGURE 11.1   *The inferential purpose when one sample's mean is computed.*

INTERVAL ESTIMATION

Of the two basic ways of applying inferential statistics to a sample mean, the **confidence interval** procedure is simpler. All the researcher will do in implementing this inferential strategy is (1) make a decision as to the level of confidence that will be associated with the interval to be built and (2) build the interval around $\overline{X}$ by using a formula that incorporates information from the sample (e.g., $\overline{X}$, *SD,* and *n*) as well as a numerical value extracted from a statistical table. The result will be an interval that extends equally far above and below the sample value of $\overline{X}$.

In Excerpt 11.1, we see an example of confidence intervals being placed around sample means. The original sample of 695 men was first split into five subsamples, each with a distinct level of lead in the blood. Then, the mean

---

Excerpt 11.1   Confidence Intervals Around Single Means

Table 2

Mean systolic and diastolic blood pressure in men classified by blood lead levels in an occupational survey in Birmingham, United Kingdom, 1981

Blood lead (µg/dl)	No.	Unadjusted blood pressure (mmHg)	95% confidence interval	Adjusted blood pressure* (mmHg)
Systolic presssure[†]				
<21	91	127	123.5–130.5	129
21–30	225	127	124.6–129.4	127
31–40	195	129	126.5–131.5	129
41–50	128	132	128.9–135.1	131
>50	65	133	128.7–137.3	1322
Diastolic pressure[‡]				
<21	91	83	80.3–85.7	85
21–30	225	84	82.2–85.8	84
31–40	195	83	81.0–85.0	82
41–50	128	86	83.6–88.4	85
>50	65	83	79.7–86.3	82

*Adjusted for age, body mass index, and alcohol intake.
[†]Unadjusted, $F = 3.3$, $p < 0.05$; adjusted, $F = 1.3$, not significant
[‡]Unadjusted, $F = 1.1$, not significant; adjusted, $F = 1.3$, not significant.

Source: R. Maheswaran, J. S. Gill, and D. G. Beevers, (1993). Blood pressure and industrial lead exposure. *American Journal of Epidemiology, 137*(6), p. 647.

---

blood pressure (both systolic and diastolic) was computed for each subsample, with a 95 percent confidence interval reported for each mean.

Note how the confidence intervals in Excerpt 11.1 turned out to be narrower for the larger subsamples and wider for the smaller subsamples. In general, a larger n will produce a confidence interval that extends a shorter distance away from $\overline{X}$. For this reason, researchers will try to increase n (when time and money permit more data to be collected), but a "point of diminishing returns" will eventually be reached. This is because the amount of increase in precision in estimating μ associated with any fixed increase in n decreases as the "base" sample size gets larger and larger. Eventually, it becomes unwise to add any more data to the existing sample.

TESTS CONCERNING A NULL HYPOTHESIS

When researchers have a single sample (and thus a single population) and have inferential interest in the mean, they can approach the data by means of the hypothesis testing procedure, significance testing, or the hybrid approach to testing H_0. Regardless of which strategy is used, a null hypothesis must be articulated. In this kind of research situation, the null hypothesis will take the form

$$H_0: \mu = a$$

where a stands for a pinpoint numerical value selected by the researcher.

After specifying H_0, researchers will proceed to apply the various steps of the inferential testing strategy they have decided to follow. (The three main strategies, in addition to the main variations of these strategies, were discussed in Chapters 7–9.) Regardless of which strategy is used, researchers assess the discrepancy between the sample mean and H_0's pinpoint value; if the difference between $\overline{X}$ and H_0's μ-value is large enough, H_0 will either (1) be rejected, if the hypothesis testing procedure is being applied, or (2) be viewed as not likely to be true due to the small value of p associated with the sample data, if significance testing is being applied.

There are several available test procedures that can be used to analyze the data of a one-sample study wherein the statistical focus is the mean. The two most popular of these test procedures are the t-test and the z-test. These two ways of testing the discrepancy between $\overline{X}$ and H_0's μ-value are identical in logic and have the same decision rule when comparing the calculated value against the critical value.[1] The only difference between the two tests is that the z-test yields a calculated value that is slightly larger than it ought to be (and a p-value that is slightly smaller than it ought to be). However, the amount of the bias is trivial when the sample size is at least 30.

---

[1] *This decision rule says to reject H_0 if the calculated value is as large as or larger than the critical value; otherwise, the null hypothesis should not be rejected.*

In Excerpt 11.2, we see a study in which the research team applied an inferential test to the mean of a single sample. Actually, this was done six times, three times with the male sample and three times with the female sample. Three tests were conducted with each sample because there were three dependent variables, or measures, of interest to the researchers. As explained in the text of the excerpt and in Note "a" beneath the table, the "expected value of each t-test was zero." In other words, zero was the pinpoint number used within each H_0 that was set up and evaluated.

Excerpt 11.2 Use of the t Statistic to Test the Mean of a Single Sample

---

To assess whether participants had overall preferences for the therapists' ethnicity, we conducted t tests for single means (Hays, 1973). The obtained means were tested against an expected value of zero, which represents the neutral point of equal preference for Mexican-American and Anglo-American therapists. We analyzed the preferences for men and women separately because the two samples were given two distinct vignettes. An examination of Table 1 reveals that for both male and female students, the means of the three preference-related ratings were significantly different from the expected value of zero and were in the direction of preferring Mexican-American therapists.

Table 1

Means, Standard Deviations, and t values of Preference-Related Ratings by Participants' Gender

Measure	*Men*				*Women*			
	n	M	SD	t[a]	n	M	SD	t[a]
Preference	53	1.32	1.40	6.88*	50	1.34	1.27	7.45*
Understanding	52[b]	1.46	1.38	7.56*	49[b]	1.86	1.55	11.26*
Competene	52[b]	1.02	1.35	5.44*	50	0.92	1.24	5.23*

Note. The rating scale ranges from *strongly prefer Anglo American, Anglo American would best understand*, and *Anglo American would be most competent* (−3) to *strongly prefer Mexican American, Mexican American would best understand*, and *Mexican American would be most competent* (+3) for the preference, understanding, and competence measures, respectively.
[a]Single-mean t tests were conducted to test the obtained means against the expected value of zero, which represents the neutral point of equal preference for Mexican-American and Anglo-American counselors. [b]One data point is missing from the subsample.
*$p < .001$.

Source: S. R. Lopez, A. A. Lopez, and K. T. Fong, (1991). Mexican Americans' initial preferences for counselors: The role of ethnic factors. *Journal of Counseling Psychology 38*(4), p. 490.

Although the researchers never stated this, we believe that they used the hybrid approach to testing each H_0. We say this because they (1) stated that each sample mean was "significantly different" from the zero value in H_0 and (2) reported each of the six test results as being $p < .001$. We highly suspect that the level of significance associated with each of the six tests was .05 but that the "more impressive" p-levels were reported to show how dramatically each sample mean differed from H_0.

One final point concerning Excerpt 11.2. In this report of the results, no degrees of freedom (df) values are reported along with the t-test calculated values. If the df values had been presented, each one would have been equal to the sample size minus 1. For example, the df for the t-test on the measure competence for the women was equal to 49.

INFERENCES CONCERNING TWO MEANS

If researchers want to compare, using inferential statistics, two samples in terms of the mean scores, they can utilize a confidence interval approach to the data or an approach that involves setting up and testing a null hypothesis. We will discuss the way in which estimation can be used with two means after we consider the way in which two means can be compared through a tested H_0. Before we do either of these things, however, we must draw a distinction between two 2-group situations: those that involve independent samples and those that involve correlated samples.

INDEPENDENT VERSUS CORRELATED SAMPLES

Whether two samples are considered to be independent or correlated is tied to the issue of the nature of the groups *before* data are collected on the study's dependent variable. If the two groups have been assembled in such a way that a logical relationship exists between each member of the first sample and one and only one member of the second sample, then the two samples are **correlated samples**. On the other hand, if no such relationship exists, the two samples are **independent samples**.

Correlated samples come into existence in one of three ways. If a single group of subjects is measured twice (e.g., to provide pretest and posttest data), then a relationship exists "in" the data because each of the pretest scores "goes with" one and only one of the posttest scores, since both come from measuring the same research subject. A second situation that produces correlated samples is **matching**. Here, each subject in the second group is recruited for the study because he or she (or it) is a good match for a particular subject in the first group. The matching could be done in terms of height, IQ, running speed, or any of a multitude of possible matching variables. The matching variable, however, is never the same as the dependent variable that will be measured and then used to compare the two samples. The third situation that produces correlated samples occurs when biological twins are split up, with one member of each pair going into the first sample and the other member going into the second group. Here, the obvious connection that ties together the two samples is genetic similarity.

Of the three situations that bring forth correlated samples, the one that involves matching is potentially confusing because subjects in the study are measured twice (once on the variable used to do the matching and once on the dependent variable). Excerpt 11.3 illustrates this matching situation, and it may help to clarify how each of the two sets of data is used. In this study, the data on the intelligence variable (see Table 3) were used simply to form the matched pairs. The researcher's primary interest was not in the intelligence scores, however, but rather in the achievement scores earned by subjects later in their educational careers, during fifth or sixth grade (see Table 5). These achievement scores correspond to the study's dependent variable, and it turned out that the children who began kindergarten at age 6 performed significantly better, on the average, in fifth or sixth grade, than did those who began kindergarten at age 5.

Excerpt 11.3   The Data on Two Variables When Correlated Samples Are Formed by Matching

---

Forty-five subjects who entered kindergarten at age 6 were matched on the basis of intelligence quotients with same-gender subjects who entered kindergarten at age 5. . . . Achievement scores were analyzed separately by gender for reading, mathematics, and the composite test battery. . . . [T]here was a significant difference ($p < .05$) in the achievement at the intermediate grade level, as measured by the composite test battery when children of similar intellectual ability (± 1 SEM) were compared.

Table 3

Female Subject Pairs Matched for Intelligence

Matched pairs	Intelligence quotients by age at kindergarten entrance	
	5 years	6 years
1	85	81
2	88	84
3	88	84
4	90	90
5	89	92

(Continued)

Excerpt 11.3 The Data on Two Variables When Correlated Samples Are Formed by Matching *(Continued)*

Matched pairs	Intelligence quotients by age at kindergarten entrance	
	5 years	*6 years*
6	102	101
7	104	102
8	99	103
9	101	106
10	102	106
11	109	106
12	107	109
13	122	119
14	120	121
15	126	121
16	122	127

Table 5

Composite Achievement Test Means Taken at Fifth or Sixth Grade, Compared by Kindergarten Entrance Age

Kindergarten entrance age	*n*	*M NCE[a]*	*SD*	Dependent *t ratio*	*p*
Females	32				
Age 5	16	55.250	15.661	2.19	<.05
Age 6	16	56.125	20.020		

[a]NCE = normal curve equivalent scores.

Source: S. L. Crosser. (1991). Summer birthdate children: Kindergarten entrance age and academic achievement. *Journal of Educational Research, 84*(3), p. 144.

If the two groups of scores being compared do not represent one of these three situations (pre–post, matched subjects, or twins), then they are considered to be independent samples. Such samples can come about in any number of ways. Subjects might be assigned to one of two groups using the method of simple randomization, or possibly they end up in one or the other of two groups because they possess a characteristic that coincides with the thing that distinguishes the two groups. This second situation is exemplified by the multitude of studies that compare males against females, students who graduate against those who don't graduate, people who die of a heart attack versus those who don't, and so on. Or, maybe one of the two groups is formed by those who volunteer to undergo some form of treatment whereas the other group is made up of folks who choose not to volunteer. A final example (of the ones to be mentioned) would be created if the researchers simply designate one of two intact groups to be their first sample, which receives something that might help them, while the second intact group is provided with nothing at all or maybe a placebo.

In Excerpts 11.4 and 11.5, we see how researchers will sometimes clarify whether the two samples of data being compared are independent samples or correlated samples. In each case, the clarification comes immediately prior to the term *t-test*.

Excerpts 11.4–11.5   Independent and Correlated Samples

An independent *t* test was used to test for differences between raters who saw Tape A and raters who saw Tape B.

Source: G. R. Sodowsky and R. C. Taffe. (1991). Counselor trainees' analyses of multicultural counseling videotapes. *Journal of Multicultural Counseling and Development, 19*(3), p. 121.

P values, based on two-tailed matched-pair *t* tests, were calculated for comparisons between the before and after study period data.

Source: L. R. Sauvage, Jr., B. M. Myklebust, J. Crow-Pan, S. Novak, P. Millington, M. D. Hoffman, A. J. Hartz, and D. Rudman. (1992). A clinical trial of strengthening and aerobic exercise to improve gait and balance in elderly male nursing home residents. *American Journal of Physical Medicine and Rehabilitation, 71*(6), p. 336.

In Excerpt 11.5, the term *matched-pair* is used instead of the word *correlated*. Some researchers use the single adjective *matched,* others use the single adjective *paired,* and a few use the adjective *dependent*; all are synonyms for the adjective *correlated*. The terms *unpaired, unmatched,* and *uncorrelated* mean the same thing as *independent*. To understand exactly what researchers did in comparing their two groups, you must develop the ability to distinguish between correlated samples and independent samples. The language used by the researchers will help to indicate what kind of samples were involved in the study. If a descriptive adjective is not used, you will have to make a judgment based on the description of how the two samples were formed.

THE INFERENTIAL PURPOSE

Before we turn our attention to the way researchers typically summarize studies that focus on two sample means, we want to underscore the fact that these comparisons of means are inferential in nature. Figure 11.2 is designed to help you "see" this important point.

Panel A in Figure 11.2 represents the case where the means of two independent samples are compared. Panel B represents the case where two

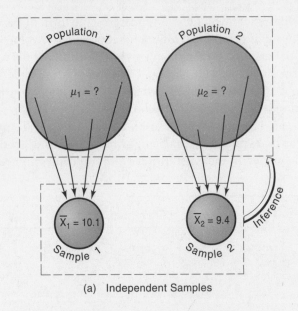

(a)   Independent Samples

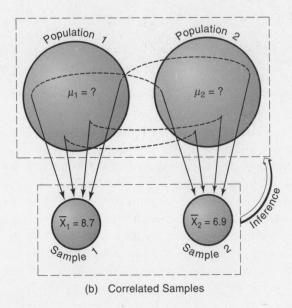

(b)   Correlated Samples

FIGURE 11.2   *Two different kinds of inferention situations involving two means.*

correlated samples of data are compared in terms of means. (In Panel B, the dotted "chains" that extend from Population 1 to Population 2 are meant to denote the pairing or matching that is characteristic of correlated samples.)

Two points about Figure 11.2 need to be highlighted. First, in both the independent-samples situation and in the correlated-samples situation, inferential statements are made about populations, not samples. Unfortunately, researchers often discuss their results as if the samples were the total focus of their investigations. If you keep Figure 11.2 in mind when you are dealing with these research summaries, you can (and should) "correct" the discussion by having all conclusions apply to the study's populations.

Our second point regarding Figure 11.2 concerns the fact that the statistical inference, in Panel A and in Panel B, extends from the full set of sample data to the study's *pair* of populations. Separate inferences are not made from each sample to its corresponding population because the purpose is to make a comparison between two things. The focus here is on how μ_1 compares with μ_2, and thus the inferential arrow in each picture points to the dotted box surrounding both populations involved in the study.

SETTING UP AND TESTING A NULL HYPOTHESIS

The null hypothesis for the two-sample case having a focus on means can be expressed in the same form regardless of whether the samples are independent or correlated. The most general way to write the null hypothesis is to state

$$H_0: \mu_1 - \mu_2 = a$$

where a represents any pinpoint number the researcher wishes to use in H_0. In most studies, researchers decide to set up a "no difference" null hypothesis, and they accomplish this goal by saying $H_0: \mu_1 - \mu_2 = 0$. Alternative ways to express the notion of "no difference" is to say $H_0: \mu_1 = \mu_2$ or to say $H_0: \sigma^2_\mu = 0$.

Unfortunately, the null hypothesis is rarely stated in studies where two means are inferentially compared using a statistical test (or in other studies, for that matter). Evidently, typical researchers assume that their readers will be able to discern the null hypothesis from the discussion of the research hypothesis and/or the way the sample data are summarized. A good rule of thumb to use when trying to decipher research reports is to presume that a test of two means revolved around a "no difference" H_0 unless it is explicitly stated that some other kind of null hypothesis was set up.

After the sample data are collected, summarized, and analyzed, the results of the statistical comparison of the two $\overline{X}$s will be presented within the text of the report and/or in a table. Excerpts 11.6 and 11.7 illustrate the way results are typically presented, with the first and second studies involving independent and correlated samples, respectively. In each case, the difference between the $\overline{X}$s being compared was so large as to make it very unlikely that the two samples of data had come from populations having the same mean. Accordingly, the null hypothesis in each study was rejected.

In Excerpts 11.6 and 11.7, we see that the data from each study were analyzed by a *t*-test. As we saw in Chapter 10, *t*-tests can be used in conjunction with inferential tests on correlation coefficients; moreover, *t*-tests can be used when a study's statistical focus is on a variety of other things (e.g., proportions and regression coefficients). Nevertheless, *t*-tests probably are used more often with means than anything else.

Excerpts 11.6–11.7   Comparison of Two Sample Means Using a *t*-Test

---

Subjects were randomly assigned to an intervention ($n = 43$) or non-intervention control group ($n = 63$). For the post-intervention prosocial choice measure, the means of the two groups were significantly different ($t = -2.20$, df $= 104$, $p < .05$).

Source: C. S. Weidman and J. M. Strayhorn, (1992). Relationships between children's prosocial behaviors and choices in story dilemmas. *Journal of Psychoeducational Assessment, 10*(4), p. 332.

Respondents were asked to recall and to rate the level of satisfaction they experienced with regard to both the instructional and noninstructional aspects of their special education assignments. Response frequencies, means, and standard deviations are shown in Table 4. Inspection of these statistics indicates that the respondents were far more satisfied with the instructional aspects of their special education experience than with the noninstructional aspects, paired $t(274) = 8.84$, $p < .001$.

Table 4

Frequencies and Percentages for Satisfaction Recollections

Aspect	1 Very satisfied	2 Satisfied	3 Somewhat dissatisfied	4 Very dissatisfied	Mean (SD)	t
Instructional	78	107	63	29	2.16	
	28.2%	38.6%	22.7%	10.5%	(.95)	
						8.82*
Noninstructional	25	84	100	66	2.75	
	9.1%	30.5%	36.4%	24.0%	(.92)	

*$p < .001$.

Source: B. S. Billingsley and L. H. Cross. (1991). Teachers' decisions to transfer from special to general education. *Journal of Special Education, 24*(4), p. 503.

Note that the authors of Excerpts 11.6 and 11.7, in reporting their *t*-test results, provide information as to the degrees of freedom associated with the tests that were conducted. These *df* values are useful because they allow us to know how much data each *t* was based on. When *t*-tests are conducted to compare the means of two independent samples, the total amount of data can be determined by adding 2 to the *t*-test's *df*. When t-tests are used to see if a significant difference exists between the means of two correlated samples of data, you can determine how many pairs of data were used by adding 1 to the *t*-test's *df*.

Although a statistical test comparing two means can be conducted using a *t*-test, it can also be accomplished by means of a **z-test** or an **F-test.** The *z*-test provides a result that is slightly biased in the sense that its probability of resulting in a Type I error is greater than the level of significance (with this bias being more pronounced when the sample sizes are small). The *F*-test, on the other hand, is not biased. The *F*-test's conclusion regarding H_0 will always be identical to the conclusion reached by a *t*-test. Hence, it really doesn't matter whether researchers compare their two means using a *t*-test or an *F*-test.

In light of the fact that (1) some researchers opt to use an *F*-test when comparing two means and (2) the results of an *F*-test are typically presented in a way that requires an understanding of concepts not yet addressed, we feel obliged to comment briefly about *F*-test results. Here we will focus our attention exclusively on the use of *F*-tests to compare the means of two independent samples. In Chapter 16, we will show how *F*-tests can be used with correlated samples.

To begin our discussion of *F*-tests applied to the means of two independent samples, consider the material in Excerpt 11.8. In this excerpt, note that two groups were being compared, that the focus was on the means of the two samples (5.73 and 6.60 for Groups 1 and 2, respectively), and that no statistically significant difference was found between these means, as indicated by notation at the end of the excerpt (*ns* for "not significant"). Also note that the calculated value turned out equal to .94 and that this value is referred to as *F*. Because of this, we know that the data were analyzed by means of an *F*-test.

Excerpt 11.8   Comparison of Means from Two Independent Samples
Using an *F*-Test

CBM teachers (Group 1 and 2) were provided initial training to implement CBM over 8 weeks, with two 2-hour after-school workshops, teacher practice, and staff observations of teachers. Then, staff met with teachers in their classrooms once every 2 to 3 weeks to help them solve implementation problems. During the study, Group 1 teachers received 5.73 visits ($SD = 2.01$); Group 2 teachers, 6.60 visits ($SD = 2.12$), $F(1,18) = .94$, *ns*.

Source: L. S. Fuchs, D. Fuchs, C. L. Hamlett, and R. M. Allinder. (1991). The contribution of skills analysis to curriculum-based measurement in spelling. *Exceptional Children, 57*(5), p. 447.

In Excerpt 11.8, also note that there are two degrees of freedom values presented along with the calculated value. The *df*s appear within a set of parentheses immediately to the right of the *F*, and they are separated by a comma. *F*-tests always have a pair of *df* values associated with them, and in this case the *df* values are equal to 1 and 18.

The *df* values presented along with the results of an *F*-test can be used to discern the amount of data used to make the statistical comparison. When an *F*-test is used as in Excerpt 11.8 to compare the means of two independent samples, all you need to do to determine the amount of data used is add the two *df* values together and then add 1 to the resulting sum. Thus, in this study the calculated value of .94 was based upon a total of 20 pieces of data. Since each piece of data corresponded to a particular teacher and the number of times he or she had a visit, we know that there were 20 teachers in this study. Although this is now purely a guess, we suspect that there were 10 teachers in Group 1 and 10 in Group 2.

Sometimes, a table will be used to present the results of the kind of *F*-test we have been discussing. An example of such a table is contained in Excerpt 11.9. The first thing to note about Excerpt 11.9 is that the phrase **analysis of**

Excerpt 11.9   *F*-Test Comparison of Two Sample Means with Results Presented in Analysis of Variance Summary Table

Table 2

Summary Data and Analysis of Variance Data for Comparisons Between Pupil Control Behavior of Public and Private School Teachers

	Teachers	
	Public School	*Private School*
Number	56	48
Mean	48.82	46.42
Standard deviation	11.89	12.15

Source	*df*	*SS*	*MS*	*F*
Between groups	1	149.47	149.47	1.02 (N.S.)
Within groups	102	14951.88	146.59	

Source: F. C. Lunenburg. (1991). Pupil control ideology and behavior as predictors of environmental robustness: Public and private schools compared. *Journal of Research and Development in Education, 24*(3), p. 16.

---

variance appears in the title of the table. This phrase is misleading, for it probably would lead an uninformed reader to think that the statistical focus was on variances. Although one could not be faulted for making such a guess, the fact of the matter is that analysis of variance focuses on *means*.[2]

The main thing "going on" in Excerpt 11.9 is a statistical comparison of the two means shown in the top half of the table, 48.82 and 46.42. Based on the table's title, it seems reasonable to guess that each of the means represents the average amount of pupil control behavior exhibited by teachers, one mean being computed from data collected in public schools and the other from data collected in private schools. The numbers immediately above and below each of the two sample means provides descriptive information concerning the number of teachers measured and the variability among the scores within each group.

The outcome of the inferential test comparing two means is presented in the lower half of the table. The calculated value is presented at the far right in the column labeled "*F*." This data-based value, 1.02, turned out to be nonsignificant, as indicated by the notation "N.S." next to the calculated value. Thus, the two sample means differed by an amount that was within the limits of chance sampling, presuming that μ_{public} and $\mu_{private}$ were equal. The null hypothesis, therefore, was not rejected.

There are two *df* values presented in the analysis of variance table. On the row labeled "Between groups," the *df* value is equal to 1; this will always be the case when two sample means are being compared. The *df* value on the row labeled "Within groups" is found first by subtracting 1 from each sample size and then by adding the resulting figures [$(56 - 1) + (48 - 1) = 102$]. Note that the sum of the *df*s for the "Between groups" and "Within groups" rows is equal to 103, one less than the total number of subjects used in the analysis.

The numbers in the **SS** column are the "sums of squares." These numbers come from a statistical analysis of the sample data, and there is really no way to make sense out of this column of the analysis of variance table. The next column is labeled **MS** for "mean squares." The first of these values was found by dividing the first row's *SS* by that row's *df* ($149.47 \div 1 = 149.47$). In a similar fashion, the second row's *MS* was found by dividing 14,951.88 by 102. Finally, the calculated value for the *F* column was computed by dividing the "Between groups" *MS* by the "Within groups" *MS* ($149.47 \div 146.59 = 1.02$).

In one sense, all of the numbers in the *df*, *SS*, and *MS* columns of the analysis of variance table are used solely as "stepping stones" to obtain the calculated value. The two *df* values are especially important, however, because the researcher must use both of these numbers (along with the selected level

---

[2]*The phrase* analysis of variance *is often abbreviated as* ANOVA.

of significance) to locate the critical value. Accordingly, the three most important numbers in the table are the two values in the *df* column and the single number in the *F* column.

INTERVAL ESTIMATION WITH TWO MEANS

As noted in Chapter 6, confidence intervals can be used to deal with a null hypothesis that a researcher wishes to test. Or, the confidence interval can be set up in studies where no test is being conducted on any H_0, with interest instead residing strictly in the process of interval estimation. Regardless of the researcher's objective, it is important to be able to decipher the results of a study in which the results are presented using a confidence interval around the difference between two means.

Consider Excerpt 11.10. Here we see that each of 129 individuals in the sample was measured in terms of (1) reported educational level and (2) functional grade level as indicated by performance on the WRAT test. A paired *t*-test compared the reported and functional grade level means, with a resulting calculated value of 12.62. Although not reported, the null hypothesis associated with this *t*-test was probably of the "no difference" variety.

Excerpt 11.10   A Confidence Interval Built Around the Difference
Between Two Sample Means

The sample was comprised of 74 males (57 percent) and 55 females (43 percent). . . . The mean grade level of reported education among subjects was grade 11 and the mean grade level according to the WRAT was grade 7, a difference of 4 grades (paired t = 12.62, 95% CI: 3.31, 4.52).

Source: C. D. Meade, J. C. Byrd, and M. Lee. (1989). Improving patient comprehension of literature on smoking. *American Journal of Public Health, 79*(10), p. 1411.

Nowhere in Excerpt 11.10 (or in any other portion of the research report) did the researchers indicate whether the result of their *t*-test was significant, nor did they present a *p*-value for the calculated value of 12.62. They do, however, indicate that a 95 percent confidence interval built around the difference between the reported and functional sample means extended from 3.31 to 4.52. Since the 95 percent confidence interval did not contain zero, we know that the null hypothesis of a zero difference between the two population means was rejected at the .05 level.

MULTIPLE DEPENDENT VARIABLES

If data are collected from one or two samples on two or more dependent variables, researchers with inferential interest in their data may build several confidence intervals or set up and test several null hypotheses, one for each dependent variable. A quick look at a few excerpts from recent studies will illustrate how researchers often talk about such analyses.

RESULTS PRESENTED IN THE TEXT

In Excerpts 11.11 and 11.12, we see two examples of how researchers often talk about their multiple tests within the text of their discussions. While both studies involved comparisons of two means, notice how the first study used correlated samples while the second used independent samples.

Excerpts 11.11–11.12   *t*-Tests with Multiple Dependent Variables, with Discussion Presented in Text

One-tailed, paired-sample *t* tests were used to test for increases from pre- to post-intervention means for benefit satisfaction and overall job satisfaction. We also tested for differences in facets of satisfaction that were *not* expected to change following implementation of the flexible plan: satisfaction with physical working conditions, co-workers, supervision, kind of work, and amount of work.

Source: A. E. Barber, R. B. Dunham, and R. A. Formisano. (1992). The impact of flexible benefits on employee satisfaction: A field study. *Personnel Psychology, 45*(1), p. 64.

t-tests for independent samples were computed. . . . Differences between the SWS and EMP group were not significant at the .05 level in years of visual impairment ($t = -.90$; $p = .37$) and years of education ($t = -1.73$; $p = .09$). Significant differences were found between the two groups on age ($t = 2.46$; $p = .017$) and age of onset of visual impairment ($t = 2.77$; $p = .008$).

Source: D. E. Sampson. (1990). Attributional styles of sheltered workshop clients and employed persons who are blind or visually impaired. *Vocational Evaluation and Work Adjustment Bulletin, 23*(2), p. 56.

RESULTS PRESENTED IN A TABLE

Excerpt 11.13 shows how a researcher may use a table to present the results of a two-sample comparison of means on several dependent variables. The numerical values in the column labeled "*t*" are the calculated values that resulted from a comparison of the two means on each row. Hence, the first calculated value of 2.4 came from a comparison of 3.25 and 3.16. Each value in the right-hand column is the *p*-value for the calculated value on the same row. When the *t*-test yielded a nonsignificant result, the letters *NS* were given rather than the actual *p*-value.

Notice that there is no statement in Excerpt 11.13 as to whether the *t*-test comparisons of girls versus boys were based on independent samples or on

Excerpt 11.13   Results of a Two-Group Comparison of Five
Dependent Variables Presented in a Table

Table 6

t-Test—Comparison of Boys and Girls (Pre-Field Trip)
(Likert-type 1–4)

Scale	Girls (N = 360)		Boys (N = 300)			
	M	SD	M	SD	t	P
Learning tool	3.25	0.41	3.16	0.47	2.4	0.02
Individualized learning	2.41	0.57	2.30	0.66	2.3	0.02
Social aspect	2.96	0.44	2.98	0.42	0.6	NS
Adventurous aspect	2.88	0.68	3.05	0.69	3.2	0.001
Environmental aspect	3.07	0.53	3.02	0.57	1.2	NS

Source: N. Orion and A. Hofstein. (1991). The measurement of students' attitudes towards scientific field trips. *Science Education, 75*(5), p. 520. © John Wiley & Sons, Inc. Reprinted by permission.

correlated samples. Although not told this directly, you can discern what kind of samples were involved from the information provided on the sample sizes. Since the two groups were not of equal size, the two samples must have been independent, not correlated. Correlated samples require the same *n* in each group.

USE OF THE BONFERRONI ADJUSTMENT TECHNIQUE

When a researcher sets up and tests several null hypotheses, each corresponding to a different dependent variable, the probability of having at least one Type I error pop up somewhere in the set of tests will be higher than indicated by the level of significance used in making the individual tests. As indicated in Chapter 8, this problem is referred to as the "inflated Type I error problem." There are many ways to deal with this problem, with the most common strategy being the application of the Bonferroni adjustment technique.

In Excerpt 11.14, we see a case in which the Bonferroni technique was used to hold down the chances of a Type I error in a study involving eight dependent variables. There were two correlated samples used in this portion of the study, with the data associated with each dependent variable analyzed by means of a *t*-test. Although the researchers did not indicate exactly how they applied the Bonferroni technique, we suspect that they divided the desired study-wide Type I error rate of .05 by the number of *t*-tests that were conducted. Thus, the comparison on each dependent variable had to produce a *p* equal to or smaller than .00625 (i.e., .05/8) before the label *significant* could be applied to the results.

In Excerpt 11.14, the Bonferroni technique was applied within a study wherein the researchers had an inferential interest in two means per dependent variable, with the data coming from correlated samples. It should be noted that the Bonferroni technique can be used in studies where there is only one sample that is measured on two or more dependent variables, or in studies where two independent samples are measured relative to two or more variables. Moreover, this procedure for handling the "inflated Type I error problem" can be used regardless of the statistical test (*z*, *t*, or *F*) used to analyze the study's data.

Excerpt 11.14   Use of the Bonferroni Adjustment Technique

Paired *t* tests comparing aggressive-rejected students with a matched group of average students indicated many individually significant differences in behavior while maintaining a family-wise alpha of .05, using Bonferroni's correction. Consistent with the procedure by which aggressive-rejected students were identified, they received more nominations than average students for "start fights," $t(15) = 7.46$, $p < .001$, but not for "easy to push around," $t(15) = 1.32$. Additionally, they received more nominations for "disrupts," $t(15) = 5.04$, $p < .001$, and for "can't take teasing," $t(15) = 3.37$, $p < .006$, and fewer nominations for "cooperates," $t(15) = 4.56$, $p < .001$; "kind," $t(15) = 3.98$, $p < .001$; and "someone you can trust," $t(15) = 4.79$, $p < .001$. They did not differ significantly on "shy," $t(15) = 2.61$.

Source: J. T. Parkhurst and S. R. Asher. (1992). Peer rejection in middle school: Subgroup differences in behavior, loneliness, and interpersonal concerns. *Developmental Psychology, 28*(2), p. 236.

A PSEUDO-BONFERRONI ADJUSTMENT

Some researchers who have multiple dependent variables attempt to hold down their total Type I error risk by using a crude technique referred to here as the **pseudo-Bonferroni adjustment procedure**. This procedure works as follows: The researchers take the normal level of significance and changes it to a popular but more rigorous level. For example, researchers who normally would set alpha equal to .05 if there were just one dependent variable might decide to use an alpha level of .01 to compensate for the inflated Type I error risk caused by multiple dependent variables. In Excerpts 11.15 and 11.16, we see two examples of this kind of alpha adjustment.

Excerpts 11.15–11.16   A Pseudo-Bonferroni Adjustment

Ratings were analyzed for differences in the [12] self-evaluations of the two groups, using the Student t test on the composite score of each self-image subscale as the dependent variable. To reduce concerns regarding the Type I error rate associated with the use of multiple t tests, only results that indicated significance at $p < .01$ were deemed statistically significant.

Source: D. E. Smith and D. W. Tegano. (1992). Relationship of scores on two personality measures: Creativity and self-image. *Psychological Reports, 71,* p. 46.

Using a significance level of p <.01 to correct for possible Type I error, dependent t tests indicated that the high-risk group made significant increments on 3 of the 12 subscales.

Source: J. N. Reich and J. W. Cleland. (1993). Children born at risk: What's happening in kindergarten. *Psychology in the Schools, 30,* p. 51.

When multiple tests are conducted, a change in the alpha level (e.g., from .05 to .01) does bring about greater control of Type I errors. We refer to it as a pseudo-Bonferroni technique, however, because the study-wide risk of falsely rejecting one or more true null hypotheses rarely will be equal to the desired (in most cases) .05 level.

POWER ANALYSIS AND STRENGTH-OF-EFFECT ESTIMATION

When dealing with one or two means using hypothesis testing or the hybrid approach to assessing H_0, many researchers pay no attention to the estimated strength of effect, power, or effect size. Those researchers seem content simply to reject or to fail-to-reject the null hypotheses that they assess, with "impressive" p-levels sometimes reported along with calculated values when the sample data "beat" the conventional .05 alpha level by a wide margin. A few researchers, however, make an effort to provide insight into their results or to set up their studies with systematic control over the probability of Type II errors. In Chapters 8 and 9, we discussed in general terms the way researchers can accomplish these goals. Now, we wish to illustrate how researchers actually do these things in studies where there is inferential interest in one or two means.

In Excerpt 11.17, we see an example where a researcher compared the means of two independent samples by means of a t-test. In addition to making a decision about H_0, the researcher (1) estimated the magnitude of the observed experimental-versus-control effect and (2) estimated the power associated with the t-test result.

Excerpts 11.18 and 11.19 illustrate the way researchers will sometimes compute a strength-of-association index. Note that eta squared was used in the first of these excerpts while omega squared was the strength-of-association index computed in the second excerpt. In each case, the index estimates the proportion of variability among the scores on the dependent variable that is explained by the independent variable (i.e., group affiliation).

Excerpt 11.17 Post Hoc Estimation of Power and Magnitude of Effect

---

Next, independent t-tests (p < .05) were used to test directional hypotheses that experimental means were significantly greater than control means for the dependent variable in each experiment. Estimates were computed for the power of each t-test and for the effect size in each experiment. . . .

Experiment 1. Experimental subjects correctly answered more of the recall items than controls when completing their six-item quiz (M_E = 3.38, M_C = 2.07; SD_E = 1.78, SD_C = 1.67). Differences between group means attained statistical significance, t(29) = 2.11, p < .05). Size of effect (0.76) was computed using a pooled variance estimate and the estimated power of the t-test equalled .65.

Source: D. McDougall and P. Cordeiro. (1992). Effects of random questioning expectations on education majors' preparedness for lecture and discussion. *College Student Journal, 26*(2), p. 196.

Excerpts 11.18–11.19 Estimating the Strength of Association

The general pattern of results was for Catholics to score lower than Protestants. The exception to this pattern was that no difference was found for the Spiritual Well-Being Scale and one of its subscales, Existential Well-Being. When we considered the magnitude of the significant effect, by looking at eta squared, the most dramatic difference between Protestants and Catholics was for the Shepherd Scale.

Source: R. L. Bassett, W. Camplin, D. Humphrey, C. Dorr, S. Biggs, R. Distaffen, I. Doxator, M. Flaherty, P. J. Hunsberger, R. Poage, and H. Thompson. (1991). Measuring Christian maturity: A comparison of several scales. *Journal of Psychology and Theology, 19*(1), p. 89.

t-tests were performed between the two groups in order to examine group differences. As can be seen, the only significant difference between the groups was in their performance on the adaptive PSI competitive listening task. The otitis-negative group had a significantly lower mean S/CM (M_{OM-} = − 9.7) than the otitis-positive group (M_{OM+} = − 6.8). In other words, otitis-positive children as a group required a more advantageous signal-to-competing message ratio than did the otitis-negative children to maintain performance at 50% sentence understanding. Moreover, using omega squared, 20% of the variance in children's performance was explained by otitis media status.

Source: J. S. Gravel and I. F. Wallace. (1992). Listening and language at 4 years of age: Effects of early otitis media. *Journal of Speech and Hearing Research, 35*(June), p. 591.

In the three excerpts we have just examined, the researchers' estimation of power, of the magnitude of the observed effect, or of the strength-of-association index was performed *after* all data were collected. As pointed out in Chapter 8, however, Type II error risk can be controlled by conducting a power analysis *before* any data are collected. The purpose of such an analysis is to determine how large the sample(s) should be so as to have a known probability of rejecting H_0 when H_0 is false by an amount at least as large as the researcher-specified effect size. In Excerpt 11.20, we see an illustration where a power analysis was conducted in a study focusing on the means of two independent samples. In this investigation, an "experimental" group and a "comparison" group were compared in terms of the degree to which subjects followed instructions for mite allergen avoidance measures. The experimental group received instruction through printed materials and computer-assisted reinforcement of the same information, while the comparison group received only the printed materials.

Excerpt 11.20   A Power Analysis in a Two-Group Study Focusing on Means

A purposive sample of 52 subjects was accessed through an allergy clinic at a tertiary medical center in a mid-Atlantic metropolitan area. The sample size was based on a power analysis utilizing: Alpha = .05, power .80, and a large effect size for the Student's two-tailed t test (Cohen, 1977).

Source: K. Huss, M. Salerno, and R. W. Huss. (1991). Computer-assisted reinforcement of instruction: Effects of adherence in adult atopic asthmatics. *Research in Nursing and Health, 14*(4), p. 261.

UNDERLYING ASSUMPTIONS

When a statistical inference concerning one or two means is made using a confidence interval or a t-, F-, or z-test, certain assumptions about the sample(s) and population(s) are typically associated with the statistical technique applied to the data. If one or more of these assumptions are violated, then the probability statements attached to the statistical results may be invalid. For this reason, well-trained researchers (1) are familiar with the assumptions associated with the techniques used to analyze their data and (2) take the time to check out important assumptions before making inferences from the sample mean(s).

For the statistical techniques covered thus far in this chapter, there are four underlying assumptions. First, each sample should be a random subset of the population it represents. Second, there should be "independence of observations" (meaning that a particular subject's score is not influenced by what happens to any other subject during the study). Third, each population should be normally distributed in terms of the dependent variable being focused upon in the study. And fourth, the two populations associated with studies involving two independent samples or two correlated samples should each have the same degree of variability relative to the dependent variable.

The assumptions dealing with the randomness and independence of observations are methodological concerns, and researchers rarely talk about either of these assumptions in their research reports. Because theoretical studies in statistics have shown that the normality assumption, when violated, is typically not disruptive to the functioning of confidence intervals or of t-, F-, and z-tests, most researchers do not do anything with their data relative to the issue of normality. The assumption of equal population variances, if violated, *can* cause a study's results to be distorted. Accordingly, you are likely to encounter a research write-up in which this assumption is discussed—and possibly tested.

When researchers test the equal variance assumption, they will use the variance estimates from the two samples to make an inference about the two population variances. This inference will be made according to the rules of hypothesis testing, significance testing, or the hybrid approach to testing a null hypothesis. Regardless of which of these testing strategies is used, the null hypothesis will be set up to say that the variance is the same in each population: H_0: $\sigma_1^2 = \sigma_2^2$

The assumption of equal variances is often referred to as the **homogeneity of variance assumption**. This term is somewhat misleading, however, since it causes many learners to think that the assumption specifies homogeneity *within* each population in terms of the dependent variable. That is not what the assumption says. If you look at the null hypothesis presented at the end of the previous paragraph, it becomes clear that the assumption can be true even when there is a large degree of variability within each population. "Homogeneity of variance" exists if σ_1^2 is equal to σ_2^2, regardless of how large or small the common value of σ^2.

When researchers test the equal variance assumption (or, for that matter, any other assumption), they hope that the sample data will *not* lead to a rejection of the null hypothesis associated with the assumption. If the sample evidence leads to a fail-to-reject decision of H_0: $\sigma_1^2 = \sigma_2^2$, then the researcher can proceed to the primary test of concern, the comparison of the two sample means. In testing H_0: $\mu_1^2 = \mu_2^2$, however, the typical researcher hopes to find a significant difference.

There are several test procedures that can be used to check on the tenability of the equal variance assumption. Some of the more frequently used tests include an F-test, Hartley's F-max test, Cochran's C test, Levene's test, and the Bartlett chi-square test. The first of these test procedures was used in the study from which Excerpt 11.21 was taken.

Excerpt 11.21   Testing the Equal Variance Assumption

The homogeneity of variance test produced a significant $F_{49,49}$ of 3.82 ($p < 0.001$). The mean age of the convicts, at time of execution, was 36.4 yr. ($SD = 8.5$ yr.). The mean age of their victims at time of death was 37.8 yr. ($SD = 16.6$ yr.).

Source: M. Snyder. (1992). Capital punishment in Texas: Comparison of some factors shared by 50 convicted murderers and their victims. *Psychological Reports, 71,* p. 754.

In Excerpt 11.21 note that there are two numbers that appear as subscripts to F. These numbers are the *df* values associated with the data, each based on one of the samples. In conducting an *F*-test to check on the equal variance assumption, each *df* value is computed by subtracting 1 from the sample size. Knowing this, you could infer that there were 50 subjects in each of the samples involved in this study.

When researchers are interested in comparing the means of two groups, they will often bypass testing the assumption of equal variances if the two samples are equally big. This is done because studies in theoretical statistics have shown that a test on means will function very much as it should even if the two populations have unequal amounts of variability *as long as* $n_1 = n_2$. In other words, *t*-, *F*-, and *z*-tests are "strong enough" to withstand a violation of the equal variance assumption if the sample sizes are equal. Stated in statistical "jargoneze," equal *n*s make these tests **robust** to violations of the homogeneity of variance assumption.

In Excerpt 11.22, we see a case in which a researcher tested the equal variance assumption before moving to the main tests of interest. These latter tests involved a comparison of Mexican-Americans versus non-Mexican-American Hispanics in terms of mean scores on three academic variables. Before *t*-tests were used to compare the means, the equal variance assumption was checked because the two *n*s were 141 and 45.

If the equal variance assumption is tested and if the data indicate that there is a statistically significant difference between the two sample variances, the

---

Excerpt 11.22   Unequal Sample Sizes Causing the Equal Variance
Assumption to Need Testing

Three *t* tests were performed to examine differences in SAT-Math scores, SAT-Verbal scores, and first-year GPA between the two Hispanic subgroups. Prior to performing the *t* tests, we tested the assumption of equal variance because the groups did not include the same number of observations.

Source: C. Arbona and D. M. Novy. (1991). Hispanic college students: Are there within-group differences? *Journal of College Student Development, 32*(4), p. 337.

---

researcher will probably take some form of "corrective action." Several options exist for handling this situation of likely unequal variances in the population. These include (1) using a special formula for computing the t, F, or z calculated value—one that is designed for the unequal variance situation; (2) using a different test procedure altogether—one that does not involve the assumption of equal variances; or (3) using a data transformation in order to "stabilize" the variances so the regular t-, F-, or z-test can be applied. In Excerpt 11.23, we see a short comment indicating that the first of these options was selected in a recent study.

Excerpt 11.23   Handling Heterogeneity of Variance Using a Special Formula for the Calculated Value

---

The t tests were unequal variance t tests.

Source: M. R. Moran. (1992). Effects of sexual orientation similarity and counselor experience level on gay men's and lesbians' perceptions of counselors. *Journal of Counseling Psychology, 39*(2), p. 250.

COMMENTS

Before concluding our discussion of inferences regarding one or two means, we want to offer four warnings that will, if you heed them, cause you to be a more informed recipient of research results. Our warnings are concerned with (1) outcomes where the null hypothesis is not rejected, (2) outcomes where H_0 is rejected, (3) the typical use of t-tests, and (4) research claims that seem to neglect the possibility of a Type I or a Type II error.

A NONSIGNIFICANT RESULT DOES NOT MEAN H_0 IS TRUE

In Chapter 7, we explained why a null hypothesis that is not rejected should *not* be considered to be true. Researchers sometimes forget this important point, especially when they compare groups in terms of pretest means. Excerpt 11.24 is a case in point.

In Excerpt 11.24, the null hypothesis that was not rejected was H_0: $\mu_1 = \mu_2$. Note that if H_0 had been set up to specify a 2-point advantage for the self-scoring group (i.e., H_0: $\mu_1 - \mu_2 = 2$), a fail-to-reject decision also would have been reached. Since the data support multiple null hypotheses that could have been set up (and that are in conflict with each other), there is no scientific justification for believing that any one of them is right while the others are wrong.

In Chapter 10, we discussed attenuation and pointed out how measuring instruments that have less than perfect reliability can function to mask true relationships that exist between two variables. The same principle applies to inferential tests that focus on things other than correlation coefficients, such

Excerpt 11.24 Misinterpretation of a Nonrejected H_0 Comparing Two Means

Table 1 gives the means and standard deviations of the pre-test scores for both self-scoring and teacher-scoring groups. No significant difference between the mean scores of the two groups was found. It was therefore assumed that at the time of pre-testing both groups were at the same level of achievement in agricultural science.

Table 1

Means and standard deviations of pre-test scores for self-scoring and teacher scoring groups

Group	N	Mean	SD	t
Self-scoring	30	44.47	9.59	
				0.85 (n.s.)
Teacher scoring	38	42.44	9.92	

Source: M. Maqsud and C. M. Pillai. (1991). Effect of self-scoring on subsequent performances in academic achievement tests. *Educational Research, 33*(2), p. 152.

as the mean. In the study from which Excerpt 11.24 was taken, the pretest used to compare the two groups was a teacher-made achievement test—an instrument that undoubtedly had lower reliability than standardized instruments constructed by testing companies. Very possibly, the pretest means of the two groups turned out to be nonsignificant because of unreliability in the data, not because $\mu_1 = \mu_2$.

A final consideration that mitigates against concluding that $\mu_1 = \mu_2$ when H_0 is "accepted" has to do with statistical power. As we have pointed out on several occasions, there is a direct relationship between sample size and the probability of detecting a situation in which H_0 is false. In Excerpt 11.24, the sample sizes of 30 and 38 are not tiny—but they certainly are not gigantic either.

For these three reasons (logic, reliability, and statistical power), be on guard for unjustified claims that H_0 is true following a decision not to reject H_0.

OVERLAPPING DISTRIBUTIONS

Suppose a researcher compares two groups of scores and finds that there is a statistically significant difference between $\overline{X}_1$ and $\overline{X}_2$. Notice that the significant difference exists between the *means* of the two groups. Be on guard for research reports in which the results are discussed without reference to the group means, thus creating the impression that every score in one group is higher than every score in the second group. Such a situation is *very* unlikely.

Consider Excerpts 11.25 and 11.26. In each case, the means of two groups were compared. But in each case, no reference is made to the means (or to the average score within each group). The impression given is that *all* prospective teachers indicated a greater willingness to act unethically than any of the veteran teachers, and that *all* of the children with handwriting difficulties had lower scores on the drawing task than any of their peers. Each of these statements is highly likely to be false because the situation of **overlapping distributions** almost always exists—even when a statistically significant difference has been found between means. In other words, it is usually the case that the highest scores in the group with the lower mean are higher than the lowest scores in the group with the higher mean.[3]

Excerpts 11.25–11.26   The Mistake of Suggesting "No Overlap" Between Two Groups of Scores

---

The hypothesis that prospective teachers were more likely to act unethically than veteran teachers was supported in terms of the Mach IV scale. Prospective teachers were significantly more willing to conduct themselves unethically (tactics) than were veteran teachers ($t_{(111)} = 3.39, p < .000$).

Source: R. L. Calabrese and C. Seldin. (1992). A conflict of value systems: Emerging adults in a traditional world. *The High School Journal, 75*(4), p. 240.

To test the hypothesis that children with handwriting difficulties will demonstrate less mature grips than their peers, a *t* test was performed to compare the two groups on the drawing task scores. The difference was significant ($t = 2.4$, $p = .02$), thus supporting this hypothesis.

Source: C. M. Schneck. (1991). Comparison of pencil-grip patterns in first graders with good and poor writing skills. *The American Journal of Occupational Therapy, 45*(8), p. 704.

Researchers ought to use the word *mean* or the phrase *on the average* when discussing the results of their statistical tests. In Excerpt 11.25, the phrase *on the average* should have appeared at the beginning of the second sentence. In Excerpt 11.26, the word *mean* should have appeared prior to the word *difference* in the second sentence.

In Excerpt 11.27, we see a rare example of a comparison of two means yielding a statistically significant result and there being absolutely no overlap between

---

[3]*Excerpt 11.7 illustrates nicely our point about overlapping distributions. Even though the t-test revealed a significant difference (at p < .001) between the two group means, 33.2 percent of the group having the lower mean were higher than the mean of the higher-scoring group, while 39.6 percent of the group having the higher mean were lower than the mean of the lower-scoring group.*

> **Excerpt 11.27** A True Case of No Overlap Between Two
> Distributions
>
> ---
>
> As expected, the experts recalled substantially more techniques than did the
> novices, with the experts recalling on average nearly twice as many techniques
> as did the novices. The mean number recalled by the experts (of a possible max-
> imum of 20) was 14.9 items ($SD = 2.0$; range, 13–16) and the mean number re-
> called by the novices was 8.3 items ($SD = 2.0$; range, 6–12). This difference is
> statistically significant [$t(28) = 11.2, p, .001$].
>
> ---
>
> *Source:* B. G. Bedon and D. V. Howard. (1992). Memory for the frequency of occurrence of karate
> techniques: A comparison of experts and novices. *Bulletin for the Psychonomic Society, 30*(2), p. 118.

the two groups of scores. By providing information concerning each group's
range of scores, the researchers made it clear that all of the experts scored better
than the highest-scoring novice. Very few studies turn out like this one.

THE TYPICAL USE OF *T*-TESTS

In the previous chapter, we saw how a *t*-test can be used to assess a null
hypothesis that focuses on a correlation coefficient. In this chapter, we saw
how a *t*-test can be used to evaluate a null hypothesis dealing with one or two
means. In future chapters, we will see how *t*-tests can be used when the researcher's statistical focus is on things other than correlation coefficients and
means. For this reason, it is best to consider a *t*-test to be a general tool that
can be used to accomplish a variety of inferential goals.

Although a *t*-test can focus on many things, it is used most often when the researcher is concerned with one or two means. In fact, *t*-tests are used so frequently to deal with means that many researchers equate the term *t-test* with the
notion of "a test focusing on the mean(s)." These researchers use a modifying
phrase to clarify how many means are involved and the nature of the samples,
thus leading to the terms "one-sample *t*-test," "independent-samples *t*-test,"
"correlated-samples *t*-test," "matched *t*-test," "dependent-samples *t*-test," and
"paired *t*-test." When any of these terms is used, a safe bet is that the *t*-test being
referred to had the concept of mean as its statistical focus. To understand why it
is important to know that *t*-tests are usually applied to means, consider Excerpts
11.28 and 11.29. In neither case is it clear that the *t*-tests were applied to means.
An educated guess has to be made that this was the case.

TYPE I AND TYPE II ERRORS

Our final comment concerns the conclusion reached whenever the hypothesis testing procedure or the hybrid approach to testing H_0 is used. Because the

---

Excerpts 11.28–11.29 A *t*-Test on Means Without Reference to Means

---

Among the youths who identified school and work as their primary stressor, younger adolescents perceived their family climate as characterized by significantly less open communication and expressiveness ($t = 3.21, p < .01$) and more rigidity with regard to rules and procedures ($t = 2.06, p < .05$) than did older adolescents.

Source: M. Stern and M. A. Zevon. (1990). Stress, coping, and family environment: The adolescent's response to naturally occurring stressors. *Journal of Adolescent Research, 5*(3), p. 298.

As hypothesized, this research shows that students requiring external discipline perceived significantly less intimacy with their families than do students who behave in generally more socially acceptable ways.

Source: P. Yelsma, J. Yelsma and A. Hovestadt. (1991). Autonomy and intimacy of self- and externally disciplined students: Families or origin and the implementation of an adult mentor program. *The School Counselor, 39*(1), p. 24.

---

decision to reject or fail-to-reject H_0 is fully inferential in nature (being based on sample data), there is *always* the possibility that a Type I or Type II error will be committed. You need to keep this in mind as you read technical research reports, for most researchers do not allude to the possibility of inferential error as they present their results or discuss their findings. In certain cases, the researcher simply presumes that you know that a Type I or Type II error may occur whenever a null hypothesis is tested. In other cases, the researcher unfortunately may have overlooked this possibility in the excitement of seeing that the statistical results were congruent with the research hypothesis.

Consider Excerpt 11.30, taken from the Discussion section of a recent article. This study was well designed and it dealt with a topic that was (and is) extremely important. In the last of the three sentences presented, note that the researcher stated only that his study *suggests* something. He did not use the word "demonstrates" or the word "confirms" or the word "proves." We believe, as a consequence, that this researcher *was* sensitive to the possibility that the three *t*-test results amount to nothing more that three Type I errors—even though this is a very remote possibility. It is the responsibility of those who read this article (and others like it) to understand the importance of the word "suggests" and to recognize that any statistically significant finding *may* be nothing more than a Type I error.

To see an example where a set of researchers neglected the possibility of a Type II error, return to Chapter 7 and take another look at Excerpt 7.40. The final sentence of that excerpt strikes us as an assertion by the researchers that they have discovered something definitive. It almost seems as if they have found a new "law of learning." Although the researchers base

---

Excerpt 11.30   A Conclusion That Seems to Neglect the Concept of a Type I Error

---

Wolchik *et al.* (1985) found that in joint custody arrangements it is possible to have high depression, high hostility, and moderately high self-esteem. The YES study contradicts the Wolchik study. It supports the findings of the majority of studies, and shows that hostility and depression have a positive relationship that is inverse to self-esteem. It also suggests that among adolescents in crisis the emotional impact of these constructs is significantly more extreme than it is among adolescents who are not in crisis (see Table I).

Table 1

Instrument	YES			Comparative sample	
	Mean	SD	t	Mean	SD
Hostility	41.3	9.8	6.62[a]	29.49	9.91
Depression	19	11.8	3.83[a]	10.3	8.41
Self-Esteem	53	17.8	−3.15[a]	63.8	16.3

[a]$p < .05$.

Source: B. E. Maxwell. (1992). Hostility, depression, and self-esteem among troubled and homeless adolescents in crisis. *Journal of Youth and Adolescence, 21*(2), pp. 144–145.

their "discovery" on a *t*-test comparison of means, it *may* be that the null hypothesis they tested was false.

Remember that *inferences* are always involved when (1) confidence intervals are placed around means or differences between means and (2) null hypotheses involving one or two means are evaluated. Nothing is *proven* by any of these techniques, regardless of the results obtained by the researcher.

REVIEW TERMS

Analysis of variance	*MS*
Confidence interval	Overlapping distributions
Correlated samples	Paired samples
Dependent samples	Pseudo-Bonferroni adjustment
df	procedure
F-test	Robust
Homogeneity of variance	SS
assumption	*t*-test
Independent samples	*z*-test
Matched samples	

REVIEW QUESTIONS

1. Of the 10 confidence intervals presented in Excerpt 11.1, how many have $\overline{X}$ positioned exactly halfway between the interval's endpoints?

2. If a researcher randomly assigns each of 100 individuals to either the experimental group or the control group, should the resulting groups be thought of as correlated samples or as independent samples?

3. What was the likely null hypothesis that was set up in connection with Excerpt 11.5?

4. In the Results section of the article from which Excerpt 11.4 was taken, the researcher stated:

   > The independent t test showed that the mean for Tape A was significantly higher ($M = 6.01$; i.e., closer to the culturally consistent perspective) than the mean for Tape B ($M = 1.84$; i.e., closer to the culturally discrepant perspective), $t(16) = 20.70$, p $<.001$, two tailed.

   Based upon the information provided in this statement, how many pieces of data was the comparison of the two means based on?

5. If an F-test is used to compare the means of two independent samples and if it turns out that $F(1,28) = 6.13, p <.05$, how many subjects were involved in the study?

6. Based on information contained in the ANOVA table presented below, what numerical value would the researchers end up with for their calculated value?

Source	df	SS	MS	F
Between groups	1	12		
Within groups	18	54		

7. Suppose two researchers analyze the same data set that came from two independent samples. Also suppose that they each decide to test the same null hypothesis; $H_0: \mu_1 = \mu_2$. The first researcher uses a confidence interval approach to assessing the difference between the two sample means, with a result that 95 percent CI: 6.7, 18.4. If the second researcher uses the hypothesis testing procedure with $\alpha = .05$, what decision regarding H_0 will be made?

8. If the researchers associated with Excerpt 11.15 had used the Bonferroni technique to make sure that their Type I error risk was equal to .05 for the *set* of comparisons conducted, what alpha level would have been used for each separate t-test?

9. (True or False) Whereas strength-of-association indices *can* be computed in studies concerned with the mean of a single sample, they *cannot* be computed in studies concerned with the means of two samples.

10. If a researcher uses sample data to test the homogeneity of variance assumption in a study involving two independent samples, what will the null hypothesis be? Will the researcher hope that this null hypothesis is rejected or not rejected?

11. With respect to Excerpt 11.9, should a check have been made on the equal variance assumption before using the ANOVA F-test to compare the two means? Why or why not?

12. If the measuring instrument used to collect data has less than perfect reliability, the confidence intervals built around a mean or the difference between two means will be _____ (wider/narrower) than would have been the case if the data had been perfectly reliable.

13. (True or False) A statistically significant difference between the means of two correlated or independent samples indicates that most of the subjects in the higher-scoring group had higher scores than any of the scores earned by subjects in the other group.

TESTS ON THREE OR MORE MEANS USING A ONE-WAY ANOVA

In Chapter 11, we considered various techniques used by researchers when they apply inferential statistics within studies focusing on one or two means. We now wish to extend that discussion by considering the main inferential technique used by researchers when their studies involve three or more means. The popular technique used in these situations is called analysis of variance and it is abbreviated **ANOVA.**

As we pointed out in the preceding chapter, the analysis of variance can be used to see if there is a significant difference between two sample means. Hence, this particular statistical technique is quite versatile. It can be used when a researcher wants to compare two means, three means, or any number of means. It is also versatile in ways that will become apparent in later chapters.

The analysis of variance is an inferential tool that is widely used in many disciplines. Although a variety of statistical techniques have been developed to help applied researchers deal with three or more means, ANOVA ranks number 1 in popularity. Moreover, there is a big gap between ANOVA and whatever ranks number 2!

In the current chapter, we focus our attention on the simplest version of ANOVA, something called a one-way analysis of variance. We will begin with a discussion of the statistical purpose of a one-way ANOVA, followed by a clarification of how a one-way ANOVA differs from other kinds of ANOVA. Then, we will turn our attention to the way researchers present the results of their one-way ANOVAs, with examples to show how the Bonferroni adjustment technique is used in conjunction with one-way ANOVAs, how the assumptions underlying a one-way ANOVA are occasionally tested, and how researchers sometimes concern themselves with power analyses, measures of association, and magnitude-of-effect estimates. Finally, we will offer a few tips that should serve to make you better able to decipher and critique the results of one-way ANOVAs.

THE PURPOSE OF A ONE-WAY ANOVA

When a study has been conducted in which focus is centered on three or more groups of scores, a **one-way ANOVA** permits the researcher to use the data in the samples for the purpose of making a single inferential statement concerning the means of the study's populations. Regardless of how many samples are involved, there is just one inference that extends from the set of samples to the set of populations. This single inference deals with the question, "Are the means of the various populations equal to one another?"

In Figure 12.1 we have tried to illustrate what is going on in a one-way ANOVA. There are three things to notice about this picture. First, we have drawn our picture for the specific situation where there are three comparison groups in the study; additional samples and populations can be added to parallel studies having four, five, or more comparison groups. Second, there is a single inference made from the full set of sample data to the group of populations. Finally, the focus of the inference is on the population means, even though each sample is described in terms of $\overline{X}$, SD, and n.

Although you will never come across a journal article that contains a picture like that presented in Figure 12.1, we hope that our picture will help you to understand what is going on when researchers talk about having applied a one-way ANOVA to their data. Consider, for example, Excerpt 12.1. After looking at our picture (in Figure 12.1), you should be able to look at Excerpt 12.1 and discern what the researcher is trying to accomplish by using a one-

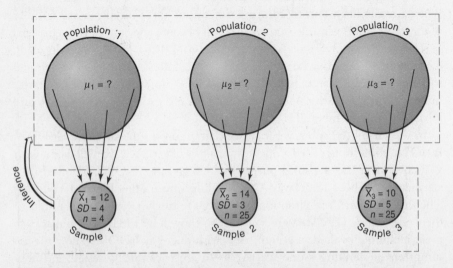

FIGURE 12.1 *Illustration of a one-way ANOVA's inferential objective.*

way ANOVA. Each column of data in Excerpt 12.1 corresponds to one of the three samples involved in the study, and the researchers' goal was to use the data from all three samples to make a single inference concerning the means of the three populations. The question being dealt with here could be stated as: "In light of the empirical information available in the samples, is it reasonable to think that mean stress level is the same in each of the three populations of mothers, with the populations being defined in terms of the kind of children paired up with each mother?"

Excerpt 12.1   Sample Data Associated with a One-Way ANOVA Study

---

The mean overall stress scores for each group are shown in Table 1. As can be seen, the mothers of children of autism reported the greatest amount of overall stress, followed by the mothers of children with cystic fibrosis, who in turn reported more stress than the control group. To test the statistical significance of these differences, an ANOVA was performed on the data.

Table 1

Analysis of variance for overall score on QRS Short Form for the autistic, cystic fibrosis, and control groups

	Group		
	Autistic	*Cystic Fibrosis*	*Control*
Mean overall scores	29.08	20.04	13.17
SD	7.3	6.7	5.1

Source: R. Bouma and R. Schweitzer. (1990). The impact of chronic childhood illness on family stress: A comparison between autism and cystic fibrosis. *Journal of Clinical Psychology, 46*(6), p. 725.

In Excerpt 12.2, we see another example where a researcher stated that a one-way ANOVA was conducted. Here again there were three comparison groups involved in the study. In subjecting the sample data to a one-way ANOVA, the researcher wanted to make a single inference to the populations associated with the samples. The question to be answered by this inferential process could be stated as, "Is the mean IRA total score the same in the population of third graders, in the population of fourth graders, and in the population of fifth graders?"

In Excerpts 12.1 and 12.2 the sample means turned out to be different from each other. Based on the fact that the $\overline{X}$s in each study were dissimilar, you might be tempted to think that there was an easy answer to the inferential question associated with each study. However, the concept of sampling

---

Excerpt 12.2   A Second Example to Illustrate the Purpose of a One-
Way ANOVA

Because of Paris and Jacobs's (1987) criterion of developmental sensitivity, we
also conducted a one-way analysis of variance to examine differences in IRA
total scores across grades. Fourth graders scored highest ($M = 30.30$, $SD =
3.82$), with fifth graders second ($M = 29.52$, $SD = 3.79$), and third graders low-
est ($M = 25.54$, $SD = 5.00$).

Source: K. V. McLain, B. E. Gridley and D. McIntosh. (1991). Value of a scale used to measure meta
cognitive reading awareness. *Journal of Educational Research, 85*(2), p. 84.

---

error makes it *impossible* to simply look at the sample means, see differences,
and then conclude that the population means are also different. Possibly, the
population means are identical, with the sample means being dissimilar simply because of sampling error. Or, maybe the discrepancy between the $\overline{\text{Xs}}$ *is*
attributable to dissimilarities among the population means. A one-way
ANOVA helps researchers to decide, in a scientific manner, whether the sample means are far enough apart to place their eggs into the second of these
two possible baskets.

THE DISTINCTION BETWEEN A ONE-WAY ANOVA AND OTHER KINDS OF ANOVA

In this chapter we are focusing our attention on the simplest kind of ANOVA,
the kind that is referred to as a **one-way ANOVA**, as a **one-factor
ANOVA**, or as a **simple ANOVA**. Since there are many different kinds of
analysis variance, it is important to clarify the difference between the kind that
we are considering in this chapter and the more complex kinds of ANOVA
that will be discussed in later chapters. (Some of the more complex kinds of
analysis of variance have the labels "two-way ANOVA," "randomized blocks
ANOVA," "repeated measures ANOVA," and "multivariate ANOVA.")

Although all ANOVAs are alike in that they focus on means, they differ in
three main respects: the number of independent variables, the number of dependent variables, and whether the samples are independent or correlated. In
terms of these distinguishing characteristics, a one-way ANOVA has *one* independent variable, it focuses on *one* dependent variable, and it involves samples that are *independent*. It is worthwhile to consider each of these defining
elements of a one-way ANOVA, because researchers sometimes use the term
ANOVA by itself without the clarifying adjective *one-way*.

When we say that there is just one independent variable, this means that
the comparison groups differ from one another, prior to the collection and
analysis of any data, in one manner that is important to the researcher. The

comparison groups can differ in terms of a qualitative variable (e.g., favorite TV show) or in terms of a quantitative variable (e.g., number of siblings) but there can be only one characteristic that defines how the comparison groups differ. Since the terms **factor** and **independent variable** mean the same thing within the context of analysis of variance, this first way in which a one-way ANOVA differs from other ANOVAs can be summed up in this manner: A one-way ANOVA has a single factor, i.e., one independent variable.

Excerpt 12.3 gives you an opportunity to see if you can tell what the independent variable was in a recent study. Since the term *one-way analysis of variance* is used within this excerpt, you know that there is only one independent variable involved, but what is it? Read the excerpt, formulate your answer, and then check our footnote to see if you're right.[1]

Excerpt 12.3   The Independent Variable in a One-Way ANOVA

Finally, as a direct assessment of construct validity, it was hypothesized that students rated by their English teachers as having different levels of social standing with peers would also exhibit significantly different levels of self-reported psychological membership. A one-way analysis of variance confirmed this hypothesis: Students rated as having high, medium, or low social standing were different in their PSSM scores (4.23, 3.87, and 3.32, respectively, $F[2,451] = 26.59$, $p < .001$).

Source: C. Goodenow. (1993). The psychological sense of school membership among adolescents: Scale development and educational correlates. *Psychology in the Schools, 30*(January), p. 85.

In Excerpt 12.3, the three comparison groups were formed by considering whether each student seemed to have a high, medium, or low social standing. Thus the comparison groups were set on the basis of one variable (or factor): apparent social standing. If each of these three groups had been subdivided on the basis of gender, there would have been six comparison groups in the study. With those six groups, there would be two independent variables—apparent social standing and gender—and a two-way ANOVA would likely become the statistical tool used to analyze the data. However, gender was not included in this study as a second independent variable and, consequently, a one-way ANOVA was applied to the data because there was only one independent variable.

Even if there is just one independent variable within a study in which the analysis of variance is applied, the ANOVA may or may not be a one-way ANOVA. The second criterion that distinguishes one-way ANOVAs from

---

[1] *The independent variable is "student level of social standing with peers, as rated by the students' English teachers."*

many other kinds of ANOVAs has to do with the number of dependent variables involved in the analysis. With a one-way ANOVA, there is always just one dependent variable. (If there are two or more dependent variables involved in the same analysis, then you are likely to see the analysis described as a multivariate ANOVA, or MANOVA.)

The **dependent variable** corresponds to the characteristic of the subjects that is measured, with the data within each group summarized using means and standard deviations. In Excerpt 12.3, no standard deviations are cited (even though they were computed), only means. Nevertheless, enough information is provided to allow us to tell that the single dependent variable was level of self-reported psychological membership, measured by the Psychological Sense of School Membership (PSSM) scale. If you review Excerpts 12.1 and 12.2, you will find that they are like Excerpt 12.3 in that only one dependent variable was associated with the one-way ANOVAs.

The third distinguishing feature of a one-way ANOVA concerns the fact that the comparison groups are independent (rather than correlated) in nature. As you will recall from the discussion in Chapter 11 of independent versus correlated samples, this means that (1) the subjects who provide the scores in any given group are different from the subjects who provide data in any other comparison group and (2) subjects are not "connected" across comparison groups because of matching or because several triplets or litters were split up (with one member of each family being put into each of the comparison groups). It is possible for an ANOVA to be applied to the data that come from correlated samples, but we will delay our discussion of that form of analysis until later in the book.

Take another look at the first three excerpts in this chapter, this time with a concern for the nature of the samples. As you will see, the samples in each of these three studies were independent, since each mother (Excerpt 12.1), schoolchild (Excerpt 12.2), and student in English (Excerpt 12.3) not only contributed a score that helped determine just one of the sample means but also was "unconnected" to anyone in the other samples.

Now, we turn our attention to the specific components of a one-way ANOVA that are relevant to those who come into contact with this popular inferential technique. We begin that effort with a consideration of the one-way ANOVA's null and alternative hypotheses.

THE ONE-WAY ANOVA'S NULL AND ALTERNATIVE HYPOTHESES

The null hypothesis of a one-way ANOVA is always set up to say that the mean score on the dependent variable is the same in each of the populations associated with the study. The null hypothesis is usually written by putting equal signs between a set of μs, with each μ representing the mean score within one of the populations. For example, if there were four comparison groups in the study, the null hypothesis would be $H_0: \mu_1 = \mu_2 = \mu_3 = \mu_4$.

If you recall our claim (in Chapter 7) that every null hypothesis must contain a pinpoint parameter, you may now be wondering how the symbolic statement at the end of the preceding paragraph qualifies as a legitimate null hypothesis since it doesn't contain any pinpoint number. In reality, there is a pinpoint number contained in that H_0 but it is simply "hidden from view." If the population means are all equal to one another, then there is no variability among those means. Therefore, we can bring H_0's pinpoint number into plain view by rewriting the null hypothesis as $H_0: \sigma_\mu^2 = 0$. As we said earlier, however, you are more likely to see H_0 written with Greek mus and equal signs and no pinpoint number (e.g., $H_0: \mu_1 = \mu_2 = \mu_3$) rather than with a sigma squared set equal to zero.

In Excerpts 12.4, 12.5, and 12.6, we see examples of one-way ANOVA null hypotheses that have appeared in research summaries. Of these three null statements, we prefer the first two because they unambiguously deal with the means of the various populations. The third null hypothesis would have been better if it had said, "There is no difference between the populations associated with the research and two control groups in terms of mean attitude toward people with disabilities. . . ."

Although we think the null hypothesis in Excerpt 12.6 could be improved, we want to applaud that author (along with the authors of Excerpts

---

Excerpts 12.4–12.6 The Null Hypothesis in a One-Way ANOVA

The null hypothesis for this study, $H_0: \mu_I = \mu_{II} = \mu_{III}$, stated that there were no differences in mean scores on the curricular need scale for each of the 30 curricular need statements among the three groups.

Source: K. W. Lambrecht. (1991). Curricular preparation needs. *Journal of Sports Management, 5*(1), p. 51.

A one-way Analysis of Variance was calculated for each socialization variable. The null hypothesis in each case was that the population means of each socialization variable were equal across [the five] levels of termination.

Source: D. E. Martin and R. A. Dodder. (1991). Socialization experiences and level of terminating participation in sports. *Journal of Sport Behavior, 14*(2), p. 121.

There is no difference between the research and [the two] control groups in their attitude toward people with disabilities as measured by the Scale of Attitudes Toward Disabled Persons (Antonak, 1982).

Source: D. D. Gilbride. Parental attitudes toward their child with a disability: Implications for rehabilitation counselors. *Rehabilitation Counseling Bulletin, 36*(3), p. 141.

12.4 and 12.5) for stating the null hypothesis associated with their one-way ANOVAs. The vast majority of researchers do not do this. They tell us about the data they collected and what happened in terms of results, but they skip over the important first step of hypothesis testing, significance testing, or the hybrid approach to testing H_0. Evidently, they assume that readers will know what the null hypothesis was.

If researchers are following the procedures of hypothesis testing or the hybrid approach to testing H_0, the null hypothesis must be accompanied by an alternative hypothesis. In other words, H_a will always say that at least two of the population means differ. Using symbols to express this thought, we get $H_a: \sigma_\mu^2 \neq 0$. Unfortunately, the alternative hypothesis is rarely included in technical discussions of research studies. Again, researchers evidently presume that their readers are familiar enough with the testing procedure being applied and familiar enough with what goes on in a one-way ANOVA to know what H_a is without being told.

PRESENTATION OF RESULTS

The outcome of a one-way ANOVA is presented in one of two ways. Researchers may elect to talk about the results within the text of their report and to present an ANOVA **summary table**. On the other hand, they may opt to exclude the table from the report and simply describe the outcome in a sentence or two of the text. (At times, a researcher wants to include the table in the report but is told by the journal editor to delete it due to limitations of space.)

Once you become skilled at deciphering the way results are presented within an ANOVA summary table, we are confident that you will have no difficulty interpreting results presented within a "tableless" report. For this reason, we begin each of the next two sections with a consideration of how the results of one-way ANOVAs are typically presented in tables. We have divided this discussion into two sections because some reports contain the results of a single one-way ANOVA while other reports present the results of many one-way ANOVAs.

RESULTS OF A SINGLE ONE-WAY ANOVA

In Excerpt 12.7, we see a pair of sentences and a table, both of which relate to a study characterized by a single independent variable, a single dependent variable, four independent samples, and a focus on means. In this excerpt, the number 3.531 is the calculated value, and it is positioned in the column labeled F. That calculated value was obtained by dividing the "Between" row's mean square by the "Within" row's mean square. Each row's **mean square** was found by dividing that row's *df* into its sum of squares, with the **sum of**

squares coming from an analysis of the sample data.[2] The *df* values, on the other hand, came from simply counting the number of groups, the number of subjects within each group, and the total number of subjects—with 1 subtracted from each number to obtain the *df* values presented in the table.[3]

Excerpt 12.7   Results of a One-Way ANOVA Presented Using Text and Table

---

The "pure restricters" obtained a mean STIC score of 44.00, which was higher than the mean STIC scores of the bulimic anorexic, normal control, and psychiatric control groups. A one-way analysis of variance of group differences on the STIC yielded a significant *F* ratio of 3.53, which indicated that there was a significant difference between groups on the STIC ($p < .01$).

Table 1

Analysis of variance: group STIC scores using only "pure restricters" in restricting anorexic group

Source	df	Sum of squares	Mean of squares	F
Between	3	453.500	151.167	3.531*
Within	35	1498.500	42.814	
Total	38	1952.000		

*$p < .05$.

Source: J. G. Woznica. (1990). Delay of gratification in bulimic and restricting anorexia nervosa patients. *Journal of Clinical Psychology, 46*(6), p. 711.

The first two *df* values were used by the researcher to locate (in the back of a statistics book) the critical value against which 3.531 was compared. We are not told how large the critical value was, but we know it must have been smaller than 3.531 because of the asterisk attached to the calculated value and the nature of the note beneath the table. While the Between and Within *df* values were useful to the researcher, the Between and Total *df*s are useful to you. By adding 1 to the Between *df*, you could determine that there were four groups being compared in this analysis. And by adding 1 to the Total *df*, you can figure out that a total of 39 subjects were involved in the study.

---

[2] *A mean square is never computed for the Total row of a one-way ANOVA or for the Total row of any other kind of ANOVA.*

[3] *The Within df was computed first by subtracting 1 from each of the four sample sizes, and then by adding the four n − 1 values.*

In Excerpt 12.8, we see another one-way ANOVA summary table that closely resembles the one we just considered, except this time the results suggest that the null hypothesis was not rejected. You can discern this from the p-level (i.e., "F prob.") presented to the right of the calculated value. Since the data-based p-level is larger than the widely used alpha level of .05, the researcher most likely concluded that the three sample means were not far enough apart to suggest differences among the three population means.

Excerpt 12.8   Another One-Way ANOVA Summary Table

Table 4

ANOVA summary table of alienation total scores across racial-ethnic groups

Group	df	Sums of squares	Mean squares	F ratio	F prob.
Between groups	2	550.806	275.403	1.95	.14
Within groups	90	1268.81	140.876		
Total	92	1253.60			

Source: R. J. Steward, S. Germain, and J. D. Jackson. (1993). Alienation and interactional style: A study of successful Anglo, Asian, and Hispanic university students. *Journal of College Student Development, 33,* p. 154.

Before leaving Excerpt 12.8, you should notice three things. To begin with, the first and second rows of numbers are labeled **Between groups** and **Within groups**, respectively (rather than simply "Between" and "Within" as was the case in Excerpt 12.7). Second, the first column of Excerpt 12.8 is labeled "Group"; this is somewhat unusual, as most researchers use the word **Source** or the term **Source of Variation** to label the names of the rows. Finally, the title of the table provides information as to the independent and dependent variables, thus allowing you to tell that racial-ethnic groups were compared in terms of mean total alienation score.

Now consider Excerpt 12.9. The authors of this excerpt provide information in the upper section of their table on the six samples that were compared and then present the results of their one-way ANOVA in the lower section of the table. This ANOVA summary table closely resembles the one we looked at in Excerpt 12.7 except for three differences. First, the SS column is positioned to the left (not the right) of the *df* column. Second, the rows are labeled "Program" and **"Error"** (rather than "Between groups" and "Within groups").[4]

---

[4]*The first row of a one-way ANOVA summary table is frequently labeled so as to correspond with the name of the independent variable. The label on the second row, "error," is a synonym for "Within groups."*

Finally, the third row, for "Total," has been omitted. Nothing is lost by having only two rows of numbers, since the total number of subjects in the study can be determined by adding the dfs from the two rows that are provided (5 + 582 = 587) and then adding 1 (587 + 1 = 588).

Excerpt 12.9   A Table Giving Information on Each of Six Samples and a One–Way ANOVA Summary Table

Table 8

Average hourly wage by program area

Program area	n	M	SD
Services	26	5.39	1.40
Medical/health	206	8.01	1.64
Child care/food	22	4.65	1.29
Secretarial/business	219	6.58	2.29
Technology	106	8.08	2.64
Production	9	8.46	3.69
Total	588	7.22	2.35

Source	SS	df	MS	F	p
Program	307	5	61.4	12.8	<.001*
Error	2,798	582	4.8		

* = statistically significant result.

Source: J. Carifio, R. Biron, and A. Shweder. (1992). Results of the vocational education data system employer follow-up survey for Massachusetts community colleges. *Community/Junior College Quarterly, 16*(3), p. 301.

The final one-way ANOVA summary table that we want you to examine appears in Excerpt 12.10. The table in this excerpt has some obvious differences from the ones considered in Excerpts 12.7–12.9, but the basic finding should be clear: The variability among the four sample means being compared was large enough to cast doubt on the null hypothesis of equal population means.

In Excerpt 12.10, notice that the title of the table indicates the two variables involved in the investigation but does not clarify which is the independent variable and which is the dependent variable. It could be that groups differing in learning style preference were compared in terms of mean orientation to reading instruction. On the other hand, it could be that groups differing in orientation to reading instruction were compared in terms of mean learning style preference. In situations like this, where the title does not

Excerpt 12.10   Another One-Way ANOVA Summary Table

Table 1

The relationship between learning style preference and orientation to reading instruction

Source	SS	df	MS	F	p
Total	8530.79	40	—	—	—
Betw groups	2140.79	3	713.6	4.132	<.025
Within grps	6390.00	37	—	—	—

Source: A. P. Wakefield. (1992). An investigation of teaching style and orientation to reading instruction. *Reading Improvement, 29*(3), p. 185.

specify what is the "grouping" variable and what is the "score" variable, you should assume that the first variable mentioned is the independent variable. That was the case in this study.

Although the results of a one-way ANOVA are sometimes presented in a table similar to those we have just considered, it is more often the case that the outcome of the statistical analysis simply will be talked about in the text of the report, with no table included. In Excerpts 12.11–12.13, we see three illustrations of a one-way ANOVA being summarized in one or two sentences.

In each of these excerpts, enough information is provided to allow you to have a sense of what the independent and dependent variables were: rotations

Excerpts 12.11–12.13   Presentation of a One-Way ANOVA's Results Without a Table

A one-way ANOVA comparing pretest total score means for each rotation found no significant difference among the five rotations.

Source: M. C. Duerson, J. W. Thomas, J. Chang, and C. B. Stevens. (1992). Medical students' knowledge and misconceptions about aging: Responses to Palmore's Facts on Aging Quizzes. *The Gerontologist, 32*(2), p. 173.

A one-way ANOVA on the interpretation measure, with condition (high arousal, low arousal, and control) as the independent variable, yielded a significant effect, $F(2,57) = 3.65, p < .05$.

Source: D. H. Olson and C. D. Claiborn. (1990). Interpretation and arousal in the counseling process. *Journal of Counseling Psychology, 37*(2), p. 135.

(Continued)

Excerpts 12.11–12.13 Presentation of a One-Way ANOVA's
Results Without a Table *(Continued)*

A one-way ANOVA of subjects' agreement with the proposition that aerosol spray cans should be banned revealed a statistically significant effect of condition, $F(2,109) = 5.13$, $p < .01$. The pattern of means was consistent with the hypothesis; the means were 0.23, 0.67 and 1.47 in the no-message control, low accessible source, and high accessible source conditions, respectively.

Source: D. R. Roskos-Ewoldsen and R. H. Fazio. (1992). The accessibility of source likability as a determinant of persuasion. *Personality and Social Psychology Bulletin, 18*(1), p. 21.

and pretest total score in Excerpt 12.11, condition and score on the interpretation measure in Excerpt 12.12, and condition and level of agreement about banning aerosol spray cans in Excerpt 12.13. You also are told, through words and *p*s, what happened to the null hypothesis in each study. And in two of the excerpts, the researchers included the calculated value.

In Excerpts 12.12 and 12.13, two numbers appear in parentheses next to each *F*. These are the *df* values taken from the Between groups and Within groups rows of the one-way ANOVA summary table. By adding 1 to the first of these *df* values, you can verify how many groups were compared. To determine how many subjects were involved in each study, you must add the two *df* values together and then add 1 to the sum. Thus, the study from which Excerpt 12.12 was taken was based on 60 subjects, whereas the study that supplied Excerpt 12.13 involved 112 subjects.

RESULTS OF TWO OR MORE ONE-WAY ANOVAS

In studies characterized by at least three comparison groups, a concern for means, and a single independent variable, data are often collected on two or more dependent variables. Although such data sets can be analyzed in various ways, many researchers choose to conduct a separate one-way ANOVA for each of the multiple dependent variables. In a small number of studies, multiple one-way ANOVAs are conducted because data on a single dependent variable are grouped in different ways to reflect the researcher's interest in multiple independent variables. Eventually, you will encounter research reports that fall into either of these two categories. Accordingly, we ought to look at some of the different ways researchers present their results when more than one one-way ANOVA has been conducted.

In Excerpt 12.14, we see two one-way ANOVAs that have been combined into a single table. Since the upper and lower halves of this table closely resemble the ANOVA summary tables we have already considered, we doubt that you will have any difficulty with either set of results. Simply stated, there were three diagnostic groups in this study, with data collected on two major dependent variables: physiological adaptation and psychological adaptation. A one-way ANOVA was conducted on the data corresponding to each dependent variable.

Excerpt 12.14   Results of Two One-Way ANOVAs Combined into One Table

---

Analysis of variance procedures were performed for selected major variables across diagnostic groups to determine whether group differences existed. There was a significant difference in physiologic adaptation (Table 1) among the three chronic illness groups, $F = 13.19, p = .0000$. However, there were no significant differences in psychological adaptation, $F = 1.85, p = .1595$ (Table 1).

Table 1

Analysis of variance of physiological adaption (PAX) and psychological adaptation (MHI) by diagnostic group

Source	df	Sum of squares	Mean squares	F ratio	p
Physiological adaptation (N = 209)					
Between groups	2	1340.19	670.09	13.19	.0000*
Within groups	207	10508.75	50.77		
Total	209	11848.94			
Psychological adaptation (N = 204)					
Between groups	2	2782.44	1391.22	1.85	.1595
Within groups	202	151691.80	750.95		
Total	204	154474.24			

*$p < .001$.

Source: S. E. Pollock, B. J. Christian, and D. Sands. (1990). Responses to chronic illness: Analysis of psychological and physiological adaptation. *Nursing Research, 39*(5), p. 302. © The American Journal of Nursing Company. Used with permission. All rights reserved.

Before leaving Excerpt 12.14, we need to point out something important that holds true for any presentation of results that contains the statistical outcome of two or more statistical tests. In such a presentation, a distinct null hypothesis is associated with each outcome that turned out to be either statistically significant or statistically nonsignificant. Hence, two null hypotheses were connected to Excerpt 12.14. Each H_0 would, on the surface, look the same: $H_0: \mu_1 = \mu_2 = \mu_3$. They differ, however, with respect to the variable represented by the three μs. In one of the ANOVAs, the variable was physiological adaptation; in the other analysis, the variable was psychological adaptation. The first H_0 was rejected whereas the second H_0 was retained.

In Excerpt 12.15, we see another case where two one-way ANOVAs were combined into one table. Each of these ANOVAs was conducted on a different dependent variable, with the results from one analysis presented on the first, third, and fifth rows (Labeled "I") while the results from the other analysis are located on the second, fourth, and sixth rows (labeled "F"). Notice how the *df* values are identical for both analyses; this was brought about by the same 37 subjects in the same three groups being used in each analysis.

Excerpt 12.15   Results of Two One-Way ANOVAs Again Combined into the Same Table

Table 3

Analysis of variance for social perspective taking in the individual (I) and friendship domains (F)

Source		*df*	*Sum of squares*	*Means squares*	*F*
Between groups	(I)	2	12.8377	6.4188	25.998*
	(F)	2	14.4479	7.2239	32.145*
Within groups	(I)	34	8.3945	0.2469	
	(F)	34	7.6408	0.2247	
Total	(I)	36	21.2322		
	(F)	36	22.0886		

*$p < .0001$.

Source: L. J. Bradley and R. C. Meredith. (1991). Interpersonal development: A study with children classified as educable mentally retarded. *Education and Training in Mental Retardation, 26*(2), p. 136.

We now turn to a table that contains the results of nine one-way ANOVAs. Although we have included in Excerpt 12.16 some of the research report's text as well as the table displaying the ANOVA results, we hope that you can decipher what is going on in the table without reading the researcher's explanation. Most importantly, we want to call your attention to the fact that the hypothesis testing procedure was used nine times, once in conjunction with each of the various CES subscales. In each case, H_0 said that the three clusters had identical population means.

Excerpt 12.16   Results of Nine One-Way ANOVAs Presented in One Table

Table 3 shows the analysis of variance (ANOVA) results with the CES dimension means . . . as dependent variables and with the three clusters of classrooms serving as levels of the independent variable. The cluster mean square figure represents the between-cluster variance, and the error mean square figure represents the within-cluster variance.

Table 3

Analyses of variance of the three clusters formed by classroom environment scales and 36 science classrooms

CES subscale	Cluster MS	df	Error MS	df	F	p <
Involvement	38.34	2	1.09	33	35.28	.001
Affiliation	5.40	2	.42	33	12.62	.001
Teacher support	26.00	2	.76	33	34.15	.001
Task orientation	5.19	2	.61	33	8.50	.002
Competition	4.13	2	.37	33	11.26	.001
Order and organization	30.75	2	1.35	33	22.72	.001
Rule clarity	6.99	2	.51	33	13.61	.001
Teacher control	6.24	2	1.20	33	5.19	.012
Innovation	13.14	2	.63	33	20.65	.001

Source: J. T. Fouts and R. E. Myers. (1992). Classroom environments and middle school students' views of science. *Journal of Educational Research, 85*(6), p. 359.

In many research reports, the results of more than one-way ANOVA are presented without any ANOVA summary table(s). We now turn our attention to a few examples where multiple one-way ANOVA results are discussed in the text of the report. These illustrations appear in Excerpts 12.17–12.19. Despite the differences among these three excerpts, notice that in each presentation of results you can determine (1) how many null hypotheses were tested, (2) what decision was made regarding each H_0, (3) what the dependent variables were, (4) how many comparison groups were involved in each analysis, and (5) how many subjects were measured. As a check on your ability to recognize these things, are you able to tell that there were four comparison groups in the study from which Excerpt 12.17 was taken, that there were 2,812 subjects used in the study from which Excerpt 12.18

Excerpts 12.17–12.19   Results of More Than One One-Way
ANOVA Presented Without Any Table

A one-way ANOVA was performed for each task, yielding a significant effect on writing $[F(3,116) = 44.86; p < .001]$ and on reading $[F(3,116) = 56.81; p < .001]$.

Source: M. A. Nippold, I. E. Schwarz, and R. A. Undlin. (1992). Use and understanding of adverbial conjuncts: A developmental study of adolescents and young adults. *Journal of Speech and Hearing Research, 35*(1), p. 112.

To examine potential differences in mean performances among grades on the two measures, separate one-way analyses of variance were conducted. Significant differences among grades for the number of correct words per minute were found for the third-grade passage, $F(5,2806) = 642.02, p < .0001$, and for the HJ Word List $F(5,2806) = 721.18, p < .0001$.

Source: K. Rodden-Nord and M. R. Shinn. (1991). The range of reading skills within and across general education classrooms: Contributions to understanding special education for students with mild handicaps. *The Journal of Special Education, 24*(4), p. 445.

Preliminary analyses were conducted to determine if there were significant racial or ethnic group differences (Whites versus Blacks versus Asians) in the life events scales. The results of these one-way ANOVAs were: Total life events, $F=1.20$, $df=2/152$, $p=.31$; Personal life events, $F=2.83$, $df=2/156$, $p=.06$; Interpersonal life events, $F=.23$, $df=2/159$, $p=.80$; and Illness life events, $F=1.91$, $df=2/159, p=.15$.

Source: F. T. L. Leong and A. Vaux. (1991). The relationship between stressful life events, psychological distress, and social desirability. *Measurement and Evaluation in Counseling and Development, 23,* p.

---

was taken, and that there were four null hypotheses tested in the study from which Excerpt 12.19 was taken?

In each of the excerpts that we have looked at in this section, multiple one-way ANOVAs were conducted because the researchers had data on multiple dependent variables. Such situations are quite typical. In Excerpt 12.20, however, we see a different situation. In this study, activity level was the dependent variable in each of two one-way ANOVAs conducted on separate independent variables. The children were first grouped into three comparison groups on the basis of how many obese parents each child had, with data on activity level analyzed. Then the same children were regrouped into two comparison groups on the basis of each child's weight, with the same data on activity level analyzed again. Actually, there were two *F*s computed in each of these analyses, because there were two measures of activity level taken (direct observation and Caltrac monitors). Altogether, four *F*s were found to be nonsignificant.

> **Excerpt 12.20** One-Way ANOVAs Conducted with Two
> Independent Variables
>
> One-way ANOVAs compared the activity levels of children as a function of the
> number of obese parents and as a function of the child's classification as normal
> weight or overweight. There were no significant effects of either the parents' or
> children's relative weight status on the children's activity levels measured by ei-
> ther direct observation or Caltrac monitors (all Fs < 1).
>
> *Source:* M. Noland, F. Danner, K. DeWalt, M. McFadden, and J. M. Kotchen. (1990). The measure-
> ment of physical activity in young children. *Research Quarterly for Exercise and Sport, 61*(2), p. 152.

THE BONFERRONI ADJUSTMENT TECHNIQUE

In the preceding section, we looked at seven examples where multiple one-
way ANOVAs were used to assess the data from two or more dependent variables. When a researcher has a situation such as this, there will be an inflated
Type I error risk unless something is done to compensate for the fact that
multiple tests are being conducted. In other words, if the data associated with
each of several dependent variables are analyzed separately by means of a one-
way ANOVA, the probability of incorrectly rejecting at least one of the null
hypotheses is greater than the common alpha level used across the set of tests.

Several statistical techniques are available for dealing with the problem of
an inflated Type I error risk. Among these, the **Bonferroni adjustment
procedure** appears to be the most popular choice among applied researchers. As you will recall from our earlier discussions of this procedure, the
researcher compensates for the fact that multiple tests are being conducted by
making the alpha level more rigorous on each of the separate tests.

In Excerpt 12.21, we see an example of the Bonferroni technique being
used in a study where several one-way ANOVAs were conducted. Each of
these ANOVAs was applied to the data associated with a different subscale of
the study's primary measuring instrument. This instrument dealt with situations related to excessive drinking, and the three comparison groups were
light, moderate, and heavy drinkers.

In the study from which Excerpt 12.21 was taken, the researcher set
alpha equal to .006 for each of the eight one-way ANOVAs that were conducted. Note that 8 times .006 approximates the desired .05 Type I error
risk for the full set of tests. If the researcher had wanted to test one or two
of the eight dependent variables with more power than the others, the alpha
level on the separate tests could be set at different levels. (e.g., .02 for two
tests, .002 for four tests, and .001 for two tests)—as long as the sum of the
separate alphas did not exceed the desired Type I error risk. Although researchers have the option of using the Bonferroni technique in this fashion,

Excerpt 12.21 The Bonferroni Adjustment Procedure Used in Conjunction with One-Way ANOVAs

Means and standard deviations for each IDS situation for light, moderate, and heavy drinkers are presented in Table 1. [Table 1 is not included here.] To determine whether the groups differed on the situations associated with excessive drinking, I performed eight separate one-way analyses of variance (ANOVAs) on the IDS scales. To control for Type I error, the Bonferroni correction was used to hold the familywise error rate to .05 (Grove & Andreasen, 1982); that is, alpha (.05) was divided by 8, and only p values less than .006 were considered significant.

Source: K. B. Carey. (1993). Situational determinants of heavy drinking among college students. *Journal of Counseling Psychology, 40*(2), p. 218.

the vast majority choose the option of using the same reduced alpha for all tests that are conducted.

There is no law, of course, that directs all researchers to deal with the problem of an inflated Type I error risk when multiple one-way ANOVAs are used, each with a different dependent variable. Furthermore, there are circumstances where it would be unwise to take any form of "corrective action." Nevertheless, we believe that you should value more highly those reports wherein the researcher either (1) does something (e.g., using the Bonferroni procedure) to hold down the chances of a Type I error when multiple tests are conducted or (2) explains why nothing was done to deal with the inflated Type I error risk. If neither of these things is done, we believe that you should downgrade your evaluation of the study.

ASSUMPTIONS OF A ONE-WAY ANOVA

In Chapter 11, we discussed the four main assumptions associated with t-tests, F-tests and z-tests: independence, randomness, normality, and homogeneity of variance. Those earlier comments apply as much now to cases where a one-way ANOVA is used to compare three or more means as they did to cases where two means are compared using a t-, F-, or z-test. In particular, we hope you recall the meaning of these four assumptions and our point about how these tests are robust to the equal variance assumption when the sample sizes of the various comparison groups are equal.

We believe that too many researchers who use a one-way ANOVA pay little or no attention to the assumptions that underlie the F-test comparison of their sample means. Consequently, we encourage you to feel better about research reports that (1) contain discussions of the assumptions, (2) present results of tests that were conducted to check on the testable assumptions,

(3) explain what efforts were made to get the data in line with the assumptions, and/or (4) point out that an alternative test was used having fewer assumptions than a regular one-way ANOVA F-test. Conversely, we encourage you to lower your evaluation of research reports that do none of those things.

To illustrate some of the steps taken by researchers relative to the assumptions of **normality** and **homogeneity of variance**, we have included five excerpts from recent studies. The first of these, Excerpt 12.22, shows how a research team was aware of the assumption of normality. It is unusual to see this assumption tested, partly because many researchers have the mistaken belief that the F-test is always robust to violations of the normality assumption and partly because others either are unaware of the assumption or don't know how to test it. In any event, we salute the researchers associated with Excerpt 12.22 for "checking their data" before conducting a one-way ANOVA F-test.

Excerpt 12.22   Testing the Normality Assumption Before Using a One-Way ANOVA

[A] one-way analysis was judged to be more appropriate in this case. Shapiro-Wilk tests were conducted to test for the normality of the data. These tests suggest that the data distribution is normal. For this reason, parametric statistical analyses assuming normality were used with more confidence.

Source: M. Boubekri, R. B. Hull, and L. L. Boyer. (1991). Impact of window size and sunlight penetration on office workers' mood and satisfaction: A novel way of assessing sunlight. *Environment and Behavior, 23*(4), p. 485.

In Excerpts 12.23 and 12.24, we see two instances where the homogeneity of variance assumption was tested. In both of these cases, the null hypothesis of equal variance was rejected using the Barlett-Box test.[5] Notice how the data in each study made it appear that the equal variance assumption was untenable. Once this was determined, the researchers transformed their data in an effort to obtain data sets that would be in agreement with the assumption. (The log and square root transformations are frequently used for this purpose, as are the inverse and arcsin transformations.)

Occasionally, a consideration of assumptions will cause a researcher to compare the sample means using a test procedure that is different from the

---

[5]*Other frequently used tests to evaluate the equal variance assumption are called Levene's test, Hartley's F-max test, Cochran's C test, and the Bartlett-Kendall Log s^2 test.*

Excerpts 12.23–12.24   Testing the Equal Variance Assumption
Before Using a One-Way ANOVA

Because the Bartlett–Box test for homogeneity of variance indicated that lack of homogeneity existed for several of the analyses of variance (ANOVAs), we performed a square-root transformation of the data to equalize the variances before calculating the F ratios. This satisfied the common variance assumption required for the ANOVAs.

Source: J. C. Wofford and V. L. Goodwin. (1990). Effects of feedback on cognitive processing and choice of decision style. *Journal of Applied Psychology, 75*(6), p. 606.

Raw scores on four of the dependent measures did not meet the homogeneity of variance assumption as determined by Bartlett's Box F test. The values on these four variables. . . were transformed by computing the base 10 logarithm of $(x + 1)$.

Source: R. J. Lueger and K. J. Gill. (1990). Frontal-lobe dysfunction in conduct disorder adolescents. *Journal of Clinical Psychology, 46*(6), p. 699.

---

one-way ANOVA F-test covered in this chapter. Excerpts 12.25 and 12.26 illustrate situations where this has been done. In the first of these studies, the decision to use a different kind of test was made after the equal variance assumption was shown to be untenable. In the second excerpt, it appears that the researchers simply made a decision at the outset to compare means using a test that did not have an equal variance assumption.

Excerpts 12.25–12.26   The Brown–Forsythe and Welch Tests as
Alternatives to the Regular One-Way
ANOVA

Several measures failed Levene's test for equality of variance. For these measures, comparisons between groups within each time period were based on Brown-Forsythe's one-way analysis of variance (Dixon, Brown, Engelman, Hill & Jennrich, 1988), which does not assume equal variance.

Source: D. M. Clark, E. Winton, and L. Thynn. (1993). A further experimental investigation of thought suppression. *Behavior Research and Therapy, 31*(2), p. 208.

We used Welch's (1951) F' test to compute univariate analyses of variance for each factor across all groups. This test does not require equal ns or homogeneity of variance.

Source: V. Moreno and F. J. diVesta. (1991). Cross-cultural comparisons of study habits. *Journal of Educational Psychology, 83*(2), p. 235.

STATISTICAL SIGNIFICANCE VERSUS PRACTICAL SIGNIFICANCE

Researchers who use a one-way ANOVA to compare three or more means can do one of four things in an effort to avoid ending up with a result that is insignificant in any practical sense even though it is statistically significant.[6] One option is to conduct a **power analysis** before any data are collected, with the outcome of the power analysis dictating how large the sample sizes should be. A second option is to estimate the strength of association (between the independent and dependent variables) after the sample data have been collected and analyzed to obtain the F-ratio. The third option is to estimate the **magnitude of the observed effect** associated with each comparison group. The final option is to compute a post hoc estimate of the power associated with the completed analysis.

Unfortunately, far fewer than 100 percent of the researchers who use a one-way ANOVA take the time to perform any form of analysis designed to address the issue of **practical versus statistical significance.** In our opinion, too many researchers simply use the simplest version of hypothesis testing, of significance testing, or of the hybrid approach to testing their one-way ANOVA's H_0. They collect the amount of data that time, money, or energy will allow, and then they anxiously await the outcome of the analysis. If their F-ratios turn out significant, these researchers quickly summarize their studies, with emphasis put on the fact that "significant findings" have been obtained.

We encourage you to upgrade your evaluation of those one-way ANOVA research reports that provide evidence that the researchers were concerned about practical significance as well as statistical significance. Examples of such reports are contained in Excerpts 12.27 and 12.28. In each of these studies, a

---

Excerpts 12.27–12.28   Efforts to Address the Statistical Significance Versus Practical Significance Issue

---

The four groups did differ significantly with respect to patient age, $F(3,56) = 6.42, p < .05, \omega^2 = .15$.

Source: T. G. Burish, S. L. Snyder, and R. A. Jenkins. (1991). Preparing patients for cancer chemotherapy: Effect of coping preparation and relaxation interventions. *Journal of Consulting and Clinical Psychology, 59*(4), p. 521.

The bivariate relationships (one-way analysis of variance) between the religious affiliation categories and retributiveness, religious identity salience, and biblical literalness are reported in Table 1.

(Continued)

---

[6] *We discussed the difference between statistical significance and practical significance in Chapters 8 and 9. You may wish to review that material before proceeding.*

Excerpts 12.27–12.28   Efforts to Address the Statistical Significance Versus Practical Significance Issue *(Contintued)*

Table 1

Bivariate relationships of religious affiliation with retributiveness, religious identity salience, and biblical literalness (N = 322)

Religious affiliation	Scale means		
	Retributiveness	Salience	Literalness
Fundamentalist prot. (43.8%)	.637	.692	1.667
No affiliation (11.5%)	−.547	−1.772	−1.747
Catholic (14.0%)	−.258	−.261	−.345
Liberal/moderate prot. (30.7%)	−.426	.032	−1.025
Eta	.226	.292	.403
$F_{3,318}$	5.685	9.914	20.573
p	<.001	<.001	<.001

Source: H. G. Grasmick, E. Davenport, M. B. Chamlin, and R. J. Bursik, Jr. (1992). Protestant fundamentalism and the retributive doctrine of punishment. *Criminology, 30*(1), p. 31.

strength-of-association index was computed. In the first of these excerpts, the index was omega squared; in the second excerpt, it was eta.

TIPS FOR DECIPHERING/CRITIQUING RESEARCH RESULTS BASED ON ONE-WAY ANOVA

Before we conclude our discussion of inferential comparisons of three or more means, we want to offer a few tips that we hope will increase your skills at deciphering and critiquing research reports based on one-way ANOVAs.

DETERMINING WHETHER A ONE-WAY ANOVA HAS BEEN USED

There are many different kinds of ANOVA used by applied researchers, with *F*-tests computed within each variation. Because of this fact and because researchers often do not use a clarifying adjective (such as "one-way" or "one-factor") to signify the specific kind of ANOVA employed, it is sometimes difficult to tell whether a researcher has used the type of statistical procedure focused upon in this chapter. We have a simple three-pronged guideline that will help you tell whether a one-way ANOVA stands in front of you as you travel through the forest of ANOVAs, ANCOVAs, and MANOVAs.

A one-way ANOVA focuses on means. Therefore, if you are looking at the results of an *F*-test, first ask yourself whether the statistical focus of the analysis was means. If so, move to our second question. Now ask yourself whether subjects were measured just once on the dependent variable dealt with by the *F*-test you think might have come from a one-way ANOVA. If the answer to this second query is affirmative, you can move to our third and final question. If you add 1 to the sum of the two *df* values associated with the *F* you are looking at, ask yourself whether you get a number that matches the total number of subjects that were measured. If you do, then you're looking at the results of a one-way ANOVA.

To illustrate how this procedure works, consider Excerpt 12.29. Although we are not told that the *F* of .07 came from a one-way ANOVA, our three-pronged litmus test will tell us whether or not it did. It's clear that the *F*-test dealt with means, so let's move on to our second question. Since the *F*-test that we are trying to interpret was based on data collected at Time 1, and since no one would measure a person's age more than once at the same time, we may presume that repeated measures on age at T1 were not collected. We therefore move to our third question. It turns out that the sum of the two *df* values plus 1 does, in fact, equal the total number of subjects. Therefore, what we are looking at is a one-way ANOVA *F*-test.

Excerpt 12.29   Checking an *F*-Ratio to See If It Came from a One-Way ANOVA

Of these 95 subjects, 12 bulimics, 20 subclinical bulimics, and 12 normals participated in the study at Time 1 (T1), Time 2 (T2), and Time 3 (T3). These 44 subjects are the focus of the present study. . . . All demographic measures were taken at T1. The mean age was 18.5 for the bulimic subjects, 18.6 for the subclinical subjects, and 18.6 for the normal subjects, $F(2,41) = .07$, *ns*.

Source: M. H. Thelen, J. Farmer, L. M. Mann, and J. Pruitt. (1990). Bulimia and interpersonal relationships: A longitudinal study. *Journal of Counseling Psychology, 37*(1), p. 86.

SIGNIFICANT AND NONSIGNIFICANT RESULTS FROM ONE-WAY ANOVAS

When researchers say that they have obtained a statistically significant result from a one-way ANOVA, this means that they have rejected the null hypothesis. Because you are unlikely to see the researchers articulate the study's H_0 (in words or symbols) or even see them use the term *null hypothesis* in discussing the results, it is especially important for you to remember (1) that a significant *F* means H_0 has been rejected, (2) what the one-way ANOVA H_0 stipulates, and (3) how to interpret correctly that decision to reject H_0.

Although a one-way ANOVA can be used to compare the means of two groups, this chapter has focused on the use of one-way ANOVAs to compare three or more means. When the data lead to a significant finding when more than two means have been contrasted, it means that the sample data are not likely to have come from populations having the same μ. This one-way ANOVA result does not provide any information as to how many of the μ values are likely to be dissimilar, nor does it provide any information as to whether any specific pair of populations are likely to have different μ values. The only thing that a significant result indicates is that the variability among the full set of sample means is larger than would be expected if all population means were identical.

Usually, a researcher wants to know more about the likely state of the population means than is revealed by a one-way ANOVA. To be more specific, the typical researcher wants to be able to make comparative statements about pairs of population means, such as "μ_1 is likely to be larger than μ_2 but μ_2 and μ_3 cannot be looked upon as different based on the sample data." To address these concerns, the researcher must move past the significant ANOVA F and apply a subsequent analysis. In the next chapter, we will consider such analyses, which are called, understandably, "post hoc" or "follow-up" tests.

Since you probably will be given information regarding the means that were compared by the one-way ANOVA, you may be tempted, if a significant result has been obtained, to consider each mean to be significantly different from every other mean. Refrain from doing this! And don't go along with researchers who discuss their results as if this can be done.

You must also be on guard when it comes to one-way ANOVAs that yield nonsignificant Fs. As we have pointed out now on several occasions, a fail-to-reject decision should not be interpreted to mean that H_0 is true. Unfortunately, many researchers make this inferential mistake when comparison groups are compared in terms of mean scores on a pretest. The researchers' goal is to see whether the comparison groups are equal to one another at the beginning of their studies, and they mistakenly interpret a nonsignificant F-test to mean that no group began with an advantage or a disadvantage.

In Excerpt 12.30, we see an example where a nonsignificant result from a one-way ANOVA applied to pretest data was misinterpreted to mean that the three comparison groups were equivalent at the outset of the study. (The sample

---

Excerpt 12.30   Improper Interpretation of a Nonsignificant One-Way ANOVA Result

---

An ANOVA conducted on the content pretests indicated that all three experimental groups entered the course with commensurate levels of content analysis skill, so that no group had "an edge" on another in terms of understanding and analyzing a sit-com.

Source: P. Hunter. Teaching critical television viewing: An approach for gifted learners. *Roeper Review,* 15(2), p. 88.

means were 47.0, 47.2, and 49.3.) We believe that two mistakes were made here. First, the focus seems to be exclusively on sample means rather than on population means. Second, the possibility of a Type II error is totally neglected.

CONFIDENCE INTERVALS

In Chapter 11, we saw how a confidence interval can be placed around the difference between two sample means. We also saw how such confidence intervals can be used to test a null hypothesis, with H_0 rejected if the null's pinpoint numerical value lies beyond the limits of the interval. As we now conclude our discussion of how researchers compare three or more means with a one-way ANOVA, you may be wondering why we haven't said anything in this chapter about the techniques of estimation.

When a study's focus is on three or more means, researchers will occasionally build a confidence interval around each of the separate sample means. This is done in situations where (1) there is no interest in comparing all the means together at one time or (2) there is a desire to probe the data in a more specific fashion after the null hypothesis of equal population means has been rejected. Whereas researchers sometimes use interval estimation (on individual means) in lieu of or as a complement to a test of the hypothesis that all μs are equal, they do not use interval estimation as an alternative strategy for testing the one-way ANOVA null hypothesis. Stated differently, you are not likely to come across research studies where a confidence interval is put around the variance of the sample means in order to test $H_0: \sigma_\mu^2 = 0$.

OTHER THINGS TO KEEP IN MIND

If we momentarily lump together the current chapter with the ones that preceded it, we can say that you have been given a slew of tips or warnings designed to help you become a more discerning recipient of research-based claims. Several of the points are important enough to repeat here.

1. The mean is focused upon in research studies more than any other statistical concept. In many studies, however, a focus on means does not allow the research question to be answered because the question deals with something other than central tendency.
2. If the researcher's interest resides exclusively in the group(s) from which data are collected, only descriptive statistics should be used in analyzing the data.
3. The reliability and validity of the researcher's data are worth considering. To the extent that reliability is lacking, it is difficult to reject H_0 even when H_0 is false. To the extent that validity is lacking, the conclusions drawn will be unwarranted because of a mismatch be-

tween what is truly being measured and what the researcher thinks is being measured with a one-way ANOVA.

4. With a one-way ANOVA, nothing is proven regardless of what the researcher concludes after analyzing the data. Either a Type I error or a Type II error always will be possible no matter what decision is made about H_0.

5. The purpose of a one-way ANOVA is to gain an insight into the population means, not the sample means.

6. Those researchers who talk about (and possibly test) the assumptions underlying a one-way ANOVA deserve credit for being careful in their utilization of this inferential technique.

7. A decision not to reject the one-way ANOVA's H_0 does not mean that all population means should be considered equal.

8. Those researchers who perform a power analysis (either before or after conducting their one-way ANOVAs) or compute strength of association indices or estimates of the magnitude of observed effects (following the application of a one-way ANOVA) are doing a more conscientious job than are those researchers who fail to do anything to help distinguish between statistical significance and practical significance.

9. The Bonferroni procedure helps to control the risk of Type I errors in studies where one-way ANOVAs are conducted on two or more dependent variables.

10. The *df* values associated with a one-way ANOVA (whether presented in an ANOVA summary table or positioned next to the calculated *F*-value in the text of the research report) can be used to determine the number of groups and the total number of subjects involved in the study.

REVIEW TERMS

ANOVA	One-factor ANOVA
Between groups	One-way ANOVA
Bonferroni adjustment procedure	Power analysis
Dependent variable	Practical significance
df	versus statistical significance
Error	Simple ANOVA
Factor	Source
F	Source of variation
Homogeneity of variance	Strength-of-association index
Independent variable	Sum of squares
Mean square	Summary table
Normality	Within groups

REVIEW QUESTIONS

1. (True or False) The purpose of a one-way ANOVA is to make an inferential statement as to the unknown value of sample means on the basis of the known value of the population means.

2. In a one-way ANOVA, how many independent variables are there? How many dependent variables?

3. In Excerpt 12.2, what were the independent and dependent variables?

4. Write out, in symbols, the null hypothesis for the one-way ANOVA that was conducted in Excerpt 12.3.

5. In Excerpt 12.8, how many comparison groups were involved, and how many subjects provided data for the one-way ANOVA?

6. With respect to Excerpt 12.9, what statistical test should have been conducted *before* the one-way ANOVA compared the six program areas in terms of mean hourly wage?

7. In Excerpt 12.10, one of the mean squares is missing. Which row of the table is missing its mean square, and what is the numerical value of the mean square that was inadvertently omitted?

8. In Excerpt 12.16, how was the first F of 35.28 computed?

9. In Excerpt 12.19, how many subjects were involved in the analysis of the data on Total life events?

10. Suppose a researcher wants to conduct 10 one-way ANOVAs, each on a separate dependent variable. Also suppose the researcher wants to conduct these ANOVAs such that the probability of making at least one Type I error is set equal to .05. To accomplish this objective, what alpha level should the researcher use in evaluating each of the F-tests?

11. What is the purpose of the Bartlett-Box F-test?

12. In Excerpt 12.28, what were the independent and dependent variable?

13. Consider again Excerpt 12.28. If the means in the first column (Retributiveness) had ended up further apart than they did, what impact would this have had on the size of the first column's eta, F, and p?

14. To determine whether an F-ratio presented in the text of a research report came from a one-way ANOVA, there are three questions to ask. (1) Did the analysis focus on means? (2) Were subjects measured just once? What is the third question?

13

Post Hoc and Planned Comparisons

In the previous chapter, we examined the setting, purpose, assumptions, and outcome of a one-way analysis of variance that compares three or more groups. In this chapter, we turn our attention to two categories of inferential procedures that are closely related to the one-way ANOVA. As with a one-way ANOVA, the procedures looked at in this chapter involve one independent variable, one dependent variable, no repeated measures, and a focus on means.

The two classes of procedures considered here are called **post hoc comparisons** and **planned comparisons**. One set of these procedures—the post hoc kind—was developed because a one-way ANOVA F, if significant, does not provide any specific insight into what caused the null hypothesis to be rejected. To know that all population means are probably not equal to one another is helpful, but differing scenarios fit the general statement that not all μs are identical. For example, with three comparison groups, it might be that two μs are equal but the third is higher, or maybe two μs are equal but the third is lower, or it could be that all three μs are different. By using a post hoc procedure, the researcher attempts to probe the data to find out which of the possible non-null scenarios is most likely to be true.

The second class of procedures considered in this chapter involves planned comparisons. These procedures were developed because researchers sometimes pose questions that cannot be answered by rejecting or failing to reject the null hypothesis of the more general one-way ANOVA H_0. For example, a researcher might wonder whether a specific pair of μs is different, or whether the average of two μs is different from a third μ. In addition to allowing researchers to answer specific questions about the population means, planned comparisons have another desirable characteristic. Simply stated, the statistical power of the tests used to answer specific, preplanned questions is higher than is the power of the more generic F-test from a one-way ANOVA. In other words, planned comparisons allow a researcher to deal with specific, *a priori* questions with less risk of a Type II error than does a two-step approach involving an ANOVA *F*-test followed by post hoc comparisons.

Researchers use post hoc comparisons more often than they do planned comparisons. For this reason, we will first consider the different test procedures and reporting schemes used when a one-way ANOVA yields a significant *F* and is followed up by a post hoc comparison. We then will turn our attention to what researchers do when they initially set up and test planned comparisons instead of following the two-step strategy of conducting a one-way ANOVA followed by a post hoc investigation. Finally, we will look at the unusual situation where planned comparisons are conducted along with a one-way ANOVA, with no post hoc investigation conducted to help explain what caused the ANOVA *F* to turn out significant.

POST HOC COMPARISONS

DEFINITION AND PURPOSE

There is confusion among researchers as to what is or is not a post hoc test. We have come across examples where researchers conducted a post hoc investigation but used the term *planned comparisons* to describe what they did. We have also come across research reports where planned comparisons were conducted by means of a test procedure that many researchers consider to be post hoc in nature. To help you avoid getting confused when you read research reports, we want to clarify what does and does not qualify as a post hoc investigation.

If a researcher conducts a one-way ANOVA and uses the outcome of the *F*-test to determine whether additional specific tests should be conducted, then such additional tests would constitute a post hoc investigation. As this definition makes clear, the defining criterion of a post hoc investigation has nothing to do with the name of the test procedure employed, with the number of tests conducted, or with the nature of the comparisons made. The only thing that matters is whether the ANOVA *F*-test must first be checked to see if further analysis of the data set is needed.

In turning to a post hoc investigation, the researcher's objective is to better understand why the ANOVA yielded a significant *F*. Stated differently, a post hoc investigation helps the researcher understand why the ANOVA H_0 was rejected. Since the H_0 specifies equality among all population means, we can say that a set of post hoc comparisons is designed to help the researcher gain insight into the pattern of μs. As we indicated at the outset of this chapter, the ANOVA *F* can turn out to be significant for different reasons—that is, because of different possible patterns of μs. The post hoc analysis helps researchers in their effort to understand the true pattern of the population means.

In light of the fact that empirical studies are usually driven by research hypotheses, it is not surprising to find that post hoc investigations are typically conducted to find out whether such hypotheses are likely to be true. Furthermore, it should not be surprising that differences in research hypotheses lead researchers to do different things in their post hoc investigations. Sometimes, for example, researchers set up their post hoc investigations to compare each sample mean against every other sample mean. On other occasions they use their post hoc tests to compare the mean associated with each of several experimental groups against a control group's mean, with no comparisons made among the experimental groups. On rare occasions, a post hoc investigation is implemented to compare the mean of one of the comparison groups against the average of the means of two or more of the remaining groups. We will illustrate each of these post hoc comparisons later in the chapter.

TERMINOLOGY

Various terms are used in a synonymous fashion to mean the same thing as the term **post hoc test**. The three synonyms that show up most often in the published literature are **follow-up test, multiple comparison test,** and *a posteriori* **test.** Excerpts 13.1–13.3 show how some of these terms have been used.

In Excerpt 13.1, notice that the term *post-hoc contrast* appears. The word **contrast** is synonymous with the term **comparison.** Hence, post hoc contrasts are nothing more than post hoc comparisons. Follow-up contrasts are nothing more than follow-up comparisons. *A posteriori* contrasts are nothing more than *a posteriori* comparisons.

It is also worth noting that the *F*-test used in the preliminary ANOVA is sometimes referred to as the **omnibus *F*-test.** This term seems appropriate

---

Excerpts 13.1–13.3 Use of the Terms *Post Hoc, Follow-Up*, and *A Posteriori*

Analyses of variance tests were conducted to analyze the data for this study. Significant *F* statistics were followed by post-hoc contrasts designed to investigate mean differences among the four coping groups.

Source: P. Mantzicopoulos. (1990). Coping with school failure: Characteristics of students employing successful and unsuccessful coping strategies. *Psychology in the Schools, 27*(2), p. 141.

In the final analysis, the relationship of context received to the quantity of support selected was examined via a one-way ANOVA comparing the five context groups. The analysis yielded $F(4,73) = 8.61, MS_e = 3.26, p < .05$. Follow-up analyses indicated that the animals-context group ($M = 5.71$) selected significantly more

(Continued)

Excerpts 13.1–13.3   Use of the Terms *Post Hoc, Follow-Up,* and *A Posteriori (Continued)*

---

items than did the clothing-context group ($M=3.64$). Other means were learner control ($M=4.33$); no-context, $M=4.25$; and sports, $M=4.06$.

Source: G. R. Morrison, S. M. Ross, and W. Baldwin. (1992). Learner control of context and instructional support in learning elementary school mathematics. *Educational Technology Research and Development, 40*(1), p. 11.

A posteriori analyses indicated that participants in the present study scored significantly higher ($p<.01$) on the questionnaire than both exercising and sedentary students. The latter two groups also differed ($p<.01$).

Source: L. Gauvin and A. Szabo. (1992). Application of the experience sampling method to the study of the effects of exercise withdrawal on well-being. *Journal of Sport and Exercise Psychologist, 14*(4), p. 367.

---

because the ANOVA's H_0 involves *all* of the population means. Since post hoc (and planned) investigations often use F-tests to accomplish their objectives, we feel it is helpful when researchers use the term *omnibus* (when referring to the ANOVA F) to clarify which F is being discussed.

Finally, the terms *pairwise* and *nonpairwise* often pop up in discussions of post hoc (and planned) comparisons. The term **pairwise** simply means that groups are being compared two at a time. For example, pairwise comparisons among three groups labeled A, B, and C would involve comparisons of A versus B, A versus C, and B versus C. With four groups in the study, a total of six pairwise comparisons would be possible.

A **nonpairwise** (or **complex**) **comparison** involves three or more groups, with these comparison groups divided into two subsets. The mean score for the data in each subset is then computed and compared. For example, suppose there are four comparison groups in a study: A, B, C, and D. A researcher might be interested in comparing the average of groups A and B against the average of groups C and D. This would be a nonpairwise comparison. So would a comparison between the first group and the average of the final two groups (with the second group omitted from the comparison).

TEST PROCEDURES FREQUENTLY USED IN POST HOC ANALYSES

A wide array of statistical procedures are employed by applied researchers in their post hoc investigations. The five most frequently used test procedures were developed by Fisher, Duncan, Newman and Keuls, Tukey, and Scheffé. The tests developed by these statisticians carry the names of their inventors—and in some cases the test's label also contains a three-letter abbreviation or a three-word phrase. Thus, you will see these five test procedures referred to by the labels **Fisher's LSD**, **Duncan's multiple range test**, **Newman-Keuls**, **Tukey's HSD**, and **Scheffé**. In Excerpts 13.4–13.8, we see cases where these tests were used by applied researchers.

Excerpts 13.4–13.8 The Five Test Procedures Used Most Frequently in Post Hoc Investigations

---

Comparisons between pairs of means were assessed with the Least-Significant Difference Test (Winer, 1971).

Source: B. U. Watson. (1992). Auditory temporal acuity in normally achieving and learning-disabled college students. *Journal of Speech and Hearing Research, 35*(1), p. 151.

Since the ANOVA tests only indicate that there is a difference between group means, Duncan's Multiple Range Tests were performed to determine which means were significantly different at the .05 level.

Source: S. J. Backman. (1991). An investigation of the relationship between activity loyalty and perceived constraints. Special issue: Leisure constraints/constrained leisure. *Journal of Leisure Research, 23*(4), p. 341.

Analysis of variance (ANOVA) procedures were used to determine whether differences existed between the three instruction groups on the various indices of reading. . . . Differences at the .05 level were followed by Newman-Keuls post hoc tests to determine which pairs of the three instruction group means differed.

Source: M. S. Wilson, J. M. Schendel, and J. E. Ulman. (1992). Curriculum-based measures, teachers' ratings and group achievement scores: Alternative screening measures. *Journal of School Psychology, 30*(1), p. 66.

Data were analyzed in one-way ANOVAs to establish overall significance. Post hoc comparisons were made with Tukey's test.

Source: L. K. Takahashi. (1992). Developmental expression of defensive responses during exposure to conspecific adults in preweanling rats. *Journal of Comparative Psychology, 106*(1), p. 74.

To determine the direction of effect on the SCAN scale, post hoc comparisons using the Scheffé technique were conducted.

Source: J. J. Summers, K. Miller, and S. Ford. (1991). Attentional style and basketball performance. *Journal of Sport and Exercise Psychology, 13*(3), p. 247.

Various test procedures have been developed because researchers differ in the degree of control they want to have over Type I errors when more than one comparison is made. For example, if all possible pairwise comparisons are made among four group means, a total of six tests must be conducted in the post hoc investigation. If each of these six tests were to be conducted at any particular alpha level, the chance of at least one Type I error being made somewhere in the set of tests would be greater than the nominal alpha level employed. (This situation is highly analogous to the problem discussed in earlier chapters where a separate test is used to see if two comparison groups are significantly different on each of multiple dependent variables.)

Instead of dealing with the problem of an inflated Type I error risk by adjusting the level of significance (as is done when the Bonferroni technique or Dunn-Sidak modification is applied), the Fisher, Duncan, Newman-Keuls, Tukey, and Scheffé procedures make an adjustment in the size of the critical value used to determine whether an observed difference between two means is significant. To compensate for the fact that more than one comparison is made, larger critical values are used. However, the degree to which the critical value is adjusted upwards varies according to which test procedure is used.

When the critical value is increased only slightly (as compared with what would have been the critical value in the situation of a two-group study), the test procedure is considered to be **liberal**. On the other hand, when the critical value is increased greatly, the test procedure is referred to as being **conservative**. Liberal procedures provide less control over Type I errors, but this disadvantage is offset by increased power (i.e., more control over Type II errors). Conservative procedures do just the opposite: They provide greater control over Type I error risk but do so at the expense of lower power (i.e., higher risk of Type II errors). In terms of relative positioning along a liberal-conservative continuum, the five procedures we have been discussing would be arranged as follows:

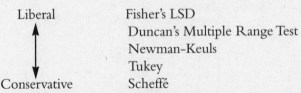

Liberal

Conservative

Fisher's LSD
Duncan's Multiple Range Test
Newman-Keuls
Tukey
Scheffé

A sixth test procedure exists that is often used in a post hoc investigation, but it is different from the Fisher, Duncan, Newman-Keuls, Tukey, and Scheffé procedures. Referred to as the **Dunnett test**, this sixth way of comparing groups allows for only a certain kind of contrast to be made. To be more specific, the Dunnett test compares the mean of a particular group in the study against each of the remaining group means. Typically, the Dunnett test is used when a researcher cares only about how each of several versions of an experimental treatment affect the dependent variable, in terms of means, as compared against a control (or placebo) group. Dunnett's test involves pairwise comparisons (C versus E_1, C versus E_2, etc.) but not all possible pairwise comparisons since contrasts are not made among the experimental groups.

Before turning our attention to the way researchers report the results of their post hoc analyses, a special comment needs to be made regarding the Scheffé test. This test procedure is the only one of those we have mentioned that can be used to make both pairwise and nonpairwise comparisons. Despite this extra versatility of the Scheffé procedure, it is used almost exclusively in studies characterized solely by pairwise comparisons.

THE NULL HYPOTHESES OF A POST HOC INVESTIGATION

In the next section, we will look at the different ways researchers present the results of their post hoc analyses. In those presentations, you will rarely see reference made, through symbols or words, to the null hypotheses that are associated with the test results. Consequently, you need to remember that all of the post hoc procedures are inferential in nature and are concerned with null hypotheses.

In any post hoc analysis, at least two contrasts will be investigated, each involving a null hypothesis. For example, in a study involving three groups (A, B, and C) and pairwise comparisons used to probe a significant result from a one-way ANOVA, three null hypotheses would be tested: H_0: $\mu_A = \mu_B$, H_0: $\mu_A = \mu_C$, and H_0: $\mu_B = \mu_C$.[1] With a similar analysis involving four groups, there will be six null hypotheses. With Dunnett's test, there will be one null hypothesis fewer than there are comparison groups.

The purpose of a post hoc analysis is to evaluate the null hypothesis associated with each contrast that is investigated. Regardless of which approach to evaluating null hypotheses is used (hypothesis testing, significance testing, or the hybrid approach to testing H_0), the results of each comparison will be presented. As mentioned earlier, the reporting schemes used by researchers to summarize the results of a post hoc analysis vary widely.

PRESENTATION OF RESULTS

Researchers sometimes summarize the results of their post hoc investigations through the text of the technical report. Usually it is not difficult to understand what the researcher concluded when the results are presented in this fashion. To see whether this claim of ours holds true for you, take a look at Excerpts 13.9–13.12 and ask yourself whether you can make sense out of each set of results.

When the results of a post hoc analysis are presented through a table, one of four formats is typically used. One of these formats involves a triangular table of mean differences, one involves means and subscripts, one involves lines drawn beneath means, and one involves lines drawn above vertical bars. Although different formats are employed for displaying the results, these four

---

[1]*Although the null hypotheses of a post hoc investigation theoretically can be set up with something other than zero as H_0's pinpoint number, we have never seen a researcher test anything except no-difference null hypotheses in a post hoc analysis.*

Excerpts 13.9–13.12 Results of Post Hoc Analyses Presented in the Text of Research Reports

The rating of work adjustment training differed on the basis of the variable years of experience, $F(2,38)=3.51$, $p=.04$. Comparisons of the groups were made using the Duncan Multiple Range Test, indicating that group three was significantly different from group two.

Source: J. Satcher and K. Dooley-Dickey. (1991). Rehabilitation counselor selections of service options for persons with learning disabilities. *Journal of Applied Rehabilitation Counseling, 22*(1), p. 35.

Newman-Keuls procedures revealed that the age group 55–74 had a significantly higher premorbid adjustment score than the other two age categories ($p<.05$). There was no significant difference between the 19- to 34- and the 35- to 54-year-olds.

Source: D. H. Flics, and W. G. Herron. (1991). Activity-withdrawal, diagnosis, and demographics as predictors of premorbid adjustment. *Journal of Clinical Psychology, 47*(2), p. 193.

A one-way analysis of variance to determine equivalence of subject groups in terms of age revealed a significant F ratio of 5.49 ($p<.01$), which indicated that there was a significant age difference between groups. A Tukey post hoc multiple comparison test indicated that there were no significant differences between the ages of restricting anorexic, bulimic anorexic, and psychiatric control groups; however, the normal group was significantly younger than the two anorexic groups (both at $p<.01$).

Source: J. G. Woznica. (1990). Delay of gratification in anorexia nervosa. *Journal of Clinical Psychology, 46*(6), p. 709.

A one-way ANOVA of the means revealed significant differences among the four groups, $F(3,76)=8.59$, $p<.001$. Follow-up with Scheffé's procedure indicated that the three older groups all scored significantly higher ($p<.05$) than the youngest group, but there were no significant differences among the three older groups. This is consistent with what Piaget would have predicted.

Source: D. W. Rainey, N. R. Santilli, and K. Fallon. (1992). Development of athletes' conceptions of sport officials' authority. *Journal of Sport and Exercise Psychology, 14*(4), p. 398.

kinds of table are identical in that they reveal where significant differences were found among the comparison groups.

To illustrate the **triangular table** format, we have constructed a table for a hypothetical study in which comparisons are made among three independent samples each containing 20 subjects. After obtaining a significant F from the one-way ANOVA [$F(2,57)=3.45$, $p<.05$], our hypothetical researcher conducts a post hoc analysis using the Tukey test. The results of this follow-up investigation—with means of 16.1, 14.9, and 13.6 for groups A, B, and C— would turn out as follows:

Group	A	B	C
A	—	1.2	2.5*
B		—	1.3
C			—

*$p < .05$.

Each numerical entry in this table is simply the difference between the means of the groups that label the row and column where the number is located. Each of these mean differences is evaluated to see if it is larger than would be expected by chance. An asterisk is positioned next to the table's entries that turn out significant. For our hypothetical study, the triangular table of results from the post hoc analysis suggests that a difference exists between the means of the populations associated with groups A and C. The differences between the A and B sample means and between the B and C sample means, however, were not large enough to permit the null hypotheses associated with the comparisons to be rejected.

In the triangular table of results from our hypothetical study, each numerical entry was computed as the difference between two means. Sometimes, researchers will set up their triangular tables such that the numerical entries are not mean differences but rather the calculated values associated with the test's comparison of each pair of means. Regardless of how its numerical entries are computed, the triangular table reveals nicely, by means of asterisks and an explanatory footnote, the nature of the inferential decisions made in the post hoc investigation.

The second format for presenting post hoc results in a table uses group means with lettered subscripts. Such a table from a real study appears in Excerpt 13.13.

Excerpt 13.13 shows six separate post hoc analyses, each conducted with respect to a separate dependent variable involved in the study. Each dependent variable corresponds to a different row of the table (labeled "Crafts," "Scientific," "The arts," etc). The title of the table, in conjunction with the column headings, makes it clear that five independent samples, each containing subjects from a different country, were compared on the first dependent variable, then on the second dependent variable, and so forth.

The note beneath the table in Excerpt 13.13 indicates which post hoc test was used in the follow-up investigation and also how to interpret the subscripts attached to the means. Focusing on the results in the top row of the table ("Crafts"), we see that the Canadian Spanish, Canadian English, and Canadian French means have a common subscript, "b." This indicates that the Scheffé test revealed no significant differences among these groups. The means of the remaining two groups have unique subscripts, showing that each of them was found to be significantly different from the other four comparison groups and also significantly different from each other. Consider now the

Excerpt 13.13   Results of a Post Hoc Analysis Presented in a Table
with Subscripts Attached to Means

Table 1

Scale means and standard deviations for five CDM editions, for students grades 10 through 12

Description of jobs		United States (N=5,646)	Canadian Spanish (N=267)	Canadian English (N=803)	Canadian French (N=342)	Australian (N=899)
Crafts	M	15.6_c	12.1_b	11.2_b	13.3_b	7.5_a
	SD	11.4	8.9	10.2	10.7	8.4
Scientific	M	12.3_a	16.1_c	$13.8_{b,c}$	$13.6_{a,b,c}$	$12.7_{a,b}$
	SD	11.2	11.3	11.8	11.2	11.2
The arts	M	12.2_b	16.2_d	13.6_c	9.9_a	$12.8_{b,c}$
	SD	10.2	10.8	11.1	8.7	10.5
Social	M	15.1_a	13.8_a	17.6_b	15.4_a	14.9_a
	SD	10.7	10.8	11.3	9.9	10.2
Business	M	14.8_a	16.0_a	$14.5_{a,b}$	12.6_b	15.5_a
	SD	9.8	10.5	9.7	7.9	9.8
Clerical	M	14.3_a	14.9_a	13.7_a	15.1_a	11.1_b
	SD	11.4	11.7	11.2	10.1	9.8

Note. Means (*M*) sharing a common subscript are not significantly different by the Scheffé test.

Source: T. F. Harrington. (1991). The cross-cultural applicability of the Career Decision-Making System. Special Issue: Career development of racial and ethnic minorities. *The Career Development Quarterly, 39*(3), p. 217.

results presented on the third row of the table. To see whether you can decipher what is being communicated by the researcher, we have one simple question for you: How many significant differences were found when the Scheffé test evaluated all possible pairwise comparisons among the five sample means on "The arts"? After considering the information in the table, you can check our answer at the bottom of this page.[2]

The third format used to present the results of a post hoc analysis utilizes lines drawn beneath the study's sample means. Excerpt 13.14 contains an example of this method. In the study from which Excerpt 13.14 was taken, subjects were asked to indicate the likelihood that they would refer a subordinate

---

[2] *A total of eight pairwise comparisons turned out to be statistically significant. More specifically, significant differences were found between 16.2 and each of the other four means, between 13.6 and each of the two smallest means, between 12.8 and 9.9, and between 12.2 and 9.9.*

to an employee assistance program. There were five different kinds of hypothetical subordinates described for the subjects, thus creating five conditions of the independent variable called "Type of Employee Problem." Each number in the table shown in Excerpt 13.14 is the mean likelihood that subjects would make an EAP referral for employees having a given problem.

Excerpt 13.14   Results of a Post Hoc Analysis Presented by Means of the Underlining Method

Table 1

Scheffé results: Employee assistance program referrals by type of employee problem

	Type of Employee Problem				
EAP Referral	*Cocaine abuse*	*AIDS[a]*	*HIV[b]*	*Alcohol abuse*	*Nonabuse*
Mean	67%	63%	49%	38%	26%

Note. Each line represents means that do not differ significantly, $p > .05$. Means that do differ significantly, $p < .05$, are not subsumed under a line.
[a]AIDS = acquired immunodeficiency syndrome. [b]HIV = human immunodeficiency virus.

Source: L.H. Gerstein and K. Duffey (1992). Workers with AIDS: Hypothetical supervisors' willingness to make EAP referrals. *Journal of Employment Counseling, 29*(3), p. 108.

As indicated by the note near the bottom of Excerpt 13.14, each of the three lines extends beneath means that were found (by the Scheffé test) not to differ from one another in a statistically significant sense. Means not underlined *by the same line* were shown to be significantly different. Therefore, only three of the full set of 10 pairwise comparisons turned out to be significant: Cocaine abuse versus Alcohol abuse, Cocaine abuse versus Nonabuse, and AIDS versus Nonabuse.

The **underlining format for presenting the results** of a post hoc investigation is very similar to the format that uses subscripts attached to means. In fact, either of these formats could be easily changed into the other by converting each line that extends beneath a subset of the group means into a set of common letter subscripts attached to that particular subset of means (or vice versa). The only difference between these two reporting schemes is that the underlining format requires that the means be arranged from high to low or low to high. This requirement often creates difficulties for the researcher in setting up a table when there are two or more dependent variables, with the rank order of the comparison group means being different for different dependent variables.[3]

The fourth format for displaying the results of a post hoc investigation uses a figure containing vertical bars, each of which corresponds to a different comparison group. The height of each bar indicates the mean score earned by the group represented by that bar. Horizontal lines are then positioned above the bars to indicate pairs of groups that were found to be significantly different from each other. An example of this format appears in Excerpt 13.15.

Excerpt 13.15   Results of a Post Hoc Analysis Presented by Means of Vertical Bars and Horizontal Lines

The T_{26} and T_{45} groups had the greatest tension outputs for back muscle (Figure 2). These values were significantly higher than for the untrained group. The T_{56} group was intermediate as to force production. No significant differences were observed between the other groups.

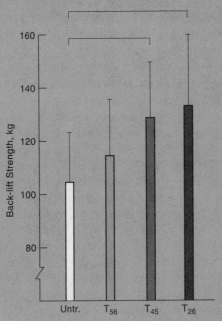

Figure 2   *Back-lift strength for the different groups of subjects, (⊢—⊣), significant difference between groups (p<0.05).*

Source: Y. Aoyagi and S. Katsuta. (1990). Relationship between the starting age of training and physical fitness in old age. *Canadian Journal of Sport Sciences, 15*(1), p. 68.

---

[3] *If you take another look at Excerpt 13.13, you will see an example of a table containing letter subscripts attached to means that could not easily be converted to the underlining method.*

Note that the horizontal lines appearing beneath means in Excerpt 13.14 have a meaning exactly opposite to that of the horizontal lines drawn above the bars in Excerpt 13.15. With underlining, each line indicates what *did not* turn out to be statistically significant. With horizontal lines above bars, each line corresponds to a result that *was* significant. Moreover, each line used in the underlining method must be interpreted in terms of *all* of the means above the line. In contrast, each horizontal line drawn above the bars in Excerpt 13.15 "points to" only two means, with the intervening means being irrelevant to the statistically significant result being displayed.

THE BONFERRONI PROCEDURE AS A POST HOC TECHNIQUE

Earlier in this chapter, we indicated that the Fisher, Duncan, Newman-Keuls, Tukey, and Scheffé tests have been designed to hold down the chances of a Type I error when comparisons are made among a set of group means. We also indicated that these test procedures are analogous in purpose to the Bonferroni technique's effort to deal with the "inflated Type I error risk problem" when comparisons are made between two groups on each of several dependent variables. The analogy is a strong one. In fact, some researchers use the Bonferroni technique in situations where others utilize the test procedures mentioned at the outset of this paragraph.

In Excerpt 13.16, we see a study where a one-way ANOVA was used to compare three experimental groups. Following a significant F, three pairwise comparisons were made with an independent-samples t-test. However, because of the increased chance of a Type I error being committed in the post hoc investigation, the Bonferroni procedure was used. Because the researcher wanted to use a .05 level of significance, each of the three t-test comparisons was conducted with an alpha set equal to .017.

Excerpt 13.16 The Bonferroni Procedure Used Within a Post Hoc Analysis

---

The difference between two means among the three experimental groups was determined by the use of analysis of variance and Student's t test with Bonferroni correction.

Source: J. M. Delehanty, N. Imai, and C. S. Liang. (1992). Effects of dichloroacetate on hemodynamic responses to dynamic exercise in dogs. *Journal of Applied Physiology, 72*(2), p. 516.

PLANNED COMPARISONS

We have discussed the comparison of group means using a two-step strategy that involves conducting a one-way ANOVA followed by a post hoc investigation. Researchers can, if they wish, bypass the ANOVA *F*-test and move directly to one or more specific comparisons of particular interest. Such comparisons among means (without reliance on a "green light" from a significant omnibus *F*-test) are called planned comparisons. Although planned comparisons are used less frequently than post hoc comparisons, they show up in the research literature often enough to make it important for you to recognize and understand this kind of statistical test on means.

In Excerpt 13.17, we see an example of a research team conducting a set of planned comparisons. In this investigation, notice that a one-way ANOVA was not conducted, that all possible pairwise comparisons were made, and that Duncan's multiple range test was used to make these comparisons.

Excerpt 13.17   A Set of Planned Comparisons

RESULTS

The mean ages at menarche, standard deviations, and ranges for nonathletes and athletes at different competitive levels are shown in Table 2. A Duncan multiple range test indicated that the nonathletes attained menarche significantly earlier ($p < .001$) than high school, college, and top athletes. The high school athletes attained menarche significantly earlier ($p < .001$) than college and top athletes. The college athletes attained menarche significantly earlier ($p < .01$) than top athletes.

Table 2

Age (yrs) at menarche in nonathletes and athletes

	n	*M*	*SD*	*Range*
NA	204	12.21	1.09	9.83–16.7
HSA	253	12.59	1.11	9.75–16.08
CA	386	12.92	1.17	9.58–17.83
YTA	40	13.48	1.32	11.25–18.50

Source: E. Hata and E. Aoki. (1990). Age at menarche and selected menstrual characteristics in young Japanese athletes. *Research Quarterly for Exercise and Sport, 61*(2), p. 179.

Earlier, in Excerpts 13.5 and 13.9, we saw examples of how the Duncan test was used within a post hoc investigation. Now, in Excerpt 13.17, we see a case in which the Duncan test was used to make specific comparisons among the group means without reliance on any ANOVA *F*-test. Collectively, these three excerpts help to make an important point. It is not the name of a test that causes it to be planned or post hoc in nature but rather the issue of whether it is applied to help explain why the omnibus F turns out to be significant. For this reason, Duncan's and the other test procedures considered in our discussion of post hoc comparisons should not be thought of as being post hoc tests. They can be used within post hoc investigations *or* they can be used to make planned comparisons.

As is the case with most post hoc investigations, the contrasts set up in planned comparisons usually are pairwise in nature. (This was the case when Duncan's test was used in Excerpt 13.17.) Researchers can, however, set up one or more of their planned comparisons in a nonpairwise fashion. Excerpt 13.18 illustrates this option.

Two aspects of Excerpt 13.18 are worth noting. First, each of the three planned comparisons was set up on the basis of theoretical predictions (i.e., on the basis of the anomaly and obstacle hypotheses). As exemplified by this investigation, nonpairwise comparisons are set up only when the researcher has a theoretical rationale for combining groups. Second, the first of the two *df* values associated with each planned comparison F-test is 1, even though five groups were involved in the first contrast and four groups were involved in the second and third contrasts. This *df* value is 1 because the contrast in each case involves only two means. The first contrast compared the original mean with the mean of the other four means; the second and third contrasts compared the mean of the data collected under the deletion and contradiction conditions with the mean of the data collected under the two

---

Excerpt 13.18   Planned Comparisons Involving Nonpairwise
                            Contrasts

RESULTS

As in Experiment 1, we computed the mean number of questions generated per problem. These means and standard deviations are presented in Table 2. As predicted by the anomaly hypothesis, the mean of the four transformed conditions combined (2.32) was significantly higher than the mean of the original condition (2.05), $F(1,156) = 4.59$, $p < .025$, one-tailed, $MS_e = 0.48$. . . . Table 2 also presents the number of transformation-relevant questions per problem. The obstacle hypothesis predicts that the deletion and contradiction conditions should produce more transformation-relevant questions than the two irrelevancy conditions; this predicted trend was supported by the data in a planned comparison between the two pairs of conditions, .68 versus .31, $F(1,117) = 23.89$, $p < .025$, $MS_e = 0.22$. . . . The bottom section of Table 2 presents the likelihood that a particular transformation was detected by the subjects, as manifested by at least one transformation-relevant question. These likelihood scores were higher for the deletion and contradiction conditions ($M = .41$) than for the two irrelevancy

(Continued)

Excerpt 13.18 Planned Comparisons Involving Nonpairwise
Contrasts *(Continued)*

conditions $(M=.27)$, $F(1,117)=9.11$, $p<.025$, $MS_e=0.08$. This outcome is consistent with the obstacle hypothesis.

Table 2

**Questions generated while solving quantitative problems:
Experiment 2**

| | | | Version of problem | | |
| | *Original* | *Deletion* | *Contradiction* | *Salient irrelevancy* | *Subtle irrelevancy* |
Measure					
Overall number of questions					
M	2.05	2.43	2.18	2.45	2.21
SD	1.49	1.88	1.37	1.53	1.45
Number of transformation-relevant questions					
M	—	0.90	0.46	0.35	0.27
SD	—	0.76	0.59	0.46	0.41
Likelihood that a subject detected a particular transformation					
M	—	.50	.31	.31	.23
SD	—	.35	.32	.34	.32

Note. Dashes indicate not applicable.

Source: A. C. Graesser and C. L. McMahen. (1993). Anomalous information triggers questions when adults solve quantitative problems and comprehend stories. *Journal of Educational Psychology, 85*(1), p. 142.

irrelevancy conditions. Since all nonpairwise comparisons have this feature of contrasting two means (even though one or both of these means will be based upon data from two or more comparison groups), they are sometimes referred to as **one degree of freedom F-tests.**

Before we conclude our discussion of planned comparisons, two final points ought to be made. The first of these has to do with terminology; the second has to do with statistical power.

Regarding terminology, it is important to know that the term **a priori contrast** means the same thing as "planned contrast." Excerpt 13.19 illustrates how you may come across this term when reading about planned comparisons. As you can see, all of the *a priori* contrasts conducted in this study were pairwise in nature.

Our second concluding point concerning planned comparisons has to do with statistical power. For any particular contrast, pairwise or nonpairwise, there

---

Excerpt 13.19 Use of the Term *A Priori Contrast*

A priori contrasts were used to compare depressed youth with each of the other three groups. . . . Compared to healthy youth, depressed youth reported more physical health, home/money, parent, extended family, and school stressors and more negative life events. Depressed youth also differed from the rheumatic disease group on each index except physical health, sibling, and boy/girlfriend stressors. Depressed youth generally reported more life stressors than did youth with conduct disorder, but the differences were significant only for home/money and parent stressors.

Source: D. Daniels and R.H. Moos. (1990). Assessing life stressors and social resources among adolescents: Applications to depressed youth. *Journal of Adolescent Research, 5*(3), p. 278.

---

is less chance of a Type II error being committed when that contrast is evaluated as a planned comparison than is the case when it is evaluated within the context of the two-stage omnibus-*F*/post-hoc strategy. This holds true for sets of contrasts as well. For example, the use of the Duncan test in Excerpt 13.17 to make all possible pairwise contrasts represented a more powerful analytic strategy than would have been the case if a one-way ANOVA had been applied first, with the Duncan test applied within a post hoc investigation. This situation is caused by the omnibus *F*-test of the one-way ANOVA being a relatively conservative screening device in the two-stage strategy. With certain data sets, a researcher will never reach the post hoc portion of the two-stage strategy (because the ANOVA yields a nonsignificant *F*), whereas the comparison(s) of interest not only would be reached but also would be declared statistically significant if the data are analyzed using one or more planned comparisons.

Although there is more statistical power associated with planned comparisons than with post hoc comparisons, researchers use the former far less frequently than the latter. This situation might be attributable to researchers being more concerned about Type I errors than Type II errors, but we honestly do not believe that is the true reason for planned comparisons being used so infrequently. It is also conceivable that researchers use the two-stage strategy because they want the freedom to set up their post hoc contrasts after examining the means of the comparison groups, a procedure that is statistically legitimate within a post hoc investigation but statistically unethical within an a priori investigation. Again, however, we do not believe that is the true explanation for the two-stage strategy being used so frequently.

In our opinion, planned comparisons are used infrequently for two reasons. On the one hand, many researchers have not learned about them. On the other hand, many of those who are aware of planned contrasts shy away from using them because they would rather end up with something in their study that is statistically significant—even if the significant contrast is related to an uninteresting research question—than run the risk of having an *a priori* investigation yield nonsignificant results on the smaller number of priority questions. We anticipate that the popularity of planned comparisons will increase as more researchers become aware of them and become less willing to allow "statistical significance on anything" to be their goal.

PLANNED COMPARISONS USED WITH A ONE-WAY ANOVA

If you come into contact with enough research reports, it is likely that you will encounter one or more cases in which planned comparisons (rather than post hoc comparisons) were used in conjunction with a one-way ANOVA. Examples of this situation are contained in Excerpts 13.20 and 13.21.

Excerpts 13.20–13.21   Planned Comparisons Used with a One-Way ANOVA

A statistical analysis of the results of Experiment 4 indicated that the three conditions were significantly different, $F(2,52)=3.70, P<.05, MS_e=.004$. A planned comparison between the ascending massed and ascending spaced conditions indicated that these two conditions were significantly different, $F(1,26)=4.84, p<.05$.

Source: J. G. Snodgrass and E. Hirshman. (1991). Theoretical explorations of the Bruner-Potter (1964) interference effect. *Journal of Memory and Language, 30*(3), p. 290.

An analysis of variance was conducted on the mean recovery scores across the four conditions (synchrony, composition, specific object-sound, and collapsed control) and indicated a significant result $(F(3,92)=3.67, p<.02)$. Planned *t* tests comparing the mean visual recovery of each of the experimental conditions $[M_{SYNC}=7.53; M_{COMP}=7.92; M_{SOS}=1.93]$ against that of the collapsed control condition $[M_{CON}=-.64]$ revealed a significant visual recovery to the change in synchrony relations $(t(52)=2.76, p < .01)$ and to the change in composition relations $(t(52)=2.68, p < .01)$, but not to the change in specific object-sound relations $(t(58)=.97, p > .1)$ with respect to the recovery observed in the control condition.

Source: L.E. Bahrick. (1992). Infants' perceptual differentiation of amodal and modality-specific audio-visual relations. *Journal of Experimental Child Psychology, 53*, p. 191.

In the reports from which these excerpts were taken, no mention was made of any post hoc analysis being conducted. Since it is "standard operating procedure" for researchers to probe their data with a post hoc investigation if an ANOVA comparison of three or more means yields a significant *F*, we are somewhat perplexed by the seemingly strange combination of analyses that are reported in Excerpts 13.20 and 13.21. Possibly, the researchers who conducted these studies mistakenly used the word *planned* when they meant to use the phrase *post hoc*. Or, maybe they really did conduct planned comparisons, but then bypassed any post hoc investigation because they obtained answers to all of their research questions from their *a priori* contrasts. (But if that was the case, we wonder why they would compute an omnibus *F*.) Then again, maybe they conducted true planned comparisons but also subjected their data to a one-way ANOVA simply because ANOVA *F*-tests show up so often in published reports of research studies. We have no way to tell which of these three possible explanations is correct.

COMMENTS

As we come to the end of this chapter on planned and post hoc comparisons, there are four suggestions we want to pass along, each of which is designed to help you become better able to decipher and critique research reports. These four concluding comments deal with assumptions, the researcher's choice of test procedure, statistical versus practical significance, and test procedures other than the ones discussed earlier in the chapter.

ASSUMPTIONS

The various planned and post hoc test procedures mentioned earlier in this chapter will function as they are supposed to function only if four underlying assumptions hold true for the populations and samples involved in the study. These assumptions are the same ones that underlie a one-way ANOVA *F*-test, and they are referred to by the terms *randomness, independence, normality,* and *homogeneity of variance*. We hope you remember the main points that we made in Chapter 12 about these assumptions.

Although the various test procedures covered so far in this chapter generally are robust to the normality assumption, the same point cannot be made regarding the equal variance assumption—especially in situations where the sample sizes are dissimilar. If researchers conduct planned comparisons, they ought to talk about the issue of assumptions. If the study's sample sizes vary, a test should be applied to assess the homogeneity of variance assumption. With a post hoc investigation, the assumptions should have been discussed in conjunction with the omnibus *F*-test; those assumptions do not have to be discussed or tested a second time when the researcher moves from the one-way ANOVA to the post hoc comparisons.

If the equal variance assumption is tested and shown to be untenable (in connection with planned comparisons or with the one-way ANOVA), the researcher will likely make some form of "adjustment" when *a priori* or post hoc contrasts are tested. This adjustment might take the form of a data transformation, a change in the level of significance employed, or a change in the test procedure used to compare means. If the latter approach is taken, you are likely to see the Welch test applied to the data (because the Welch model does not assume equal population variances).

Many of the test procedures for making planned or post hoc comparisons were developed for the situation where the various samples are the same size. When used in situations where samples vary in size, researchers may indicate that they used a variation of one of the main techniques. For example, Kramer's extension of Duncan's multiple range test simply involves a modification of the regular Duncan test procedure to make it usable in studies where the ns vary. Don't let such extensions or modifications cause you to shy away from deciphering research reports in the same way you would if the "regular" planned or post hoc test had been used.

THE RESEARCHER'S CHOICE OF TEST PROCEDURE

As we pointed out near the outset of this chapter, the various post hoc procedures differ in terms of how liberal or conservative they are. Ideally, a researcher ought to choose among these procedures after considering the way they differ in terms of power and control of Type I errors. Realistically, however, the decision to use a particular test procedure is probably influenced most by what computer programs are available for doing the data analysis or by what procedure was emphasized in a specific textbook or by a specific instructor.

Regardless of the reasons why the researcher chooses to use a particular test procedure, you are in full control of how *you* interpret the results presented in the research report. If a researcher uses a test procedure that is too liberal or too conservative for *your* taste, remember that you have the undisputed right to accept only a portion of the researcher's full set of conclusions. Or, you may want to reject *everything* that is "discovered" in the research study because your position on the liberal/conservative continuum is quite different from that of the researcher who performed the data analysis.

To illustrate our point, we must first point out that we generally consider the Scheffé procedure to be too conservative for situations where all pairwise contrasts are tested. For this reason, we are sometimes unwilling to accept the conclusions drawn by a researcher when the Scheffé test yields one or more nonsignificant results. For example, in Excerpt 13.12, we are somewhat hesitant to accept the research team's assertion that "there were no significant differences among the three older groups." Very possibly, a less conservative test procedure used in the post hoc investigation might have revealed statistically significant differences among those three groups.

The important point we are trying to make here can be summed up in this simple caution: Do not allow researchers to reify their significant (or nonsignificant) findings into more than what they truly are. The results obtained in many areas of statistics, and particularly in the arena of post hoc investigations, depend upon a variety of choices made by the researcher. These involve, among other things, level of significance, sample size, quality of instruments used to collect data, and the nature of the test procedure employed. If you are dissatisfied with any of the choices made by the researcher, do not accept the conclusions drawn from the study.

STATISTICAL SIGNIFICANCE VERSUS PRACTICAL SIGNIFICANCE

We have discussed the distinction between statistical significance and practical significance in earlier chapters. Our simple suggestion at this point is to keep this distinction in mind when you come into contact with the results of planned and post hoc comparisons.

To illustrate the importance of keeping this distinction in mind, consider once again the results contained in Excerpt 13.17. In that study, nonathletes and three different kinds of athlete were compared, using all possible pairwise contrasts, within a set of planned comparisons. The dependent variable was age at menarche, and each group's mean turned out to be significantly different from each of the other three group means. When we look at the group means, however, we do not think that all differences between groups are meaningful. In particular, the differences between 12.21 and 12.59 and between 12.59 and 12.92 seem to us to be small in magnitude.

In Excerpt 13.17, the sample sizes (for three of the four groups) are extremely large. Moreover, comparisons between groups were made by means of the Duncan test, a procedure that is relatively liberal compared with the other test procedures examined in this chapter. These two factors function to make differences that are small to the naked eye seem large from the perspective of the statistical test used to compare the means. If a power analysis had been conducted before the collection and analysis of data, it is more likely that the naked eye and the statistical test would have seen the same thing.

OTHER TEST PROCEDURES

In this chapter, we have discussed several test procedures that researchers use when comparing means within planned and post hoc investigations. We have seen how Fisher's LSD, Duncan's multiple range test, the Newman-Keuls test, the Tukey test, Scheffé's test, and Dunnett's test are used to hold down the chances of a Type I error when two or more contrasts were evaluated. We also saw how this same objective is sometimes achieved by using the Bonferroni technique to adjust the level of significance used in planned or post hoc tests.

Although a variety of test procedures have received our attention in this chapter, there are additional test procedures that we have not discussed. The tests mentioned in the preceding paragraph are the ones we believe you will encounter most often when you read research reports. However, you may come across one or more techniques not discussed in this text. For example, Ryan's method of adjusted significance levels or Gabriel's simultaneous test procedure (STP) might be mentioned by the researchers who conducted the research report you are reviewing. If this happens, we hope you will not be thrown by the utilization of a specific test procedure different from those considered here. If you understand the general purpose served by the planned and post hoc tests we *have* considered, we think you will have little difficulty understanding the purpose and results of similar test procedures that we have *not* considered.

REVIEW TERMS

A posteriori test	Omnibus *F*-test
A priori	One-degree-of-freedom *F*-test
Comparison	Newman-Keuls
Complex comparison	Nonpairwise (or complex) comparison
Conservative	Pairwise comparison
Contrast	Planned comparisons
Duncan's multiple range test	Post hoc comparisons
Dunnett test	Scheffé
Fisher's LSD	Triangular table method for presenting results
Follow-up test	Tukey's HSD
Liberal	Underline method for presenting results
Multiple comparison test	

REVIEW QUESTIONS

1. Do the authors of this book consider the Tukey test to be planned or post hoc in nature?

2. What are the differences among these three terms: post hoc comparison, follow-up comparison, *a posteriori* comparison?

3. Are the comparisons discussed in Excerpt 13.3 pairwise or nonpairwise in nature?

4. What adjective is sometimes used in conjunction with the term "*F*-test" to clarify that the *F*-test compared *all* of the comparison group means?

5. Will a conservative test procedure or a liberal test procedure more likely yield statistically significant results?

6. In Excerpt 13.9, Duncan's multiple range test was used in a post hoc investigation. How many null hypotheses were associated with this post hoc investigation? What were they?

7. If, in Excerpt 13.9, the underlining method had been used to summarize the outcome of the post hoc investigation, what would the results look like?

8. If, in Excerpt 13.15, the underlining method had been used to summarize the outcome of the post hoc investigation, how many lines would be positioned under the four group means, and how many means would be above each of these lines?

9. When conducting post hoc investigations, do researchers ever use the Bonferroni technique in conjunction with t-tests as a way of dealing with the inflated Type I error problem?

10. In Excerpt 13.18, what would the null hypothesis look like for the first nonpairwise contrast that was evaluated?

11. The term _____ *comparison* means the same thing as *planned comparison*.

12. Do researchers set up and test planned comparisons more often or less often than they set up and test post hoc comparisons?

13. If a researcher uses a test procedure in a planned or post hoc investigation that is, in your opinion, too liberal or too conservative, do you have the right to reject the researcher's conclusions?

14. What might cause a conservative test procedure (e.g., Scheffé's) conducted at a rigorous alpha level to yield results indicating that statistically significant differences exist among groups when those differences are of little practical significance?

Two-Way Analyses of Variance

In Chapters 11 and 12, we saw how one-way ANOVAs can be used to compare two or more sample means in studies involving a single independent variable. In this chapter, we want to extend our discussion of analysis of variance to consider how this extremely popular statistical tool is used in studies characterized by two independent variables. It should come as no surprise that the kind of ANOVA to be considered here is referred to as a two-way ANOVA. Since you may have come across the term *multivariate analysis of variance* or the abbreviation *MANOVA*, it is important to clarify that this chapter does not deal with multivariate analyses of variance. The first letter of the acronym *MANOVA* stands for the word *multivariate*, but the letter *M* indicates that multiple dependent variables are involved in the same unitary analysis. Within the confines of this chapter, we will look at ANOVAs that involve multiple independent variables but only one dependent variable. Accordingly, the topics in this chapter (along with those of earlier chapters) fall under the general heading **univariate analyses**.

Similarities Between One-Way and Two-Way ANOVAs

Like any one-way ANOVA, a two-way ANOVA focuses on group means. (As you will soon see, a minimum of four $\overline{X}$s are involved in any two-way ANOVA.) Because it is an inferential technique, any two-way ANOVA is actually concerned with the set of μ values that correspond to the sample means that are computed from the study's data. The inference from the samples to the populations will be made through hypothesis testing, significance testing, or the hybrid approach to evaluating null hypotheses. Statistical assumptions may need to be tested, and the research questions will dictate whether planned and/or post hoc comparisons are used in conjunction with (or in lieu of) the two-way ANOVA. Despite these similarities between one-way and two-way ANOVAs, the kind of ANOVA to which we now turn is substantially different from the kind we examined in Chapter 12.

FACTORS, LEVELS, AND CELLS

A two-way ANOVA always involves two independent variables. Each independent variable, or **factor**, is made up of, or defined by, two or more elements called **levels**. When looked at simultaneously, the levels of the first factor and the levels of the second factor create the conditions of the study to be compared. Each of these conditions is referred to as a **cell**.

In Excerpts 14.1–14.5, we see several examples of how researchers describe the framework of their two-way ANOVAs by saying something about the factors and/or the levels of the factors involved in their studies. Notice that only in the first of these excerpts is there a description of both factors *and* levels. (One factor, gender, is made up of two levels: male and female; the other factor, parenting style, is made up of four levels: authoritarian, democratic, permissive, and uninvolved.) In the second and third excerpts, only the names of the factors are given; however, the number that precedes each factor name indicates how many levels make up each factor. In Excerpt 14.4, the information in parenthesis corresponds to the names of the levels making up

---

Excerpts 14.1–14.5   Delineation of Factors and Levels in Two-Way ANOVAs

---

A two-way analysis of variance was conducted using gender (male or female) and parenting style (authoritarian, democratic, permissive, or uninvolved) as the independent variables and codependency as the dependent variable.

Source: J. L. Fischer and D. W. Crawford. (1992). Codependency and parenting styles. *Journal of Adolescent Research,* 7(3), p. 357.

Posttest achievement was analyzed via a 5(context) $\times$ 3(support) ANOVA.

Source: G. R. Morrison, S. M. Ross, and W. Baldwin. (1992). Learner control of context and instructional support in learning elementary school mathematics. *Educational Technology Research and Development,* 40(1), p. 9.

Although it was not the primary purpose of the present study, we looked at the relation among gender-typed toy choice, sex, and age to see whether it is manifested in our design. A 2(sex) $\times$ 3(age level) ANOVA was computed on the toy-choice score.

Source: T. E. Lobel and J. Menashri. (1993). Relations of conceptions of gender-role transgressions and gender constancy to gender-typed toy preferences. *Developmental Psychology, 29,* p. 153.

(Continued)

Excerpts 14.1–14.5   Delineation of Factors and Levels in Two-Way
ANOVAS (*Continued*)

A 2(first version/second version) × 2(same/different scheme) analysis of variance produced no significant main effects.

Source: H. S. Waters, F. Hou, and Y. Lee. (1993). Organization and elaboration in children's repeated production of prose. *Journal of Experimental Child Psychology, 55*(1), p. 43.

To test the first hypothesis, a 2(Gender) × 2(Personal/Impersonal Real-Life Dilemma) analysis of variance with ECI total scores as the dependent variable was conducted.

Source: E. E. Skoe and A. Gooden. (1993). Ethic of care and real-life moral dilemma content in male and female early adolescents. *Journal of Early Adolescence, 13,* p. 161.

---

each factor, with neither factor name provided. In Excerpt 14.5, we are given the name of one factor (Gender) along with the names of the levels that constitute the other factor (Personal/Impersonal Real-Life Dilemma).

The cells of a two-way ANOVA correspond to the comparison groups of the study, and each cell is created by combining a level of the first factor with a level of the second factor. The full array of cells comes into being when each and every level of the first factor is combined, separately, with each and every level of the second factor. Excerpt 14.6 shows how this combining of levels produces cells. Since there were two levels of gender (male, female) and two levels of CSES effect (higher, lower), the two-way ANOVA involved four cells.

Excerpt 14.6   The Creation of Cells by Combining Levels of Factors

---

Gender and CSES effects were examined by organizing subjects' TCT scores into a four-cell paradigm—lower CSES male, higher CSES male, lower CSES female, and higher CSES female. A two-way analysis of variance (ANOVA) for independent samples was used to analyze the data.

Source: D. Richard. (1991). Intransitivity of paired comparisons related to gender and community socioeconomic setting. *Journal of Experimental Education, 59*(2), p. 200.

We believe that it will be easy for you to see the cells of any two-way ANOVA if you think of (or actually sketch) a square or rectangle that is partitioned into rows and columns. The specific number of rows and columns will be determined by the number of levels in the two factors. Each place where a row intersects with a column is a cell, and it represents a separate comparison group involved in the study.

To illustrate how easy it is to "see" the cells of a two-way ANOVA, consider again Excerpt 14.1. Although the cells were not specifically described in the original article and although no picture of the ANOVA design was provided, you can easily set up a picture, on paper or in your mind, that looks like this:

PARENTING STYLE

		Authoritarian	*Democratic*	*Permissive*	*Uninvolved*
GENDER	*Male*				
	Female				

This picture shows clearly how each of the cells came into being by combining each level of gender with each level of parenting style. Because such pictures will help immensely when we go about the task of interpreting the results of a two-way ANOVA, we strongly encourage you to visualize or sketch this kind of rectangle whenever you encounter a discussion of a two-way ANOVA.

Before completing our discussion of factors, levels, and cells, we ought to clarify something about terms such as 2 × 2 ANOVA, 3-by–3 ANOVA, 4 × 5 ANOVA, and 2-by–2-by–2 ANOVA. Whenever researchers use a term like this to describe their ANOVA, the number of numbers that precede the acronym ANOVA indicates how many independent variables (i.e., factors) were involved, while the specific value of each number indicates how many levels made up each factor. Accordingly, a 3 × 3 ANOVA is a two-way ANOVA (with three levels of each of the two factors) whereas a 2 × 2 × 2 ANOVA is not a two-way ANOVA because there are three factors. The picture that appears near the top of this page corresponds to a 2 × 4 ANOVA.

ACTIVE VERSUS ASSIGNED FACTORS AND THE FORMATION OF COMPARISON GROUPS

Although all two-way ANOVAs are the same in that the levels of the two factors jointly define the cells of the ANOVA design, there are different ways to "fill" each cell with a group of subjects. In any given study, one of three possible procedures for forming the comparison groups will be used depending upon the nature of the two factors. Since any factor can be classified as being "assigned" or "active" in nature, a two-way ANOVA could be set up to involve two assigned factors, two active factors, or one factor of each type.

An **assigned factor** deals with a characteristic of the study's subjects that they bring with them to the investigation. Examples include gender, handedness, birth order, intellectual capability, color preference, GPA, and personality type. When such a variable corresponds to a factor in a two-way ANOVA, no effort is made to change any subject's status on the variable. With assigned factors, each subject's status on the variable is determined entirely by the nature of the subject upon entry into the study. Furthermore, the presumption is made that subjects will not alter their status on such variables during the time frame of the investigation.

Whereas the status of a subject on an assigned factor is influenced totally by the subject, the subject's status on an **active factor** is determined wholly by the researcher. This is because active factors deal with conditions of the study that are under the control of the researcher. Simply put, this means the researcher can decide which level of the factor any subject will experience. Examples of active factors include time allowed to practice a task, type of diet given to the subject, gender of the counselor to whom the subject is assigned, and kind of reward given following the occurrence of desirable behavior being emitted by the subject. The hallmark of these and all other active factors is that the researcher gets to decide which level of the factor any subject will experience during the investigation.

If a two-way ANOVA involves two assigned factors, the researcher simply will put the available subjects into the various cells of the design based upon the characteristics of the subjects. This situation is exemplified by Excerpt 14.1, the study in which the two factors were gender and parenting style. In that study, the comparison groups were formed by putting each subject into one of the eight cells based upon a joint consideration of whether the subject was a male or female and whether the subject's parenting style was authoritarian, democratic, permissive, or uninvolved.

If a two-way ANOVA involves two active factors, the researcher will form the comparison groups by using the technique of randomization to allocate the available subjects to the various cells of the design. This situation is exemplified by Excerpt 14.7. In this study, the conditions of high and low ego involvement were not characteristics of the subjects as they entered the study

---

Excerpt 14.7 Creating Comparison Groups When There Are Two Active Factors

---

Subjects were randomly assigned to one of six conditions in a 2 × 3 (Ego involvement: high, low × Outcome: success, failure, no feedback) design.

Source: B. W. Brewer, J. L. Van Raalte, D. E. Linder, and N. S. Van Raalte. (1991). Peak performance and the perils of retrospective introspection. *Journal of Sport & Exercise Psychology, 13,* p. 234.

but rather mental states that were induced by the researcher. Accordingly, ego involvement was an active factor, and subjects could be randomly assigned to the high and low conditions (as well as to the success, failure, and no feedback levels of the outcome factor).

If a two-way ANOVA involves one active factor and one assigned factor, the researcher will form the comparison groups by taking the subjects who correspond to each level of the assigned factor and randomly assigning them to the various levels of the active factor. This third way of forming the comparison groups was used in the study from which Excerpt 14.8 was taken. In this study, the assigned factor was gender. The male subjects were randomly assigned to the three levels of the active factor (information conditions), as were the female subjects.

Excerpt 14.8   Creating Comparison Groups When There Is One Assigned Factor and One Active Factor

---

During the 1992 spring semester, subjects within each of five classes received one of three packets. The three packets were randomly distributed within each class. The packet contained a cover sheet, an article (for the two information groups), the measure of attitude toward homosexuals, and a check sheet for recording age and gender. . . . The scores [on the attitude inventory] were analyzed in a 3 (information condition) $\times$ 2 (gender) analysis of variance.

Source: J. Piskur and D. Degelman. (1992). Effect of reading a summary of research about biological bases of homosexual orientation on attitudes toward homosexuals. *Psychological Reports, 71,* pp. 1221–1222.

SAMPLES AND POPULATIONS

The samples associated with any two-way ANOVA are always easy to identify. There will be as many samples as there are cells, with the subjects who share a common cell creating each of the samples. Thus, there will be 4 distinct samples in any 2 $\times$ 2 ANOVA, 6 distinct samples in any 2 $\times$ 3 ANOVA, 12 distinct samples in any 3 $\times$ 4 ANOVA, and so on.

As is always the case in inferential statistics, a distinct population is associated with each sample in the study. Hence, the number of cells designates not only the number of samples (i.e., comparison groups) in the study, but also the number of populations involved in the investigation. While it is easy to tell how many populations are involved in any two-way ANOVA, care must be exercised in thinking about the nature of these populations, especially when one or both factors are active.

Simply put, each population in a two-way ANOVA should be conceptualized as being made up of a large group of people, animals, objects, or ideas that are similar to those in the corresponding sample represented by one of the cells. Thus, in the study in which the factors were gender and parenting style, one of the populations was authoritarian male parents, a second of the eight populations was democratic male parents, and the remaining six populations were defined in a similar fashion. If the researchers extracted each of their eight samples from a larger group of potential subjects, then each of the eight populations could be concrete or tangible in nature. If, on the other hand, the researchers simply used all available subjects, assigning each subject to one of the eight cells, then the populations are abstract in nature.[1]

If a two-way ANOVA involves one or two active factors, the populations associated with the study will definitely be abstract in nature. To understand why this is true, consider once again Excerpt 14.8. In this study, male and female students were randomly assigned to three information conditions. Each of the six populations was abstract in nature because it is characterized by students like those who were together in one of the cells *following "application" of the active factor.* Although there were lots of males similar to the ones who served as subjects in this investigation, there were probably no males outside of the study who were similar to the ones who experienced the same information conditions used in this study. Thus, the six populations of this investigation were abstract, made up of male and females like the ones used here who might, in the future, receive the same information conditions as those used in this study.

THREE RESEARCH QUESTIONS

To gain an understanding of the three research questions that are focused upon by a two-way ANOVA, consider the recently completed study in which each of 100 college students (50 male, 50 female) was asked to identify as many of the 48 contiguous states as possible on an outline map of the United States. Twenty-five of the male subjects and 25 of the female subjects were randomly assigned to an experimental condition in which they were given only the outline map; the other half of each gender group performed the same task with the aid of an alphabetized list of the 48 state names. There was a 20-minute time limit to perform the state-labeling task, with the dependent variable being the total number of state outlines correctly identified.

The table of results shown in Excerpt 14.9 summarizes the performance of the 100 subjects involved in this study. As you can see, the rows of this table are labeled so as to correspond with the levels of the gender factor whereas the two main columns—"Map Only" and "Map with Name Aid"—are labeled so as to correspond with the levels of the second factor. While the name of this second factor is not given in the table, it was referred to as "Condition" in the

---

[1] *We discussed the difference between concrete and abstract populations in Chapter 5.*

text of the research report. With two levels in each of the two factors, there are four cells of data in this table, each containing a mean and a standard deviation.

When the researchers applied a two-way ANOVA to the data provided by the 100 subjects, they obtained answers to three research questions. Although these three research questions were tied to the specific independent and dependent variables involved in this study, the nature of their questions was identical to the nature of the three research questions that are posed and answered in any two-way ANOVA. These three questions, in their generic form, can be stated as follows: (1) Is there a statistically significant main effect for the first factor? (2) Is there a statistically significant main effect for the second factor? (3) Is there a statistically significant interaction between the two factors?

The first research question in the study dealing with identifying states asked whether there was a statistically significant main effect for gender. To get a feel for what this first research question was asking, you must focus your attention on the **main effect means** for gender. These means are not provided in Excerpt 14.9, but they are easy to compute. The main effect mean for males is simply the overall mean for all 50 males involved in the study. Since 25 males were in the Map Only condition and 25 were in the Map with Name Aid condition, the main effect mean for males is simply the arithmetic average of 37.48 and 32.96, or 35.22. We suggest that you write this main effect to the right of the two cells on the top row of information in Excerpt 14.9. The main effect mean for females, computed in a similar fashion, turns out equal to 29.88. It should be positioned to the right of the two cells on the bottom row.

In any two-way ANOVA, the first research question asks whether there is a statistically significant **main effect** for the factor that corresponds to the

---

Excerpt 14.9   Cell Means from the Study Dealing with Identifying States on an Outline Map

Table I

Mean number of state outlines identified correctly

Gender	Map Only		Map with Name Aid	
	Mean	SD	Mean	SD
Males	37.48	9.25	32.96	11.64
Females	31.92	10.82	27.84	10.42

Source: H. R. Straub and B. E. Seaton. (1993). Relationship between gender and knowledge of U.S. state names and locations. *Sex Roles, 28,* p. 626.

rows of the two-dimensional picture of the study. Stated differently, the first research question is asking whether the main effect means associated with the first factor are further apart from each other than would be expected by chance. There will be as many such means as there are levels of the first factor. In the study we are considering, there were two levels (male, female) of the first factor (gender), with the first research question asking whether the difference between 35.22 and 29.88 was larger than could be accounted for by chance. In other words, the first research question asked, "Is there a statistically significant difference between the mean performance on the state-labeling-task of the 50 males and that of the 50 females?"

The second research question in any two-way ANOVA asks whether there is a significant main effect for the factor that corresponds to the columns of the two-dimensional picture of the study. The answer to this question will be "yes" if the main effect means for the second factor turn out to be further apart from each other than would be expected by chance. In the study we are considering, there are two such main effect means, one for Map Only and one for Map with Name Aid. These means turned out equal to 34.70 and 30.40, respectively, and we suggest that you write these means beneath the columns of Excerpt 14.9. Simply put, the second research question in the state-labeling study asked, "Is there a statistically significant difference between the mean performance of the 50 subjects who identified states without the aid of a list of state names as compared with the 50 subjects who were given such a list?"

The third research question in any two-way ANOVA asks whether there is a statistically significant **interaction** between the two factors involved in the study. The interaction deals with the cell means of the study, and we have reproduced here the four cell means of Excerpt 14.9:

		CONDITION	
		Map Only	Map with Name Aid
GENDER	Males	37.48	32.96
	Females	31.92	27.84

Interaction exists to the extent that the difference between the levels of the first factor changes when we move from level to level of the second factor. To illustrate, consider the cell means from the study on labeling states. The difference between the male and female subjects who performed the task in the Map Only condition was 5.56, with the upper left-hand cell being larger than the lower left-hand cell. If this difference of 5.56 were to show up again when we examine the cell means in the right-hand column of the cell means (with the same ordering of the means in terms of magnitude), there would be absolutely no interaction. That is not the case, however. Although the mean on the top row in the right-hand column is larger than the mean beneath it (as was the case with the means in the left-hand column), the difference between the means in the right-hand column is 5.12, not 5.56. Hence, there is some interaction between the gender and condition factors. But is the amount of interaction contained in the cell means more than what one would expect by chance? If so, then it can be said that a statistically significant interaction exists between the two factors of the study.

It should be noted that the interaction of a two-way ANOVA can be thought of as dealing with the difference between the levels of the row's factor as one moves from one level to another level of the column's factor, or it can be thought of as dealing with the difference between the levels of the column's factor as one moves from one level to another level of the row's factor. To illustrate, consider once again the cell means of the study involving labeling states. The difference between the two cell means on the top row is 4.52 (with the left-hand mean being larger than the right-hand mean) whereas the difference between the two cell means on the bottom row is 4.08 (again with the left-hand mean being larger). Although these two differences (4.52 and 4.08) are not the same as the differences discussed in the preceding paragraph (5.56 and 5.12), note that in both cases the difference between the differences is exactly the same: .44. Our point here is simply that there is only one interaction in a two-way ANOVA; the order in which the factors are named (or are used to compare cell means) makes no difference whatsoever.

THE THREE NULL HYPOTHESES (AND THREE ALTERNATIVE HYPOTHESES)

There are three null hypotheses examined within a two-way ANOVA. One of these null hypotheses is concerned with the main effect of the row's factor, the second is concerned with the main effect of the column's factor, and the third is concerned with the interaction between the two factors.

To explain how each of these null hypotheses should be conceptualized, we must reiterate that the group of subjects that supplies data for any cell of the two-way ANOVA is only a sample. As we pointed out earlier in this chapter, a population is connected to each cell's sample. Sometimes each of these populations will be concrete in nature, with subjects randomly selected from a finite pool of potential subjects. In many studies, each population will be abstract in nature, with the nature of the population tailored to fit the nature of the group within each cell and the condition under which data are collected from the subjects in that group.

In the 2×2 ANOVA dealing with identifying states on an outline map of the United States, four populations were involved. Since the "conditions" factor of this study was active in nature (with subjects randomly assigned to the Map Only and Map with Name Aid conditions), the populations were abstract in nature. One of these populations should be conceptualized as being made up of male college students similar to the ones used in this study who are given 20 minutes to identify states on the outline map used in this study. A second population should be conceptualized as being made up of male college students like those used in the study who perform the same state-identifying task with the aid of an alphabetized list of the 48 contiguous states. The third and fourth populations are like the first two except they should be conceptualized as being made up of female college students like those used in this study.

The first null hypothesis in any two-way ANOVA deals with the main effect means associated with the rows' factor of the study. This null hypothesis asserts that the population counterparts of these sample-based main effect means are equal to each other. Stated in symbols for the general case, this null hypothesis is as follows: $H_0: \mu_{ROW1} = \mu_{ROW2} = \cdots = \mu_{BOTTOM\ ROW}$. For the study dealing with identifying states on an outline map, this null hypothesis took the form $H_0: \mu_{MALES} = \mu_{FEMALES}$.

The second null hypothesis in any two-way ANOVA deals with the main effect means associated with the columns factors. This null hypothesis asserts that the population counterparts of these sample-based main effect means are equal to each other. For the general case, the null hypothesis says $H_0: \mu_{COLUMN_1} = \mu_{COLUMN_2} = \cdots = \mu_{LAST\ COLUMN}$. For the study dealing with the outline map, this null hypothesis took the form $H_0: \mu_{MAP\ ONLY} = \mu_{MAP\ +\ LIST}$.

Before we turn our attention to the third null hypothesis of a two-way ANOVA, we need to clarify the meaning of the μs that appear in the null hypothesis for the main effects. Each of these μs, like the data-based sample mean to which it is tied, actually represents the average of cell means. For example, $\mu_{ROW\ 1}$ is the average of the μs associated with the cells on row 1, while $\mu_{COLUMN\ 1}$ is the average of the μs associated with the cells in column 1. Each of the other main effect μs similarly represents the average of the μs associated with the cells that lie in a common row or in a common column. This point about the main effect μs is important to note because (1) populations are always tied conceptually to samples and (2) the samples in a two-way ANOVA are located *in* the cells. Unless you realize that the main effect μs are conceptually derived from averaging cell μs, you might find yourself being misled into thinking that the number of populations associated with any two-way ANOVA can be determine by adding the number of main effect means to the number of cells. Hopefully, our earlier and current comments will help you to see that a two-way ANOVA has only as many populations as there are cells.

The third null hypothesis in a two-way ANOVA specifies that there is no interaction between the two factors. This null hypothesis deals with the cell means, not the main effect means. In other words, this null hypothesis asserts that whatever differences exist among the population means associated with the cells in any given column of the two-way layout are equal to the differences among the population means associated with the cells in each of the other columns. Stated differently, this null hypothesis says that the relationship among the population means associated with the full set of cells is such that a single pattern of differences describes accurately what exists within any column.[2]

To express the interaction null hypothesis using symbols, we must first agree to let j and j' stand for any two different rows in the two-way layout, and to let k and k' stand for any two different columns. Thus, the intersection of row j and column k designates cell jk, with the population mean associated with this cell being referred to as μ_{jk}. The population mean associated with a different cell in the same column would be symbolized as $\mu_{j'k}$. The population means associated with two cells on these same rows, j and j', but in a different column, k', could be symbolized as $\mu_{jk'}$ and $\mu_{j'k'}$, respectively. Using this notational scheme, we can express the interaction null hypothesis of any two-way ANOVA as follows:

$$H_0: \mu_{jk} - \mu_{j'k} = \mu_{jk'} - \mu_{j'k'}, \text{ for all rows and columns}$$
$$\text{(i.e., for all combinations of both } j \text{ and } j', k \text{ and } k')$$

To help you understand the meaning of the interaction null hypothesis, we have constructed sets of hypothetical population means corresponding to a 2×2 ANOVA, a 2×3 ANOVA, and a 2×4 ANOVA. In each of the hypothetical ANOVAs, the interaction null hypothesis is completely true.

$\mu = 20$	$\mu = 40$
$\mu = 10$	$\mu = 30$

$\mu = 10$	$\mu = 30$	$\mu = 29$
$\mu = 5$	$\mu = 25$	$\mu = 24$

$\mu = 2$	$\mu = 12$	$\mu = 6$	$\mu = 24$
$\mu = 4$	$\mu = 14$	$\mu = 8$	$\mu = 26$

Before turning our attention to the alternative hypotheses associated with a two-way ANOVA, it is important to note that each H_0 we have considered is independent from the other two. In other words, any combination of the three null hypotheses can be true (or false). To illustrate, we have constructed three sets of hypothetical population means for a 2×2 layout. Moving from

[2] *The interaction null hypothesis can be stated with references to parameter differences among the cell means within the various rows (rather than within the various columns). Thus, the interaction null hypothesis asserts that whatever differences exist among the population means associated with the cells in any given row of the two-way layout are equal to the differences among the population means associated with the cells in each of the other rows.*

left to right, we see a case in which only the row means differ, a case in which only the interaction null hypothesis is false, and a case in which the null hypotheses for both the row's main effect and the interaction are false:

$\mu = 10$	$\mu = 10$
$\mu = 5$	$\mu = 5$

$\mu = 20$	$\mu = 10$
$\mu = 10$	$\mu = 20$

$\mu = 10$	$\mu = 30$
$\mu = 20$	$\mu = 0$

Because the three null hypotheses are independent of each other, a conclusion drawn (from sample data) concerning one of the null hypotheses is specific to that particular H_0. The same data set can be used to evaluate all three null statements, but the data must be looked at from "different angles" in order to address all three null hypotheses. This is accomplished by computing a separate F-test to see if each H_0 is likely to be false.

If the researcher who conducts the two-way ANOVA evaluates each H_0 by means of hypothesis testing or by means of the hybrid approach to testing null hypotheses, there will be three alternative hypotheses. Each H_0 is set up in a nondirectional fashion, and they assert that:

1. The row μs are *not* all equal to each other;
2. The column μs are *not* all equal to each other;
3. The pattern of differences among the cell μs in the first column (or the first row) *fails* to describe accurately the pattern of differences among the cell μs in at least one other column (row).

PRESENTATION OF RESULTS

The results of a two-way ANOVA can be communicated through a table or within the text of the research report. We begin our consideration of how researchers present the findings gleaned from their two-way ANOVAs by looking at the results of the study dealing with identifying states on an outline map. We then consider how the results of several other two-way ANOVAs were presented. Near the end of this section, we will look at the various ways researchers organize their findings when two or more two-way ANOVAs have been conducted within the same study.

RESULTS OF THE TWO-WAY ANOVA STUDY ON IDENTIFYING STATES

In the research report of the study dealing with identifying states on an outline map, the findings were not presented in a two-way ANOVA summary table. If such a table had been prepared, it probably would have looked like Table 14.1. Notice that this summary table is similar to the summary table for a one-way ANOVA in terms of (1) the number and names of columns included in the table, (2) each row's MS being computed by dividing the row's df into its SS, (3) the total df being equal to one less than the number of subjects used in the investigation, and (4) calculated values being presented in the *F* column. Despite these similarities, one-way and two-way ANOVA summary tables differ in that the latter contains five rows (rather than three) and three *F*-ratios (rather than one). Note that in the two-way summary table, the *MS* for the next-to-the-bottom row (which is usually labeled *Error* or *Within groups*) was used as the denominator in computing each of the three *F*-ratios: $712.89/111.68 = 6.38$, $462.25/111.68 = 4.14$, and $1.21/111.68 = .01$.

TABLE 14.1

Source	df	SS	MS	F
Gender	1	712.89	712.89	6.38*
Condition	1	462.25	462.25	4.14*
Interaction	1	1.21	1.21	.01
Error	96	10,720.82	111.68	
Total	99	23,794.34		

*$p < .05$

There are three values in the *F* column of a two-way ANOVA summary table because there are three null hypotheses associated with this kind of ANOVA. Each of the three *F*s addresses a different null hypothesis. The first two *F*s are concerned with the study's main effects; in other words, the first two *F*s deal with the two sets of main effect means. The third *F* deals with the interaction between the two factors, with the focus of this *F* being on cell means.

Shortly, we will show you several two-way ANOVA summary tables that appeared in published research reports. Before doing that, however, we want to show you how the authors of the study dealing with labeling states presented their results. Their findings appear in Excerpt 14.10. There, the numbers in parentheses to the right of each *F* are the degrees of freedom associated with that *F*. The first of each pair of *df* values came from the row of the ANOVA summary table that contained the calculated value being reported, while the second *df* value came from the next-to-bottom row in the ANOVA summary table. In this study, each of the three *F*s has 1 and 96 *df*. Whereas the *df* value of 96 came from the same place in the summary table, the *df* values of 1 came from different rows.

In Excerpt 14.10, note that the main effect *F* for gender turned out to be slightly larger than the main effect *F* for condition. If you take another look at Excerpt 14.9, you will see why this happened. The main effect means for gender were 35.22 and 29.88, whereas the main effect means for condition were 34.70 and 30.40. Because the first two of these means were further apart from each other than were the second two means, the sample data argue a bit

Excerpt 14.10   Results of the Two-Way ANOVA from the Study
Dealing with Labeling States on an Outline Map

A 2(Condition—Map Only/Map with Name Aid) $\times$ 2(Gender) analysis of
variance (ANOVA) with number of states identified correctly as the dependent
variable yielded a significant main effect for condition $[F(1,96) = 4.14, p < .05]$
and a significant main effect for gender $[F(1,96) = 6.38, p < .05]$, but no significant interaction $[F(1,96) = 0.01, p > .10]$. Students in the Map Only condition
identified more states correctly than did students in the Map with Name Aid
condition. Males named correctly more state outlines than did females.

Source: H. R. Straub and B. E. Seaton. (1993). Relationship between gender and knowledge of U.S.
state names and locations. *Sex Roles, 28*, p. 626.

more strongly against the gender null hypothesis than against the condition
null hypothesis. Nevertheless, the discrepancy between the two condition
means (like the discrepancy between the two gender means) was so large that
the null hypothesis could be rejected at the .05 level.

In Excerpt 14.10, the researchers report that the interaction between gender and condition was not significant. This result is understandable in light of
the cell means reported in Excerpt 14.9. The difference between the mean
scores earned by the 25 males and the 25 females who performed the state-
identifying task under the Map Only condition is very similar to the difference between the other males and females who were given the outline map
plus the list of state names. In both cases, males identified, on the average,
about 5 more states than did females. Because the difference between the
male and female means changes very little across the two conditions of the
study, the interaction F was not even close to being significant.

RESULTS FROM VARIOUS TWO-WAY ANOVA STUDIES

In Excerpts 14.11–14.13, we see the summary tables from three separate
studies in which a 2 $\times$ ANOVA was used to analyze the data.

Note the differences among the summary tables in Excerpts 14.11–14.13.
Only the first one has a row for Total, thus allowing us to tell that 48 subjects
were involved in the study. (We can determine how many subjects were involved
in the other two ANOVAs, but to do so we must add the *df*s in each table to obtain the total—and then add 1.) In Excerpt 14.12, the interaction row of the
table is labeled A $\times$ B (following a designation of the main effect rows as A and
B). Finally, note in Excerpt 14.13 that a column of *p*-values is positioned to the
right of the *F*-values; in the other two tables, an asterisk and an explanatory note
beneath the table was used to reveal the outcome of the *F*-tests.

Excerpts 14.11–14.13   Three 2 × 2 ANOVA Summary Tables

Table 4

Summary of 2 (hearing status) by 2 (age) Analysis of Variance of Conservation Scores

Source of variation	Sum of squares	Degrees of freedom	Mean square	F
Hearing status	17.9	1	17.9	12.2*
Age	2.7	1	2.7	1.8
Hearing status × age	0.6	1	0.6	0.4
Error	64.8	44	1.5	
Total	86.0	47		

* $p < .01$

Source: D. S. Cates and F. C. Shontz. (1990). Social and nonsocial decentration in hearing-impaired and normal hearing children. *Journal of Childhood Communication Disorders, 13,* p. 176.

Table 3

ANOVA for a competitive learning preference

Source	Sum of squares	df	MS	F
Academic achievement (A)	25.68	1	25.68	0.73
Gender (B)	87.44	1	87.44	0.21
A × B	238.43	1	238.43	7.21*
Error	4365.98	132	33.08	

* $p < .05$.

Source: C. Johnson and G. Engelhard. (1992). Gender, academic achievement, and preferences for cooperative, competitive, and individualistic learning among African-American adolescents. *The Journal of Psychology, 126,* p. 391.

A 2 × 2 (Type of Card × Field Style) analysis of variance (ANOVA) was performed comparing the total time spent in study (see Table 2). Type of Card was the only effect that reached a level of significance ($p = .003$, $df = 1,50$, $F = 9.80$). Subjects using the instructor–designed cards spent an average of 217 minutes in study; those making their own cards, an average of 329 minutes.

(Continued)

Excerpts 14.11–14.13   Three 2 × 2 ANOVA Summary Tables

Table 2

Analysis of variance for total study time

Source	Sum of Squares	df	Mean Square	F	p
Type of Card	192209.56	1	192209.56	9.80	.003
Field Style	59766.66	1	59766.66	3.05	.09
Card × Field	37589.36	1	37589.36	1.92	.17
Error	980447.69	50	19608.95	—	—

Despite the differences among Excerpts 14.11–14.13, these ANOVA summary tables are similar in several respects. In each case, the title of the table reveals what the dependent variable was. In each case, the names of the first two rows reveal the names of the two factors. In each case, the *df* values for the main effect rows of the table allow us to know that there were two levels in each factor. In each case, the mean square values were computed by dividing each row's *df* into its sum of squares. And in each case, three calculated *F*-values are presented, one of which addresses each of the three null hypotheses associated with the two-way ANOVA.

Not all two-way ANOVAs, of course, are of the 2 × 2 variety. In Excerpt 14.14, we see the summary table for a 2 × 4 ANOVA. Although there were two levels of the Status factor and four levels of the Time since loss factor, the two-way ANOVA still yields three *F*-ratios, one for each of the two main effects and one for the interaction between the two factors.

In reporting the outcome of their two-way ANOVAs, researchers often talk about the results within the text of the research report without including a summary table. Earlier, in Excerpt 14.10, we saw an example of this typical way of presenting the results of a two-way ANOVA. In Excerpt 14.15, we see another example. Based on the information presented here, you should be able to figure out what the independent and dependent variables were, what the three null hypotheses were (and what decision was made relative to each H_0), and how many clients were involved in the study.[3]

---

[3]*If you said to yourself that 78 clients were involved in this study, try again to come up with the correct answer!*

Excerpt 14.14   Summary Table for a 2 × 4 ANOVA

Table 3

Summary of two-way analysis of variance between self-esteem scores and status, time since loss, and their interaction

Source	SS	DF	MS	F
Status	.4096	1	.4096	6.18*
Time since loss	.2694	3	.0898	1.35
Status × Time since loss interaction	.4867	3	.1622	2.45
Within	13.9930	211	.0663	

* $p < .05$.

Source: J. Farnsworth, M. A. Pett, and D. A. Lund, (1992). The influence of self-esteem on the loss-management and subjective well-being of older divorced and widowed adults. *Family Perspective, 26,* p. 108.

Excerpt 14.15   Results of a Two-Way ANOVA Presented Without a Summary Table

A 2×2 (Training Condition × Counselor Race) analysis of variance (ANOVA) was performed on the number of counselor sessions attended by each client. A significant main effect for training was found, $F(1,76) = 52.80, p < .001$. An examination of the means (2.88 for the culture sensitivity training condition and 1.90 for the control condition) revealed that clients assigned to counselors in the culture sensitivity training group returned for more sessions than did clients assigned to counselors in the control condition.

Source: P. Wade and B. L. Bernstein. (1991). Culture sensitivity training and counselor's race: Effects on Black female clients' perceptions and attrition. *Journal of Counseling Psychology, 38,* p. 12.

When there are two or more dependent variables in a study along with two independent variables, many researchers choose a strategy for data analysis that involves conducting a separate two-way ANOVA on the data from each dependent variable. When this is done, three *F*-tests will be computed for each dependent variable, one for each main effect and one for the interaction. An example of this kind of data analysis situation is presented in Excerpt 14.16. Here, each row presents the descriptive and inferential results for a different dependent variable. The final six numbers on each row are the three *F*-values and corresponding *p*-values for the tests of the two main effects and

Excerpt 14.16   Results of Several Two–Way ANOVAs, Each Involving the Same Independent Variables but a Different Dependent Variable

Table 2

Means, standard deviations, and ANOVA results of substance abuse and psychiatric patients on the new DAB scales

| DAB Scales | Boys | | | | Girls | | | | Setting[e] | | Gender | | Interaction | |
| | Substance Abuse[a] | | Psychiatric[b] | | Substance Abuse[c] | | Psychiatric[d] | | | | | | | |
	M	SD	M	SD	M	SD	M	SD	F	p	F	p	F	p
AOB	81.50	21.52	73.86	23.93	75.51	19.65	64.83	20.79	32.46	.001	20.75	.001	.89	ns
WTB	41.31	13.65	41.11	15.18	41.50	13.87	44.86	14.62	1.27	ns	3.20	ns	2.65	ns
PB	23.16	5.57	26.18	7.52	23.86	6.72	22.74	5.44	6.03	.01	7.32	.007	19.14	.001
NDB	23.27	7.16	19.10	6.14	24.47	6.21	20.32	6.16	70.90	.001	5.85	ns	0	ns
HI	16.34	6.60	16.03	5.62	21.80	7.44	18.83	7.34	8.76	.003	65.98	.001	6.76	.01

Note. All *df* = 1,733.

[a]*n* = 267. [b]*n* = 153. [c]*n* = 137. [d]*n* = 180. [e]Substance abuse setting compared with psychiatric setting.

Source: C. L. Williams, Y. S. Ben-Porath, C. Uchiyama, N. C. Weed, and R. P. Archer. (1990). External validity of the new Devereaux Adolescent Behavior Rating Scales. *Journal of Personality Assessment, 55,* p. 79.

the interaction. The initial eight numbers on each row are the means and standard deviations for the four cells of the 2 × 2 Setting-by-Gender ANOVA. The four cells for each of the two-way ANOVAs are lined up in a single row rather than being presented in a box having two rows and two columns. You can, however, easily rearrange the cell means into the more familiar row-by-column format. To illustrate, we have done this for the fourth dependent variable, the NDB scale of the DAB:

		GENDER	
		Boys	*Girls*
SETTING	*Substance Abuse*	23.27	24.47
	Psychiatric	19.10	20.32

This arrangement of the four means for the NDB variable ought to provide you with some insights as to why the Setting main effect turned out to be significant while the Gender main effect and the Setting-by-Gender Interaction turned out to be nonsignificant.

In Excerpt, 14.17, we see another example of how the descriptive and inferential results associated with several two-way ANOVAs, each involving the same independent variables but a different dependent variable, can be combined into a single table. Note that the portion of this table that presents the results of the inferential tests provides information only as to the researcher's decision regarding each null hypothesis. Although we are told which F-tests turned out to be significant, we are not told how large the F-ratios were or the value of p associated with each F. Although we are not even told what level of

---

Excerpt 14.17 Another Table Containing the Results of Several Two-Way ANOVAs, Each Conducted on a Different Dependent Variable

---

Table 1 presents the responses obtained from the husbands and wives of both family types on the survey of family activities. For each item on the list, the subject was asked to estimate the number of hours that would be spent pursuing that activity "in an average week." These estimates were then analyzed in a series of 2×2 (Family Type × Sex of Respondent) ANOVAs with $df = 1,76$ for all comparisons. The results of the statistical analyses are also summarized in Table 1.

(Continued)

Excerpt 14.17   Another Table Containing the Results of Several
Two-Way ANOVAs, Each Conducted on a Different
Dependent Variable *(Continued)*

Table 1

Means, *SDs*, and summaries of ANOVA results for estimates of hours spent per week in different activities

Activity		Male-tilted		Female-tilted		Results
		Husbands	Wives	Husbands	Wives	
Working outside the home	$\overline{X}$	52.10	15.05	46.15	18.70	b
	SD	(12.02)	(11.75)	(16.19)	(17.12)	
Alone with spouse	$\overline{X}$	15.75	13.70	16.15	15.90	N.S.
	SD	(17.30)	(7.52)	(13.90)	(13.13)	
Engaged in conversation with children	$\overline{X}$	8.95	16.25	8.60	14.65	b
	SD	(9.98)	(9.37)	(5.89)	(12.48)	
Engaged in recreational activity with children	$\overline{X}$	8.70	8.55	5.55	7.15	a
	SD	(4.90)	(4.59)	(3.80)	(6.83)	
Engaged in social activities only with other members of same sex	$\overline{X}$	3.45	3.75	4.20	3.35	N.S.
	SD	(4.37)	(2.49)	(4.16)	(2.25)	
Engaged in social activities with mixed-sex company	$\overline{X}$	4.75	4.30	5.15	4.20	N.S.
	SD	(3.81)	(1.56)	(4.70)	(2.38)	
Helping children with school work	$\overline{X}$	1.45	3.10	1.25	2.40	b
	SD	(1.39)	(2.02)	(1.02)	(2.41)	
Engaged in a recreational activity alone	$\overline{X}$	3.05	4.85	6.90	2.95	a $\times$ b
	SD	(2.82)	(4.58)	(5.76)	(2.86)	

Note. The Results column indicates the comparisons that are statistically significant.
a = Main effect of Family Type.
b = Main effect of Sex of Respondent.
a $\times$ b = Interaction effect of Family Type $\times$ Sex of Respondent.
N.S. = Not Significant.

Source: C. W. Falconer, K. G. Wilson, and J. Falconer. (1990). A psychometric investigation of gender-tilted families: Implications for family therapy. *Family Relations,* 39, p. 10. © by the National Council on Family Relations, 3989 Central Ave. NE, Suite 550, Minneapolis, MN 55421. Reprinted by permission.

significance was used in conjunction with these tests, we probably would be correct if we made a guess that the alpha level was set equal to .05 for each test.

If multiple two-way ANOVAs are conducted, each on a separate dependent variable, the researcher may choose to summarize the results within the text of the research report without any table. Excerpt 14.18 illustrates how this can be done.

Excerpt 14.18   Results of Several Two-Way ANOVAs Presented Within the Text of the Research Report

Gender differences in pride following success and in shame and a desire to hide one's paper following failure were analyzed with 2×2 ANOVAs, with gender and grade as the two independent variables. For pride in success, the gender main effect, $F(1,287) = 6.16$, $MS_e = 1.75$, $p < .01$, was significant, but the Gender × Grade interaction was not. . . . Neither the gender main effect, $F(1,178) = 1.18$, nor the Gender × Grade interaction, $F(1,178) = .07$, was significant for the emotion shame following a poor outcome. For "feel like hiding my paper," the gender main effect, $F(1,178) = 10.29$, $MS_e = 2.11$, $p < .01$, was significant, but the Gender × Grade interaction effect was not.

Source: D. J. Stipek and J. H. Gralinski. (1991). Gender differences in children's achievement-related beliefs and emotional responses to success and failure in mathematics. *Journal of Educational Psychology, 83*(3), p. 365.

FOLLOW-UP TESTS

If none of the two-way ANOVA *F*s turns out to be significant, no follow-up test will be conducted. On the other hand, if at least one of the main effects is found to be significant, or if the interaction null hypothesis is rejected, you may find that a follow-up investigation is undertaken in an effort to probe the data. We will discuss first the follow-up tests used in conjunction with significant main effect *F*-ratios. Then, we will consider the post hoc strategy typically employed when the interaction *F* turns out to be significant.

FOLLOW-UP TESTS TO PROBE SIGNIFICANT MAIN EFFECTS

If the *F*-test for one of the factors turns out to be significant and if there are only two levels associated with that factor, no post hoc test will be applied. In this situation, the outcome of the *F*-test indicates that a significant difference exists between that factor's two main effect means, and the only thing the researcher needs to do to determine where the significant difference lies is to look at the two row (or two column) means. Whichever of the two means is larger is significantly larger than the other mean. If you take another look at Excerpt 14.15, you will see an example where the two main effect means associated with a two-level factor were simply included in the text of the research report after it was reported that this factor's *F*-ratio turned out to be significant.

If the two-way ANOVA yields a significant *F* for one of the two factors, and if that factor involves three or more levels, the researcher is likely to conduct a **post hoc** investigation in order to compare the main effect means associated with the significant *F*. This is done for the same reasons that a post hoc investigation is typically conducted in conjunction with a one-way

ANOVA that yields a significant result when three or more means are compared. In both cases, the omnibus F that turns out to be significant needs to be "probed" so as to allow the researcher (and others) to gain insight into the pattern of population means.

Excerpt 14.19 illustrates how a post hoc investigation can help to clarify the meaning of a significant main effect. Notice how the Scheffé test helped to explain why the main effect of grade turned out significant.

Excerpt 14.19   A Post Hoc Investigation Used to Clarify a Significant Main Effect F

A 2×5 (gender × grade) analysis of variance (ANOVA) was performed for the total group on the MASC scores. The results showed that there were significant differences in mathematics anxiety among students in different grades [$F(4,552)$ = 14.38, $p < .05$], but there were no differences between boys and girls. The interaction effect between gender and grade was also not significant. Subsequent to the 2×5 ANOVA, the Scheffé method was used to make all comparisons between means of different grade levels. The results showed that the eighth graders scored significantly lower than the fifth graders, sixth graders, and seventh graders. No other comparisons between grade levels were significant.

Source: L. Chiu and L. L. Henry. (1990). Development and validation of the Mathematics Anxiety Scale for Children. *Measurement and Evaluation in Counseling and Development, 23*, p. 125.

If each of the factors in a two-way ANOVA turns out significant and if each of those factors contains three or more levels, then it is likely that a separate post hoc investigation will be conducted on each set of main effect means. The purpose of the two post hoc investigations would be the same: to identify the main effect means associated with each factor that are far enough apart to suggest that the corresponding population means are dissimilar. When both sets of main effect means are probed by means of post hoc investigations, the same test procedure (e.g., Tukey's) will be used to make comparisons among each set of main effect means.

FOLLOW-UP TESTS TO PROBE A SIGNIFICANT INTERACTION

When confronted with a statistically significant interaction, researchers will typically do two things. First, they will *refrain* from interpreting the F-ratios associated with the two main effects. Second, post hoc tests will be conducted and/or a graph will be prepared to help explain the specific nature of the interaction within the context of the study that has been conducted. Before turning our attention to the most frequently used follow-up strategies employed by researchers after observing a statistically significant interaction, we want to say a word or two about what they *do not do*.

Once the results of the two-way ANOVA become available, researchers will usually first look to see what happened relative to the interaction *F*. If the interaction turns out to be nonsignificant, they will move their attention to the two main effect *F*s and will interpret them in accordance with the principles outlined in the previous section. If, however, the interaction turns out to be significant, little or no attention will be devoted to the main effect *F*-ratios. This is because conclusions based on main effects can be quite misleading in the presence of significant interactions.

To illustrate how the presence of interaction renders the interpretation of main effects problematic, consider the three hypothetical situations presented in Figure 14.1. The number within each cell of each diagram is meant to be a sample mean, the numbers to the right of and below each diagram are meant to be main effect means (assuming equal cell sizes), and the abbreviated summary table provides the results that would be obtained if the samples were large enough or if the within-cell variability was small enough.

In situation 1, both main effect *F*s turn out nonsignificant. These results, coupled with the fact that there is no variability within either set of main effect means, might well lead one to think that the two levels of factor A are equivalent and to think that the three levels of factor B are equivalent. An inspection of the cell means, however, shows that those conclusions based on main effect means would cause one to overlook potentially important findings. The two levels of factor A "produced" different means at the first and third levels of factor B, and the three levels of factor B were dissimilar at each level of factor A.

To drive home our point about how main effect *F*s can be misleading when the interaction is significant, pretend that factor A is gender (males on the top row, females on the bottom row), that factor B is a type of headache medicine given to relieve pain (brands X, Y, and Z corresponding to the first, second, and third columns, respectively), with each subject asked to rate the effectiveness of his or her medication on a 0–40 scale (0 = no relief; 40 = total relief) 60 minutes after being given a single dose of one brand of med-

(1)

	B			
A	10	15	20	15
	20	15	10	15
	15	15	15	

Source	F
A	ns
B	ns
A × B	*

(2)

	B			
A	5	10	15	10
	25	20	15	20
	15	15	15	

Source	F
A	*
B	ns
A × B	*

(3)

	B			
A	10	10	10	10
	10	10	40	20
	10	10	25	

Source	F
A	*
B	*
A × B	*

FIGURE 14.1 *Hypothetical results from three two-way ANOVAs*

ication. If one were to pay attention to the main effect *F*s, one might be tempted to conclude that men and women experienced equal relief and that the three brands of medication were equally effective. Such conclusions would be unfortunate, because the cell means suggest strongly (1) that males and females differed, on the average, in the reactions to headache medications X and Z, and (2) that the three medications differed in the relief produced (with Brand X being superior for females, Brand Z being superior for males).

In the second of our hypothetical situations, notice again how the main effect *F*s are misleading because of the interaction. Now, the main effect of factor A is significant, and one might be tempted to look at the main effect means and draw the conclusion that males experienced less relief from their headache medicines than did females. However, inspection of the cell means clearly shows that no difference exists between males and females when given Brand Z. Again, the main effect *F* for factor B would be misleading for the same reason as it would in the first set of results.

In the final hypothetical situation, both main effect *F*s are significant. Inspection of the cell means reveals, however, that the levels of factor A do not differ at the first or at the second levels of factor B, and that the levels of factor B do not differ at the first level of factor A. Within the context of our hypothetical headache study, the main effect *F*s, if interpreted, would lead one to suspect that females experienced more relief than males and that the three medicines differed in their effectiveness. Such conclusions would be misleading, for males and females experienced differential relief only when given Brand Z, and the brands seem to be differentially effective only in the case of females.

When the interaction *F* turns out to be significant, the main effect *F*s must be interpreted with extreme caution—or not interpreted directly at all. This is why most researchers are encouraged to look at the interaction *F* first when trying to make sense out of the results provided by a two-way ANOVA. The interaction *F* serves as a guidepost that tells the researchers what to do next. If the interaction *F* turns out to be *non*significant, this means that they have a "green light" and may proceed to interpret the *F*-ratios associated with the two main effects. If, however, the interaction *F* *is* significant, this is tantamount to a "red light" that says "Don't pay attention to the main effect means but instead focus your attention on the cell means."

One of the strategies used to help gain insight into a statistically significant interaction is a **graph of the cell means**. Such a graph is contained in Excerpt 14.20. Most researchers set up their graphs like the one in Excerpt 14.20 in that (1) the ordinate represents the dependent variable, (2) the points on the abscissa represents the levels of one of the two independent variables, and (3) the lines in the graph represent the levels of the other independent variable. (Either of the two independent variables can be used to label the abscissa. In Excerpt 14.20, if the Education factor had been put on the abscissa, there would have been three points on the baseline—one for 11–12, one for 13–16, and one for +17—with two lines in the graph—one for reference information being present and one for reference information being absent.)

Notice how the graph in Excerpt 14.20 displays nicely the basic idea of a statistical interaction. Recall that an interaction means that the difference between the levels of one factor changes as we move from one level to another level of the other factor. In Excerpt 14.20, the height difference between the endpoints of the three lines is not the same; it is greatest for the oldest subjects and smallest for the youngest subjects. Considered as a whole, this graph sug-

---

Excerpt 14.20   The Graph of a Significant Interaction

A significant interaction was also found between education and reference information on the comprehension variable. . . . Figure 4 depicts this interaction. As presented there, reference information dramatically increases the comprehension accuracy (from $\overline{X} = 2.49$ to $\overline{X} = 1.02$) of subjects with some graduate education (+17 years). Reference information also increases the comprehension accuracy (from $\overline{X} = 2.53$ to $\overline{X} = 1.52$) of university-level subjects (13–16 years), but less dramatically than for those with some graduate education. Finally, reference information slightly reduces comprehension accuracy (from $\overline{X} = 2.25$ to $\overline{X} = 2.27$) of consumers with high school educations only (11–12 years).

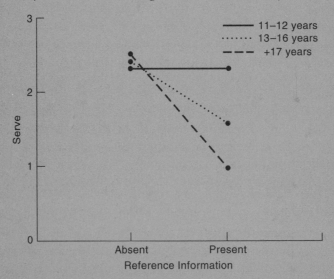

Figure 4   *The interaction of reference information and education on comprehension accuracy.*

Source: R. S. Lee. (1991). The effect of reference information and education on comprehension accuracy. *Journal of Marketing Research,* May, p. 371.

gests that the degree to which reference information aids comprehension accuracy varies depending upon the educational level of the subjects.[4]

Another strategy used by researchers to help understand the nature of a significant interaction is a statistical comparison of cell means. Such comparisons will normally be performed in one of two ways. Sometimes all of the cell means will be compared simultaneously in a pairwise fashion using one of the test procedures discussed in Chapter 13. In other studies, cell means will be compared in a pairwise fashion one row and/or one column at a time using a post hoc strategy referred to as a simple main effects analysis. In the following two paragraphs, excerpts from actual studies are used to illustrate each of these post hoc strategies.

In Excerpt 14.21, we see a case in which the strategy for "probing" a statistically significant interaction involved a simultaneous pairwise comparison of all cell means. The Scheffé test was used to make these comparisons. There were six dependent variables and a separate 2×2 ANOVA was conducted on each such variable. Whenever the interaction from one of these two-way ANOVAs produced a significant F, the Scheffé test was used to compare the four cell means in a pairwise fashion.

Excerpt 14.21 Pairwise Comparisons of All Cell Means Following a Rejection of the Interaction Null Hypothesis

---

Each dimension of power was first explored in a separate statistical analysis. A 2×2 (Gender $\times$ Type of Sport) ANOVA was used to examine each of the following dependent variables: resource access, comparative access, status access, AD interaction, AD input, and advance information access. . . . As a follow-up to analyses that produced a significant interaction effect, we conducted a post hoc Scheffé test across the four groups created by Gender $\times$ Type of Sport.

Source: A. Knoppers, B. B. Meyer, M. Ewing, and L. Forrest. (1990). Dimensions of power: A question of sport or gender? *Sociology of Sport Journal, 7*, pp. 372–373.

Instead of simultaneously making all possible pairwise comparisons among all cell means, many researchers will probe a significant interaction via **tests of simple main effects**. When this is done, the various levels of one factor are compared in such a way that the other factor is "held constant." This is accomplished by comparing the cell means on individual rows and/or in individual columns of the two dimensional arrangement of cell means. This

---

[4]*Notice that the three lines in Excerpt 14.20 are not parallel. If the interaction F turns out to be significant, this will cause the lines in the graph to be nonparallel to a degree greater than what one expects by chance. For this reason, some authors define interaction as a departure from parallelism.*

strategy is exemplified in Excerpt 14.22, and what was done will be easy to understand if you consider the following picture:

GRADE

		4th	6th	8th
SCHOOL	*Urban*	4.06	4.10	4.13
	Rural	4.25	4.07	3.87

The second sentence of Excerpt 14.22 indicates that one test of the simple main effects of Grade compared the three cell means on the top row while a second test of the simple main effects of Grade compared the three cells on the bottom row. We suspect that each of these tests resembled a one-way ANOVA, and since there are three means on each row we also suspect that a test such as Tukey's HSD was used to obtain the results presented in the last portion of the second sentence. The third sentence of Excerpt 14.22 indicates that additional tests of simple main effects were conducted, this time looking at School differences. The Urban and Rural means were compared first at Grade 4, then at Grade 6, and finally at Grade 8; each of these comparisons involved only two means and can thus be considered analogous to a *t*-test.

Excerpt 14.22 Tests of Simple Main Effects

An ANOVA for the SFT composite yielded a significant disordinal Grade $\times$ School interaction, $F(2,589) = 8.19$, $p < .001$. No grade differences in SFT were observed for urban students; but, consistent with previous findings (Clifford, 1988; Clifford, Lan, Chou, & Qi, 1989), a steady developmental decrease was evidenced for rural students (4.25, 4.07, 3.87), with fourth graders scoring significantly higher than eighth graders. In addition, rural fourth graders had significantly higher SFT scores than their urban counterparts (4.25 vs. 4.06), whereas rural eighth graders had significantly lower SFT scores than their urban counterparts (3.87 vs. 4.13).

Source: M. M. Clifford, F. C. Chou, K. Mao, W. V. Lan, and S. Kuo. (1990). Academic risk taking, development, and external constraint. *Journal of Experimental Education, 59*, p. 57.

ASSUMPTIONS ASSOCIATED WITH A TWO-WAY ANOVA

The assumptions associated with a two-way ANOVA are the same as those associated with a one-way ANOVA: randomness, independence, normality, and homogeneity of variance. As we hope you recall from the discussion of assumptions contained in Chapter 12, randomness and independence are methodological concerns; they are dealt with (or *should* be dealt with) when a study is set up, when data are collected, and when results are generalized beyond the subjects and conditions of the researcher's investigation. Although the randomness and independence assumptions can ruin a study if they are violated, there is no way to use the study's sample data to test the validity of these prerequisite conditions.

The assumptions of normality and homogeneity of variance *can* be tested and in certain circumstances *should* be tested. The procedures used to conduct such tests are the same as those used by researchers to check on the normality and equal variance assumptions when conducting *t*-tests or one-way ANOVAs. Two-way ANOVAs are also similar to *t*-tests and one-way ANOVAs in that (1) violations of the normality assumption usually do not reduce the validity of the results, and (2) violations of the equal variance assumption are problematic only when the sample sizes differ.

Many researchers, in an effort to have the *F*-tests of their two-way ANOVAs be robust to violations of the equal variance assumption, will set up their studies such that the cell *n*s are equal. Frequently, however, it is impossible to achieve this goal. On occasion, a researcher will start out with equal cell sizes but will end up with cell *n*s that vary because of equipment failure, subject dropout, or unusable answer sheets. On other occasions, the researcher will have varying sample sizes at the beginning of the study but will not want to discard any data so as to create equal *n*s because such a strategy would lead to a loss of statistical power. For either of these reasons, a researcher may end up with cell sizes that vary, thus making it important to test the homogeneity of variance assumption.

In Excerpts 14.23 and 14.24, we see two examples of the **equal variance assumption** being tested. In the first example, use of the Cochran and Box tests yielded results that did not cast doubt upon the equal variance assumption. In Excerpt 14.24, however, Hartley's *F* max test *did* yield a significant result. Such a result suggests that the two-way ANOVA *F*-tests (for the two main effects and the interaction) would be biased. That **bias** can be negative or positive in nature, thus causing the ANOVA's *F*-tests to turn out either too small or too large, respectively. Notice that the authors of Excerpts 14.24 argue that the heterogeneity of variance within their study created a negative bias, thus causing their *F*-tests to be depressed as compared with what they should have been. As pointed out in Excerpt 14.24, this means that any finding that was labeled statistically significant was actually even "more significant" than indicated by the computed *F*-test.

In Excerpt 14.25, we see a case in which the researcher was concerned about the equal variance assumption not because of varying cell sizes (even though the cell *n*s did differ) but rather because of the way the sample data were summarized. In this study, the two-way ANOVA was applied to percentages rather than to means, thus making it unlikely that the equal variance

Excerpts 14.23–14.24   Testing the Equal Variance Assumption in
Two-Way ANOVAs

Cochran C and Box's M tests of homogeneity indicated that the variance for the dependent variables did not differ significantly across grade and sex groups.

Source: R. Larson and M. Ham. (1993). Stress and "storm and stress" in early adolescence: The relationship of negative events with dysphonic affect. *Developmental Psychology, 29*(1), 133.

The F max test (Hartley, 1940, 1950) indicated heterogeneity of variance between cells. Examination of cell sizes and variances suggested a negative bias (Milligan, Wong, & Thompson, 1987); therefore, the effect is likely to be slightly more significant than indicated.

Source: R. Ludwick-Rosenthal and R. W. J. Neufeld. (1993). Preparation for undergoing an invasive medical procedure: Interacting effects of information and coping style. *Journal of Consulting and Clinical Psychology, 61*(1), 161.

Excerpt 14.25   Applying a Data Transformation to Stabilize Cell
Variances

Because the data were available in percentages, there was concern about the violation of the homogeneity of variance assumption for the analysis of variance statistical procedure. Because these data were analyzed using a two-way ANOVA (Grade $\times$ Sociability) to investigate their effects (singly and together) upon task-relevant private speech, the arcsine transformation was calculated. Therefore the means are adjusted arcsine transformed means. . . . The two-way ANOVA (Grade $\times$ Sociability) revealed a significant main effect for grade level, $F(4, 98) = 12.08$, $p < .0001$. No main effect was noted for sociability. In addition, the interaction between grade level and sociability was not significant.

Source: B. H. Manning, and C. S. White. (1990). Task-relevant private speech as a function of age and sociability. Private speech. *Psychology in the Schools, 27*, p. 369.

---

assumption would be true. As a consequence, the arcsine transformation was used in an effort to stabilize the variances (of the transformed percentages).

As we have just seen, researchers can demonstrate their concern for the equal variance assumption in a number of different ways. They can indicate that they consciously did not test this assumption because of equal sample sizes, they can test the assumption and conclude that the assumption seems tenable, they can examine the relationship between the cell sizes and sample variances and then discuss the direction of bias of the two-way ANOVA's F-tests, or they can transform their sample data (either because a test of the assumption yielded a significant result or because the nature of the data calls for a transformation). Unfortunately, many researchers do none of these things.

Because heterogeneity of variance causes F-tests to be biased when sample sizes are dissimilar, you should downgrade any research report based on a two-way ANOVA when the cell ns vary unless the researcher indicates (1) that some kind of action was taken so as to lessen (or eliminate) the bias or (2) that the bias is of such a nature as to not cloud the obtained results. When the researcher indicates neither of these things, you have a right—even an obligation—to receive the researcher's end-of-study claims with a big grain of salt. In our opinion, this means that you have a right to discount a researcher's findings if no attention is given to the equal variance assumption in situations where such attention is essential.

ESTIMATED MAGNITUDE OF EFFECT, POWER ANALYSES, AND STRENGTH OF EFFECT MEASURES IN TWO-WAY ANOVAS

As indicated in Chapter 8, various techniques have been developed to help researchers assess the extent to which their results are significant in a practical sense. It is worth repeating that such techniques serve a valuable role in quantitative studies wherein null hypotheses are tested, for it is possible for a result to end up being declared statistically significant even though it is totally unimportant from a practical standpoint. Earlier, we saw how these techniques have been used in conjunction with t-tests and one-way ANOVAs. We now wish to consider their relevance to two-way ANOVAs.

In Excerpt 14.26, we see a case in which the researchers computed effect sizes for the results that turned out to be significant in their two-way ANOVAs. As indicated earlier, we believe that the term **estimated magnitude of effect** is more appropriate when the researcher uses sample data to make an inference as to the size of an effect in the population. Despite this difference of opinion as to the best term to use to describe the values of .41 and .28 that appear in the final paragraph of this excerpt, we wish to commend

---

Excerpt 14.26 Estimated Magnitude of Effects in a Two-Way ANOVA

Specifically, we predicted that men with relatively negative attitudes toward traditional, one-to-one counseling would prefer a brochure describing alternative formats for providing assistance. We explored this question in two 2×2 tables (Table 4).

We first attempted to discover whether there was an interaction involving attitudes toward traditional counseling and the type of brochure. Therefore, in the first 2×2 analysis, the independent variables were two levels of Fisher-Turner scores

(Continued)

Excerpt 14.26 Estimated Magnitude of Effects in a Two-Way ANOVA *(Continued)*

and the two brochure types. We used the upper and lower quarters of the distribution to increase sensitivity, thus reducing the number of subjects in the analysis to 209. The dependent variable in the table was the brochure evaluation score. An analysis of variance revealed a strong main effect for Fisher-Turner group, $F(1,205) = 35.922, p < .01$, but no main effect for brochure group and no interaction.

In the second 2×2 analysis, the independent variables were brochure type and upper and lower quarters of the GRCS-I scores (the combined scores of the Restrictive Emotionality and Success, Power, and Competition Scales). The purpose of this analysis was to explore any interaction between attitudes toward masculinity and attitudes toward the two brochures. This analysis, based on 219 subjects, also appears in Table 4. The analysis showed a significant interaction, $F(1,215) - 3.896, p < .05.$ . . . No main effects were observed.

To provide a frame of reference for the substantive meaning of these results, we computed effect sizes (Cohen, 1988). Effect size is a measure of "the degree to which the phenomenon is present in the population" (Cohen, 1988, p. 9). As a guide to interpreting the results of an analysis of variance, Cohen proposed that a "small" effect size is .10; a "medium" effect size is .25, and a "large" effect size is .40 (Cohen, 1988, pp. 284–286). On the basis of Cohen's formulas, the effect size for the main effect for the Fisher-Turner group was .41, a large effect, and the effect size of the interaction of GRCS-I (upper and lower quarters) and brochure group was .28, a medium effect.

Table 4

Mean ratings of the brochure evaluation questionnaire

Subsample	Counseling brochure group			Services brochure group		
	n	M	SD	n	M	SD
Fisher-Turner level						
Highest quarter	49	60.4	17.8	52	61.3	16.5
Lowest quarter	59	43.9	15.9	49	49.8	16.8
GRCS-I level						
Highest quarter	58	50.2	18.2	53	56.4	16.7
Lowest quarter	52	54.4	20.2	56	51.8	19.1

Note. The dependent variable is the mean score on the brochure evaluation questionnaire. High Fisher-Turner scores indicate a more positive attitude toward traditional counseling. High GRCS-I scores indicate highly masculine attitudes.

Source: J. M. Robertson and L. F. Fitzgerald. (1992). Overcoming the masculine mystique: Preferences for alternative forms of assistance among men who avoid counseling. *Journal of Counseling Psychology, 39*(2), p. 244.

these researchers for making a systematic effort to provide their readers with "a frame of reference for the substantive meaning of their results."

A second technique for dealing with the issue of statistical versus practical significance involves conducting a **power analysis**. While a power analysis can be performed either prior to the collection and analysis of data (to see if sufficient power exists to make the study worth doing) or following the data analysis (to see if there was sufficient power associated with the completed statistical tests), there are obvious advantages to the first of these two kinds of power analyses. In Excerpt 14.27, we see an example of how such a power analysis was performed in conjunction with a two-way ANOVA.

Excerpt 14.27 A Power Analysis in a Two-Way ANOVA

A power analysis was conducted using the method suggested by O'Brien and Lohr (1984) to determine whether the design was sufficiently powerful to allow detection of an interaction effect. This analysis assumed 10 observations per cell in the four cells created by the groups versus individuals and type of matrix factors. On the basis of past research (Insko et al., 1990), the noncentrality parameter was calculated using means for the number of cooperative choices of 10 (out of 20) for groups and 19 (out of 20) for individuals. On the assumption that the PDG-Negative matrix would eliminate discontinuity, those means were set at 19 for both groups and individuals. Also on the basis of past research, the value of 3.0 was conservatively used to estimate the population standard deviation. Given these conditions, the power to detect a significant interaction (alpha = .05, two-tailed) is .99.

Source: J. Schopler, C. A. Insko, K. A. Graetz, S. M. Drigotas, and V. A. Smith. (1991). The generality of the individual-group discontinuity effect: Variations in positive-negativity of outcomes, players' relative power, and magnitude of outcomes. *Personality and Social Psychology Bulletin, 17*(6), p. 616.

The third way that researchers confront the issues of statistical versus practical significance is by computing a **strength of effect index**. As you will recall, such indices are similar to the square of a correlation coefficient in that (1) they can range anywhere from 0 to 1.0 and (2) the resulting value indicates the percent of variability in the dependent variable that is explained by the independent variable. In a two-way ANOVA, such an index can be computed for each of the main effects and also for the interaction. (If post hoc tests are applied to main effect means or to the cell means, strength of effect indices can be computed there as well.)

As pointed out in Chapter 8, several different strength of effect measures have been developed. The ones used most frequently are called **eta squared**, and **omega squared**. In Excerpt 14.28, we see a study in which the researchers used the eta squared statistic as an aid to interpreting their results. In this study, a 2 × ANOVA was used to see if the subjects (school children) who evaluated the circumstances surrounding a hypothetical student who was suspended from school would consider the disciplinary action of suspension as more or less effective depending upon the reputation of the transgressor (well-behaved versus misbehaved) and/or the severity of the problem (fighting versus disrupting the classroom).

Excerpt 14.28 Strength of Effect Indices for Main Effects and Interaction

---

As predicted, reputation exerted a substantial influence on effectiveness ratings, $F(1,116) = 67.15, p < .001. . . .$ [S]uspension was perceived to be less effective for the misbehaved transgressor than for the well-behaved transgressor. However, contrary to our hypothesis that suspension would be perceived as equally effective for both fighting and disturbing the classroom, a significant main effect for problem severity was found, $F(1,116) = 6.43, p < .05.$ This effect was qualified by the significant Problem Severity × Reputation interaction, $F(1,116) = 5.72, p < .05. . . .$ While statistically significant, the main effect of problem severity and the interaction effect of problem severity and reputation were of minor practical importance. Based on the partial eta square statistic, each accounted for only 5% of the variance. Reputation, in contrast, accounted for 37% of the variance in predicted effectiveness ratings.

Source: L. M. Bear and J. Fink. (1991). Fairness and effectiveness. *School Psychology Quarterly, 6,* p. 93.

In Excerpt 14.28, notice how three *F*-ratios turned out to be significant, yet two of these were labeled by the authors as being of only minor practical significance. Clearly, these researchers (as well as those who conducted the studies appearing in Excerpts 14.26 and 14.27) were aware of the fact that a single inferential result can turn out to be, at the same time, both significant from a statistical perspective and nonsignificant from a practical perspective. They deserve credit for conducting their data analyses with this important distinction in mind, and even further credit for incorporating this distinction into the written summaries of their investigations. Unfortunately, most researchers address formally only the concept of statistical significance, with the notion of practical significance automatically (and incorrectly) superimposed on each and every result that turns out to be statistically significant. In your reading of research reports, remain vigilant for instances of this unjustified interpretation of results.

THE FAMILYWISE ERROR RATE IN FACTORIAL ANOVAS

When data are subjected to a standard two-way ANOVA, three *F*-values are computed—one for each main effect and one for the interaction. If the same level of significance (e.g., .05) is used in assessing each F-value, you may have been thinking that the probability of a Type I error occurring somewhere among the three F-tests is greater than the alpha level used to evaluate each F-value. Accordingly, you may have been expecting us to point out how conscientious researchers make some form of adjustment to avoid having an inflated Type I error rate associated with their two-way ANOVAs.

Although it is clear that the computation of three F-values in a two-way ANOVA leads to a greater-than-alpha chance that one or more of the three null hypotheses will be incorrectly rejected, the vast majority of applied researchers do not adjust anything in an effort to deal with this "problem." This is because most applied researchers consider each F-test separately rather than look at the three F-tests collectively as a set. When the F-tests are viewed in that manner, the Type I error risk is *not* inflated, for the researcher's alpha level correctly specifies the probability that any given F-test will cause a true H_0 to be rejected.

When a given level of significance is used to evaluate each of the three F-values, it can be said that the **familywise error rate** is set equal to the alpha level. Each "family" is defined as the set of contrasts represented by an F-test and any post hoc tests that might be conducted if the F turns out to be statistically significant. The familywise error rate is equal to the common alpha level employed to evaluate all three F-tests because the chances of a Type I error, *within each family,* are equal to the alpha level.

If a researcher analyzes the data from two or more dependent variables with separate two-way ANOVAs, you may find that the Bonferroni procedure is used to adjust the alpha level. For example, if separate two-way ANOVAs are used to analyze the data from two dependent variables, a ".05" researcher might use the .025 level of significance to evaluate all six of the F-values. With five dependent variables and five separate two-way ANOVAs, that same researcher would likely use the .01 level of significance to evaluate each F-test. In these examples, the Bonferroni technique is used to adjust for multiple dependent variables, not for multiple F-tests within the same analysis.

In the next three chapters, you will see examples of how ANOVA can be used in studies where there are three or more independent variables. In these "higher-order" factorial ANOVAs, you will again see how the familywise error rate is typically used to evaluate the multiple F-values yielded by the analysis. Thus, the practice of using an alpha level such as .05 with each F-value in the ANOVA summary table is not restricted to two-way ANOVAs.

A FEW WARNINGS CONCERNING TWO-WAY ANOVAS

Before concluding this chapter, we want to offer a few cautionary comments that we hope you will tuck away in your memory bank and then bring up to consciousness whenever you encounter a research report based upon a two-way ANOVA. Although we have touched upon some of these issues in previous chapters, your ability to decipher *and* critique research summaries may well improve a bit if we deliberately reiterate a few of our earlier concerns.

EVALUATE THE WORTH OF THE HYPOTHESES BEING TESTED

We cannot overemphasize how important it is to critically assess the worth of the hypotheses being tested within any study based upon a two-way ANOVA. No matter how good the study may be from a statistical perspective and no matter how clear the research report is, the study cannot possibly make a contribution unless the questions being dealt with are interesting. In other words, the research questions that prompt the investigator to select the factors and levels of the two-way ANOVA must be worth answering and must have no clear answer before the study is conducted. If these things do not hold true, then the study has a fatal flaw in its foundation that cannot be overcome by large sample sizes, rigorous alpha levels, impressive reliability and validity estimates, impressive *F*-ratios that are statistically significant, elaborate post hoc analyses, tests of assumptions, and power analyses. The old saying that "you can't make a silk purse from a sow's ear" is as relevant here as anywhere else.

To see an example of a two-way ANOVA that deals with questions that could be answered, we believe, *without* an empirical investigation, consider once again Excerpt 14.26. After citing evidence showing that "American men are generally hesitant to seek counseling. . . and do not become clients as often as women," the researchers conducted two 2 × 2 ANOVAs in an effort to evaluate their prediction that "men with relatively negative attitudes toward traditional, one-to-one counseling would prefer a brochure describing alternative formats for providing assistance." Would anyone contest this prediction and doubt that it would be supported by the empirical evidence? If we are correct in asserting that no sensible person would disagree with the prediction, then the study's worth must be questioned—and the study's findings, though statistically significant, do not add very much to what we already knew.

REMEMBER THAT TWO-WAY ANOVAS FOCUS ON MEANS

As with *t*-tests and one-way ANOVAs, the focus of a two-way ANOVA is on means. The main effect means and the cell means serve as the focal points of the three research questions associated with any two-way ANOVA. When the main effect and interaction *F*-tests are discussed, it is essential for you to keep in mind that conclusions should be tied to means.

To illustrate our concern, consider Excerpt 14.29. In this study, a two-way ANOVA was used in which the factors were Gender (male and female) and Grade (3rd versus junior high). The subjects were asked to answer several questions regarding how they felt about mathematics (e.g., grade expected), with a 2 × 2 ANOVA being performed on the data collected in response to each question.

Excerpt 14.29   The Focus of Two-Way ANOVAs on Means

There were significant gender main effects for all four variables. As predicted, in comparison with girls, boys on average rated their competence in mathematics higher, $F(1, 469) = 11.64$, $MS_e = 0.73$, $p \le .001$, expected a higher grade, $F(1, 469) = 16.84$, $MS_e = 5.82$, $p \le .001$, and expected to do better relative to their classmates, $F(1, 469) = 6.44$, $MS_e = .81$, $p \le .01$. Girls claimed that mathematics was more difficult than did boys, $F(1, 469) = 6.20$, $MS_e = .90$, $p \le .001$. The absence of significant Grade × Gender interaction effects indicates that, contrary to predictions, these gender differences were not weaker in third grade than in junior high school.

Source: D. J. Stipek and J. H. Gralinski. (1991). Gender differences in children's achievement-related beliefs and emotional responses to success and failure in mathematics. *Journal of Educational Psychology, 83*(3), p. 364.

In the second sentence of Excerpt 14.29, the words *on average* make it clear that (1) some of the girls may have rated their competence in mathematics higher than some of the boys, (2) some of the girls may have expected a higher grade than did some of the boys, and (3) some of the girls may have expected to outperform their classmates whereas some of the boys may not have had such expectations. In contrast, now consider the next-to-the-last sentence in Excerpt 14.29. With the phrase *on average* absent from this sentence, the impression is given that every girl said that mathematics is more difficult than any of the boys. This, most likely, was not the case, for the girls' and boys' distributions of scores surely overlapped one another.

Many researchers fail to note that their statistically significant findings deal with means, and the literal interpretation of the researchers' words says that all of the folks in one group outperformed those in the comparison group(s). If the phrase *on average* or some similar wording does not appear in the research report, make certain that you insert it as you attempt to decipher and understand the statistical findings. If you don't do this, you will end up thinking that comparison groups were far more different from one another than was actually the case.

THE INTERPRETATION OF MAIN EFFECTS

Earlier in this chapter, we pointed out that each H_0 in a two-way ANOVA is independent of the other two null hypotheses. This means, as we have previously explained, that any pattern of results is possible when the F-tests are examined. If only one of the F-tests turns out to be significant, the one that is significant could be either of the two main effects or it could be the interaction. If two Fs turn out significant, the ones that show up as significant could be both main effects or they could be one of the main effects and the interaction. It is also possible, of course, to have both main effects *and* the interaction end up being significant.

Although the two factors that come together to define any two-way ANOVA have main effect *F*-tests associated with them that are independent, the interpretation of each of these *F*-tests cannot be made properly unless the other factor is considered. Thus, the two main effect *F*-tests are *not* independent when it comes time to draw conclusions from the study.[5] Simply stated, each factor provides an important "context" that must be noted when you try to interpret results pertaining to the other factor's main effect.

To help clarify this important point we are trying to make, imagine that a little experiment is conducted in which the dependent variable is operationalized as the number of simple math problems (e.g., $2 + 7 = ?$ and $12 \div 4 = ?$) solved within a 60-second time period. Subjects are run through this experiment one at a time, with the math problems presented by means of slides projected on a screen. Each subject responds orally to each problem (with answers recorded on tape to document correct responses), with the subject controlling the rate at which the slides are presented by means of a hand-held remote that can advance to the next slide.

In our little experiment, suppose that one of the factors is Gender. The other factor is Figure-Ground, with half of the subjects seeing slides in which each math problem appears in black type on a white background while the other half of the subjects see the same problems presented in white type on a black background. Since Gender is an assigned factor whereas Figure-Ground is active in nature, subjects would be randomly assigned to the levels of the Figure-Ground factor from within their respective levels of the Gender factor.

Suppose the 2×2 ANOVA, when applied to the data of this study, produces a statistically significant *F* for Gender. The other two *F*s turn out to be nonsignificant. Given this pattern of results, what conclusions legitimately can be drawn from the study? Or stated in the negative form, what limitations are there to the generalizability of the results?

Looked at from the perspective of concerns regarding the generalizability of the study's findings, a claim that males probably differ from females would be restricted to subjects similar to those used as subjects in the study. For example, if all subjects were college freshmen, it would be inappropriate to extrapolate the statistically significant Gender main effect to folks not represented in the study (e.g., second graders or Ph.D.s in physics). In addition, any conclusion drawn about males differing from females would be restricted to the study's dependent variable. For obvious reasons, the statistically significant Gender main effect obtained in our study would be restricted to

---

[5] *In a strict statistical sense, the three F-tests of a two-way ANOVA are not even independent in terms of how they are computed. This is because each of the three F-ratios is determined by using MS_{ERROR} as the denominator. If MS_{ERROR} is small (or large), all three of the F-ratios will be large (or small).*

simple math problems like those presented to the subjects. Based on the results of this study, it would be totally inappropriate to think that males and females differ with respect to any variable except the one represented by the data that were collected and analyzed.

Although it is relatively easy to see how the generalizability of a statistically significant main effect is limited by the nature of the subjects involved in the study and the nature of the dependent variable, it is more difficult to see how the conclusions drawn about that significant main effect must also take into consideration the nature of the other factor. In our hypothetical study, it would be inappropriate to conclude simply that the males and females of the study were found to differ significantly with respect to their performance on the simple math problems that they saw. This conclusion would be too broad because it does not indicate the specific way in which the simple math problems were presented to the subjects. For one thing, those problems were presented through slides projected on a screen. But more than that, the levels of the Figure-Ground factor define what was seen on those slides. Taking these things into consideration, we must qualify our study's finding by saying that our males differed significantly from our females in terms of mean performance on the simple math problems they saw when those problems were presented through slides *with half having white type on a black background and the other half having black type on a white background*. The results do not generalize to paper-and-pencil tests, nor do they generalize to slides in which different colors are used as figure and ground.

At this point, let us turn our attention to a real study that is not unlike the hypothetical experiment we have just considered. The real study that we want to review is the investigation dealing with labeling states on an outline map, discussed earlier in this chapter (see Excerpt 14.10). In that study, the analysis yielded a significant main effect for gender (with males naming more states correctly than females). The important point that we want to make is that the gender effect suggested by this investigation is limited to the situation where the task involves labeling states on an outline map (either with or without the aid of an alphabetized list of states). If subjects had been asked to respond orally to questions about state locations (e.g., "What state is located north of Illinois?" or "The Mississippi River terminates in what state?"), it might be that no gender effect would exist—or possibly it would be females who would outperform males.

The main point of this discussion can be summed up in a single sentence: The generalizability of a significant main effect is limited not only by the nature of the subjects used in the investigation and by the nature of the task that produces the study's data but also by the nature of the levels that make up the *other* factor. When you read research reports, be on guard for instances when this interdependence between the two factors is overlooked when conclusions are drawn concerning one or both of the main effects. Unfortunately, many researchers overgeneralize their results when they talk about their significant main effects.

REMEMBER THE POSSIBILITY OF TYPE I AND TYPE II ERRORS

The fourth warning that we want to offer is not new. You have encountered it earlier in our discussions of *t*-tests and one-way ANOVAs. Simply stated, we want to encourage you to remember that regardless of how the results of a two-way ANOVA turn out, there is always the possibility of either a Type I or Type II error whenever a decision is made to reject or fail-to-reject a null hypothesis.

Based upon the words used by many researchers in discussing their results, we believe that the notion of "statistical significance" is quite often amplified (incorrectly) into something on the order of a firm discovery—or even proof. Far too seldom do we see the word *inference* or the phrase *null hypothesis* in the technical write-ups of research investigations wherein the hypothesis testing procedure has been used. Although you do not have the ability to control what researchers say when they summarize their investigations, you most certainly *do* have the freedom to adjust the research summary so as to make it more accurate.

Sooner or later, you are bound to encounter a research report wherein a statement is made on the order of (1) "Treatment A works better than Treatment B" or (2) "Folks who possess characteristic X outperform those who possess characteristic Y." Such statements will come from researchers who temporarily forgot not only the difference between sample statistics and population parameters but also the ever-present possibility of an inferential error when a finding is declared either significant or nonsignificant. You can avoid making the mistake of accepting such statements as points of fact by remembering that no *F*-test *ever* proves anything.

BE CAREFUL WHEN INTERPRETING NONSIGNIFICANT F-TESTS

In Chapter 7, we explained why it is wrong to consider a null hypothesis to be true simply because the hypothesis testing procedure results in a fail-to-reject decision. To recapitulate, any of several factors (e.g., small sample sizes, unreliable measuring instruments or too much within-group variability) can cause the result to be nonsignificant, even if the null hypothesis being tested is actually false. This is especially true when the null hypothesis is false by a small amount.

To see an example where a fail-to-reject decision was misinterpreted, consider once again Excerpt 14.29. The last sentence in this excerpt says, "The absence of significant Grade $\times$ Gender interaction effects [when a 2×2 ANOVA was conducted on each of four dependent variables] indicates that, contrary to predictions, these gender differences were not weaker in third grade than in junior high school." This sentence, taken literally, means that there is *no* interaction.

In one of the ANOVAs summarized in Excerpt 14.29, the sample means were as follows: third grade girls = 3.40, third grade boys = 2.78, junior high girls = 5.78, junior high boys = 4.56. Here, the difference between boys and girls at third grade is only about half as large as is the gender difference in junior high school. But even if the sample means had turned out such that the gender difference in third grade was identical to that observed in junior high school, it *still* would be wrong to say that the nonsignificant interaction result means that the difference between boys and girls is the same at the two grade levels. The only legitimate thing to say here is that the *F*-test for the Grade × Gender interaction was not sufficiently large to permit a rejection of the interaction null hypothesis.

Almost all researchers who engage in hypothesis testing have been taught that it is improper to conclude that a null hypothesis is true simply because the hypothesis testing procedure leads to a fail-to-reject decision. Nevertheless, many of these same researchers use language in their research reports suggesting that they have completely forgotten that a fail-to-reject decision does not logically permit one to leave a study believing that the tested H_0 is true. In your review of studies that utilized two-way ANOVAs (or, for that matter, any procedure for testing null hypotheses), remain vigilant to erroneous statements as to what a nonsignificant finding means.

REVIEW TERMS

Active factor	Interaction
Assigned factor	Level
Biased *F*-test	Main effect *F*
Cell	Main effect mean
Equal variance assumption	Omega squared
Estimated magnitude of effect	Post hoc tests
Eta squared	Power analysis
Factor	Simple main effect
Familywise error rate	Univariate analysis
Graph of an interaction	

REVIEW QUESTIONS

1. How many independent variables will there be in any univariate two-way ANOVA? How many dependent variables?

2. How many cells are there in the study that appears in Excerpt 14.14?

3. If researchers report that they utilized a 2 × 2 × 2 ANOVA, does this indicate that a two-way ANOVA was used?

4. In Excerpt 14.3, how many of the independent variables were assigned factors?

5. Suppose the factors of a 2 × 2 ANOVA are referred to as Factor A and Factor B. How will subjects be put into the cells of this study if Factor A is assigned while Factor B is active?

6. How many of the research questions dealt with by a two-way ANOVA are concerned with main effects? How many are concerned with interaction?

7. Suppose a 2 (Gender) × 3 (Handedness) ANOVA is conducted, with the dependent variable being the number of nuts that can be attached to bolts within a 60-second time limit. Suppose further that the mean scores for the six groups, each containing 10 subjects, turn out as follows: right-handed males = 10.2, right-handed females = 8.8; left-handed males = 7.8, left-handed females = 9.8; ambidextrous males = 9.0, and ambidextrous females = 8.4. Given these results, what are the main effect means for handedness equal to? How many scores is each of these means based on?

8. (True or False) There is absolutely no interaction associated with the sample data presented in question 7.

9. (True or False) In order for the interaction F to be statistically significant, both main effect Fs must also be statistically significant.

10. How many different mean squares serve as the denominator when the F-ratios are computed for the two main effects and the interaction?

11. Based on the information presented in Excerpt 14.19, how many subjects were involved in the study?

12. In a 2 × 2 ANOVA, the degrees of freedom for the two main effects and the interaction are equal to 1, 1, and 1, respectively. Collectively, the degrees of freedom for these three sources add up to 3. Is it possible for a two-way ANOVA to have the degrees of freedom for its main effects and the interaction add up to 7?

13. In Excerpt 14.13, how many of the F-ratios would have turned out to be statistically significant if the .10 level of significance had been used to evaluate the results?

14. (True or False) You should not expect to see a post hoc test used to compare the main effect means of a 2 × 2 ANOVA, even if the F-ratios for both main effects turn out to statistically significant at a rigorous alpha level.

15. In Excerpt 14.11, which of the three F-ratios should be looked at first as the researchers (or we) try to make sense out of the results contained in the two-way ANOVA summary table?

16. If the statistically significant interaction obtained in Excerpt 14.12 were to be graphed, how many lines would there be in the graph?

17. How many simple main effects are there for Factor A in a 2 × 3 (A × B) ANOVA?

15

Three-Way Analysis of Variance

In Chapter 14, we considered how a two-way ANOVA can be used when two independent variables jointly define the comparison groups in a researcher's study. Now, we want to extend this discussion by looking at the ways in which analysis of variance techniques can be used when three independent variables are involved. Not surprisingly, the term **three-way ANOVA** is used to denote the kind of analysis of variance considered in this chapter.

As you will see, two-way and three-way ANOVAs differ from each other in a number of important ways. (For example, the typical three-way ANOVA helps the researcher deal with more than twice as many null hypotheses as does the typical two-way ANOVA.) Despite these differences, many of the concepts covered in our earlier discussion of two-way ANOVAs are fully relevant to three-way ANOVAs. In particular, the concepts of factor, level, and cell serve as the "building blocks" of both two-way and three-way ANOVAs. Moreover, the distinction between assigned factors and active factors is just as relevant to three-way ANOVAs as to two-way ANOVAs. Finally, the ANOVAs to be considered here, like those considered in the previous chapter, are univariate in nature and focus on group means. Because of these similarities, the bulk of Chapter 14 constitutes an important "preface" to our treatment of three-way ANOVAs.

In discussing three-way ANOVAs, we have four primary objectives. We want to (1) clarify the nature of the null hypotheses associated with this form of analysis of variance, (2) examine the various mechanisms used by researchers to present their findings, (3) consider how planned and post hoc tests can be used to help the researcher zero in on specific contrasts of interest, and (4) point out that anyone who uses a three-way ANOVA ought to be concerned about several related and important topics (such as the distinction between statistical and practical significance). Before doing these things, however, we first want to consider how researchers indicate that a three-way ANOVA has been used.

LABELS DENOTING USE OF THE THREE-WAY ANOVA

To indicate that a three-way ANOVA has been used, researchers can choose any of several available terms, including *three-factor ANOVA, an ANOVA with three independent variables, a completely between-subjects three-way ANOVA*, and *a completely randomized three-way ANOVA.* The phrase **completely between-subjects** simply clarifies that each score entered into the analysis comes from a different subject.[1] The phrase **completely randomized** simply indicates that all three factors are active (rather than assigned) in nature.

Many researchers indicate the number of levels in each of the three factors by means of a label such as 2 × 3 × 4 ANOVA. Others clarify the nature of their ANOVAs by citing the names of the three factors. A few create a label that contains both the factor names and the number of levels in each factor.

Excerpts 15.1–15.5 illustrate how researchers use various labeling schemes to communicate that a data set has been subjected to a three-way ANOVA. Notice how the fourth of these excerpts clarifies the nature of the dependent variable that was used: self-esteem. Excerpt 15.5 is a bit more challenging, because there is no direct indication that a three-way ANOVA is being discussed even though it is.

Excerpts 15.1–15.5   Different Ways to Indicate That a Three-Way ANOVA Has Been Used

---

Subjects' recall of the presented attributes was subjected to a 3 × 2 × 3 (Initial Processing Goals × Time of Judgment × Expertise) between-subjects ANOVA.

Source: D. Sanbonmatsu, F. Kardes, and C. Sansone, (1991). Remembering less and inferring more: Effects of time of judgment on inferences about unknown attributes. *Journal of Personality and Social Psychology, 61*(4), p. 548.

Culture (2) × Grade (2) × Sex (2) analyses of variance (ANOVA) were conducted.

Source: D. R. Rolandelli, K. Sugihara, and J. C. Wright. (1992). Visual processing of televised information by Japanese and American children. *Journal of Cross-Cultural Psychology, 23*(1), p. 12.

(Continued)

---

[1]*In Chapters 16 and 17, you will see how ANOVAs that are completely or partially "within-subjects" in nature involve repeated measurements taken from each subject.*

Excerpts 15.1–15.5   Different Ways to Indicate That a Three-Way
ANOVA Has Been Used *(Continued)*

A 2 × 2 × 2 (problem severity × interventionist × effectiveness information) independent-groups factorial analysis of variance was used to analyze IRP–15 scores.

Source: D. H. Tingstrom. (1990). Acceptability of time-out: The influence of problem behavior severity, interventionist, and reported effectiveness. *Journal of School Psychology, 28*(2), p. 167.

A 2 × 2 × 3 analysis of variance was performed to examine the effect of life-satisfaction, sex, and age on self-esteem.

Source: S. Hong, M. A. Bianca, M. R. Bianca, and J. Bollington. (1993). Self-esteem: The effects of life-satisfaction, sex, and age. *Psychological Reports, 72*, p. 97.

An analysis of variance was performed with grade, sex, and occupational choice (traditional, non traditional, or androgynous) as the independent variables. Because of missing data, grades 9 and 10, and 11 and 12 were grouped together respectively for the analysis. Achievement test (Math, Reading, Total) and SET scores were the dependent variables.

Source: J. Wilson and D. Fasko. (1992). Self-esteem, achievement, and career choices of rural students. *Journal of Humanistic Education and Development, 30*, p. 134.

THE DATA LAYOUT

To understand the research questions dealt with by a three-way ANOVA, you must be able to create a mental picture (or an actual sketch on paper) that shows how the levels of the three factors come together to form the cells of the study. Although such a picture is easy to build, we cannot overemphasize how important it is. Simply stated, the statistical questions posed within a three-way ANOVA (as well as the answers provided to those questions) cannot be discussed or understood without reference to a picture showing the factors, the levels, and the cells.

To demonstrate how to "diagram" the structure of a three-way ANOVA, we want to consider an interesting study dealing with personal space and distance estimation. In this study, each of the 64 undergraduate volunteers who served as a subject stood at one end of a straight line that had been painted on the cement floor of an outdoor plaza at a university. One of the study's three experimenters then stood either "close to" or "far away" from the subject, with these distances being 70 centimeters (approximately 2.3 feet) and 210 centimeters (approximately 6.9 feet), respectively. The experimenter moved very slowly down the line, either toward the subject (if the two had started out far apart) or away from the subject (if the two had started out close together). The subject's task was to say "stop" when the experimenter had moved to a point 140 cm away from the subject. Of course, no distance markings appeared on the line painted on the cement.

One of the three factors in this study on distance estimation was "Condition," and it had two levels: "Approaching" and "Departing." That factor was concerned with whether the experimenter moved toward or away from any given subject. The second factor was "Subject's Sex," with half of the subjects representing each of the obvious levels of this factor. The final factor was "Experimenter's Sex," with the two levels of this factor corresponding to the gender of the person who moved toward or away from the subject. Each subject contributed one score to the data set—the measured distance between him or her and the experimenter after the subject told the experimenter to stop.

Our picture of this study appears in Figure 15.1. Each open box is meant to represent one of the study's eight cells. (The number of cells in any three-way ANOVA can be determined by multiplying the number of levels in the three factors; here, $2 \times 2 \times 2 = 8$.) Each of these cells corresponds to a different subgroup of the subject pool. For example, the upper left-hand cell represents the male subjects who had to stop a male experimenter who started out far away and moved toward the subject. The bottom right-hand cell represents female subjects who had to stop a female experimenter who began close by and moved away from the subject. In this study, there were eight subjects in each cell. Since each subject was measured only once, you should be able to imagine that eight scores ended up inside each cell.

A diagram like that in Figure 15.1 does not reveal how subjects were put into the various cells of the three-way ANOVA. The Procedure section of the journal article will normally explain how this was done. In the report of the study we have been discussing, the researchers pointed out that "four males and four females were assigned at random to each of the eight experimental conditions." This randomization procedure was necessary because one of the three factors (subject's sex) was **assigned** in nature.

If a table of cell means is included in the research report, such a table can serve as the needed diagram of the study. Consider, for example, Excerpt

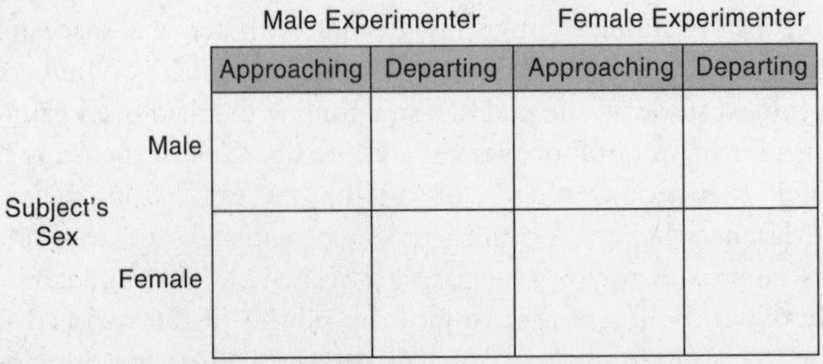

Figure 15.1 *Diagram of a 2 × 2 × 2 ANOVA on distance estimation.*

Excerpt 15.6   Table of Means Serving as a "Diagram" of a Three-Way ANOVA

Table 1

Means of the measured distances (in centimeters)

Condition		*Female subject*		*Male subject*		
		Male Exp.	*Female Exp.*	*Male Exp.*	*Female Exp.*	*Comb.*
Approaching from 210-cm start	$M=$ 177.12	187.12	172.11	174.42	177.62
Departing from 70-cm start	$M=$ 151.75	167.50	156.66	156.00	158.00
Combined	$M=$ 164.43	177.31	164.38	165.21	

Note—$n = 8$ in each cell. Exp. = experimenter.

Source: D. Zakay, L. A. Hayduk, and Y. Tsal. (1992). Personal space and distance misperceptions: Implication of a novel observation. Bulletin of the Psychonomic Society, 30(1), p. 34. (adapted slightly for presentation here.)

15.6. This table appeared in the journal article on estimating distances. It shows the size of each cell's mean. Also shown are six "combined means."

   If you compare Excerpt 15.6 with Figure 15.1, you will note that the position of the three factors is not the same in the two "diagrams." Such differences in how the diagram is set up have no influence on the structure of the study or the results of the statistical analysis. There are 18 different ways to set up a two-dimensional diagram of a three-way ANOVA, and the one you construct or the one you look at in a research report represents nothing more than someone's personal preference.[2] Tables like the one in Excerpt 15.6 may help you to "see" the structure of a study. You have the right, however, to rearrange the table in your mind or on paper—and we encourage you to do this if it will assist you in understanding the procedures and/or results of the study your are reading.

---

[2]*When a three-way ANOVA involves both assigned and active factors, we prefer to set up our diagram with the assigned factor(s) as rows and the active factor(s) as columns. The table in Excerpt 15.6 was set up as it was because the researchers wanted to accentuate the difference between the combined means for the approaching and departing conditions.*

SAMPLES AND POPULATIONS

As is the case with two-way ANOVAs, the samples associated with a three-way ANOVA are easy to identify. This is because the subjects who "share" a common cell constitute each of the samples. The total number of samples can be determined quickly by multiplying together the three numbers indicating how many levels are in the three factors. Thus, there are eight samples in any $2 \times 2 \times 2$ ANOVA, 24 samples in any $2 \times 3 \times 4$ ANOVA, 60 samples in any $3 \times 4 \times 5$ ANOVA, and so on.

Associated with each cell's sample is a population. Each of these populations should be conceptualized as being made up of a large group of people, animals, or objects similar to those in the corresponding sample represented by one of the cells. As with a two-way ANOVA, the populations of a three-way ANOVA can be concrete or abstract in nature depending on (1) how the subjects made their way into the study and (2) whether any of the factors are active. In the study on personal space and estimating distance, each of the eight populations was abstract (because two of the three factors were active).

SEVEN QUESTIONS CONCERNING MAIN AND INTERACTION EFFECTS

A standard three-way ANOVA permits the researcher to answer seven questions. Three of these questions deal with main effects while four deal with interactions. These seven questions are conceptually connected to the diagram of the three-way ANOVA. Since Excerpt 15.6 contains the sample means for the study on personal space and estimating distance, we will refer to that study as we explain how the seven questions consider the various populations "from different angles."

In Excerpt 15.6, four cells are associated with the approaching condition and four cells are associated with the departing condition. The data-based main effect mean for each of these levels of the Condition factor are presented in the right-hand column labeled "Combined." The first of these combined means (177.62) was based on the scores from 32 subjects and it represents the best estimate of how the four populations corresponding to the four approaching samples would score on the study's task if those four populations were to be lumped together. Similarly, the second of the combined means for the Condition factor (158.00) was based on the scores from the other 32 subjects and it constitutes the best estimate of how the four departing populations, if lumped together, would score. The first question is concerned with the relative status of the μs estimated by these two data-based main effect means, with the first null hypothesis of the three-way ANOVA stipulating that they are equal.

To conceptualize the second and third questions of a three-way ANOVA, you should think about the main effect means associated with the second and third factors, respectively. For example, the question concerning the main effect of Subject's Sex asks whether the mean score produced by lumping together the four populations of females is different from the mean score produced by lumping together the four populations of males. The data-based counterparts of these two means are 170.87 and 164.80, respectively.[3] The question concerning the main effect of Experimenter's Sex similarly deals with two μs, with the data-based estimates being 166.41 and 171.26 (for the male and female levels, respectively).[4]

Whereas there is only a single interaction question in a two-way ANOVA, there are four such questions in a three-way ANOVA. Three of these interaction questions consider the factors two at a time. These two-way interactions are sometimes referred to as the **first-order interactions**. The fourth interaction considers all three factors together, and it is sometimes referred to as the **second-order interaction** (or the **triple interaction**). We will explain what these interactions deal with by looking further at the study on personal space.

To get a feel for what any two-way interaction deals with, the diagram of the three-way ANOVA should be collapsed across levels of the factor not involved in the interaction being considered. For example, the interaction between Condition and Subject Sex is concerned with the following "reduction" of Excerpt 15.6:

	Female Subject	Male Subject
Approaching	182.12	173.27
Departing	159.63	155.33

The numbers inside the cells of this two-dimensional matrix represent the data-based estimates of the μs focused upon by this interaction question. (Each value shown, of course, was derived by averaging two of the means displayed in Excerpt 15.6). The question concerning a possible interaction between Condition and Subject Sex is the same as it would have been if the study had been conducted with these two factors as the only independent variables. This question asks whether the difference between the μs for females and males

---

[3] $170.87 = (177.12 + 151.75 + 187.12 + 167.50)/4$; $164.80 = (172.11 + 156.66 + 174.42 + 156.00)/4$.

[4] $166.41 = (177.12 + 151.75 + 172.11 + 156.66)/4$; $171.26 = (187.12 + 167.50 + 174.42 + 156.00)/4$.

varies across the approaching and departing conditions. The null hypothesis stipulates that it does not.

The remaining two-way (i.e., first-order) interaction questions are similar to the one just considered except a different pair of factors is "retained" as the diagram is collapsed across levels of one of the factors. These two questions thus are tied to the following "reductions" of Excerpt 15.6:

	Male Exp.	Female Exp.			Male Exp.	Female Exp.
Approaching	174.62	180.77		Female Subject	164.43	177.31
Departing	154.21	161.75		Male Subject	164.38	165.21

Each of these two-way interaction questions, like the first one we considered, is focused on the μs associated with the data-based means that appear here. In each case, the question concerning a possible interaction asks whether those μs are such that the difference between levels of one factor remains constant across levels of the other factor. In each case, the null hypothesis stipulates that it does.

The final question dealt with by a three-way ANOVA concerns the possibility of a three-way interaction. To understand what this question is getting at, you must focus your attention simultaneously on all cells of the study's diagram. Moreover, you must keep in mind that this question, like the six we have already considered, is concerned with population means.

To help us with the discussion of three-way interaction, we have extracted the eight cell means from Excerpt 15.6 and arranged them as follows:

DATA FROM FEMALE SUBJECTS				**DATA FROM MALE SUBJECTS**		
	Male Exp.	Female Exp.			Male Exp.	Female Exp.
Approaching	177.12	187.12		Approaching	172.11	174.42
Departing	151.75	167.50		Departing	156.66	156.00

For the moment, let's pretend that each of these eight sample means is identical to the mean of its corresponding population. (Each $\overline{X}$, of course, would most likely be *different* from its corresponding μ; we will pretend that they are identical solely to facilitate discussion of the triple interaction.)

If you focus on the data provided by the female subjects, you will note that the difference between the cell means on the top row is not equal to the difference between the cell means on the bottom row. Although each row's mean in the right-hand column is larger, this difference shifts from 10.00 on the top row to 15.75 on the bottom row. Accordingly, there is some interaction in this 2×2 matrix. Since this matrix shows the interaction of two of the factors *at* one particular level of the third factor, it is referred to as one of the **simple interactions** between Condition and Experimenter's Sex.

A triple interaction exists if the nature of the simple interaction between two factors varies across levels of the third factor. To see if such an interaction exists (as we still pretend that each sample mean is identical to its μ), we shift our focus to the data provided by the male subjects. Again we find that the difference between the cell means on the top row is not the same as the difference between the cell means on the bottom row. Note, however, that the pattern of these differences has changed from the pattern we first saw when examining the females' matrix. With males, the differences between the means in each row are smaller, the larger difference is on the top row, and the larger mean on the bottom row is in the left-hand column. If the means we have been looking at were truly μs, the three-way interaction null hypothesis would not be true, since this H_0 stipulates that the pattern of the simple interaction between two factors remains stable across levels of the third factor.

Once the results of the three-way ANOVA become available, the researcher will have access to tentative, data-based answers to the seven questions concerning main and interaction effects. Surprisingly, the answers to the four interaction questions do not really answer questions about which there is inherent interest. Instead, the answers to the two-way and three-way interactions function more as "signposts" that tell researchers where to turn in their effort to draw sound inferential conclusions based upon the sample evidence.

Most researchers first consider the answer to the three-way interaction question. If the sample evidence does not suggest the presence of a second-order interaction, the researcher will then consider the answers to the three two-way interaction questions. If these first-order interactions also appear to be nonexistent or weak, the researcher will consider the three main effect questions.

If the sample evidence suggests that a three-way interaction *does* exist, the researcher will likely refrain from paying much attention to the questions concerning main and two-way interaction effects. Instead, the researcher will probably examine the simple interaction of two of the factors *at* each level of the third factor. This is a sensible thing to do because the pattern of these simple interactions is not constant if a triple interaction exists, and the only way to see how the pattern changes is to examine directly each of the simple interactions. The two-dimensional matrix of means associated with each simple interaction would be dealt with as if it were a separate two-way ANOVA.

A researcher's sample evidence may suggest, of course, that the triple interaction is nonexistent (or weak) while one of the first-order interactions is present in the relevant populations. If this combination of answers were to be supplied by the three-way ANOVA, the typical researcher will probably pay little attention to the results concerning the main effects of the factors involved in the two-way interaction. Instead, those two factors would be examined within the two-dimensional matrix defined by the factors involved in the two-way interaction, with the data of that matrix reanalyzed as if they had come from a regular two-way ANOVA. The factor *not* involved in the interaction would be dealt with as a main effect.

We recognize that the inferential strategies discussed in the preceding four paragraphs are probably not easy to understand for anyone who is considering three-way ANOVAs for the first time. The concepts involved here are relatively complex, and folks are often confused when they first are told that there are seven questions associated with a standard three-way ANOVA; but then informed that the answers to certain questions may never be considered depending upon the answers provided to other questions. However, we feel confident that the material contained in the next set of excerpts presented in this chapter will help clarify the points we have just covered.

PRESENTATION OF RESULTS

THE ANOVA SUMMARY TABLE

The researchers who conducted the study on personal space presented the results of their three-way ANOVA exclusively in two sentences of their journal article. These two sentences appear in Excerpt 15.7.

Although an ANOVA summary table was not included in the journal article, we have reconstructed it on the basis of the study's means and standard deviations (Table 15.1).

Excerpt 15.7   Results from the Study on Personal Space

Analyzing [our] data with a three-way analysis of variance (Subject's Sex $\times$ Experimenter's Sex $\times$ Approaching-Departing) located no interactions and only one significant main effect. The subjects halted the experimenter at significantly larger distances in the approaching than in the departing condition [$F(1,56) = 28.01, p < .01$].

Source: D. Zakay, L. A. Hayduk, and Y. Tsal. (1992). Personal space and distance misperception: Implications of a novel observation. *Bulletin of the Psychonomic Society, 30*(1), p. 34.

TABLE 15.1

ANOVA SUMMARY TABLE FOR THE PERSONAL SPACE STUDY

Source	df	SS	MS	F
Condition	1	6,159.11	6,159.11	28.01
Subject sex	1	590.49	590.49	2.69
Exp. sex	1	751.86	751.86	3.42
Condition × Subject sex	1	123.65	123.65	.56
Condition × Subject sex	1	7.73	7.73	.04
Subject sex × Exp. sex	1	580.81	580.81	2.64
Condition × Subject sex × Exp. sex	1	76.04	76.04	.35
Error	56	12,313.82	219.89	
Total	63	20,603.51		

In interpreting their results, the researchers who conducted the personal space study probably considered first the F-value for the three-way interaction. Since this F-value was not large enough to warrant rejection of the three-way interaction null hypothesis, the researchers next considered the three F-values for the two-way interactions. Because none of these F-values was sufficiently large to argue against the null hypotheses associated with the first-order interactions, the researchers finally turned their attention to the main effect F-values. One of these Fs was found to be so large that its associated null hypothesis was rejected. The researchers were justified in doing this because the data-based main effect means for Condition (177.62 and 158.00) were much further apart than one would expect if the main effect means in the population had been the same.

As Excerpt 15.7 and Table 15.1 make clear, none of the null hypotheses except the one for Condition was rejected. It may seem odd that six of the seven F-values turned out to be nonsignificant, since the sample means seem, on the surface, to be inconsistent with all seven null hypotheses. For example, we saw in the previous section that the main effect means for Subject Sex were 170.87 and 164.80. We also saw that male and female subjects produced almost identical means (164.43 and 164.38) when halting the male experimenter but produced quite different means (177.31 and 165.21) when halting the female experimenter. Moreover, we saw that the simple interaction of Condition × Experimenter Sex took a different form for male subjects than it did for female subjects. "Why," you might ask, "didn't the sample data lead to a rejection of all seven null hypotheses?"

Although it may seem that there is a large discrepancy between the data-based means and the μs set forth in any of the seven null hypotheses, you must keep in mind that the statistical "yardstick" used to evaluate such discrepancies is influenced by the magnitude of the standard deviations within the cells. When these *SD*s are large, the "statistical yardstick" is large; when the *SD*s are small, the "statistical yardstick" is small. In the study on personal space, these *SD*s were quite large. Because of this within-cell variability, the discrepancy between the data and H_0, in six of seven tests, was evaluated statistically as being within the limits of chance expectation.

To continue our discussion of how researchers present the results of their three-way ANOVAs, let's consider the summary table from a different study. This table is presented in Excerpt 15.8. From the information here, you can determine quite a lot about the study being summarized. First, the table's title informs us that data analyzed were CTBS math scores. Second, the top three *df* values allow us to discern that there were two levels of the Grade factor, two levels of the Sex factor, and three levels of the Careers factor. Third, the full column of *df* values allows us to figure out that this 2 × 2 × 3 ANOVA involved 173 subjects. Finally, the notes beneath the table tell us that the sample evidence is not consistent with (1) what one would expect if the Careers main effect were true or (2) what one would expect if the triple interaction null hypothesis were true.

Excerpt 15.8   ANOVA Summary Table

Table 1

Analysis of variance of math scores on the CTBS

Source	Sum of squares	df	Mean square	F
Grade (G)	1601.59	1	1601.59	0.68
Sex (S)	4534.67	1	4534.67	1.91
Careers (C)	15416.85	2	7708.42	3.25*
G × S	1358.54	1	1358.54	0.57
G × C	2278.36	2	1139.18	0.48
S × C	1629.92	2	814.96	0.34
G × S × C	13906.63	2	6953.32	2.93**
Error	381808.12	161	2371.48	

*p = .04; **p = .06.

Source: J. Wilson and D. Fasko. (1992). Self-esteem, achievement, and career choices of rural students. *Journal of Humanistic Education and Development, 30,* p. 134.

PRESENTATION OF RESULTS WITHOUT AN ANOVA SUMMARY TABLE

Although ANOVA summary tables can help readers understand certain key elements of researchers' studies, such tables usually are not included in research reports. When results are presented exclusively within the text of the report, you may want to construct an ANOVA summary table (either on scratch paper or in your mind) so you can better understand the three-way ANOVA. For example, consider the material in Excerpt 15.9. Here, we are told that the data were analyzed by a 2 × 3 × 2 ANOVA. This fact allows us to determine that the *df* values for the three main effects were 1, 2, and 1. Multiplying these numbers two at a time, we can also determine that the *df* values for the three first-order interactions were 2, 2, and 1. Multiplying all three main effect *df* values yields 2, the *df* value for the second-order interaction. The second of the two *df* values next to the reported *F*-value is 257, and this is the *df* value for "error" (or what some researchers call "within groups" or "residual"). The sum of these various *df* values gives us 268, the *df* for Total. Adding 1 allows us to know that this ANOVA was based on data from 269 subjects. (You may profit from constructing a table showing these *df*s.)

Excerpt 15.9   Results of a Three-Way ANOVA Presented Without an ANOVA Summary Table

---

A 2×3×2 (Group × Age × Gender) ANOVA was performed on the mean Total Fear scores. The mean Total Fear scores for the visually impaired ($M = 130.51$, $SD = 25.94$) and normally sighted children ($M = 134.59$, $SD = 25.12$) were not significantly different. The Total Fear score ($M = 137.14$, $SD = 26.08$; $M = 130.24$, $SD = 28.39$; $M = 130.97$, $SD = 23.70$) for the three age groups (8–10 years; 11–13 years, and 14–16 years, respectively) were not significantly different. However, Total Fear scores for girls and boys ($M = 143.53$, $SD = 25.41$; $M = 125.71$, $SD = 24.12$, respectively) were significantly different, $F(1, 257) = 30.82$, $p < .0001$. There were no significant two-way or three-way interactions.

Source: N. J. King, E. Gullone, and C. Stafford. (1990). Fears in visually impaired and normally sighted children and adolescents. *Journal of School Psychology, 28*(8), p. 227.

SIGNIFICANT MAIN EFFECTS AND POST HOC TESTS

Even though the ANOVA in Excerpt 15.9 yielded a significant *F*, no post hoc test was needed because only two means were being compared by that *F*. If a significant main effect involves three or more levels, however, researchers will typically conduct a post hoc investigation in an effort to localize the cause of the significant finding. In Excerpt 15.10, we see a study in which the Newman-Keuls procedure was used to accomplish this objective.

Excerpt 15.10 Use of a Post Hoc Test to Probe a Significant Main Effect

A three-way analysis of variance (ANOVA), Orientation of the Counselor (nonsexist-humanist, liberal feminist, or radical feminist) $\times$ Statement of Values (implicit or explicit) $\times$ Orientation of Subject (nonfeminist or feminist) was conducted on the single-item measure of the subjects' rating of counselor feminist orientation. Significant main effects for all three factors were uncovered $F(2, 137) = 61.87, p < .001, F(1, 137) = 11.89, p < .01,$ and $F(1, 137) = 10.59, p < .01,$ for counselor orientation, value statement, and feminist orientation of the subject, respectively. No significant interactions were found.

Post hoc comparisons with the Newman-Keuls procedure (Winer, 1971) with an alpha level of .01 revealed significant differences for counselor orientation between all three conditions in the expected direction, which confirms that subjects accurately perceived the experimental manipulation.

Source: C. A. Enns and G. Hackett. (1990). Comparison of feminist and nonfeminist women's reactions to variants of nonsexist and feminist counseling. *Journal of Counseling Psychology, 37*(1), p. 36.

SIGNIFICANT FIRST-ORDER INTERACTIONS AND TESTS OF SIMPLE MAIN EFFECTS

So far, we have examined actual studies in which all interactions turned out to be nonsignificant. Now, we want to consider what researchers typically do when a first-order interaction null hypothesis is rejected. To accomplish this task, let's take a look at a recent investigation that focused on "old flames" (i.e., past romantic relationships).

In the study we want to consider, over 100 college students were each asked to write about a past relationship. Each student was given one of eight sets of instructions, with these sets generated by combining three two-level factors. In other words, there were eights cells located in a $2 \times 2 \times 2$ ANOVA design. Each of the three factors was active in nature, thus allowing each subject to be randomly assigned to any of the eight cells.

On the day of the investigation, each of the subjects was given one of eight packets of materials. The instructions inside each packet told the subject to think about either (1) a relationship that was understood (i.e., one in which the relationship's development made sense) or (2) a relationship that did not make sense. The instructions then directed the subject to concentrate on either (1) the beginning of the relationship (i.e., when they fell in love) or (2) the end of the relationship (i.e., when they fell out of love). Finally, the instructions told each subject to focus on the details of either (1) how or (2) why the relationship began (or ended).

Data on several dependent variables were collected and analyzed, because each student had to do several things after writing about his or her "old flame." Each subject had to rate several mood adjectives, list as many events as possible connected to the relationship that had been described, and then generate as many reasons as possible why the relationship began (or ended). A separate page of the packet was allocated for each of these tasks. The final page of the packet asked each student to indicate how well he or she understood why the relationship ended. A seven-point rating scale was used to collect these data, with 7 and 1 indicating complete and no understanding, respectively.

The data from the seven-point rating scale served as a **manipulation check** to see if subjects had followed the directions asking them to think of a relationship that either was or was not understood. Those data were subjected to a $2 \times 2 \times 2$ ANOVA, and the results are presented in Excerpt 15.11.

To help explain what was done in Excerpt 15.11, we have constructed two "pictures" of the study on "old flames," one showing the sample means for all cells of the full $2 \times 2 \times 2$ ANOVA design and the other showing the

---

Excerpt 15.11   Tests of Simple Main Effects Following a Statistically Significant First-Order Interaction

---

A 2 (understood, not understood) $\times$ 2 (how-focus, why-focus) $\times$ 2 (in love, out of love) between-participants ANOVA was conducted on the manipulation check for prior understanding. . . . [P]articipants who were prompted to recall an understood relationship indeed reported more understanding of why that relationship turned out as it did ($M = 5.62$) than participants who recalled relationships they did not understand ($M = 4.88$), $F(1, 106) = 5.96, p < .02$.

In addition, there was a significant interaction between prior understanding and thought focus, $F(1, 106) = 4.21, p < .04$. Simple main effects follow-up analyses indicated that, under the why-focus conditions, participants reported relatively high understanding of the relationship's demise irrespective of their prior understanding ($Ms = 5.31$ and 4.50 for prior understanding and no prior understanding, respectively). How-focused participants who discussed an understood relationship reported more understanding of the relationship's ending ($M = 6.00$) than participants who discussed a relationship they did not understand ($M = 4.81$). It is possible that because this measure was assessed after the task for generating a list of reasons, why-focused individuals in the no prior understanding condition felt they ought to have figured out why the relationship turned out as it did.

Source: L. F. Clark and J. E. Collins II. (1993). Remembering old flames: How the past affects assessments of the present. *Personality and Social Psychology Bulletin, 19*(4), pp. 404–405.

Prior Understanding	Experience Valence	Thought Focus Why	How
Understood	Falling in love	4.50	5.75
Understood	Falling out of love	6.13	6.25
Not understood	Falling in love	4.50	5.38
Not understood	Falling out of love	4.50	4.25

		Thought Focus Why	How
Prior Understanding	Understood	5.31	6.00
Prior Understanding	Not Understood	4.50	4.81

FIGURE 15.2 *Original cell means from the "old flames" study and the derived means involved in the significant two-way interaction.*

means involved in the interaction between Prior Understanding and Thought Focus. These two sets of means are contained in Figure 15.2, and it should be apparent that the means in the 2×2 matrix were derived by "collapsing" the $2 \times 2 \times 2$ matrix across levels of the factor not involved in the significant first-order interaction. For example, the top right-hand number in the 2×2 matrix (6.00) came from averaging the numbers 5.75 and 6.25 that appear in the $2 \times 2 \times 2$ matrix.

When the researchers conducted their simple main effects follow-up analysis, they focused on means in the 2×2 matrix of Figure 15.2 and performed two statistical tests. First, they compared the two means in the left-hand column (5.31 versus 4.50). These are the simple main effect means of Prior Understanding at the first level of Thought Focus. The null hypothesis associated with this test was not rejected. Second, the researchers compared the means in the right-hand column (6.00 versus 4.81), with results leading to a rejection of the null hypothesis of equal population means.

The tests of simple main effects discussed in Excerpt 15.11 involved comparing the means located in a common column of the 2×2 matrix shown in Figure 15.2. Since each of those columns contain only two means, the tests of simple main effects conducted in the "old flames" study are analogous to *t*-tests. In some studies, there will be more than two means involved in any test of simple main effects. For example, if there had been three levels of Prior Understanding (e.g., understood well, understood a little, and not understood at all), the two-dimensional matrix in Figure 15.2 would have three rows, not two. If a test of simple main effects is conducted within each column of that 3×2 matrix, an F-test analogous to a one-way ANOVA is likely be computed first. If the F-test produces a significant result, a post hoc analysis will probably be used to compare the means within the columns.

We need to make one final point about tests of simple main effects. Such tests can be applied to the means of the two-dimensional matrix in one of two ways. Comparisons can be made (1) among the means that reside within each separate column of the matrix or (2) among the means that reside within each separate row of matrix.[5] In choosing between these two options, a researcher should consider the nature of the study and the research questions being considered. At times, those considerations will make it clear that one of the two options makes far more sense than the other. In Excerpt 15.11, for example, the manipulation check necessitated that the means for the two levels of Prior Understanding be compared at each level of Thought Focus.

INTERPRETING A SIGNIFICANT TRIPLE INTERACTION

As we explained earlier in this chapter, the second-order interaction is concerned with (1) the original cell means of the three-dimensional layout and (2) a set of simple interactions. As we hope you recall, a simple interaction is nothing more than the interaction between two of the factors at a particular level of the third factor. If the sample data indicate that the simple interactions vary from one another more than would be expected by chance, then the F-value for the triple interaction will be large, the p-value for this effect will be small, and the researcher will interpret the sample evidence as providing little support for the null hypothesis of no variability among the simple interactions.

If the triple interaction turns out to be statistically significant, a researcher will probably conduct some form of post hoc investigation in an effort to pinpoint the source of the significant finding. Such post hoc investigations can be done in many different ways. In this portion of our discussion of three-way ANOVAs, we will consider three of the techniques you are likely to see used when researchers talk about significant three-way interactions.

Since the core essence of a triple interaction is connected to the concept of simple interactions, researchers will sometimes conduct a post hoc investigation that formally examines the simple interactions. In Excerpt 15.12, we see an example where this was done.[6]

---

[5]*In some studies, tests of simple main effects are conducted both ways.*
[6]*In the article from which Excerpt 15.12 was taken, Table 2 contained the means for three dependent variables. Only the means for one of those dependent variables, rated likelihood, are presented here.*

Excerpt 15.12   Tests of Simple Interactions

Table 2

Likelihood Judgments for Case Study Outcomes as a Function of Discrediting and Dogmatism, Experiment 2

	No discrediting		Discrediting	
	Outcome A	Outcome B	Outcome A	Outcome B
High Dogmatics	3.18	7.13	3.90	6.93
	($n = 11$)	($n = 12$)	($n = 10$)	($n = 10$)
Low Dogmatics	3.05	7.35	4.80	5.86
	($n = 10$)	($n = 10$)	($n = 10$)	($n = 11$)

Of particular relevance to the hypotheses under investigation was the significant three-way interaction of Reported Outcome × Discrediting × Dogmatism, $F(1, 76) = 4.27, p < .05$. Simple effects analyses revealed that this three-way interaction was due to a significant simple interaction of dogmatism and reported outcome in the discrediting condition, $F(1, 76) = 6.13, p < .02$, but not in the no-discrediting condition, $F < 1$. In the discrediting condition, the outcome B-outcome A difference was 3.03 for high-dogmatic individuals but only 1.06 for low-dogmatic individuals (see Table 2), whereas in the no-discrediting condition, the outcome B-outcome A difference was similar for high-dogmatic individuals (3.95) and low-dogmatic individuals (4.30).

Source: M. F. Davis. (1993). Dogmatism and the persistence of discredited beliefs. *Personality and Social Psychology Bulletin, 19*(6), p. 693.

Some researchers, in their efforts to understand the cause of a statistically significant three-way interaction, focus on the simple interactions but do not directly apply tests of such interactions. Instead, the cell means within each simple interaction are compared in a pairwise fashion using one of the test procedures discussed in Chapter 13. Excerpt 15.13 contains an example of this form of post hoc analysis. The graph of the three-way interaction displayed in this excerpt shows nicely the simple interactions focused upon by the researchers.

Since a statistically significant three-way interaction means, by definition, that the simple interactions vary from one another more than would be expected by chance, some researchers will simply graph the simple interactions without conducting any post hoc tests. Excerpt 15.14 illustrates this third way of interpreting a triple interaction.

Excerpt 15.13   Pairwise Comparisons of Means Within Simple Interactions

The three-way interaction, personalization by sex by item type, was also statistically significant, $F(1,67) = 5.79$, $p < .05$. This interaction revealed a pattern similar to the two-way one in that males in the standard group scored lower than both males and females in the other three treatment conditions on both one-step and two-step problems. Males under the standard treatment scored more than two items correct lower than subjects in each of the other three treatment combinations on one-step problems and more than 1.4 items lower on two-step problems. Simple effects analyses using Newman-Keuls revealed that scores for males in the standard treatment were significantly lower at the .05 level than scores of the other three groups on both one-step and two-step problems, whereas scores of the other three groups did not differ significantly from each other on either type of problem. The three-way interaction showing these differences is diagrammed in Figure 1.

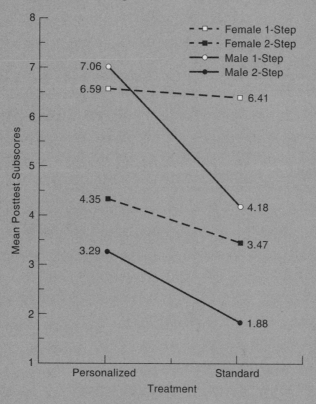

Figure 1. *Treatment by sex by item-type interaction.*

Source: C. L. Lopez and H. J. Sullivan. (1991). Effects of personalized math instruction for Hispanic students. *Contemporary Educational Psychology, 16*(1), pp. 98–99.

Excerpt 15.14 Graphing the Simple Interactions

The breakdown of the second-order interaction indicated that the high school girls in the treatment and control groups showed the greatest differences in attitudes; the girls in the treatment group scored much higher. However, the experimental group of high school boys scored slightly lower than the control group of high school boys. Elementary school treatment groups of both boys and girls showed similar higher scores than their respective control groups (See Table 1 and Fig. 1).

Table 1

Means and Standard Deviations of Sentence-Completion Test Scores by Treatment, School Level, and Gender

Variable	Control			Experimental		
	N	M	SD	N	M	SD
Elementary school						
Girls	14	9.79	1.72	15	10.07	1.94
Boys	18	7.89	2.05	19	8.79	2.25
High school						
Girls	13	6.69	2.18	12	10.33	2.31
Boys	14	7.07	2.98	8	6.50	3.12

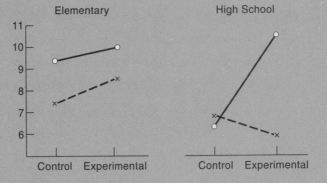

Figure 1. *Mean scores on the sentence-completion test for elementary and high school students as a function of treatment and gender.*

Source: D. P. Couper, N. W. Sheehan, and E. L. Thomas. (1991). Attitude toward old people: The impact of an intergenerational program. *Educational Gerontology, 17*, pp. 45–47.

RELATED ISSUES

When you encounter a research report in which the findings are based upon a three-way ANOVA, you should not be surprised if the researchers do more than simply discuss how the seven main *F*-tests and any post hoc tests turned out. To be more specific, you will find that competent researchers will discuss underlying assumptions, utilize the Bonferroni (or Dunn-Sidak) adjustment procedure, comment on the practical significance of findings that are statistically significant, and conduct planned comparisons. Although we have discussed these topics in earlier chapters, it may prove helpful to show how they are also relevant to three-way ANOVAs.

ASSUMPTIONS

A three-way ANOVA involves the same underlying assumptions as does a one-way ANOVA or a two-way ANOVA. These assumptions can be summed up in four phrases: random samples, normally distributed populations, equal population variances, and independence of observations. When researchers discuss these assumption—explaining why an assumption seemed tenable, why a test of an assumption was not needed, or what happened when a test of an assumption was conducted—you should upgrade your evaluation of the study.

In Excerpt 15.15, we see an example of a study that deserves high marks for considering the equal variance assumption. As illustrated here, researchers regularly use the arcsine transformation when their data are in the form of proportions; such a transformation helps to make the sample variances more similar across the comparison groups.

Excerpt 15.15   Concern over the Equal Variance Assumption

First, the responses to all of the previously described cognitive and affective tasks were analyzed for age, sex, and SES differences with a series of $2\times2\times2$ analyses of variance (ANOVAs). For this analysis, statistics on proportional scores were computed on arc sine transformations of the proportions. This procedure was included to stabilize the variance and to pass the homogeneity of variance test.

Source: P. G. Ramsey. (1991). The salience of race in young children growing up in an all-white community. *Journal of Educational Psychology, 83*(1), p. 31.

THE BONFERRONI ADJUSTMENT PROCEDURE

If a researcher collects data on two or more dependent variables and then performs a separate three-way ANOVA on each dependent variable's data, the true probability of a Type I error will exceed the nominal familywise level of significance. Although various techniques can be used to avoid having multiple analyses fall prey to an "inflated Type I error rate," most researchers use the Bonferroni adjustment procedure or the Dunn-Sidak modification to circumvent this problem. In Excerpt 15.16, we see a case in which the Bonferroni procedure was used within each of three sets of analyses.

Excerpt 15.16 Use of the Bonferroni Adjustment Procedure

A total of 27 outcome measures were obtained from each respondent. These included 13 vocational preferences, 7 professional activities preferences, and 7 perceived levels of competence. Thus, a total of 27 three-way factorial analyses of variance (program by sex by candidacy status) were computed to determine statistically significant differences and interactions among preferences for the 13 vocational settings and the seven professional activities and for perceived levels of self-efficacy for the seven professional activities. Because of the number of analyses done, the Bonferroni adjustment of alpha level (Keppel, 1982) was used for determination of statistical significance for each of the three subsets of analyses. Thus, the alpha level for the first subset of 13 vocational settings was $p < .004$ (.05/13). An alpha level of $p < .007$ (.05/7) was used for the remaining two subsets of preferred professional activities and perceived levels of self-efficacy.

Source: J. M. Poidevant, L. C. Loesch, and J. Wittmer. (1991). Vocational aspirations and perceived self-efficacy of doctoral students in the counseling professions, *Counselor Education and Supervision, 30,* p. 293.

CONCERN FOR PRACTICAL SIGNIFICANCE

In earlier chapters, we pointed out that the concepts of statistical significance and practical significance are not interchangeable. We have tried to make this point as often as possible because (1) it is possible for an inferential test to yield results that are significant in a statistical sense but not in a practical sense and (2) many researchers pay no attention whatsoever to the concept of practical significance when interpreting their results. When you come across a research report that *does* address the issue of practical significance, you should upgrade your evaluation of the investigation.

In Excerpt 15.17, we see a case in which the researchers utilized a strength-of-association measure to assess the meaningfulness of their statisti-

---

Excerpt 15.17 Concern over the Practical Significance of Results

The ANOVA on the number of behavior-relevant sex-typed traits in the subjects' descriptions also showed a main effect for behavior type [$F(1, 69) = 105.2$, $p < .001$], a reliable two-way interaction between behavior type and load [$F(1, 69) = 3.49, p = .001$], and reliable three-way interaction [$F(1, 69) = 3.49, p = .02$]. The means . . . clearly show a large effect for behavior type, which accounts for 54% of the variance, with male typed behavior sets producing more masculine than feminine traits and conversely for female-typed behavior sets. This effect is present at $p < .001$ in both load conditions, but is larger in the

(Continued)

Excerpt 15.17   Concern over the Practical Significance of Results
(Continued)

---

nonoverload condition $\eta^2 = 69.7\%$) than in the overload condition ($\eta^2 = 41.5\%$), resulting in the two-way interaction. The three-way interaction does not essentially modify this result.

Source: F. Prato and J. A. Bargh. (1991). Stereotyping based on apparently individuating information: Trait and global components of sex stereotypes under attention overload. *Journal of Experimental Social Psychology, 27*(1), p. 36.

---

cally significant results. By using the eta squared index, the researchers provided evidence to back up their claim that there was "a large effect" for the main effect of behavior type. The researchers also used the strength-of-association index as an aid in interpreting the first-order interaction that turned out to be statistically significant.

PLANNED COMPARISONS

In many investigations where there are three factors, the data will be analyzed in the manner illustrated by the excerpts you have seen thus far in this chapter. In such studies, a "standard" three-way ANOVA is first used to help procure answers to the seven "basic" research questions. Post hoc tests are then used to clarify the meaning of significant main effects having three or more levels and any significant interaction.

Although the two-step data-analysis strategy alluded to in the preceding paragraph is quite popular, you are likely to encounter research reports wherein the results of planned comparisons are discussed. Researchers who know how to set up planned comparisons often use them in conjunction with or instead of a standard three-way ANOVA. They do this for one or both of two reasons. On the one hand, planned comparisons are more powerful than the seven "omnibus" F-tests of the standard three-way ANOVA, thus making it less likely that a Type II error will be made. On the other hand, researchers who set up and evaluate sensible, planned comparisons come across as knowing their field more thoroughly than if just a "standard" three-way ANOVA is used.

To illustrate how planned comparisons can be used in place of the standard ANOVA's F-tests, we want to show you what a group of researchers did in a recent investigation involving bicycles. In this study, the human subjects were first tested to see how much they knew about the parts of a bicycle and were then subdivided into three groups: high knowledge, moderate knowledge, and low knowledge. Next, one-third of the subjects in each of these "expertise" groups was assigned to each of the three "information processing" conditions of the study. These conditions were created by giving each subject a promotional document on a "newly developed" bicycle along with one of three sets of instructions (to evaluate the new bike's ride/handling, to evaluate the new bike's overall quality, or to memorize the information describing the new bike). After reading the promotional material, each subject was tested either immediately or after a week's delay to see how many of the new bike's attributes could be recalled. The results appear in Excerpt 15.18.

Excerpt 15.18 Planned Comparisons in a Three-Way ANOVA

Subjects' recall of the presented attributes was subjected to a $3\times2\times3$ (Initial Processing Goals $\times$ Time of Judgment $\times$ Expertise) between-subjects ANOVA. Not surprisingly, the number of attributes recalled was considerably lower after a delay ($M = 3.27$), $F(1, 241) = 256.23$, $p < .01$. Initial processing set also affected recall, $F,(2, 241) = 5.38$, $p < .01$. A Newman-Keuls test indicated that subjects instructed to form a specific judgment ($M = 2.10$) recalled fewer attributes than subjects in the memory set ($M = 2.55$) and the global evaluation set ($M = 2.41$), although the latter difference was marginally significant.

As expected, recall varied as a function of subjects' prior knowledge of bicycles. Planned comparisons indicated that immediately after stimulus presentation, high knowledge subjects ($M = 3.71$) recalled a greater number of the presented attributes than low knowledge subjects ($M = 3.10$), $t(241) = 2.65$, $p < .01$, but not moderate knowledge subjects ($M = 3.40$), $t(241) = 1.35$, ns. After a delay, however, high knowledge subjects ($M = 1.92$) recalled more of the presented attributes than both low knowledge subjects ($M = 1.08$), $t(241) = 3.65$, $p < .01$, and moderate knowledge subjects ($M = .86$), $t(241) = 4.61$. $p < .01$.

Source: D. Sanbonmatsu, F. Kardes, and C. Sansone. (1991). Remembering less and inferring more: Effects of time of judgment on inferences about unknown attributes. *Journal of Personality and Social Psychology, 61*(4), p. 548.

Although a three-way ANOVA was used in the conventional manner to investigate the main effects, notice what the researchers did and did not report in the second paragraph. Instead of presenting the results of any of the interaction tests that could have been conducted, the researchers discuss their planned comparisons. Evidently, the researchers had an *a priori* interest in comparing the high-knowledge subjects against the moderate- and low-expertise groups at the immediate and delayed points of data collection.

A FEW WARNINGS CONCERNING THREE-WAY ANOVAS

Before concluding this chapter, we want to offer four warnings concerning three-way ANOVAs. The first three of these warnings actually apply to *any* analysis of variance, including those considered in Chapters 11, 12, and 14. In a similar fashion, the warnings offered at the end of those chapters are relevant to three-way ANOVAs. Accordingly, we encourage you to review the final sections of those earlier chapters. (The comment in Chapter 14 concerning the proper way to interpret the *F*-tests of main effects is especially relevant to three-way ANOVAs.) After reviewing those earlier warnings, return here to read about our new tips for being a critical consumer of the research literature.

"EYEBALLING" GRAPHS OF INTERACTIONS

Graphs of significant first- and second-order interactions will help you understand the results obtained in the ANOVA summary table. However, it is important to remember that neither you nor the researcher has the ability to simply look at the graph and determine, for any pair of the plotted means, whether the mean difference is statistically significant. The reason why this cannot be done is related to the fact that the "yardstick" used to establish statistical significance is based upon the standard deviations in the various cells. Graphs of interactions almost never contain information on within-cell variability, thus making it impossible to judge whether any two means are further apart than would be expected by chance.

When you read research reports, try to remember that claimed differences between means should be based upon statistical evidence, not simply a visual examination of the graph. To illustrate why this is important, take another look at Excerpt 15.14. In discussing their statistically significant three-way interaction, the researchers make several statements about pairs of means. The terms *much higher*, *slightly lower*, and *higher* are used to describe some of the specific differences focused upon by the researchers. However, no evidence is presented concerning a statistical comparison of these mean differences. Accordingly, we really don't know whether any of those differences is large enough to warrant rejection of the implied null hypothesis.

Our warning about the danger of "eyeballing" graphs of interactions becomes even more legitimate once you recognize the arbitrary manner in which such graphs are set up. Again, we ask you to consider Figure 1 in Excerpt 15.14. If the ordinate had been set up with scores going from 0 to 11 (instead of 6 to 11) and if the abscissa had been set up with a larger distance between Control and Experimental, the pairwise comparisons focused upon by the researchers would not have seemed as large. This graph, therefore, provides a clear example of why you must be vigilant when considering what researchers have to say about their graphed interactions.

THE INFLUENCE OF LARGE SAMPLE SIZES

With a three-way ANOVA (as well as with most other inferential procedures), a direct relationship exists between statistical power and the amount of data being analyzed. In other words, researchers are more likely to reject false null hypotheses if their sample sizes are large. While this fact might prompt you to think that researchers should base their analysis on as much data as possible, we must remind you that giant sample sizes make it quite likely that a null hypothesis will end up being rejected, even if the discrepancy between the sample evidence and H_0 is very small. Simply stated, comparisons based on enormous amounts of data can lead to statistical significance despite the full absence of any practical significance.

To illustrate why readers of the research literature should pay attention to the size of samples used in group comparison studies, consider the three-way ANOVA summary table in Excerpt 15.19. All seven F-tests turned out to be

---

Excerpt 15.19   A Three-Way ANOVA Based upon an Enormous Amount of Data

Table 3

Analysis of variance summary of household production by employment status, sex and nationality

Source	SS	DF	MS	F	Probability
Employment (A)	24,728.43	2	12,364.21	62.98	***
Sex (B)	131,506.76	1	131,506.76	669.89	***
Nationality (C)	893.32	1	893.32	4.55	*
A × B	7,875.18	2	3,937.59	20.25	***
A × C	3,643.58	2	1,821.79	9.28	***
B × C	5,816.14	1	5,816.14	29.63	***
A × B × C	3,269.86	2	1,634.93	8.32	***
Error	108,563,632.00	5,877	196.31		
Total	230,967,980.00	5,888	39,220.23		

***Significant at 0.001 level; *Significant at 0.05 level.

Source: L. M. Kirjavainen and N. A. Barclay. (1990). Household production time by sex and employment status: A cross-national comparison between Finland and the U.S.A. *Journal of Consumer Studies and Home Economics, 14*(4), p. 310.

---

statistically significant, with six achieving significance at an "impressive" .001 level. But consider the amount of data used in this analysis: The ANOVA results are based upon scores from 5889 subjects!! As a result, many of the F-tests were statistically significant even though the differences in the sample data were exceedingly small.

Earlier in this chapter (as also in preceding chapters), we discussed techniques available to researchers for assessing the practical significance of their findings. Such techniques are especially important in studies where large amounts of data either are available for a pending analysis or have been used in a completed analysis. You should upgrade your evaluation of research reports when such techniques are utilized.

Gender (or Sex) as a Factor

In this and earlier chapters, we have presented many excerpts in which one of the factors of the ANOVA has been gender (or sex). In most studies, gender will be an assigned (rather than active) factor. In such studies, many subjects will be grouped together under the male and female levels of the gender factor, with each subject's affiliation with one or the other of the two levels determined exclusively by that subject's status on the gender variable.

In some studies, however, gender is an active factor. This occurs when the researcher controls the gender of the person the subject evaluates or interacts with during the study. Such studies are, by definition, experiments, because the researcher (1) will randomly assign subjects to the male and female conditions of the study and (2) is interested in finding out whether scores on the dependent variable are influenced by the gender variable. Such experiments are conducted when a researcher wants to see if a gender bias exists in the hiring process or in the awarding of financial aid. Two versions of a set of credentials are created, with both versions identical except for the gender of the hypothetical person being evaluated. Half the subjects are given the male version of the credentials while the remaining subjects are given the female version. A statistically significant difference between the gender main effect means is then interpreted to mean that a gender bias exists in the evaluations.

In the "personal space" study considered earlier in this chapter, we saw a case where gender was an active factor that involved real people. The subjects in that investigation had to stop an approaching or departing person who began walking toward the subject from a distance of 210 cm or who began moving away from the subject from a starting distance of 70 cm. In each case, the subject was instructed to halt the other person when a distance of 140 cm separated them.

As you may recall from our earlier discussion of the "personal space" study, the person who walked toward or away from each subject was one of the experimenters. Accordingly, one of the factors in the three-way ANOVA was Experimenter's Sex. That factor was not statistically significant as a main effect or in any of the interactions that were computed. That was also the case with the factor called Subject's Sex, and thus the researchers concluded that "the absence of sex effects implies that the effects produced by approaching or departing hold for all pairings of the sex of the subject and the experimenter."

Although we are fully confident that the male and female versions of hypothetical applicants do, in fact, differ in gender, and although we are fully confident that the male and female conditions of the "personal space" study really did involve a male or female person walking toward or away from each subject, we are concerned about the generalizability of any results concerning gender in studies such as these. To be more precise, we believe that a study's results involving an active gender factor have very limited generalizability if a single person, real or hypothetical, "represents" each level of the gender factor.

In the "personal space" study, 32 male subjects were used along with 32 female subjects. We highly suspect that the 32 individuals who represented each level of the Subject Sex factor were quite heterogeneous even though they were all undergraduate students at a single university. They undoubtedly varied in height, weight, attractiveness, and a whole host of other characteristics. But when we consider the factor of Experimenter Sex, we find that a single male experimenter represented "maleness" and a single female experimenter represented "femaleness." We do not think any human being can perform such a task in a way that produces generalizable results.

In the "personal space" study, the researchers state that the effects associated with approaching or departing "hold for all pairing of the sex of the subject and the experimenter." We contend that this statement probably needs to be qualified by a consideration of the perceived attractiveness of the person who is approaching or departing. Since we have no idea as to how attractive the subjects considered the male and female experimenters to be, we cannot predict how the results might change if two *different* people were to approach or depart from a similar group of subjects. However, we are absolutely confident that the results from such a replication might be drastically different from those reported in the original study.

This third warning that we have been discussing can be summed up as follows: Be very cautious when you are considering the results of a study in which gender is an active factor. If only one person was used to create the male condition and only one person used to create the female condition, downgrade your evaluation of the study unless there is an extremely detailed description of those two individuals. Upgrade your evaluation of the investigation if the study was conducted in such a way that each of several different males in turn created the male condition for some of the subjects while each of several different females created the female condition for the other subjects.

More Complex ANOVAs

Our final warning of the chapter concerns the fact that ANOVAs involving more than three factors are often used by researchers. Excerpts 15.20 and 15.21 show that four-way and five-way ANOVAs can be, and have been, used by applied researchers. Space considerations make it impossible for us to discuss such higher-order ANOVAs in detail. All we can do here is suggest that readers who understand three-way ANOVAs are in a good position to understand almost everything that is involved in an ANOVA involving more than three factors. To see whether this claim applies to you, consider the ANOVA summary table presented in Excerpt 15.22. Based upon your knowledge of three-way ANOVAs, you should be able to look at this table and determine how many factors there were, how many levels made up each factor, how many subjects were involved in the study, and which of the F-tests turned out to be statistically significant. We also suspect that you have the skills to explain the meaning of each of the F-tests that was significant, the order in which the researchers examined their significant results, and the kind of post hoc tests that may have been used by the researchers.

Excerpts 15.20–15.21   ANOVAs Involving Four and Five Factors

The major analysis concerned a 2×2×2×6 between-subjects factorial ANOVA using the total number of individual responses made in each condition as the dependent measure, with ethnicity, gender, feedback (cooperative, competitive), and ingroup/outgroup (I/O) ratio (1:5, 2:4, 3:3, 4:2, 5:1, 6:0) as independent variables.

Source: R. T. Garza and S. J. Santos. (1991). Ingroup/outgroup balance and interdependent interethnic behavior. *Journal of Experimental Social Psychology, 27*(2), p. 130.

A 2 (Gender of Defendant) × 2 (Ethnicity) × 2 (Gender of Judge) × 5 (Attractiveness Level) × 3 (Degree) unequal N, between-groups ANOVA on bail/fine amounts yielded neither main nor interaction effects for any of the variables, except for an expected main effect for degree of felony, $F(2, 305) = 512.21, p < .0001$.

Source: A. C. Downs and P. Lyons. (1991). Natural observations of the links between attractiveness and initial legal judgments. *Personality and Social Psychology Bulletin, 17*(5), p. 544.

Excerpt 15.22 A Four-Way ANOVA Summary Table

Table 1

Analysis of variance for cross-cultural counseling inventory total scores

Source	Sum of squares	df	MS	F
Participant acculturation level (A)	0.03	1	0.03	0.00
Counselor condition (B)	2,508.67	1	2,508.67	19.55***
Counselor ethnicity (C)	990.98	1	990.98	7.72**
Participant gender (D)	93.95	1	93.95	0.73
A × B	215.51	1	215.51	1.68
A × C	1.42	1	1.42	0.01
A × D	2.47	1	2.47	0.02
B × C	569.81	1	569.81	4.44*
B × D	217.44	1	217.44	1.70
C × D	29.94	1	29.94	0.23
A × B × C	50.93	1	50.93	0.04
A × B × D	431.54	1	431.54	3.36
A × C × D	13.83	1	13.83	0.11
B × C × D	959.42	1	959.42	7.48**
A × B × C × D	86.50	1	86.50	0.67
Error	10,905.51	85	128.30	

*p<.05. **p<.01. ***p<.001.

Source: R. H. Gim, D. R. Atkinson, and S. J. Kim. (1991). Asian-American acculturation, counselor ethnicity, cultural sensitivity, and ratings of counselors. *Journal of Counseling Psychology, 38,* p. 59.

REVIEW TERMS

Between-subjects factor
Cell
Completely between-subjects ANOVA
Completely randomized ANOVA
First-order interaction

Manipulation check
Second-order interaction
Simple interactions
Three-way ANOVA
Triple interaction

REVIEW QUESTIONS

1. Is a 3 × 3 ANOVA a two-way ANOVA or a three-way ANOVA? What about a 2 × 2 × 2 ANOVA?

2. (True or False) There are 12 cells in a 2 × 3 × 2 ANOVA, with each cell representing a different sample of subjects.

3. In a $3 \times 3 \times 3$ ANOVA in which there are 10 subjects per cell, how many scores will each main effect mean be based on?

4. How many first-order interactions are there in a three-way ANOVA? How many second-order interactions?

5. If a researcher were to talk about a particular first-order interaction from a three-way ANOVA like that discussed in Question 3, how many means would be involved in that first-order interaction? How many scores would each of those means be based on?

6. (True or False) The null hypothesis associated with the triple interaction stipulates that all three first-order interactions have the same pattern.

7. If an $A \times B \times C$ ANOVA produces a statistically significant main effect for factor A and a statistically significant $A \times B$ interaction, which of these effects is likely to receive the most attention from the researchers as they attempt to interpret the results?

8. How many subjects provided data for the three-way ANOVA summarized in Excerpt 15.10?

9. Look at the means in the 2×2 matrix in Figure 15.2. Suppose you were given the freedom to change the mean in the upper left-hand cell from 5.31 to any other value of your choosing. Also suppose that you were asked to change that cell mean so as to totally eliminate the interaction in the 2×2 matrix. If you accepted this challenge, what new number would you substitute for 5.31?

10. (True or False) The null hypothesis associated with the triple interaction in a three-way ANOVA stipulates that the pattern of the simple interactions between any two of the factors will not vary across levels of the third factor.

11. Look at the graph of the three-way interaction displayed in Excerpt 15.13. If the mean for the males in the two-step, personalized condition had turned out equal to 5.00 (rather than 3.29), would the F-value for the three-way interaction have turned out larger or smaller than it actually did?

12. If the sample sizes vary across the cells of a three-way ANOVA, should the researcher test the homogeneity of variance assumption?

13. Look at the Excerpt 15.18. Are the mean scores presented in the second paragraph of this excerpt main effect means, cell means from the original three-dimensional diagram, or are they cell means from a two-dimensional diagram that had been collapsed across one of the factors?

14. (True or False) The two-level factor Gender (or Sex) will always take the form of an assigned factor, because it is impossible to randomly assign subjects to the male and female conditions of this variable.

15. How many cells were there in the four-way ANOVA summarized in Excerpt 15.22?

FULLY REPEATED MEASURES ANALYSES OF VARIANCE

In this chapter, we consider different ANOVAs that are characterized by repeated measures. In particular, the focus here is on one-way ANOVAs with repeated measures, two-way ANOVAs with repeated measures, and three-way ANOVAs with repeated measures. Although there are other kinds of ANOVAs that could be discussed within the context of this chapter (e.g., a five-way fully repeated measures ANOVA), the three types considered here are the ones you are most likely to encounter.

The one-way, two-way, and three-way ANOVAs examined in this chapter are similar, in many respects, to the ANOVAs considered in Chapters 12, 14, and 15. The primary difference between the ANOVAs of this chapter and those looked at in earlier chapters is that the ANOVAs to which we now turn our attention involve data characterized by repeated measures across all factors in the ANOVA. In other words, instead of having just one score per subject (as was the case in the one-way, two-way, and three-way ANOVAs considered earlier), we now have multiple scores for each subject. To be more specific, the ANOVAs focused upon in this chapter are characterized by each subject being measured once under each level (or under each combination of levels) of the factor(s) involved in the ANOVA.

Perhaps an example will help to distinguish between the ANOVAs considered in earlier chapters and their repeated measures counterparts examined in this chapter. If a researcher has a 2×3 design characterized by no repeated measures, each subject in the study can be thought of (1) as being located inside *one* of the six cells of the factorial design and (2) as contributing *one* score to the data set. In contrast, if a researcher has a 2×3 design characterized by repeated measures across both factors, each subject can be thought of (1) as being in *each of the six* cells and (2) as contributing *six* scores to the data set.

Researchers often use the terms *between-subjects* and *within-subjects* to distinguish between factors that do or don't involve repeated measures. With a **between-subjects factor,** each subject provides just one score, with that score coming from the single level of the factor under which the subject is measured. With a **within-subjects factor,** on the other hand, each subject provides multiple scores, with one score coming from each of the levels that make up the factor. In Excerpts 16.1 and 16.2, we see examples of how these terms are used.

Excerpt 16.1–16.2   Within-Subjects and Between-Subjects Factors

A within-subject factor design was used . . . in this study. The training session was treated as the within-subject factor.

Source: A. M. Genuidy, T. Gupta, and A. Alshedi. (1990). Improving human capabilities for combined manual handling tasks through a short and intensive physical training program. *American Industrial Hygiene Association Journal, 51* (November), p. 612.

The study uses a between subjects, single factor design where the factor is complexity of topological floor plan layout (ICD).

Source: M. J. O'Neill. (1991). Evaluation of a conceptual model of architectural legibility. *Environment and Behavior, 23*(3), p. 273.

Before turning our attention to the specific ANOVAs considered in this chapter, we need to make three final introductory comments. First, each of the ANOVAs looked at in this chapter will be fully repeated measures in nature. The phrase *fully repeated measures* means that there will be repeated measures across the levels of each and every factor involved in the ANOVA. As you will see in Chapter 17, it is possible to combine, in the same ANOVA, one or more between-subjects factors *and* one or more within-subjects factors. Such so-called mixed ANOVAs will not be considered here, since our focus now is on completely within-subjects ANOVAs.

Our next-to-last introductory point involves the assertion that only univariate ANOVAs are considered in this chapter. Even though subjects are measured repeatedly within each of the ANOVAs that we will soon examine, these statistical procedures are univariate—not multivariate—in nature because each subject provides only one score to the data set for each level (or combination of levels) of the factor(s) involved in the study. The ANOVAs of this chapter could be turned into multivariate ANOVAs if each subject were measured repeatedly within each cell of the design, with these within-cell repeated measurements corresponding to different dependent variables. Such multivariate repeated measures ANOVAs, however, are not considered in this chapter.

The final introductory point that we need to make involves the distinction between (1) two or more separate ANOVAs, each conducted on the data corresponding to a different dependent variable, with all data coming from the same set of subjects, and (2) a single unified ANOVA in which there are repeated measures across levels of the factor(s) of the study. In Chapters 12, 14, and 15, you have seen many examples of multiple but separate ANOVAs being applied to different sets of data, each corresponding to a unique dependent variable. The ANOVAs to which we now turn our attention are different from those referred to in the preceding sentence in that the ones to be considered here always involve a single, consolidated analysis. This will be the case even when one of the within-subjects factors is made up of levels that correspond to what might be thought of as different dependent variables.

ONE-WAY REPEATED MEASURES ANOVA
DIFFERENT-LABELS FOR THIS KIND OF ANOVA

A variety of different terms are used by researchers to designate a one-way repeated measures ANOVA. Some researchers will use the label **one-factor within-subjects ANOVA**, some will use the label **treatments-by-subjects ANOVA**, and some will use the label **randomized blocks ANOVA**. Since all these terms refer to the same kind of ANOVA, you will be better able to decipher research reports if you can recognize each of these labels as referring to a **one-way repeated measures ANOVA**.

In Excerpts 16.3–16.6, we see examples of how different researchers have used varying terms to refer to the same thing. In each case, what is being referred to is a one-way repeated measures ANOVA.

Excerpts 16.3–16.6   Different Labels for a One-Way Repeated Measures ANOVA

A univariate one-way analysis of variance for repeated measures was used for the statistical analysis.

Source: C. W. Conoley, J. C. Conoley, D. C. Ivey, and M. J. Scheel. (1991). Enhancing consultation by matching the consultee's perspectives. *Journal of Counseling & Development, 69* (July/August), p. 548.

The changes in dose were analyzed over a 1-year period by using one-factor ANOVA for repeated measures method.

Source: J. Meythaler, W. D. Steers, S. M. Tuel, L. L. Cross, and C. S. Haworth. (1992). Continuous intrathecal baclofen in spinal cord spasticity: A prospective study. *American Journal of Physical and Medical Rehabilitation, 71*(6), p. 324.

(Continued)

Excerpts 16.3–16.6   Different Labels for a One-Way Repeated
Measures ANOVA *(Continued)*

A one-way within-subjects ANOVA on threshold savings yielded . . . .

Source: J. G. Snodgrass and K. Feenan. (1990). Priming effects in picture fragment completion: Support for the perceptual closure hypothesis. *Journal of Experimental Psychology: General, 119*(3), p. 283.

A randomized block ANOVA revealed . . . .

Source: M. J. A. Buekers. (1991). The time structure of the block in volleyball: A comparison of different step techniques. *Research Quarterly for Exercise and Sport, 62*(2), p. 233.

PURPOSE

The purpose of a one-way repeated measures ANOVA is identical to the purpose of a one-way ANOVA not having repeated measures. In each case, the researcher is interested in seeing whether (or the degree to which) the sample data cast doubt upon the null hypothesis of the ANOVA. That null hypothesis, for the within-subjects case as well as the between-subjects case, states that the μs associated with the different levels of the factor do not differ. Since the researcher who uses a one-way within-subjects ANOVA is probably interested in gaining an insight into how the μs differ, post hoc tests are normally used (as in a between-subjects ANOVA) if the overall null hypothesis is rejected and if three or more levels compose the ANOVA's factor.[1]

To illustrate, suppose a researcher collects reaction-time data from six subjects on three occasions: immediately upon awakening in the morning, one hour after awakening, and two hours after awakening. Each of the six subjects would be measured three times, with a total of 18 pieces of data available for analysis. In subjecting the data to a one-way repeated measures ANOVA, the researcher would be asking whether the three sample means, each based on six scores collected at the same "time" during the day, are far enough apart to call into question the null hypothesis that says that all three population means are equivalent. In other words, the purpose of the one-way repeated measures ANOVA in this study would be to see if the reaction time of folks similar to the six subjects used in the study varies depending upon whether they are tested 0, 60, or 120 minutes after awakening.

It is usually helpful to think of any one-way repeated measures ANOVA in terms of a two-dimensional matrix. Within this matrix, each row corresponds

---

[1] *Of course, planned comparisons can be used instead of or in addition to the two-stage strategy of testing an overall null hypothesis first and then following up with post hoc tests. Such planned comparisons, however, are used by only a small minority of researchers.*

Hours Since Awakening

	Zero	One	Two
Subject 1	1.7	1.1	1.7
Subject 2	1.8	0.9	1.5
Subject 3	1.6	1.2	1.4
Subject 4	2.3	1.5	1.8
Subject 5	2.0	1.5	1.3
Subject 6	2.0	1.0	1.9
	$\bar{X} = 1.9$	$\bar{X} = 1.2$	$\bar{X} = 1.6$

FIGURE 16.1 *Illustration of the data setup for the one-way repeated measures ANOVA in the hypothetical reaction-time study.*

to a different subject and each column corresponds to a different level of the study's factor. A single score is entered into each cell of this matrix, with the scores on any row coming from the same subject. Such a matrix, created for our hypothetical reaction-time study, is presented in Figure 16.1. Such illustrations normally do not appear in research reports. Therefore, you will need to create such a picture (in your mind or on a piece of scratch paper) when trying to decipher the results of a one-way repeated measures ANOVA. This will usually be easy to do, because you will be given information as to the number of subjects involved in the study, the nature of the repeated measures factor, and the sample means that correspond to the levels of the repeated measures factor.

PRESENTATION OF RESULTS

The results of a one-way repeated measures ANOVA may be presented in an ANOVA summary table. In Table 16.1, we have prepared such a table for our hypothetical study on reaction time. This summary table is similar in some ways to the one-way ANOVA summary tables contained in Chapter 12, yet it is similar, in other respects, to the two-way ANOVA summary tables included in Chapter 14. Table 16.1 is like a one-way ANOVA summary table in that a single *F*-ratio is contained in the right-hand column of the table. (Note that this *F*-ratio is computed by dividing the *MS* for the study's factor by the *MS* for residual.) It is like a two-way ANOVA summary table in that (1) the row for Subjects functions, in some respects, as a second factor of the study and (2) the numerical values on the row for Residual are computed in the same way as if this were the interaction from a two-way ANOVA. (Note that the *df* for Residual are computed by multiplying together the first two *df* values.) In fact, we could have used the term *Hours × Subjects* to label this row instead of the term *Residual*.

TABLE 16.1

ANOVA SUMMARY TABLE FOR THE REACTION-TIME DATA CONTAINED IN FIGURE 16.1

Source	df	SS	MS	F
Hours since awakening	2	1.48	.74	16.34*
Subjects	5	.47	.09	
Residual	10	.45	.05	
Total	17	2.40		

*$p < .01$.

Regardless of whether Table 16.1 resembles more closely the summary table for a one-way ANOVA or a two-way ANOVA, it contains useful information for anyone trying to understand the structure and the results of the investigation. First, the title of the table indicates what kind of data were collected. Second, we can tell from the Source column that the study's factor was Hours since awakening. Third, the top two numbers in the df column inform us that the study involved three levels ($2+1=3$) of the factor and six subjects ($5+1=6$). Fourth, the bottom number in the df column indicates that a total of 18 pieces of data were analyzed ($17+1=18$). Finally, the note beneath the table reveals that the study's null hypothesis was rejected, with .01 being either the level of significance used by the researcher (if hypothesis testing was used) or the most rigorous alpha level "beaten" by the data (if the hybrid approach to evaluating the null hypothesis was used).

In our hypothetical study on reaction time, Table 16.1 indicates that the null hypothesis of equal population means is not likely to be true. To gain an insight into the pattern of the population means, a post hoc investigation would probably be conducted. Most researchers would set up this follow-up investigation such that three pairwise contrasts are tested, each involving a different pair of means ($\overline{X}_0$ versus $\overline{X}_1$, $\overline{X}_0$ versus $\overline{X}_2$, and $\overline{X}_1$ versus $\overline{X}_2$).

In Excerpt 16.7, we see the results from a real study that used a one-way repeated measures ANOVA. Note that only one F-ratio appears in the ANOVA summary table, since there is only one true factor in this study, Testing.

Although it is helpful to be able to look at the ANOVA summary table, researchers often must delete such a table from their reports because of space considerations. In Excerpt 16.8, we see how the results of a one-way repeated measures ANOVA were presented wholly within the text of the report. Based upon these results, can you figure out how many subjects provided data for this analysis?[2]

---

[2] *You should have come up with 12.*

Excerpt 16.7   Results of a One-Way Repeated Measures ANOVA Presented with a Summary Table

Repeated measures analysis of variance (ANOVA) [was] used to test the hypothesis that a workshop intervention on childhood cancer would increase knowledge. . . . Summary scores from prior to the workshop, immediately after the workshop, and one week after the workshop were compared.

A significant increase ($F = 63.42, p = 0.0001$) in knowledge about childhood cancer after the workshop was found for the total sample (see Table 2). Mean scores on the knowledge questionnaire were 13.59 on the pre-test, 17.92 on the post-test, and 17.94 on the post-test one week after the workshop. A significant difference existed between the pre- and initial post-test and the pre- and final post-test as demonstrated by the Scheffé's tests. No significant differences were noted between initial and final post-test scores.

Table 2

Repeated measures ANOVA, knowledge subscale: pre-, post-, and final post-test

Source	df^a	Sum of squares	Mean square	F-test	p value
Subjects	34	829.96	24.41	—	—
Testing	2	451.79	225.90	63.42	0.0001
Residual	68	242.21	3.56	—	—
Total	104	1523.96	—	—	—

[a]df = degrees of freedom.

Source: Reproduced with permission of the Association for the Care of Children's Health, 7910 Woodmont Ave., Suite 300, Bethesda, MD 20814, from A. E. Benner, and L. S. Marlow. (1991). The effect of a workshop on childhood cancer on students' knowledge, concerns, and desire to interact with a classmate with cancer, *Children's Health Care, 20*(2), p. 104.

Excerpt 16.8   Results of a One-Way Repeated Measures ANOVA Presented Without an ANOVA Summary Table

Preliminary analyses were conducted to verify that performance scores differed across the three performance categories. Results of a one-way repeated measures ANOVA indicated that there were significant differences among categories, $F(2,22) = 40.22, p < .001$. Follow-up comparisons using Tukey's HSD procedure revealed that shooting scores for the optimal category ($M = 83.75$) differed significantly ($p < .01$) from the acceptable category ($M = 78.66$). The acceptable category also differed significantly ($p < .01$) from the worst category ($M = 72.58$).

Source: H. Prapavessis and J. R. Grove. (1991). Precompetitive emotions and shooting performance: The mental health and zone of optimal function models, *The Sport Psychologist, 5*(5), p. 227.

Sometimes researchers will apply a one-way repeated measures ANOVA more than once within the same study. They do this for one of two reasons. On the one hand, each subject in the study may have provided two or more pieces of data at each level of the repeated measures factor, with each of these scores corresponding to a different dependent variable. Given this situation, the researcher may utilize a separate one-way repeated measures ANOVA to analyze the data corresponding to each dependent variable. On the other hand, the researcher may have two or more groups of subjects, with just one score collected from each subject at each level of the within-subjects factor. Here, the researcher may decide to subject the data provided by each group to a separate one-way repeated measures ANOVA. Excerpt 16.9 illustrates the second of these two situations.

Excerpt 16.9 Two One-Way Repeated Measures ANOVAs Used in the Same Study

A repeated measures analysis of variance revealed that, for women, there was a statistically sig n ificant difference, $F(1,24) = 13.53, p < .0012$, in the harassment sensitivity scores between the sexual ($M = 4.36$) and nonsexual ($M = 3.90$) conditions. A second repeated measures analysis of variance revealed that, for men, there was also a statistically significant difference, $F(1,107) = 122.49$, $p < .001$, in the average harassment sensitivity score between sexual ($M = 4.53$) and nonsexual ($M = 3.90$) conditions. Thus, both women and men showed greater sensitivity to sexual rather than nonsexual harassing behaviors.

Source: L. A. Lee and P. P. Heppner. (1991). The development and evaluation of a sexual harassment inventory. *Journal of Counseling and Development, 69*(July/August), p. 514.

THE PRESENTATION ORDER OF LEVELS OF THE WITHIN-SUBJECTS FACTOR

The factor in a one-way repeated measures ANOVA can take one of three basic forms. In some studies, the within-subjects factor corresponds to time, with the levels of the factor indicating the different points in time at which data are collected. The second kind of within-subjects factor corresponds to different treatments or conditions given to or created for the subjects, with a measurement taken on each subject "under" each treatment or condition. The third kind of within-subjects factor is found in validity studies where the levels of the factor correspond to different versions of the same measuring device that may (or may not) measure the same thing.

If the one-way repeated measures ANOVA involves data collected at different points in time, there is only one order in which the data can be collected. If, however, the within-subjects factor corresponds to treatment conditions or different versions of a measuring device, then there are different ways in which the data can be collected. When an option exists regarding the order in which the levels of the factor are presented, the researcher's decision regarding this aspect of the study should be taken into consideration when *you* make a decision as to whether or not to accept the researcher's findings.

If the various treatment conditions (or the various versions of a measuring device) are presented in the same order to all subjects, then a systematic bias may creep into the study and function to make it extremely difficult—or impossible—to draw clear conclusions from the statistical results. The systematic bias might take the form of a **practice effect**, with subjects performing better as they "warm up" or learn from what they have already done; a **fatigue effect**, with subjects performing less well on subsequent tasks simply because they get bored or tired; or **confounding** with things that the subjects do or learn outside the study's setting between the points at which the study's data are collected. Whatever its form, such bias can cause different treatment conditions (or the different versions of a measuring device) to look different when they are really alike or to look alike when they are really dissimilar.

To prevent the study from being wrecked by practice effects, fatigue effects, and confounding due to order effects, a researcher should alter the order in which the treatment conditions (or the different versions of a measuring device) are presented to subjects. This can be done in one of three ways. One design strategy is to randomize the order in which the levels of the within-subjects factor are presented to subjects. A second strategy is to utilize all possible presentation orders, with an equal proportion of the subjects assigned randomly to each possible order. The third strategy involves a subset of the full array of all possible presentation orders, with the specific orders selected in such a way as to create a desired kind of balance, or symmetry, in the subset of orders actually used in the study.[3]

In Excerpts 16.10 and 16.11, we see two examples of how the researchers altered the order in which the levels of the repeated measures factor were presented. In the first of these excerpts, the technique of individually randomizing orders across subjects was used. In the second excerpt, the researchers reported that the order of experimental conditions was counterbalanced. This **counterbalancing** may have been set up such that four subjects were assigned to each of three possible orders (control, waist, feet; waist, feet, control; feet, control, waist) or it may have been set up such that two subjects were assigned to each of the six possible orders (control, waist, feet; control, feet, waist; waist, control, feet; waist, feet, control; feet, control, waist; feet, waist, control). Although we cannot tell for certain which of these two forms of counterbalancing was used in the second of these excerpts, we believe that the researchers in both of these studies deserve credit for designing their studies to avoid the potential bias created when treatments are presented in the same order.

---

[3] *Normally, a special chart called a Latin Square is referred to or developed so the researcher can achieve the desired balance.*

Excerpts 16.10–16.11   Randomizing the Presentation Order of the
Levels of the Within-Subjects Factor

The order of step techniques was randomized across subjects.

Source: M. J. A. Buekers. (1991). The time structure of the block in volleyball: A comparison of different step techniques. *Research Quarterly for Exercise and Sport, 62*(2), p. 233.

Twelve adult students and researchers, 6 women and 6 men, between the ages of 21 and 46 (*M* = 30 years) participated in the experiment. . . . The experimental conditions, whose order was counterbalanced, were the same as in the first experiment: the control condition; the waist condition, in which the subject wore a diving belt around the waist; and the feet condition, in which loads were tied to each foot.

Source: M. Bonnard, and J. Pailhous. (1991). Intentional compensation for selective loading affecting human gait phases. *Journal of Motor Behavior, 23*(1), p. 8.

THE SPHERICITY ASSUMPTION

In order for a one-way repeated measures ANOVA to yield an *F*-test that is valid, an important assumption must hold true. This is called the **sphericity assumption**, and it should be considered by *every* researcher who uses this form of ANOVA. Even though the same amount of data will be collected for each level of the repeated measures factor, the *F*-test of a one-way repeated measures ANOVA is *not* robust to violations of the sphericity assumption. To be more specific, the *F*-value from this ANOVA will turn out to be too large to the extent that this assumption is violated.

The sphericity assumption says that the population variances associated with the levels of the repeated measures factor, in combination with the population correlations between pairs of levels, must represent one of a set of acceptable patterns. One of the acceptable patterns is for all the population variances to be identical and for all the bivariate correlations to be identical. There are, however, other patterns of variances and correlations that adhere to the requirements of sphericity.

The sample data collected in any one-factor repeated measures investigation can be used to test the sphericity assumption. This test was developed by J. W. Mauchley in 1940, and researchers now refer to it as the Mauchley sphericity test. If the application of **Mauchley's test** yields a statistically significant result (thus suggesting that the condition of sphericity does not exist), there are various things the researcher can do in an effort to help avoid making a Type I error when the one-way repeated measures ANOVA is used to test the null hypothesis of equal population means across the levels of the repeated measures factor. The two most popular strategies both involve using a smaller pair of *df* values to determine the critical *F*-value used to evaluate the calculated F-value. This adjustment results in a larger critical value and a greater likelihood that a fail-to-reject decision will be made when the null hypothesis of the one-way repeated measures ANOVA is evaluated.

One of the two ways to adjust the df values is to use a simple procedure developed by two statisticians, S. Geisser and S. W. Greenhouse. Their procedure involves basing the critical F-value on the df values that would have been appropriate if there had been just two levels of the repeated measures factor. This creates a drastic reduction in the critical value's dfs, because it presumes that the sphericity assumption is violated to the maximum extent. Thus, the **Geisser-Greenhouse** approach to dealing with significant departures from sphericity creates a **conservative F-test** (since the true Type I error rate will be smaller than that suggested by the level of significance).

The second procedure for adjusting the degrees of freedom involves first using the sample data to estimate how extensively the sphericity assumption is violated. This step leads to ε, a fraction that turns out to be smaller than 1.0 to the extent that the sample data suggest that the sphericity assumption is violated. Then, the "regular" df values associated with the F-test are multiplied by ε, thus producing adjusted df values and a critical value that are tailor-made for the study being conducted.

In Excerpt 16.12, we see a case in which the authors deserve credit for being concerned about the sphericity assumption. Notice that they employed the first of the two strategies just discussed. Mauchley's test was first applied to the sample data, followed by the utilization of the Geisser-Greenhouse conservative df values because the Mauchley test turned out significant.

Excerpt 16.12   The Geisser-Greenhouse Conservative F-Test Procedure Applied Following Significant Results from Mauchley's Sphericity Test

---

The first set of hypotheses was tested by conducting a separate repeated measures, one-way analysis of variance (ANOVA) [for each dependent variable]. . . . Geisser and Greenhouse's (1958) procedure was used to adjust the degrees of freedom for all F tests because the Mauchley sphericity tests were significant (i.e., the homogeneity of variance assumption was violated: Jaccard and Ackerman, 1985).

Source: M. V. Ellis. (1991). Critical incidents in supervision: Assessing supervisory issues. *Journal of Counseling Psychology, 38*(3), p. 345.

It is possible for researchers to demonstrate a concern for the sphericity assumption *without* applying the Mauchley test to their data sets. They can do this by applying a simple three-step strategy. First, they compare the calculated F-value against a critical F based on unadjusted df values. If this comparison produces a fail-to-reject decision, then the researcher can stop and be confident that the null hypothesis should not be rejected, because this comparison is positively biased in assuming that the sphericity assumption is fully true. If this first step reveals that the calculated F is equal to or larger than the critical value, then the calculated value is reassessed, this time using the conservative Geisser-Greenhouse df values for locating the critical value. If this second step produces a reject decision, then the researcher can stop and be confident that the null hypothesis should be rejected, for this comparison is negatively biased since it assumes maximum violation of the sphericity assumption. If the second step is reached and it turns out that the calculated F-value is smaller than the conservative critical F-value, the researcher can then use the sample data to compute ε and compare the calculated F-value against a more proper critical value. This strategy for dealing with the sphericity assumption is nice, because it often allows the researcher to make a quick, confident decision about the null hypothesis being tested at the end of the first or second step.

In Excerpt 16.13, we see an example of how a pair of researchers described the use of the three-step approach to dealing with the sphericity assumption.

Excerpt 16.13   Dealing with the Sphericity Assumption Without Applying Mauchley's Test

To control for the liberalization of the F test when the sphericity assumption is not met, the adjusted F test three-step decision making procedure recommended by Greenhouse and Geisser (1959) was employed (for details, see Kirk, 1982, pp. 500–505). In this report, the use of the conventional F test, the conservative F test, and the Greenhouse-Geisser epsilon correction for the lack of sphericity will be indicated by F_{conv}, F_{cons}, and F_{eps}, respectively.

Source: M. Bouffard, and A. E. Wall. (1991). Knowledge, decision making, and performance in table tennis by educable mentally handicapped adolescents. *Adapted Physical Education Quarterly, 8*, p. 64.

Regardless of which strategy is used to deal with the sphericity assumption, we want to reiterate our earlier statement that this is an important assumption for the ANOVAs being discussed in this chapter (and also the ANOVAs in Chapter 17). If a researcher conducts a repeated measures ANOVA and does not say anything at all about the sphericity assumption, the conclusions drawn from that investigation probably ought to be considered with a *big* grain of salt. If the data analysis produces a statistically significant finding when no test of sphericity is conducted or no adjustment is made to the critical value's *df*, we believe that you should disregard the inferential claims made by the researcher.

TWO-WAY REPEATED MEASURES ANOVA
DIFFERENT LABELS FOR THIS KIND OF ANOVA

It would be nice if everyone used the same label when referring to a **two-way repeated measures ANOVA,** but they don't. Most researchers use the term **two-way within-subjects ANOVA** or **two-way ANOVA with repeated measures on both factors.** A few researchers, however, use the term **multiple treatments-by-subjects ANOVA** or **treatments-by-treatments-by-subjects ANOVA** when referring to the same kind of analysis. You will need to recognize these labels as being synonymous, because it is unlikely that any rule will soon be passed forcing researchers to use the same label when referring to the ANOVA to which we now turn our attention.

In Excerpts 16.14–16.15, we see the way different labels have been used in connection with the ANOVA considered in this section of the chapter. Notice how the term *within-group analyses* was used in the second of these excerpts. It is very similar to the term *within-subjects analyses,* and it means the same thing.

Excerpts 16.14–16.15 Different Labels for a Two-Way Repeated Measures ANOVA

Data from the CIRP with all students ($N = 48$) were analyzed by means of a 2×2 [(condition: large vs. small) $\times$ (time: pretest vs. posttest)] ANOVA, with repeated measures across both factors.

Source: E. S. Shapiro and R. Goldberg. (1990). *In vivo* rating of treatment acceptability by children: Group size effects in group contingencies to improve spelling performance. *Journal of School Psychology, 28,* p. 245.

Analyses of variance were conducted separately for the auditory and visual conditions for central sites F_z, C_z, P_z, and O_z. These were 2×4 two-way within-group analyses, crossing repetition condition (repeated words vs. non-repeated words) with electrode site.

Source: P. Domalski, M. E. Smith, and E. Halgreen. (1991). Cross-modal repetition effect on the N4. *Psychological Science, 2*(3), p. 174.

PURPOSE

The purpose of a two-way repeated measures ANOVA is identical to the purpose of a two-way ANOVA not having repeated measures. In each case, the researcher uses inferential statistics to help assess three null hypotheses. The first of these null hypotheses deals with the main effect of one of the two factors.

The second null hypothesis deals with the main effect of the second factor. The third null hypothesis deals with the interaction between the two factors.

Although two-way ANOVAs with and without repeated measures are identical in the number and nature of null hypotheses that are evaluated, they differ in two main respects. In terms of the way data are collected, the kind of two-way ANOVA considered in Chapter 14 requires that each subject be "positioned in" a single cell, with only one score per subject going into the data analysis. In contrast, a two-way repeated measures ANOVA requires that each subject "travel" across all cells created by the two factors, with each subject being measured once within *each* cell. The second main difference between two-way ANOVAs with and without repeated measures involves the ANOVA summary table. We will return to this second difference in the next section when we consider how researchers present the results of their two-way repeated measures ANOVAs. Right now, we want to concentrate on the three null hypotheses dealt with by this ANOVA and the way the necessary data must be collected.

To accomplish the dual goals of this section, we wish to look at a portion of a real study that used a two-way repeated measures ANOVA. The study we want to examine comes from the field of motor behavior, an area of research where researchers investigate the way in which humans perform movement tasks. As you will see from the study we want to examine, research in the field of motor behavior often involves tightly controlled laboratory experiments that focus on arm movements and reaction time.

In our example study, 12 right-handed undergraduate college students were used as subjects. On each of eight separate days, each subject sat in front of a table when performing the motor behavior task. On top of the table were three round brass disks affixed to the table in a row parallel to the front edge of the table. The disk on the subject's right was the "starting" disk, and the subject began by resting the tip of a penlike stylus on this disk. Upon hearing an auditory stimulus (a loud tone), the subject's task involved quickly moving the stylus to the left and tapping either one or both of the so-called "target" disks. The brass disks were connected, by wires beneath the table, to clocks that could record (in milliseconds) how long it took the subject to (a) get the stylus off the first disk after hearing the tone and (b) complete the task by tapping the target disk(s). The clocks were connected to the auditory stimulus such that they began timing the subject as soon as the auditory stimulus was given.

On each of the eight days, or sessions, of data collection, each of 12 subjects performed the motor behavior task 150 times, with 75 trials involving instructions that the subject tap only the target disk located immediately to the left of the starting disk and with the other 75 trials involving instructions that told the subject to tap both of the target disks. Four of the eight sessions were set up such that the 75 one-target trials came first, followed by the 75 two-target trials; the other four sessions were arranged such that the two sets of trials occurred in the opposite order. One of the dependent variables of the study was reaction time, operationalized as the length of time the stylus remained on the "starting" disk after the auditory stimulus was provided. The data gathered during each session were collapsed across trials by computing the mean reaction time for each set of 75 trials. Thus, each subject provided two reaction time scores (each a mean) per session, one indicating performance on the one-target task and the other indicating performance on the two-target task.

In the part of the study dealing with reaction time, the researchers used a two-way repeated measures ANOVA to help them investigate three questions. First, they wondered whether there would be a main effect for Target Condition (and they predicted that reaction time would be slower when subjects were told to tap both the target disks). Next, they wondered whether there would be a main effect for Sessions (with no prediction made as to whether reaction time would improve—or possibly become worse—over the eight sessions of the study). Finally, the researchers wondered whether there would be an interaction between Target Condition and Sessions (and they predicted that any difference between the reaction time to the one- and two-target conditions would evaporate by the end of the eighth session).

In Excerpt 16.16, we see a table presenting the descriptive statistics for the portion of the motor behavior study just described. Each of the means

Excerpt 16.16   Cell Means from the Two-Way Repeated Measures Study on Reaction Time

Table 2

Descriptive statistics of RT data (in ms) as a function of target conditions and test sessions, experiment 2

| | Target condition | | | |
| | One target | | Two targets | |
Session	M	SD	M	SD
1	181	30	192	41
2	164	26	172	24
3	156	19	165	17
4	151	12	162	16

(Continued)

Excerpt 16.16 Cell Means from the Two-Way Repeated Measures Study on Reaction Time *(Continued)*

	Target condition			
	One target		*Two targets*	
Session	*M*	*SD*	*M*	*SD*
5	148	12	155	16
6	147	15	156	19
7	148	15	158	15
8	147	8	153	14

Source: M. G. Fischman, and C. Lim. (1991). Influence of extended practice on programming time, movement time, and transfer in simple target-striking responses. *Journal of Motor Behavior, 23*(1), p. 42. (Adapted slightly for inclusion here.)

contained in this table is based on 12 scores, each of which was itself the mean of 75 reaction time values. The first important thing to realize about Excerpt 16.16 is that the same 12 subjects provided the data upon which each of the 16 means was based. The second important thing to notice about the data in Excerpt 16.16 is that each of the 16 means corresponds to a cell within a two-dimensional matrix. One dimension (i.e., factor) is Target Condition; the other dimension, or factor, is Session.

In trying to understand the way the data from the reaction time study (or *any* two-way repeated measures ANOVA study) were collected and arranged for analysis, we suggest that you construct, either in your mind or on paper, a picture similar to that contained in Figure 16.2. Such a picture shows how many subjects were involved, what the two factors were, and what levels went together to form each factor. In addition, this kind of picture conveys the idea that each subject is measured repeatedly across the levels of both factors.[4]

Illustrations such as that presented in Figure 16.2 rarely appear in research reports. Nevertheless, it is quite easy to construct such pictures when trying to decipher the results of a two-way repeated measures ANOVA. This picture-constructing task is easy because you will be given information as to (1) the factors and levels involved in the study, (2) the nature of the dependent variable, and (3) the sample means that were computed.

---

[4]*A picture showing how the data were arranged for analysis may not reflect accurately how the data were collected. For example, if you will recall the procedures associated with the reaction time study, the ordering of the two target conditions was reversed on half the sessions.*

		Session 1		Session 2			Session 8	
		One Target	Two Target	One Target	Two Target	...	One Target	Two Target
	1	158	159	144	149		144	150
	2	228	287	166	182		149	145
	3	229	239	229	225		157	165
	4	166	153	162	165		144	146
	5	180	171	174	164		145	156
Subjects	6	160	202	146	167		154	154
	7	224	209	175	182		149	169
	8	184	212	170	190		147	160
	9	178	178	178	178		151	161
	10	149	161	145	165		151	161
	11	142	143	120	125		124	116
	12	174	194	163	176		147	159
Means=		181	192	164	172	...	147	153

FIGURE 16.2 *A picture showing how the data from the two-way repeated measures reaction time study were collected and arranged.*

PRESENTATION OF RESULTS

Occasionally, the results of a two-way repeated measures ANOVA will be presented using an ANOVA summary table. In Table 16.2, we have prepared such a table to correspond with the results of the motor behavior study on reaction time.

TABLE 16.2

ANOVA SUMMARY TABLE FOR THE MOTOR BEHAVIOR STUDY ON REACTION TIME

Source	df	SS	MS	F
Subjects	11	39,515.08	3,592.28	
Target conditions	1	3,852.08	3,852.08	28.41*
Target conditions × subjects	11	1,491.27	135.57	
Sessions	.7	26,114.00	3,730.57	10.78*
Sessions × subjects	77	26,654.90	346.17	
Target conditions × sessions	7	99.25	14.18	0.21
Target conditions × sessions × subjects	77	5,229.34	67.91	
Total	191	102,955.92		

*$p < .001$.

The summary table shown in Table 16.2 is similar in some ways to the two-way ANOVA summary tables contained in Chapter 14, yet it is similar, in other respects, to the three-way ANOVA summary tables contained in Chapter 15. Table 16.2 is like a two-way ANOVA summary table in that three F-values are contained in the table's right-hand column. It is like a three-way ANOVA summary table in that (1) the row for Subjects functions, in some respects, like a third factor of the study and (2) the numerical values on the third, fifth, and seventh rows of the table are computed in the same way as would be the case if this were a three-way ANOVA.

Although Table 16.2 contains certain features that might make it seem, on first glance, to have come from a three-way ANOVA, it definitely shows the results of a two-way repeated measures ANOVA. You can determine this by noting that only three F-values are presented, one for each main effect (Target Conditions and Sessions) and one for the interaction between the two factors. No F-value is computed for the "main effect" of Subjects or for any of the "interactions" that involve Subjects. In fact, if you will look closely at how the mean squares on the third, fifth, and seventh rows were used, you will see that these MS values were divided into the MS values on the second, fourth, and sixth rows, respectively, in order to obtain the three F-values contained in the table. In other words, the sources that have Subjects involved in an apparent interaction are actually three different errors. Each is used solely to help compute one of the three calculated F-values used to answer the research questions of the two-factor study.

If you ever encounter a summary of results like that presented in Table 16.2, do not overlook the valuable information sitting in front of you. From such a table, you can determine how many subjects were involved in the study ($11 + 1 = 12$), what the dependent variable was (reaction time), what the two factors were (Target Conditions and Sessions) and how many levels made up each factor ($1 + 1 = 2$ and $7 + 1 = 8$, respectively), how many total pieces of data were involved in the data analysis ($191 + 1 = 192$), and which of the F-values turned out to be statistically significant.

In Excerpt 16.17, we see the way the results from the reaction time study were actually presented in the journal article that summarized the study. Notice that a working knowledge of degrees of freedom should allow you to construct much of Table 16.2 simply on the basis of the information presented here.

In this study on reaction time, no post hoc test was needed to probe the statistically significant main effect of Target Condition, since there were only two levels of this factor. In contrast, a follow-up test was applied in an effort to pinpoint the reasons for the significant main effect of Sessions. The post hoc test was needed here because there were more than two levels in the Sessions factor.

In Excerpt 16.17, the main effect F-values were interpreted by the researchers because the interaction F turned out to be nonsignificant. If the in-

---

Excerpt 16.17   Results from the Text of the Study on Reaction Time

---

A 2 × 8 (Target Condition × Test Session) ANOVA, with repeated measures on both factors, revealed a significant main effect for target condition, $F(1, 11) = 28.41$, $p < .001$, indicating that overall RT for the one-target condition ($M = 155$ms, $SD = 21$) was faster than for the two-target condition ($M = 164$ ms, $SD = 24$). . . .

The main effect for test session was also significant, $F(7, 77) = 10.78$, $p < .001$, and a Tukey WSD follow-up test at the .05 level revealed that RT on Session 1 was slower than on Sessions 3 to 8, and there were no RT differences between Sessions 1 and 2 or Sessions 2 through 8. Finally, the interaction between factors was not significant, $F(7, 77) = < 1$.

Source: M. G. Fischman, and C. Lim. (1991). Influence of extended practice on programming time, movement time, and transfer in simple target-striking responses. *Journal of Motor Behavior, 23*(1), pp. 44–45.

---

teraction null hypothesis had been rejected, the researchers probably would have paid very little attention to the main effects. Instead, they most likely would have focused their post hoc investigation on the cell means. They probably would have done this in one of two ways, either through tests of simple main effects or through a full set of pairwise comparisons constrasting each cell mean against each of the other cell means.

In Excerpt 16.18, we see an example where a post hoc investigation was conducted on the cell means because the interaction null hypothesis was rejected. It is unclear, we feel, precisely how the post hoc test was conducted. It may have

---

Excerpt 16.18   A Post Hoc Investigation to Probe a Significant
                    Interaction

Statistical analyses of averaged data were accomplished using a 2×4 (Condition × Weight) analysis of variance, with repeated measures on both factors. Post hoc analyses were done using the Tukey's HSD test. . . . There were significant main effects for weight, $F(3,27) = 17.57$, $p < .0001$, and condition, $F(1,9) = 10.52$, $p = .0101$, and significant Weight × Condition interaction, $F(3,27) = 5.88$, $p = .0032$. Post hoc analysis (Tukey's HSD) for the interaction revealed that in the random condition, presentation of the 410-g dowel resulted in longer movement times than the 20-, 55-, and 150-g dowels; whereas in the blocked condition, the movement time to the 410-g dowel was significantly longer than to the 20-g dowel. For each weight, the blocked trials were significantly faster than the random trials.

Source: P. L. Weir, C. L. MacKenzie, R. G. Marteniuk, S. L. Cargoe, and M. D. Frazer. (1991). The effects of object weight on the Kinematics of Prehension. *Journal of Motor Behavior, 23*(3) p. 194.

been that six Tukey tests were applied to probe the simple main effects, with each Tukey test comparing the cell means located on one of the rows or on one of the columns of the 2 × 4 matrix of cells. Or, it may have been that a single Tukey test compared all eight cells in a pairwise fashion. Regardless of how the Tukey test was applied, we wish to commend the researchers for using the significant interaction as a signal calling for additional examination of the data.

THE PRESENTATION ORDER OF DIFFERENT TASKS

Earlier in this chapter, we indicated how a repeated measures factor can take one of three basic forms: different points in time, different treatment conditions, or different versions of a measuring instrument. With a two-way repeated measures ANOVA, any combination of these three kinds of factors is possible. The most popular combinations, however, involve either (1) two factors, each of which is defined by different versions (i.e., levels) of a treatment, or (2) one treatment factor and one factor that involves measurements taken at different points in time. The study in Excerpt 16.18 illustrates the use of two treatment-type factors, while the study in Excerpt 16.17 is representative of the kind of two-way repeated measures ANOVA in which there is one treatment-type factor and one time-type factor.

If both of the factors involve measuring subjects at different points in time (e.g., at 8:00 A.M., noon, 4:00 P.M., and 8:00 P.M. on each of six consecutive days), there is only one way in which to order the levels of each factor. If, however, at least one of the factors is made up of different treatment conditions or different versions of a measuring instrument, certain problems (such as a practice effect, fatigue effect, sequence effect, or carry-over effect) may occur and may hinder clear interpretations regarding any of the F-values that appear in the ANOVA summary table or in any post hoc investigation. For this reason, researchers typically present the levels of the repeated measures factor(s) in different orders—that is, in different sequences—when possible.

In Excerpts 16.19–16.20, we see cases in which studies were set up such that varying presentation orders of treatments were built into the research design. Notice that in the first of these studies, both factors contained levels that represented different treatment conditions; in the second study, however, only one of the two factors allowed for different presentation orders of its levels. Also notice that the technique of randomizing the orders for individual subjects was used in the first study whereas the order of the treatment conditions in the second study were purposefully "balanced" (thus assuring that each subject experienced each of the two possible orders on half of the sessions).[5]

---

[5] *Although this is not explicitly stated in the journal article, we highly suspect that half of the subjects performed the one-target task first on any given day while the remaining subjects performed the two-target task first.*

Excerpts 16.19–16.20   Different Presentation Orders in Two-Way Repeated Measures ANOVAS

A repeated measures design was used in which each subject completed the three patterns for one, three, four, and five cycles. Each pattern/cycle combination was completed during a separate session, such that 12 sessions were required to collect all of the data. The order in which the subjects completed the 12 combinations was randomized. Thus, no two subjects received the same combination on consecutive days.

Source: P. VanDonkelaar and I. M. Franks. (1990). Reaction time and reproduction accuracy in tapping movements with varying temporal structure. *Journal of Human Movement Studies, 18*(2), p. 54.

Subjects performed 50 trials each of the one-target and two-target conditions on 8 separate days, with not more than 4 days between testing sessions. The order of the conditions was balanced over days for each subject so that on 4 days the subject performed 50 trials of the one-target condition first, followed by the two-target condition, and on the alternating 4 days, this order was reversed.

Source: M. G. Fischman, and C. Lim. (1991). Influence of extended practice on programming of extended practice on programming time, movement time, and transfer in simple target-striking responses. *Journal of Motor Behavior, 23*(1), p. 41.

THE SPHERICITY ASSUMPTION

The calculated F-values that are computed in a two-way repeated measure ANOVA will turn out to be too large unless the population variances and correlations that correspond to the sample data conform, collectively, to one or more acceptable patterns. This is the case even though the sample variances and correlations in a two-way repeated measures ANOVA are based upon sample sizes that are equal (a condition brought about by measuring the same subjects repeatedly). Therefore, it is important that researchers, when using this kind of ANOVA, attend to the assumption concerning population variances and correlations. This assumption is popularly referred to as the sphericity assumption.

Any of three strategies can be used when dealing with sphericity assumption. As is the case with a one-way repeated measures ANOVA, the researcher can (1) subject the sample data to Mauchley's test for sphericity, (2) bypass Mauchley's test and instead use the Geisser-Greenhouse conservative *df*s for locating the critical value needed to evaluate the calculated F-values, or (3) utilize the sample data to compute ε (the index that estimates how badly the sphericity assumption is violated) and then reduce the critical value(s) *df*s to the extent indicated by the ε index.

Although the second of these strategies is the easiest to implement, it carries with it the disadvantage of producing overly conservative F-tests, since it reduces critical value dfs too much (because it assumes the worst-case scenario in terms of the sphericity assumption). The third strategy, in which ε is used, is more difficult to implement but seems to us to be the best strategy. We would not use the first strategy, in which the Mauchley test is conducted, because we would want to utilize ε to reduce critical value dfs *regardless of the outcome.*[6]

Even though we consider certain of the strategies for dealing with the sphericity assumption to be preferable to the others, we consider *any* of the strategies to be far superior to the "strategy" of paying no attention at all to the assumption of sphericity. Unfortunately, many researchers use two-way repeated measures ANOVAs without attending to this important assumption. When you encounter a study wherein the sphericity assumption *is* consid-

---

Excerpt 16.21   Concern for the Sphericity Assumption in a Two-Way Repeated Measures ANOVA

A multiple treatments-by-subjects analysis of variance (ANOVA) design was used to determine whether changes occurred in T_{re}, T_{sk}, HR and RPE between the experimental conditions (2 menstrual phases) and/or during the exercise bouts (6 time period). . . . If the ANOVA sphericity assumption was not met, appropriate adjustments in degrees of freedom were made.

Source: J.M. Pivarnik, C.J. Marichal, T. Spillman, and J. R. Morrow Jr. (1992). Menstrual cycle phase affects temperature regulation during endurance exercise. *Journal of Applied Physiology, 72*(2), p. 544.

---

ered, as exemplified in Excerpt 16.21, we believe that you ought to upgrade your evaluation of the completed investigation.

FULLY REPEATED MEASURES THREE-FACTOR ANOVA

Just as it is possible to have three or more factors in an ANOVA, all of which are between-subjects factors, it is possible to have more than two factors in a completely within-subjects factorial ANOVA. In this section, we want to consider the case of a three-way fully repeated measures ANOVA. Evidence that such ANOVAs are used by researchers is presented in Excerpts 16.22–16.24.

---

[6]*Remember, failing-to-reject a null hypothesis should not be interpreted to mean that the null hypothesis is true.*

Excerpts 16.22–16.24   Use of Three-Way Repeated Measures ANOVAs

---

Data were analyzed using a 3×2×6 (Segment × Acquisition Phase × Block) ANOVA, with repeated measures on all factors.

Source: S. P. Swinnen, C. B. Walter, M. B. Beirinckx, and P. F. Muegens. (1991). Dissociation of bimanual movement. *Journal of Motor Behavior, 23*(4), p. 268.

Prolonged tie score was included in two 2×3×2 within-subjects factorial ANOVAs.

Source: Bar-Eli et al. (1991). Perceived team performance. *Journal of Applied Sport Psychology, 3,* p. 167.

The hypothesis thus to be tested was whether the inclusion of basic data with MLCs in the form specified by the expository process model would affect readers' ratings of the statements. Additionally, tests of whether readers might rate statements differently depending on whether they were based on cognitive or behavioral MLCs and whether they were rated on credibility or persuasiveness were also carried out. The sum of ratings for each condition was used as the unit of measurement. Thus, there were two levels of each of these variables, analyzed in a repeated measures, within-subjects, three-way ANOVA design.

Source: R. L. Ownby, (1990). A study of the expository process model in school psychological reports. *Psychology in the Schools, 27,* p. 356.

PURPOSE

In using a three-way repeated measures ANOVA, a researcher normally wants to find out whether differential effects are associated with one or more of the three factors involved in the study. This general research question typically is broken down into seven specific questions, each of which is assessed using an *F*-test. If we let A, B, and C stand for the three factors involved in the study, these seven specific questions deal with three main effects (A, B, and C), three two-way interactions (A × B, A × C, and B × C), and one three-way interaction (A × B × C).[7]

In order to understand the results yielded by a three-way repeated measures ANOVA, you must first have the ability to conceptualize the way in which the data of the study were collected. For this reason, we want you to consider an extremely small-scale hypothetical study. This study involves eight insomniacs who serve as subjects in an experiment designed to compare the effectiveness of two brands of over-the-counter sleeping medication.

---

[7] *Two-way and three-way interactions are sometimes referred to as first-order and second-order interactions, respectively.*

	Excedrin PM				Tylenol PM			
	1 Pill		2 Pills		1 Pill		2 Pills	
	W[a]	M[b]	W	M	W	M	W	M
Subject 1	7	6	9	7	6	8	8	6
Subject 2	5	5	8	6	7	9	9	7
Subject 3	4	4	7	5	5	7	7	5
Subject 4	4	6	8	8	6	4	8	6
Subject 5	3	5	7	7	5	3	7	7
Subject 6	4	4	7	5	7	9	9	7
Subject 7	3	3	6	4	4	6	6	4
Subject 8	4	4	7	5	3	5	8	8

[a]W = water, [b]M = milk

FIGURE 16.3 *Hypothetical data for our make-believe three-factor fully within-subjects experiment.*

In our little study on restful sleep, we'll set things up such that there are three factors, each of which has two levels. The first factor is Brand (Excedrin PM versus Tylenol PM), the second factor is Dosage (1 pill versus 2 pills), and the third factor is Liquid (Milk versus Water). Our study lasts for eight nights, with each subject on each night consuming either one or two pills of either Excedrin PM or Tylenol PM with eight ounces of either milk or water immediately before going to bed.[8] The dependent variable will be self-rating, on a 0-to-10, scale of the quality of sleep experienced during the night, with these ratings collected at 8:00 A.M. on the morning following each night of the study.

The data from our hypothetical study might turn out as indicated in Figure 16.3. (Although the data in this figure have been arranged so as to facilitate not only the data analysis but also an understanding of the results, it should be noted that Figure 16.3 does *not* indicate how our study would actually be conducted. To prevent sequence or carry-over effects from affecting the results, we would present the eight treatment conditions to the subjects in different orders, either by using randomized orders or by using a systematic set of orders ensuring that each night of the experiment involved four pills of each brand, four levels of each dosage, and four kinds of each liquid.)

---

[8]*To standardize things a bit in our study, all subjects would be asked to engage in the same work, leisure, and exercise activities during the study. They also would be given the same amount and kind of food, and they all would be told to retire at the same time each night.*

The hypothetical researcher associated with our little experiment on insomniacs would be able to answer seven questions after looking at the results of the data analysis. Each of these questions takes the same form: "Should the null hypothesis of _____ be rejected?" The blank in this question would be filled seven times. The "inserts" are as follows: (1) no difference between the two brands, (2) no difference between the two dosage levels, (3) no difference between the two liquids, (4) no interaction between brand and dosage, (5) no interaction between brand and liquid, (6) no interaction between dosage and liquid, and (7) no interaction between brand, dosage, and level. Each of these seven questions, of course, would have relevance to the dependent variable of the study, self-rating of sleep quality.

PRESENTATION OF RESULTS

The results of a three-way repeated measures ANOVA can be (and sometimes are) displayed in an ANOVA summary table. To illustrate what such a table looks like, we have analyzed the hypothetical data from our make-believe study on insomniacs and put the results in Table 16.3.

TABLE 16.3
RESULTS FROM THE HYPOTHETICAL STUDY ON INSOMNIACS

Source	df	SS	MS	F
Subjects	7	44.61	6.37	
Brand	1	13.14	13.41	4.72
Brand × subjects	7	19.48	2.78	
Dosage	1	43.89	43.89	22.37*
Dosage × subjects	7	13.73	1.96	
Liquid	1	2.64	2.64	18.78*
Liquid × subjects	7	.98	.14	
Brand × dosage	1	4.52	4.52	4.45
Brand × dosage × subjects	7	7.11	1.02	
Brand × liquid	1	.39	.39	0.24
Brand × liquid × subjects	7	11.23	1.06	
Dosage × liquid	1	19.14	19.14	29.88*
Dosage × liquid × subjects	7	4.48	.64	
Brand × dosage × liquid	1	.39	.39	0.52
Brand × dosage × liquid × subjects	7	5.23	.74	
Total	63			

*$p < .01$.

Note that *F*-values are computed for the main and interaction effects of Brand, Dosage, and Liquid. No *F* is computed for the "main effect" of Subjects or for any of the "interactions" that involve Subjects. As is the case in a two-way repeated measures ANOVA, the mean square for each "interaction" involving Subjects is used as the denominator in forming one of the *F*-values. For example, the *MS* for Brand was divided by the *MS* for Brand × Subjects in order to obtain the *F*-value for Brand.

As indicated in Table 16.3, the results from our hypothetical study on insomniacs would permit the researcher to reject (at $\alpha = .01$) the null hypothesis concerning the main effect of Dosage, the main effect of Liquid, and the first-order interaction of Dosage × Liquid. Our hypothetical researcher would probably pay more attention to the third of these three significant results, with a post hoc investigation most likely applied to compare the two liquids at each dosage level (or vice versa).

In Excerpt 16.25, we see the ANOVA summary table from a real study in which a three-way repeated measures ANOVA was used. Notice how there are seven Error rows in the table, each containing a MS used in the computation of one of the seven *F*-values. Each of these rows could have been labeled "Subjects × _____," with the blank filled with the source of the preceding row. No problem is created by using the term *Error* to label each of these rows, since no one familiar with three-way repeated measures ANOVAs

---

Excerpt 16.25 Summary Table for a Three-Way Repeated Measures ANOVA

Table 1

Manual dexterity analysis of variance with three levels of repeated measures[a]

Source	Sum of squares	DF	Mean square	F
Sessions	165.44	2	82.72	70.20**
Error	44.78	38	1.18	
Jebsen Hand Function				
Subtests[b]	11,376.56	6	1,896.09	337.70**
Error	640.07	114	5.61	
Orthotic conditions	91.08	4	22.77	33.50**
Error	51.66	76	0.68	
Sessions × Jebsen				
Subtests	13.72	12	1.14	2.07*
Error	126.15	228	0.55	

(Continued)

Excerpt 16.25 Summary Table for a Three-Way Repeated Measures ANOVA *(Continued)*

Source	Sum of squares	DF	Mean square	F
Sessions × orthotic conditions	9.73	8	1.22	1.60
Error	115.56	152	0.76	
Jebsen Subtests × orthotic conditions	44.96	24	1.87	4.23**
Error	201.88	456	0.44	
Sessions × Jebsen Subtests × conditions	19.42	48	0.40	0.87
Error	426.18	912	0.47	

[a](Sessions × Jebsen Subtests × Orthotic Conditions). [b](Jebsen, Taylor, Trieschmann, Trotter, & Howard, 1969).

*$p < .05$. **$p < .01$.

Source: E. B. Stern. (1991). Wrist extensor orthoses: Dexterity and grip strength across four styles, *American Journal of Occupational Therapy, 45*(1), p. 45.

would think that all seven of these Error rows are supposed to be filled with the same numerical values.

In Excerpt 16.26, you will find the text that accompanied the ANOVA summary table we just considered. We highly recommend that you read this passage closely because it provides an excellent illustration of how post hoc tests are often applied within a three-way ANOVA to probe a significant two-way interaction.

Excerpt 16.26 Discussion of the Results Contained in Excerpt 16.25 and Yielded by Subsequent Post Hoc Tests

RESULTS

Manual Dexterity. A 3 × 7 × 5 (Sessions × Jebsen Subtests × Orthotic Conditions) analysis of variance (ANOVA) was performed with the Biomedical Data Processing Statistical Software Package, Program 2V (Dixon, 1983). Each of the three main effects (sessions, subtests, and orthotic conditions) was significant at the $p < .01$ level, indicating that all three variables significantly influence the speed of manual dexterity (see Table 1 [not shown]).

Total dexterity showed significant improvement ($p < .01$) across the three sessions, with the seven individual subtests also showing significantly different practice effects ($p < .05$). The practice effect was not significantly different across orthotic styles.

(Continued)

Excerpt 16.26 Discussion of the Results Contained in Excerpt 16.25 and Yielded by Subsequent Post Hoc Tests *(Continued)*

Because practice similarly influenced the dexterity afforded by the five orthotic conditions, the influence that practice had on dexterity was not of particular importance to the primary question in this study. The significant practice effect, however, does raise questions of the Jebsen test's test-retest reliability in clinical practice. A post hoc analysis of total dexterity across the three sessions was performed with the Newman-Keuls Multiple Comparisons Test (the computer program was based on Winer, 1971). It showed improvement in total test times across the three sessions, with the third session being significantly faster than the second ($p < .01$) and the second significantly faster than the first ($p < .01$).

Concerning the primary research question, the ANOVA demonstrated significant difference in the dexterity trends for the orthotic conditions (i.e., free hand, Futuro, thumbhole, connector bar, and dorsal) across the seven Jebsen subtests ($p < .01$). . . . A post hoc Newman-Keuls test was therefore performed on this interaction effect.

The Newman-Keuls test compares each orthotic condition to every other orthotic condition. It is therefore possible to have a situation in which two orthoses do not differ significantly from each other, yet only one of these two orthoses differs significantly from a third orthosis.

Reviewing each subtest separately, the free hand mean time (8.73 sec) was significantly faster ($p < .01$) than that of all of the orthoses in the writing task. The dorsal (9.52 sec), connector bar (9.61 sec), and thumbhole (9.62 sec) orthoses did not differ significantly in speed, whereas the Futuro orthosis was significantly slower (9.95 sec).

In the card turning subtest, the free hand mean time (3.38 sec) was significantly faster than the Futuro ($p < .05$) as well as significantly faster than that of all of the custom-made orthoses. The Futuro (3.63 sec) and connector bar (3.78 sec) orthoses were next fastest, not differing significantly from each other in the dexterity that they afforded. The thumbhole (3.91 sec) and dorsal (4.00 sec) orthoses were significantly slower than both the Futuro ($p < .05$) and free hand ($p < .01$), but did not differ significantly from the connector bar orthosis.

Concerning the moving of small objects, the free hand mean time (5.34 sec) was significantly faster than that of all of the orthoses ($p < .01$). Next fastest in that task were the Futuro (5.78 sec) and connector bar (5.91 sec) orthoses, which did not differ significantly in their speeds. The dorsal (6.20 sec) and thumbhole (6.21 sec) orthoses did not differ significantly in their speeds. Both of these orthoses, however, were significantly slower than the Futuro ($p < .01$) and connector bar ($p < .05$) orthoses.

In the simulated feeding subtest, the free hand mean time (6.17 sec) was significantly faster than all orthoses ($p < .01$). The Futuro (6.66 sec) and dorsal

(Continued)

Excerpt 16.26   Discussion of the Results Contained in Excerpt 16.25 and Yielded by Subsequent Post Hoc Tests *(Continued)*

(6.87 sec) orthoses' speeds were not significantly different. The dorsal, connector bar (7.00 sec), and thumbhole (7.01 sec) orthoses showed no significant difference in their speeds. The connector bar and thumbhole orthoses were, however, significantly slower than the Futuro ($p < .05$) and free hand ($p < .01$).

The Futuro (310 sec) and free hand (2.96 sec) mean speeds did not differ significantly for the task of stacking checkers. The connector bar (3.25 sec), dorsal (3.31 sec), and thumbhole (3.39 sec) orthoses were significantly slower than the free hand ($p < .05$, $p < .05$, and $p < .01$, respectively), but did not differ significantly from each other or from the Futuro orthosis.

In the large light objects subtest, dexterity did not differ significantly across the five conditions (free hand, 2.65 sec; Futuro, 2.81 sec; connector bar, 2.89 sec; dorsal, 2.92 sec; thumbhole, 2.92 sec). A similar lack of significant difference was found among the speeds for moving large heavy objects (free hand, 2.75 sec; Futuro, 2.83 sec; connector bar, 2.94 sec; thumbhole, 2.94 sec; dorsal, 2.95 sec).

Source: E. B. Stern. (1991). Wrist extensor orthoses: Dexterity and grip strength across four styles. *American Journal of Occupational Therapy, 45*(1), pp. 45–46.

DISCUSSION

In this final section of our consideration of fully repeated measures analyses of variance, we wish to raise a few issues—some new, some old—that you should keep in mind when you encounter research claims based upon this kind of ANOVA. Focusing on these issues will put you in the position of being able to critique the research studies upon which such claims are based. In some cases, you may end up deciding that the conclusions drawn from the study are not justified on the basis of how data were collected and/or analyzed.

REPEATED MEASURES ANOVAS: ADVANTAGES AND DISADVANTAGES

Researchers usually have the option of (1) measuring each subject just once, under a single level of each factor involved in the study or (2) measuring each subject repeatedly, with a score collected under each level (or combination of levels) of the factor(s) involved in the study. In other words, researchers usually have the option of structuring their studies such that any factor turns out to be either between-subjects or within-subjects in nature. It is helpful to know the advantages and disadvantages associated with these two ways of designing studies.

As compared with studies in which each subject contributes a single score to the data analysis, investigations leading to a fully repeated measures

ANOVA are typically more efficient when it comes to sample sizes. In other words, the latter kind of study usually allows the researcher to assess the same null hypothesis(es) with the same level of statistical power but with a smaller number of subjects. Accordingly, fully repeated measures ANOVAs are frequently used by researchers who have a limited number of subjects available for use. Although lots of data can be collected from a small sample of subjects when all factors are within-subjects in nature, the type of population corresponding to that sample is typically narrow in nature because of the small sample size. Accordingly, the generalizability of the results from fully repeated measures ANOVAs is likely to be more limited than from a similar study using the same amount of data but set up such that each subject is measured just once.

A second way between-subjects studies and within-subjects studies differ concerns the possibility, in the latter kind of study, that either the treatment given or the measurement taken at one point in time will influence the data collected subsequently. As indicated earlier, researchers need to be sensitive to the possibility of such carry-over or sequence effects (and also sensitive to the possibility of practice or fatigue effects) whenever they collect data from the same subjects across the various levels of a factor. You should also be sensitive to the possibility of such effects when you examine a research report that involved repeated measures, and you should downgrade your evaluation of the study if various presentation orders were needed but not used. This concern, of course, never arises in studies that are fully between-subject in nature.

A third difference between ANOVAs that either do or don't involve repeated measures is that the former are generally more powerful than the latter. This means that if we hold everything else constant, fully within-subjects ANOVAs are less likely to produce inferential errors of the Type II variety than are fully between-subjects ANOVAs. This advantage associated with repeated measures ANOVAs is connected to a disadvantage, because such ANOVAs are based upon an underlying assumption that is not relevant to fully between-subjects ANOVAs. This assumption is frequently referred to as the sphericity assumption, and it should *always* be dealt with whenever a researcher uses a repeated measures ANOVA.

ADDITIVE VERSUS NONADDITIVE MODELS

With two-way or three-way repeated measures ANOVAs, we saw that the F-values in the ANOVA summary table are computed by using different MSs as the denominators in forming the calculated Fs. In some ANOVA summary tables, the rows containing these MSs will be labeled with phrases that make them look like interactions (e.g., Conditions $\times$ Subjects); in other summary tables, each of these rows carries the same one-word label, *Error*. Regardless of how the rows containing these denominator MSs are labeled, the point is that the *F*-values contained in each of the two-way and three-way summary tables in this chapter were computed by using more than one *MS* as the denominator.

When the *F*-values are computed as were those appearing in each of the two-way and three-way summary tables presented in this chapter, the ANOVA summary table is said to be based on a **nonadditive model**. This term simply means that a separate row of the ANOVA summary table is set up for each of the possible "interactions" involving the Subjects "factor." Although this is the typical way that such ANOVA summary tables will be set up, it is possible for a researcher to base the ANOVA computations on an **additive model**. If this is done, all of the "Subjects $\times$ _____" rows of the summary table are lumped together into a single row that is called "Residual."

If a fully within-subjects ANOVA is based on an additive model, all *F*-values are computed by using the *MS* for residual as the denominator. This denominator, *if the additive model is legitimate,* will be smaller than the denominator *MS*s associated with the nonadditive model, thus causing the *F*-test of the main and interaction effects to be more powerful. Although some researchers may be tempted to base their ANOVAs on the additive rather than the nonadditive model, they should do this *only* after statistical tests are conducted to see whether the additive model is reasonable. If you ever come across a research report that includes a fully repeated measures ANOVA based on an additive model, you should check to see whether the preliminary tests were conducted. Such preliminary tests typically are not required when a nonadditive model is used, since the *F*-tests here are conservative in the situation where no "interactions" with Subjects exist.

THE POSSIBILITY OF INFERENTIAL ERROR

Many researchers discuss the results of their fully repeated measures ANOVAs in such a way that it appears they have discovered Ultimate Truth. Stated differently, the language used in many research reports causes us to feel as if sample statistics and the results of inferential tests are being reified into population parameters and definitive claims. Such language ought to make you wonder whether the researchers who talk in this fashion ever were taught about Type I and Type II errors. We cannot overemphasize our concern that *you* should not forget about the possibility of inferential error whenever results are based on hypothesis testing, statistical testing, or the hybrid approach to assessing null hypotheses.

PLANNED COMPARISONS

In each of the one-way, two-way, and three-way repeated measures ANOVAs considered in this chapter, the data analysis involved a general two-step procedure. First, all main effect and interaction F-tests were computed. Then, a post hoc investigation was conducted whenever three or more means were the focus of any F-test that turned out to be statistically significant.

As we have seen in earlier chapters, researchers can conduct planned comparisons instead of (or in addition to) the general two-step strategy that seems so popular. Since planned comparisons typically allow researchers (1) to answer the precise research questions that caused their studies to be carried out and (2) to test null hypotheses with a lower probability of a Type II error, we believe that many studies can be criticized, legitimately, because planned comparisons were not used.

Because the editorial boards of most research journals rarely will publish studies in which all statistical tests yield nonsignificant results, it might appear that our concern about planned comparisons ought to be directed solely toward unpublished studies. However, the vast majority of published studies present the results of multiple statistical tests. The typical study will have "mixed" results in the sense that some of the tested null hypotheses are rejected while other null hypotheses are retained. In these studies, the failure to use planned comparisons where they could have been used may have resulted in an unnecessary Type II error.

Because planned comparisons force researchers to think carefully about what is likely to happen in their studies before any data are analyzed and because of the increased statistical power associated with planned comparisons, we feel that you should upgrade your evaluation of research reports that contain discussions of planned comparisons. This recommendation is relevant, of course, for all ANOVAs, not just those that are characterized by repeated measures on all factors.

REVIEW TERMS

Additive model

Between-subjects factor

Confounding

Counterbalancing

ε

Fatigue effect

Geisser-Greenhouse conservative
    F-test

Mauchley's test

Multiple treatments-by-
    subjects ANOVA

Nonadditive model

One-factor within-
    subjects ANOVA

One-way repeated measures ANOVA

Practice effect

Randomized blocks ANOVA

Sphericity assumption

Three-way repeated measures ANOVA

Treatments-by-treatments-by-subjects
    ANOVA

Treatments-by-subjects ANOVA

Two-way ANOVA with repeated
    measures on both factors

Two-way repeated measures ANOVA

Two-way within-subjects ANOVA

Within-subjects factor

REVIEW QUESTIONS

1. If a 2×2 ANOVA were conducted on the data supplied by 16 subjects, how many individual scores would be involved in the analysis if both factors were between-subjects in nature? What would be the answer if both factors were within-subjects in nature?

2. (True or False) Since the data analyzed in a fully repeated measures ANOVA come from subjects who are measured multiple times, the term *multivariate ANOVA* is used to describe the various analyses considered in this chapter.

3. How does the null hypothesis of a between-subjects one-way ANOVA differ from the null hypothesis of a within-subjects one-way ANOVA?

4. How many subjects were involved in the study summarized in Excerpt 16.7?

5. Why wasn't a post hoc investigation applied in Excerpt 16.9, since the F-tests turned out to be statistically significant?

6. If the two treatments of a one-way repeated measures ANOVA are presented to subjects in a counterbalanced order, how many presentation orders will there be?

7. (True or False) If a one-way repeated measures ANOVA is applied to a data set in which the sample means are all based upon the same amount of data, the researcher does not have to worry about the sphericity assumption.

8. What happens when the Geisser-Greenhouse conservative F-test procedure is used?

   a. The *df* associated with the calculated value are increased.

   b. The *df* associated with the critical value are increased.

   c. The *df* associated with the calculated value are decreased.

   d. The *df* associated with the critical value are decreased.

9. If 8 subjects are to be measured repeatedly across the 3 levels of factor A and the 4 levels of factor B, how many *df* will be associated with each source in the ANOVA summary table?

10. How many subjects provided data for the results presented in Excerpt 16.18?

11. The ANOVA summary table presented below is nearly identical to one that recently appeared in a journal article. Based on the information contained in this table, determine (a) the number of subjects involved in the study, (b) the number of times each subject was measured, and (c) the total number of scores used in the analysis.

Source	Sum of squares	df	Mean square	F
A	2,339.91	4	584.98	28.24**
Error	1,574.44	76	20.72	
B	122.65	2	61.32	4.61*
Error	505.47	38	13.30	
A × B	176.37	8	22.05	3.57**
Error	937.51	152	6.17	

$*p<.05$ $**p<.01$.

12. How many F-values appear in the summary table for a three-way repeated measures ANOVA?

13. In the sixth paragraph of Excerpt 16.26, five sample means are presented. How many pieces of data was each of these means based on?

14. (True or False) Although repeated measures ANOVAs allow researchers to collect lots of data from a small group of subjects, they involve F-tests that are more likely to result in Type II errors than is the case when the same amount of data is collected in a fully between-subjects design.

15. Are most two-way and three-way repeated measures ANOVAs based on an additive model or a nonadditive model?

Mixed ANOVAs

In Chapters 14 and 15, we considered two-way and three-way completely between-subjects ANOVAs. In Chapter 16, we looked at two-way and three-way completely within-subjects ANOVAs. Now we want to consider the ANOVAs used by researchers when their studies contain at least one between-subjects factor and at least one within-subjects factor. Not surprisingly, the analyses of variance that fall into this category are called **mixed ANOVAs**.

We focus our attention on the three kinds of mixed ANOVA used most frequently by applied researchers. These include (1) a two-way ANOVA in which there is one between-subjects factor and one within-subjects factor, (2) a three-way ANOVA in which there are two between-subjects factors and one within-subjects factor, and (3) a three-way ANOVA in which there is one between-subjects factor and two within-subjects factors. Although mixed ANOVAs can take other, more complicated forms (e.g., a five-way ANOVA with two between-subjects factors and three within-subjects factors), our focus on two-way and three-way mixed ANOVAs will give you a familiarity with the vast majority of mixed ANOVAs you are likely to encounter—and it also will provide you with a solid foundation for trying to understand the higher-order mixed ANOVAs that are sometimes used.

Two-Way Mixed ANOVAs

We begin our examination of mixed ANOVAs with a consideration of the simplest case of this kind of ANOVA, the two-factor case. With this form of ANOVA, one of the two factors is between-subjects in nature while the other factor is within-subjects.

LABELS FOR THIS KIND OF ANOVA

Various terms are used to denote the kind of ANOVA considered in this section. These labels include the following: a **two-way ANOVA with repeated measures on one factor**, a **two-way mixed ANOVA,** an **ANOVA with _____ as the between-subjects factor and _____ as the within-subjects factor**, a **two-way between-within ANOVA**, a **two-factor split-plot ANOVA**, and a **Lindquist Type I ANOVA**. In Excerpts 17.1–17.5, we see examples of how different researchers have used many of these labels. As you look at these excerpts, note that a two-way mixed ANOVA was used multiple times in three of the studies, because each of these studies involved data on multiple dependent variables. In two of the studies, there was only one set of data analyzed by the two-way mixed ANOVA.

Excerpts 17.1–17.5   Different Labels for a Two-Way Mixed ANOVA

Two-factor (Condition × Time Delay) mixed analyses of variance (ANOVAs) were calculated on the basis of these aggregated SRF scores.

Source: J. D. Berger and L. G. Herringer. (1991). Individual differences in eyewitness recall accuracy. *The Journal of Social Psychology, 131,* p. 811.

First, as a rough check on the possibility of differential levels of treatment induced stress, the daily weights of the animals were analyzed by computing a 3 (treatments) × 10 (days) factor analysis of variance with repeated measures on the second factor (days).

Source: J. Puentes, J. Bautista, R. Mistry, N. Phillips, and R. A. Hicks. (1992). The effects of REM sleep deprivation on the metabolic rates of male rats. *Bulletin of the Psychonomic Society, 30*(1), p. 40.

A repeated measures analysis of variance (ANOVA), with conditions (high and low arousal) as the between-subjects variable and time (five repeated measures) as the within-subjects variable, yielded . . . .

Source: D. H. Olson and C. O. Claiborn. (1990). Interpretation and arousal in the counseling process. *Journal of Counseling Psychology, 37,* p. 134.

To analyze the long-term effects of writing, a series of 2 (Condition) × 2 (Day) between-within repeated-measures ANOVAS were performed on the various blood values and personality measures of interest. In addition, absentee days were analyzed using a 2 (Condition) × 5 (Period) between-within repeated-measures ANOVA.

Source: S. M. Levy and G. Muchow. (1992). Provider compliance with recommended dietary fluoride supplement protocol. *American Journal of Public Health, 6*(4), p. 283.

(Continued)

> **Excerpts 17.1–17.5**   Different Labels for a Two-Way Mixed ANOVA
> *(Continued)*
>
> ---
>
> Three split-plot factorial analyses of variance (ANOVAs) (Kirk, 1982) were
> conducted to analyze scores obtained on the cognitive, social, and school-appro-
> priate behavior domains of the Teachable Pupil Survey. These ANOVAs had one
> between- and one within-group factor.
>
> ---
>
> *Source:* L. J. Johnson, and M. C. Pugach. (1991). Peer collaboration: Accommodating students with
> mild learning and behavior problems. *Exceptional Children, 57,* p. 458.

You will occasionally encounter the term *two-way repeated measures
ANOVA*. Such an ANOVA could be fully repeated measures in nature (like
the kind considered in the previous chapter) or it could be of the mixed variety. Normally, the nature of the two factors will allow you to make an educated guess as to which kind of ANOVA is being discussed. For example, we
would guess that the ANOVA discussed in Excerpt 17.6 was a two-way
mixed ANOVA. We suspect that Time was a within-subjects factor and that
Gender was a between-subjects factor.

> **Excerpt 17.6**   Use of the Generic Term *Repeated Measures ANOVA* to
> Describe a Two-Way Mixed ANOVA
>
> ---
>
> A commitment-to-running index was computed by summing, on a 5-point
> Likert scale, 12 questions that asked runners to rate their general feelings about
> running. Scores for this index ranged from 12 to 60, with 60 representing the
> highest amount of commitment. These scores were then analyzed in a 2 × 5
> (Gender × Time) repeated measures ANOVA.
>
> ---
>
> *Source:* D. L. Feltz, C. D. Lirgg, and R. R. Albrecht. (1992). Psychological implications of competitive
> running in elite young distance runners: A longitudinal analysis. *The Sport Psychologist, 6*(2), p. 132.

DATA LAYOUT AND PURPOSE

To understand the results of a two-way mixed ANOVA, you must be able to
conceptualize the way the data were arranged prior to being analyzed.
Whenever we deal with this kind of ANOVA, we always think of (or actually
draw) a picture similar to the one displayed in Figure 17.1. Our picture is set
up for an extremely small-scale study, but it illustrates how each subject is
measured repeatedly across levels of the within-subjects factor but not across
levels of the between-subjects factor. In our picture, of course, the between-
subjects factor is Gender and the within-subjects factor is Time of Day. The
scores are hypothetical, and they are meant to reflect the data that might be

Gender		Time of Day		
		8 A.M.	2 P.M.	8 P.M.
Male	Subject 1	6	9	5
	Subject 2	7	6	6
	Subject 3	4	7	6
	Subject 4	9	8	3
	Subject 5	5	7	9
Female	Subject 6	6	8	10
	Subject 7	8	7	2
	Subject 8	5	8	4
	Subject 9	8	7	7
	Subject 10	7	4	6

FIGURE 17.1 *Picture of the data layout for a 2 × 3 mixed ANOVA.*

collected if we asked each of five males and five females to give us a self-rating of his or her typical energy level (on a 0–10 scale) at each of three points during the day: 8 A.M., 2 P.M., and 8 P.M.

Although a two-way mixed ANOVA always involves one between-subjects factor and one within-subjects factor, the numbers of levels in these factors will vary from study to study. In other words, the dimensions and labeling of Figure 17.1 only "match" our hypothetical two-way mixed ANOVA in which there is a two-level between-subjects factor, a three-level within-subjects factor, and five subjects per group. Our picture can easily be adapted to fit *any* two-way mixed ANOVA, because we can change the number of main rows and columns, the number of mini-rows (to indicate the number of subjects involved), and the terms used to reflect the names of the factors and levels involved in the study.

The purpose of a two-way mixed ANOVA is identical to that of a completely between-subjects two-way ANOVA or of a completely within-subjects two-way ANOVA. In general, that purpose can be described as examining the sample means to see if they are further apart than would be expected by chance. Most researchers take this general purpose and make it more specific by setting up and testing three null hypotheses. These null hypotheses, of course, focus on the populations relevant to the investigation, with the three null statements asserting that (1) the main effect means of the first factor are equal to one another, (2) the main effect means of the second factor are equal to one another, and (3) the two factors do not interact.

If the data in Figure 17.1 were subjected to a two-way mixed ANOVA, one research question would be tied to the main effect of Gender. To answer this question, the mean of the 15 scores provided by the 5 males would be compared against the mean of the 15 scores provided by the 5 females. The second research question, which concerns the main effect of Time of Day, would be addressed through a statistical comparison of the 8 A.M., 2 P.M. and 8 P.M. means (each of which would be based on the scores from all 10 subjects). The third research question, dealing with the interaction between Gender and Time of Day, would be dealt with by focusing on the six cell means (each based on 5 scores) and would ask whether the difference between the male and female means at 8 A.M. is similar, within the limits of chance sampling, to the male/female differences at 2 P.M. and at 8 P.M.

Although information such as that contained in Figure 17.1 is never included in a research report, tables showing the main effect and cell means sometimes are provided. In Excerpt 17.7, we see such a table. Tables like this help to clarify what questions are being dealt with by two-way mixed ANOVAs. In Excerpt 17.7, for example, it is easy to see that the main effect F for Adaptation group was concerned with the four means presented in the Total column on the right side of the table. It is also easy to see that the main effect F for Time focused on the two means presented in the row labeled "Total." Finally, this table allows us to see the eight cell means focused upon by the interaction F (and also to see that the first three adaptation groups had a higher mean at Time 2 than at Time 1 while the reverse was true for the fourth adaptation group).

Excerpt 17.7 Cell and Main Effect Means for a Two-Way Mixed ANOVA

Table 4

Adaptation group × time repeated measures ANOVA mean level of ego development

Adaptation group	n	Time 1	Time 2	Total
Low[→]high	13	5.46	5.92	5.69
Low[→]low	32	6.22	6.50	6.36
High[→]high	33	6.03	6.21	6.12
High[→]low	16	5.81	5.56	5.69
Total		5.88	6.05	

Note. ANOVA = analysis of variance. For adaptation group, $F(3,90) = 3.48$, $p < .05$; for time, $F(1,90) = 4.47$, $p < .05$; for Adaptation Group × Time ANOVA, $F(3,90) = 3.59$, $p < .05$.

Source: K. Bursik. (1991). Adaptation to divorce and ego development in adult women. *Journal of Personality and Social Psychology, 60,* p. 305.

PRESENTATION OF RESULTS

If the results of a two-way mixed ANOVA are presented in an ANOVA summary table, three *F*-values will be presented—two for the main effects and one for the interaction—just as is the case in the ANOVA summary tables for completely between-subjects and completely within-subjects ANOVAs. However, the ANOVA summary table is set up differently from those associated with the ANOVAs considered in earlier chapters. A typical summary table from a two-way mixed ANOVA is shown in Excerpt 17.8

Excerpt 17.8   Summary Table for a Two-Way Mixed ANOVA

Table 4

Summary of repeated-measures ANOVA influence of external agencies by administrative level

Effect	DF	SS	MS	F
Between subjects				
Administrative level	1	6.40	6.40	1.43
Error	50	223.22	4.46	
Within subjects				
Influence of external agencies	5	832.59	166.52	88.33*
Administrative level × influence of external agencies	5	16.13	3.23	1.71
Error	250	471.27	1.89	

*$p < .001$.

Source: S. Inglis. (1990). Influence in and around interuniversity athletics. *Journal of Sport Management, 4*(2), p. 27.

As Excerpt 17.8 shows, the summary table for a mixed ANOVA has an upper section and a lower section. These two sections are often labeled **Between subjects** and **Within subjects**, respectively. In the upper section, there will be two rows of information, one concerning the main effect of the between-subjects factor and the other for the Error that goes with the between-subjects main effect. In the lower section of the summary table, there will be three rows of information. The first of these rows is for the main effect of the within-subjects factor, the second is for the interaction between the two factors, and the third provides information for the within-subjects error term. As you can see from Excerpt 17.8, the *MS* for the first Error was used as a denominator in computing the *F*-value in the upper section of the summary table, while the *MS* for the second error was used as the denominator in computing the two *F*-values in the lower section.

The information contained in Excerpt 17.8 allows us to understand the structure of the study, which is necessary to understand if the results are to have any meaning. First of all, the *df* values for the two main effects allow us to know that there were two different administrative groups of subjects involved in this study, with each subject measured six times. Each of the six scores from each subject corresponded to a different level of the repeated measures factor, Influence of External Agencies. Second, we can figure out how many subjects were involved in this 2 × 6 study by adding 1 to the sum of the *df* values shown in the *upper* section of the table. Finally, we can use the *F*-values (in combination with the note beneath the table) to see that the data provided by the 52 subjects have brought about a rejection of the null hypotheses concerning the main effect of the within-subjects factor. Evidently, there was more variability among the six Influence-of-External-Agency main effect means, each based on the scores from all 52 subjects, than could be explained by chance. In contrast, the null hypotheses concerning the main effect of Administrative level and the interaction were not rejected.

In Excerpt 17.9, we see another summary table for a two-way mixed ANOVA. There are two primary differences between this summary table and the one presented in Excerpt 17.8. First, the upper and lower sections of the summary table are not distinguished from each other by means of rows

---

Excerpt 17.9   Another Summary Table for a Two–Way Mixed
ANOVA

Table 5

Two-way analysis of variance of post-feedback ratings for three groups and five worker traits with repeated measures for traits

Source	Sum of Squares	df	Means Squares	F
Groups	1713.09	2	857.55	7.87*
Subjects within groups	5004.00	46	108.78	
Traits	397.99	5	79.60	5.81*
Groups by traits	475.00	10	47.50	3.47*
Traits by subjects within groups	3151.19	230	13.70	

*$p < 0.05$.

Source: S. Kravetz, V. Florian, and E. Nofer. (1990). The differential effects of feedback of trait ratings on worker traits in vocational rehabilitation workshops in a correctional institution, *Vocational Evaluation and Work Adjustment Bulletin,* Summer, p. 52.

carrying the labels "Between Subjects" and "Within Subjects." (Nothing is really lost by not having these two rows, since they do nothing more than *label* the two sections.) Second, the two error rows are called different things in Excerpt 17.9 than was the case in Excerpt 17.8. Here, the rows containing the *MS* values used as denominators in forming the *F*-values are called "Subjects within groups" and "Traits by subjects within groups."

As illustrated in Excerpts 17.8 and 17.9, different terms are sometimes used to label the two rows that contain the *MS* values used as the denominators for the *F*s. In addition to the labels used in the summary tables just considered, you may encounter ANOVA summary tables in which these two rows are labeled Error 1 and Error 2, Error(a) and Error(b), or Error(b) and Error(w). The "b" and the "w" in the final labeling scheme, of course, stand for "between" and "within", the two sections of the summary table in which these error terms are positioned.

Although we like to look at ANOVA summary tables when trying to decipher and critique research reports, such tables are usually not included in journal articles. Instead, the results are typically presented strictly within one or more paragraphs of textual material. To illustrate, consider Excerpt 17.10, wherein the results of a two-way mixed ANOVA are presented without a summary table.

Excerpt 17.10   Results of a Two-Way Mixed ANOVA Presented in the Text of the Research Report

---

A 2×4 (Blood Pressure Group × Trials) repeated measures analysis of variance was conducted to evaluate possible trial-dependent interactions. Results revealed a significant main effect for blood pressure group, $F(1, 38) = 6.14, p < .02$; mean values indicated that, across trials, the EBP group performed more poorly than did normotensive control subjects. A significant main effect was also apparent for trials, $F(3, 114) = 29.01, p < .0001$. Post hoc comparisons (Tukey's honestly significant difference) [Tukey's HSD] between successive trials indicated that across all subjects, performance improved significantly only from Trial 1 to Trial 2 ($p < .05$). The Group × Trials interaction did not reach significance.

Source: S. R. Waldstein, C. M. Ryan, S. B. Manuck, D. K. Parkinson, and E. J. Bromet. (1991). Learning and memory function in men with untreated blood pressure elevation. *Journal of Consulting and Clinical Psychology, 59*, p. 515.

Excerpt 17.10 is worth looking at closely because it illustrates how a post hoc investigation will usually be applied when there are three or more levels associated with a significant main effect (but not be applied when there are only two levels).[1] It also provides us with an opportunity to show how to utilize the *df* values contained in such presentations. If we add 1 to the first of the two *df* values located in parentheses next to each main effect *F*, we obtain

---

[1]*John Tukey has developed several post hoc tests. The most popular of these tests is referred to as Tukey's HSD or as Tukey's honestly significant difference test.*

the numbers 2 and 4. These numbers indicate the number of levels in the between-subjects and within-subjects factors, respectively. The second df associated with each F comes from the error row that contained the MS used as a denominator when computing that F. Thus, there were 38 df for the error row in the upper section of the ANOVA summary table and 114 df associated with the lower section's error row. Knowing where the various df values came from, we can tell that there were 40 subjects involved in this study by adding 1 to the sum of the two numbers in parentheses next to the F for the main effect of the between-subjects factor.

The two-way mixed ANOVA summarized in Excerpt 17.10 allowed the researchers to reject the null hypothesis associated with each main effect. Each set of main effect means could be examined because the interaction F turned out to be nonsignificant. In Excerpt 17.11, however, we see how researchers will usually refrain from paying attention to the main effect means when there is a significant interaction. Instead, attention is focused on the cell means. In Excerpt 17.11, we see that the researchers used the popular two-step approach to dealing with their cell means; tests of simple main effects were first conducted, with a graph of the interaction provided to assist readers in understanding the results.

If there are two or more dependent variables involved in the same study, a researcher may decide to subject the data collected on each dependent variable to a separate two-way mixed ANOVA. In Excerpt 17.12, we see how the results of such a study were combined within a single ANOVA summary table.

Excerpt 17.11   Test of Simple Main Effects and a Graph of the Interaction

---

Results of a two-way ANOVA of self-preference ratings yielded no significant main effects for either the between-subjects worldview factor, $F(1, 59) = 0.851$, $p = .36$, or the within-subjects counseling approach factor, $F(2, 118) = 1.96$, $p = .14$. The interaction of the two factors, however, was significant, $F(2, 118) = 5.28$, $p < .01$. The form of this interaction is shown in Figure 2. A comparison of the simple main effects revealed that (a) participants with an organismic worldview ($M = 4.8$) exhibited a significant preference for constructivist counseling as compared with those with a commitment to mechanism ($M = 3.76$), $t(58) = 1.97$, $p < .05$; and (b) participants with a mechanistic worldview ($M = 5.28$) significantly preferred behavioral counseling as compared with persons with an organismic worldview ($M = 4.30$), $t(58) = 1.88$, $p < .05$. Organicists and mechanists did not significantly differ in their preferences for rationalist counseling.

(Continued)

Excerpt 17.11 Test of Simple Main Effects and a Graph of the
Interaction *(Continued)*

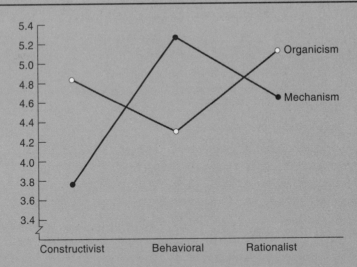

Figure 2 *Mean preference ratings for self: Type of counseling approach by worldview.*

Source: W. J. Lyddon and L. A. Adamson. (1992). Worldview and counseling preference: An analogue study. *Journal of Counseling & Development, 71,* p. 45.

Excerpt 17.12 Results of Three Two–Way Mixed ANOVAs
Presented in a Single Summary Table

Table 2

Mean scores of participating teachers on the teachable pupil survey

	Intervention Group				Comparison Group			
	Pre		Post		Pre		Post	
Domain	$\overline{X}$	SD	$\overline{X}$	SD	$\overline{X}$	SD	$\overline{X}$	SD
Cognitive	4.62	.80	4.31	.80	4.35	1.10	4.45	1.00
School-appropriate behavior	5.09	.71	4.94	.62	4.92	.88	4.85	.77
Social	4.74	.69	4.45	.82	4.51	.92	4.55	.83

(Continued)

Excerpt 17.12   Results of Three Two-Way Mixed ANOVAs
Presented in a Single Summary Table *(Continued)*

Table 3

ANOVA summary table for scores of teachers in intervention and comparison groups

Source	df	Cognitive		School Appropriate Behavior		Social	
		MS	F	MS	F	MS	F
Between groups							
Group	1	.20	.15	.77	.91	.22	.23
Error	89	118.24	—	74.97	—	84.84	—
Within groups							
Time	1	.58	1.49	.63	2.33	.85	2.29
Group by time	1	1.89	4.85**	.07	.26	1.24	3.35*
Error	89	35.07	—	24.24	—	33.25	—
Total	181	155.98					

*$p < .08$.
**$p < .05$.

Source: L. J. Johnson and M. C. Pugach. (1991). Peer collaboration: Accommodating students with mild learning and behavior problems. *Exceptional Children, 57,* p. 458.

Excerpt 17.13 shows how the results of two separate two-way mixed ANOVAs can be presented strictly within the text of the research report. [The next-to-the-last sentence should have contained the phrase "was no main effect" rather than "were no main effects," since there is only one main effect being referred to in this sentence; the final sentence should have said "no significant findings for either main effect (group or conceptualization) or for the interaction."]

Excerpt 17.13   Results of Two Two-Way Mixed ANOVAs, Each
Using Data on a Different Dependent Variable,
Presented in the Text of the Research Report

The two dependent measures, the behavioral problem description and self-perceived helpfulness, were analyzed in separate 2×2 ANOVAs with repeated measures. The independent variables were group (consultation trained versus

(Continued)

Excerpt 17.13   Results of Two Two-Way Mixed ANOVAs, Each Using Data on a Different Dependent Variable, Presented in the Text of the Research Report (*Continued*)

behavior analysis trained) by conceptualization type (medical model versus behavioral problem conceptualization). The behavioral description measure revealed a significant main effect for the type of conceptualization, $F(1, 16) = 13.00$, $p < .002$. There were no main effects for group, nor was there a significant interaction. . . . The perceived helpfulness measure analysis indicated no significant findings for main effects for group, conceptualization, or interaction.

Source: C. W. Conoley, J. C. Conoley, and W. B. Gumm, II. (1992). Effects of consultee problem presentation and consultant training on consultant problem definition. *Journal of Counseling and Development, 71,* p. 61.

RELATED ISSUES

In Chapter 16, we indicated how the levels of within-subjects factors sometimes can and should be presented to subjects in varying orders. That discussion applies to mixed ANOVAs as well as to fully repeated measures ANOVAs. In Excerpt 17.14, we see a case in which the technique of **counterbalancing** the order of the two levels of the within-subjects factor allowed the researchers to make sure that any effects associated with this factor were not confounded with an order effect.

Excerpt 17.14   Counterbalancing the Order of the Levels of the Within-Subjects Factor

Each participant engaged in two interactive role plays: one with a pregnant manager and one with a manager who was not pregnant. This yielded a 2×2 repeated measures design with one within-subjects factor, the pregnant (P) or "nonpregnant" (NP) condition of the manager, and one between-subjects factor, the gender—male (M) or female (F)—of the participant. The order in which the participant encountered the pregnant versus the nonpregnant manager was counterbalanced, with participants distributed as follows: P followed by NP for 20 men and 20 women, and NP followed by P for 21 men and 20 women.

Source: J. J. Corse. (1990). Pregnant managers and their subordinates: The effects of gender expectations on hierarchical relationships. *The Journal of Applied Behavioral Science, 26*(1), p. 32.

A second issue that you should keep in mind when examining the results of two-way mixed ANOVAs is the important assumption of **sphericity**. We discussed this assumption in Chapter 16 when we considered fully repeated measures ANOVAs. It is relevant to mixed ANOVAs as well—but only the

F-tests located in the within-subjects portion of the ANOVA summary are based upon the sphericity assumption. Thus, the *F*-value for the main effect of the between-subjects factor is unaffected by a lack of sphericity in the populations connected to the study. In contrast, the *F*-values for the main effect of the within-subjects factor and for the interaction will be positively biased (i.e., turn out larger than they ought to) to the extent that the sphericity assumption is violated.

Researchers who recognize the importance of the sphericity assumption to the validity of their within-subjects *F*-tests will follow one of the options discussed in Chapter 16. One option is to subject the sample data to Mauchley's test of sphericity, a second option is to use the three-step procedure for evaluating calculated *F*s with regular and conservative *df* values, and the third option is to compute ε and then reduce the critical values' *df*s to offset the extent to which the sphericity assumption appears to be violated. In Excerpts 17.15 and 17.16, we see examples where the sphericity assumption was dealt with by means of the first two of these strategies.

Excerpts 17.15–17.16   The Sphericity Assumption in Two-Way Mixed ANOVAs

---

It should be noted that the validity of the within-subjects *F* ratios in Table 3 [a summary table for a two-way mixed ANOVA], which were calculated using the univariate approach to repeated measures, depends on the assumption of sphericity of the covariance matrix for the four measures across years. In this regard, Mauchley's statistic for testing sphericity was .936, and the associated chi-square approximation was $\chi^2 = 5.17, p = .39$.

Source: G. K. Mandeville. (1992). Does achievement increase over time? Another look at the South Carolina PET program. *The Elementary School Journal, 93*(2), p. 124.

Trial-block means for the two dependent measures were calculated in blocks of 25 trials. The 250 acquisition trials were analyzed with a 4×10 (Learning Strategy × Trial Block) ANOVA with repeated measures on the last factor. Alpha was set at .05 for all statistical tests. Note that the present results were significant with both the traditional *F* values and the conservative degrees of freedom adjustments (Greenhouse & Geisser, 1959; Huynh & Feldt, 1970).

Source: R. N. Singer, R. Lidor, and J. H. Cauraugh. (1993). To be aware or not aware? What to think about while learning and performing a motor skill. *The Sport Psychologist, 7*(1), p. 25.

A third issue to keep in mind when you encounter the results of two-way mixed ANOVAs concerns the distinction between statistical significance and practical significance. We first talked about this distinction in Chapter 7, and we have tried to bring up this issue as often as possible since then. We have done this because far too many researchers conduct studies that yield one or more findings that have very little practical significance even though a very low probability level is associated with the calculated value produced by their statistical test(s).

Most researchers who conduct two-way mixed ANOVAs fail to address the question of practical significance. However, some researchers do this— and they deserve credit for performing a more complete analysis of the study's data than is usually the case. In Excerpt 17.17, we see one of these studies. In this investigation, **omega squared** was used to assess the extent to which variability in the data was attributable to the interaction.

Excerpt 17.17   Concern for Practical Significance

A two-way analysis of variance (ANOVA), with group membership as the between-groups factor and CTS held as the within-subject factor, was used to check actual group differences on these scales after group membership was assigned. There was a significant interaction effect between group membership and CTS, $F(6, 206) = 12.18$, $p < .0001$. The omega-squared statistic indicated that 47% of the variability in CTS scores was attributable to actual group membership.

Source: J. W. Fantuzzo, L. M. DePaola, L. Lambert, T. Martino, G. Anderson, and S. Sutton. (1991). The effects of interparental violence on the psychological adjustment and competencies of young children. *Journal of Consulting and Clinical Psychology, 59*, p. 260.

A fourth issue to keep in mind when dealing with two-way mixed ANOVAs (and also all other inferential test procedures) is the inflated Type I error risk generated by the separate analysis of two or more dependent variables. As indicated in previous chapters, the most frequently used technique for dealing with this situation is the Bonferroni adjustment procedure. In Excerpt 17.18, we see an example of how this general procedure was used in a study where eight two-way ANOVAs were conducted, each focusing on the data of a different dependent variable. The operational alpha level (.006) was determine by dividing .05 by 8.

Excerpt 17.18   Use of the Bonferroni Technique in Conjunction
with Two-Way Mixed ANOVAs

Two-way repeated measures ANOVAs (split-plot design) were used to test the significance of changes on the eight dependent measures (two scales from the ECBI, three scales from the PAT, and three scales from the PSI). The alpha level for the ANOVAs was adjusted to $p < .006$ using the Bonferroni technique to control for Type I error.

Source: R. W. Thompson, C. R. Grow, P. R. Ruma, D. L. Daly, and R. V. Burke. (1993). Evaluation of a practical parenting program with middle- and low-income families. *Family Relations, 42*, p. 23.

THREE-WAY MIXED ANOVAS

Although two-way mixed ANOVAs are all the same in that they all contain one between-subjects factor and one within-subjects factor, three-way mixed ANOVAs can take one of two forms. Simply stated, these higher-order mixed ANOVAs can involve repeated measures on either one or two of the factors in the study. In this section, we will consider both kinds of three-way mixed ANOVAs.

Since we covered three-way ANOVAs in Chapters 15 and 16 and since you now know what is meant by a mixed ANOVA, there are only a few things that need to be said here about three-way mixed ANOVAs. This is the case because the purpose of the ANOVAs focused upon in this section is identical to the purpose of the three-way ANOVAs considered earlier. In each case, seven null hypotheses are evaluated by means of analyzing the sample data. Three of these null hypotheses deal with main effects, three deal with two-way (i.e., first-order) interactions, and one deals with the three-way (i.e., second-order) interaction. Additional similarities also exist, such as the way post hoc tests are applied following rejection of any null hypothesis, the importance of the sphericity assumption to any within-subjects F-tests, the way the Bonferroni procedure can be applied to help protect against Type I errors, and the availability of various techniques to address the issue of practical versus statistical significance.

Although three-way ANOVAs are exceedingly similar regardless of the number of within-subjects factors involved, we need to consider two features of three-way mixed ANOVAs that make them different from three-way ANOVAs having either no repeated measures at all or repeated measures on all three factors. These two features involve the way the data are collected and organized for analysis, on the one hand, and the way the results are presented in the ANOVA summary table, on the other hand. Before turning to these topics, however, we need to consider the way researchers distinguish between the two kinds of three-way mixed ANOVAs. This is an important distinction, because the form of the ANOVA summary table varies depending upon whether one or two within-subjects factors are involved.

DISTINGUISHING BETWEEN THE TWO KINDS OF THREE-WAY MIXED ANOVAS

Because a three-way mixed ANOVA can have two between-subjects factors combined with one within-subjects factor, or one between-subjects factor combined with two within-subjects factor, the term **three-way mixed ANOVA** is not specific enough to let anyone know the precise form of the ANOVA. As a consequence, researchers will almost always include an indication of how many of their factors involved repeated measures. In Excerpts 17.19–17.22, we see four examples of how this was done.

> ## Excerpts 17.19–17.22   Clarifying Which Kind of Three-Way Mixed ANOVA Was Used
>
> The percentages correct on the two tasks were subjected to a 3 (Grade) × 2 (Reader Group) × 2 (Task) analysis of variance with repeated measures on task (Short vs. Long).
>
> *Source:* D. P. Hurlford and A. Shedelbower. (1993). The relationship between discrimination and memory ability in children with reading disabilities. *Contemporary Educational Psychology, 18*(1), p. 106.
>
> The data were submitted to an analysis of variance with target beverage (7-Up vs. Perrier) and context manipulation (taste vs. social impressiveness question-naire) as between-subjects variables and thought category (taste-related vs. social impression thoughts) as a within-subject variable.
>
> *Source:* S. Shavitt and R. H. Fazio. (1991). Effects of attribute salience on the consistency between attitudes and behavior predictions. *Personality and Social Psychology Bulletin, 17*(5), p. 510.
>
> A repeated measures analysis of variance (ANOVA) of responses to targets (hits) was carried out with two within-subject factors, response type ("know" and "remember") and word valence (threat and nonthreat), and one between-subject factor of group (anxious vs. control).
>
> *Source:* K. Mogg, J. M. Gardiner, A. Stavrou, and S. Golombok. (1992). Recollective experience and recognition memory for threat in clinical anxiety states. *Bulletin of the Psychonomic Society, 30*(2), p. 111.
>
> Data from the acceptability rating were analyzed by means of a 2 × 3 × 4 [(group: Group 1, Group 2) × (time: pretest, Phase B, Phase C) × (treatment condition; interdependent-large, interdependent small, dependent-large, dependent-small)] ANOVA with repeated measures across the last two factors.
>
> *Source:* E. F. Shapiro and R. Goldberg. (1990). *In vivo* rating of treatment acceptability by children: Group sizes effects, group contingencies to improve spelling performance. *The Journal of School Psychology, 28,* p. 240.

DATA LAYOUT AND TABLES OF MEANS

It is extremely helpful, we believe, to be able to conceptualize the way in which data are arranged prior to being subjected to a three-way mixed ANOVA. If you can do this, then you will be better able to interpret the results associated with any of the seven main *F*-tests (or any planned or post hoc tests that are conducted). For this reason, we want to consider the data layouts for both kinds of three-way mixed ANOVAs.

Figure 17.2 contains the data layout for two 2 × 2 × 2 mixed ANOVAs. In each layout, the factors are denoted by the letters A, B, and C while the levels within each factor are designated by the subscripts 1 and 2. For the purposes of illustration, we have set up each hypothetical study such that only eight subjects are involved. Although each data set contains hypothetical scores,

			C_1	C_2
A_1	B_1	Subject 1	7	8
		Subject 2	4	9
	B_2	Subject 3	5	5
		Subject 4	3	6
A_2	B_1	Subject 5	6	4
		Subject 6	9	7
	B_2	Subject 7	7	6
		Subject 8	5	9

			C_1		C_2	
			B_1	B_2	B_1	B_2
A_1		Subject 1	2	2	3	6
		Subject 2	3	1	5	7
		Subject 3	4	3	5	7
		Subject 4	3	4	3	4
A_2		Subject 5	8	7	7	7
		Subject 6	9	8	5	6
		Subject 7	9	9	7	8
		Subject 8	7	8	7	6

FIGURE 17.2 *Data layouts for three-way mixed ANOVAs having one within-subjects factor (upper picture) or two within-subjects factors (lower picture).*

both layouts should convey the impression that each subject has been measured repeatedly resulting in the scores appearing in his or her row. It should be clear that the upper section of Figure 17.2 represents the case of a mixed ANOVA having two between-subjects factors (A and B) and one within-subjects factor (C), whereas the lower section corresponds to the situation where there is one between-subjects factor (A) and two within-subjects factors (B and C).

Although information like that presented in Figure 17.2 will rarely appear in research reports, tables of mean scores often *are* included to help the reader understand the results. Such tables are similar to the data layouts shown in Figure 17.2 except that sample means are reported (usually with standard deviations) instead of individual raw scores for each cell created by a combination of the three factors. In Excerpt 17.23, we see such a table, this one coming from a study in which there were two between-subjects factors and one within-subjects factor.

Excerpt 17.23 Table of Means and Standard Deviations for a Three-Way ANOVA Having Repeated Measures on One Factor

Table 2 illustrates the results of subjects' performance on the pseudoword task in terms of rhyming and rhyming control errors. A 2 Age (young, old) $\times$ 2 Ability (poor, good readers) $\times$ 2 Trial Type (rhyming target, rhyming control) analysis of variance was conducted with trial type as the within-subject factor.

Table 2

Means and standard deviations of percentage rhyming and rhyming control errors on the pseudoword task

| | Good readers | | | | Poor readers | | | |
| | Young | | Older | | Young | | Older | |
Variables:	M	(SD)	M	(SD)	M	(SD)	M	(SD)
% Rhyming	44.6	(13.8)	35.4	(11.5)	39.6	(19.5)	45.8	(14.3)
% Rhyming control	13.8	(15.4)	10.0	(10.0)	13.3	(14.0)	12.5	(10.0)

Source: B. Waterman and L. Lewandowski. (1993). Phonologic and semantic processing in reading-disabled and non-disabled males at two age levels. *Journal of Experimental Child Psychology, 55*(1), p. 95.

If we had constructed the table in Excerpt 17.23, we would have reversed the positioning of rows and columns, so that the two between-subjects factors would have corresponded with the table's rows and the within-subjects factor would correspond with columns. Then, the structure of the table would have been identical to what appears in the upper section of Figure 17.2. Factors A, B, and C would then have represented good and poor readers, younger and older subjects, and scores on the two trial types, respectively. Even though we would have set up the table differently, you must develop the ability to decipher research reports as the authors decide to arrange their results. Unfortunately, different authors arrange their results in different ways.

In Excerpt 17.24, we see a table of means for a three-way mixed ANOVA in which there are two within-subjects factors. The structure of this table is identical to that of the data layout shown in the lower section of Figure 17.2. A, B, and C correspond to the group, materials, and time of testing factors, respectively. The only difference is that we now have three levels of Factor C (time of testing) instead of two. Despite this minor difference, it should be clear in Excerpt 17.24 that the means on any row of the table were based on the same group of subjects.

Excerpt 17.24   Table of Means and Standard Deviations for a Three-Way ANOVA Having Repeated Measures on Two Factors

---

The results for recall of concrete and abstract words were analyzed with a 3 (group: multifactorial, unifactorial, control) × 3 (time of testing: pretest, posttest 1, posttest 2) × 2 (materials: concrete words, abstract words) ANOVA, with repeated measures on the last two factors.

Table 2

Means and standard deviations for recall of concrete and abstract words across group and time of testing

Group	Pretest Concrete	Pretest Abstract	Posttest 1 Concrete	Posttest 1 Abstract	Posttest 2 Concrete	Posttest 2 Abstract
Multifactorial	6.09	5.00	8.27	5.55	9.27	6.64
	(2.43)	(1.38)	(2.60)	(1.29)	(2.67)	(2.06)
Unifactorial	6.67	4.92	7.46	5.46	8.42	6.08
	(1.80)	(1.04)	(2.78)	(1.32)	(2.70)	(2.32)
Control	6.27	4.27	6.04	4.81	6.85	5.38
	(2.69)	(1.81)	(2.14)	(2.16)	(2.17)	(2.27)

Note. Maximum score = 16.

Source: L. Backman and A. S. Neely. (1993). Maintenance of gains following multifactorial and unifactorial memory training in late adulthood. *Educational Gerontology, 19*(2), p. 113.

PRESENTATION OF RESULTS

Because a three-way mixed ANOVA has the same purpose as three-way fully between-subjects ANOVAs and three-way fully within-subjects ANOVAs, it should not come as any surprise that the two kinds of mixed ANOVAs being considered here each lead to seven F-tests. These F-tests on the main and interaction effects are conceptually the same as the corresponding F-tests considered in earlier chapters when we looked at other kinds of three-way ANOVAs. Although the number and meaning of these F-tests remains the same regardless of what kind of three-way ANOVA has been conducted, the form of the summary table varies depending upon how many within-subjects factors are involved.

Excerpt 17.25 Summary Table for a Three-Way ANOVA with Repeated Measures on One Factor

Table 1

Repeated measures analysis of variance of the effects of counseling style, acculturation level, and time of test on the rating of peer counselor effectiveness

Analysis/source	df	SS	MS	F
Between subjects	48	—	—	—
Counseling style (CS)	1	288.09	288.09	1.68
Acculturation level (AL)	1	56.35	56.35	0.33
CS × AL	1	1,027.52	1,027.52	5.99*
Error between	45	7,725.44	171.68	—
Within subjects	49	—	—	—
Time of test (TT)	1	52.33	52.33	1.92
CS × TT	1	0.68	0.68	0.02
AL × TT	1	56.20	56.20	2.06
CS × AL × TT	1	10.51	10.51	0.39
Error within	45	1,227.42	27.28	—
Total	97	—	—	—

Note. Peer counseling effectiveness was rated with the Counselor Effectiveness Rating Scale. Dashes indicate not applicable.

*$p < .05$.

Source: R. Merta, J. Ponterotto, and R. Brown. (1992). Comparing the effectiveness of two directive styles in the academic counseling of foreign students. *Journal of Counseling Psychology, 39*(2), p. 216.

Excerpt 17.25 illustrates what the standard ANOVA summary table looks like when there are two between-subjects factors and one within-subjects factor. As you can see, three F-values are positioned in the upper portion of the summary table while four are located in the lower section of the table. These two sections will be called "Between subjects" and "Within subjects," respectively.

The rule of thumb for deciding where to position any main or interaction effect in the summary table is simple. If the effect being tested is a main effect of a between-subjects factor or an interaction between factors that are solely between-subjects in nature, then the row of information for that effect is positioned in the upper section of the table. The lower section is reserved for the main effect of the within-subjects factor and all interactions that involve the within-subjects factor. Getting each row of information positioned correctly is quite important, because each section of the summary table contains its own MS for error, the numerical value that functions as the denominator when each F-value is computed. Note that these two error terms have MS values that are very different (171.68 versus 27.28).

The information contained in Excerpt 17.25 not only allows us to see what happened to each of the seven null hypotheses dealt with by the ANOVA, it also tells us about the structure and size of the study. Based on the dfs associated with the main effects, we can easily determine that there were two levels of each factor. By adding 1 to the between-subjects df value, we can also figure out that 49 subjects provided the data upon which these results were based.

Excerpt 17.26 shows the summary table for a three-way mixed ANOVA having repeated measures on two factors. This summary table is somewhat unusual because each of the seven rows containing an F-value is positioned *below* the row containing the MS value used as the denominator when computing the F-value. There are only four error-term rows—labeled *Within Cells, Within Cells (1), Within Cells (2),* and *Within Cells (3)*—because the MS value in three of these rows was used to compute two F-values.

Except for the unusual positioning of the four error-term rows, the summary table in Excerpt 17.26 is like those set up by other researchers who analyze data using a three-way mixed ANOVA with repeated measures on two factors. The main effect for the between-subjects factor is located in the upper section of the summary table while the other two main effects along with all four interactions are positioned in the lower section of the table. The df values from the main effect rows allow us to discern the structure of the study, the combined dfs in the top portion of the table help us know how many subjects were used, and the F-values (coupled with the notes beneath the table) give us the results of the analysis. From Excerpt 17.26, you therefore should be able to figure out that each of 27 subjects, a member of one of the three Original Form groups, was measured across the six combinations of

Excerpt 17.26 Summary Table for a Three-Way Mixed ANOVA Having Repeated Measures on Two Factors

Table 3

Repeated measures ANOVA source table

Source of Variation	SS	DF	MS	F
Between subjects				
Within cells	20.16	24	0.84	
Original form	4.86	2	2.43	2.89*
Within subjects				
Within cells(1)	2.00	24	0.08	
Training	0.03	1	0.03	0.34
Original by training	0.24	2	0.12	1.46
Within cells (2)	4.09	48	0.09	
Graphic mode	1.56	2	0.78	9.15**
Original by graphic mode	0.62	4	0.16	1.83
Within cells (3)	2.98	48	0.06	
Training by graphic mode	0.10	2	0.05	0.79
Original by training by graphic mode	0.06	4	0.01	0.23

*$p = .07$.
**$p < .001$.

Source: C. O. Sweedler-Brown. (1992). The effect of training on the appearance bias of holistic essay graders. *Journal of Research and Development in Education, 26*(1), p. 28.

Training and Graphic Mode factors, with results indicating that the three main effect means for Graphic Mode were much further apart than could be expected by chance, while the main effect of Original Form was of borderline significance.

As noted earlier, because the summary table for a three-way mixed ANOVA can end up being so large and because space is at a premium in most journals, researchers often summarize their results within the text of their articles. In Excerpt 17.27, we see how this is typically done. The contents of this excerpt are worth examining, because you will see a nice example of how tests of simple main effects are usually applied in an effort to help understand a statistically significant first-order interaction.

Excerpt 17.27 Results of a Three-Way Mixed ANOVA Presented Without a Summary Table

RESULTS

Subject's ratings of own and other's behaviors were analyzed by a 2 (Order) $\times$ 2 (Target of Judgment: own vs. other's behavior) $\times$ 2 (Dimension of Judgment: morality vs. intelligence) ANOVA with repeated measures for the last two factors. This analysis revealed two significant effects. In line with the idea that people would view themselves as more desirable than others, we found a main effect for target of judgment, $F(1, 85) = 8.80$, $p < .005$. As can be seen from Table 1, own behavior was rated as more desirable than another person's behavior. More important, we also found a significant interaction between target and dimension of judgment, $F(1, 85) = 6.02$, $p < .02$. Consistent with the Muhammad Ali effect (Allison et al., 1989), the extent to which own behavior was judged as more desirable than another person's behavior was greater for morality than for intelligence judgments.

Tests for simple main effects were conducted to examine the interaction of target and dimension of judgment more closely. These analyses revealed that subjects judged their own behavior as more moral, $F(1, 86) = 14.09$, $p < .001$, but not as significantly more intelligent, $F(1, 86) = 1.67$, n.s., than the other person's behavior. In addition, subjects judged their own behavior as more moral than intelligent, $F(1, 86) = 6.09$, $p < .02$, but did not judge the other's behavior as less moral than intelligent, $F(1, 86) = 1.09$, n.s. This suggests that the Muhammad Ali effect is primarily due to differences in the morality and intelligence judgments of own behavior, rather than those of other's behavior.

Table 1

Mean ratings of own and other's behavior on morality and intelligence

Target of Judgment	Dimension of judgment		
	Morality	Intelligence	Mean
Self	5.92	5.55	5.74
Other	5.11	5.29	5.20
Mean	5.52	5.42	

Note. Ratings could range from 1 to 7; higher numbers indicate judgments of greater goodness or intelligence.

Source: P. A. M. Van Lange. (1991). Being better but not smarter than others: The Muhammad Ali effect at work in interpersonal situations. *Personality and Social Science Bulletin, 17*(6), p. 691.

RELATED ISSUES

Near the end of the section on two-way mixed ANOVAs, we considered four issues that you should keep in mind when evaluating research claims based upon ANOVAs having one between-subjects factor and one within-subjects factor. Those issues are just as relevant to three-way mixed ANOVAs. We encourage you, therefore, to review our earlier comments about varying presentation orders, the sphericity assumption, the distinction between practical significance and statistical significance, and the possibility of inflated Type I error rates. In this section, we will revisit two of these issues and then raise a third not discussed earlier.

The assumption of sphericity, if violated, will cause some of the calculated F-values to turn out too large. The ones that are affected are the F-values located in the lower section of the ANOVA summary table. To prevent these F-tests from being positively biased, researchers can implement any of the three strategies originally discussed in Chapter 16. Unfortunately, most researchers neither test the sphericity assumption nor make an adjustment in dfs associated with their critical values.

If the sphericity assumption is dealt with through a reduction in dfs, it should be noted that this adjustment will be made only for the within-subjects F-tests. The validity of the between-subjects F-test(s) is not tied to the sphericity assumption—but the assumption of homogeneity of variance *is* associated with these F-tests. Accordingly, researchers ought to discuss the equal variance assumption before interpreting the between-subjects F-test(s) with confidence. If there are equal numbers of subjects across levels of the between-subjects factor(s), then the equal variance assumption is of minor importance (since equal ns function to make F-tests robust to violations of the assumption). If, however, the groups of subjects are of varying size, homogeneity of variance *is* important to the between-subjects F-test(s). You have a right to downgrade your evaluation of a study if nothing is said about this assumption when the ns vary.

Turning to the distinction between practical and statistical significance, researchers have a variety of techniques at their disposal for assessing the degree to which statistically significant results are nontrivial. When you come across a study in which one of these techniques has been used in conjunction with a three-way mixed ANOVA, give the researcher(s) credit for having gone beyond the basics in analyzing the study's data. In Excerpt 17.28, we see an example of such a study.

The third and final issue that we want to address concerns planned comparisons. As we pointed out in Chapter 13, researchers sometimes investigate specific contrasts instead of (or in addition to) computing the more general, "omnibus" F-tests associated with the analysis of variance. We tend to think more highly of the studies that involve planned comparisons, because researchers cannot throw together such comparisons in an undisciplined, hap-

---

Excerpt 17.28   Use of a Strength-of-Association Index to Assess
Practical Significance

A two-by-two-by-two mixed design analysis of variance examined the effects of
applicant's gender, applicant's hearing status, and child's gender on the ratings of
the applicant's suitability to adopt a child. For each significant effect, a modified
η^2 statistic (Tabachnick & Fidell, 1983) was calculated as an indicator of strength
of association. There was a significant two-way interaction between the child's
gender and the applicant's gender ($F_{1,50} = 28.64$, $p<0.0001$; $\eta^2 = .36$)....
There was also a significant three-way interaction between applicant's gender,
applicant's hearing status, and child's gender ($F_{1,50} = 4.35$, $p<0.05$; $\eta^2 = .08$).

Source: B. M. Rienz, K. S. Levinson, and D. J. Scrams. (1992). University students' perceptions of deaf
parents. *Psychological Reports, 71,* p. 765.

---

hazard fashion. Instead, they must truly understand what is going on in their
study in order to set up meaningful planned comparisons. For this reason,
planned comparisons are generally found in studies that have a more extensive connection to a theoretical framework and/or to the empirical results of
earlier investigations.

In Excerpt 17.29, we see a study where the data could have been analyzed
by means of a three-way mixed ANOVA having one repeated measures factor. However, the seven "generic" F-tests conducted within such an analysis
would not have helped to answer the three primary research questions posed
by the researchers. Consequently, three sets of planned contrasts were set up
and tested. Although a great deal of space in the research article was devoted
to the rationale behind these planned contrasts, we have not included that
discussion in Excerpt 17.29. Our effort here is solely to show that planned
comparisons can be set up and tested instead of the seven more traditional
null hypotheses of a three-way ANOVA.

Excerpt 17.29   Use of Planned Comparisons in a Study Involving
Two Between-Subjects Factors and One Within-
Subjects Factor

Although designed as a $3 \times 2 \times 16$ factorial, the experiment addressed specific
questions about group differences on Day 11, across Days 11–15, and on Day
16. Three sets of planned, nonorthogonal contrasts were written to determine
the significance of differences in latencies between the groups on Day 11, across
Days 11–15, and on Day 16. The first set of contrasts written for the analysis of
the results from Day 11 was generated from the interest in simple and interaction effects between the groups. The second set of contrasts written to analyze

(Continued)

Excerpt 17.29   Use of Planned Comparisons in a Study Involving
Two Between-Subjects Factors and One Within-
Subjects Factor *(Continued)*

---

the results across Days 11–15 was used to test for differential decreases in latencies in the rats that were given morphine. The final set of contrasts written to
analyze the results from Day 16 were used to test for simple effects. In each of
these analyses, the Bonferroni decision rule was used to calculate the critical Fs.

Source: H. Foo. (1992). The hypoalgesia conditioned by a heat stressor with naloxone is nonopioid:
Implications for hypoalgesias conditioned by shock. *Psychobiology, 20*(1), p. 57.

A FINAL COMMENT

In this chapter we have considered two-way and three-way mixed ANOVAs.
Although we have not discussed mixed ANOVAs involving four or more factors, you should be able to extrapolate from what you have learned here so as
to understand most (or all) of the results derived from these higher-order
mixed ANOVAs. Evidence that such ANOVAs are used is found in Excerpts
17.30–17.33.

Excerpts 17.30–17.33   Use of Mixed ANOVAs Involving Four or
More Factors

A $3 \times 2 \times 3 \times 10$ (Groups $\times$ Gender $\times$ Condition $\times$ Trials) mixed design was
used in the analysis. Group and gender were the between-subjects factors, and
the conditions and trials were the within-subjects factors. Repeated measures
ANOVA were performed for each of the four dependent variables of premotor
time, motor time, total reaction time, and movement time.

Source: W. E. Davis, W. A. Sparrow, and T. Ward. (1991). Fractionated reaction times and movement
times of Down Syndrome and other adults with mental retardation. *Adapted Physical Activity
Quarterly, 8*, p. 225.

The main analysis was a mixed model univariate analysis of variance. Variables
were Group (BC1 vs. BC2 vs. BC3 vs. Control), Behavior (TB vs. OB), Scale
(Severity vs. Manageability vs. Tolerability), and Trial (Pre- vs. Post-intervention), with repeated measures on the last three variables.

Source: D. Fuchs and L. S. Fuchs. (1989). Exploring effective and efficient prereferral interventions:
A component analysis of behavioral consultation. *School Psychology Review, 18*(2), p. 268.

(Continued)

Excerpts 17.30–17.33   Use of Mixed ANOVAs Involving Four or
More Factors *(Continued)*

A 3 (response mode) $\times$ 2 (laterality) $\times$ 2 (visual field) $\times$ 2 (memory set) $\times$ 2 (response assignment) mixed design analysis of variance was performed on the data.

Source: M. A. Adkins, W. A. Hilli, and J. W. Brown. (1992). The effects of response mode and stimulus laterality on reaction time in a Sternberg task. *Bulletin of the Psychonomic Society, 30*(2), p. 106.

Analyses of variance (ANOVAs) with three between-subjects variables (age, sex, and presentation order) and two within-subject variables (stimulus and period) were performed on each variable for the mother group and stranger group, respectively.

Source: C. P. Ellsworth, D. W. Muir, and S. M. J. Hains. (1993). Social competence and person-object differentiation: An analysis of the still-face effect. *Developmental Psychology, 29*, p. 66.

REVIEW TERMS

Between subjects
Bonferroni technique
Counterbalancing
Lindquist Type I ANOVA
Mixed ANOVA
Omega squared
One between, one within ANOVA

One between, two within ANOVA
Sphericity
Split-plot ANOVA
Three-way mixed ANOVA
Two between, one within ANOVA
Two-way mixed ANOVA
Within subjects

REVIEW QUESTIONS

1. What is the difference between a 3 $\times$ 3 mixed ANOVA and a 3 $\times$ 3 split-plot ANOVA?

2. How many null hypotheses are typically associated with a two-way mixed ANOVA? What do these null hypotheses usually say?

3. If each of 10 males and 10 females is measured on three occasions with the resulting data analyzed by a two-way mixed ANOVA, how many main effect means would there be for Gender and how many scores would each of these sample means be based on?

4. In Excerpt 17.7, which pair of *df* values in the note beneath the table can be used to verify that the two-way mixed ANOVA was based on the data supplied by 94 subjects?

5. (True or False) In Excerpt 17.11, the *df* values associated with the between-subjects factor are consistent with the single *df* value associated with each of the *t*-tests conducted during the simple main effects investigation.

6. In the ANOVA summary table shown in Excerpt 17.8, which of the *F*-values would be too large if the sphericity assumption was violated?

7. In Excerpt 17.18, where did the number .006 come from?

8. (True or False) There is no difference between (a) a two-way ANOVA with one between-subjects factor and one within-subjects factor and (b) a two-way ANOVA with one within-subjects factor and one between-subjects factor.

9. (True or False) There is no difference between (a) a three-way ANOVA with two between-subjects factors and one within-subjects factor and (b) a three-way ANOVA with one between-subjects factor and two within-subjects factors.

10. What is a 33.2 split-plot factorial ANOVA? (To help you answer this question, we will tell you that the two-way mixed ANOVAs in Figure 17.1 and Excerpt 17.7 could be referred to as 2.3 and 4.2 split-plot factorial ANOVAs, respectively, while the data layouts shown in the upper and lower portions of Figure 17.2 could be referred to as 22.2 and 2.22 split-plot factorials, respectively.)

11. In Excerpt 17.23, what are the numerical values of the main effect means for the Age factor, assuming that all cells contained the same amount of data?

12. In Excerpt 17.24, the main effect means for the first level of the Group factor could be computed by averaging what numbers contained in the table?

13. How many *F*-values will appear in the between-subjects section of the summary table for a three-way mixed ANOVA having repeated measures on one factor? What would the answer to this question be if there are repeated measures on two factors?

14. Take a look at any two or three ANOVA summary tables presented in this chapter. How does the size of the *MS* for the between-subjects error term compare with the size of the *MS* for the within-subjects error term(s)?

15. In Excerpt 17.27, why are only four cell means presented (rather than eight, since a $2 \times 2 \times 2$ ANOVA was applied to the data)?

16. Look at the ANOVA summary table contained in Excerpt 17.12. There are two things wrong with this table. Can you identify them?

THE ANALYSIS OF COVARIANCE

In the previous seven chapters, we looked at several different kinds of analysis of variance. We focused our attention on one-way, two-way, and three-way ANOVAs, with consideration given to the situations where (1) each factor is between-subjects in nature, (2) each factor is within-subjects in nature, and (3) both between-subjects and within-subjects factors are combined in the same study. Distinguished from one another by the number and nature of the factors, nine different kinds of ANOVA were closely examined. Additional higher-order ANOVAs were alluded to, since more than three factors can be (and often are) incorporated into the same study.

We now turn our attention to an ANOVA-like inferential strategy that can be used instead of any of the ANOVAs examined or referred to in earlier chapters. Called the **analysis of covariance** and abbreviated by the six letters **ANCOVA**, this statistical technique can be used in any study regardless of the number of factors involved or the between-versus-within nature of the factor(s). Accordingly, the analysis of covariance is best thought of as an option to the analysis of variance. For example, if a researcher's study involves one between-subjects factor, data can be collected and analyzed using a one-way ANOVA *or* a one-way ANCOVA. The same option exists for any of the other eight situations examined in earlier chapters (or for any of the higher-order situations not considered in detail). Simply stated, there is an ANCOVA counterpart to any ANOVA.

In Excerpts 18.1–18.4, we see how researchers typically indicate that their data were subjected to an analysis of covariance. Note how these excerpts illustrate the way ANCOVA can be used as an option to ANOVA regardless of the number of factors involved in the study or the between-versus-within nature of any factor.

Excerpts 18.1–18.4   The Versatility of the Analysis of Covariance

Performance in the treatment conditions for tutors was analyzed by a one-way analysis of covariance.

Source: M. Beirne-Smith. (1991). Peer tutoring in arithmetic for children with learning disabilities. *Exceptional Children, 57,* p. 334.

We carried out a 3(time of menarche) × 2(school type) analysis of covariance (ANCOVA) using the summary index of familiarity with peer delinquency at age 13 as the outcome variable.

Source: A. Caspi, D. Lynam. T. E. Moffitt, and P. A. Silva. (1993). Unraveling girls' delinquency: Biological, dispositional, and contextual contributions to adolescent misbehavior. *Developmental Psychology, 29*(1), p. 24.

A 3 × 3 × 2 ANCOVA was performed, with group (positional analysis group, sequential analysis group, and control group), intelligence level (high, medium, or low), and grade (1 or 2) as independent variables.

Source: A. Lie. (1991). Effects of a training program for stimulating skills in word analysis in first-grade children. *Reading Research Quarterly, 26*(3), p. 244.

A mixed model, repeated measures (3 × 2 × 2) analysis of covariance (R-ANCOVA) was used to analyze data. . . . Mattress type was the three-level between groups factor, with position and site as the repeated measures.

Source: S. Sideranko, A. Quinn, K. Burns, and R. D. Froman. (1992). Effects of position and mattress overlay on sacral and heel pressures in a clinical population. *Research in Nursing & Health, 15,* p. 248.

THE PURPOSE OF ANCOVA

Like the analysis of variance, the analysis of covariance allows researchers to make inferential statements about main and interaction effects in the populations of interest. In that sense, these two statistical procedures have the same objective. The primary difference between ANOVA and ANCOVA, however, is that the latter procedure was developed to reduce the probability of a Type II error—the kind of mistake that is committed whenever a false H_0 is not rejected. In other words, ANCOVA permits the researcher to investigate main and interaction effects with a higher level of statistical power than can be attained through the application of a comparable ANOVA.

To accomplish its main purpose, ANCOVA necessitates that each subject be measured not only on the dependent variable but also on one or more **covariate variables.**[1] Hence, there will be three kinds of variables in any ANCOVA study: (1) one or more independent variables (i.e., factors) that serve to create

---

[1] *The term* **concomitant variable** *is synonymous with the term* covariate variable.

the comparison groups of the investigation, (2) a dependent variable that gives meaning to the μs contained in the main effect and interaction null hypotheses, and (3) one or more covariate variables (on which subjects are measured) that provide the basis for increasing the investigation's statistical power.

In Excerpts 18.5–18.8, we see examples of how researchers will talk about the three kinds of variables involved in their ANCOVA studies. Note that none of these excerpts makes explicit reference to the independent, dependent, and covariate variables. In each case, however, all three kinds of variables are mentioned. For example, the independent and dependent variables in Excerpt 18.5 are student category and home score, respectively. In Excerpt 18.8, the independent variable is patient subgroup, the dependent variable is T_1 (INSPIRIT score), and the covariate variables are gender, age, and education.

In addition to its primary purpose of increasing the power of statistical tests, the analysis of covariance accomplishes a second objective. This second feature of ANCOVA can be summed up by the word *control*. If you consider Excerpt 18.8 once again, you will see that gender, age, and education were used as control variables. When ANCOVA is used for this second purpose, the covariate variable(s) is (are) the control variables.

Excerpts 18.5–18.8   Three Kinds of Variables in Any ANCOVA Study

---

Analysis of covariance (ANCOVA) on home score by students category (LD, EBD, EMR, NH) with SES as the covariate was conducted.

Source: S. L. Christenson. (1990). Differences in students' home environments: The need to work with families. *School Psychology Review, 19*(4), p. 512.

We examined the data using a 2×6 (Eyes × Emotions) factorial analysis of covariance (ANCOVA), with EEA for emotions as the dependent measure and EEA for neutral expressions as the covariate.

Source: M. K. Mandal, R. Pandey, and S. H. Madam. (1992). Exposed eye area (EEA) in the expression of various emotions. *The Journal of General Psychology, 119*(4), p. 387.

The WAIS-R Digit Symbol test results were analyzed using an analysis of covariance procedure with initial condition results as the covariate and group and diagnostic categories used as the independent variables.

Source: J. E. Gilliam. (1991). The effects of Baker–Miller pink on physiological and cognitive behavior of emotionally disturbed and regular education students. *Behavior Disorders, 17*(1), p. 51.

An ANCOVA comparing INSPIRIT scores (T_1) among the patient subgroups was performed. Demographic data (gender, age, education) were utilized as control variables.

Source: J. D. Kass, R. Friedman, J. Leserman, P. C. Zuttermeister, and H. Benson. (1991). Health outcomes and a new index of spiritual experience. *Journal for the Scientific Study of Religion, 30*(2), p. 206.

The logic behind the control feature of ANCOVA is simple. The comparison groups involved in a study are likely to differ from one another with respect to one or more variables that the researcher may wish to "hold constant." In an attempt to accomplish this objective, the researcher could use subjects who have identical scores on the variable(s) where control is desired. That effort, however, would normally bring forth two undesirable outcomes. For one thing, only a portion of the available subjects would actually be used, thus *reducing* the statistical power of inferential tests. Furthermore, the generalizability of the findings would be greatly restricted as compared with the situation where the analysis is based upon a more heterogeneous group of subjects.

To bring about the desired control, ANCOVA adjusts each group mean on the dependent variable. Although the precise formulas used to make these adjustments are somewhat complicated, the rationale behind the adjustment process is easy to understand. If one of the comparison groups has an *above-average* mean on the *control variable* (as compared with the other comparison groups in the study), then that group's mean score on the *dependent variable* will be *lowered*. In contrast, any group having a *below-average* mean on the *covariate* will have its mean score on the *dependent* variable *raised*. The degree to which any group's mean score on the dependent variable is adjusted depends upon how far above- or below-average that group stands on the control variable. By adjusting the mean scores on the dependent variable in this fashion, ANCOVA provides the best estimates of how the comparison groups would have performed if they all had possessed identical means on the control variable(s).

To illustrate the way ANCOVA adjusts group means on the dependent variable, consider Excerpt 18.9. In the article from which this excerpt was taken, the researchers explained that three groups of children with learning disabilities were compared on how well they could perform mathematics problems. The independent variable in this study was Treatment Method, with one group

Excerpt 18.9   Adjusted Means on the Dependent Variable

Table 5

Mean number of problems correct: Tutees

Treatment method	Pretest	Posttest	Adjusted Posttest
A	23.8	40.8	40.1
B	23.1	37.9	38.1
C	22.9	25.9	26.3

Source: J. Beirne-Smith. (1991). Peer tutoring in arithmetic for children with learning disabilities. *Exceptional Children, 57,* p. 334.

(Group A) of students given a particular kind of peer tutoring, a second group (Group B) given a different kind of peer tutoring, and a third group (Group C) given no peer tutoring. The dependent variable was posttest performance, measured as the number of math problems computed correctly. The control, or covariate, variable was beginning math ability, as measured by the pretest.

With 10 subjects in each of the three comparison groups, it is easy to show that the mean score of all 30 subjects on the covariate was 23.3. Knowing this, you can see that Group A began the study with an above-average pretest mean while groups B and C each began with a below-average pretest mean. Compared with Group B, Group C was even further behind at the outset of the study. To acknowledge the existence of these differences among the groups on the covariate, ANCOVA adjusted the posttest means. If you examine the three sets of means contained in Excerpt 18.9, you will see (1) why each group's posttest mean was adjusted so as to become larger or smaller and (2) why the largest adjustment was made to group A's posttest mean while the smallest adjustment was made to group B's posttest mean.

It should be noted that the two purposes of ANCOVA—increased power, on the one hand, and control of extraneous variables, on the other hand—occur simultaneously. If a researcher decides to use this statistical procedure solely to gain the increased power that ANCOVA affords, the means on the dependent variable will automatically be adjusted to reflect differences among the group means on the covariate variable. If, on the other hand, the researcher applies ANCOVA solely because of a desire to exert statistical control on a covariate variable, there will be, automatically, an increase in the statistical power of the inferential tests.[2] In other words, ANCOVA accomplishes two objectives even though the researcher may have selected it with only one objective in mind.

At the beginning of this section, we stated that ANCOVA allows the researcher to make inferential statements about main and interaction effects in the populations of interest. Since we have explained how data on the covariate variable(s) make it possible for the researcher to control one or more extraneous variables, we can now point out that ANCOVA's inferential statements are based upon the adjusted means. The data on the covariate and the dependent variable are used to compute the adjusted means on the dependent variable, with ANCOVA's focus resting on these adjusted means whenever a null hypothesis is tested.

NULL HYPOTHESES

As typically used, ANCOVA will involve the same number of null hypotheses as would be the case in a comparable ANOVA. Hence, you will usually find that there will be one, three, and seven null hypotheses associated with

---

[2]*This statement is true only when a "good" covariate variable is used. We will shortly explain what we mean by "good."*

ANCOVAs having one, two, or three factors, respectively. The nature of these ANCOVA null hypotheses is the same as the null hypotheses we talked about in earlier chapters when we considered various forms of ANOVA, except that the μs in any covariance H_0 must be considered to be adjusted means.[3]

Although null hypotheses rarely appear in research reports that contain ANCOVA results, they sometimes are referred to. Two examples to illustrate this are contained in Excerpts 18.10 and 18.11. The first of these excerpts explicitly talks about adjusted means, and our only suggested modification would be the inclusion of the word *population* between the words *adjusted* and *means*. Excerpt 18.11, in contrast, contains the word *population* but lacks the word *adjusted*. (The omission of the word *adjusted* in Excerpt 18.11 is surprising, since it was taken from the same research summary that provided us with Excerpt 18.9).

Excerpts 18.10–18.11　　The Null Hypothesis in ANCOVA

The statistical hypothesis tested, stated in the null form, was the following: There are no differences between supported employment-change countries and non-system-change countries in adjusted means of supported-employment closures.

Source: E. M. Szymanski, C. Hanley-Maxwell, J. L. Schaller, R. M. Parker, and S. Kidder. (1992). Impact of a system-change initiative on supported employment in Wisconsin. *Rehabilitation Counseling Bulletin, 35*(4), p. 214.

A one-way analysis of covariance using pretest scores as the covariate was used to test the hypothesis that the means of the treatment populations were equal.

Source: M. Beirne-Smith. (1991). Peer tutoring in arithmetic for children with learning disabilities. *Exceptional Children, 57*, p. 334.

THE COVARIATE VARIABLE(S)

In many studies, the covariate variable is set up to be an indication of each subject's status at the outset of the investigation. When this is done, the data associated with the covariate variable will be referred to as the pretest or baseline measure. Such covariates, of course, will be measured using the same measuring instrument as that used to measure the dependent variable. Excerpts 18.7 and 18.9 illustrate the use of this kind of covariate variable.

There is no rule, however, that forces the researcher to use pretest-type data to represent the covariate variable. In many studies, the covariate variable

---

[3]*In a completely randomized ANCOVA where each factor is active in nature, the adjusted population means on the dependent variable are logically and mathematically equal to the unadjusted means.*

is entirely different from the dependent variable. For example, consider again Excerpt 18.5. In that study, the dependent variable was measured by administering the Home Rating Scale while the covariate variable, socioeconomic status, was measured by using Hollingshead's four-factor index of social status. In the study from which Excerpt 18.4 was taken, the dependent variable was defined as the pressure exerted on mattresses by immobilized intensive care patients, while the covariate variable was defined as each patient's body mass. Clearly, home rating scores are dealing with a different variable than socioeconomic status, and measured pressure on a mattress with a different variable than body mass.

Regardless of whether the covariate and dependent variables are the same or different, the adjustment process of ANCOVA is basically the same. First, the mean covariate score of all subjects in all comparison groups is computed. Next, each comparison group's covariate mean is compared against the grand covariate mean to see (1) if the former is above or below the latter, and (2) how much of a difference there is between these two means. Finally, each group's mean on the dependent variable is adjusted up or down (depending on whether the group was below- or above-average on the covariate), with larger adjustments made when a group's covariate mean is found to deviate further from the grand covariate mean.

Although the logic behind ANCOVA's adjustment of group means on the dependent variable is easy to follow, the statistical procedures used to make the adjustments is quite complicated. We will not present the formula used to do this because you do not need to understand the intricacies of the adjustment formula in order to decipher and critique ANCOVA results. The only thing we will say here is that the adjustment process involves far more than (1) determining how far each group's covariate mean lies above or below the grand covariate mean and (2) adding or subtracting that difference to the group's mean on the dependent variable. Based upon the information presented in Excerpt 18.9, you may have concluded that this is the way the covariance adjustment actually works. It is extremely unusual, however, for the ANCOVA adjustments to be equal in magnitude to the deviations between each group's mean on the covariate and the grand covariate mean. We doubt that you (or we) will ever again see a set of results like those contained in Excerpt 18.9!

As indicated earlier, more than one covariate variable can be included within the same ANCOVA study. In other words, data on two or more covariate variables can be used in an effort to increase statistical power and/or to control extraneous variables. Although it might seem as if ANCOVA would work better when lots of covariate variables are involved, the researcher has to "pay a price" for each such variable. We will discuss this point later in the chapter. For now, all we want you to know is that most ANCOVAs are conducted with only one or two covariate variables.

PRESENTATION OF RESULTS

You will occasionally encounter research reports containing ANCOVA summary tables. In Excerpt 18.12, we see such a table for an ANCOVA that was applied to the data of a three-factor, fully between-subjects study.

Excerpt 18.12   Summary Table for a Three-Way ANCOVA

Table 3

Analysis of covariance for scores on the postinterview willingness to see a counselor scale

Source	SS	df	MS	F
Predicate (A)	0.548	1	0.548	0.109
Proficiency (B)	27.281	1	27.282	5.422*
Sex (C)	3.738	1	3.738	0.743
A × B	13.696	1	13.696	2.722
A × C	4.268	1	4.268	0.848
B × C	9.969	1	9.969	1.981
A × B × C	8.530	1	8.530	1.695
Residual	1086.800	216	5.031	
Total	1631.427	224	7.283	

*$p < .05$.

Source: E. Goldin, and R. E. Doyle. (1991). Counselor predicate usage and communication proficiency on ratings of counselor empathic understanding. *Counselor Education and Supervision, 30*(3), p. 221.

The table of results contained in Excerpt 18.12 has the same basic form as the three-way ANOVA summary tables presented in Chapter 15. There are seven F-values (three for main effects, three for two-way interactions, and one for the triple interaction), each computed by dividing the Residual MS into the MS for the effect being tested. Moreover, each MS was computed in the usual manner—by dividing each row's SS by its df. In fact, this table is so similar to a three-way ANOVA summary table that it requires a careful reading of the table's title to realize that the results come from an ANCOVA, not an ANOVA.

The interpretation of an ANCOVA summary table is almost identical to the interpretation of an ANOVA summary table. For example, we can determine from the table in Excerpt 18.12 that there were two levels of each factor, that the dependent variable was postinterview willingness to see a counselor, and that the only statistically significant result is associated with the main effect of Proficiency. There are only two things that must be done differently with this table. First, you must keep in mind that all F-values are focused on *adjusted* means. Second, to figure out how many subjects were involved in the study, you must add 1 to the Total *df* (as you would if the data had been subjected to an ANOVA) *plus* 1 for each covariate variable involved in the ANCOVA. Since the table in Excerpt 18.12 does not reveal how many covariates were used, all we can do is surmise that at least 226 subjects were used in the counseling study.

In Excerpt 18.13, we see the results of the one-way ANCOVA that was applied to the data presented earlier in Excerpt 18.9. This summary table, on first glance, does not resemble a one-way ANOVA summary table because there are four rows of information and two *F*-values. However, if you disregard the row called Regression and if you recognize that the row called Tutor method could have been labeled Between groups, then the table becomes highly similar to the one-way ANOVA summary tables considered in Chapter 12.

In Excerpt 18.13, notice how a post hoc investigation was conducted using the Tukey HSD procedure. This was done because a statistically significant

---

Excerpt 18.13   ANCOVA Results for Tutoring-on-Mathematics
Study

Table 4

Summary table for analysis of covariance: Tutees

Source	Adjusted SS	df	MS	F
Regression	6236.09	1	6236.09	114.23
Tutor method (A vs. B vs. C)	1104.37	2	552.18	10.11*
Within	1419.30	26	54.58	
Total	8759.77	29		

*$p = .0006$.

Performance in the treatment conditions for tutees was analyzed using a one-way analysis of covariance. As shown in Table 4, the effects of peer tutoring were significantly different, $F(2, 26) = 10.1, p = .0006$. . . . The influence of counting-on and rote memorization peer tutoring was examined using Tukey's HSD post hoc test. When peer tutoring was contrasted with no peer tutoring, a significant difference was found between groups. When Method A peer tutoring was contrasted with Method B peer tutoring, no significant difference was found. When Method A peer tutoring was contrasted with Method C, the no-treatment control group, a significant difference was found. Finally, when Method B peer tutoring was contrasted with Method C, a significant difference was found.

Source: M. Beirne-Smith. (1991). Peer tutoring in arithmetic for children with learning disabilities. *Exceptional Children, 57,* p. 334.

F-value (of 10.11) was obtained when the three groups were compared. Like the overall F-test, Tukey's test involved a comparison of adjusted posttest means.

Before leaving Excerpt 18.13, we need to say a thing or two about the top row of information in the summary table. Earlier, we suggested that you disregard this row. Many researchers will make it easy for you to do this, since the regression row of the ANCOVA summary table usually will be deleted when the results are presented. That was the case in Excerpt 18.12 and will be the case with all but one of the other summary tables in this chapter.

When you see an ANCOVA summary table that contains a row labeled Regression (or Covariate), you can safely assume that the data analysis was performed by a computer and that the researchers have given you what the computer gave them. We believe that the inclusion of the Regression row of information provides little useful information and may actually confuse those who are trying to understand the results of analysis. From our point of view, the only possible benefit brought about by including this row is related to the fact that the total df number in the ANCOVA summary table is 1 less than the number of subjects involved in the analysis. Hence, when the Regression row is included, you can use the same method to figure out how many subjects were involved in the study as you can with any ANOVA. If the Regression row is deleted, however, you will need to add 2 to the total df, not 1.

In Excerpt 18.14, we see a table that presents the results of three separate one-way ANCOVAs, each computed for a different dependent variable. Notice how each row of this table represents just the top row of a complete ANCOVA summary table. In other words, the table in Excerpt 18.14 presents the "between groups" row of information from each of the ANCOVAs, with no information from the "within groups" or "total" rows of any of the three analyses given to us.

Excerpt 18.15 (on page 494) is like Excerpt 18.14 in that the results of three separate one-way ANCOVAs are presented. Moreover, these two tables are similar in that two groups were compared within each study. Despite these commonalities, notice how different these two tables are. Whereas the table in Excerpt 18.14 shows the between-groups SS, df, and MS from each analysis, the table in Excerpt 18.15 presents each group's mean and standard deviation on the covariate and dependent variables, along with the adjusted means compared in each analysis.[4]

---

[4] *Of these two ways of displaying the results of several independent ANCOVAs, we prefer the reporting scheme used in Excerpt 18.15. In this table, we see the F-test results along with the means involved in each comparison. With the adjusted means in front of us, we can make a judgment on our own about the practical significance of the findings.*

Excerpt 18.14   Results of Three Separate One-Way ANCOVAs
Combined into One Table

Table 1

**Comparison of three body image scales for normal-weight and
overweight groups: ANCOVA[a]**

Body image scale	For normal-weight and overweight groups:				
	SS	df	MS	F	F probability
Nash	1384.98	1	1384.98	28.03	.0001[*]
BIPT pre–	253.96	1	253.96	6.18	.0143
BIPT video	938.40	1	938.40	11.58	.0009[*]

[a]Age and education were used as covariates; $N = 120$.
[*]Statistically significant at .001 level.

Source: S. Popkess-Vawter and N. Banks. (1992). Body image measurement in overweight females.
Clinical Nursing Research, 1(4), p. 411.

The results of an ANCOVA, of course, often are presented strictly within
the text of the research report. In Excerpt 18.16 (on page 495), we see what
happened when a 2×5 mixed ANCOVA was used to investigate the effects
of an acute psychological stress on a measure of immune function, lymphocyte proliferation in the blood. Subjects were randomly assigned to one of
two conditions: experimental (where they watched a gruesome combat
surgery film) or control (where they watched a film of African landscape
scenes with calming background music). Blood samples were taken at five
points during the study: prior to the film (baseline), halfway through the
film, and then 30, 60, and 90 minutes after the film. Condition (experimental versus control) was the between-subjects factor, the baseline blood sample
provided the covariate data, and the remaining four blood samples represented the levels of the within-subjects factor, Time.

The degrees of freedom that appear in Excerpt 18.16 are worth noting.
Because the means were adjusted on the basis of the first blood sample, one *df*
was "used up" from the between-subjects error term. Thus, to determine how
many subjects were involved in this study, you must add the two *df* values next
to the first *F*, and then add 2. Hence, a total of 25 subjects provided the data
for this ANCOVA. As a check on this claim, note that the second of the two
df values next to the first *F* would have been equal to 23 if data from the final

Excerpt 18.15 A Different Way of Presenting the Results of Three One–Way ANCOVAs

Analysis of covariance was used to compare the groups on the three posttests with the pretest used as a covariate. Table 1 displays the means, standard deviations, adjusted means, and *f* values for the written arithmetic word-problem test and the two interview measures.

Table 1

Means, standard deviations, adjusted means, and *f* values for the arithmetic word problem pretest and the three posttests

| Achievement measure | Maximum possible | CGI | | Non–CGI | | *f value* |
		Mean (SD)	Adjusted mean	Mean (SD)	Adjusted mean	
Written problem–solving pretest	14	2.26 (1.04)		1.25 (.56)		
Written problem–solving posttest	14	9.67 (1.76)	9.41	2.92 (.94)	3.18	87.60[*]
Interview word problems	6	5.54 (.35)	5.44	2.83 (.61)	2.93	114.45[*]
Interview number facts	5	4.76 (.47)	4.68	2.92 (.56)	3.00	46.47[*]

Note. N = 24
[*]*p < .001.*

Source: A. Villasenor, and H. A. Kepner. (1993). Arithmetic from a problem-solving perspective: An urban implematation. *Journal of Research in Mathematics Education, 24(1)*, p. 67.

four blood samples had been analyzed with an ANOVA; the second *df* next to the second *F* matches the answer you get from multiplying 23 by 3.[5,6]

Excerpt 18.17 contains the results from another two-factor mixed AN-COVA, this one conducted within a study set up to investigate the impact of people's preconceptions of their abilities on the development of competen-

---

[5]*You may want to review the material in Chapter 17 for two-factor mixed ANOVAs if you have trouble understanding the rationale behind our little check.*

[6]*In mixed ANCOVAs, data on the covariate will sometimes be collected immediately prior to when data (on the dependent variable) are collected at each level of the within-subjects factor. When this happens, the covariance adjustment uses up 1 df from each of the error terms.*

Excerpt 18.16   Results of a Mixed ANCOVA Presented Solely
Within the Text of the Research Report

To determine whether stress affected lymphocyte proliferation, repeated measures ANCOVAs were performed (again covarying for baseline). Overall, experimental subjects exhibited weaker proliferative response than did control subjects, . . . $F(1, 22) = 5.32, p < .05$. There was also a significant time effect, indicating that lymphocyte proliferation increased during the 2-hour period in both groups, $F(3, 69) = 4.44, p < .01$. . . . The Treatment $\times$ Time interaction was not significant, indicating that, after controlling for baseline, . . . the effects of the stressor, although most dramatic during the stressor session, persisted throughout the study.

Source: S. G. Zakowski, C. G. McAllister, M. Deal, and A. Baum. (1992). Stress, reactivity, and immune function in healthy men. *Health Psychology, 11*(4), p. 228.

cies. In this study, 48 subjects were randomly assigned to one of two conditions. Half of the subjects were told that ability for the experiment's task was an acquirable skill, while the remaining subjects were told that performance ability was determined by inherited aptitude. The "pursuit rotor task" in the study involved asking subjects to keep a penlike stylus on the target area of a revolving disk, with measurements taken both before students were given the differing instructions and then during three post-instruction sessions. The two factors were called Conditions and Phases.

In Excerpt 18.17, note that no post hoc comparisons were made of the three adjusted main effect means for phases (even though the main effect for phases was statistically significant). In "probing" the interaction, tests of simple main effects were applied in such a way as to compare (1) each group's performance across the three phases and (2) the two groups against each other at each phase. Also note that the Bonferroni procedure was used in conjunction with the intragroup comparison because more than one comparison was made of each group's performance across the three phases.[7]

Excerpt 18.17   Two-Factor Mixed ANCOVA with a Post Hoc
Investigation

The significance of the changes produced by the treatment conditions was evaluated using a 2×3 analysis of covariance (ANCOVA), with conception of ability as a between-subjects variable, phases as a within-subjects, repeated measures

(Continued)

---

[7] *In Chapter 13, we indicated that the Bonferroni procedure can be used in situations where there are multiple dependent variables or in situations where there are multiple contrasts investigated. In Excerpt 18.17, we see the latter kind of application of the Bonferroni procedure.*

Excerpt 18.17   Two-Factor Mixed ANCOVA with a Post Hoc
Investigation *(Continued)*

variable, and prefatory performance as the covariate. . . . The analysis yielded
highly significant main effects for conditions, $F(1, 45) = 10.82$, $p<.002$, and
phases, $F(2, 92) = 20.41$, $p<.0001$. These effects were qualified by a highly significant interaction between treatment conditions and phases, $F(2, 92) = 8.08$,
$p<.001$.

In the intragroup contrasts, using the Bonferroni procedure, subjects in the
inherent-aptitude condition achieved no performance gains across adjacent
phases; their counterparts in the acquirable-skill condition raised their performance from the first to the second phase, $p<.07$, and achieved even larger performance improvements between the second and the third phase, $p<.001$. The
intergroup difference in performance attainments was significant beyond the
$p<.001$ level at each of the three phases of the experiment.

Source: F. J. Jourden, A. Bandura, and J. T. Banfield. (1991). The impact of conceptions of ability on
self-regulatory factors and motor skill acquisition. *Journal of Sport and Exercise Psychology, 13*(3), p. 213.

THE STATISTICAL BASIS FOR ANCOVA'S POWER ADVANTAGE AND ADJUSTMENT FEATURE

In order for ANCOVA to provide increased power (over a comparable
ANOVA) and to adjust the group means, the covariate variable(s) must be
correlated with the dependent variable. Although the correlation(s) can be
either positive or negative in nature, ANCOVA will not achieve its power
and adjustment objectives unless at least a moderate relationship exists between each covariate variable and the dependent variable. Stated differently,
"nuisance" variability within the dependent variable scores can be accounted
for to the extent that a strong relationship exists between the covariate(s) and
the dependent variable.[8]

There are many ways to consider the correlation in ANCOVA, even when
data have been collected on just one covariate variable. Two ways of doing
this involve (1) looking at the correlation between the covariate and dependent variables for all subjects from all comparison groups thrown into one
large group, or (2) looking at the correlation between the covariate and dependent variables separately within each comparison group. The second of
these two ways of considering the correlation is appropriate, because
ANCOVA makes its adjustments (of individual scores and of group means)
on the basis of the pooled within-groups correlation coefficient. If re-

---

[8]*When two or more covariate variables are used within the same study, ANCOVA works best when the
covariates are unrelated to each other. When the correlations among the covariate variables are low, each
such variable has a chance to account for a different portion of the nuisance variability in the dependent
variable.*

searchers provide evidence in an effort to show that the correlation was high enough to justify using ANCOVA, they should report on the pooled within-group r, not the r based on all subjects thrown together. Unfortunately, the information in a computer's ANCOVA's summary table called "regression" or "covariate" (with 1 df) deals with the latter, not the former.

One final point is worth making about the correlation between the covariate and dependent variables. Regarding the question of how large the pooled within-groups r needs to be before the covariate can "make a difference" in terms of increasing power, statistical theory responds by saying that the absolute value of this r should be at least .20. If r is smaller than this, the power of ANCOVA will be *lower* than that associated with a comparable ANOVA. This is the case because the researcher must "pay a price" for using information on a covariate variable within the analysis. That price takes the form of 1 df being "lost" from the within-groups row of the ANCOVA summary table. Losing df from within-groups is harmful, because the within-groups df value is divided into the within-groups SS in order to obtain the MS that is used as the denominator of the F-test. The researcher does not want to "give up" that df unless, in return, the covariate brings about a proportionately greater reduction in the within-groups SS. When the absolute value of the pooled within-groups r exceeds .20, ANCOVA is advantageous because this trade-off makes it more likely that a false H_0 will be rejected. If r is between $-.20$ and $+.20$, however, more is lost than is gained.[9]

ASSUMPTIONS

The statistical assumptions of ANCOVA include all the assumptions that are associated with ANOVA, plus three that are unique to the situation where data on a covariate variable are used in an effort to make adjustments and increase power. All three of these unique-to-ANCOVA assumptions must be met if the analysis is to function in its intended manner, and the researcher (and you) should consider these assumptions whenever ANCOVA is used—even in situations where the comparison groups are equally large. In other words, equal ns do *not* cause ANCOVA to be robust to any of the assumptions we now wish to consider.

THE INDEPENDENT VARIABLE SHOULD NOT AFFECT THE COVARIATE VARIABLE

The first of these three new assumptions stipulates that the study's independent variable should not affect the covariate variable. In an experiment (where the independent variable is an active factor), this assumption clearly

---

[9]*Although we have used r in this paragraph, it is actually the population parameter ρ that needs to exceed ± .20 in order for ANCOVA to have a power advantage.*

will be met if the data on the covariate variable are collected before the treatments are applied. If the covariate data are collected after the treatments have been applied, the situation is far more murky—and the researcher should provide a logical argument on behalf of the implicit claim that treatments do not affect the covariate. In nonexperimental (i.e., descriptive) studies, the situation is even *more* murky, since the independent variable very likely may have influenced, prior to the study, each subject's status on the covariate variable. We will return to this issue—of covariance being used in nonrandomized studies—in the next major section.

HOMOGENEITY OF WITHIN-GROUP CORRELATIONS (OR REGRESSION SLOPES)

The second unique assumption associated with ANCOVA stipulates that the correlation between the covariate and dependent variables is the same within each of the populations involved in the study. This assumption usually is talked about in terms of regression slopes rather than correlations, and hence you are likely to come across ANCOVA research reports that contain references to the **assumption of equal regression slopes** or to the **homogeneity of regression slope assumption.** The data of a study can be employed to test this assumption—and it should *always* be tested when ANCOVA is used. As is the case when testing other assumptions, the researcher will be happy when the statistical test of the equal slopes assumption leads to a fail-to-reject decision. That outcome is interpreted as a signal that it is permissible to analyze the study's data using ANCOVA procedures.

In Excerpts 18.18 and 18.19, we see cases in which the assumption of equal regression slopes was tested. In each case, the tested null hypothesis was not rejected, thus indicating that the data did not argue convincingly against the important assumption of common regression slopes (or common correlations) in the populations being compared. Accordingly, the researchers who conducted these tests moved on to what they wanted to do from the outset—a comparison of their various group means through a covariance analysis.

If the equal-slopes H_0 is rejected, there are several options open to the researcher. In that situation, the data can be transformed and then the assumption can be tested again using the transformed data. Or, the researcher can turn to one of several more complicated analyses (e.g., the Johnson–Neyman technique) developed specifically for the situation where heterogeneous regressions exist. Or, the researcher can decide to pay no attention to the covariate data and simply use an ANOVA to compare groups on the dependent variable. These various options come into play only rarely, either because the equal-slopes assumption is not rejected when it is tested or because the researcher wrongfully bypasses testing the assumption.

Excerpts 18.18–18.19   Testing the Assumption of Equal Regression
Slopes

The homogeneity of group regressions assumption for ANCOVA was tested. The F test for heterogeneous regressions of number of supported employment closures on changes in outcomes for other populations was not significant, $F(1, 66) = .42, p = .53$. Therefore, ANCOVA was deemed feasible.

Source: E. M. Szymanski, C. Hanley-Maxwell, J. L. Schaller, R. M. Parker, and S. Kidder. (1992). Impact of a system-change initiative on supported employment in Wisconsin. *Rehabilitation Counseling Bulletin, 35*(4), p. 214.

To ensure the appropriate application of analysis of covariance, the total scores were analyzed to determine if the regression coefficients of the treatment groups were homogeneous. For each of the three tests [one performed for each dependent variable], it was determined that there was not a significant difference between the coefficients for the treatment groups.

Source: F. E. Fischer. (1992). A part-part-whole curriculum. *Journal for Research in Mathematics Education, 21*(3), p. 213.

LINEARITY

The third assumption connected to ANCOVA (but not ANOVA) stipulates that the within-group relationship between the covariate and dependent variables should be linear.[10] A statistical test exists that makes it possible to check out this **linearity** assumption, but not many applied researchers who use ANCOVA discuss the application of this test. When no evidence is presented to show that the test on linearity was conducted, you have no option but to conclude that no attention was devoted to the linearity assumption. Since the impact of nonlinearity is to lower the statistical power of tests on the adjusted means, you have a right to be suspicious of any claims based on *nonsignificant* ANCOVA F-tests when nothing is said about linearity.

OTHER "STANDARD" ASSUMPTIONS

As indicated earlier, the "standard" assumptions of ANOVA (e.g., normality, homogeneity of variance, sphericity) underlie ANCOVA as well. You should upgrade or downgrade your evaluation of a study depending upon the attention given to these assumptions in the situations where F-tests are biased when assumptions are violated. To illustrate this point, consider the ANCOVA results presented in Excerpt 18.20. The brief note beneath the table

---

[10]*We first discussed the notion of linearity in Chapter 3; you may want to review that earlier discussion if you have forgotten what it means to say that two variables have a linear relationship.*

Excerpt 18.20   Concern for the Sphericity Assumption in a Four-Way Mixed ANCOVA

Table 5

Repeated measures analysis of covariance for willingness to see counselor ratings

Source	SS	df	MS	F
Gender (A)	9.045	1	9.045	6.36*
Acculturation (B)	7.538	1	7.538	5.30*
Ethnicity (C)	7.183	4	1.796	1.26
A × B	0.060	1	0.060	0.04
A × C	7.517	4	1.879	1.32
B × C	2.840	4	0.710	0.50
A × B × C	3.887	4	0.972	0.68
Covariate	1,622.175	1	1,622.175	1,140.59
Error	1,006.936	708	1.422	
Concerns (D)	68.650	7	9.807	22.46**
D × A	5.427	7	0.775	1.78
D × B	2.563	7	0.366	0.84
D × C	11.030	28	0.394	0.90
D × A × B	2.828	7	0.404	0.92
D × A × C	8.438	28	0.301	0.69
D × B × C	7.018	28	0.251	0.57
D × A × BC	5.753	28	0.205	0.47
Covariate	2,885.320	1	2,885.320	6,606.49
Error	2,167.104	4962	0.437	

Note. The Geisser-Greenhouse conservative test was applied to all F values that involved the repeated factor.

*p < .05. **p < .0001.

Source: R. H. Gim, D. R. Atkinson, and S. Whiteley. (1990). Asian-American acculturation, severity of concerns, and willingness to see a counselor. *Journal of Counseling Psychology, 37*, 284.

causes us to *upgrade* our confidence in the conclusions drawn by the researchers.

ANCOVA USED WITH INTACT GROUPS

In a randomized experiment, the various population means on the covariate variable can be considered identical. This is the case because of the random assignment of subjects to the comparison groups of the investigation.

Granted, the sample means for the comparison groups on the covariate variable will probably vary, but the corresponding population means are identical.

When ANCOVA is used to compare **intact groups** (i.e., groups that are formed in a nonrandomized fashion), the population means on the covariate variable cannot be assumed to be equal. For example, if a study is set up to compare sixth-grade boys with sixth-grade girls on their ability to solve word problems in mathematics, a researcher might choose to make the comparison using ANCOVA, with reading ability used as the covariate variable. In such a study, the population means on reading ability might well differ between the two gender groups.

Although our concern over the equality or inequality of the covariate population means may initially seem silly (because of the adjustment feature of AN-COVA), this issue is far more important than it might at first appear. We say this because studies in theoretical statistics have shown that the ANCOVA's adjusted means turn out to be biased in the situation where the comparison groups differ with respect to population means on the covariate variable. In other words, the sample-based adjusted means on the dependent variable do not turn out to be accurate estimates of the corresponding adjusted means in the population when the population means on the covariate variable are dissimilar.

Because ANCOVA produces adjusted means, many applied researchers evidently think that this statistical procedure was designed so as to permit intact groups to be compared. We say this because we repeatedly come across research reports in which the researchers talk as if ANCOVA has the magical power to equate intact groups and thereby allow valid inferences to be drawn from comparisons of adjusted means. Excerpts 18.21–18.23, we believe, illustrate this view held by many applied researchers that ANCOVA works well with intact groups.

Besides ANCOVA's statistical inability to generate unbiased adjusted means when intact groups are compared, there is a second, logical reason why you should be on guard whenever you come across a research report in which ANCOVA was used in an effort to "equate" intact groups. Simply stated, the covariate variable(s) used by the researcher may not address one or more important differences between the intact groups. In Excerpt 18.21, for

---

Excerpts 18.21–18.23   The Use of ANCOVA to Compare Intact Groups

---

At baseline, the emotionally disturbed subjects differed from the regular education subjects on systolic blood pressure and on the WAIS-R-Digit Symbol test scores. . . . The analysis of covariance statistical procedure was implemented to correct for these differences.

Source: J. E. Gilliam. (1991). The effects of Baker-Miller pink on physiological and cognitive behavior of emotionally disturbed and regular education students. *Behavior Disorders, 17*(1), p. 51.

(Continued)

Excerpts 18.21–18.23 The Use of ANCOVA to Compare Intact
Groups *(Continued)*

Controlling for pre-existing differences in SES level for this school-identified
sample of students was critical to address the research question, "To what extent are there differences in home environments for different categories of
mildly handicapped students and nonhandicapped students?" . . . The covariate
(SES) was significantly different for the four student groups, $F(3, 67) = 4.453$,
$p < .007$.

Source: S. L. Christenson. (1990). Differences in students' home environments: The need to work
with families. *School Psychology Review, 19*(4), p. 512.

Because the experimental and control groups were not formed randomly, analysis of covariance (ANCOVA) was used to examine the results, with auditory linguistic ability and letter knowledge as covariates. Analysis of covariance reduces
the effect of initial group differences statistically by making compensating adjustments on the final means for the dependent variable.

Source: A. Lie. (1991). Effects of a training program for stimulating skills in word analysis in first-
grade children. *Reading Research Quarterly, 26*(3), p. 244.

example, ANCOVA was used because the two intact groups had been found
to differ, at baseline, with respect to systolic blood pressure and performance
on the Digit Symbol portion of the WAIS-R intelligence test. But isn't it
quite possible that the comparison groups *also* differed at the outset with respect to other important characteristics that were not measured? If so,
ANCOVA would have no way to "correct" for such differences because no
data on such variables were collected.

In summary, we suggest that you be extremely cautious when confronted
with research claims based upon the use of ANCOVA with intact groups. If
an important covariate variable was overlooked by those who conducted the
study, pay no attention whatsoever to the conclusions based upon the data
analysis. Even in the case where data on all important covariate variables
were collected and used, you *still* should be tentative in your inclination to
"buy into" the claims made by the researchers.

RELATED ISSUES

Near the beginning of this chapter, we asserted that any ANCOVA is, in several respects, like its ANOVA counterpart. We have already considered many
of the ways in which ANOVA and ANCOVA are similar, such as the way
post hoc tests are typically used to probe significant F-tests in the summary
table. At this point, we want to point out three additional ways in which
ANCOVA is akin to ANOVA.

As with ANOVA, the Type I error rate will be inflated if separate ANCOVAs are used to analyze the data corresponding to two or more dependent variables. To deal with this problem, the conscientious researcher will implement one of several available strategies. The most frequently used strategy for keeping the operational Type I error rate in line with the stated alpha level is the **Bonferroni adjustment technique**, and it can be used with ANCOVA as easily as it can with ANOVA.

In Excerpt 18.24, we see a case where the Bonferroni procedure was used in conjunction with a covariance analysis. The authors of this investigation deserve credit for being sensitive to a problem that would have existed if each of the four ANCOVAs had been conducted as if it were the only one in the study.

The second issue that has a common connection to both ANOVA and ANCOVA is the important distinction between **statistical significance** and **practical significance.** Since it is possible, in either kind of analysis, for the data to produce a finding that is significant in a statistical sense but not in a practical sense, you should upgrade your evaluation of any ANCOVA study wherein the researcher conducts a power analysis, estimates the magnitude of observed effects, or computes a strength–of–association index. Excerpts 18.25 and 18.26 contain examples of how the second and third of these approaches were used in recent studies to address concerns about the practical significance of the obtained results.

The third point we want to make in this section is simple: **Planned comparisons** can be used in ANCOVA studies just as easily as they can be used in ANOVA studies. Excerpt 18.27 illustrates the use of such comparisons to test three specific hypotheses not directly addressed by any of the main or interaction F-tests of the 3×2 ANCOVA. One of the factors, Time of Menarche, was made up of three levels: early maturers, on–time maturers, and late maturers. The other factor, School Type, had two levels: all–girl schools and mixed–sex schools.

Excerpt 18.24 Use of the Bonferroni Adjustment Procedures in an ANCOVA Analysis

---

All four dependent variables were highly correlated with each other at both pretest and posttest ($p<.0001$). Univariate rather than multivariate ANCOVAs were used, however, in order to examine each dependent variable separately (rather than as a composite) and thus not obscure any differences in outcome due to rater–versus–patient perspective. Because treatment and therapist effects were expected, . . . [F-tests] were conducted according to the modified Bonferroni Test (Keppel, 1983) in order to control for familywise error rate.

Source: L. R. Propst, R. Ostrom, P. Watkins, T. Dean, and D. Mashburn. (1992). Comparative efficacy of religious and nonreligious cognitive-behavioral therapy for the treatment of clinical depression in religious individuals. *Journal of Consulting and Clinical Psychology, 60*(1), p. 97.

Excerpts 18.25–18.26   Dealing with the Issue of the Practical
Significance of Results

[One-way] analyses of covariance were used with the General Mathematics, Mathematical Word Problem, and Number Competence Tests as the respective dependent variables. . . [and] Language as the independent variable. . . . In each case, there was a significant effect for Language. . . . The amount of variance explained by Language for General Mathematics, Mathematical Word Problem, and Number Competence respectively was 44%, 51%, and 39% after the effects of the covariates had been removed.

Source: P. C. Clarkson, and P. Galbraith. (1992). Bilingualism and mathematics learning: Another perspective. *Journal of Research in Mathematics Education, 23/24,* p. 43.

Effect sizes comparing the two CBM groups were .02 for words read correctly, .14 for questions correct, .55 for total words written on the recall, .54 for matched words written on the recall, .16 for number of maze correct, and 0 for percentage of maze correct.

Source: L. S. Fuchs, D. Fuchs, C. L. Hamlett, and C. Ferguson. (1992). Effects of expert system consultation within curriculum-based measurement, using a reading maze task. *Exceptional Children,* 58(5), p. 445.

When we first looked at the material in Excerpt 18.27, we thought that the researchers had actually conducted a post hoc (rather than planned) investigation, since the first sentence says that the 3 × 2 ANCOVA was "*followed by* planned comparisons" (our emphasis). However, after closely examining what was done, we concluded that the three *t*-tests discussed in the second paragraph conform fully to the definition of planned comparisons we presented in Chapter 13. We take this position because the comparison of the girls from the two different school types at each of the three maturational levels was performed even though the *F*-test for the interaction turned out to be

Excerpt 18.27   The Investigation of Planned Comparisons in an
ANCOVA Study

To explore these questions, we carried out a 3×2 ANCOVA followed by planned comparisons to test the hypothesized effects by using self-reported illegal delinquency at age 15 as the outcome variable. Once again, we introduced social class and external behaviors in late childhood as covariates into the analysis. . . . The results revealed a significant main effect for time of menarche, $F(2, 261) = 3.81, p < .05$. . . . The main effect for school type was not significant,

(Continued)

Excerpt 18.27   The Investigation of Planned Comparisons in an
ANCOVA Study *(Continued)*

$F(1, 261) = 1.88$ *ns.* The interaction effect in this preliminary analysis was not significant, $F(2, 261) = 1.06$, *ns.*

As before, we used a set of planned contrasts to compare our specific predictions with the obtained data. The first prediction was supported: . . . early-maturing girls in mixed-sex schools engaged in significantly more delinquent activities than did their counterparts in all-girl schools (3.16 vs. 1.78), $t(261) = 2.02, p<.05$. The second prediction received marginal support: . . . on-time maturers in mixed-sex schools engaged in slightly more delinquent activities than their all-girl school counterparts (3.49 vs. 2.45), $t(261) = 1.78, p<.10$. The third prediction was confirmed: late maturing girls in mixed-sex schools did not differ significantly in terms of their self-reported delinquency from their counterparts in all-girl schools (1.26 vs. 1.51), $t<1$.

Source: A. Caspi, D. Lynam, T. E. Moffitt, and P. A. Silva. (1993). Unraveling girls' delinquency: Biological, dispositional, and contextual contributions to adolescent misbehavior, *Developmental Psychology, 29*(1), p. 24.

---

nonsignificant. If these comparisons, which are essentially tests of simple main effects, had been approached from strictly a post hoc perspective, they never would have been investigated. That is because such tests, if post hoc in nature, require the interaction F to be significant in order for a simple main effects investigation to be justified.

A FEW WARNINGS

Before concluding our discussion of ANCOVA, we want to offer a few warnings about deciphering research reports that present results from this form of statistical analysis. As you consider our comments, however, do not forget that ANCOVA legitimately can be thought of as a set of statistical procedures made possible by adding covariate data to an ANOVA-type situation. Because of this fact, all the tips and warnings offered at the conclusions of Chapters 12–17 should be kept in mind when you consider the results from a study that used ANCOVA. In addition to being aware of the concerns focused upon in those earlier chapters, you should also remain sensitive to the following three unique-to-ANCOVA cautions when considering research claims based on covariance analyses.

THE STATISTICAL FOCUS: ADJUSTED MEANS

In a covariance analysis, all F-tests (other than those concerned with underlying assumptions) deal with adjusted means on the dependent variable, not the unadjusted means. This holds true for the F-tests contained in the ANCOVA summary table, the F-tests involved in any planned comparisons, and the F-tests involved in any post hoc investigation. For this reason, adjusted means should be presented—either in a table or within the textual discussion—whenever the researcher attempts to explain the meaning of any F-test result. It is helpful, as we have seen, to have access to the means on the covariate variable and the unadjusted means on the dependent variable. However, it is the adjusted means on the dependent variable that constitute the central statistical focus of any ANCOVA.

Unfortunately, many researchers fail to present the adjusted means in their research reports. When this happens, you are boxed into a corner where you cannot easily decide for yourself whether a statistically significant finding ought to be considered significant in a practical sense. Since making this kind of decision is one of the things we believe consumers of the researcher literature ought to do on a regular basis, we must encourage you to downgrade your evaluation of any ANCOVA-based study that fails to contain the adjusted means that "go with" the F-test(s) focused upon by the researcher.

THE IMPORTANCE OF UNDERLYING ASSUMPTIONS

ANCOVA's F-tests that compare adjusted means function as they are supposed to function only if various underlying assumptions are valid. Moreover, the condition of equal sample sizes does not bring about a situation where the assumptions are rendered unimportant. In other words, equal ns do not cause ANCOVA to become robust to its underlying assumptions.

Whenever you consider research claims based upon ANCOVA, check to see whether the researcher says anything about the statistical assumptions upon which the analysis was based. Upgrade your evaluation of the research report when there is expressed concern over the assumption of equal regression slopes, the assumption of a linear relationship between the covariate and dependent variables, and the assumption that scores on the covariate variable are not influenced by the independent variable. If these assumptions are not discussed, you should downgrade your evaluation of the study.

If an assumption is tested, give the researchers some bonus credit if they use a lenient rather than rigorous alpha level in assessing the assumption's H_0. We say this because researchers deserve credit if they perform statistical tests in such a way that the "deck" is "stacked against them" in terms of what they would like to show. Since the typical researcher who uses ANCOVA wants the linearity and equal-slopes assumptions to be met, a lenient level of significance (such as .10, .15, .20, or even .25) gives the data more of a chance to reveal an improper situation than would be the case if alpha is set equal to .05, .01, or .001. When testing assumptions, Type II errors are generally considered to be more serious than "errors of the first kind," and the level of significance should be set accordingly.

ANCOVA VERSUS ANOVA

Our final warning has to do with your general opinion of ANCOVA-based studies as compared with ANOVA-based studies. Because ANCOVA is more complex (due to the involvement of a larger number of variables and assumptions), many consumers of the research literature hold the opinion that data-based claims are more trustworthy when they are based upon ANCOVA rather than ANOVA. We strongly encourage you to *refrain* from adopting this unjustified point of view.

Although ANCOVA (as compared with ANOVA) does, in fact, involve more complexities in terms of what is involved both on and beneath the surface, it is an extremely delicate instrument. To provide meaningful results, ANCOVA must be used very carefully—with attention paid to important assumptions, with focus directed at the appropriate set of sample means, and with concern over the correct way to draw inferences from ANCOVA's *F*-tests. Because of its complexity, ANCOVA affords its users more opportunities to make mistakes than does ANOVA.

If used skillfully, ANCOVA can be of great assistance to applied researchers. If not used skillfully, however, ANCOVA can be dangerous. We say that because of the unfortunate tendency of many people to think of complexity as being an inherent virtue. In statistics, that is often *not* the case. As pointed out earlier in the chapter, the interpretation of ANCOVA *F*-tests is problematic whenever the groups being compared have been formed in a nonrandom fashion—and this statement holds true even if (1) multiple covariate variables are involved and (2) full attention is directed to all underlying assumptions. In contrast, it would be much easier to interpret the results generated by the application of ANOVA to the data provided by subjects who have been randomly assigned to comparison groups. Care is required, of course, whenever you attempt to interpret the outcome of *any* inferential test. Our point is simply that ANCOVA, because of its complexity as compared to ANOVA, demands a higher—not lower—level of care on your part when you encounter its results.

REVIEW TERMS

Adjusted means	Homogeneity of regression slopes
Analysis of covariance	Linearity
ANCOVA	Intact groups
Assumption of equal regression slopes	Planned comparison
Bonferroni adjustment technique	Post hoc investigation
Concomitant variable	Practical significance
Covariate variable	Statistical significance

REVIEW QUESTIONS

1. ANCOVA was developed to help researchers decrease the probability that they will make Type _____ errors when they test null hypothesis.

2. What are the three kinds of variables involved in any ANCOVA study?

3. (True or False) If data from two or more covariate variables are used within the analysis (as was done in Excerpt 18.8), the resulting ANCOVA should be considered to be multivariate in nature.

4. In Excerpt 18.6, the data on which variable were used as a basis for making adjustments? Those adjustments were made in the group means on which variable?

5. (True or False) The number of null hypotheses associated with any ANCOVA can be determined by multiplying the number of covariate variables times the number of independent variables.

6. In ANCOVA studies, is it possible for something other than a pretest (or baseline measure) to serve as the covariate?

7. In Excerpt 18.14, how large was the within-groups mean square in the ANCOVA performed on the BIPT video data?

8. In Excerpt 18.15, why aren't there any adjusted means presented for the first achievement measure?

9. For ANCOVA to achieve its objectives, should there be a strong or weak correlation between each covariate variable and the dependent variable?

10. When ANCOVA is used, 1 df is "used up" (or "lost") for each covariate variable included in the analysis. What is the source of this/these "lost" df(s)?

11. (True or False) Like ANOVA, ANCOVA is robust to violations of its underlying assumptions if the sample sizes are equal.

12. One of ANCOVA's assumptions states that the _____ variable should not affect the _____ variable.

13. In testing the assumption of equal homogeneous regression slopes, does the typical researcher hope that the null hypothesis will be rejected or not rejected?

14. Where does ANCOVA work best, in randomized experiments or in studies comparing intact groups?

15. (True or False) Because ANCOVA involves data on one or more covariate variables, the Bonferroni procedure cannot be used when separate analyses are performed on different dependent variables.

16. Would it make more sense for a researcher to set alpha equal to .01 or .1 when conducting a test of the equal slopes assumption?

INFERENCES ON PERCENTAGES, PROPORTIONS, AND FREQUENCIES

In your journey through the previous nine chapters, you have examined a variety of inferential techniques that are used when at least one of the researcher's variables is quantitative in nature. The bulk of Chapter 10, for example, dealt with inferences concerning Pearson's r, a bivariate measure of association designed for use with two quantitative variables. Beginning in Chapter 11, you saw how inferential techniques can be used to investigate one or more groups in terms of means (and variances), with the dependent variable in such situations obviously being quantitative in nature.

In the present chapter, your journey takes a slight turn, for you will now look at an array of inferential techniques designed for the situation where *none* of the researcher's variables are quantitative. In other words, the statistical techniques discussed in this chapter are used when all of a researcher's variables involve questions concerning membership in categories. For example, a researcher might wish to use sample data to help gain insights as to the prevalence of AIDS in the general population. Or, a pollster might be interested in using sample data to predict how each of three political candidates competing for the same office would fare "if the election were to be held today." In these two illustrations as well as in countless real studies, the study's data do not reflect *the extent* to which each subject possesses some characteristic of interest but instead reveal how each subject has been classified into one of the categories established by the researcher.

When a study's data speak to the issue of group membership, the researcher's statistical focus will be on frequencies, on percentages, or on proportions. For example, the hypothetical pollster referred to in the previous paragraph might summarize the study's data by reporting, "Of the 1,000 voters who were sampled, 428 stated that they would vote for candidate A, 381 stated that they would vote for candidate B, and 191 reported that they would vote for candidate C." Instead of providing us with **frequencies** (i.e., the number of people in each response category), the same data could be summarized through **percentages**. With this approach, the researcher would report that "candidates A, B, and C received 42.8 percent, 38.1 percent, and 19.1 percent of the votes, respectively." Or, the data could be converted into **proportions**, with the researcher asserting that "the proportionate popularity of candidates A, B, and C turned out to be .428, .381, and .191, respectively." The same information, of course, is communicated through each of these three ways of summarizing the data.

Regardless of whether the data concerning group membership are summarized through frequencies, percentages, or proportions, it can be said that the level of measurement used within this kind of study is nominal (rather than ordinal, interval, or ratio). As we pointed out in Chapter 3, a researcher's data *can* be nominal in nature. In focusing on inferential techniques appropriate for means, we spent the last several chapters dealing with procedures that are useful when the researcher's data are interval or ratio in nature. In the present chapter, however, we restrict our consideration to statistical inferences appropriate for nominal data.

Although a multitude of inferential procedures have been developed for use with nominal-level data, we will consider here only six of these procedures that permit researchers to evaluate null hypotheses. These procedures are the sign test, the binomial test, Fisher's Exact Test, the chi-square test, McNemar's test, and Cochran's test. These are the most frequently used of the test procedures designed for nominal-level data, and a knowledge of these procedures will put you in a fairly good position to understand researchers' results when their data take the form of frequencies, percentages, or proportions.

We will also illustrate how *z*-tests and *t*-tests can be used, in certain situations, to answer the same kinds of research questions as those posed by the six basic test procedures considered in this chapter. Moreover, we will show how the Bonferroni technique can be used with any of these test procedures so as to control against an inflated Type I error rate. Finally, we will examine a few cases in which confidence intervals have been built around sample percentages or proportions.

THE SIGN TEST

Of all inferential tests, the **sign test** is perhaps the simplest and easiest to understand. It requires that the researcher do nothing more than classify each subject of the study into one of two categories. Each of the subjects put into one of these categories receives a plus sign (i.e., a "+"); in contrast, a minus sign (i.e., a "−") is given to each subject who falls into the other category.

The hypothesis testing procedure is then used to evaluate the null hypothesis that says the full sample of subjects comes from a population in which there are as many pluses as minuses. If the sample is quite "lopsided" with far more pluses than minuses (or far more minuses than pluses), the sign test's H_0 will be rejected. On the other hand, if the frequencies of pluses and minuses in the sample are equal or nearly equal, the null hypothesis of the sign test will be retained.

In Excerpt 19.1, we see a case in which the sign test was used within a study dealing with people who had a phobia about flying in airplanes. Each of 13 subjects was measured in terms of both heart rate and self-reported anxiety at five measurement periods: upon arriving at the airport, sitting in the airplane prior to take-off, five minutes after take-off, five minutes prior to landing, and sitting in the airplane after landing. For each subject, heart rate and anxiety were correlated across the five time periods. The data used in the sign test were simply the signs of these correlation coefficients. A positive sign indicated a tendency, within a given subject, for heart rate and anxiety to be directly related; a negative sign indicated an inverse relationship.

Excerpt 19.1   A Sign Test

Synchrony/desynchrony was investigated by correlating heart rate and anxiety over the five measurement occasions of the flight for each subject separately. Heart rate and self-reported anxiety covaried positively (mean $r = .58$, median $r = .75$; range $= -0.27–.95$). Only one of 13 subjects exhibited a negative correlation (sign test, $Z = 3.05$, $P < .003$).

Source: J. Beckham, S. Vrana, J. May, D. Gustafson, and G. Smith. (1990). Emotional processing and fear measurement synchrony as indicators of treatment outcome in fear of flying. *Journal of Behavior Therapy and Experimental Psychology, 21*(3), p. 159.

As indicated in the last sentence of Excerpt 19.1, the intrasubject correlation between the physiological and self-report measures of anxiety was greater than zero for 12 of the 13 subjects. The "lopsided" nature of sample data (12 pluses, 1 minus) is quite improbable if the population contains as many pluses as minuses. Hence, the data suggest that intraindividual measures of heart rate and self-reported anxiety covary positively in the population, at least when such measures are taken before, during, and after an airplane ride.

As is the case with all of the test procedures considered in this chapter, researchers can evaluate the sign test's null hypothesis through hypothesis testing, statistical testing, or the "hybrid" approach discussed in Chapters 7–9. Based on the information presented in Excerpt 19.1, we believe that the sign test was conducted either in accord with statistical testing (where a data-based *p* is computed and interpreted without regard to any preset level of significance) or in accord with the hybrid approach to evaluating H_0 (where the alpha level is initially set, most likely at .05, but then "adjusted" so as to become more rigorous if the data-based p-level turns out to be small enough to beat other standard alpha levels—such as .01). We doubt that the researchers who conducted the airplane phobia study used the hypothesis testing procedure with alpha set equal to .003!

One final comment may help to clarify the technical information in Excerpt 19.1. Within the final set of parentheses, the researchers provide the numerical value of their calculated value: $z = 3.05$. When n is 12 or more, the sample data can be put into a formula producing a calculated value that can be referred to the normal curve. With other tests considered later in this chapter and in Chapter 20, we will come across further examples of the researcher's calculated value being presented as a z-value. Such situations simply represent what is referred to as the **large-sample approximation** to whatever test is being conducted, but you do not need to be concerned about the formula used to obtain the calculated value. You should, however, make every effort to understand, for any test, the null hypothesis being evaluated as well as the legitimate statistical interpretation that can be drawn from the data analysis.

The sign test that we have been discussing up until this point is often referred to as a one-sample sign test. The sign test can be used just as easily and with absolutely no change in logic in situations where a single group of subjects is measured on two occasions (e.g., both before and after an intervention) or where two related samples are compared. If the researcher is interested solely in assigning plus and minus signs to indicate the nature of change over time or to indicate which member of a matched pair performed better, then the sign test will probably be the statistical tool used to evaluate the null hypothesis. With the sign test, that null hypothesis is always a statement of equally present pluses and minuses in the population.

THE BINOMIAL TEST

The binomial test is similar to the sign test in that (1) the data are nominal in nature, (2) only two response categories are set up by the researcher, and (3) the response categories must be mutually exclusive. The binomial test is also like the sign test in that it can be used with a single group of subjects who are measured just once, with a single group of subjects who are measured twice (e.g., pre-intervention and post-intervention), or with two groups of subjects who are matched or are related in some logical fashion (e.g., husbands and wives). The binomial and sign tests are even further alike in that both procedures lead to a data-based p-level that comes from tentatively considering the null hypothesis to be true.

The only difference between the sign test and the binomial test concerns the flexibility of the null hypothesis. With the sign test, there is no flexibility.

This is because the sign test's H_0 always says that the objects in the population are divided evenly into the two response categories. With the binomial test, on the other hand, researchers have the flexibility to set up H_0 with any proportionate split that they wish to test.

In Excerpts 19.2 and 19.3, we see two cases that illustrate the versatility of the binomial test. In the study from which Excerpt 19.2 was taken, young children in nursery school, first grade, and third grade were asked to indicate what month it was. The responses from the children in each group were evaluated by two separate binomial tests. In the first use of the binomial test, a child's response was considered to be correct only if the then-current month of November was mentioned. The same responses were subjected to a second binomial test, this time with October, November, and December considered to be correct answers. The null hypothesis for each binomial test was set up to conform to what one would expect by chance if the children (in the population) were to guess randomly among the 12 months when answering the "current month" question. A chart in the research report showed what the null hypothesis specified for each of these binomial tests: 1/12 "correct" and 11/12 "incorrect" when only November was counted as correct; 1/4 "correct" and 3/4 "incorrect" when any of the final three months of the year was counted as a positive response.

Excerpts 19.2–19.3   The Binomial Test

Few of the nursery children and nearly all from the other groups knew the current month. The nursery group exceeded chance levels on the more lenient criterion of being within 1 month of the current month, November.

Source: W. J. Friedman. (1991). The development of children's memory for the time of past events. *Child Development, 62*(1), p. 151.

Subjects were presented one of three randomized orders of 16 personality-descriptive words drawn at regular intervals from Plutchik's (1980, p. 193) circumplex of such terms. Subjects were asked to assign a category of "typically masculine" or "typically feminine" to each of the 16 words. When the binomial test was applied to each of the words (two-tailed, $p < .05$), eight words were identified as significantly more feminine and five words as significantly more masculine.

Source: C. Whissell and G. Chellew. (1994). The position of sex-typical words in two-dimensional emotion space psychological reports. *Psychological Reports, 74*(1), p. 4.

In Excerpt 19.3, the proportionate split in the binomial test's null hypothesis was "even," thus indicating that 50 percent of the people in the population would say that any of the 16 words was typically masculine while the other 50 percent would say that the word was typically feminine. When the binomial test's null hypothesis is set up in this fashion (with H_0 specifying a 50–50 split in the population), the binomial test and the sign test are one and the same. Hence, the inferential test used in Excerpt 19.3 could have been referred to as a sign test.

FISHER'S EXACT TEST

The sign test and the binomial tests, as we have seen, can be used when the researcher has dichotomous data from either a single sample or from two related samples. However, researchers often conduct studies for the purpose of comparing two independent samples with respect to a dichotomous dependent variable. In such situations, Fishers' Exact Test often serves as the researcher's inferential tool.[1]

The null hypothesis of Fisher's Exact Test is highly analogous to the typical null hypothesis of an independent-samples t-test. With that kind of t-test, most researchers evaluate a null hypothesis that says $H_0: \mu_1 = \mu_2$ (or alternatively as $H_0: \mu_1 - \mu_2 = 0$). Using the symbols P_1 and P_2 to stand for the proportion of cases (in the first and second populations, respectively) that fall into one of the two dichotomous categories of the dependent variable, the null hypothesis of Fisher's Exact Test can be expressed $H_0 : P_1 = P_2$ (or alternatively as $H_0: P_1 - P_2 = 0$).

In Excerpt 19.4, we see an example of Fisher's Exact Test being used to compare a treatment group against a control group in terms of the proportion of subjects who experienced exacerbations. As you look at this excerpt, keep in mind that Fisher's Exact Test was used to compare the two sample groups

---

Excerpt 19.4 Fisher's Exact Test

Fisher's Exact Test was used to look for [differences] between the placebo and methotrexate treatments [in] the proportion of subjects having exacerbations. . . . During treatment a total of three exacerbations occurred in two of the nine exacerbation-remitting methotrexate patients over a period of 150 treatment months, for a mean of one exacerbation per 50 months. Seven of the 11 placebo patients had 12 exacerbations during 169 total group treatment months, a mean of one per 14 months. The difference in proportion of patients having exacerbations is not significant (p = 0.09).

Source: R. Currier, A. Haerrer, and E. Maydreth. (1993). Low dose methotrexate treatment of multiple sclerosis: A pilot study. *Journal of Neurology, Neurosurgery, and Psychiatry, 56*, p. 1218.

---

[1] *The word* exact *in the title of this test gives the impression that the Fisher test is superior to other test procedures. This is unfortunate, since many other tests (e.g., the sign test and the binomial test) possess just as much "exactness" as does Fisher's test.*

in terms of proportions, not means. Those sample proportions of .22 (2 out of 9 patients in the treatment group) and .64 (7 out of 11 patients in the placebo group) were not sufficiently different to permit H_0 to be rejected at the .05 level of significance.

It should be noted that certain researchers, in discussing their use of Fisher's Exact Test, use words and phrases suggesting that they tested a correlation coefficient to see if it was significantly different from zero. For example, the words *relationship* and *association* that appear in Excerpts 19.5 and 19.6 are very "correlational" in flavor. This way of talking about Fisher's Exact Test is legitimate and should not throw you when you encounter it. If the two sample proportions turn out to be significantly different, then there is a nonzero relationship (in the sample data) between the dichotomous variable that "creates" the two comparison groups and the dichotomous dependent variable. Hence, the use of Fisher's Exact Test accomplishes the same basic goal as does a test of significance applied to a phi or tetrachoric correlation coefficient.[2]

Excerpts 19.5–19.6   Fisher's Exact Test as a Test of "Relationship" or "Association"

Among High Comprehension readers, subjects linked target information causally 11 times out of a possible 20 (.55 of the cases in which sufficient target information was recalled). Among Low Comprehension readers, subjects linked target information only once in 9 times (.11 of possible cases). A Fisher Exact Probability test proved this relationship significant, with $p = .032$.

Source: S. Zinar. (1990). Fifth-graders' recall of propositional content and causal relationships from expository prose. *Journal of Reading Behavior, 22*(2), p. 193.

All subjects who showed this outcome bias in a given case also rated commissions worse than omissions for that case. The association between the outcome bias and the omission bias is significant by Fishers' exact test for case 1 (p 5 .027).

Source: M. Spranca, E. Minsk, and J. Baron. Omission and commission in judgment and choice. *Journal of Experimental Social Psychology, 27*(1), p. 85.

CHI-SQUARE TESTS: AN INTRODUCTION

Although inferential tests of frequencies, percentages, or proportions are sometimes made using the sign test, the binomial test, or Fisher's Exact Test, the most frequently used statistical tool for making such tests is called

---

[2]*Again we have a parallel between Fisher's Exact Test and the independent-samples t-test, since the t-test's comparison of the two sample means is mathematically equivalent to a test applied to the point-biserial correlation coefficient that assesses the relationship between the dichotomous grouping variable and the dependent variable.*

chi square. As you will see, the chi-square procedure can be used, in certain circumstances, instead of the sign, binomial, or Fisher tests. In addition, the chi-square procedure can be used to answer research questions that cannot be answered by any of the inferential techniques covered thus far in this chapter. Because the chi-square test is so versatile and popular, it is important for any reader of the research literature to become thoroughly familiar with this inferential technique. For this reason, we feel obliged to consider the chi-square technique in a careful and unhurried fashion.

DIFFERENT CHI-SQUARE TESTS

The term *chi-square test* technically describes any inferential test that involves a critical value being pulled from and/or a data-based *p*-value being tied to one of the many chi-square distributions. Each such distribution is like the normal and *t* distributions in that it (1) has one mode, (2) is asymptotic to the baseline, (3) comes from a mathematical formula, and (4) helps applied researchers decide whether to reject or fail-to-reject null hypotheses. Unlike the normal and *t* distributions (but like any *F* distribution), each chi-square distribution is positively skewed. There are many chi-square distributions simply because the degree of skewness tapers off as the number of degrees of freedom increases. In fact, the various chi-square distributions are distinguished from one another solely by the concept of degrees of freedom.

Certain of the inferential tests that are called chi square (because they utilize a chi-square distribution) have nothing to do with frequencies, proportions, or percentages. For example, a comparison of a single sample's variance against a hypothesized null value is conducted by means of a chi-square test. However, these kinds of chi-square tests are clearly in the minority. Without a doubt, most chi-square tests *do* involve the type of data being focused upon throughout this chapter. In other words, it is a relatively safe bet that any chi-square test that you encounter will be dealing with nominal data.

Even when we restrict our consideration of chi square to those cases that involve nominal data, there still are different types of chi-square tests. One type is called a one-sample chi-square test (or a chi-square goodness-of-fit test), a second type is called an independent-samples chi-square test (or a chi-square test of homogeneity of proportions), and the third type is called a chi-square test of independence. We will consider each of these chi-square tests shortly, and then later in the chapter we will see how a chi-square test can also be used with related samples. Before we look at any of these chi-square tests, however, it is appropriate first to consider how to tell that a researcher is presenting results of a chi-square test.

CHI-SQUARE NOTATION AND LANGUAGE

Excerpts 19.7–19.13 illustrate the variation in how applied researchers refer to the chi-square tests used in their studies. Although the studies from which these excerpts were taken differ in the number of samples being compared and the number of nominal categories in the data, it should be noted that each of these studies had the same statistical focus as all of the other tests considered in this chapter: frequencies, proportions, or percentages.

Excerpts 19.7–19.13   Different Ways of Referring to Chi Square

---

To determine whether these differences were significant, the chi-square test was used.

Source: R. Silver. (1988). Screening children and adolescents for depression through Draw-A-Story. *American Journal of Art Therapy, 26*, p. 120.

Significance testing using the statistical package for the social sciences (SPSSX) for differences between the workshop and control groups was undertaken using chi-squared tests.

Source: J. Corner and J. Wilson-Barnett. (1992). The newly registered nurse and the cancer patient: An educational evaluation. *International Journal of Nursing Studies, 29*(2), p. 182.

No differences were found between groups for age or gender of the handicapped children (Kibbutz: 32 males and 11 females; City: 30 males and 18 females; χ^2 (1, N=91) = .99, ns).

Source: M. Margalit, D. Ankonina, and Y. Avraham. (1991). Community support in Israeli Kibbutz and city families of children with disabilities: Family climate and parental coherence. *Journal of Special Education, 24*(4), p. 431.

The gifted group responded significantly more often without probes on questions 1 (chi^2(1) = 4.37, $p < .05$) and 3 (chi^2(1) = 5.56, $p < .05$).

Source: A. Dover and B. Shore. (1991). Giftedness and flexibility on a mathematical set-breaking task. *Gifted Child Quarterly, 35*(2), p. 103.

As expected, more men expressed a positive attitude toward interracial dating than did women (c^2 = 9.54, $df = 2, p = .0085$).

Source: J. Todd, et al. (1992). Attitudes toward interracial dating: Effects of age, sex, and race. *Journal of Multicultural Counseling and Development, 20*(October), p. 205.

Since the interest was in students' positive and negative perceptions of science activity, the two positive and negative response categories were combined to provide one response [category] for both positive and negative. The category of indifference (middle response) was eliminated from data analysis as it indicated neither a negative or positive perception. The positive and negative frequencies

(Continued)

> **Excerpts 19.7–19.13** Different Ways of Referring to Chi Square
> *(Continued)*
>
> ---
>
> were then utilized for data analysis. Thus, the initial item analysis involved a 2 × 3 (response category × treatment) contingency table per questionnaire item.
>
> ---
>
> *Source:* D. P. Shepardson and E. L. Pizzini. (1993). A comparison of student perceptions of science activities within three instructional approaches. *School Science and Mathematics, 93*(3), p. 129.
>
> Pearson chi-square (fields) $= 14.53, 4$ *df*, $p = .006$.
>
> ---
>
> *Source:* J. E. Cote and C. G. Levine. (1992). The genesis of the humanistic academic: A second test of Erikson's theory of ego identity formation. *Youth and Society, 23*(4), p. 403.

Excerpt 19.7 is clear-cut, since the author used the phrase *chi-square test*. In Excerpt 19.8, we see a slight variation in the name given to this test: *chi-squared*.[3] The Greek symbol for chi square, χ^2, is shown in Excerpt 19.9. Two infrequently seen abbreviations appear in Excerpts 19.10 and 19.11. The term **contingency table** appears in Excerpt 19.12; the use of this term strongly suggests (but does not guarantee) that a chi-square test was used. In Excerpt 19.13 we come across the term **Pearson chi-square**. The adjective *Pearson* is the technically correct way to indicate that the chi-square test has been applied to frequencies (rather than, for example, to variances). However, very few applied researchers use this adjective (or the more formal label, *Pearson's approximation to chi square*). Accordingly, it's fairly safe to presume that any chi-square test you encounter is like those considered in this chapter, even though the word *Pearson* does not appear in the test's label. (Of course, this would not be a safe bet if the term *chi-square test* is used within a context where it is clear that the test's statistical focus deals with something other than frequencies, proportions, or percentages.)

THREE MAIN TYPES OF CHI-SQUARE TESTS

We now wish to turn our attention to the three main types of chi-square tests used by applied researchers—the one-sample chi-square test, the independent samples chi-square test, and the chi-square test of independence. Although applied researchers typically refer to all three using the same label (*chi-square test*), the null hypotheses of these tests differ. Accordingly, you need to know

---

[3]*From a technical standpoint, the term* chi-squared *is more accurate than* chi-square. *However, most applied researchers use the latter label when referring to this inferential test.*

which kind of chi-square test has been used in order to understand what is meant by a statistically significant (or nonsignificant) finding.

THE ONE-SAMPLE CHI-SQUARE TEST

With this kind of chi-square test, the various categories of the nominal variable of interest are first set up and considered. Second, a null hypothesis is formulated. The H_0 for the **one-sample chi-square test** is simply a specification of what proportion of the population being considered falls into each category. Next, the researchers determine what proportion of their sample falls into each of the established categories. Finally, the hypothesis testing procedure is used to determine whether the discrepancy between the set of sample proportions and those specified in H_0 is large enough to permit H_0 to be rejected.

In Excerpt 19.14, we see an application of the one-sample chi-square test. In this study, entitled "Born to Play Ball," the researchers wanted to see whether Major League baseball players' birthdays are spread out evenly throughout the year. Two null hypotheses were set up, one having the 12 months as the categories of the nominal variable and the other having four three-month quarters (beginning with August, September, and October as the first quarter) as the categories. The researchers set up the first null hypothesis to say that one-twelfth of the population of ballplayers had birthdays in each month, while the second null hypothesis was set up to say that one-fourth of the population had birthdays in each quarter. These two null hypotheses were tested twice, once with sample data gathered from 682 ballplayers in 1985 and then again with sample data collected from 837 ballplayers in 1990.

It should be noted that the null hypothesis in a one-sample chi-square test can be (and often is) set up such that the null population proportions across the various categories of the nominal variable are not all identical. In fact, for the two chi-square tests in Excerpt 19.14 that examined ballplayers' births within the 12 months, we believe that the researchers should have set up each H_0 to reflect the fact that some months have more days than others. If this had been done, the null proportions for months containing 28, 30, and 31 days would have been .0767, .0822, and .0849, respectively.

Because the one-sample chi-square test compares the set of observed sample proportions with the corresponding set of population proportions specified in H_0, this kind of chi-square analysis is often referred to as a **goodness-of-fit test**. If these two sets of proportions differ by an amount that can be attributable to sampling error, then there is said to be a "good fit" between the observed data and what would be expected if H_0 were true. In this situation, H_0 is retained. On the other hand, if sampling error cannot adequately explain the discrepancies between the observed and null proportions, then a "bad fit" is said to exist and H_0 is rejected. The researcher's level

Excerpt 19.14   A One-Sample Chi-Square Test

Birth dates for all players were simply tabulated by month across a year beginning in August and ending in July. Chi-square statistical tests were applied to the
data in order to determine the significance of deviations from the expected
number of births per month. Since the proportion of live births differs very little from month to month (Barnsay & Thompson, 1988), expected values were
calculated on the basis of an even distribution of births. . . . The results of the
simple birth-month analyses are shown in Table 1. Also shown are the same data
tabulated by quarter-year (i.e., Quarter 1 = August, September, and October;
Quarter 2 = November, December, and January; etc.). As indicated in Table 1,
the analyses by quarter produced statistically significant results for both 1985
and 1990, with the proportion of players born in each quarter diminishing consistently from the beginning to the end of each sport year.

Table 1

Birthdate by month and by quarter for the 1985
reanalysis and for 1990 Major League players

	A	*S*	*O*	*N*	*D*	*J*	*F*	*M*	*A*	*M*	*J*	*J*
					Month of birth							
1985 (n = 682)												
Month	64	57	74	68	60	58	60	51	47	47	45	51
Quarter*	195			186			158			143		
	28.6%			27.3%			23.2%			21.0%		
1990 (n = 837)												
Month	80	76	88	68	76	67	64	65	65	61	65	62
Quarter**	244			211			194			188		
	29.2%			25.2%			23.2%			22.5%		

*χ^2 (1985) = 10.28, df = 3, $p < .02$;
**χ^2 (1990) = 9.06, df = 3, $p < .05$.

Source: A. Thompson, R. Barnsley, and G. Stebelsky. (1990). "Born to play ball": The relative age effect and major league baseball. *Sociology of Sport Journal,* 7(2), p. 149.

of significance, in conjunction with the data-based *p*-value, makes it easy to
determine what action should be taken whenever this chi-square goodness-
of-fit test is applied.

On occasion, researchers will use the chi-square goodness-of-fit test to see
if it is reasonable to presume that the sample data have come from a normally
distributed population. Of course, for researchers to have this concern, their
response variable must be quantitative, not qualitative. If researchers have data

that are interval or ratio in nature and if they want to apply this kind of a test of normality, the baseline beneath the theoretical normal distribution can be subdivided into segments, with each segment assigned a proportion to reflect the proportion of cases in a true normal distribution that would lie within that segment. These proportions are then put into H_0. Then, the sample is examined to determine what proportion of the observed cases fall within each of the predetermined segments, or categories. Finally, the chi-square goodness-of-fit test compares the observed and null proportions across the various categories to see whether sampling error can account for any discrepancies.[4]

THE INDEPENDENT-SAMPLES CHI-SQUARE TEST

Researchers frequently wish to compare two or more samples on a response variable that is categorical in nature. Since the response variable can be made up of two or more categories, we can set up four different kinds of situations to which the **independent-samples chi-square test** can be applied: (1) two samples compared on a dichotomous response variable, (2) more than two samples compared on a dichotomous response variable, (3) two samples compared on a response variable having three or more categories, and (4) more than two samples compared on a response variable having three or more categories. As you will see, considering these four situations one by one will allow you to generate some valuable insights about chi square and its relationship with other inferential tests we have covered.

When two independent samples are compared with respect to a dichotomous dependent variable, the chi-square test can be thought of as analogous to an independent-samples t-test. With the t-test, the null hypothesis usually tested is $H_0: \mu_1 = \mu_2$. With the chi-square test, the null hypothesis is $H_0: P_1 = P_2$, where the notation P_1 and P_2 stand for the proportion of cases (in the first and second populations) that fall into one of the two response categories. Thus, the null hypothesis for this form of the chi-square test simply says that the two populations are identical in the percentage split between the two categories of the response variable.

In Excerpts 19.15–19.17, we see three examples of this first kind of independent-samples chi-square test. In each case, two groups were compared in terms of the way the subjects were spread out between the two categories of the response variable. And in each case, the null hypothesis was rejected.

When this kind of chi-square test is used, it is important to note that the null hypothesis does *not* specify that each population has a 50–50 split between the two categories of the response variable. Instead, H_0 says that the

---

[4]*The Kolmogorov-Smirnoff one-sample test is another goodness-of-fit procedure that can be used as a check on normality. It has several properties that make it superior to chi square in situations where concern rests with the distributional shape of a continuous variable.*

Excerpts 19.15–19.17   Two-Group Independent-Samples Chi-Square Test with a Dichotomous Response Variable

---

There was a significant difference in the proportion of homesick students in the American and Turkish groups χ^2 (1, N = 144) = 32.10; p < .0001. Whereas 14 or 18.67% of the 75 American students were classified as being homesick during the first 3 weeks of the term, the corresponding figures for the Turkish students were 53 or 76.81% (n = 69).

Source: A. Carden and R. Feicht. (1991). Homesickness among American and Turkish college students. *Journal of Cross Cultural Psychology, 22*(3), p. 421.

A chi-square analysis revealed that significantly more public schools returned surveys than did private ones ($\chi^2_{(2)}$ = 29.23, p < .01).

Source: K. A. Lattal, J. M. McFarland, and J. H. Joyce. (1990). What is happening in psychology of learning courses. *The Behavior Analyst, 13*(2), p. 123.

Among minority students, 40.9% perceived jobs as an important reason to study FL [Foreign Language]; only 26.9% of the Caucasian students mentioned this argument (see Table VI.)

Table VI

Importance of jobs by race/ethnic heritage

Race	Ignored jobs	Mentioned jobs
Minorities (n = 88)	59.1	40.9
Caucasian (n = 458)	73.1	26.9

Chi square significance = .00787

Source: L. Pavian. (1992). Attitudes of entering university freshmen toward foreign language study: A descriptive analysis. *The Modern Language Journal, 76*(3), p. 280.

---

two populations are *identical to each other* in the proportion, or percentage, of cases that fall into each of the two categories. Hence, the null hypothesis would not have been rejected in Excerpt 19.15 if the same or about the same percentage of American and Turkish students had been homesick, regardless of whether that percentage was 18.67, 76.81, or any other value. Similarly, the null hypothesis associated with Excerpt 19.16 simply stipulated that the "return rate" from public and private schools would be the same; however, that common return rate in H_0 could be high, low, or anywhere in between.

It is instructive to look at the table in Excerpt 19.17, since the data of an independent-samples chi-square analysis can always be organized in this manner. Such an arrangement of the sample data is referred to as a **contingency table**, and there will always be two rows and two columns in such tables for the kind of chi-square test we are now considering. In Excerpt 19.17, the two rows have been set up to correspond to the two comparison groups while the two columns represent the two categories of the response variable. As you will note, the two percentages on each row add up to 100, a necessary result in light of the fact that each subject either did or did not mention jobs as a reason to study foreign language.

Earlier, we stated that a chi-square test that compares two groups on a dichotomous response variable is analogous to an independent t-test. This kind of chi square is even more similar to Fisher's Exact Test, since these two tests have the same null hypothesis and also utilize the same kind of data. Because of these similarities, you may have been wondering why some researchers choose to use a Fisher's Exact Test while others subject their data to an independent-samples chi-square test. Although we will address this question more fully later in the chapter, suffice it to say that Fisher's test works better when the researcher has a small number of subjects.

The second kind of independent-samples chi-square test to consider involves a comparison of three or more samples with respect to a dichotomous response variable. Excerpt 19.18 illustrates the use of this kind of chi-square test. In the study from which this excerpt was taken, three groups were compared in terms of the percentage (or proportion) of students referred to special education by their teachers. The three groups differed in terms of what was done during the year to try to help the students. One group of 24 students received a short version of the intervention, a second group of 24 students received a long version of the intervention, and the third group of 12 students received no intervention.

Excerpt 19.18   Three-Group Independent-Samples Chi-Square Test with a Dichotomous Response Variable

---

Of 24 students in the long and short groups, respectively, 3 (13%) and 2 (8%) were referred to special education at the end of the school year. Among 12 control pupils, 6 (50%) were referred to special education. Chi square analysis, using a three (group) by two (referred/not referred) contingency table, revealed a significant relation between group membership and referral status, χ^2 (2, $N = 60$) = 10.19, $p < .01$.

Source: D. Fuchs, L. Fuchs, and M. Bahr. (1990). Mainstream assistance teams: A scientific basis for the art of consultation. *Exceptional Children, 57*(1), p. 137.

Although a 3 × 2 "contingency table" is mentioned in Excerpt 19.18, such a table was not included in the journal article. However, enough information was presented to allow us to construct it on our own and fill each of the six cells with an observed frequency:

	Referred	Not Referred
Long (n = 24)	3	21
Short (n = 24)	2	22
Control (n = 12)	6	6

GROUPS

Or, if the contingency table were to be set up with an observed proportion in each of the six cells, it would look like this:

	Referred	Not Referred
Long (n = 24)	.125	.875
Short (n = 24)	.083	.917
Control (n = 12)	.500	.500

GROUPS

With three or more groups being compared, this second version of the independent-samples chi-square test is analogous to a one-way analysis of variance. Whereas a one-way ANOVA focuses on means, this kind of chi-square test focuses on proportions. Thus, whereas the null hypothesis in a three-group one-way ANOVA would state $H_0: \mu_1 = \mu_2 = \mu_3$, the null hypothesis in a three-group chi-square of the kind being considered would state $H_0: P_1 = P_2 = P_3$, where P stands for the proportion of cases in the population that fall into the first of the two available response categories (and where each subscript number designates a different population). The numerical value of the common P in the chi-square null hypothesis is not specified by the researcher but instead is determined by the data and can be any value between 0 and 1. Thus, the null hypothesis in Excerpt 19.18 would have been retained if the proportion of referred students had turned out to be

Excerpts 19.19–19.20 Two-Group Independent-Samples Chi-Square with a Multicategory Response Variable

The distribution of participants by the four personality types (see Table 4) for first-time offenders was significantly different from the distribution of repeat offenders, $\chi^2 (3, N = 236) = 19.91, p < .0001$. In both groups, the majority of offenders were extroverts. The repeat offenders, however, consisted of few change-oriented types, and the relative proportion of stability-oriented introverts was greater among repeat offenders.

Table 4

Distribution of participants by personality type and offender group

| | Offenders | | | |
| | First-time | | Repeat | |
Personality type	n	%	n	%
Stability-oriented extravert	68	39.5	34	53.1
Change-oriented extravert	49	28.5	4	6.3
Stability-oriented introvert	34	19.8	23	35.9
Change-oriented introvert	21	12.2	3	4.7
Total	172	100.0	64	100.0

Note. $\chi^2 (3, N = 236) = 19.91, p < .0001$.

Source: J. R. Reynolds, J. T. Kunce, and C. S. Cope. (1991). Personality differences of first-time and repeat offenders arrested for driving while intoxicated. *Journal of Counseling Psychology, 38*(3), p. 293.

Within the client sample, men and women differed from each other only in respect of occupation, $\chi^2 (7, N = 196) = 71.48, p < .001$, with more women in the home duties, professional, unemployed, and armed service (police, army, and prison officers) categories and more men in the managerial, trades, laboring, and shop assistant positions.

Source: D. G. McKinnon. (1990). Client-preferred therapist sex role orientations. *Journal of Counseling Psychology, 37*(1), p. 214.

.125 in each of the three groups, .50 in each of the three groups, or any other common value in each of the three groups.[5]

The third kind of independent-samples chi-square test we wish to consider involves two comparison groups and a response variable having three or

---

[5]*The null hypothesis would also be retained if these three sample proportions were all "slightly" different, with "slightly" defined as "within the expected limits of sampling error presuming that H_0 is true."*

more categories. Excerpts 19.19 and 19.20 provide illustrations of how this kind of statistical procedure can be used to help researchers in making inferential statements about the populations of interest. In the first of these excerpts, two groups of drivers arrested for drunken driving (first-time offenders versus repeat offenders) were compared in terms of a four-category response variable dealing with Personality Type. In the second of these excerpts, men and women were compared with respect to how they were distributed across eight occupational categories.

Whenever a chi-square test compares two groups on a response variable having more than two categories, the null hypothesis states simply that the two populations are distributed in the same fashion across the various response categories. Thus, the null hypothesis for the chi-square test in Excerpt 19.19 specified that the population of first-time offenders had the same proportionate breakdown of personality types as did the population of repeat offenders. As with the other kinds of independent-samples chi-square tests being considered, the null proportions for the various categories of the response variable do not have to be specified by the researcher at the outset of the hypothesis testing procedure, because H_0 simply says that "whatever is the case in the first population is also the case in the second population." This means, of course, that H_0 can be true even though the proportions vary in size across the response categories; however, the way they vary must be the same in each population if H_0 is true.

As is the case with most other inferential tests (including t-tests and F-tests), researchers rarely indicate, in words or symbols, the nature of the null hypothesis associated with their chi-square tests. When a contingency table is included in the research report, it is somewhat easy to discern the nature of the tested (but unstated) H_0. Often, however, no contingency table will be available to look at. That was the case in the journal article from which Excerpt 19.20 was taken. In such situations, you must generate on your own, either on paper or in your mind, the structure of the contingency table if you hope to understand the nature of the H_0 being tested.

For Excerpt 19.20, the picture that we visualize has two columns (one for men, the other for women) and eight rows (one for each of the eight occupational categories). We don't know the numerical values of the observed sample proportions in the 16 cells of the contingency table, but we do know that for four of these categories (i.e., for four rows of our picture) the male proportion was larger while for the other four categories the female proportion was larger. Some or all of these differences, between the male and female sample proportions, were so large that the data-based p-value turned out to be very small. Thus, the sample data were highly inconsistent with the null hypothesis stating that the population of men has the same proportionate distribution across the eight occupational categories as the population of women.

The fourth kind of independent-samples chi-square test involves three or more comparison groups and a response variable made up of three or more categories. An example of this kind of chi-square test appears in Excerpt 19.21.

The null hypothesis in this fourth kind of independent-samples is very much like the H_0 for a one-way ANOVA except that the one-way ANOVA focuses on means whereas the chi-square test focuses on proportions (or percentages). With the chi-square test, the null hypothesis simply says that the various populations are identical to one another in the way

---

Excerpt 19.21   An Independent-Samples Chi-Square Test Involving Three Comparison Groups and a Three-Category Response Variable

A significant difference was found in the use of different types of instructional units between teachers with different dominant theoretical orientations ($\chi^2 = 95.89, df = 4, p < .01$).

Table 2

Frequencies for type of instructional units used by teachers with different theoretical orientations

Type of Instructional Unit		Teacher by Theoretical Orientation		
		Skill-based	Rule-based	Function-based
Skill-based	n	29	9	0
	%	69.1	20.5	0
Rule-based	n	5	24	3
	%	11.9	54.5	6.5
Function-based	n	8	11	43
	%	19.0	25.0	93.5
Total	N	42	44	46

Source: K. Johnson. (1992). The relationship between teachers' beliefs and practices during literacy instruction for non-native speakers of English. *Journal of Reading Behavior, 24*(1), p. 97.

---

subjects are distributed across the various categories of the response variable. Hence, if the percentages within the second or third columns of the table in Excerpt 19.21 had been identical to or only slightly different from the percentages in the first column, the chi-square calculated value would have been small, the data-based p-value would have been large, and the null hypothesis would have been retained. Such was not the case, however, because each column of percentages is quite dissimilar from the other two.

CHI SQUARE AS A CORRELATIONAL PROBE

In many studies, a researcher is interested in whether a nonchance relationship exists between two nominal variables. In such studies, a single sample of subjects is measured, with each subject classified into one of the available categories of the first variable and then classified once more into each of the categories of the second variable. After the data are arranged into a contingency table, a chi-square test can be used to determine whether a statistically significant relationship exists between the two variables.

In Excerpt 19.22, we see an example of chi square being used to help a researcher determine whether a nonchance relationship exists between two variables. If the two variables in this study—goal and inference rule—are unrelated in the population, we would expect the frequencies on each row to be

---

Excerpt 19.22 Chi Square Used as a Correlational Probe

As in previous studies (Elliott and Dweck, 1988; Leggett, 1985, 1986; Leggett and Dweck, 1987), chi square analyses were conducted to test the relationship between the variables. The results revealed a significant tendency for those who endorse an inverse rule of reasoning about effort and ability, that is, effort discredits ability, to be performance-goal oriented; whereas those who endorsed a positive rule of reasoning about effort and ability, that is, effort activates ability, tended to be learning-goal oriented. This result was significant at the $p < .05$ level (see Table 1).

Table 1

Frequency of students with each inference rule and each goal

Inference rule	Performance to validate abilities	Learning to develop abilities
Positive (effort activates ability)	22	37
Inverse (effort discredits ability)	34	26

$\chi^2 (1, N = 119) = 4.48 \, p < .05.$

Source: J. M. Livengood. (1992). Students motivational goals and beliefs about effort and ability as they relate to college academic success. *Research in Higher Education, 33*(2), p. 253. (Adapted slightly for inclusion here.)

spread out, proportionately, in approximately the same fashion. Similarly, we would expect the frequencies within each column to be spread out, proportionately, in about the same fashion. Such sample frequencies, if they had turned out in this way, would suggest a zero correlation between the goal and inference rule variables, since knowing a student's status on one of the variables would not improve your chances of guessing that student's status on the other variable.

In Excerpt 19.22, however, the sample data suggest that the variables of inference rule and goal *are* related. This is the case because more of the students with a positive inference rule had a learning goal whereas more of the students with an inverse inference rule had a performance goal. It also is the case in Excerpt 19.22 that more of the students with a performance goal were classified as having an inverse inference rule whereas more of those with a learning goal were classified as having a positive inference rule.

When a chi-square test is used as a correlational probe, it does not produce an index that estimates the strength of the relationship between the two variables that label the contingency table's rows and columns. Instead, the chi-square test simply addresses the question, "In the population of interest, are the two variables related?" Focusing on the sample data, this question takes the form, "In the contingency table, is there a nonchance relationship between the two variables?"

To illustrate what we mean by "nonchance relationship," imagine that we go out and ask each of 100 people to name a relative. (If anyone responds with a gender-free name like Pat, we would ask the respondent to indicate whether the relative is a male or a female). We would also keep track of each respondent's gender. After collecting these two pieces of information from our 100th subject, we might end up with sample data that looks like this:

**GENDER OF
THE RELATIVE**

		Male	Female
GENDER OF THE SUBJECTS	Male	30	20
	Female	23	27

In the 2 × 2 contingency table for our little hypothetical study, there is a relationship between the two variables—subject's gender and relative's gender. More of the male subjects responded with the name of a male relative while more of the female subjects thought of a female relative. (Or, we could say that there was a tendency for male relatives to be thought of by male subjects while female relatives were thought of by female subjects.) But is this relationship something other than what would be expected by chance?

If there were *no* relationship in the population between the two variables in our gender study, the population frequencies in all four cells of the contingency table would be identical. But a sample extracted from that population would not likely mirror the population perfectly. Instead, sampling error would likely be "in" the sample data, thus causing the observed contingency table to have dissimilar cell frequencies. In other words, we would expect a relationship to pop up in the sample data even if there were no relationship in the population. Such a relationship, in the sample data, would be due entirely to chance. Although we should expect a "null population" (i.e., one in which there is no relationship between the two variables) to yield sample data in which a relationship *does* exist between the two variables, such a relationship ought to be small, or weak. It *is* possible for a null population to yield sample data suggesting a strong relationship between the two variables, but this is *not* very likely to happen. Stated differently, if researchers end up with a contingency table in which there is a meager relationship, they have only weak evidence for arguing that the two variables of interest are related in the population. If, in contrast, a pronounced relationship shows up in the contingency table built with the sample data, the researchers possess strong evidence for suggesting that a relationship does, in fact, exist in the population.

Returning to our little gender study, the chi-square test can be used to label the relationship that shows up in the sample data as being either "meager" or "pronounced." Using the hypothesis testing procedure in which the level of significance is set equal to .05, the null hypothesis of no relationship in the population cannot be rejected. This means that the observed relationship in the contingency table could easily have come from a sample pulled from a population characterized by H_0. This means that the observed relationship is not of the nonchance variety. In contrast, the sample data in the contingency table contained in Excerpt 19.22 allowed the researcher to argue that the two variables were related.

When researchers use a chi-square test to investigate the relationship between two variables, they will often use the phrase **test of independence** to describe what they are doing. Additionally, you are likely to see the terms *relationship* and *association* used in conjunction with this application of chi square. Excerpts 19.23–19.25 illustrate the use of these terms.

In addition to using a chi-square test to see if a nonchance relationship exists in the sample data, researchers can convert their chi-square calculated value into an index that estimates the strength of the relationship that exists in the population. By making this conversion, the researcher obtains a numerical value that is analogous to the correlation coefficient generated by Pearson's or Spearman's technique. Several different conversion procedures have been developed.

Excerpts 19.23–19.25 Terms Used in Conjunction with the Use of Chi Square as a Correlational Probe

The chi-square test of independence for the two variables, continuation to Calculus II and secondary school background, is significant ($p < .001$).

Source: J. Ferrini-Mundy, and M. Gaudard. (1992). Secondary school calculus: Preparation or pitfall in the study of college calculus? *Journal of Research in Mathematics Education, 23*(1), p. 67.

Chi square value showed a significant relationship between serum albumin and nutritional status of the children ($P < .05$).

Source: R. O. Abidoye, and A. A. Abidoye. (1993). Comparative haematological screening of urban and rural pregnant women attending antenatal clinics in Layos and its environs. *Early Child Development and Care, 67*, p. 90.

A significant association was found between what children reported they do when they see bullying and their attitudes to bullying, $\chi^2 (6, N = 293) = 18.5$, $p < 0.01$; for those children that did report helping victims, more than expected said that bullying upsets them (27.1 per cent) and fewer than expected that they could understand why some children pick on others (27.8 per cent), whereas for those who did not help, fewer than expected said that it upsets them (7.9 per cent) and more than expected said that they could understand why children pick on others (49.2 per cent).

Source: M. J. Boulton and K. Underwood. (1992). Bully/victim problems among middle school children. *British Journal of Educational Psychology, 62*(Part 1), p. 79.

The phi coefficient can be used to measure the strength of association in 2 × 2 contingency tables. We discussed this correlational procedure in Chapters 3 and 11 and pointed out in those discussions how phi is appropriate for the case of two dichotomous variables. Now, we can extend our discussion of phi by pointing out its connection to chi square. If a chi-square test has been applied to a 2 × 2 contingency table, the phi index of association can be obtained directly by putting the chi-square calculated value into this simple formula:

$$\text{phi} = \sqrt{\frac{\chi^2}{N}}$$

where N stands for the total sample size.

For contingency tables having more than two rows or columns, researchers can convert their chi-square calculated value into a measure of association called the **contingency coefficient**. This index of relationship is symbolized by

C, and the connection between C and chi square is made evident by the following formula for C:

$$C = \sqrt{\frac{\chi^2}{N + \chi^2}}$$

In Excerpt 19.26, we see an illustration of how the contingency coefficient can be computed following a chi-square test of independence.[6]

Excerpt 19.26 The Contingency Coefficient

As previously noted, the two levels of the worldview factor were obtained by dividing the total sample into thirds with the upper and lower thirds defining a worldview commitment to organicism ($M = 18.6$) and mechanism ($M = 11.8$). Of the sample of 60 participants, the frequency of first-choice preferences for rationalist, constructivist, or behavioral counseling as a function of one's worldview commitment were placed in a contingency table for analysis. A subsequent test of the relationship between worldview and first-choice preference for type of counseling yielded a significant result, $\chi^2(2) = 8.37, p < .025$. These data and a moderate contingency coefficient ($C = .35$) suggest a significant relation between worldview and first-choice counseling approach.

Source: W. Lyddon and L. A. Adamson. (1992). Worldview and counseling preference: An analogue study. *Journal of Counseling & Development, 71*(September/October), p. 44.

The formulas for phi and C show that these indices of association will turn out equal to zero when there is no relationship in the contingency table (since in that case, the calculated value of χ^2 will itself turn out equal to zero) and that they will assume larger values for larger values of χ^2. What these formulas do not show is that these indices usually cannot achieve a maximum value of 1.00 (as is the case with Pearson's r, Spearman's rho, and other correlation coefficients). This problem can be circumvented easily if the researcher computes **Cramer's measure of association**, because Cramer's index is simply equal to the computed index of relationship divided by the maximum value that the index could assume, given the contingency table's dimensions and marginal totals.

ISSUES RELATED TO CHI-SQUARE TESTS

Before we conclude our discussion of chi-square tests, a few related issues need to be addressed. Unless you are aware of the connection between these issues and the various chi-square tests we have covered, you will be unable to fully understand and critique research reports that contain the results of chi-square tests. Accordingly, it is important for you to be sensitive to the following issues.

---

[6]*A variation of C is called the mean square contingency coefficient. This index of relationship uses the same formula as that presented for phi.*

Chi Square's Degrees of Freedom

In our earlier discussion of t-tests we pointed out how the test's df is determined by the number of subjects in the study's samples(s). With F-tests, the situation is the same with respect to the df for error. In each case, the df value will be large to the extent that the study is characterized by large sample size(s).

With chi-square tests, the df value is determined by the number of categories into which the data are classified rather than by the number of pieces of data that are classified. In that sense, chi square's df is like the first of the two df values associated with an F-test, since the df value for the source being tested by any F-test is influenced only by the number of comparison groups (and not by the size of the groups).

For one-sample chi-square tests, the researcher computes the df simply by subtracting 1 from the number of response categories associated with the data. Thus, there were 3 df associated with the chi-square test included in Excerpt 19.14 because each of the baseball players was classified into one of four categories based on the quarter of the year in which he was born. (If the subjects in that study had been classified, by birthdate, into the 12 months of the year rather than into three-month quarters, the chi-square test would have involved 11 df.)

For independent-samples chi-square tests or for the situation where chi square is used to probe the relationship between two variables, the test's df value is computed from the contingency table. The researcher does this simply by multiplying one less than the number of rows by one less than the number of columns. For example, there were 4 df associated with the chi-square test shown in Excerpt 19.21 because the contingency table contained 3 rows and 3 columns.

Occasionally, researchers will indicate their chi-square's df value in a totally clear fashion, as was done in Excerpts 19.14 and 19.21. More typically, however, researchers will report the number of df associated with their test without using the letters df. In other words, when you see a number inside a set of parentheses immediately to the right of the symbol for chi square (or positioned as a subscript on that symbol), you can presume that the researchers are reporting the df value associated with their chi-square test. Examples of this manner of reporting chi square's df appear in 8 of the most recent 12 excerpts in this chapter. We suggest that you take a look at a few of these excerpts to make sure that you can see where the df number is typically positioned and how it is determined from the dimensions of the contingency table.

Post Hoc Tests

If an independent-samples chi-square test is used to compare two groups, interpretation of the results is straightforward regardless of what decision is made regarding the null hypothesis. If there are three or more comparison groups involved in the study, the results can be interpreted without difficulty so long as H_0 is not rejected. If, however, the independent-samples chi-square test leads to a rejection of H_0 when three or more groups are contrasted, the situation remains unclear.

When three or more samples are compared, a statistically significant outcome simply indicates that it is unlikely that all corresponding populations are distributed in the same way across the categories of the response variable. In other words, a rejection of H_0 suggests that at least two of the populations differ, but this outcome by itself does not provide any insight as to which specific populations differ from one another. To gain such insights, the researcher must conduct a post hoc investigation.

In Excerpt 19.27, we see a case where a post hoc investigation was conducted in conjunction with an independent-samples chi-square test. In this study, there were three comparison groups and a dichotomous response variable. After the overall null hypothesis was rejected, the post hoc investigation was performed by using separate independent-samples chi-square tests to compare the samples in a pairwise fashion. As you can see, the researchers provide us with the calculated value that was obtained when a chi-square test was applied to the data of a 2×2 contingency table set up for each of the three pairwise comparisons.

Excerpt 19.27 Post Hoc Investigation Following a Significant Chi-Square Test

Using the dichotomous criterion of presence versus absence of 12-month continuous abstinence yielded similar results. Nine of 31 in the moderate-SER subgroup (29.0%) abstained throughout the follow-up period, compared with 4 of 32 (12.5%) in the High-SER subgroup and 3 of 32 (9.4%) in the low-SER subgroup. Taken as a whole these proportions differed significantly, $\chi^2(2, N = 95) = 5.00, p < .05$. Pairwise comparisons were nonsignificant for high versus moderate, $\chi^2(1, N = 63) = 2.63, p > .10$, and high versus low subgroups, $\chi^2(1, N = 64) = 0.16, p > .10$, significant for moderate versus low, $\chi^2(1, N = 63) = 3.95, p < .05$.

Source: D. A. F. Haaga and B. L. Stewart. (1992). Self-efficacy for recovery from a lapse after smoking cessation. *Journal of Consulting and Clinical Psychology, 60*(1), p. 26.

Whenever two or more separate chi-square tests are performed within a post hoc investigation, with each incorporating the same level of significance as that used in the initial (omnibus) chi-square test, the chances of a Type I error being made somewhere in the post hoc analysis will exceed the nominal level of significance. This is not a problem in those situations where the researcher judges Type II errors to be more costly than Type I errors. Be that as it may, the scientific community seems to encourage researchers to guard against Type I errors. Consequently, the kind of post hoc analysis illustrated in Excerpt 19.27 would not receive high marks from those who advocate tight control over Type I errors.

Procedures have been developed that permit a post hoc investigation to be conducted without creating an inflated Type I error rate. One such procedure is called the simultaneous confidence-interval procedure, and it performs the same basic function as does the Tukey or Scheffé strategy when applied following an omnibus F-test comparison of means. Although we cannot be positive that Excerpt 19.28 illustrates this post hoc procedure, it is our opinion that pairwise comparisons were conducted in this study through simultaneous confidence intervals. The phrase *analysis of contrasts* in the final sentence leads us to this opinion.

Excerpt 19.28   A Post Hoc Investigation Using an Analysis of
                     Contrasts

We anticipated that rates of refusal to participate and reasons for declining participation might vary across treatment conditions. These data were important to determine the extent to which random assignment was violated and also were informative regarding school and parent concerns surrounding the various models. Our initial analyses confirmed that refusal rates differed significantly across treatments, $\chi^2(3, n = 108) = 14.15, p < .01$. An analysis of contrasts verified that C/I refusals (53%) were significantly higher than those for C/D (22%) and RRI (12%), and approached significance in the comparison with RR2 (30%).

Source: A. C. Schulte, S. Osborne, and J. D. McKinney. (1990). Academic outcomes for students with learning disabilities in consultation and resource programs. *Exceptional Children, 57*(2), p. 167.

Another procedure for exerting control over Type I errors in a post hoc investigation is the Bonferroni adjustment technique. The Bonferroni technique simply adjusts the level of significance that is used within the post hoc investigation, and thus it can be used just as easily following an omnibus chi-square test as following an omnibus F-test. It is an extremely versatile technique.

We are somewhat puzzled when a researcher indicates awareness of the inflated Type I error-rate problem but does nothing to help make the results more interpretable. This situation is exemplified in Excerpt 19.29. In this study, three groups of students were compared in terms of how they responded to eight questions dealing with attitudes toward science. Each question had five response options (Strongly Agree, Agree, Undecided, Disagree, and Strongly Disagree), and thus the data for each item formed a 3 × 5 contingency table that was subjected to an independent-samples chi square.

Excerpt 19.29   Advising "Caution" in Connection with a Post Hoc
Investigation

The questionnaire was designed and administered to obtain individual item responses, not a cumulative score. Therefore, a chi-square item analysis was conducted with follow-up chi-square comparisons made for each item that was
statistically significant ($p < .05$). Caution is required in the interpretation of the
individual chi-square analysis because as the number of nonindependent tests of
significance increase so does the probability of obtaining one or more significant
results or a Type I error.

Source: D. P. Shepardson and E. L. Pizzini. (1993). A comparison of student perceptions of science activities within three instructional approaches. *School Science and Mathematics, 93*(3), p. 128.

Although the researchers who authored the report from which Excerpt
19.29 was taken deserve credit for knowing about the inflated Type I error-
rate problem, we believe that they could have done more than simply tell us
that "caution is required" when trying to make sense out of the results. Since
the simultaneous confidence interval technique or the Bonferroni procedure
could have been used during the data analysis phase of this study, we wonder
why the researchers didn't deal with the potential Type I error-rate problem
on the front end. Did they expect their readers to be willing or able to apply
one of these procedures when reading their article?

SMALL AMOUNTS OF SAMPLE DATA

To work properly, the chi-square tests discussed in this chapter necessitate
sample sizes that are not too small. Actually, it is the **expected frequencies**
that must be sufficiently large for the chi-square test to function as intended.
An expected frequency exists for each category into which the sample objects are classified, and each one is nothing more than the proportion of the
sample data you would expect in the category if H_0 were true and if there
were absolutely no sampling error. For example, if we were to perform a taste
test in which each of 20 individuals is asked to sip four different beverages
and then indicate which one is the best, the expected frequency for each of
the four options would be equal to 5 (presuming that H_0 specifies equality
among the four beverages). If this same study were to be conducted with 40
subjects, each of the four expected values would be equal to 10.

If researchers have a small amount of sample data, the expected values associated with their chi-square test will also be small. If the expected values are
too small, the chi-square test should not be used. Various rules of thumb have
been offered over the years to help applied researchers know when they
should refrain from using the chi-square test because of "small" expected val-

ues, with the current rule saying that chi square should not be used if the average expected frequency is less than 2.[7]

In Excerpts 19.30 and 19.31, we see examples where researchers chose to analyze their data by means of Fisher's Exact Test because of small sample sizes. (In the first of these excerpts, an older and more conservative way of defining "small expected frequencies" is cited as the reason for choosing not to use the chi-square test.)

Excerpts 19.30–19.31 Use of Fisher's Exact Test Rather than Chi Square Because of Small Expected Frequencies

---

The correlation between the different types of ventilatory impairment observed in the exposed and the control groups with explanatory variables like age, sex, smoking habit, and length of exposure was tested by using the chi square test. Nonparametric Fisher's Exact Test was applied where the expected call frequencies were less than five.

Source: B. Gupta, S. Rastogi, T. Husain, N. Mathur, and B. Pangley. (1991). A study of respiratory morbidity and pulmonary function among solderers in the electronics industry. *American Industrial Hygiene Association, 52*(February), p. 46.

Two-sided chi square tests were used to compare categorical variables; Fisher's Exact Test was used if a cell contained less than 10 subjects.

Source: M. Holmes, S. Safyer, N. Bickell, S. Vermund, D. Hanff, and R. Phillips. (1993). Chlamydial cervical infection in jailed women. *American Journal of Public Health, 83*(4), p. 552.

The option of turning to Fisher's Exact Test when the expected frequencies are too small is available in those situations where the sample data create a 2 × 2 contingency table. This option does not exist, however, if their researcher is using (1) a one-sample chi-square test with three or more categories or (2) one that involves a contingency table that has more than two rows and/or more than two columns. In these situations, the problem of "small" expected frequencies will be solved by the researcher's redefining of the response categories such that two or more of the original categories can be collapsed together. For example, if men and women are being compared regarding their responses to a five-option Likert-type question, the researcher might convert the five original categories into three new categories by (1) merging together the "strongly agree" and "agree" categories into a new single category called "favorable response," (2) leaving the "undecided" category unchanged, and (3) merging together the "disagree" and "strongly disagree"

---

[7] *This rule of thumb appears on page 88 of Gene V Glass and Kenneth D. Hopkins' text,* Statistical Methods in Education and Psychology *(Englewood Cliffs, NJ: Prentice-Hall, 1984).*

categories into a new single category called "unfavorable response." By so doing, the revised contingency table might not have any expected frequencies that are too small.

YATES' CORRECTION FOR CONTINUITY

When applying a chi-square test to situations where $df = 1$, some researchers use a special formula that yields a slightly smaller calculated value than would be the case if the regular formula is employed. When this is done, it can be said that the data are being analyzed using a chi-square test that has been **corrected for discontinuity**. This special formula was developed by a famous statistician named **Yates**, and occasionally the chi-square test has Yates' name attached to it when the special formula is used. The first footnote beneath the table in Excerpt 19.32 illustrates the use of Yates' correction.

Excerpt 19.32   Yates' Correction for Discontinuity

Table 2

Lifetime psychiatric diagnoses in anorectic and control probands

	AN (N = 34)		Control (N = 34)		
	N	(%)	N	(%)	χ^{2*}
SUD	5	(15)	1	(3)	1.65[†]
Mood disorder[‡]	23	(68)	9	(26)	9.98[§]
Other disorders	3	(9)	2	(6)	0.00[†]
Total[¶]	24	(71)	11	(32)	8.48[§]

[*]Calculated with one degree of freedom, with Yates' correction for discontinuity. P values are not significant at the .05 level, except where otherwise specified.

[†]Since the expected frequencies for these comparisons are less than 5, Fisher's exact test would give a more accurate value for P. Note, however, that P values would be even less significant with this test.

[‡]Probands were diagnosed as having a mood disorder if they had a definite or probable RDC diagnosis of either major mood disorder (manic disorder or major depressive disorder) or minor mood disorder (hypomanic disorder, minor depressive disorder, intermittent depressive disorder, or cyclothymic personality). Nineteen of the anorectic and five of the control probands had a lifetime diagnosis of major mood disorder.

[§]$P < .005$.

[¶]Probands with more than one type of psychiatric disorder were counted only once for total.

Source: S. Stern, K. Dixon, R. Sansone, M. Lake, E. Nemzer, and D. Jones. (1992). Psychoactive substance use disorder in relatives of patients with Anorexia Nervosa. *Comprehensive Psychiatry, 33*(3), p. 209.

Statistical authorities are not in agreement as to the need for using Yates' special formula. Some argue that it should *always* be used in situations where $df = 1$ because the regular formula leads to calculated values that are too large (and thus to an inflated probability of a Type I error). Other authorities take the position that the Yates adjustment causes the pendulum to swing too far in the opposite direction, because Yates' correction makes the chi-square test overly conservative (thus increasing the chances of a Type II error). Ideally, researchers should clarify why the Yates formula either was or wasn't used on the basis of a judicious consideration of the different risks associated with a Type I or a Type II error. Realistically, however, you are most likely to see the Yates formula used only occasionally and, in those cases, used without any explanation as to why it was employed.

McNemar's Chi Square

Earlier in this chapter, we saw how a chi-square test can be used to compare two independent samples with respect to a dichotomous dependent variable. If the two samples involved in such a comparison are related rather than independent, chi square can still be used to test the **homogeneity of proportions** null hypothesis. However, both the formula used by the researchers to analyze their data and the label attached to the test procedure are slightly different in this situation where two related samples are compared. Although there is no reason to concern ourselves here with the unique formula used when correlated data have been collected, it *is* important that you become familiar with the way researchers refer to this kind of test.

In Excerpts 19.33 through 19.36, we see four different ways that researchers have labeled their chi-square test of related samples. The common element across all these labels is the word McNemar. Here again we have a situation where a statistical test is named in honor of the individual who invented it.

McNemar's chi-square test is very much like a correlated-samples *t*-test in that two sets of data being compared can come either from a single group that is measured twice (e.g., in a pre-post sense) or from matched samples that are measured just once. All four of these excerpts fall into the first of these categories, including the fourth excerpt, where each subject evaluated two blood glucose monitoring strips (one presented to the subject in its regular size, the other presented after being cut in half). To see how McNemar's test can be used with a matched sample, consider Excerpt 19.35 once again and imagine that the children are first matched on IQ and then tested such that one member of each matched pair is given the Untimed Minitest while the other member of the pair is given the Ten-Digit Test.

Although the McNemar chi square is similar to a correlated *t*-test with respect to the kind of sample(s) involved in the comparison, the two tests differ dramatically in terms of the null hypothesis. With the *t*-test, the null

Excerpts 19.33–19.36 McNemar's Chi-Square Test

Baseline and follow-up values for dichotomous questions were compared by contingency table analysis, using the McNemar test.

Source: D. A. Calsyn, C. Meinecke, A. J. Saxson, and V. Stanton. (1992). Risk reduction in sexual behaviors: A condom giveaway program in a drug abuse treatment clinic. *American Journal of Public Health, 82*(11), p. 1536.

In order to compute McNemar change tests (Marascuilo & McSweeney, 1977) on the percentages of children in the subset who offered correct labels for the genitals at both pre- and posttesting, we coded all slang, private part, and incorrect/"don't know" responses as incorrect.

Source: S. K. Wurtele, A. M. Melzer, and L. C. Kast. (1992). Preschoolers' knowledge of and ability to learn genital terminology. *Journal of Sex Education and Therapy, 18*(2), p. 119.

On the pretest 10% of the instructed sample met the criterion on the Untimed Minitest, and on the posttest 96% of the children met this criterion. This shift for the Ten-Digit Test was from 5% on the pretest to 90% meeting the criterion on the posttest. Both of these changes were significant, McNemar's test of correlated proportions chi-square = 674 and 659, $p < .0001$.

Source: K. C. Fuson, and D. J. Briars. (1992). Using a base-ten blocks learning/teaching approach for first- and second-grade place-value and multidigit addition and subtraction. *Journal for Research in Mathematics Education, 21*(3), p. 199.

Using a McNemar's chi-square test for paired data to compare whole and bisected readings, $\chi^2(1, N = 32)$ was .78 (not significant [NS] for patients and 8.06 ($p < .01$) for RNs.

Source: B. Wakefield, D. S. Wakefield, and B. M. Booth. (1992). Evaluating the validity of blood glucose monitoring strip interpretation by experienced users. *Applied Nursing Research, 5*(1), p. 15.

hypothesis involves population means; in contrast, the null hypothesis of McNemar's chi-square test is concerned with population proportions. In other words, the null hypothesis of McNemar's test always takes the form $H_0: P_1 = P_2$ while the *t*-test's null hypothesis always involves the symbol μ (and it usually is set up to say $H_0: \mu_1 = \mu_2$).

THE COCHRAN Q TEST

A test developed by Cochran is appropriate for the situation where the researcher wishes to compare three or more related samples with respect to a dichotomous dependent variable. This test is called the **Cochran Q test,** with the letter Q simply being the arbitrary symbol used by Cochran to label the calculated value produced by putting the sample data into Cochran's formula. This test just as easily could have been called Cochran's chi-square test inasmuch as the calculated value is compared against a chi-square critical value to determine whether the null hypothesis should be rejected.

The Cochran Q test can be thought of as an "extension" of McNemar's chi-square test, since McNemar's test is restricted to the situation where just two correlated samples of data are compared while Cochran's test can be used when there are any number of such samples. Or, the Cochran Q test can be likened to the one-factor repeated-measures analysis of variance covered in Chapter 16; in each case, multiple related samples of data are compared. (That ANOVA is quite different from the Cochran test, however, because the null hypothesis in the former focuses on μs whereas Cochran's H_0 involves Ps.)

In Excerpt 19.37, we see a case in which the Cochran Q test was used to see what happened to the academic eligibility of 91 high school athletes from Dallas during the fall semesters of 1984, 1985, and 1986. This study was conducted because of interest in discerning the impact of a new "no pass, no play" regulation. Under the new rule each student had to pass all courses taken in order to play.

Excerpt 19.37 Cochran's Q Test

Using nonprobability purposive sampling procedures (Kerlinger, 1986), subjects (N, 91) were selected from 19 of the 32 high schools in the Dallas Independent School District (DISD). Informed consent was obtained from the Director of Research, Evaluation, and Information Systems and the DISD with the stipulation that race would not be identified. The other 13 schools had no male and/or female interscholastic athletic teams. Subjects were female interscholastic volleyball and basketball players (Grades 9–12), treated as a single group of participants for the purposes of this study. Subjects selected were enrolled and competed on an interscholastic volleyball and/or basketball team in the DISD in the fall semesters of 1984, 1985, and 1986.

The investigator then secured . . . a working document on each of the 91 subjects. Each working document contained the following data: subjects' home address, parents' name, birthdate, and transcripts for fall 1984 through fall 1986. . . . The data from the transcripts were statistically treated using a Cochran Q test to find whether there was a difference in the number of female volleyball and basketball athletes from 1984 to 1985 to 1986 who failed one or more courses versus those who passed all courses in the DISD. . . . The Cochran Q test yielded a significant difference ($\chi^2 = 75.20, \chi^2[2] = 5.99, p < .05$) in the number of subjects able to play throughout the fall semesters among the 1984–85, 1985–1986, and 1986–87 school years.

Source: D. S. Espinosa. (1990). The effect of the "no pass, no play" provision on girls' volleyball and basketball eligibility. *Research Quarterly for Exercise and Sport, 61*(4), pp. 403–404.

The null hypothesis associated with the Cochran Q test in Excerpt 19.37 could be stated as H_0: $P_{1984} = P_{1985} = P_{1986}$. As it turned out, this null hypothesis was rejected at the .05 level of significance. (Of the two χ^2 numerical values presented near the end of the excerpt, the first one is the calculated value while the second is the critical value; the number in brackets is simply the degrees of freedom for the Cochran test, computed as the number of sets of data less 1.)

When Cochran's test leads to a rejection of the null hypothesis, the researcher will probably conduct a post hoc investigation within which pairwise comparisons are set up and tested. Although this kind of post hoc investigation could be accomplished by applying a McNemar test to each pair of data sets, it is better to make such comparisons with a follow-up test specifically developed for use with the Cochran Q test. In Excerpt 19.38, we see how this more tailor-made test was used within the study in Dallas comparing academic eligibility in 1984, 1985, and 1986.

Excerpt 19.38   The Cochran Q Post Hoc Test

Due to the significance found in the Cochran Q test, a post-hoc analysis was accomplished by utilizing the Cochran Q Post Hoc Test. The output was a series of pairwise comparisons among the fall semesters studied. . . . The series of pairwise comparisons indicated a significant difference between all comparisons except the last two years, 1985–86 versus 1986–87.

Source: D. S. Espinosa. (1990). The effect of the "no pass, no play" provision on girls' volleyball and basketball eligibility. *Research Quarterly for Exercise and Sport, 61*(4), p. 404.

THE USE OF z-TESTS WHEN DEALING WITH PROPORTIONS

As you may recall from Chapter 11, researchers will sometimes use a z-test (rather than a t-test) when their studies are focused on either the mean of one group or the means of two comparison groups. It may come as a surprise that researchers will sometimes apply a z-test when dealing with dependent variables that are qualitative rather than quantitative in nature. In other words, you are likely to come across cases where a z-test has been used by researchers when their data take the form of proportions, percentages, or frequencies.

If a researcher wishes to contrast two unrelated groups on a dichotomous dependent variable, such a comparison can be made either by an independent-samples chi-square test or by a z-test. The choice here is immaterial, since these two tests are mathematically equivalent and will always lead to the same decision regarding H_0. This is because the data-based p-value will be the same regardless of which test is used.

In Excerpts 19.39 and 19.40 we see two cases in which a z-test was used to compare two groups with respect to the percentage of each group that fell

---

Excerpts 19.39–19.40   Comparing Two Unrelated Samples on a
Dichotomous Variable Using a z-Test

A comparison of students who were unemployed and students who worked
during their senior year in high school revealed a significant difference in the
percentage of students in the top 10 percent of their high school class.
Specifically, 33.3 percent of the unemployed students were in the top 10 percent
of their high school class while only 22.7 percent of those who worked during
their senior year were in the top 10 percent irrespective of the number of hours
worked per week. This difference is statistically significant ($Z = 2.37, p < .01$).

Source: R. High and J. W. Collins. (1992). High school student employment at what cost. *The High
School Journal*, Dec./Jan., pp. 91–92.

A z-test was used to compare differences in percentages of 1984 and 1991 respondents who collected accountability data. A statistically significant difference
did not exist between the percentage of current (57.8%) and previous (60%) respondents involved in accountability activities.

Source: T. N. Fairchild and J. E. Zins. (1992). Accountability practices of school psychologists. *School
Psychology Review*, 21(4), p. 623.

---

into the categories of a dichotomous dependent variable. In each case, the
null hypothesis could be stated as $H_0: P_1 = P_2$, where the subscripts represent
the two groups being compared and where the letter P stands for the proportion (or percentage) of cases in each population that fall into one of the
two response categories. Thus, the null hypothesis in Excerpt 19.39 states that
the two populations of interest (unemployed and employed students) have
the same percentage representation in the top tenth of their class. In the
study from which Excerpt 19.40 was taken, the null hypothesis again says
that the two populations have an equivalent split, in terms of percent, across
the two categories of the response variable (involvement or noninvolvement
in accountability activities).

Whereas the z-test we have just discussed and the chi-square test covered
earlier (for the case of two independent samples and a dichotomous response
variable) are mathematically equivalent, there is another z-test that represents
a "large sample approximation" to some of the tests examined in earlier sections of this chapter. To be more specific, researchers will sometimes use a z-
test, if they have large samples, where you might expect them to use a sign
test, a binomial test, a one-sample chi-square test, or a McNemar test.

In Excerpt 19.41 and Excerpt 19.42, we see two cases in which there was
a single sample of subjects and a two-category response variable. Because of
the large samples ($n = 250$ in the first study; $n = 68$ in the second study), the
researchers elected to apply a z-test to their data.

> **Excerpts 19.41–19.42**   Using a *z*-Test as a Normal Approximation to the Binomial Test
>
> With the sexual scenario, 63% of the clinicians responding said that they would do what they felt they should do, and 37% said that they would do less than they felt they should do. Applying the binomial expansion to these data provides a significant normal approximation to distribution of proportions: $Z(1) = 9.08$, $p < .001$.
>
> *Source:* J. Bernard, M. Murphy, and M. Little. (1987). The failure of clinical psychologists to apply understood ethical principles. *Professional Psychology Research and Practices, 18*(5), p. 490.
>
> Seventy-four percent of all experimenters preferred live rats over computer rats, while 26% preferred computer rats over live rats (Binomial $z = 3.88$, $p < .01$).
>
> *Source:* J. E. Roeckelein. (1994). GPA and preference in conditioning live vs. computer rats. *Psychological Reports, 74*, p. 246.

A FEW FINAL THOUGHTS

As you have seen, a wide variety of test procedures have been designed for situations where the researcher's data take the form of frequencies, percentages, or proportions. Despite the differences among these tests (in terms of their names, the number of groups involved, and whether repeated measures are involved), there are many commonalities that cut across the tests we have considered. These commonalities exist because each of these tests involves the computation of a data-based *p*-value that is then used to evaluate a null hypothesis.

In using the procedures considered in this chapter within an applied research study, a researcher will follow the various steps of hypothesis testing, statistical testing, or the hybrid approach to evaluating null hypotheses. Accordingly, many of the "side issues" dealt with in Chapters 7–9 are relevant to the proper use of any and all of the tests we have just discussed. In an effort to help you keep these important concerns in the forefront of your consciousness as you read and evaluate research reports, we feel obliged to conclude this chapter by turning our attention to a few of these more generic concerns.

Our first point is simply a reiteration that the data-based *p*-value is always computed on the basis of a tentative belief that the null hypothesis is true. Accordingly, the statistical results of a study are always tied to the null hypothesis. If the researcher's null hypothesis is silly or articulates something that no one would defend or expect to be true, then the rejection of H_0, regardless of how "impressive" the *p*-value, does not signify an important finding.

If you think that our first point is simply a "straw man" that has no connection to the real world of actual research, consider once again Excerpt 19.21. In that excerpt, you will see that a chi-square test was used to compare three groups of teachers in terms of the types of instructional units they used. The data strongly suggest that skill-based instructional units tend to be used by teachers who possess a skill-based theoretical orientation, that rule-based instructional units tend to be used by teachers who possess a rule-based theoretical orientation, and that function-based instructional units tend to be used by teachers who possess a function-based theoretical orientation. It does not seem to us very surprising that the chi-square null hypothesis (of no relationship between teachers' theoretical orientation and type of instructional unit used) was found to be inconsistent with the data. In our opinion, the null hypothesis could have been rejected, without the chi-square test, simply on the basis of common sense!

The second point we wish to reiterate is that the chances of a Type I error increase above the researcher's nominal level of significance in the situation where multiple null hypotheses are evaluated. Although there are alternative ways of dealing with this potential problem, you are likely to see the Bonferroni technique employed most often to keep control over Type I errors. Excerpt 19.43 illustrates the use of this technique in conjunction with the chi-square test.

Excerpt 19.43 The Bonferroni Technique Used with Chi Square

Several preliminary analyses were calculated to assess the demographic equivalence of the four subject groups. Specifically, ANOVA's were calculated for the dependent variables of age, number of children, and ages of children. Chi square analyses were conducted for the dependent variables of living situation (with partner versus separate from partner), ethnicity (white versus non-white), educational level (less than high-school, high-school, college), income source (work, public assistance, partner support), and marital status (married or cohabitating, divorced or widowed, single). Given the number of preliminary analyses, alpha levels were set at .006 (i.e., .05/8) to adjust for Type I Error.

Source: K. Wilson, R. Vercella, C. Brems, D. Benning, and N. Renfro. (1992). Levels of learned helplessness in abused women. *Women & Therapy, 13*(4), p. 58.

Our third point concerns the distinction between statistical significance and practical significance. As we hope you recall from our earlier discussions, it is possible for H_0 to be rejected, with an "impressive" data-based p-value (e.g., $p < .0001$), even though the computed sample statistic does not appear to be very dissimilar from the value of the parameter expressed in H_0. We also hope you remember our earlier contention that conscientious researchers will either design their studies and/or conduct a more complete analysis of their data with an eye toward avoiding the potential error of figuratively making a mountain out of a molehill.

There are several ways researchers can demonstrate sensitivity to the distinction between practical significance and statistical significance. In our examination of *t*-tests, *F*-tests, and tests on correlation coefficients, we have seen that these options include (1) computing, in the design phase of the investigation, the proper sample size; (2) calculating, after the data have been collected, the magnitude of the discrepancy between the estimated and null values of the population parameter; and (3) computing, once again after the data have been gathered, a strength-of-association index. These three options are as readily available to researchers who use the various test procedures covered in this chapter as they are to those who conduct *t*-tests, *F*-tests, or tests involving one or more correlation coefficients.

Excerpt 19.44 shows how a more complete analysis can assist with statistical inferences based on proportions. In the study from which this ex-

---

Excerpt 19.44   Computation of Effect Size Indices When Comparing Two Percentages

Statistical analysis indicated that the proportion of unusual PVIs on the Verbal scale was significantly greater for patients than for control subjects when the Full Scale IQ was ≤ 79, $z = 2.56$, $p < .01$. Likewise, with Full Scale IQs between 90 and 109, the frequency of abnormal PVIs on the Verbal scale was significantly larger for neurological compared with normal individuals, $z = 2.50$, $p < .05$. The effect size (ES) associated with each statistically reliable difference was small (ES $\leq .34$; Cohen, 1988) and unimpressive.

Table 3

Percentage of brain-damaged subjects with scatter ranges and profile variability indexes (PVIs) at the $\leq 5\%$ level of abnormality

Measure	≤ 79 (n = 68)			80–89 (n = 72)			90–109 (n = 71)			110–119 (n = 5)		
	V	P	F	V	P	F	V	P	F	V	P	F
Range	10.3	1.5	5.9	5.6	0.0	11.1	7.0	5.6	2.8	0.0	0.0	0.0
PVI	14.7[a]	1.5	2.9	6.9	0.0	1.4	11.3[b]	7.0	2.8	0.0	0.0	0.0

Note. The following abbreviations refer to measures of the Wechsler Adult Intelligence Scale—Revised: V = Verbal; P = Performance; and F = Full Scale.

[a]Different from standardization subjects at $p < .01$ using two-tailed test.
[b]Different from standardization subjects at $p < .05$ using two-tailed test.

Source: J. J. Ryan, A. M. Paolo, and A. J. Smith. (1992). Wechsler Adult Intelligence Scale-Revised intersubtest scatter in brain-damaged patients: A comparison with the standardization sample. *Psychological Assessment, 4*(1), p. 65.

cerpt was taken, the researchers collected data to assess the widely held view among psychologists that "intersubtest scatter" on the WAIS-R intelligence test is suggestive of brain damage. (Intersubtest scatter is said to exist when an examinee scores much better or worse on some subtests than on others.) The researchers located 216 subjects known to have brain damage and tested them with the WAIS. These subjects were then compared against a standardization sample of so-called normals to see if these two groups were different in the percentage of examinees who had high levels of intersubtest scatter. As the table in Excerpt 19.44 shows, the 216 brain-damaged subjects were divided into four subgroups, with a z-test used to compare each subgroup against its corresponding section of the standardization sample with respect to the two measures of intersubtest scatter: "range" and "PVI."

As the last sentence in Excerpt 19.44 shows, the researchers estimated the magnitude of effect for each of the two comparisons that turned out to be statistically significant. Note that these indices were so small that the researchers labeled them as "unimpressive." With six of the eight z-tests leading to a retention of the null hypothesis and the remaining two tests yielding statistically significant results that were too small to be meaningful, the researchers concluded that "interpresentations of marked intersubtest scatter as a sign of brain damage appears unwarranted."

In Excerpt 19.45, we see a case where a chi-square test of independence was applied to the data of a 4×2 contingency table. Note how the researchers who conducted this study first computed the power associated with their chi-square test and then estimated the strength of association (between the two variables of problem area and gender) by means of Cramer's V. These researchers should be applauded for demonstrating a concern about statistical power and the practical significance of their findings.

Excerpt 19.45   Computation of Power and Cramer's V in Conjunction with a Chi-Square Test of Independence

---

The statistical power of the analysis was taken into consideration in this study to qualify the interpretation of the data. For a 4 (problem area) $\times$ 2 (gender) chi-squared test of independence at $\alpha = .05$, the power for detecting practical medium-size differences ($\omega^2 = 0.09$) was 0.86 (Cohen, 1988).. . . The hypothesis of no association was rejected for the obtained data [χ_3^2 ($n = 139$) = 21.1, $p < .001$, $V = 0.39$]. The effect size, as measured by Cramer's V, indicates a moderately strong relationship between gender and problem area.

Source: V. Vara, and I. W. Kelly. (1994). Commonly reported problems in middle-school children. *Perceptual and Motor Skills, 78*(2), p. 1284.

Our fourth and final point concerns the fact that it is possible to build confidence intervals around sample proportions and percentages. Such intervals serve the same basic purpose as those built around means and correlation coefficients, and they can be used in one of two ways. They can be used simply to estimate the percentage (or proportion) value in the population, or as a vehicle for assessing null hypotheses that have been set up concerning the populations of interest.

In Excerpt 19.46, we see a case where a confidence interval was built around the prevalence rate of HIV infection in a sample of 62 men discharged from a shelter psychiatry program in New York City. The computed incidence of the HIV infection in the sample was 19.4 percent, and the 95 percent confidence interval extended from 9.5 percent to 29.2 percent. This interval was used simply to estimate the prevalence of HIV in the relevant population, and no null hypothesis was tested.

Excerpt 19.46   Building a Confidence Interval Around a Sample Percentage

---

Among the 62 men whose HIV status was known, the prevalence was 19.4% (n = 12) (95% CI = 9.5%, 29.2%).

Source: E. Susser, E. Valencia, and S. Conover. (1993). Prevalence of HIV infection among psychiatric patients in a New York men's shelter. *American Journal of Public Health, 83*(4), p. 569.

In Excerpt 19.47, we see a case where two sample percentages were compared by means of a confidence interval. Here, a null hypothesis was involved, and it could be stated as H_0: $P_e = P_c$ (where the subscripts "e" and "c" stand for the experimental and control groups, respectively. Because the confidence interval (which was built for the difference between the two sample percentages) did not overlap zero, the researchers had a right to reject the hypothesis.

Excerpt 19.47   Using a Confidence Interval to Compare Two Sample Percentages

---

More experimental than control group women attended classes in preparation for childbirth and parenthood, 83.1 and 63.9 percent, respectively (95% CI$_{diff}$ 14.1 – 24.2, $P < 0.001$).

Source: U. Waldestrom and C. Nilsson. (1993). Women's satisfaction with birth center care: A randomized, controlled study. *Birth, 20*(1), p. 7.

REVIEW TERMS

Binomial test	Large-sample approximation
Chi square	McNeman's chi square test
Cochran Q test	Observed frequency
Contingency coefficient	One-sample chi-square test
Contingency table	Pearson chi-square
Cramer's measure of association	Percentages
Expected frequency	Proportions
Fisher's Exact Test	Sign test
Frequencies	Test of independence
Goodness-of-fit test	Test of normality
Homogeneity of proportions	Yates' correction for continuity
Independent-samples	

REVIEW QUESTIONS

1. (True or False) Whenever the sign test is used, the null hypothesis says that the sample data will contain an equal number of observations in each of the two response categories (i.e., as many "pluses" as "minuses").

2. Look at Excerpt 19.4. If only six (rather than seven) of the placebo patients had been classified as having had at least one exacerbation, would the data-based p-value have turned out to be smaller than .09, larger than .09, or equal to .09?

3. Look at Excerpt 19.5. If this paragraph had presented information on the proportion of each group that *failed* to link target information, the two "key" numbers in this passage would have been .45 and .89 for the high comprehension and low comprehension readers, respectively. Had Fisher's Exact Test been used to compare these two proportions, would the resulting p-value turn out to be smaller than .032, larger than .032, or equal to .032?

4. What symbol is used to represent chi square?

5. In Excerpt 19.14, how many proportions would there have been in H_0 if the year had been divided into thirds (rather than into quarters)? Had the researchers done this, what numerical values in H_0 would have been associated with these proportions?

6. (True or False) If you were asked to change the sample percentages in the sentence of Excerpt 19.17 so as to make them perfectly consistent with the null hypothesis of the chi-square test, you would have to change 40.9 to 50 and 26.9 to 50.

7. Look at Excerpt 19.19. If the numbers of repeat offenders in the change-oriented extravert and stability-oriented introvert categories had turned out to be reversed from what they actually were, how would this change affect the p-value?

8. In Excerpt 19.16, could it be said that the chi-square test is assessing the relationship between two variables? If so, what are those two variables?

9. (True or False) A positive relationship exists between χ^2 and C, between χ^2 and phi, and between χ^2 and Cramer's measure of association.

10. Based upon the information contained in Excerpt 19.15, build a contingency table that shows an observed frequency for each cell.

11. In Excerpt 19.14, 837 baseball players in 1990 were classified into 12 groups based on their birth month. If the chi-square test had been used with these 12 groups (rather than combining groups to form four "quarters"), how many degrees of freedom would there have been?

12. Suppose a researcher goes out and asks each of 200 people two questions: (1) What is your blood type (A, B, AB, O)? and (2) Would you like to be taller, shorter, or your current height? If the data produced by these two questions are analyzed by a chi-square test to see if a relationship exists between blood type and satisfaction with one's current height, how many degrees of freedom would there be?

13. What are the two features of Excerpt 19.18 that jointly call for a post hoc test?

14. Whose name is often associated with the special chi-square formula that carries the label "correction for continuity"?

15. McNemar's chi-square test is appropriate for comparing _____ (two/more than two) groups of data, where the samples are _____ (independent/correlated), and where the response variable contains _____ (two/more than two) categories.

16. If some researchers got ready to subject their data to a one-factor repeated measures ANOVA but stopped after realizing that the data were dichotomous, what statistical test could they turn to in order to complete the data analysis?

17. In Excerpts 19.41 and 19.42, a single-sample z-test was used as a normal approximation to the binomial test. In each case, the null hypothesis being tested specified that $P = 50$ percent. Why did the study with the larger z-value have sample data closer to H_0, whereas the other study, with a smaller z, had sample data more divergent from H_0?

18. In Excerpt 19.46, we saw that 19.4 percent of the 62 subjects were infected by HIV. The confidence interval extended from 9.5 percent to 29.2 percent. If a larger sample had been used, with 19.4 percent still turning up as being HIV-positive, would the "width" of the confidence interval be smaller, larger, or the same as it was when n was 62?

STATISTICAL TESTS ON RANKS (NONPARAMETRIC TESTS)

In the previous chapter, we examined a variety of test procedures designed for data that are qualitative, or nominal, in nature. Whether dealing with frequencies, percentages, or proportions, those tests involved response categories devoid of any quantitative meaning. For example, when a chi-square test was used in Excerpt 19.20 to compare men against women in terms of occupation, neither the grouping variable (gender) nor the response variable (occupation) involved categories that had any numerical relationship to each other.

We now turn our attention to a group of test procedures that utilize the simplest kind of quantitative data: ranks. In a sense, we are returning to this topic (rather than starting from ground zero), since in Chapter 10, we pointed out how researchers can set up and evaluate null hypotheses concerning Spearman's rho and Kendall's tau. As we hope you recall, each of these correlational procedures involves an analysis of ranked data.

Within the context of this chapter, we consider five of the many test procedures that have been developed for use with ordinal data. These procedures are the median test, the Mann–Whitney U test, the Kruskal-Wallis one-way analysis of variance of ranks, the Wilcoxon matched-pairs signed-ranks test, and the Friedman two-way analysis of variance. Excerpts 20.1–20.5 provide proof that each of these tests has been used in a recent study.

The five test procedures considered in this chapter are not the only ones that involve ranked data, but they are the ones used most frequently by applied researchers. Because these five tests are used so often, we will discuss each one separately, clarifying (we hope) the research "setting" for which each test is appropriate, the typical format used to report the test's results, and the proper meaning of a rejected null hypothesis. First, however, we need to consider the three ways in which a researcher can obtain the ranked data needed for any of the five tests.

Excerpts 20.1–20.5   The Five Test Procedures That Involve Ranked Data

---

Significantly more important ($p < .05$) by Median test.

Source: S. H. Schwartz. (1990). Individualism-collectivism: Critique and proposed refinements. *Journal of Cross-Cultural Psychology, 21*(2), p. 146.

A Mann-Whitney U test was performed on the income levels of the women, which indicated that there was not a statistically significant difference by race for participants' income level.

Source: R. E. Fassinger, and B. S. Rice. (1994). Being the best: Preliminary results from a national study of the achievement of prominent Black and White women. *Journal of Counseling Psychology, 41*(2), p. 197.

The Kruskal-Wallis test showed no difference in candidates' sentence complexity scores ($H = .1697; p = .92$).

Source: M. Leon. (1993). Revealing character and addressing voters' need in the 1992 presidential debates: A content analysis. *Argumentation and Advocacy, 30*, p. 93.

Statistical comparisons between groups were performed by means of a nonparametric within-subject test of significance (Wilcoxon signed-ranks test) because we used the one-to-one subject-matching procedure.

Source: D. Grossi, J. T. Becker, and L. Trojand. (1994). Visuospatial imagery in Alzheimer disease. *Perceptual and Motor Skills, 78*(3), p. 870.

A Friedman test demonstrated significant ordering of the ten qualities by all participants, $\chi^2 (9, N = 188) = 603.22, p < .001$.

Source: D. A. Stiles, J. L. Gibbons, and J. L. G. Schnellmann. (1990). Opposite-sex ideal in the U.S.A. and Mexico as perceived by young adolescents. *Journal of Cross-Cultural Psychology, 21*(2), p. 186.

OBTAINING RANKED DATA

One obvious way for a researcher to obtain ranked data is to ask each subject to rank a set of objects, statements, ideas, or other things. In Excerpt 20.6, we see a case where this was done. In the study from which this excerpt was drawn, the subjects were 9th-grade students in St. Louis and Mexico City, with each subject given a questionnaire containing ten desirable human characteristics.

A second way for a researcher to obtain ranks is to observe or arrange the study's subjects such that each one has an ordered position within the group. For example, we could go to the Boston Marathon, stand near the finish line with a list of all contestants' names, and then record each person's standing (first, second, third, or whatever) as he or she completes the race.

Excerpt 20.6   Obtaining Ordinal Data by Having Subjects Rank a
Set of Things

The participants completed the "Characterizing the Ideal Man & Woman"
questionnaire from the textbook *Activities and Readings in Learning and
Development* (Clifford, Grandgenett, & Bardwell, 1981). Participants were instructed to rank 10 characteristics of the ideal man or woman such as "he is kind
and honest" or "she is intelligent."

Source: D. A. Stiles, J. L. Gibbons, and J. L. G. Schnellmann. (1990). Opposite-sex ideal in the U.S.A.
and Mexico as perceived by young adolescents. *Journal of Cross-Cultural Psychology, 21*(2), p. 182.

Or, we might go into a classroom, ask the students to line up by height, and
then request that the students "count off" beginning at the "tall" end of the
line.[1]

The third way for a researcher to obtain ranks involves a two-step
process. First, each subject is independently measured on some variable of
interest with a measuring instrument that yields a score indicative of that
subject's absolute standing with respect to the numerical continuum associated with the variable. Then, the scores from the group of subjects are compared and converted into ranks to indicate each subject's relative standing
within the group.

In Excerpt 20.7, we see a case in which this two-step process was used. In
the study from which this excerpt was taken, 12 rats were trained to run
through a maze. All of the rats were given the same number of "acquisition
trials" to learn how to navigate through the maze, but half had all such training in one day (MT = massed trials) while the other half had the acquisition
trials spread out over four days (ST = spaced trials). Following the four days
of training, five "test trials" were conducted. During these test trials, one of
the measures taken was how long it took each rat to climb out (CO) of the
maze's goal box, because during these test trials the cover on the goal box was
raised thus permitting the rat to climb out. Comparisons were made between
the two groups of rats on each of the five test trials.

Using a stopwatch to measure how long it took each rat to climb out of
the goal box, the researcher obtained ratio-level data. However, those scores
(on the last test trial) were converted to ranks, with each rat's rank determined by comparing it against the other 11 rats. These ranks were then used

---

[1] *Although none of the tests discussed in this chapter could be applied to just the ranks obtained in our
running or line-up-by-height examples, two of the tests could be used if we simply classified each subject
into one of two or more subgroups (e.g., gender) in addition to noting his or her order on the running speed
or height variable.*

Excerpt 20.7   Converting Ratio-Level Data into Ranks

For the CO measure, there was no significant difference between the massed and spaced treatments on the initial test trial, with the MT animals averaging 12.5 min. and the ST animals averaging 11.24 min. Over successive test trials, however, the MT animals were decreasingly willing to climb out, and on the fifth test trial all of the animals in that group stayed in the goalbox for the maximum duration allowed (16.67 min.). In contrast, the ST animals decreased the amount of time it took them to climb out, and on the fifth test trial they took an average of 6.09 min. to do so. Using the Mann–Whitney U test, the difference between the two groups on the last test trial was significant [$U(6,6) = 3, p < .05$].

Source: H. Babb. (1992). Goal aversiveness after escape training with short and long intertrial intervals. *Bulletin of the Psychonomic Society, 30*(2), p. 151.

---

within a Mann–Whitney U test to see if a significant difference existed between the two groups.[2]

REASONS FOR CONVERTING SCORES ON A CONTINUOUS VARIABLE INTO RANKS

It may seem odd that researchers sometimes engage in the two-step, data-conversion process whereby subjects' scores on a variable of interest are converted into ranks. Since the original scores typically are interval or ratio in nature whereas the ranks are ordinal, such a conversion might appear to be ill-advised in that it brings about a "loss of information." There are, however, three reasons why researchers might consider the benefits associated with the scores-to-ranks conversion to outweigh the loss-of-information liability.

One reason why researchers often change raw scores into ranks is that the test procedures developed for use with ranks involve fewer assumptions than do the test procedures developed for use with interval- or ratio-level data. For example, the assumptions of normality and homogeneity of variance that underlie t- and F-tests do not serve as the basis for some of the tests considered in this chapter. As Excerpts 20.8–20.11 make clear, researchers sometimes convert their raw scores into ranks because the original data involved nonnormality and/or heterogeneity of variance.[3]

---

[2] *Because all six rats in the MT group as well as one rat from the ST group had identical times (since they stayed in the goalbox for the maximum time allowed), each of these seven rats was given a rank of 9, the average of the seven ranks (6, 7, 8, 9, 10, 11, 12) that would have been assigned if no "ties" had occurred.*

[3] *In three of the four excerpts presented here, the term* nonparametric *appears. This term is simply a label for the various test procedures that involve ranked data. In contrast, the term* parametric *is used to denote those test (e.g., t and F) that are built upon a more stringent set of assumptions about the population(s) associated wtih the study's sample(s).*

Excerpts 20.8–20.11 Skewness and Heterogeneous Variances as
Reasons for Converting Scores to Ranks

The time spent in aggressive behavior was analyzed with the Mann–Whitney U
test, in view of the data's skewed distribution.

Source: L. A. Hilakivi-Clark and R.G. Lister. (1992). Are there pre-existing behavioral characteristics
that predict the dominant status of the male NIH Swiss Mice (*Mus musculus*)? *Journal of Comparative
Psychology, 106*(2), p. 185.

Results of Kruskal–Wallis test. This nonparametric test was used because an
analysis of variance test of means did not meet the test of homogeneity of variance, an assumption necessary for using parametric analysis of variance procedures.

Source: W. B. Hammitt and M. B. Patterson. (1991). Coping behavior to avoid visitor encounters: Its
relationship to wildland privacy. *Journal of Leisure Research, 23*(3), p. 235.

Finally, statistical evaluation of differences between the introverts and extroverts
was performed using the Kruskal–Wallis one way analysis of variance (Hollander
and Wolfe, 1973), a nonparametric conservative procedure which makes no assumptions about normality and homogeneity of the variance in the population
sample.

Source: M. A. Wilson, and M. L. Langus. (1990). A topographical study of differences in the P300 between introverts and extroverts. *Brain Topography, 2*(4), pp. 270–271.

Since assumptions concerning normality and homogeneity of the population
group variances could not be met by the present data, analysis was carried out
by means of Kruskal–Wallis nonparametric analysis of variance.

Source: B. Seginer. (1992). Future orientation: Age-related differences among older adolescents.
Journal of Youth and Adolescence, 21(4), p. 429.

A second reason why researhcers convert raw scores to ranks is related to
the issue of sample size. As you will recall, t- and F-tests tend to be robust to
violations of underlying assumptions when the samples being compared are
the same size. When the ns differ, however, nonnormality and/or heterogeneity of variance in the population(s) can cause the t- or F-test to function differently than intended. For this reason, some researchers will turn to one of
the five test procedures discussed in this chapter if their ns differ. In Excerpt
20.12, different sample sizes prompted a pair of researchers to convert self-esteem scores into the ranks needed for the Mann–Whitney U test.

In Excerpt 20.12, the researchers indicate that they used the Mann–
Whitney U test because "sample sizes were small and uneven." It seems legitimate to ask what these researchers would have done if their study had
involved ns that were equal but small. This question is very difficult to answer
because applied researchers have been given two conflicting rules of thumb

---

Excerpt 20.12   Turning to the Mann-Whitney *U* Test Because of Sample Sizes

---

Possible differences in self-esteem scores between boys and girls on all subscales as well as the total score in this replication sample were computed using the Mann-Whitney *U*-Test since sample sizes were small and uneven.

Source: H. E. Rawson, and D. McIntosh. (1991). The effects of therapeutic camping on the self-esteem of children with severe behavior problems. *Therapeutic Recreation Journal, 25*(4), p. 47.

---

by mathematical statisticians. According to one statistician, researchers should use nonparametric tests if their sample size is 6 or less, even if all samples are the same size. According to a different statistician, parametric tests can be used with very small samples as long as the *n*s don't differ. We mention this controversy simply to alert you to the fact that some researchers use nonparametric tests because they have small sample sizes, even though the *n*s are equal.[4]

The third reason for converting raw scores to ranks is related to the fact that raw scores sometimes appear to be more precise than they really are. In other words, a study's raw scores may provide only ordinal information about the study's subjects even though the scores are connected to a theoretical numerical continuum associated with the dependent variable. In such a case, it would be improper to treat the raw scores as if they indicate the absolute distance that separates any two subjects having different scores when in fact the raw scores only indicate, in a relative sense, which subject has more of the measured characteristic than the other.

Consider, for example, the popular technique of having subjects respond to a **Likert-type attitude inventory**. With this kind of measuring device, each subject indicates a level of agreement or disagreement with each of several statements by selecting one of four or five options that typically include "strongly agree" and "strongly disagree" on the ends. In scoring a respondent's answer sheet, consecutive integers are typically assigned to the response options (e.g., 1, 2, 3, 4, 5) and then the respondent's total score is obtained by adding together the individual scores "earned" on each of the inventory's statements. In this fashion, two subjects in a study might end up with total scores of 32 and 29.

With Likert-type attitude inventories, the total scores derived from the subjects' responses are probably only ordinal in nature. For one thing, the arbitrary assignment of consecutive integers to the response options does not likely correspond to any subject's view of how the response options relate to another. Moreover, it is probably the case that certain of the inventory's statements are more highly connected than others to one's reason for holding a

---

[4] *The two statisticians referred to in this paragraph are Sidney Siegel and John Gaito.*

positive or negative attitude toward the topic being focused on—yet all statements are equal in their impact on a respondent's total score. For these reasons, it is not very plausible to presume that the resulting total scores possess the characteristic of "equal intervals" that is embodied in interval (and ratio) levels of measurement.

In Excerpt 20.13, we see a case in which a researcher points out that her reason for using the Mann-Whitney and Kruskal-Wallis tests is based upon the ordinal nature of her data. In the study from which this excerpt was taken, a Likert-type attitude inventory was not used to collect the data. However, the method of data collection that was employed produced raw scores that were clearly devoid of any semblance of equal intervals.

Excerpt 20.13   Using Nonparametric Tests Because the Data Are Ordinal

---

Because of their ordinal nature, data were analyzed using a non-parametric Mann-Whitney U (Z) or a Kruskal-Wallis one-way analysis of variance (H) test.

Source: W. Z. Hultsman. (1993). The influence of others as a barrier to recreation participation among early adolescents. *Journal of Leisure Research, 25*(2), p. 154.

Now that we have discussed how and why a researcher might end up with ranked data, let us take a look at each of the five test procedures that deserve the label "popular nonparametric test." As noted earlier, these test procedures are the median test, the Mann-Whitney U test, the Kruskal-Wallis one-way ANOVA, the Wilcoxon matched-pairs signed-ranks test, and the Friedman two-way ANOVA. In looking at each of these test procedures, we want to focus our attention on the nature of the research "setting" for which the test is appropriate, the way in which the ranked data are used, the typical format for reporting results, and the meaning of a rejected null hypothesis.

THE MEDIAN TEST

The **median test** is designed for use when a researcher wishes to compare two or more independent samples. If two such groups are compared, the median test is a nonparametric analog to the independent-samples t-test. With three or more groups, it is the nonparametric analog to a one-way ANOVA.

A researcher might select the median test in order to contrast two groups defined by a dichotomous characteristic (e.g., males versus female, or experimental versus control) on a dependent variable of interest (e.g., throwing ability, level of conformity, or anything else the researcher wishes to measure). Or, the median test might be selected if the researcher wishes to compare three or more groups (that differ in some qualitative fashion) on a measured dependent variable. An example of this latter situation might involve comparing football players, basketball players, and baseball players in terms of their endurance while riding a stationary bicycle.

The null hypothesis of the two-group version of the median test can be stated as $H_0: M_1 = M_2$, where the letter M stands for the median in the population and the numerical subscripts serve to identify the first and second populations. If three or more groups are compared using the median test, the null hypothesis takes the same form except that there would be additional Ms involved in H_0. The alternative hypothesis says that the two Ms differ (if just two groups are being compared) or that at least two of the Ms differ (in the situation where three or more groups are being contrasted).

To conduct a median test, the researcher follows a simple three-step procedure. First, the comparison groups are temporarily combined and a single median is determined for the entire set of scores. (This step necessitates that ranks be assigned either to all subjects or at least to those subjects who are positioned near the "middle of the pack.") In the second step, the comparison groups are reconstituted so that a contingency table can be set up to indicate how many subjects in each comparison group lie above and below the "grand median" identified in the first step. This contingency table will have as many columns as there are comparison groups, but it will always have two rows (one labeled "above the median," the other labeled "below the median"). Finally, an independent-samples chi-square test is applied to the data in the contingency table to see if the samples differ (in the proportion of cases falling above the combined median) by more than what would be expected by chance alone, presuming that H_0 is true.

In Excerpt 20.14, we see a case in which the median test was used to compare a group of service station dealers against a group of priests. As indicated in the excerpt, the median test was used four times: once to compare the two groups in terms of their overall individualistic scores derived from Rokeach's survey, and then three more times to compare the two groups on subscales of individualistic values. The table shown in this excerpt gives the impression that two medians were computed for each of the four comparisons of the two groups. In reality, each median test used a single median (computed from the scores of both groups being combined) and then a 2×2 contingency table to show how many members of each group were above and below that single median. For each of the four comparisons, it turned out that the service station dealers and priests were quite dissimilar in the proportion of group members on each side of the combined group median.

In trying to interpret the results of the median test, one should recognize that the "grand median" computed from the sample data is unlikely to match the common median found in H_0. Because of this, the actual null hypothesis being tested is not that the populations being compared have the same median but rather that the various populations have the same proportion of scores above the value of the median of the combined *samples*. With larger

---

Excerpt 20.14 The Median Test

In studies of American priests and of American gasoline service station dealers, using Rokeach's 36-value survey, service station dealers gave higher priority overall than priests to individualistic values (Rokeach, 1973, p. 153–158). This finding conforms with the image of the priesthood as an occupation that forgoes selfish concerns and of service station owners as individualistic entrepreneurs. Examination of group differences in the three types of individualistic values measurable with the Rokeach survey, however, reveals that an important distinction is obscured by the overall comparison (Table 2). Service station dealers gave higher priority to enjoyment and achievement values, reflecting their greater self-serving occupations. They gave substantially lower priority, however, to the third individualistic value type—self-direction.

Table 2

Median value rankings by American priests and service station dealers[a]

	Number of values in index	Service station dealers (N = 235)	Priests (N = 80)
Individualist values overall	(12)	10.40[*]	11.16
Subtypes			
Enjoyment	(4)	7.81[*]	11.55
Achievement	(4)	8.50[*]	11.43
Self-direction	(4)	14.88	10.50[*]

[a] Data from Rokeach (1973, p. 153–158). 1 = ranked most important, 18 = ranked least important.
[*]Significantly more important ($p < .05$) by Median test.

Source: S. H. Schwartz. (1990). Individualism-collectivism: Critique and proposed refinements. *Journal of Cross-Cultural Psychology*, 21(2), pp. 145–146.

samples, of course, there is likely to be a smaller discrepancy between the median value used to set up the contingency table and the common value of M hypothesized to exist in the populations. With small samples, however, it turns out that the median test (despite its name) is not really a test of equal population medians.

Occasionally, a researcher will conduct what might be thought of as a "double" median test. The setting for this kind of test always involves a single group of subjects, interval or ratio measurements of each subject on each of two variables, and researcher interest in the relationship between the two variables on which measurements have been collected. Once the data are available, the researcher (1) independently ranks the subjects on each measure,

(2) determines for each variable whether a subject is above or below the median, (3) sets up a 2 × 2 contingency table wherein each subject is positioned to reflect his or her standing relative to the two medians, and (4) applies a chi-square test to the frequency data of the contingency table. A statistically significant result would suggest that there is either a positive or negative relationship, in the relevant population, between the two variables.

In Excerpt 20.15 we see an example of this "double" median test. The findings point toward a positive relationship between the two sets of measures, since the chi-square test turned out to be significant because of the large number of boys who were either above the median on both response dimensions or below both medians.

Excerpt 20.15   A "Double" Median Test

Subjects were also rank ordered on their weighted average ESs separately for overall MPH and BM response, and median splits were performed on the two dimensions. Boys were assigned to the resulting four cells (above or below the median in response to each treatment). Twenty-one boys were either above or below the median on both response dimensions, $\chi^2 (1, N=27) = 8.3, p < .005$.

Source: W. E. Pelham, C. Carlson, S. E. Sams, G. Vallano, M. J. Dixon, and B. Hoza. (1993). Separate and combined effects of methylphenidate and behavior modification on boys with attention deficit-hyperactivity disorder in the classroom. *Journal of Consulting and Clinical Psychology, 61*(3), p. 511.

THE MANN–WHITNEY U TEST[5]

The **Mann-Whitney U test** is like the two-sample version of the median test in that both tests allow a researcher to compare two independent samples. While these two procedures are similar in that they are both considered to be nonparametric tests, the Mann-Whitney U test is the more powerful of two. In other words, if the two comparison groups truly do differ from each other, the Mann-Whitney U test (as compared to the median test) is less likely to produce a Type II error. This superiority of the Mann-Whitney test comes about because it utilizes more information from the subjects than does the median test.

When using the Mann-Whitney U test, the researcher examines the scores made available by measuring the subjects on the variable of interest. Initially, the two comparison groups are lumped together. This is done so that each subject can be ranked to reflect his or her standing within the combined group. After the ranks have been assigned, the researcher reconstitutes the

---

[5] *This test is also referred to as the Wilcoxon test, as the Wilcoxon rank-sum test, and as the Wilcoxon-Mann-Whitney test.*

two comparison groups. The previously assigned ranks are then examined to see if the two groups are significantly different.

If the two samples being compared came from identical populations, then the **sum of ranks** in one group ought to be approximately equal to the sum of ranks in the other group. For example, if there were four subjects in each sample and if H_0 were true, we would not be surprised if the ranks in one group were 2, 4, 5, and 8 while the ranks in the other group were 1, 3, 6, and 7. Here, the sum of the ranks are 19 and 17, respectively. It *would* be surprising, however, to find (again assuming that H_0 is true) that the sum of the ranks are 10 and 26. Such an extreme outcome would occur if the ranks of 1, 2, 3, and 4 are located in one of the samples while the ranks of 5, 6, 7, and 8 are located in the other sample.

To perform a Mann-Whitney U test, the researcher computes a sum-of-ranks value for each sample and then inserts these two numerical values into a formula. It is not important for you to know what that formula looks like, but it *is* essential that you understand the simple logic of what is going on. The formula used to analyze the data will produce a calculated value called U. Based on the value of U, the researcher (or a computer) can then derive a p-value that indicates how likely it is, under H_0, to have two samples that differ as much or more than do the ones actually used in the study. Small values of p, of course, are interpreted to mean that H_0 is unlikely to be true.

In Excerpt 20.16, we see a case in which the Mann-Whitney U test was used to compare two experimental groups in terms of the subjects' preference for doing a particular activity (as compared to doing other activities). The subjects were young children, and all of them were exposed to the same set of game activities. With one game, however, the children in one group were encouraged to positively perceive their ability to perform and to anticipate satisfaction, whereas the children in the other group were provided external reinforcement for performing well. The two groups of children were compared

---

Excerpt 20.16   The Mann-Whitney U Test

We performed another analysis, using the Mann-Whitney U test, to compare the preference for the manipulated activities of the two experimental groups at the two postmanipulation measurement times. The results of this analysis showed that immediately following the manipulation, the cognitive restructuring group ranked the manipulated activity higher than did the behavioral reinforcement group ($U = 86$, $p < .001$, one-tailed). Similar results were found at the 2-week follow-up ($U = 57.5$, $p < .001$, one-tailed).

Source: A. Barak, S. Shiloh, and O. Haushner. (1992). Modification of interests through cognitive restructuring: Test of a theoretical model in preschool children. *Journal of Counseling Psychology, 39*(4), p. 494.

twice, once immediately following their exposure to the full set of games and then again two weeks later.

Although it is quite easy for a researcher to obtain a calculated value for U from the sample data and to compare that data-based number against a tabled critical value, the task of interpreting a statistically significant result is a bit more difficult, for two reasons. First, the null hypothesis being tested deals not with the ranks used to compute the calculated value but rather with the continuous variable that "lies behind" or "beneath" the ranks. For example, if we used a Mann-Whitney U test to compare a sample of men against a sample of women with respect to their order of finish after running a 10-kilometer race, the data collected might very well simply be ranks, with each person's rank indicating his or her place (among all contestants) upon crossing the finish line. The null hypothesis, however, would deal with the continuous variable that lies beneath the ranks, which in our hypothetical study is running speed.

The second reason why statistically significant results from Mann-Whitney U tests are difficult to interpret is related to the fact that the rejected null hypothesis says that the two populations have identical distributions. Consequently, rejection of H_0 could come about because the populations differ in terms of their central tendencies, their variabilities, and/or their distributional shapes. In practice, however, the Mann-Whitney test is far more sensitive to differences in central tendency, so a statistically significant result is almost certain to mean that the populations have different average scores. But even here, an element of ambiguity remains because the Mann-Whitney U test could cause H_0 to be rejected because the two populations differ in terms of their means, or in terms of their medians, or in terms of their modes.

In the situation where the two populations have identical shapes and variances, the Mann-Whitney U test focuses on means, and thus $H_0: \mu_1 = \mu_2$. However, applied researchers rarely know anything about the populations involved in their studies. Therefore, most researchers who find that their Mann-Whitney U test yields a statistically significant result legitimately can conclude only that the two populations probably differ with respect to their averages. Another way of drawing a proper conclusion from a Mann-Whitney U test that causes H_0 to be rejected is to say that the scores in one of the populations tend to be larger than scores in the other population. This statement could only be made in a tentative fashion, however, since the statistically significant finding might well represent nothing more than a Type I error.

If you return to Excerpt 20.16 and try to make sense out of the results, you will find this more difficult than you probably would like. The statistically significant result produced by the Mann-Whitney U test simply means that the populations associated with the two samples likely differ in terms of their average scores on the continuum that underlies the ranks. Since we are not able to say that the two populations probably differ with respect to any specific measure of central tendency, it is best to conclude that the cognitive restructuring treatment seems to be more potent than the behavioral reinforcement treatment, at least when used with children and activities like those used in this study.

One other feature of the Mann–Whitney *U* test is worth mentioning. By contrast with most statistical tests (e.g., *t*, *F*, and χ^2), the null hypothesis associated with the Mann–Whitney *U* test is rejected when the researcher's data-based calculated value turns out to be equal to or *smaller than* the tabled critical value. For example, the unreported critical *U*-value associated with each of the tests reported in Excerpt 20.16 was 88. Because the calculated values turned out to be 86 and 57.5 in the two tests that were conducted, each null hypothesis was rejected.

THE KRUSKAL–WALLIS *H* TEST

In those situations where a researcher wishes to use a nonparametric statistical test to compare two independent samples, the Mann–Whitney *U* test is typically used to analyze the data. When researchers wish to compare three or more such groups, they more often than not utilize the **Kruskal–Wallis *H* test**. Hence, the Kruskal–Wallis procedure can be thought of as an "extension" of the Mann–Whitney procedure in the same way that a one-way ANOVA is typically considered to be an "extension" of an independent-samples *t*-test.[6]

The fact that the Kruskal–Wallis test is like a one-way ANOVA shows through when one considers the mathematical derivation of the formula for computing the test's calculated value. On a far simpler level, the similarity between these two test procedures shows through when we consider their names. The parametric test we considered in Chapter 12 is called a one-way ANOVA whereas the nonparametric analog to which we now turn our attention is called the Kruskal–Wallis one-way ANOVA of ranks. Excerpt 20.17 shows how the notion of an analysis of variance pops up in the way researchers describe the Kruskal–Wallis test.

Excerpt 20.17 The Kruskal–Wallis Test Referred to as an Analysis of Variance

Kruskal–Wallis analysis of variance by ranks indicated no significant differences among groups before training as to use of listening skills or feelings about the interviews.

Source: B. Baum, and J. J. Gray. (1992). Expert modeling, self-observation using videotape, and acquisition of basic therapy skills. *Professional Psychology: Research and Practice, 23*(3), p. 222.

---

[6] *When just two groups are compared, the ANOVA F-test and the independent-samples t-test yield identical results. In a similar fashion, the Kruskal-Wallis and Mann-Whitney tests are mathematically equivalent when used to compare two groups.*

The Kruskal-Wallis test works very much as the Mann-Whitney test does. First, the researcher temporarily combines the comparison groups into a single group. Next, the subjects in this one group are ranked on the basis of their performance on the dependent variable. Then, the single group is subdivided so as to reestablish the original comparison groups. Finally, each group's sum of ranks is entered into a formula that yields the calculated value. This calculated value, in the Kruskal-Wallis test, is labeled H. When the data-based H "beats" the critical value or when the p-value associated with H turns out to be smaller than the level of significance, the null hypothesis is rejected.

In Excerpt 20.18, we see a case in which the Kruskal-Wallis test was used to compare three groups. In this excerpt, notice that the number 2 appears inside a set of parentheses immediately to the right of the letter H. This number is the single df number for the Kruskal-Wallis test, and it is computed as one less than the number of comparison groups.

Excerpt 20.18   Results of a Kruskal-Wallis H Test

A Kruskal-Wallis nonparametric analysis of variance was used to compare the frequency of F responses for this control group and groups S and X. F responses were those for which the child initially responded "don't know" but then selected the correct response when presented with three alternatives. There was no difference between the three groups in the frequency of such responses ($H(2) = 0.89$).

Source: D. V. M. Bishop and C. Adams. (1992). Comprehension problems in children with specific language impairment: Literal and inferential meaning, *Journal of Speech and Hearing Research, 35*(1), p. 125.

The Kruskal-Wallis H test and the Mann-Whitney U test are similar not only in how the subjects are ranked and in how the groups' sum-of-ranks values are used to obtain the test's calculated value but also in the null hypothesis being tested and what it means when H_0 is rejected. Technically speaking, the null hypothesis of the Kruskal-Wallis H test is that the populations associated with the study's comparison groups are identical with respect to the distributions on the continuous variable that lies beneath the ranks used within the data analysis. Accordingly, a rejection of the H_0 could come about because the population distributions are not the same in central tendency, in variability, and/or in shape. In practice, however, the Kruskal-Wallis test focuses primarily on central tendency. In fact, two well-known statisticians—Leonard Marascuilo and Maryellen McSweeney—recently asserted that "the Kruskal-Wallis test is not too sensitive to differences in spread or form" and that "rejection of H_0 via the H statistic is almost certain to be equivalent to differences in mean, median, center, or some other measure of shift."[7]

---

[7] *L. A. Marascuilo and M. McSweeney. (1977).* Nonparametric and distribution-free methods for the social sciences. *Monterey, California: Brooks/Cole, p. 305.*

While the Mann–Whitney and Kruskal–Wallis tests are similar in many respects, they differ in the nature of the decision-rule used to decide whether H_0 should be rejected. With the Mann–Whitney test, H_0 is rejected if the data-based U turns out to be smaller than the critical value. In contrast, the Kruskal–Wallis H_0 is rejected when the researcher's calculated H is *larger* than the critical value.[8] In Excerpt 20.18, therefore, it was the small value of H, 0.89, that prompted the researchers to conclude that there was "no difference" among the three groups.

Whenever, the Kruskal–Wallis H test leads to a rejection of H_0, there remains uncertainty as to which specific populations are likely to differ from one another. In other words, the Kruskal–Wallis procedure functions very much as an "omnibus" test. Consequently, when such a test leads to a rejection of H_0, the researcher will normally turn to a post hoc analysis so as to derive more specific conclusions from the data. Within such post hoc investigations, comparison groups are typically compared in a pairwise fashion.

The post hoc procedure used most frequently following a statistically significant H test is the Mann–Whitney U test. In Excerpts 20.19 and 20.20, we see two illustrations of how the U test was utilized to probe the data following an H test.

In Excerpt 20.20, note that the level of significance associated with the post hoc test was changed from .05 to .0083. This change in alpha came about because applied researchers have been advised by statisticians to employ the

---

Excerpts 20.19–20.20 Use of the Mann–Whitney U Test Within a Post Hoc Investigation

---

Thus, to compare the results of the FBF-3 among the types of schizophrenia, nonparametric techniques were used (Kruskal–Wallis test). When statistically significant differences were found, the Mann–Whitney U test was applied with the aim of evaluating from which groups statistical significance was attained.

Source: V. Peralta, M. J. Cuesta, and J. De Leon. (1992). Positive versus negative schizophrenia and basic symptoms. *Comprehensive Psychiatry, 33,* p. 204.

The six IES instructional clusters and the total IES scores ratings were analyzed using the Kruskal–Wallis one-way analysis of variance by ranks to test for differences between the categories LD, EBD, EMR-R, and EMR-S in special education classrooms. A .05 level of significance was adopted for the analyses. Post-hoc follow-up tests used the Mann–Whitney U test at a .0083 (.05/6) level of significance.

Source: J. E. Vsseldyke, M. Thurlow, S. Christenson, and P. Muyskens, (1991). Classroom and home learning differences between students labeled as educable mentally retarded and their peers. *Education and Training in Mental Retardation, 26*(March), p. 9.

---

[8] *If U or H turns out equal to the critical value, H_0 is rejected. Such an outcome, however, is quite unlikely.*

Bonferroni adjustment technique when using the Mann-Whitney test within a post hoc investigation. In Excerpt 20.20, .05 was divided by 6 because six pairwise comparisons were needed in order to compare the four groups (LD, EBD, EMR-R, and EMR-S) against each other two at a time.

THE WILCOXON MATCHED-PAIRS SIGNED-RANKS TEST

Researchers frequently wish to compare two related samples of data generated by measuring the same subjects twice (e.g., in a pre-post sense) or by measuring two groups of matched subjects just once. If the data are interval or ratio in nature and if the relevant underlying assumptions are met, the researcher will probably utilize a correlated t-test to compare the two samples. On occasion, however, that kind of parametric test cannot be used because the data are ordinal or because the t-test assumptions are untenable (or considered by the researcher to be a nuisance). In such situations, the two related samples are likely to be compared using the **Wilcoxon matched-pairs signed-ranks test**.

In conducting the Wilcoxon test, the researcher must do five things. First, each pair of scores is examined so as to obtain a "change" score (for the case where a single group of subjects has been measured twice) or a "difference" score (for the case where the members of two matched samples have been measured just once). These scores are then ranked, either from high to low or from low to high. The third step involves attaching a "+" or a "−" sign to each rank. (In the one-group-measured-twice situation, these signs will indicate whether a subject's second score turned out to be higher or lower than the first score. In the two-samples-measured-once situation, these signs will indicate whether the subjects in one group earned higher or lower scores than their counterparts in the other group.) In the fourth step, the researcher simply looks to see which sign appears less frequently and then adds up the ranks that have that sign. Finally, the researcher labels the sum of the ranks having the least frequent sign as T, considers T to be the calculated value, and compares T against a tabled critical value.

In Excerpt 20.21, we see a case where the Wilcoxon matched-pairs signed-ranks test was used in a study wherein the subjects of three independent samples were each measured on three occasions: before a treatment was administered, immediately after receiving the treatment, and two weeks later. The Wilcoxon test was used to compare each group's pretest data with each of the later sets of data procured from that group.

In using the Wilcoxon test, the researcher's conclusion either to reject or to retain H_0 is based on a decision-rule like that used within the Mann-Whitney U test. Simply stated, that decision-rule gives the researcher permission to reject H_0 when the data-based value of T is equal to or smaller than the tabled critical value. This is because a direct relationship exists be-

---

Excerpt 20.21   Wilcoxon's Matched-Pairs Signed-Ranks Test

We used the Wilcoxon matched-pairs signed-ranks test to test the significance of the changes in performance order within each group. The results of these analyses (all one-tailed) showed (a) a significant increase in the ranked position of the cognitive restructuring manipulated activity both immediately after the manipulation ($T = 15$, $N = 17$, $p < .01$) and 2 weeks later ($T = 30$, $N = 17$, $p < .05$); (b) a significant decrease in preference position of behaviorally reinforced activities both immediately after manipulation ($T = 17.5$, $N = 13$, $p < .05$) and 2 weeks later ($T = 9.0$, $N = 13$, $p < .01$); and (c) no significant changes in the control participants' preferences, in either the second or the third preference.

Source: A. Barak, S. Shiloh, and O. Haushner. (1992). Modification of interests through cognitive restructuring: Test of a theoretical model in preschool children. *Journal of Counseling Psychology, 39*(4), p. 493.

---

tween T and p. You can see this relationship in operation by examining the calculated values and p-levels presented in Excerpt 20.21.

Although it is easy to conduct a Wilcoxon test, the task of interpreting the final result is more challenging. The null hypothesis says that the populations associated with the two sets of sample data are each symmetrical around the same common point. This translates into a statement that the population of change (or difference) scores is symmetrical around a median value of zero. Interpreting the outcome of a Wilcoxon matched-pairs signed-ranks test is problematic because the null hypothesis could be false because the population of change/difference scores is not symmetric, because the population median is not equal to zero, or because the population is not symmetrical around a median other than zero. Accordingly, if the Wilcoxon test leads to a statistically significant finding, neither you nor the researcher will know the precise reason why H_0 has been rejected.

There are two different ways to clarify the situation when one wants to interpret a significant finding from the Wilcoxon test. First, such a test can be interpreted to mean that the two populations, each associated with one of the samples of data used to compute the difference/change scores, are probably not identical to each other. That kind of interpretation is not too satisfying, since the two populations could differ in any number of ways. The second interpretation one can draw if the Wilcoxon test produces a small p-value is that the two populations probably have different medians. (This is synonymous to saying that the population of difference/change scores is probably not equal to zero.) This interpretation is legitimate, however, only in the situation where it is plausible to assume that both populations have the same shape.

FRIEDMAN'S TWO-WAY ANALYSIS
OF VARIANCE OF RANKS

The **Friedman test** is like the Wilcoxon test in that both procedures were developed for use with related samples. The primary difference between the Wilcoxon and Friedman tests is that the former test can accommodate just two related samples whereas the Friedman test can be used with two or more such samples. Because of this, the Friedman test can be thought of as the nonparametric equivalent of the one-factor repeated-measures ANOVA that we considered in Chapter 16.[9]

To illustrate the kind of situation to which the Friedman test could be applied, suppose you and several other individuals were asked to independently evaluate the quality of the five movies nominated for this year's "Best Picture" award from the Academy of Motion Pictures. We might ask you and the other subjects in our little study to rank the five movies on the basis of whatever criteria you typically use when evaluating movie quality. Or, we might ask you to rate each of the movies (possibly on a 0-to-100 scale), thus providing us with data that we could convert into ranks. One way or the other, we could end up with a set of five ranks from each person indicating his or her opinion of the five movies.

If the five movies being evaluated are equally good, we would expect the movies to be about the same in terms of the sum of the ranks assigned to them. In other words, movie A ought to receive some high ranks, some medium ranks, and some low ranks if it is truly no better or worse than the other movies up for the big award. That would also be the case for each of the other four movies. The Friedman test treats the data in just this manner, because the main "ingredient" is the sum of ranks assigned to each movie.

Once the sum of ranks are computed for the various things being compared, they are inserted into a formula that yields the test's calculated value. We will not discuss here the details of that formula, or even present it. Instead, we want to focus on three aspects of what pops out of that formula. First, the calculated value is typically symbolized as χ_r^2 (or sometimes simply as χ^2). Second, large values of χ_r^2 suggest that H_0 is not true. Third, the value of χ_r^2 is referred to a null distribution of such values so as to determine the data-based p-value and/or to decide whether or not the null hypothesis should be rejected.

In Excerpt 20.22, we see a case where the Friedman test was used with 188 boys and girls who were individually asked to order 10 qualities in terms of their importance in the opposite sex. These 10 characteristics included "being kind and honest," "being of average weight," and "having lots of money." As indicated in Excerpt 20.22, the results indicated a "significant or-

---

[9] *Although the Friedman and Wilcoxon tests are similar in that they both were designed for use with correlated samples of data, the Friedman test actually is an extension of the sign test.*

Excerpt 20.22   Friedman's One-Way Analysis of Variance of Ranks

---

A Friedman test demonstrated significant ordering of the ten qualities by all participants, $\chi^2 (9, N = 188) = 603.22, p < .001$.

Source: D. A. Stiles, J. L. Gibbons, and J. L. G. Schnellmann. (1990). Opposite-sex ideal in the U.S.A. and Mexico as perceived by young adolescents. *Journal of Cross-Cultural Psychology, 21*(2), p. 186.

---

dering of the ten qualities." In other words, the null hypothesis (of the 10 qualities being of equal importance) was rejected.

If the Friedman test leads to a rejection of the null hypothesis when three or more things (such as movies in our hypothetical example or personal qualities in Excerpt 20.22) are compared, you are likely to see a post hoc follow-up test utilized to compare the things that have been ranked. Although many test procedures can be used within such a post hoc investigation, you will likely see the Wilcoxon matched-pairs signed-ranks test employed to make all possible pairwise comparisons. In using the Wilcoxon test in this fashion, the researcher should use the Bonferroni adjustment procedure to protect against an inflated Type I error-rate.

LARGE-SAMPLE VERSIONS OF THE TESTS ON RANKS

Near the end of Chapter 19, we pointed out how researchers will sometimes conduct a z-test when dealing with frequencies, percentages, or proportions. Whenever this occurs, researchers put their data into a special formula that yields a calculated value called z, and then the data-based p-value is determined by referring the calculated value to the normal distribution. Any z-test, therefore, can be conceptualized as a "normal curve test."

In certain situations, the z-test represents nothing more than an option available to the researcher, with the other option(s) being mathematically equivalent to the z-test. In other situations, however, the z-test represents a **large-sample approximation** to some other test. In Chapter 19, we pointed out how the sign, binomial, one-sample chi-square, and McNemar procedures can be performed using a z-test if the sample sizes are large enough. The formula used to produce the z calculated value in these large-sample approximations varies across these test procedures, but that issue is of little concern to consumers of the research literature.

Inasmuch as tests on nominal data can be conducted using z-tests when the sample(s) are large, it should not be surprising that "large-sample approximations" exist for several of the test procedures considered in the present chapter. To be more specific, you are likely to encounter studies in which the calculated value produced by the Mann-Whitney U test is not U, studies in which the calculated value produced by the Kruskal-Wallis one-way analysis of variance of ranks is not H, and studies in which the calculated value produced by the Wilcoxon matched-pairs signed-ranks test is not T. Excerpts 20.23–20.25 illustrate such cases.

Excerpts 20.23–20.25   Large-Sample Versions of the Mann–Whitney, Kruskal–Wallis, and Wilcoxon Tests

---

In order to ascertain the relationship of the adult child's sex to the level of support received by the parents, a Mann–Whitney U test was performed. As shown in Table 5, male children provided significantly more services ($Z = -2.517$, $p = .0118$.).

Source: C. L. Wright and J. W. Maxwell. (1991). Social support during adjustment to later-life divorce: How adult children help parents. *Journal of Divorce and Remarriage, 15*(3/4), p. 33.

Means and *SD*s (in parentheses) were .52 (.28) and .67 (.17) for the high school and college groups, respectively (the Kruskal–Wallis $\chi^2[df = 1] = 4.40$, $p < .05$).

Source: R. Seginer. (1992). Future orientation: Age-related differences among adolescent females. *Journal of Youth and Adolescence, 21*(4), p. 431.

While the K-ABC ACH and MRT correlated significantly ($r = .49, p < .01$), Wilcoxon's Matched-Pairs Signed-Ranks Test revealed that children in this study found the K-ABC ACH significantly more difficult than the MRT ($z = 7.00, p < .001$).

Source: S. Zucker and J. Rioridan. (1990). One-year predictive validity of new and revised conceptual language measurement. *Journal of Psychoeducational Assessment, 8*(1), p. 5.

In Excerpts 20.23–20.25, we see that the calculated value in the large-sample versions of the Mann–Whitney and Wilcoxon tests is a z-value. In contrast, the calculated value for the large-sample version of the Kruskal–Wallis test is a chi-square value. These excerpts thus illustrate nicely the fact that many of the so-called large-sample versions of nonparametric tests yield a p-value that is based upon the normal distribution. Certain of these tests, however, are connected to the chi-square distribution.

The Friedman test procedure—like the Mann–Whitney, Kruskal–Wallis, and Wilcoxon procedures—can be conducted using a "large sample approximation." Most researchers do this by comparing their calculated value for χ_r^2 against a chi-square distribution in order to obtain a p-value. If you look again at Excerpt 20.22, you will see a case in which the Friedman test was conducted in this fashion.

It should be noted that the median test is inherently a large-sample test to begin with. That is the case because this test requires that the data be cast into a 2×2 contingency table from which a chi-square calculated value is then derived. Because this chi-square test requires sufficiently large expected cell frequencies, the only option to the regular, "large-sample" median test is

Fisher's Exact Test. Fisher's test, used within this context, could be construed as the "small-sample" version of the median test.

Before concluding our discussion of the large-sample versions of the tests considered in this chapter, it seems appropriate to ask the simple question, "How large must the sample(s) be in order for these tests to function as well as their more exact, small-sample counterparts?" The answer to this question varies depending upon the test being considered. The Mann-Whitney z-test, for example, works well if both ns are larger than 10 (or if one of the ns is larger than 20) while the Wilcoxon z-test performs adequately when its n is greater than 25. The Kruskal-Wallis chi-square test works well when there are more than 3 comparison groups or when the ns are greater than 5. The Friedman chi-square test functions nicely when there are more than 4 things being ranked or more than 10 subjects doing the ranking.

Although not used very often, other large-sample procedures have been devised for use with the Mann-Whitney, Kruskal-Wallis, Wilcoxon, and Friedman tests. Some involve using the ranked data within complex formulas. Others involve using the ranked data within t- or F-tests. Still others involve the analysis of the study's data through two different formulas, the computation of an average calculated value, and then reference to a specially formed critical value. Although not now widely used, some of these alternative procedures may gain popularity among applied researchers in the coming years.

TIES

Whenever researchers rank a set of scores, they may encounter the case of **tied observations**. For example, there are two sets of ties in this hypothetical set of 10 scores: 8, 0, 4, 3, 5, 4, 7, 1, 4, 5. Or, ties can occur when the original data take the form of ranks. Examples here would include the tenth and eleventh runners in a race crossing the finish line simultaneously, or a judge in a "taste test" indicating that two of several wines equally deserve the blue ribbon.

With the median test, tied scores do not create a problem. If the tied observations occur within the top half or the bottom half of the pooled group of scores, the ties can be disregarded since all of the scores are easily classified as being above or below the grand median. If the scores in the middle of the pooled data set are tied, the "above" and "below" categories can be defined by a numerical value that lies adjacent to the tied scores. For example, if the 10 scores in the preceding paragraph had come from two groups being compared using a median test, "high" scores could be defined as anything above 4 while "low" scores could be defined as ≤ 4. (Another way of handling ties at the grand median is simply to drop those scores from the analysis.)

If tied observations occur when the Mann-Whitney, Kruskal-Wallis, or Wilcoxon tests are being used, researchers will typically do one of three things. First, they can apply "average" ranks to the tied scores. (The second footnote in this chapter illustrates how this technique was used in conjunction with a Mann–Whitney U test.) Second, they can drop the tied observations from the data set and subject the remaining, untied scores to the statistical test. Third, they can use a special version of the test procedure developed so as to handle tied observations.

In Excerpts 20.26–20.28, we see three cases in which the third of these three options was used. In two of these three cases, the phrase *corrected for ties* is an unambiguous signal that the tied scores were left in the data set and that

---

Excerpts 20.26–20.28   Using Special Formulas to Accommodate Tied Observations in the Data

Table 3

Psychiatric symptom index: Median standardized scores by cocaine use

Psychiatric symptom index factor	Cocaine users $n = 24$	Nonusers $n = 131$	p^*
Depression	43.3	36.7	.44*
Anger	54.2	33.3	.16
Anxiety	31.8	24.2	.12
Cognitive disturbance	25.0	16.7	.23
Total index	41.4	27.6	.15

*Wilcoxon–Mann–Whitney test, corrected for ties.

Source: D. R. Neuspiel and S. C. Hamel. (1992). Cocaine use, *post partum* symptoms. *Psychological Reports, 70,* p. 55. © *Psychological Reports.*

The Kruskal–Wallis statistic was applied to compare frequencies of methods of suicide for each sex by nation. . . . Most women in Japan used hanging, strangulation, or suffocation, and then poisoning (H corrected for ties = 138.1, $p < .001$).

Source: M. L. Snyder. (1994). Methods of suicide used by Irish and Japanese samples: A cross-cultural study from 1964 to 1979. *Psychological Reports, 74,* p. 128.

Between the ratings of the different tests often appeared zero differences which are omitted for the Wilcoxon signed-ranks test (Wilcoxon test). We preferred the modification of Pratt (1959) which includes zero differences in the ranking (Wilcoxon–Pratt test).

Source: F. L. Mertesdorf. (1994). Cycle exercising in time with music. *Psychological Reports, 78,* p. 1127.

a special formula was used to compute the calculated value. In the third excerpt, we see the phrase **Wilcoxon–Pratt test**; that particular label simply indicates that the Wilcoxon matched-pairs signed-ranks test has been conducted in a corrected-for-ties fashion.

Ties can also occur within the Friedman test. This could happen, for example, if a judge were to report that two of the things being judged were equally good. Such tied observations are not discarded from the data set, since that would necessitate tossing out all the data provided by that particular judge. Instead, the technique of assigning average ranks would be used, with the regular formula then employed to obtain the calculated value for the Friedman test.

THE RELATIVE POWER OF NONPARAMETRIC TESTS

It is widely believed that nonparametric procedures are inferior to parametric techniques because the former supposedly have lower power than the latter. This concern about power is appropriate, since any test having low power is likely to lead to a Type II error when H_0 is false. It is unfortunate, however, that nonparametric tests have come to be thought of as being less able to detect true differences between populations. We say this because nonparametric tests, in certain situations, are *more* powerful than their parametric counterparts.

If researchers have collected interval- or ratio-level data from two independent samples, they could compare the two groups by means of a parametric test (say an independent-samples t-test) or by means of a nonparametric test (say the Mann–Whitney U test). Similar statements could be made for the cases where data have been collected from three or more independent samples, from two correlated samples, or from a single sample that is measured in a repeated-measures sense. For these situations where data can be analyzed either with a parametric test or with a nonparametric test, it is possible to compare the power of one test procedure versus the power of a different test procedure. Such comparisons allow us to talk about a test's **relative power**.

If the assumptions of normality and homogeneity of variance are valid, then t- and F-tests will be more powerful than their nonparametric counterparts. On the other hand, if these assumptions are violated, nonparametric tests can, in certain circumstances, provide researchers with greater protection against Type II errors. As illustrated earlier in Excerpts 20.8–20.11, researchers often explain that they utilized a nonparametric test because their data sets were skewed and/or had nonequivalent variances. By deciding to use nonparametric procedures, these researchers may have increased the sensitivity of their tests over what would have been the case if they had used t- or F-tests.

The relative power of any nonparametric test as compared with its parametric counterpart varies depending upon the distributional shape in the population(s) associated with the study. Because of this, we believe that applied researchers should explain why they decided to use whatever techniques they employed. The issue of relative power ought to be included in such explanations. We say this because the typical applied research investigation suffers from inadequate power, and consequently it behooves the researcher to utilize the most powerful analytical technique available.

A Few Final Comments

As we approach the end of this chapter, four final points need to be made. These points constitute our typical end-of-chapter "warnings" to those who come into contact with technical research reports. By remaining sensitive to these cautions, you will be more judicious in your review of research conclusions that are based upon nonparametric statistical tests.

Our first warning concerns the quality of the research question(s) associated with the study you find yourself examining. If the study focuses on a trivial topic, no statistical procedure has the ability to "turn a sow's ear into a silk purse." This is as true of nonparametric procedures as it is of the parametric techniques discussed earlier in the book. Accordingly, we once again urge you to refrain from using data-based p-levels as the criterion for assessing the worth of empirical investigations.

Our second warning concerns the important assumptions of random samples and independence of observations. Each of the nonparametric tests considered in this chapter involves a null hypothesis concerned with one or more populations. The null hypothesis is evaluated with data that come from one or more samples that are assumed to be representative of the population(s). Thus, the notion of randomness is just as essential to any nonparametric test as it is to any parametric procedure. Moreover, nonparametric tests, like their parametric counterparts, are based upon an assumption of **independence**. Independence simply means that the data provided by any subject is not influenced by what happens to any other subject in the study.[10]

Our third warning concerns the term **distribution-free**, a label that is sometimes used instead of the term *nonparametric*. As a consequence of these terms being used as if they are synonyms, many applied researchers are under the impression that nonparametric tests work equally well no matter what the shape of the population distribution(s). This is not true for the two reasons we have touched upon earlier. On the one hand, the power of each and every nonparametric test varies depending upon the shape of the population distribution(s). On the other hand, the proper meaning of a rejected null

---

[10] *With the Median, Mann-Whitney, and Kruskal-Wallis tests, independence is assumed to exist both within and between the comparison groups. With the Wilcoxon and Friedman tests, the correlated nature of the data causes the independence assumption to apply only in a between-subjects sense.*

hypothesis is frequently influenced by what is known about the distributional shape of the populations.

Our final warning concerns the fact that many nonparametric procedures have been developed besides the five focused upon within the context of this chapter. Such tests fall into one of two categories. Some are simply alternatives to the ones we have discussed, and they utilize the same kind of data to assess the same null hypothesis. For example, the Quade test can be used instead of the Friedman test. The other kind of nonparametric test not considered here has a different purpose. The Jonckheere-Terpstra test, for instance, allows a researcher to evaluate a null hypothesis that says a set of populations is ordered in a particular way in terms of their average scores. We have not discussed such tests simply because they are used infrequently by applied researchers.

REVIEW TERMS

Distribution-free	Nonparametric test
Friedman two-way analysis of variance	Parametric test
	Relative Power
Independence	Sum of ranks
Kruskal–Wallis one-way analysis of variance by ranks	Tied Observations
	Wilcoxon–Mann–Whitney test
Large-sample approximation	Wilcoxon matched-pairs signed-ranks test
Likert-type attitude inventories	Wilcoxon–Pratt test
Mann–Whitney U test	Wilcoxon rank-sum test
Median split	Wilcoxon test
Median test	

REVIEW QUESTIONS

1. Why do researchers sometimes use nonparametric tests with data that are interval or ratio in nature?

2. The median test can be used with _____ (independent/related) samples of data.

3. If the median test is used to compare two samples, how many medians will the researcher need to compute based upon the sample data?

4. (True or False) When the data used within a nonparametric test are ranks, the null hypothesis cannot deal with means or medians.

5. Look at Excerpt 20.15. If the beginning of the final sentence had said "Seventeen boys" (rather than "twenty-one boys"), would the calculated value have turned out to be larger or smaller than 8.3?

6. (True or False) Both the median and Mann-Whitney tests require that the researcher compute a sum-of-ranks value for each comparison group involved in the study.

7. If the Mann–Whitney U test is used to compare two samples that have been selected from populations having identical shapes and variances, how could the null hypothesis be written?

8. What letter is used to stand for the calculated value in a Kruskal–Wallis test?

9. If a post hoc investigation is conducted in an effort to help clarify the meaning of a significant result from a Kruskal–Wallis comparison of four groups, what test is likely to be used to make these follow-up comparisons?

10. Other things held constant, is the relationship between the Wilcoxon test's T and the resulting p-value direct or indirect in nature?

11. Which of the nonparametric tests involves a calculated value that is usually symbolized as χ_r^2?

12. (True or False) The large-sample versions of the Mann–Whitney, Kruskal–Wallis, and Wilcoxon tests all involve a calculated value that is labeled z.

13. (True or False) Because they deal with ranks, the tests considered in this chapter have lower power than their parametric counterparts.

14. Are random samples important to nonparametric tests?

PRINCIPLES OF RESEARCH DESIGN

Near the beginning of any empirical investigation, one or more research questions are posed by the researcher. Near the end of the investigation, the data are analyzed, summarized, and interpreted. Between these two points, the researcher must make several decisions regarding how to implement the study. To be more specific, the researcher must decide what kind(s) of subjects (and how many) will be used, what the subjects will be asked to do, how many comparison groups (if any) will be involved, which dependent variable(s) will be focused on, how and when the subjects will be measured, and where the study will be conducted. When dealing with these questions, the researcher is engaged in the important task of planning the investigation. The resulting plan is referred to as the study's **research design**.

The issue of research design is exceedingly important to each empirical investigation. Clearly, if a study is poorly designed, the entire effort is wasted. Even if a study is characterized by (1) clear and important research questions and (2) sophisticated and appropriate statistical analyses, the entire study will be incapable of achieving its intended objective(s) if the design is faulty. In a very real sense, therefore, the issue of design assumes the role of a link in a chain that connects the research question(s) to the data-based conclusions. If the design link is weak, the chain breaks.

Although we wish to focus exclusively on a variety of design concerns in this final chapter, it should be noted that certain aspects of research design were considered in earlier chapters. For example, the issue of measuring instrument quality (i.e., reliability and validity) was examined in Chapter 4, the notion of random samples was discussed in Chapter 5, and the technique of counterbalancing the order of tasks or tests when measuring subjects repeatedly was presented in Chapter 16. Because earlier chapters touched on elements of research design, the current chapter represents a focused attempt to build on those initial discussions of design-related topics.

The material of this chapter is divided into five main sections. The first three sections deal with the three obvious components involved in *any* investigation: the subjects, the data, and the context in which the study is conducted. Within these initial sections, we clarify the distinction between descriptive and experimental studies, and also underscore the importance of internal and external validity. In the fourth section, three main classes of experimental design are distinguished from one another. In the final section, we conclude by offering some design-oriented warnings intended to help you become a more discerning consumer of others' research reports.

DESIGN ISSUES CONCERNING THE SUBJECTS

The design issues related to a study's subjects become clear when we consider four important questions about any empirical study:

Where did the subjects come from?

How many of the intended subjects actually supplied data that were analyzed?

If the study involved two or more comparison groups, how were such groups formed?

To what extent were the subjects motivated to perform any tasks asked of them during the study?

In the paragraphs that follow, we want to consider each of these questions in detail.

THE SOURCE OF SUBJECTS

When researchers are concerned only about the subjects involved in their studies, the data will be analyzed with statistical procedures that are descriptive (not inferential) in nature, and the issue of who the subjects represent is irrelevant. Most empirical studies, however, are not of this variety. The majority of researchers have an interest that extends beyond the subjects who supply the data, for inferential procedures are almost always used in conjunction with research data. Such analyses necessarily imply that the true focus is with the population(s) that corresponds to the study's sample(s). Accordingly, whenever researchers build a confidence interval or assess a null hypothesis, it is important to ask whether their sample(s) represents the intended population(s).

As we indicated in Chapter 5, the best way for a researcher to draw a sample from a concrete population is to select individuals randomly out of the larger, available pool of potential subjects. As indicated in Excerpt 21.1, this technique is actually used in certain studies.

Excerpt 21.1   Random Selection of a Sample from a Larger Group

---

A random sample of 350 licensed, practicing teachers of the behaviorally disordered from two states in the upper midwest were mailed a two-page survey along with an explanatory cover letter and a return envelope.

Source: P. L. Beare. (1991). Philosophy, instructional methodology, training, and goals of teachers of the behaviorally disordered. *Behavior Disorders, 16*(3), p. 212.

Whereas samples are sometimes created by **random selection** of subjects from an available population, it is frequently the case that the group of subjects used in a study is nothing more than a convenience sample. If the individuals who serve as subjects are used simply because they are nearby and willing to participate, then there may well be a sizable discrepancy between the intended population and the sample actually used. To illustrate how a deep and wide gulf can exist between these two groups, consider Excerpt 21.2, which presents two of the four research questions along with a description of the study's subjects.[1]

Excerpt 21.2   Mismatch Between the Intended Population and the
Convenience Sample

The main research questions [included the following] . . .

1. Is there any difference between training in sequential analysis and training in positional analysis in short- and long-term effects on reading and spelling?

2. Will children of low intelligence profit more from training in word analysis than children with average intelligence?

METHOD

Subjects

The subjects were 208 students enrolled in first-grade classes in Halden (Norway) at the time of the study.

Source: A. Lie. (1991). Effects of a training program for stimulating skills in word analysis in first grade children. *Reading Research Quarterly, 26*(3), p. 239.

As we pointed out in Chapter 5, many researchers collect data from individuals who are readily available rather than those who have been selected from a larger group. When the data collected from these individuals are analyzed via inferential procedures, the implied population is abstract in nature.

---

[1] *We maintain that the research questions simply cannot be answered from this study because the sample is so homogeneous in terms of age and geographical location.*

It is abstract because it exists only in the researcher's (and your) mind, with the population being created—or better yet, imagined—on the basis of the known characteristics of the sample.

When a researcher uses inferential statistics with a convenience sample, there must be a clear description of that sample for you to be able to imagine what kind of population fits the sample. Unfortunately, many researchers fail to provide such descriptions in their research reports, thus making it nearly impossible for anyone to have a sense as to the characteristics of the population involved in the study. Consider, for example, the material in Excerpt 21.3 which is the *complete* description of the subjects used in a recent study.

Excerpt 21.3   An Extremely Brief Description of a Convenience Sample

---

The subjects were 24 females and 24 males drawn from introductory psychology courses. They ranged from 17 years to 39 years, with a mean of 20.1 years.

Source: F. J. Jourden, A. Bandura, and J. T. Banfield. (1991). The impact of conceptions of ability on self-regulatory factors and motor skill acquisition. *Journal of Sport and Exercise Psychology, 13*(3), p. 216.

On the basis of the information presented in Excerpt 21.3, you *do* know that the researcher's subjects were human beings, that they were enrolled in an introductory psychology course, that males and females were equally represented, and that most (but not all) of the subjects were between the ages of 17 and 20. Despite these facts, there is an enormous amount of information that you do *not* know. To be more specific, you are completely in the dark with respect to the kind of university or college attended by these 48 subjects, the size of the psychology class, the full-time/part-time status of the students, the intellectual levels of the students, and the reasons these students agreed to participate in the investigation. Simply stated, it is next to impossible to generate the proper abstract population involved in the study because of the limited information provided about the sample.

Our concern about the appropriate population in any study that involves inferential statistics is motivated by our belief that researchers should keep the concept of **external validity** clearly in mind when they design (and summarize) their investigations. A study is said to possess external validity to the extent that its results can be generalized beyond the confines of the particulars of the actual study. One aspect of external validity is concerned with the extent to which results can be generalized beyond the actual subjects who supplied data, and it is precisely this kind of generalization that becomes relevant when we ask the simple question, "Where did the subjects come from?"

We believe that any researcher who uses inferential statistics should (1) design his or her study with external validity as a clear objective and (2) discuss the issue of external validity when summarizing the study's findings. In Excerpt 21.1, we saw a case in which the technique of random selection was used in the design phase of an investigation. In Excerpts 21.4 and 21.5, we see two examples of how conscientious researchers will bring up the issue of external validity when discussing their findings.

Excerpts 21.4—21.5   Expressed Concern for External Validity

The reader is reminded that the results and conclusions are based on data from a voluntary or "convenience" sample, a factor that limits the external validity of the research.

Source: R. T. Roessler, K. F. Schriner, and P. Price. (1992). Employment concerns of people with head injuries. *Journal of Rehabilitation, 58*(1), p. 18.

The results of this study have limited external validity because the sample was drawn from one community college and was not representative of the population of part-time students attending the college.

Source: M. Okun, L. Ruehlman, and P. Karoly. (1991). Application of investment theory to predicting part-time community college student interest and institutional presistence/departure behavior. *Journal of Educational Psychology, 83*(2), p. 218.

Targeted Subjects Versus Data-Supplying Subjects

The second of our four main questions about a study's subjects asked, "How many of the intended subjects actually supplied the data that were analyzed?" This is an important question because the legitimate population involved in any inferential study is tied to the group of subjects from whom data are collected. If some of the subjects in the researcher's sample drop out of the study before it is completed, the population appropriate to the sample will change. Likewise, consider what can (and often does) happen when a researcher collects data by having subjects respond to inventories, questionnaires, or tests sent through the mail. The nature of the statistical population will change from what it was at the outset (after the subjects were identified but before anything was sent to them) if there is a systematic difference between those who do or don't choose to send back completed forms.

In Excerpt 21.1, we considered a study in which a two-page survey was mailed to 350 practicing teachers of behaviorally disordered children. Consider now, in Excerpt 21.6, what happened *after* these surveys were mailed. Because the **response rate** was so low, the nature of the relevant population changed. Whereas the original population was defined to be "teachers of the behaviorally disordered from two states in the upper midwest," the actual population involved in this study became "teachers of the behaviorally disordered from two states in the upper midwest who were concerned enough about the study to complete the survey and then send it back to the researcher."

Excerpt 21.6 Additional Information from the Study from Which Excerpt 21.1 Was Taken

---

Completed surveys were returned by 206 teachers or 59%.

Source: P. L. Beare. (1991). Philosophy, instructional methodology, training, and goals of teachers of the behaviorally disordered. *Behavior Disorders, 16*(3), p. 212.

If certain subjects drop out of a study by not returning for subsequent treatment or data-collection sessions, by ceasing to participate in the middle of a session, or by not returning mailed surveys, the generalizability of the study's results may become severely limited. In other words, the external validity of the study may well be threatened by the occurrence of subject dropout. This particular threat to external validity is referred to as **mortality** or **attrition**. Experienced researchers, in designing their studies, will try to prevent mortality from damaging their studies. It is unethical, of course, to force someone to remain in a study against his or her will. However, several ethical design strategies can be implemented in an effort to reduce the likelihood that undesirable mortality will occur.

In evaluating research reports, you should give a few bonus points to those researchers who indicate that they considered the issue of mortality as they planned their studies. In studies involving mailed surveys, for example, the researcher can send follow-up materials to those who do not initially respond, make the mailed materials short and easy to use, and explain the importance of the study in a cover letter. In studies where the researcher has direct contact with the subjects and asks them to perform one or more tasks, the researcher can spend time explaining the importance of the study, alert subjects to any potentially difficult or boring tasks, and use placebo conditions involving interesting but irrelevant activities rather than pure control (do nothing) conditions. In studies involving two or more data-collection sessions, the researcher can schedule all sessions at convenient times for the subjects, remind subjects (via mail, phone, or e-mail) of subsequent sessions, and provide some form of remuneration to compensate subjects for their willingness to spend time with the researcher.

Regardless of what researchers do in an effort to prevent attrition from occurring, it may be the case that a portion of the subjects drops out before an investigation is concluded. When faced with attrition, conscientious researchers will try to figure out whether dropouts are systematically different (on any important variable) from those subjects who remained in the study.

Excerpt 21.7 nicely illustrates how such a comparison can be made. Notice how (1) the first sentence of this excerpt clearly articulates the researcher's objective in conducting an extra set of statistical tests, and (2) how the final sentence presents the researcher's conclusions. In our opinion, researchers who demonstrate this kind of concern for attrition deserve positive marks when you are evaluating their reports.

Excerpt 21.7 Investigating Attrition

Two sets of analyses were conducted to determine whether the subjects who dropped out of the study were different from those who remained. First, I examined the descriptive sample characteristics. There were no age differences between subjects that remained and those that dropped out, $t(128) = 0.11$, $p > .05$. Results of chi-square analyses revealed that the distribution of men and women was not significantly different in the two groups, $\chi^2 (1, N = 130) = 1.8$, $p > .05$. The longitudinal freshmen group also did not differ from the attrition group with respect to college major, $\chi^2(4, N = 101) = 3.9, p > .05$. I conducted multivariate analyses comparing independence from mother and independence from father (PSI subscales) and college adjustment, as based on SACQ subscale scores. I used listwise deletion of missing data for these and all subsequent analyses. No significant differences emerged between longitudinal and attrition freshmen on the measures, $F(11, 115) = 0.99$, $p > .05$. Thus, the subjects who remained in the study appeared to be no different from those who dropped out, in terms of subject characteristics or scores on the measures of interest.

Source: K. G. Rice. (1992). Separation-individualization and adjustment to college: A longitudinal study. *Journal of Counseling Psychology, 39*(2), p. 206.

FORMING COMPARISON GROUPS

The third of our four questions about a study's subjects asked, "If there are two or more comparison groups, how were such groups formed?" In dealing with this question, we need to distinguish studies that are descriptive in nature from those that have an experimental thrust. While neither type of study is inherently superior to the other, the distinction between these two classes of empirical investigation is extremely important. We say this because the design strategies and concerns over the validity of findings vary depending on whether a study is descriptive or experimental.[2]

In **descriptive studies,** the nature of subjects' characteristics determines which particular subjects end up in each comparison group. In such studies,

---

[2]The meaning of the word descriptive when used in this context should not be confused with the meaning of this adjective when it is used in reference to a kind of statistical technique. The data from a descriptive study can be analyzed with either descriptive or inferential techniques. Likewise, the data from an experimental study can be analyzed with either descriptive or inferential techniques.

researchers have the full authority to decide which particular independent variable(s) will be used to establish the comparison group categories, how many subjects will be in each comparison group, and where the subjects will come from. In terms of forming the comparison groups, the researcher will decide which subjects go where; however, such decisions will be made solely by noting the relevant characteristic(s) of each subject and then putting that subject into the proper category.

In Excerpt 21.8, we see an example of a descriptive study involving six comparison groups. Although it is true that it was the researchers who formed the six groups of subjects, they did so simply by noting each subject's status on the gender (male or female) and sex role (androgynous, traditional, and undifferentiated) independent variables. Each of the 17 males who had higher-than-average scores on both the masculine and feminine scales of the Bem Inventory *had* to be put into the male/androgynous comparison group. In a similar fashion, the remaining subjects were put into the other five groups strictly because of their gender and standing on the Sex Role Inventory.

Excerpt 21.8   A Descriptive Study

Based on the Bem Sex Role Inventory (BSRI; Bem, 1974), 164 participants (79 males, 85 females) were categorized into three groups: (1) *androgynous* (scores above the median on both the masculine and feminine scales; 17 males and 29 females), (2) *traditional* (scores for females above the median on only the feminine scale; males above the median on only the masculine scale; 36 males and 39 females), or (3) *undifferentiated* (scores below the median on both scales; 26 males, 17 females).. . .

A 2 (sex) $\times$ 3 (sex role) analysis of variance (ANOVA) was conducted on the dependent variables of total network size, number of female friends, and number of male friends.

Source: D. C. Jones, N. Bloys, and M. Wood. (1990). Sex roles and friendship patterns. *Sex Roles,* 23(3/4), pp. 137, 138.

Whereas descriptive studies are undertaken to *describe* the preexisting group(s) of the investigation, **experiments** are conducted to see whether the independent and dependent variables are linked together in a *cause-and-effect* manner. Stated differently, experiments are undertaken to see whether the independent variable affects the dependent variable.[3] Excerpt 21.9 illustrates such a study. In this investigation, the independent variable was feedback and the dependent variable was intrinsic motivation.

---

[3] *There are many synonyms for the important word* affects — *including influences, imparts, brings about, determines, improves, and creates. When any of these terms are used in a statement that also contains a specification of the independent and dependent variables, you should presume that cause-and-effect was the focus of the study.*

Excerpt 21.9 An Experimental Study

This study was a test of Deli and Ryan's (1985) cognitive evaluation theory in a fitness testing situation. More specifically, it was a test of proposition 2 of that theory, which posits that external events that increase or decrease perceived competence will increase or decrease intrinsic motivation. Seventh and eighth grade school children ($N = 105$) volunteered for an experiment that was ostensibly to collect data on a new youth fitness test (the Illinois Agility Run). After two untimed practice runs, a specially adapted version of the Intrinsic Motivation Inventory (IMI) was administered as a pretest of intrinsic motivation. Two weeks later when subjects ran again, they were apparently electronically timed. In reality the subjects were given bogus feedback. Subjects in a positive feedback condition were told their scores were above the 80th percentile, while those in a negative feedback condition were told their scores were below the 20th percentile. Those in a control condition received no feedback. The IMI was again administered to the subjects after their runs. [Statistical tests revealed that] positive feedback enhanced all aspects of intrinsic motivation, whereas negative feedback decreased them.

Source: J. R. Whitehead, and C. B. Corbin. (1991). Youth fitness testing: The effects of percentile-based evaluative feedback on intrinsic motivation. *Research Quarterly for Exercise and Sport, 62*(2), p. 225.

While there are many research strategies that can be used when interest lies in cause-and-effect relationships, experiments constitute the most rigorous way of looking to see whether the independent variable affects the dependent variable. Experiments have the potential to yield results that are clearer than those derived from other kinds of cause-and-effect probes because researchers can, if they are careful when conducting an experiment, set up the study so that everything is held constant, prior to the collection of data on the dependent variable, except the independent variable being examined. The independent variable is purposefully made to vary within the experiment. After the data on the dependent variable are collected, the researcher will use statistical techniques to see whether a greater than chance relationship exists between the independent and dependent variables. If it does, the researcher can justifiably conclude that the independent variable appears to affect the dependent variable.

To vary an independent variable in an experiment, the researcher will set up comparison groups that are different in terms of what they do (or what is done to them) during the study. For example, in the investigation that tested Deli and Ryan's cognitive evaluation theory in a fitness situation (see Excerpt 21.9), the researchers established three different feedback groups: positive feedback, negative feedback, and no feedback. It is, of course, the researchers who decide, in any experiment, which independent variable will be varied and how it will be varied. For these reasons, it can be said that the researcher "has control over" the independent variable or that this variable is "manipulated" by the researcher.[4]

This process of forming groups in an experiment is exceedingly important because it is here that the researcher can control many of the extraneous variables that would ruin the investigation if they were allowed to vary. Consider, for example, the dilemma that would exist if in Excerpt 21.9 the variable of intelligence had been confounded with the independent variable. To be more specific, suppose the most intelligent of the schoolchildren ended up in the positive feedback group, while those with the least intelligence ended up in the negative feedback group. Had this been the case, the results would be extremely murky because there would be no way to tell whether the scores on dependent variable turned out as they did (1) solely because the feedback conditions had a causal impact on intrinsic motivation, (2) solely because intelligence and intrinsic motivation are related, or (3) because intrinsic motivation is both influenced by prior feedback *and* related to intelligence.

To control many of the extraneous variables that would destroy the study if not controlled, researchers usually will randomly assign subjects to the various comparison groups of the investigation. By doing this, researchers create a situation where the comparison groups can be considered equivalent (in a probabilistic sense)—at the time the groups are formed—on any and all variables. If the comparison groups are equivalent to begin with, and if the study is carefully conducted so that nothing differentially influences the groups except the independent variable manipulated by the researcher, the data analysis will speak directly and clearly to the issue of a possible cause-and-effect relationship between the independent and dependent variables.

The process of **randomly assigning** subjects to comparison groups is thus a very important part of experiments. In fact, it is a defining characteristic of experiments. With very few exceptions, it can be said that a research study *is* an experiment even if the word *experiment* does not appear in the report—so long as the comparison groups were formed by assigning subjects randomly to those groups. Conversely, a study most likely is *not* an experiment, even if the word *experiment* does appear in the research report, if it is the case that subjects were not randomly assigned to the comparison groups.

In Excerpt 21.10, we see two passages from the physical fitness study on feedback and intrinsic motivation, the first from the Procedures section of the published research report and the second from the Design and Statistics section. Taken together, these passages (1) clarify the way in which the three

---

[4]*In this and the preceding paragraph, we have talked as if experiments have just one independent variable. Sometimes they do, as illustrated in Excerpt 21.9. However, two or more independent variables can easily be built into the same investigation. Most experiments are characterized by multiple independent variables.*

> **Excerpt 21.10** Formation of Comparison Groups in the Physical Fitness Study on Feedback and Intrinsic Motivation
>
> In Phase 1 of the study subjects were allowed to practice runs without timing for the sake of familiarization. The IMI was then administered as a pretest of intrinsic motivation. In Phase 2 of the study (2 weeks later) the timer appeared to be connected to a portable computer, and the subjects were told that this time the [running] test was "for real." In reality, the computer was programmed to give bogus feedback according to which treatment condition (positive, negative, or no feedback) the subjects had been randomly assigned prior to their attempt.
>
> A simple randomized experimental design was used with subjects assigned to the positive, negative, or no feedback groups prior to the Phase 2 testing. This was done separately by gender so that group numbers would be balanced.
>
> *Source:* J. R. Whitehead, and C. B. Corbin. (1991). Youth fitness testing: The effect of percentile-based evaluative feedback on intrinsic motivation. *Research Quarterly for Exercise and Sport, 62*(2), pp. 226–227.

comparison groups of this study were formed and (2) confirm that the use of the term *experiment* in Excerpt 21.9 was justified.

When researchers randomly assign subjects to comparison groups, they do something that helps their studies gain **internal validity**. Earlier, we said that the results of the data analysis will speak clearly and directly to the issue of a possible cause-and-effect relationship between the independent and dependent variables if (1) the comparison groups are as equivalent as possible at the outset and (2) the study is conducted so that nothing differentially influences the groups except the independent variable manipulated by the researcher.[5] When these two conditions are met, an experiment is considered to have high internal validity. By randomly assigning subjects to comparison groups, researchers convincingly address the first of these two concerns of internal validity. Later, we will discuss how researchers can take steps when designing their studies so as to address the second concern of internal validity.

Before concluding our remarks concerning the formation of comparison groups, we need to make four additional points. First, the technique of forming groups by matching subjects (or groups) is not very good compared to the technique of random assignment. Second, randomly assigning intact groups is not nearly as good as randomly assigning individuals (unless several intact groups are randomly assigned to each treatment condition). Third, forming some (but not all) of the comparison groups through random assignment creates problems that would not exist if subjects were randomly

---

[5]*In making this statement, we presume that the study's measuring instrument is reliable and valid, that assumptions underlying the statistic test are tenable, that power is sufficiently high to detect important nonnull situations, and that the ever-present possibility of inferential error is noted.*

assigned to *all* of the treatment conditions. Fourth, randomly assigning some (but not all) of the subjects to the comparison groups is not the same as randomly assigning *all* of the subjects. Excerpts 21.11 through 21.13 illustrate three of these four situations.

Excerpts 21.11–21.13 Less-Than-Satisfactory Mechanisms for Forming Comparison Groups in an Experiment

---

Intact classes were randomly placed in one of four groups: (a) captioned TV (*n* = 32), (b) traditional TV without captions (*n* = 37), (c) reading along and listening to text (*n* = 32), and (d) textbook only (*n* = 28).

Source: S. B. Neuman, and P. Koskinen. (1992). Captioned television as comprehensible input: Effects of incidental word learning from context for language minority students. *Reading Research Quarterly, 27*(1), p. 99.

Three groups of students (*N* = 151) were exposed to one of three conditions. The subjects in two experimental conditions were randomly assigned to view a music-videotape having either a romantic or erotic theme. A third group only received the [posttest] survey.

Source: M. S. Calfin, J. L. Carroll, and J. Schmidt. (1993). Viewing music-videotapes before taking a test of premarital sexual attitudes. *Psychological Reports, 72*, pp. 475.

Twelve grade 10 geography teachers from the same four districts involved in the earlier phases of the project participated in Experiment 3; only 2 had taught correlational reasoning before. Teachers who had a preference (i.e., those who had previously committed to a particular sequence of course topics) assigned themselves to treatment and wait-list control groups. The remaining teachers were randomly assigned.

Source: J. A. Ross, and J. B. Cousins. (1993). Patterns of student growth in reasoning about correlational problems. *Journal of Educational Psychology, 85*(1), p. 61.

SUBJECT MOTIVATION

Our final question concerning a study's subjects deals with their motivational level to perform the tasks of the study. Such tasks might involve reading or listening to directions, observing something presented visually or auditorially, performing a visual-motor activity, adhering to a new at-home routine, competing against a time limit or other subjects, responding to verbal probes as to thoughts or feelings, or answering test questions. For obvious reasons, a study has no chance to achieve its objectives if subjects have low (or no) motivation to perform such tasks. Even though subjects may be physically present during the study, they are psychological dropouts if they are unmotivated to cooperate, to try their best, and to respond with honesty and candor.

It should be noted that our concern about subject motivation is relevant to both descriptive and experimental investigations. For example, in the descriptive study from which Excerpt 21.8 was taken, the subjects were classified into six gender/sex-role groups, with scores from the Bem Sex Role Inventory used to tag each subject as being androgynous, traditional, or undifferentiated. In light of the fact that the 164 subjects in this study were "volunteers recruited from introductory psychology courses at a large, public university . . . [who] were given course credit for responding to the friendship and sex role questionnaires," we feel that it is quite legitimate to be concerned about these students' motivational level. We say this because students have told us how they or others have been in similar studies and have had such a strong desire to earn their course credit *quickly* that answer sheets were filled in without reading the questions!

Now consider Excerpt 21.14, taken from an experimental study in which subjects were asked to learn and remember several rhyming word pairs (e.g., number-lumber). Perhaps all of the subjects used in this investigation were highly motivated as they listened to the directions and then attempted to learn the word pairs. However, it may have been the case that some (or many) of the 20 subjects were not motivated very much at all because they were fulfilling a course requirement. We are quite sure that credit for participating was not contingent on how well one did on the experimental task; we highly suspect that subjects either were told this directly or surmised this on their own. If the subjects possessed the competitive drive associated with Type A personalities, maybe they tried hard even though they were fulfilling a course requirement with no sanctions for doing poorly. If, on the other hand, the

---

Excerpt 21.14 An Experiment in Which Subject Motivation May Not Have Been High

SUBJECTS

Twenty students enrolled in an introductory psychology course at the State University of New York at Binghamton participated as one method of fulfilling a class requirement for research experience.

DESIGN

The experiment was a 2 (List: A vs. B) $\times$ 2 (Task: Read vs. Generate) mixed design with the fact of list being manipulated between-subjects and task varied within-subjects (and within lists).

Source: A. Grosofsky, D. G. Payne, and K. D. Campbell. (1994). Does the generation effect depend upon selective displaced rehearsal? *American Journal of Psychology, 107*(1), p. 57.

subjects disliked the course (or instructor), if they felt imposed on by the required research experience, or if they possessed Type B personalities, their level of motivation could very well have been quite low.

Because an otherwise well-designed study can be rendered useless if the subjects are unmotivated to cooperate, be honest, or try their best, researchers should design their investigations in such a way that subject motivation is likely to be high. In addition, researchers should, whenever possible, collect evidence in an effort to document the extent to which their subjects were motivated while participating in the study. There are several things researchers can do in each of these areas.

The strategies used by a conscientious researcher to promote subject motivation often must be tailored to the specific nature of the investigation being conducted. Accordingly, it is important for you to consider the specifics of a study before concluding that the researcher either did or didn't do what should have been done to gain the full cooperation of the subjects. By considering the next few excerpts, you should improve your ability to think about subject motivation when reading research reports.

Excerpt 21.15 illustrates the strategy of concealing the study's true purpose from the subjects. In the study from which this excerpt was taken, two efforts at concealment were made. First, the subjects were given a bogus reason why the study was being conducted. Then, three of the four stimuli presented to the subjects were identical for all subjects and used simply to conceal the study's objective.

Excerpt 21.15   Concealing the Purpose of the Study

Subjects were recruited under the guise of participating in a study of how people react to new products. Each subject was exposed to four product labels. One contained a vivid (or nonvivid) product warning message. Three neutral, nonexperimental product labels were included in the study to disguise the purpose of the experiment.

Source: C. A. Kelly, W. C. Gaidis, and P. H. Reingen. (1989). The use of vivid stimuli to enhance comprehension of the content of product warning labels. *Journal of Consumer Affairs, 23*(2), p. 249.

It should be noted that it is sometimes quite unethical to conceal from subjects the true objectives of an investigation. Most researchers are now required to submit their research plans to review boards that look to see if the subjects will be put at risk by participating. When that is the case, full disclosure of the study's objectives and procedures is required. In the experiment concerning product labels, no risk of harm was involved because (1) fictitious products were used and (2) subjects rated but did not use any product. For these reasons, the concealment involved in Excerpt 21.15 did not violate any ethical standards.

In Excerpt 21.16, we see one of two popular strategies used by researchers in an effort to procure candid responses from subjects. These strategies involve a pledge from the researcher that the subjects' data either (1) will be collected in an anonymous fashion or (2) will be kept confidential. In Excerpt 21.16, the second of these strategies was used (because code numbers were used to match up subjects and answer forms).

Excerpt 21.16   Pledging Confidentiality to Subjects in an Effort to Obtain Candid Responses

---

The completion of the forms was confidential. A code number was assigned to each participant and entered on the forms. After completing each form, participants were asked to place the forms in a mailing envelope and seal it before handing it to the investigator.

Source: C. Duncan, and W. B. Pryswansky. (1993). Effects of race, racial identity development, and orientation style on perceived consultant effectiveness. *Journal of Multicultural Counseling and Development, 21*(2), p. 91.

Regarding pledges of anonymity and confidentiality, we believe that researchers sometimes make the mistake of thinking that such pledges will automatically bring forth honest responses from subjects. If subjects view the study as dealing with a sensitive topic and if they think that their responses might somehow be identified (e.g., because of their unusual handwriting) or used against them, subjects are likely to refrain from sharing honestly what they believe. Motivating them to open up in such situations is difficult, and researchers deserve credit when they recognize this problem and devise ethical strategies for achieving this important objective.

When researchers include control groups in their experimental studies, one of two potential problems can develop in terms of the motivational level of the subjects assigned to the control group. If these subjects know that they have been put into a group that will not receive the treatment, they may "throw in the towel" (thinking that there is no hope for success because the thought-to-be-good treatment is withheld from them). Or, these subjects may become supermotivated to do well (because they want to show that they can succeed without benefit of the treatment). Should either of these situations develop, the motivational levels of the experimental and control groups will be confounded with the study's independent variable. If the subjects in the control group are discouraged because they are being used as controls, their low performance on the study's test(s) may make an inert treatment appear to be beneficial. On the other hand, if the control group subjects try extra hard to overcome their disadvantage, a truly beneficial treatment may end up looking as if it has no positive impact (or even a negative impact).[6]

In Excerpt 21.17, we see a case where the motivational level of the control group's subjects may have been different from that of the subjects in the experimental group. This may have occurred, we feel, because (1) all subjects volunteered in order to get something useful out of the project and (2) those in the control group knew that they were getting nothing while those in the experimental group were receiving the desired training.

Excerpt 21.17   Possible Motivational Differences Between Those in the Control Group and Those in the Experimental Group

---

The nature and purpose of the project was described to juniors and seniors by the head guidance counselor, and any students who were interested in learning more about the stress-management project were asked to attend an orientation meeting. Originally, 30 youths attended this orientation meeting, during which the research was described in full by Hains and parental and youth consent forms were distributed. Twenty-four youths returned signed consent forms and volunteered for the project. These youths were randomly assigned to either the experimental group that received training or a waiting list control group.

Source: A. A. Hains, and M. Szyjakowski. (1990). A cognitive stress-reduction intervention program for adolescents. *Journal of Counseling Psychology, 37*(1), p. 80.

One design strategy that sometimes helps the researcher maintain equivalent motivational levels in the comparison groups of an experiment is the use of placebo groups rather than pure no-treatment control groups. Another strategy involves giving each comparison group a different treatment, followed by the collection of data on multiple dependent variables targeted toward the unique benefits associated with each treatment. When using this second strategy, each group is considered to be the experimental group for one of the dependent variables but then considered to be the control group when the focus shifts to the other dependent variable(s). We applaud those researchers who use either of these design strategies because they want subject motivation to be equivalent across the comparison groups of their studies.

Excerpt 21.18 constitutes our final example to illustrate how conscientious researchers can be sensitive to their subjects' motivational levels. We are quite impressed with what the researchers did in this study. We say this because the researchers thought about their procedures, realized that a necessary intrusion during the playing of a videotape would likely be disruptive to

---

[6]*The two problems discussed in this paragraph are often referred to by means of the labels* **resentful demoralization** *and* **compensatory rivalry**.

Excerpt 21.18 Informing Subjects of Necessary Data-Collection "Intrusions"

We made several choices regarding methodology in designing the study. Because previous research has shown that the accuracy of judgments improves when more sensory modalities are used (Weiss, Marmar, & Horowitz, 1988), we used videotapes rather than audiotapes for the reviews in this study. Furthermore, we were aware that to obtain an estimate of participant experience during sessions, we had to intrude on sessions to collect data. Such intrusion undoubtedly changes the nature of therapeutic interactions, making it difficult to generalize findings to naturally occurring therapy. We hoped that by preparing participants for the intrusion, we would minimize the effects on the therapy experience and participants' judgments.

Source: C. E. Hill, K. E. O'Grady, V. Balenger, W. Busse, D. R. Falk, M. Hill, P. Rios, and R. Taffe. (1994). Methodological examination of videotape-assisted reviews in brief therapy: Helpfulness ratings, therapist intentions, client reactions, mood, and session evaluation. *Journal of Counseling Psychology, 41*(2), p. 238.

the subjects, and then decided to warn the subjects about the impending intrusion. We wish more researchers would follow this example of thinking about the plight of those who serve as subjects.

In addition to designing studies with subject motivation in mind, researchers can and should collect evidence in an effort to document the extent to which subjects were motivated while participating in the study. There are several kinds of evidence that can speak to the issue of subject motivation. We wish to discuss three of these in the following paragraphs.

Researchers should examine the data they collect in order to identify cases where it is obvious that a subject was distorting the truth, was trying to be funny, or was unable to understand the directions associated with a task or test. Obviously, if the scores from such subjects are not identified and extracted from the rest of the data, results will be distorted. Most researchers give no evidence of screening their data and we must presume they did not take the time to do so. In Excerpt 21.19, we see an example of where such care *was* exercised, and we think all researchers should follow the example provided here.

The second strategy for checking on subjects' motivational level is referred to as a **manipulation check**. This strategy is appropriate for experiments in which a manipulated independent variable is intended to create a mind-set which then in turn may (or may not) have a causal impact on the dependent variable. When researchers conduct a manipulation check, they are simply looking to see whether they were successful in having the independent variable take hold in the minds of the subjects. Unless that effort is successful,

> **Excerpt 21.19**   Screening the Data Set for Cases Where Subjects Did Not Understand the Task (or Did Not Try)
>
> ---
>
> A hand review of the results identified one outlier for which it was obvious that the subject did not understand the task. The data from this subject were removed prior to the analyses.
>
> ---
>
> *Source:* K. S. McGrew, S. R. Murphy, and D. J. Knutson. (1994). The development and investigation of a graphic system for obtaining derived scores for the *WJ-R* and other tests. *Journal of Psychoeducational Assessment, 12*(1), p. 37.

there is little point in investigating the potential causal link between the independent and dependent variables.

Excerpt 21.20 presents an illustration of a manipulation check in an experiment dealing with career interests. In this study, one of the four factors was called *career valence*. There were three levels of this manipulated independent variable, created by having subjects look at a list of 60 occupational titles and then circle 12 relevant occupations or 12 irrelevant occupations or 6 relevant and 6 irrelevant occupations. Later in the study, subjects were asked to do several things, one of which involved rating their occupations on a grid provided by the researchers. These ratings did not correspond to the study's dependent variable, but instead permitted the researchers to see if subjects followed directions in selecting their 12 occupations.

> **Excerpt 21.20**   Conducting a Manipulation Check
>
> ---
>
> Before the primary analysis along the measure of vocational differentiation, we conducted a check along valence scores to verify the effectiveness of the manipulation of career valence. Valence scores consisted of the proportion of positive ratings (3, 2, and 1) on each grid and therefore indicated how favorably participants perceived their set of 12 occupations.
>
> The analysis of valence scores revealed a significant main effect for relevance, $F(2, 386) = 70.04$, $P < .001$. Highly relevant occupations were rated more positively ($M = 61.05$) than were mixed ($M = 46.91$) and irrelevant occupations ($M = 22.80$, $Ps < .05$), indicating the effectiveness of the occupational relevance manipulation.
>
> ---
>
> *Source:* J. Parr, and G. J. Neimeyer. (1994). Effects of gender, construct type, occupational information, and career relevance on vocational differentiation. *Journal of Counseling Psychology, 41*(1), p. 30.

The third strategy for checking on subjects' motivational level involves **debriefing** the subjects at the end of the study and asking them about how motivated they were in performing tasks and completing tests. Because this is such a simple thing to do, we are dumbfounded as to why more researchers do not ask their subjects to reflect on the thoughts they had during the investigation. In Excerpt 21.21, we see another excerpt from the experiment conducted to assess Deli and Ryan's cognitive evaluation theory in a fitness testing situation. (We initially considered this study in Excerpt 21.9.) In this portion of the research report, we are informed that subjects were debriefed and that the bogus feedback was believed.

Excerpt 21.21   Debriefing Subjects

Immediately after the second run each subject was again asked to complete the IMI as a posttest of intrinsic motivation. The questionnaires were administered in another room by an assistant who was briefed to prevent subject interaction and to watch for signs of skepticism about the veracity of the feedback. None were observed, and this treatment plausibility was confirmed the following day when a debriefing was conducted. Several subjects even commented on how much they had believed the bogus results.

Source: J. R. Whitehead, and C. B. Corbin. (1990). Youth fitness testing: The effect of percentile-based evaluative feedback on intrinsic motivation. *Research Quarterly for Exercise and Sport, 62*(2), p. 227.

DESIGN ISSUES CONCERNING THE DATA

In any empirical investigation, the data collected by the researcher have an obvious impact on the success of a study. If everything about a study is perfect but the data are deficient, it will be difficult (if not impossible) for either the researcher or you to draw meaningful conclusions from the investigation. Accordingly, it is fully appropriate that we consider several design issues connected to the data of empirical investigations.

The five concerns we will examine deal with (1) instrument quality, (2) the question/data match, (3) independence of observations, (4) the person who collects the data, and (5) median splits. There are many additional data-related issues that would have been covered here had it not been for space limitations. Even though our discussion is restricted to the five concerns listed above, you will be in a fairly good position to evaluate critically the data component of research reports after completing this section of material.

INSTRUMENT QUALITY

In Chapter 4, we discussed the concepts of reliability and validity as well as a variety of procedures that can be used by researchers to assess these two characteristics of their measurements. Because the reliability and validity of research data are so important, all researchers should address these two concepts in a competent manner when describing the instruments used to collect data. Unfortunately, many researchers fail to do this.

Excerpt 21.22 contains the complete description of a measuring instrument used to collect subjective age measures. As you can see, there is absolutely no discussion of reliability and validity. When confronted with passages such as this, you have a right to downgrade your evaluation of this investigation.

Excerpt 21.22   Description of a Measuring Instrument Without Reliability and Validity Being Discussed

---

Subjective Age Measures. Respondents' subjective age perceptions were assessed by asking them to indicate on a 7-point bipolar scale with endpoints labeled (1) a lot younger than my age and (7) a lot older than my age, the age that most closely corresponded to (a) the way they felt (Felt Age), (b) the way they looked (Look Age), (c) the age of the person whom their interests and activities were most like (Act Age), (d) the age that they would like to be if they could pick out their age right now (Desired Age), (e) how old they thought their parents treated them (Parental Age), and (f) how old opposite-sex peers treated them (Opposite-Sex Age). In addition to providing scale responses, respondents were asked to indicate, in actual years, the age that best represented how old they regarded themselves along the aforementioned dimensions.

Source: J. M. Montepare. (1991). Characteristics and psychological correlates of young adult men's and women's subjective age. *Sex Roles, 24*(5/6), p. 326.

Excerpt 21.23 stands in sharp contrast to the excerpt we just considered. Here, we see a passage concerning the questionnaires used in a different study. The researchers who conducted the study from which this excerpt was taken deserve high marks for investigating the reliability and validity of the self-report data collected in their study.

Excerpt 21.23   Expressed Concern for Both Reliability and Validity

---

Self-report, especially where recall procedures are involved, is subject to error due to poor memory and possible false reporting. For these reasons, we have examined the reliability and validity of all our questionnaires. A convenience sample of 30 adults similar in social characteristics to respondents in the larger study completed the questionnaire twice, one week apart, as a test-retest estimate of reliability. . . . Our measures of exercise also appear valid. Construct validity was supported by strong associations with other measures of exercise (Sallis et al., 1989).

Source: C. R. Hofstetter, M. F. Hovell, C. Macera, J. F. Sallis, V. Spry, E. Barrington, L. Callender, M. Hackley, and M. Rauh. (1991). Illness, injury, and correlates of aerobic exercise and walking: A community study. *Research Quarterly in Exercise and Sport, 32*(1), p. 2.

In Chapter 4, we pointed out that the properties of reliability and validity reside not in the measuring instrument itself but rather in the scores that come into being once the measuring instrument is used. The importance of this fact is that an instrument that has been shown to provide quality data in a given context with a certain kind of examinee or subject potentially will *fail* to yield quality data when used at some later time. Many researchers evidently do not understand this, because they simply cite someone else's reliability and validity evidence. When using previously developed instruments, conscientious researchers will assess the reliability and validity of their own data sets even though others have previously done the same thing. In Excerpt 21.24, we see a case where this was done.[7]

Excerpt 21.24 Conducting a "Fresh" Evaluation of the Quality of
Data Produced by an Existing Instrument

Trust. The interpersonal trust scale of Johnson-George and Swap (1982) was used to assess three types of trust: emotional trust, truthfulness, and reliableness. The scale was modified so that the sense of trust in male friends and female friends were each assessed separately with 13 items. Responses varied on a scale from *strongly disagree* (0) to *strongly agree* (4), were summed across each subscale, and a mean subscale score calculated. Internal reliabilities were moderate and ranged from .63 to .76. These reliabilities are comparable to, although slightly lower than, those reported by Johnson-George and Swap (1982).

Source: D. C. Jones, N. Bloys, and M. Wood. (1990). Sex roles and friendship patterns. *Sex Roles, 23*(3/4), p. 137.

THE DATA/QUESTION MATCH

Even if the data in a study are reliable and valid, a critical concern still exists: "Do the data address the question(s) posed by the researcher?" In most studies, the answer to this question will be "yes." You should, however, remain on guard for situations where a mismatch exists between the stated objectives of the investigation and the nature of the empirical evidence.

To illustrate our point, consider Excerpt 21.25. The researchers conducted this study to investigate two research questions, one of which was stated as follows: "How favorable are undergraduates' attitudes toward FL literature study?" The researchers dealt with this question by considering how their subjects (175 undergraduates enrolled in French and Spanish) responded to two items in a Likert-type questionnaire. Putting aside our concern that

---

[7]*Although we applaud the researchers associated with this excerpt for conducting their own assessment of reliability, we must point out that they chose not to say a thing about validity. Because data can be reliable without being valid, researchers should demonstrate concern for both features of their data.*

Excerpt 21.25   Data/Question Mismatch

To answer the first research question, concerning the general tenor of under-graduate attitudes toward the study of FL literature, we calculated the percent-age of responses to the second and third items on the questionnaire, which operationally defined a positive attitude toward the study of FL literature as: (1) the feeling that such study is "personally rewarding"; and (2) the belief that lan-guage departments should encourage their majors and minors to take literature courses.

Source: C. G. Davis. (1992). Readers and foreign language: A survey of undergraduate attitudes to-ward the study of literature. *The Modern Language Journal, 76*(3), p. 322.

---

these 175 students cannot be viewed as representative undergraduates, we want to focus on the second of the two questionnaire items. That item stated, "I feel majors and minors should be encouraged to take literature courses in the FL Department." We believe that responses to this question could be both reliable and valid *without* providing information to help answer the re-search question. We say this because it seems quite plausible that respondents may have indicated strong *agreement* with this statement even though they *disliked* FL literature study.

INDEPENDENCE OF OBSERVATIONS

In our earlier discussion of statistical tests, we pointed out that several of these tests are built on an assumption of independence. As you may recall, this as-sumption says that the score provided by any given subject should not be in-fluenced either by the scores provided by other subjects or by what happens to those other subjects while they are involved in the study. You may also re-call our earlier statement that the assumption of independence is not some-thing that gets tested once the data are collected (as is the case with the assumption of equal regression slopes in the analysis of covariance) but in-stead is a methodological concern that ought to receive attention when a study is being planned.

The best way to assure that independence is built into an empirical inves-tigation is to (1) have subjects individually experience the treatment condi-tions to which they are assigned (if the study is an experiment) and (2) collect data in such a way that subjects cannot see or hear one another dur-ing any testing, or gain knowledge of anyone else's score. A few researchers achieve these objectives because their subjects are animals, because they con-tact subjects exclusively through the mail or over the phone, or because the subjects must be dealt with individually due to the complexities of the study's procedures. Most researchers, however, apply treatment conditions to groups of human subjects and/or collect data from such subjects when they are gathered together in the same room.

When human subjects can hear others' solicited or unsolicited comments, can see how hard others are working (and when they finish), and can observe others' nonverbal communication, the assumption of independence is of questionable validity. To illustrate such a situation, consider Excerpt 21.26. Although we cannot say for certain what did or did not happen when certain of the subjects in this study watched the videotapes in small groups, we highly suspect that communication took place between the subjects. (In this study, the fact that some subjects viewed the videotapes individually while others viewed them in small groups was not prompted by researcher interest either in what happened within the small groups or in a possible individual/group difference on the dependent variable, sexual attitudes.)

Excerpt 21.26   A Likely Case of Nonindependence of Observations

The subjects in the two experimental conditions were randomly assigned to view a music-videotape having either a romantic or an erotic theme. Subjects in Group 1 viewed a nonerotic, romantic video ("Baby, Baby" by Amy Grant). In this music-videotape, Grant is seen as flirting with and being pursued, in a nonthreatening manner, by a handsome man whom she eventually embraces. Subjects in Group 2 viewed a videotape with varied erotic scenes such as homosexuality, group sex, masturbation, and cross-dressing ("Justify My Love" by Madonna). The subjects viewed the videotape individually or in groups of two or three.

Source: M. S. Calfin, J. L. Carroll, and J. Schmidt. (1993). Viewing music-videotapes before taking a test of premarital sexual attitudes. *Psychological Reports, 72,* p. 476.

In these situations where subjects are together in groups during the study, conscientious researchers can do one of two things to demonstrate their sensitivity to the independence assumption. One strategy is actively to suppress communication among subjects. That strategy was used in the study from which Excerpt 21.21 was taken, because the assistant who administered the questionnaires was briefed by the researchers to prevent subject interaction. The second thing that can be done is to consider groups of subjects (rather than individual subjects) to be the **unit of analysis**. When this strategy is used, some measure of each group (usually the mean) is entered into the data analysis rather than the individuals' scores. So long as the groups are kept separate during the study, the group-based data summaries are independent from one another.

THE DATA COLLECTOR

Most researchers have hunches as to what will be revealed by their empirical investigations. If these hunches are strong and if it is the researcher who deals directly with subjects, the researcher may unwittingly convey his or her thoughts and wishes to the subjects. If this occurs, subjects may consciously (or unconsciously) provide responses that are driven by a desire to provide data that support the researcher's hunch. Or, subjects with negative attitudes about the study or the researcher might purposely provide data that will support the opposite of any perceived hunches.

Because it is disruptive when a study's data are contaminated by subjects trying to help or hurt the researcher, any hunches or hypotheses about the investigation should not be shared with subjects. The best way to accomplish this objective is to have the researcher refrain from having any oral or visual contact with the subjects. Instead of the researcher explaining directions, administering treatments, and collecting data, these tasks are best executed by someone who is naive to the researcher's hunches and hopes.

Excerpt 21.27 illustrates how people naive to the researcher's hypotheses can be used to help gather data. We salute this researcher for going to the trouble to do this, for this effort strengthened the quality of the data.

Excerpt 21.27   Using People Naive to the Research Questions to Help Gather Data

---

Finally, each product thought (product referent and evaluative criteria) was coded as to its "location" (in either prepurchase, postpurchase, or satisfaction) relative to both the interviewer's question and to the respondent's reference point in time. Both locations were necessary because consumers' responses did not always reflect the point in time that the interviewer probed (e.g., a consumer might digress to talk about prepurchase while responding to a postpurchase probe).

The two coders were independent of the research team and had no knowledge of product evaluation theory or research questions.

Source: S. F. Gardiel. (1994). Comparing consumers' recall of prepurchase and postpurchase product evaluations, experiences. *Journal of Consumer Research, 20*(4), p. 553.

MEDIAN SPLITS

Researchers will often create comparison groups by (1) examining subject scores on a characteristic that the subjects bring with them to the study and (2) dividing the total pool of subjects into two subgroups by considering all subjects above or below the median score to have a standing on the characteristic that is either high or low, respectively. After performing this **median**

split, the two groups are then compared with respect to their scores on the study's dependent variable. For example, an independent-samples *t*-test might be used to compare the mean income of those possessing IQ scores above the computed median against the mean income of those with IQ scores below that median.

The possible problem associated with median splits is that the meaning of "high" and "low" on the variable used to form the two groups is dependent on the nature of the full pool of subjects. Sometimes, these high and low labels will not correspond to the normal meanings of these terms. That would be the case, for example, if a median split on IQ were to be done in a study where all subjects come from Mensa, an exclusive organization that restricts membership to those who have performed exceedingly well on reputable intelligence tests.

In Excerpt 21.28, we see a case where a pair of researchers warned their readers that their median split created a problem. Although we are quite impressed with these researchers' concern for the meaning of high and low, we wonder why they didn't use an external criterion for creating these two groups rather than perform a median split on the hospitals' total scores.

Excerpt 21.28   A Possible Problem with Median Splits

For each hospital, a total score was computed by summing all of the items pertinent to the marketing orientation. The lowest and highest possible scores are 24 and 99, respectively. The actual scores are in the range of 24 to 97 with a median of 63. The total score of each responding hospital reflects the degree of marketing orientation of that hospital. The higher the hospital score, the greater the marketing orientation of that hospital.

Though we use the median score of 63 as the dividing point to indicate low and high marketing orientation for hypothesis testing, 63 is not really high enough to indicate a serious marketing orientation.

Source: G. M. Naidu, and C. L. Narayana. (1991). How marketing oriented are hospitals in a declining market? *Journal of Health Care Marketing, 11*(1), p. 25.

DESIGN ISSUES CONCERNING THE STUDY'S CONTEXT

No study exists in a vacuum. Every empirical investigation must be conducted within a given space and during a given time frame. Moreover, certain aspects of the study itself are components of the context for what subjects do and the data they provide. Unless this context is taken into consideration when the study is being planned, the results may have very limited (or no) connection to the questions that prompted the study's undertaking. Researchers, therefore, should consider context as they design their investigations and interpret their findings. Because this is not always done, you need to be alert to issues of context as you evaluate the merits of any research report.

In an effort to sensitize you to the way in which context can influence what findings can legitimately be derived from the statistical results, four aspects of context are discussed in the paragraphs that follow. These issues deal with (1) the physical setting of the study, (2) pretest sensitization, (3) the nature of treatment conditions, and (4) the subjects' thoughts about the study. There are other aspects of context that cannot be covered here because of space limitations. However, our discussion of the four issues to which we now turn will provide you with a firm foundation for evaluating studies from the perspective of context.

THE STUDY'S PHYSICAL SETTING

Many researchers conduct their investigations within a laboratory setting. Such settings typically allow researchers to exert greater control over (1) any independent variables that are to be manipulated and (2) all extraneous variables that should be prevented from becoming confounded with the independent variable(s). Studies conducted in the researcher's domain also make it likely that data will be collected from all subjects, thus reducing or eliminating problems of attrition.

Although laboratory studies have certain advantages over those conducted in the places where subjects normally live, work, and play, there is one main disadvantage associated with studies conducted in a laboratory setting. This limitation is associated with what we might call **setting generalizability**. Simply stated, setting generalizability is concerned with the degree to which research findings hold true for settings other than that (or those) used within the research investigation. As you probably have already guessed, setting generalizability is an element of external validity, just as is the notion of **3**

Our claim that laboratory studies often have limited setting generalizability is based primarily on our knowledge that we and most other people behave differently depending on the setting. When we find ourselves in familiar surrounding with close friends, we usually behave and talk differently than when we are in unfamiliar surroundings with strangers. Moreover, research has substantiated a phenomenon referred to as the **Hawthorne Effect**, the tendency of people to behave differently when they know they are subjects in a research investigation.[8]

---

[8]*The Hawthorne Effect, of course, can rear its ugly head in studies conducted in the field. However, the atypical surroundings of a research laboratory usually serve to make subjects blatantly aware that they are involved in a study. When the study is conducted in a more natural setting, subjects are more inclined to talk and act as they normally do.*

In Excerpt 21.29, we see an example of a study conducted in a laboratory setting. The use of videotapes, one-way mirrors, and the administration of the Inventory of Interpersonal Problems (IIP) and the Working Alliance Inventory (WAI) cause us to doubt that the subjects in this study talked and behaved as they typically would in a normal counseling setting.

Excerpt 21.29   A Study with Questionable Setting Generalizability

Fifteen students selected from a pool of 60 students who were enrolled in an undergraduate child psychology course were recruited to serve as "clients" in this study because they indicated an interest in talking to a counselor-in-training about a personal concern. Fifteen students, selected from a pool of 60 students who were enrolled in a prepracticum counseling skills class in a master's level counseling program, served as counselors in this study.

Counselors were paired with a recruited volunteer client for four counseling interviews. Before the initial interviews, clients completed the IIP. Clients were asked to discuss a real personal concern or problem during each of the 50-minute interviews. Each counseling session was videotaped. . . . After each session, the clients filled out the WAI. Raters were graduate students in counseling psychology. Two raters watched each session from behind a one-way mirror.

Source: D. M. Kivlighan, and P. J. Schmitz. (1992). Counselor technical activity in cases with improving working alliances and continuing poor working alliances. *Journal of Counseling Psychology, 39*(1), pp. 33–34.

PRETEST SENSITIZATION

Many researchers routinely pretest the subjects in the comparison groups of their experimental investigations. Evidence of this practice can be seen in Excerpts 21.30 and 21.31.

As indicated in Chapter 18, pretest data can be used within a covariance analysis to help increase statistical power. Pretest data can also be used to compare dropouts (if there are any) against subjects who stay in the study until its completion. Although pretest data can be used to accomplish these two important objectives, use of a pretest sometimes creates a problem. This problem is referred to as **pretest sensitization**, and its presence will cause the context of the study to be artificial.

When a pretest is used, it may function to alert or tip off subjects in the experimental group as to what they should attend to when they are given the treatment. Because these subjects have been sensitized, the treatment might turn out to be beneficial to them (or to anyone else who similarly is pretested before receiving the treatment). However, this same treatment, when given to

Excerpts 21.30–21.31   The Common Use of Pretests in Experimental Studies

Pretest and posttest data were gathered from both treatment and control groups.

Source: B. A. McBride. (1991). Parent education and support programs for fathers: Outcome effects on parental involvement. *Early Child Development and Care,* 67(February), p. 76.

Experimental and control subjects were pretested the week prior to initiating training.

Source: D. K. Openshaw, T. A. Mills, G. R. Adams, and D. D. Durso. (1992). Conflict resolution in parent-adolescent dyads: The influence of social skills training. *Journal of Adolescent Research,* 7(4), p. 462.

similar individuals, could potentially have no impact whatsoever if the pretest is not present to "prime the pump."

Many researchers seem to be either unaware of the possibility of pretest sensitization or unconcerned about how their treatments will function when practitioners use them in nonexperimental settings. We say this because a particular research design can be used first to determine whether subjects are sensitized by the pretest and then to see how the treatment will likely work when it is used without the pretest. This design is called the **Solomon Four-Group Design**, and its use is illustrated in Excerpt 21.32.

As shown in Table 7 of Excerpt 21.32, only two of the four groups in the Solomon Design receive the pretest and only two groups receive the experimental treatment, but all four groups receive the posttest. The four sets of posttest scores are cast into a 2 × 2 table and then analyzed by means of a two-way analysis of variance. The interaction *F*-ratio in the ANOVA summary table speaks to the issue of pretest sensitization. If the interaction is not significant, pretest sensitization will be viewed as a nonproblem and the *F* comparing the main effect means of the experimental and control groups will be examined. If the interaction *F* shows up as significant, the researcher will just compare the simple main effect means of the unpretested experimental and control groups to get a feel for whether the treatment will likely have a benefit when used outside the investigation.

Excerpt 21.32   Checking on Pretest Sensitization

There was no interaction between pretesting and the experimental condition which indicated that the pretest did not sensitize participants so that they scored better on the posttest, a desirable finding which allows for further comparison of the four conditions, since those that were pretested did not have an unfair advantage.

(Continued)

Excerpt 21.32 Checking on Pretest Sensitization *(Continued)*

Table 7

2 × 2 Table of Posttest C.K.A.Q. Mean Scores

	Pretest	*No Pretest*
Experimental	78.2	75.7
Control	72.1	73.3

Table 8

2 × 2 Factorial Analysis of Posttest C.K.A.Q. Scores (N = 398)

Source	*df*	*Mean Square*	*F-Ratio*	*Probability*
Experiment	1	1771.1	6.23	0.013★
Pretest	1	1.29	0.005	0.94
Exp × Pretest	1	363.8	1.275	0.26
Error	394	284.5		

★Statistically significant.

Source: L. M. Tutty. (1992). The ability of elementary school children to learn child sexual abuse prevention concepts. *Child Abuse and Neglect, 16*(3), p. 379.

THE TREATMENT CONDITIONS

In the typical published experiment, one treatment is identified as being superior to the other condition(s) against which it is compared. Before jumping on the researcher's bandwagon and concluding that the superior treatment is as potent as suggested in the research report, you should carefully consider the nature of *all* conditions involved in the study. It is important to do this because (1) most statistical tests provide only a relative assessment of treatment worth and (2) researchers sometimes consciously or unconsciously "stack the deck" in favor of a particular treatment by including one or more worthless comparison conditions in the study.

To see the importance of considering what kinds of comparison group(s) were involved in a study, take a look at Excerpt 21.33. As you will note, the men in this study's treatment group received 10 two-hour sessions in which they (1) participated in a discussion about paternal involvement with children and (2) engaged in father-child play. The comparison group involved father-child dyads that did nothing during this 10-week time period.

We believe that a different kind of comparison group would have made the results of this investigation more meaningful. To be more specific, we believe the

Excerpt 21.33   A Potentially Weak "Control" Condition

Fifteen father-child dyads from the treatment group participated in a 10-week parent education and support program. Fifteen control group father-child dyads then participated in a similar 10-week program upon completion of data collection for the 10-week experimental treatment (wait-list control design). . . . Treatment group father-child pairs participated in one of two parent education/play group programs that met for 2 hours on 10 consecutive Saturday mornings. The 10-week program had two major components: group discussion and father-child play time.

Source: B. A. McBride. (1991). Parent education and support programs for fathers: Outcome effects on paternal involvement. *Early Child Development and Care, 67,* p. 76.

results of this study would have been more interesting if the control group had received training for only one hour each week, training for two hours each week for five weeks, or training for two hours each week devoted to a movie presentation about father-child relationships. In our opinion, the nothing nature of the control condition served to exaggerate the worth of the treatment condition.

In designing experimental investigations, researchers should try to make the different comparison groups comparable on everything except the manipulated independent variable. That objective is hard enough to achieve. However, conscientious researchers will go one step further. They set up their studies so that the independent variable involves a small component of a larger treatment package instead of designing an all-or-none situation where some subjects receive the full, multi-element package while others receive nothing at all.

Excerpt 21.34 illustrates how researcher concern for the nature of the comparison groups can lead to a better study. Notice how the three video-

Excerpt 21.34   Demonstrating Concern for the Comparison Groups

This study used a 3×2×2 factorial design: Orientation of Counselor (nonsexist-humanist, liberal feminist, or radical feminist) × Statement of Values (implicit or explicit) × Subject's Identification with Feminism (feminist or nonfeminist). The three counseling conditions, nonsexist-humanist, liberal, and radical feminist, were depicted by 10-minute videotape vignettes of a second counseling session between a female counselor and a female client. . . . The three scripts and subsequent videotapes underwent a series of manipulation checks by expert and naive raters to ensure their representativeness, believability, and comparability across all dimensions other than the experimental manipulations.

Source: C. Z. Enns, and G. Hackett. (1990). Comparison of feminist and nonfeminist women's reactions to variants of nonsexist and feminist counseling. *Journal of Counseling Psychology, 37*(1), p. 35.

tapes in this study were checked to see if they were similar except for the manipulated independent variable of counselor orientation. Note also that two different kinds of raters performed this task. Because of the care and concern directed in this study to the comparison groups, the findings were both more specific and more meaningful.

Our final concern about a study's context is germane only to experimental investigations, and it is something we discussed previously when considering factorial ANOVAs. In that earlier discussion, we pointed out that results from studies involving two or more manipulated independent variables (i.e., active factors) must be interpreted with extreme care. This is because the levels of one factor establish a context for the findings associated with the main effect(s) of the other factor(s). To illustrate our point, consider Excerpt 21.35.

Excerpt 21.35   The Creation of Context in Multifactor Experimental Investigations

The design was a 2×2×2 between-subjects factorial, varying the amount of individual-item processing (high, low), mode of learning (incidental, intentional), and pacing of the orienting task (self-paced, experimenter-paced). The 12 subjects in each of the eight conditions were students enrolled in General Psychology at Furman University who received course credit for participating. . . . Each of the memory measures [free recall, clustering, and recognition] was evaluated with a 2×2×2 (individual-item processing condition × mode of learning × pacing of the orienting task) analysis of variance (ANOVA).

Source: M. J. Guynn, G. O. Einstein, and R. R. Hunt. (1992). Detecting the organization of materials: Perceiving the forest despite the trees. *Bulletin of the Psychonomic Society, 30*(2), p. 146.

As indicated in Excerpt 21.35, there were three manipulated independent variables in this study. The researchers were interested most in one of their three factors: individual-item processing. The subjects assigned to the low level of this factor were shown 80 target words, each accompanied by one property (e.g., mansion—groundskeeper); those assigned to the high level were shown the same target words, but each was accompanied by three properties (e.g., mansion—rich, columns, groundskeeper). There were three dependent variables, each a distinct measure of how well the target words could be remembered.

The results of the first two analyses indicated that (1) "free recall was reliably higher in the three-property ($M = 25.75$) than in the one-property ($M = 17.10$) conditions (F [1, 88] $= 37.04$, $MS_e = 48.43$)," with nothing else statistically significant, and (2) "clustering did not differ between the three-property ($M = .42$) and the one-property ($M = .37$) conditions ($F <$ 1)," with the only statistically significant effect being associated with the main effect of pacing orientation. In each of these two analyses, the finding associated with the main effect of individual-item processing must be interpreted in terms of the context created by the other two factors. This is the case because each of the 95 subjects received either one- or three-property stimulus pairs with a particular kind of pacing (self or experiment) and a particular mode of learning (incidental or intentional). If the nature of these other two factors were to be changed (say by using a group-determined pace), the results found in this study for the main effect of individual-item processing might not show up as they did here.

THE SUBJECTS' THOUGHTS ABOUT THE STUDY

When the subjects of an empirical investigation are human beings, a context usually exists in the subjects' minds. This context has reference to the subjects' thoughts as to why the investigation is being conducted and whether they are told (or figure out) what the researcher hopes to discover. This aspect of a study's context is highly important because the subjects' thoughts can make an enormous difference in the results obtained. For this reason, we are surprised to see so little attention devoted to this element of research design.

We have presented excerpts from several studies in which the subjects were kept blind to the researchers' true objectives. Sometimes this was done by not telling the subjects anything at all regarding the study's goals; in other studies, subjects were given a bogus explanation as to what the researchers were trying to accomplish. The important point we would like to make is that the subjects used in most studies in the behavioral sciences are thinking human beings who may discern what is really going on even when no explanation (or a bogus explanation) is provided.

Many of the excerpts presented in this book come from studies in which the subjects were college students. Frequently, the subjects were drawn from undergraduate psychology courses. Because students learn about the purposes and methodologies of research in their coursework in psychology (as well as about the topics psychologists study), we feel safe in asserting that few of these studies utilized subjects who were totally naive to what was going on. Instead, we suspect that many of these subjects not only figured out what variables were being investigated but also made private guesses as to what hypotheses were in the minds of the researchers. Whether these guesses were correct or incorrect is not the issue. Regardless of their accuracy, such guesses contribute to the context that exists in the minds of the subjects.

Several design techniques exist for dealing with the potential problems caused by researchers thinking incorrectly that their subjects are naive to a study's purpose(s). With one strategy, the researcher openly and candidly tells the subjects about the study's variables, comparison groups, intended statistical analyses, and research hypotheses. For ethical reasons, this strategy ought to be used whenever the study involves an assessment of new medical or psychological interventions developed for use with individuals who suffer from illnesses, problems, or abnormalities. In such investigations, the subjects are dealt with almost as if they are co-investigators, with subjects knowingly contributing their time so something can be learned to help others in the future (and possibly those who serve as subjects).

While certain studies ethically require that subjects be fully informed of the variables, comparison groups, data, and hypotheses, other investigations clearly would have no chance of achieving their objectives if these things were disclosed to subjects. When a study falls into this latter category, researchers have a variety of options from which to choose. One option involves giving subjects a plausible but bogus explanation as to what is going on in the study. This option was used in the studies from which Excerpts 21.9 and 21.15 were taken. A second option involves the use of **unobtrusive measures** whereby data are collected from subjects without those subjects being aware of their contributions to the data set. When ethical considerations permit their use, unobtrusive measures solve the problem of subject mind-set because subjects do not even know they are involved in a study. A third option involves telling the subjects very little before or during the investigation but then debriefing them after the formal study is completed. During the debriefing session, subjects can be asked to share their thoughts as to why the study was undertaken and what the researcher expected to find.

It is our impression that researchers pay scant attention to the element of context that deals with subjects' thoughts about their studies. This is unfortunate because the generalizability of results cannot be fully assessed without considering what the subjects thought about the study. When reviewing research reports, give the authors high marks for attending to this neglected yet important aspect of research design.

THREE CLASSES OF EXPERIMENTAL DESIGN

Earlier in the chapter, we distinguished between two main kinds of empirical investigations, those that are descriptive and those that are experimental. We hope you recall that experiments are characterized by researcher interest in causal relationships and control over at least one independent variable. At this point, we want to clarify the way in which three categories of experimental designs differ from one another.

PSEUDO-EXPERIMENTAL DESIGNS

The first set of research designs used to probe possible cause-and-effect relationships has the label **pseudo-experimental designs**.[9] There are three

---

[9] *The term* **pre-experimental designs** *is also used as a label for the research designs in this first category.*

specific designs housed in this category: the one-shot case study, the one-group pretest-posttest design, and the static-group comparison. As suggested by the label for this first category, these three designs are not really full-fledged experiments. Because they lack a control group and/or have comparison groups that are formed nonrandomly, these three designs yield results that are usually hard to interpret.

The **one-shot case study** involves a single group of subjects that receives (1) a treatment or intervention of some type and (2) a posttest. If diagrammed, this design would look like this

$$X \ O$$

where X represents the treatment or intervention and O represents the collection of data on the posttest measure. The obvious problem with this design is that there is no way to attach a meaningful connection between X and O. Even if all of the subjects in the group score high on the posttest, someone might argue that they would have scored just as high without X. There is no empirically-based way to defend the study against such a criticism.

The second pseudo-experimental design is the **one-group pretest-posttest design**. The diagram for this design looks like this

$$O \ X \ O$$

and shows that a single group is first pretested and then posttested following receipt of the treatment. In certain applications, this design can provide results based on a comparison of pretest and posttest data that speak clearly to the cause-and-effect connection between the treatment and the data. In most situations, however, the results provided by this design are murky. This is due to the likely existence of one or more plausible threats to internal validity. In other words, there may well be some unplanned event or phenomenon confounded with the treatment, thus making it possible (1) for an inert treatment to appear beneficial (or harmful), (2) for a worthwhile treatment to look as if it has no effect (or a detrimental impact), or (3) for a harmful treatment to show up as having no impact (or a positive impact).

In a one-group pretest-posttest design, there are several **rival hypotheses** that may compete, plausibly, with X as reasons why there was (or wasn't) a statistically significant difference between the pretest and posttest scores. For example, maybe the subjects simply mature (physically or psychologically) over the time period of the study. Or maybe the subjects experience something other than X between the two testings. Or maybe subjects do better on the posttest simply because they took the pretest. Or maybe the measuring instrument itself (or the person who uses it) changes over the course of the study. Or maybe certain kinds of subjects drop out of the study, thus allowing complete data to be collected only from those who benefited (or did not benefit) from X. Or maybe the use of subjects who scored high (or low) on a screening test allow regression-toward-the-mean to depress (or inflate) the posttest scores.[10] Usually one or more of these rival hypotheses will be plausible enough to threaten the internal validity of a study that uses a one-group pretest-posttest design.

The third pseudo-experimental design is the **static-group comparison**. With this design, a posttest is administered to each of two groups, one of which receives X while the other serves as a control group. When diagrammed, this design appears as follows

$$X \ O$$
$$O$$

with X and O carrying the same meaning as in the two previous designs, and with each row of symbols standing for a different group of subjects.

The central problem with the static-group comparison is the unknown status of the two groups prior to the time X is administered. If the analysis of the posttest data reveals a statistically significant difference between the two groups, such a difference *may* have been brought about by X being given to one of the two groups. However, such a difference *may* simply be a reflection of an initial difference between the two groups. The latter explanation is possible because the groups in a static-group comparison are *not* formed by randomly assigning subjects to the comparison groups. Instead, the experimental and control groups in this design come into being because subjects self-select themselves into the groups or because two intact groups are used or because a matched control subject from a nontreatment setting is paired up with each subject who is located in the setting where X is provided. These procedures for forming groups in the static-group comparison create the rival hypothesis that the comparison groups are unequal at the outset of the investigation.[11]

In Excerpt 21.36, we see how one of the pseudo-experimental designs was used in a recent study. As you will quickly detect from reading this excerpt, a one-group pretest-posttest design was used.

Excerpt 21.36 A Pseudo-Experimental Design

Whether a social cognitive theory AIDS prevention intervention would increase intentions to use condoms among 109 sexually active inner-city black female adolescents was tested. The first hypothesis was that the AIDS intervention

(Continued)

---

[10]*In the order given, these six rival hypotheses are often referred to by the terms* maturation, history, testing, instrumentation, mortality, *and* regression.

[11]*This particular threat to internal validity is referred to as* selection.

Excerpt 21.36 A Pseudo-Experimental Design *(Continued)*

would have an ameliorative effect on self-efficacy to use condoms and outcome expectancies regarding condom use—the social cognitive theory variables the intervention was designed to influence. The second hypothesis was that the women would report significantly stronger intentions to use condoms after receiving the intervention than before the intervention. Analyses revealed that the women scored higher in intentions to use condoms, AIDS knowledge, outcome expectancies regarding condom use, and self-efficacy to use condoms after the intervention than before the intervention.

Source: L. S. Jemmott, and J. B. Jemmott. (1992). Increasing condom-use intentions among sexually active black adolescent women. *Nursing Research, 41*(5), p. 273.

TRUE EXPERIMENTAL DESIGNS

Whereas pseudo-experimental designs typically yield results that are murky, a second class of research designs usually provides more trustworthy evidence. These designs are called **true experimental designs**, and they are characterized by (1) researcher interest in a possible causal link between the independent and dependent variables, (2) the random assignment of subjects to comparison groups, and (3) a reduced set of potential threats to internal validity. In the following paragraphs, we want to consider the three main kinds of true experimental design used by applied researchers.

1. POSTTEST-ONLY DESIGNS INVOLVING A SINGLE INDEPENDENT VARIABLE
There are several different kinds of posttest-only true experimental designs that can be used when there is a single independent variable manipulated by the researcher. The diagrams for the four most popular ones look like this

R X O	R X O	R X O	R X O
R O	R Y O	R Y O	R Y O
		R O	R Z O
(a)	(b)	(c)	(d)

where R stands for random assignment of subjects to the comparison groups; X, Y, and Z stand for different versions of the treatment; and O stands for the collection of data on the dependent variable. Diagrams (c) and (d) can, of course, be extended to accommodate studies where there are additional versions of the treatment.

As indicated by our four diagrams, a control (or placebo) group is an option. The question as to whether such a group should be used in a given study cannot be answered without a careful consideration of the research question(s), the nature and number of available subjects, and the likelihood that subjects from one group will converse with those in another group. Unfortunately, some researchers do not give very much thought to these issues, and the result is a design characterized by either the absence of a needed control (or placebo) group or the inclusion of one that is fully superfluous.

In Excerpt 21.37, we see an example of a randomized posttest-only design. Although the data collected in this study were used primarily to assess the internal consistency and validity of a newly developed measuring instrument (focusing on children's prosocial choice), the collected evidence was also used to compare the two groups involved in the investigation.

Excerpt 21.37 A Two-Group Posttest-Only Design

Parents of all children enrolled in nine Head Start classrooms were invited to participate in a study that involved an intervention designed to increase the prosocial behavior of the participants. Subjects were assigned randomly to an intervention ($N = 63$) or non-intervention control group ($N = 131$). For the post-intervention prosocial choice measure, the means of the two groups were significantly different ($t = -2.20, p < .05$). This result indicated that the intervention had some effect on the children's response to the prosocial choice measure.

Source: C. S. Weidman, and J. M. Strayhurn. (1992). Relationships between children's prosocial behaviors and choices in story dilemmas. *Journal of Psychoeducational Assessment, 10*(4), p. 332.

---

2. PRETEST-POSTTEST DESIGNS INVOLVING A SINGLE INDEPENDENT VARIABLE

The research designs in this category are similar to those discussed in the preceding section. The only difference is the addition of pretest data. Accordingly, the most frequently used designs from this category appear as follows when diagrammed

```
R O X O        R O X O        R O X O        R O X O
R O   O        R O Y O        R O Y O        R O Y O
                              R O   O        R O Z O
```

where the various symbols mean the same things as they did in the preceding section.

Diagrams of research designs appear infrequently in research reports, but occasionally they are displayed. Excerpt 21.38 contains such a diagram, although the notation is slightly different from that used by us in this chapter. When no diagram is presented (as in Excerpt 21.39), we doubt that you will have any trouble creating, in your mind, your own picture of the design.

Excerpts 21.38–21.39 References to Pretest-Posttest Designs Both with and Without a Diagram

We used a randomized pretest–posttest control group design (Campbell & Stanley, 1963, p. 9).

	Pretest	Treatment	Posttest
EG_1	T_1, T_2, T_3, T_4	X_a	T_1, T_2, T_3
EG_2	T_1, T_2, T_3, T_4	X_b	T_1, T_2, T_3
CG	T_1, T_2, T_3, T_4	X_c	T_1, T_2, T_3

EG_1 represents Experimental Group 1, using the problem-solving approach (X_a); EG_2 represents Experimental Group 2, using the computer-simulated experiment approach (X_b); and CG represents the Control Group, using the conventional approach (X_c). T_1 represents the Chemistry Achievement Test, T_2 the Science Process Skill Test, T_3 the Chemistry Attitude Scale, and T_4 the Logical Thinking Ability Test.

Source: O. Geban, P. Askar, and I. Ozkan. (1992). Effects of computer simulations and problem-solving approaches on high school students. *Journal of Educational Research, 86*(1), p. 7.

[The subjects] were randomly assigned to either the experimental group that received training or a waiting list control group. . . . All [subjects] in both experimental and control groups were given pre- and postassessments in 1-hour group sessions.

Source: A. A. Hains, and M. Szyjakowski. (1990). A cognitive stress-reduction intervention program for adolescents. *Journal of Counseling Psychology, 37*(1), p. 80.

3. FACTORIAL DESIGNS True experimental designs can be set up to accommodate two or more manipulated independent variables. They can also be set up to handle cases where researchers wish to combine manipulated and nonmanipulated independent variables within the same study. In either situation, the structure of the investigation will take the form of a factorial design.

Excerpt 21.34 (presented earlier) came from an experimental investigation in which a $3 \times 2 \times 2$ factorial design was used. In that study, a 10-minute videotape of a counseling session was shown to each subject. The researchers manipulated two of the three independent variables (or factors), because there were actually six versions of the videotape. These six versions were created by mixing the counselor's orientation (which was nonsexist-humanistic, liberal–feminist, or radical feminist) with the counselor's statement of values (which was either implicit or explicit). The third factor—not manipulated by the researchers—was the viewer's orientation toward feminism (which was either positive or negative).

Factorial designs can be used either with or without pretest data being collected from the subjects. Moreover, they can be set up with just between-subjects factors, with just within-subjects factors, or with a combination of these two kinds of factors. The study referred to in the preceding paragraph was completely between-subjects in nature. An example of a 2 × 2 mixed design was seen earlier in Excerpt 21.14.

QUASI-EXPERIMENTAL DESIGNS

The third category of designs used by researchers to investigate cause-and-effect relationships carries the label **quasi-experimental designs.** These designs are usually characterized by internal validity that is higher than that of pseudo-experimental designs but lower than that of true experimental designs. Because of this situation, you must be on guard for the possible and plausible rival hypotheses that might weaken any quasi-experimental study you are considering.

The most frequently used quasi-experimental design is the **nonequivalent control group design.** This design is almost the same as the pretest-posttest designs considered earlier. The difference is that random assignment of subjects to groups is not a feature of the nonequivalent control group design. The availability of pretest data makes this design better than the static-group comparison; the absence of randomization, however, makes this design weaker than the pretest-posttest true experimental design.

Because the nonequivalent control group design can be used with two or more groups of subjects and with or without a no-treatment (or placebo) group, there are actually many variations of this quasi-experimental design. The diagrams for the most frequently used variations look like this

```
O X O        O X O        O X O        O X O
O   O        O Y O        O Y O        O Y O
                          O   O        O Z O
```

where the symbols carry the same meaning as in the diagrams considered earlier.

In Excerpt 21.40, we see how a nonequivalent control group design was used to assess the relative effects of two nutritional therapy programs. The key element of this study that causes the research design to be quasi-experimental rather than true experimental in nature is the way subjects were assigned to the two groups.

The fact that subjects are not randomly assigned to the comparison groups in the nonequivalent control group design is a liability, and it is the reason why this design is considered to be quasi-experimental in nature. Unfortunately, many researchers make the logical error of thinking that the comparison groups can be considered equivalent at the outset of the study if a statistical comparison of the groups' pretest scores leads to the retention of a no-difference null hypothesis. This line of reasoning is faulty because (1)

Excerpt 21.40   A Nonequivalent Control Group Design

We conducted a pilot study using a two-group quasi-experimental design to assess the effectiveness of nutrition therapy by analyzing the differences in alcohol craving, hypoglycemic symptoms, nutrition intake, and length of sobriety of two treatment groups enrolled in an existing psychological/sociological/spiritual inpatient alcohol rehabilitation program based on the 12-step program of Alcoholics Anonymous.

Pretreatment data were collected from the control group, which comprised the first 18 patients admitted to the traditional treatment program. The traditional therapy program included a regular hospital diet and a basic nutrition education class. The next 20 patients admitted were assigned to the experimental group, called the nutrition therapy group. Pretreatment data were collected. Nutrition therapy included diet modifications and three individualized nutrition counseling sessions. All outside food sources were eliminated.

Source: J. R. Biery, J. H. Williford, and E. A. McMullen. (1991). Alcohol craving in rehabilitation: Assessment of nutrition therapy. *Journal of the American Dietetic Association, 91*(4), p. 464.

---

reaching a fail-to-reject decision when testing any H_0 does not justify believing that the null hypothesis is true, and (2) even if the groups were known to be equivalent in terms of the variable focused on by the pretest, the groups could still differ on one or more other variables not tapped by the pretest.

It should be noted that the problem of nonrandomization in the nonequivalent control group design cannot be swept away by using the pretest data as the covariate in an analysis of covariance. The second of the two points made at the end of the preceding paragraph provides one reason why a covariance analysis is incapable of making up for nonrandomization. Additionally, the analysis of covariance has been shown to remove only a portion of any existing pretest inequality. In other words, it underadjusts when used in situations where subjects are not randomly assigned to groups.

In addition to the nonequivalent control group design, several other quasi-experimental designs have been invented. They include the cross-lagged panel analysis, the separate-samples pretest-posttest design, and several versions of the time-series design. These designs will not be discussed because they are used infrequently as compared with the other designs we have examined.

A FEW DESIGN-ORIENTED WARNINGS

As we come to the end of this chapter, we want to offer four warnings related to the general topic of research design. These cautionary comments are needed because several research articles based on poorly designed studies slip through the screening process that is supposed to prevent them from being published or presented orally at professional meetings. Therefore, you must be careful when considering such reports, because a researcher's conclusions and claims may well have been built on a very weak foundation. If you heed the advice offered here, you will be a more discerning consumer of quantitatively based research reports and will, at times, choose to disbelieve any alleged discoveries.

RESEARCH DESIGN IS NOT INDEPENDENT FROM STATISTICAL ANALYSIS

A wise researcher does not consider the issue of research design to be unconnected to the techniques of data analysis. Even though the research design of most studies is fixed prior to the collection of data whereas statistical techniques cannot be applied until the data are in, there are many linkages between these two elements of any quantitative study. Conscientious researchers demonstrate awareness of these linkages.

As we have pointed out repeatedly throughout this book, a null hypothesis that is false by a large margin is not likely to be rejected if the sample size is too small. Conversely, if the sample size is too large, trivial deviations from the null will be declared statistically significant. Therefore, researchers ought to consider the power of their statistical techniques as they plan their studies and decide what sample sizes to use. Only a minority of researchers actually do this.

The connection between design and analysis can also be seen once you realize that the researcher decides (1) what kind(s) of data to collect and (2) what kind(s) of statistical analyses to use in analyzing the data. As we have tried to point out on several occasions, the nature of one's data set (in terms of level of measurement, distributional shape, linearity, sphericity, etc.) must be taken into consideration before the proper statistical technique can be selected. The research design associated with any study has an obvious influence on the nature of the data. Unfortunately, researchers sometimes set up a design that brings about a set of scores that calls for a particular kind of statistical analysis, yet some other inappropriate technique is used on the data. It's as if a square peg is being crammed into a round hole.

As we have seen in this chapter, there is a connection between the nature of the comparison groups in a study and the likelihood that a statistically significant result will be obtained. If an odd-ball group is thrown into a study along with more legitimate comparison groups, the null hypothesis will be rejected—but nothing at all unexpected will be revealed. Conscientious researchers refrain from designing their studies solely to impress those who confuse statistical significance with practical significance.

Although a study's research design and data analysis techniques ought to be seen as interconnected elements of the investigation, we cannot overemphasize the point that sophisticated statistical analyses cannot undo the damage created by poor design. In this chapter, you have seen us argue that the analysis of covariance does not magically move a nonequivalent control group design from the quasi-experimental category into the true experimental classification. In Chapter 16, we pointed out how a multi-factor repeated-measures ANOVA involving one or more manipulated within-subjects factors will likely yield hard-to-interpret results if all subjects receive the levels of such factors in the same order. Our warning here is simple: Don't be duped into thinking that a study is good just because fancy statistical techniques were used to analyze the data.

RANDOMIZATION SOMETIMES ISN'T REALLY RANDOM

The notion of randomization is an exceedingly important cornerstone of research design. Researchers are advised, for example, to select their subjects *randomly* from the appropriate target populations, to assign subjects *randomly* to comparison groups in experimental investigations, to consider *randomly* ordering the treatments for each subject in a repeated measures design, and (in some certain studies) to select *randomly* a small number of levels of a treatment factor from a larger pool of available levels. In a very real way, randomization becomes the tool by which the foundations of internal and external validity are built into a study.

Unfortunately, the terms *randomly selected* and *randomly assigned* are sometimes used by researchers when they did not actually do what is required to create true randomization. We say this because (1) many people have only a loose sense of what randomization means, and (2) the criteria associated with randomization are quite stringent. When researchers report that they used the technique of randomization in their studies, you should feel better than when they fail to mention that randomization was used. However, even when the researcher uses phrases such as *randomly selected* or *randomly assigned*, you cannot be completely confident that proper randomization took place.

The only way to know that a study's subjects or treatments had an equal chance of being selected or assigned is to have information concerning the actual process used to accomplish the selection or assignment objectives. In other words, you need to know *how* the researcher did the randomization. Accordingly, we believe researchers deserve some extra bonus from your evaluation of their studies when they explain precisely how the randomization was achieved. Phrases such as "by the flip of a coin," "using a table of random number," and "drawing cards from a shuffled deck" are what you should look for when trying to decide whether the researcher has described *how* the randomization was done.

THE LABELS FOR EXPERIMENTAL DESIGNS

When a research project is focused on cause and effect and is viewed as being experimental in nature, it will often be tagged with one of three labels: pseudo-experimental, true experimental, or quasi-experimental. The impression given by these labels is that the findings of true experimental designs can be trusted fully, that the conclusions from quasi-experimental designs should be looked at with skepticism, and that claims based on pseudo-experimental designs should be tossed aside. If you wish to become a competent evaluator of research reports, you must resist the temptation to be influenced by these category labels.

Under certain circumstances, convincing causal claims can come from a pseudo-experimental design. It all depends on whether the *possible* rival hypotheses associated with such a study are *plausible.* In a one-group pretest-posttest design, for example, the rival hypothesis of history is not a plausible threat to the study's internal validity if the subjects experience nothing except their treatment, control, or placebo condition between the two testings. Similarly, maturation would not be a problem if the dependent variable deals with a characteristic that is unlikely to change over time. If in a given study based on this pseudo-experimental design, these and other threats to internal validity are judged to be implausible, then a statistically reliable change in the subjects' scores from pretest to posttest *can* be attributed to the influence of the intervening treatment.

And what about the findings that come from studies using true experimental designs? Should they be trusted because they are somehow "true"? Absolutely not. Plausible rival hypotheses can sabotage a study that uses a true experimental design despite the fact that subjects are randomly assigned to comparison groups. This is the case because the random assignment of subjects serves to control only *some* of the threats to internal validity. Other rival hypotheses uncontrolled by random assignment can operate to make a truly impotent treatment appear to be effective (or damaging) or to make a truly effective (or damaging) treatment appear to have no impact at all.

Earlier in this chapter, we considered how subjects in a control group may try extra hard or may not try at all if they know that other subjects are receiving a treatment thought to provide benefits to those who receive it. These threats to internal validity (of compensatory rivalry or resentful demoralization) are not prevented by randomly assigning subjects to groups. Nor is the possible problem of **diffusion,** which occurs when subjects in the treatment group share the treatment with subjects in the control or placebo group(s).

When evaluating research reports, we applaud those researchers who show evidence of having considered potential threats to internal validity that are not controlled by randomization. In Excerpts 21.41 and 21.42, we see two cases that exemplify this concern on the part of the researchers.

Excerpts 21.41–21.42   Concerns About Diffusion

There is a possibility of some "contamination" of the experimental conditions. For example, three of the five classrooms in the in-service group were located in schools in which comparable classrooms were taught by teachers with intensive staff development. Thus, it is possible that students whose teachers had in-service staff development interacted with students whose teachers had intensive staff development concerning the content of drug education classes.

Source: K. A. Allison, G. Silverman, and C. Dignam. (1990). Effects on students of teacher training in use of a drug education curriculum. *Journal of Drug Education, 20*(1), p. 36.

Finally, measures assessing handedness and possible contamination from discussion of the experiment with classmates were collected.

Source: C. Janiszewski. (1990). The influence of print advertisement organization on affect toward a brand name. *Journal of Consumer Research, 17*(1), p. 61.

True experimental designs can suffer not only from plausible threats to internal validity but also from legitimate limitations to external validity. The random assignment of subjects to the comparison groups of an experiment does nothing to help establish the generalizability of the findings to other subjects, other settings, or other treatment conditions. Hence, researchers' claims based on true experimental designs may be unjustified because of the way the study was designed; thus, such claims may not be very true at all. How nice it is to come across research summaries that contain comments like that shown in Excerpt 21.43, for they indicate researcher awareness of ever-present limitations to external validity.

Excerpt 21.43   Threats to External Validity in True Experimental
                    Designs

With respect to external validity (i.e., generalization), the present investigation examined a large sample of experienced, practicing counselors and psychotherapists who were professionally engaged in the day-to-day activities of counseling. It is, of course, important to note that the size of our sample and its sex composition did not allow us to analyze the data for possible gender effects, effects that have sometimes been shown to occur in studies of reactions to female clients. Our inferences are also limited to White therapists who are responding to a White male client. The possible influence of alternate racial or cultural backgrounds, of either counselor or client, is unknown.

Source: J. Robertson, and L. F. Fitzgerald. (1990). The (mis)treatment of men: Effects of client gender role and life-style on diagnosis and attribution of pathology. *Journal of Counseling Psychology, 37*(1), p. 7.

RESEARCH DESIGN AND THE STUDY'S QUESTION(S)

We began this chapter with a metaphor of a chain. In that chain, research design constitutes a link that connects the research question(s) to the data-based conclusions. We argued (and would still argue) that if the design link is weak, the chain breaks. We hope the ideas covered in this chapter allow you to see clearly now why the research design in some studies can be thought of as a strong or a weak link.

Our final warning concerns the relative importance of the question element of our imaginary chain as compared with the design link. Although a study's research design is vital to the success of the project, the maximum level of success that can be achieved is determined by the quality of the research question(s). In the same sense that fancy statistical analyses cannot salvage a study characterized by a deficient research design, a complex and carefully developed research design cannot function as a magic wand that spins straw into gold. As we have stated repeatedly throughout this book, the worth of the research question(s) is of paramount importance. If given the choice to examine either (1) a study characterized by a perfect research design and impeccable statistics but an uninteresting question or (2) a study characterized by an imperfect design and simple statistical procedures but a worthwhile question, we would always choose the second study. It would, of course, be more fun to look at a study that is perfect on all counts. We have never seen such a study, however, and we doubt that we will anytime soon!

REVIEW TERMS

Attrition	Pre-experimental designs
Compensatory rivalry	Pretest-post test designs
Debriefing	Pretest sensitization
Descriptive study	Pseudo-experimental designs
Diffusion	Quasi-experimental designs
Experiments	Random assignment
External validity	Random selection
Factorial design	Research design
Hawthorne Effect	Resentful demoralization
Independence of observations	Response rate
Internal validity	Rival hypothesis
Manipulation check	Setting generalizability
Median split	Solomon Four-Group Design
Mortality	Static-group comparison
Nonequivalent control group design	Subject generalizability
One-group pretest-posttest design	True experimental design
One-shot case study	Unit of analysis
Posttest-only design	Unobtrusive measure

REVIEW QUESTIONS

1. Researchers often use convenience samples instead of randomly selecting subjects from defined populations. When this is done, what must be provided in the research report so you can decide whether the findings generalize to the people you know?

2. What kind of validity becomes diminished if the response rate to a mailed survey is low?

3. What two terms refer to the situation in which subjects drop out of a study?

4. In an experiment, is it the independent variable or the dependent variable that gets manipulated by the researcher?

5. In an experimental investigation, what technique is typically used to control extraneous variables and thereby keep such variables from becoming confounded with the independent variable(s)?

6. Take a look at Excerpts 21.9 and 21.10, both of which came from the same research report. In light of the way the subjects were assigned to the three comparison groups, is it appropriate to conclude that this study had high internal validity?

7. In the study from which Excerpt 21.15 was taken, is it possible that some of the subjects figured out what was truly going on in the experiment?

8. In terms of its effect on the data collected in an experiment, is diffusion more like resentful demoralization or compensatory rivalry?

9. In the study from which Excerpts 21.9, 21.10, and 21.21 were taken, how was a manipulation check conducted at the end of the investigation?

10. When using an existing measuring instrument to collect data, researchers can do something that is better than simply reporting reliability and validity evidence from others' studies. What can they do?

11. Which research design can be used to see whether pretest sensitization is operating to affect the posttest data of those subjects who receive a pretest prior to being given the treatment?

12. Experimental efforts at establishing cause-and-effect relationships can be classified into what three categories?

EPILOGUE

The warnings sprinkled throughout this book were offered with two distinct groups of people in mind. Our principal objective in raising these concerns has been to help those who are on the *receiving* end of research claims. However, we strongly believe that these same warnings should also be considered by those who are *doing* research. If both parties are more careful in how they "interact" with research studies, fewer invalid claims will be made, encountered, and believed.

We have two final warnings. The first has to do with the frequently heard statement that begins with these three words, "Research indicates that . . . . " The second is concerned with the power of replication. All consumers of research in addition to all doers of research should firmly resolve to heed the important messages contained in these last two admonitions.

First, you must protect yourself against those who use research to intimidate others in discussions (and arguments) over what is the best idea, the best practice, or the best anything. Because most folks (1) are unaware of the slew of problems that can cause an empirical investigation to yield untenable conclusions and (2) make the mistake of thinking that statistical analysis creates a direct pipeline to truth, they are easily bowled over when someone else claims to have "research evidence" on his or her side. Don't let this happen to you! When you encounter people who defend their points of view by alluding to research ("Well, research has shown that . . . "), ask them politely to tell you more about the research project(s) to which they refer. Also ask them if they have seen the actual research report(s). Also ask them if the researchers discussed threats to internal and external validity, if the researchers attended to the important assumptions associated with the statistical techniques used to analyze the data, and if the researchers distinguished between statistical and practical significance.

Second, be impressed with researchers who replicate their own well-designed investigations. The logic behind this admonition is simple and can be expressed in the question: Who are you most willing to believe, someone who demonstrates something once or someone who demonstrates something twice? Most researchers do not take the time to replicate their findings before they race off to publish their results. We admire those who do . . . and we place *far* more trust in their findings.

Answers to Review Questions

Chapter 1

1. Near the front of the article; a statement of the study's objective, participants, procedures, and results
2. Statement of purpose
3. *Ss*
4. Yes
5. Replicate the investigation
6. Intelligence
7. (a) Paragraphs of text, (b) tables, and (c) figures
8. In the Discussion section
9. Because it was presented in the Abstract
10. References
11. No
12. Subjects
13. Mean and standard deviation
14. Commended
15. All six

Chapter 2

1. Size of the data set; mean; standard deviation, median, upper quartile point, standard deviation, range, standard deviation, middle quartile point (or median), variance, lower quartile point, variance, mean.
2. 24
3. Bar graph
4. Positively skewed
5. 9 years
6. False
7. Because the range requires that we know the specific value of the high and low values in the data set. All we know about the youngest male case is that he is under 50 years old; likewise, we didn't know the specific ages of the four oldest members of this group.

8. Because the ordering of the columns in a bar graph is arbitrary.

9. 3

10. 20

11. The interquartile range

12. The mean was 62; the standard deviation was 4.1

13. Stem-and-leaf display

14. False

15. Distributional shape

CHAPTER 3

1. High-high, low-low

2. 20

3. $r = +.13$

4. .307

5. $-.04$

6. (a) Pearson's product-moment correlation (b) Spearman's rank-order correlation (c) Phi (d) Point-biserial

7. The exact value of r_s is $+.62$, but any guess between .30 and .90 would be considered by us to be a good guess.

8. Point-biserial

9. While both of these correlational techniques are designed for the case where the data corresponding to each variable take the form of ranks, Kendall's tau is appropriate when there are ties among the ranks associated with one (or both) of the variables.

10. Cramer's V

11. False

12. .4225 (or simply .42 if we round to two decimal places)

13. False

14. The path of the data points must be straight, but the path itself can be narrow or wide; linearity does *not* require that all data points lie on a straight line (although the relationship would be linear if this were to occur).

15. Pearson; Spearman

CHAPTER 4

1. Consistency

2. Test-retest; alternate-forms

3. 1.00

4. The length of the time interval between the two testings

5. Internal consistency

6. Cronbach's alpha is not restricted to situations where the data are dichotomous.

7. Ranks

8. Probably not (See our first "warning" about reliability.)

9. The scores obtained by using the measuring instrument

10. Estimated

11. Criterion-related

12. Construct

13. No

14. A lousy criterion

15. Between .03 and .07, depending on which criterion measure is used (We obtained these numerical values by squaring .17 and .26.)

CHAPTER 5

1. Parameter

2. From sample to population

3. Some of the individuals in the sample may refuse to participate in the study—or they may drop out prior to the time the study is completed.

4. The population is made up of students similar to the 188 students from whom data were collected.

5. A nonprobability sample (and, more specifically, a convenience sample)

6. Poor

7. Random

8. No

9. Does not

10. How the 728 male detainees were selected—that is, using names in a hat, coin flips, dice rolls, or a table of random numbers

11. Inasmuch as only 54 usable responses were returned, the actual sample size was 54, not 100! (See Excerpt 5.17, which came from the same journal article.)

12. The researcher must decide whether the sample data will be summarized so as to obtain a mean, median, mode, range, standard deviation, product-moment correlation coefficient, or any of a wide assortment of other possible indices.

13. The population is *not* BHCs located in all 50 states and the District of Columbia but rather the medium and large BHCs located in these areas. BHCs having total assets of less then $300 million were not included in the population to which inferences were made.

CHAPTER 6

1. Sampling error
2. That a "1" will turn up something other than 6 times
3. False
4. A sampling distribution
5. Standard error
6. Mean
7. 95 and 99
8. False (The parameter either will or will not fall within the confidence interval.)
9. It depends upon the size of the sample.
10. Point
11. Point estimation
12. False

CHAPTER 7

1. $H_0: \sigma_\mu^2 = 0$
2. In the relevant populations, the average (i.e., mean) number of explanatory thoughts generated by high and low need-for-cognition individuals is the same.
3. False (Nondirectional null hypotheses are evaluated with two-tailed tests.)
4. It is the researchers' calculated value.
5. .01
6. It is *not* possible for a researcher to commit both kinds of mistakes at the same time. (If H_0 is rejected, a Type II error is rendered impossible because a false null hypothesis can be overlooked only if a fail-to-reject decision is made; conversely, a Type I error is logically impossible if H_0 is not rejected because one cannot misclassify a true null hypothesis unless it is rejected.)

7. False. Null hypotheses always have reference to population parameters, not sample statistics. Accordingly, the researcher's null hypothesis should be set up to say $H_0: p = 0.00$.

8. Inconsistent

9. $H_0: \mu_1 = \mu_2$, where the subscripts "1" and "2" stand for the mean of the 14 counseling values and the mean of the general-psychology values, respectively. (One could also say $H_0: \mu_1 - \mu_2 = 0$ or $H_0: \sigma_\mu^2 = 0$.)

10. The critical values usually *does not* appear in the research summary.

11. Rejected (If p turns out to be equal to or smaller than the alpha level, H_0 will be rejected.)

12. A fail-to-reject decision should not be interpreted to mean that H_0 is likely to be true, because the same fail-to-reject decision would have been reached for several different pinpoint values (other than H_0's actual value) that could have been set forth in Step 1 of the hypothesis testing procedures. For example, consider question 7 once again. If the sample data produced a fail-to-reject decision because $r = .09$, one could not logically argue that H_0's pinpoint value of zero is likely to be true, because H_0 would *also* have been retained if the null's pinpoint value had been set equal to .01, .04, .10, or a whole host of values. Any of these values might well equal the true value of ρ.

13. Because the null hypothesis may have been set up to say something that everyone would agree, at the outset, is highly likely to be false. For example, we would consider it to be quite unimportant if a researcher conducts a study that leads to a decision to reject a null hypothesis that says intelligence and shoe size have a product-moment correlation in the population equal to $+.80$.

14. A Type III error

15. One-half the alpha level, or .025 in the case where $\alpha = .05$

CHAPTER 8

1. Yes

2. The group means were 21.21 and 22.61, yielding a mean difference of 1.40. The notation $p < .05$ indicates that there was a statistically significant difference between the two means. Although significant, the difference does not seem to be important, for eta was only .21.

3. True

4. Increase (Larger sample sizes bring about higher power.)

5. Before looking at the sample data

6. A larger number of subjects

7. .50 $[(55 - 50)/10 = 5/10 = .50]$

8. Small $= .20$, medium $= .50$, large $= .80$

9. False (In such cases, a power analysis is still recommended since it might reveal that the probability of rejecting important non-null cases is so low as to make it silly to conduct the study.)

10. No; no matter how high the statistical power might be, there is still a chance that a true H_0 will be rejected.

11. H_0 would be rejected because the confidence interval does not overlap H_0's pinpoint number of 30.

12. $10. [There are three ways your friend could win (tail, tail; head, tail; tail, head) but only one way you could win (head, head).]

13. Each separate test would have to be conducted at the .01 level of significance $(.05/5 = .01)$.

14. .0007 (This is the result obtained by dividing .01 by 14.)

15. The Bonferroni technique

CHAPTER 9

1. True

2. Although the null hypothesis does not appear in the excerpt (nor in the full article from which the excerpt was taken), we would guess that $H_0: \mu_{w.m.} = \mu_{b.m.}$, where $\mu_{w.m.}$ stands for the average age at death (in the population) of white males and $\mu_{b.m.}$ stands for the average age at death (in the population) of black males.

3. The data-based p-value would have turned out larger than 0.11 if the two means had been more similar.

4. Because there is no alpha-based critical value against which the calculated value can be compared. No critical value is available because no level of significance is specified in significance testing.

5. No

6. Because each of these excerpts has a clear indication of the level of significance that was used. In significance testing, the researcher does not specify an alpha level.

7. c. the hybrid approach to testing H_0

8. c. $p = .054$

9. a. $p = .003$

10. We could guess one asterisk, but we wouldn't wager very much money on our guess. As indicated by Excerpts 9.20–9.23, different researchers use different numbers of asterisks for the same p result.

11. Because so many researchers set $\alpha = .05$, you could be fairly confident that they have rejected H_0 if they report that $p < .05$. However, you should not be totally confident in this interpretation of what happened. If they set alpha equal to .01 or if they used the Bonferroni technique to adjust an originally set .05 level, a result that says $p < .05$ would indicate that H_0 was not rejected.

12. False

13. It is impossible to answer this question strictly on the basis of the p-values. If there were only a few subjects in the study conducted by Researcher A in comparison with a gigantic number of subjects in the study conducted by Researcher B, it could be that the difference between the sample means in the former study was larger than that in the latter study.

14. False—so long as your alpha-level standard (e.g., .01) is not influenced by the way someone's data turned out.

CHAPTER 10

1. $H_0: p = 0.00$

2. True

3. Twenty-two (We arrived at this answer by adding 2 to the reported degrees of freedom associated with each correlational test, 20.)

4. Two-tailed

5. The hybrid approach to testing H_0

6. Nine (For each correlation coefficient that either does or does not turn out significant, there must be a null hypothesis.)

7. Since there would be a total of 10 bivariate correlations computed from the data collected on five variables, the Bonferroni technique would dictate that each test be conducted with alpha set equal to .005.

8. Yes (Moreover, the answer remains the same even if we change the value of the reliability coefficient from .25 to .15 or even closer to zero, the likely value in H_0.)

9. The null hypothesis stated that in the relevant population, the K–BIT Vocabulary scores correlate equally with both the Verbal and Performance IQ scores from the WISC-R. Stated in symbols, $H_0: \rho_{KV} = \rho_{KP}$, where K stands for the K–BIT Verbal score, V = the WISC-R Verbal IQ score, and P = the WISC-R Performance IQ score.

10. Yes (The null hypothesis of a zero correlation in the population was not rejected.)

11. Yes, if the sample size is large enough. See Excerpt 10.28 for a good example.

12. (b) Equal variances

13. False (No matter how small the p-value, correlation coefficients normally do not speak to the issue of causality.)

14. Less likely

CHAPTER 11

1. All 10

2. Independent samples

3. H_0: $\mu_{before} = \mu_{after}$. (This same null hypothesis could be written as H_0: $\mu_{before} - \mu_{after} = 0$.)

4. 18

5. 30

6. 4

7. H_0 will be rejected.

8. .0041

9. False

10. H_0: $\sigma_1^2 = \sigma_2^2$. The researcher will be happy if this null hypothesis is not rejected.

11. Yes, because a test comparing two means is not robust to violations of the equal variance assumption when the two sample sizes are unequal.

12. Wider

13. False

CHAPTER 12

1. False

2. One of each

3. The independent variable was grade level; the dependent variable was total score on the IRA.

4. H_0: $\mu_{HIGH} = \mu_{MEDIUM} = \mu_{LOW}$. (or, H_0: $\sigma_\mu^2 = 0$)

5. Three groups; 93 subjects

6. Because the sample sizes are so discrepant, the homogeneity of variance assumption should have been tested.

7. The "Within groups" row ought to contain a mean square; it is 172.7.

8. The Cluster MS of 38.34 was divided by the Error MS of 1.09.

9. There were 155 subjects.

10. The alpha level should be set equal to .005.

11. It is one of the test procedures that researchers can use to check on the homogeneity of variance assumption.

12. The independent variable was Religious affiliation (made up of four comparison groups) and the dependent variables were Retributiveness, Salience, and Literalness.

13. Eta and F would have become larger while p would have become smaller. (This answer assumes that the only things that change in the original data are the means; if the unreported standard deviations were to change as well, it is possible that eta and F would decrease in size while p would increase.)

14. If 1 is added to the sum of the F's df values, does the result equal the number of subjects involved in the analysis?

CHAPTER 13

1. Neither. It depends upon whether the researcher who uses the Tukey test first examines the ANOVA F-test to see if it is "okay" to compare means using the Tukey test. If this *is* the case, the use of the Tukey test causes it to be employed in a post hoc sense. If, however, this is *not* the case, then the Tukey test is being used in a planned sense.

2. Nothing; they are synonyms.

3. Pairwise

4. Omnibus

5. A liberal test procedure

6. Three: (1) $H_0: \mu_1 = \mu_2$; (2) $H_0: \mu_1 = \mu_3$; (3) $H_0: \mu_2 = \mu_3$.

7. $\underline{\overline{X}_2 \, \overline{X}_1} \, \overline{X}_3$ or $\overline{X}_3 \, \underline{\overline{X}_1 \, \overline{X}_2}$

8. Two lines would be necessary. One line would have Untr. and T_{56} above it. The other line would have T_{56}, T_{45}, and T_{26} above it.

9. Yes (see Excerpt 13.16).

10. 10 $H_0: \mu_{ORIG.} = (\mu_{DELET.} + \mu_{CONTRA.} + \mu_{SAL.IRREL.} + \mu_{SUB.IRREL.})/4$

11. A priori

12. Less often

13. Yes

14. Extremely large sample sizes

CHAPTER 14

1. Two; one

2. Eight

3. No. (The notation $2 \times 2 \times 2$ indicates that a three-way ANOVA was used.)

4. Both.

5. First, the subjects defined by the first level of Factor A will be randomly assigned to the two levels of Factor B; then, the subjects defined by the second level of Factor A will be randomly assigned to the two levels of Factor B. Most likely, this will be done such that one-fourth of the subjects end up in each of the four cells of the 2×2 ANOVA.

6. Two; one

7. The main effect means would be equal to 9.5, 8.8 and 8.7 (for right-handed, left-handed, and ambidextrous subjects, respectively). Each would be based upon 20 scores.

8. False

9. False

10. One; it is the mean square for error. (Sometimes this mean square is labeled Within, Within groups, Residual, or Remainder.)

11. 562 (The total df was equal to $1 + 4 + 4 + 552$; $561 + 1 = 562$.)

12. No

13. Two

14. True

15. The F for the interaction between Hearing status and Age

16. Two

17. Three—one comparing the two levels of A at B_1, one comparing the two levels of A at B_2, and one comparing the two levels of A at B_3.

CHAPTER 15

1. A 3×3 ANOVA is a two-way ANOVA; a $2 \times 2 \times 2$ ANOVA is a three-way ANOVA.

2. True

3. 90 (9 cells with 10 scores each)

4. Three; one

5. Nine; 30

6. False. This null hypothesis stipulates that the *simple* interactions of any two of the three factors have the same pattern.

7. The A × B first-order interaction.

8. 149

9. You should put 5.69 in the upper left-hand cell of the 2 × 2 matrix. (This would make the difference between the means in the left-hand column identical to the difference between the means in the right-hand column.)

10. True

11. It would have turned out to be smaller. Changing 3.29 to 5.00 means that the pattern for sex-by-personalization simple interaction would be nearly the same for the one-step item as for the two-step item.

12. Yes

13. The six means in this paragraph come from the cells of the 3 × 2 (Expertise-by-Time of Judgment) matrix that had been collapsed across the three levels of the third factor (Initial Processing Goals).

14. False (see Excerpts 15.6 and 15.7).

15. 16 (2 × 2 × 2 × 2 = 16).

CHAPTER 16

1. 16; 64

2. False

3. They do not differ in any way whatsoever.

4. 35

5. No post hoc investigation was needed because there were only two levels of the factor in each one-way repeated measures ANOVA.

6. Two

7. False. (The *F*-test of this ANOVA is not robust to the sphericity assumption.)

8. d

9. Subjects, 7; A, 2; A × Subjects, 14; B, 3; B × Subjects, 21; A × B, 6; A × B × Subjects, 42; Total, 95.

10. 10

11. (a) 20 subjects each measured (b) 15 times for a total of (c) 300 scores.

12. Seven

13. Each of these means was based upon 60 scores.

14. False

15. Most are based on a nonadditive model.

CHAPTER 17

1. Nothing. These two terms are synonymous.

2. Three. These null hypotheses, of course, are concerned with population means. One H_0 states that the main effect means associated with the between-subjects factor are equal to one another. The second H_0 states that the main effect associated with the within-subjects factor are equal to one another. The third H_0 states that the between-subjects factor and the within-subjects factor do not interact.

3. Two; 30

4. The df values associated with the F for adoption group, the between-subjects factor.

5. False. The df values associated with the between-subjects F make it appear that 61 subjects were involved in the study. In contrast, the df values associated with the t-tests make it appear that there were 60 subjects.

6. Both of the F-values located in the Within subjects section of the summary table.

7. The operational alpha level of .006 was obtained by dividing .05 by 8, the number of dependent variables.

8. True

9. False

10. This would be a three-way mixed ANOVA with two between-subjects factors, each made up of three levels, and one two-level within-subjects factor.

11. The main effect mean for the Young level of the Age factor turned out equal to 55.65 while the main effect mean for the Older level turned out equal to 51.95.

12. 6.09, 5.00, 8.27, 5.55, 9.27, and 6.64

13. Three; one

14. In each instance, the MS for the between-subjects error term is larger.

15. Because the table contained in Excerpt 17.27 was prepared to help readers understand the two-way interaction between Target of Judgment

and Dimension of Judgment. Each of the cell means shown is really the average of two cells in the original $2 \times 2 \times 2$ layout, since the data have been "collapsed" across levels of the third factor, Order.

CHAPTER 18

1. II

2. Independent, dependent, and covariate variables

3. False. (ANCOVA is univariate in nature so long as there is a single dependent variable.)

4. Data on the covariate variable, EEA for neutral expressions, were used to make the adjustments. Those adjustments showed up in group means on the dependent variable, EEA for emotions.

5. False. [The number of null hypotheses is the same as would be the case if the data on just the dependent variable are subjected to an ANOVA, with the independent variable(s) used to clarify the nature of the comparison groups.]

6. Yes

7. 81.03

8. Because the first achievement measure was used as the covariate, and ANCOVA never computes adjusted means on the covariate variable(s).

9. Strong

10. In ANCOVA, each covariate variable causes the *df* for the within-groups source of variation to be lowered by 1. *

11. False

12. The independent variable should not affect the covariate variable.

13. Not rejected

14. ANCOVA works best in randomized experiments.

15. False

16. Setting alpha equal to .1 would be more sensible, since in testing this (or any other) assumption, Type II errors are considered to be worse than Type I errors.

*In mixed designs, a single covariate variable that is measured just once will cause 1 df to be lost only from the between-subjects error term; if, however, that single covariate variable is measured once for each level of the repeated measures factor, 1 df is lost from the between-subjects error term and 1 df is lost from the within-subjects error term.

CHAPTER 19

1. False. (The null hypothesis for the sign test is a statement about population parameters, not sample statistics.)

2. Larger than .09

3. Equal to .032. Note that the difference between the two groups' proportions is the same regardless of whether the proportions come from one of the response categories (did link target information) or the other possible response category (did not link target information).

4. χ^2

5. There would have been three proportions in H_0. Each proportion would have been set equal to .33.

6. False. (To accomplish the task, you could change to two sample proportions to *any* common numerical value. Setting both sample percentages equal to 50 percent would do the trick, but so would a change of either group's sample percentage to the observed value in the other group.)

7. The *p*-value would assume a larger (i.e., less significant) value.

8. Yes. The two variables are type of school (public versus private) and a school's compliance in returning the survey (yes or no).

9. True

10.

		Homesick?		
		Yes	*No*	
Groups	American	14	61	75
	Turkish	53	16	69

11. Eleven. (This is one less than the number of categories.)

12. Six. (This comes from multiplying one less than the number of blood types times one less than the number of options to the height question.

13. First, there were more than two comparison groups in the study. Second, the chi-square test comparing these groups produced a statistically significant result.

14. Yates

15. Two groups of data; correlated samples; two categories in the response variable

16. Cochran's Q test

17. The sample sizes in the two studies were different. In Excerpt 19.41, there were 250 clinicians whereas in Excerpt 19.42 there were only 68 experimenters. Because of this difference in *n*, the 63–37 split in the

first study was more inconsistent with H_0 than was the 74–26 split in the second study. This is why the first study produced a larger z and a smaller p.

18. Under the conditions specified, a larger sample size would cause the confidence interval to be narrower. In other words, the two ends of the interval would be closer to the sample value of 19.4 percent.

CHAPTER 20

1. Nonparametric procedures are sometimes used with interval or ratio data because the researcher knows (or suspects) that the normality and/or equal-variance assumptions are untenable, especially in the situation when the sample sizes are dissimilar.

2. Independent

3. One

4. False

5. Smaller

6. False. (No sum-of-ranks value is computed when groups are compared using a median test.)

7. $H_0: \mu_1 = \mu_2$

8. H

9. The Mann-Whitney U test (with the Bonferroni correction)

10. This relationship is direct, since small values of T are associated with small values of p.

11. Friedman's two-way analysis of variance of ranks

12. False. (The Kruskal-Wallis test, when conducted with large samples, yields a calculated value symbolized as χ^2.)

13. False. (Depending upon the nature of the populations associated with the comparison groups in a study, the power advantage of parametric and nonparametric tests can reside on either side of the fence.)

14. Yes

CHAPTER 21

1. A complete and detailed description of the subjects used in any researcher's study

2. External validity

3. "Mortality" and "attrition"

4. The independent variable

5. Random assignment of subjects to comparison groups

6. No. (High internal validity requires more than just the random assignment of subjects to groups.)

7. Yes

8. Compensatory Rivalry

9. Subject debriefing assessed with the bogus feedback had been believed

10. They can (and should) estimate the reliability and validity of the data collected in their own investigations

11. The Solomon four-group design

12. Pseudo-experimental designs, true experimental designs, and quasi-experimental designs

CREDITS

INDEX

Note: All numbers appearing in Roman type refer to pages; all numbers appearing in bold italics refer to Excerpts.